NEW DOCUMENTS
ILLUSTRATING EARLY CHRISTIANITY 11A:
TEXTS FROM EPHESUS

NEW DOCUMENTS ILLUSTRATING EARLY CHRISTIANITY

General Editor
James R. Harrison

Editorial Board
Edwin A. Judge
Paul McKechnie
Edwina Murphy
Alanna Nobbs

NEW DOCUMENTS ILLUSTRATING EARLY CHRISTIANITY 11A: TEXTS FROM EPHESUS

Edited by

James R. Harrison and Bradley J. Bitner

Atlanta

Copyright © 2024 by Macquarie University of Sydney, Australia

All rights reserved. No part of this work may be reproduced or transmitted in any form or by any means, electronic or mechanical, including photocopying and recording, or by means of any information storage or retrieval system, except as may be expressly permitted by the 1976 Copyright Act or in writing from the publisher. Requests for permission should be addressed in writing to the Rights and Permissions Office, SBL Press, 825 Houston Mill Road, Atlanta, GA 30329 USA.

Library of Congress Control Number: 2024944367

Contents

Abbreviations ix
Overview of the New Series xxiii

Introduction

Ephesus in Documentary Perspective
  James R. Harrison 1

Translation and Commentaries

The Gods

1. The Inviolate *temenos* of Artemis
   Bradley J. Bitner 35

2. The Fruitfulness of Demeter and the Fruitfulness of Believers
   James R. Harrison 47

3. The Blessings of Harmonia: A Happy Married Life
   James R. Harrison 57

4. Epiphanic Protocols and the Pastoral Epistles
   Bradley J. Bitner 65

Androklos, The Founder of Ephesus

5. Androklos, Founder of Ephesus
   James R. Harrison 87

Rome and Its Rulers

6. Long Live Rome!
   James R. Harrison 107

7. Hadrian Coenthroned with Dionysos: Perspectives from
   Ephesians and Revelation
   James R. Harrison 117

8. The Economic Conflagration of the Sacred Cult and Early
   Christian Preservation of Sacred Funds
   Isaac T. Soon 125

The Ephesian Elites

9. Noble and Well Born
   Bradley J. Bitner..135

10. An Incomparable Secretary: Acts 19:35 in Perspective
    James R. Harrison 141

11. Pontius Pilate and the Ephesian "Friends of Caesar"
    James R. Harrison 157

12. Julius the Jewish *archiatros*: On Being the "Chief Physician"
    at Ephesus
    James R. Harrison 169

13. "Ambassador in Chains" (Eph 6:20): What Might Ephesian
    Auditors Have Heard?
    James R. Harrison 179

The Centrality of Honor and Its Disruption

14. "They Love to Have the Place of Honor": Ephesian Priority
    Seating and Early Christian Honorific Culture
    Isaac T. Soon 197

15. A Seafarer's Reward: The Imperial Allocation of Honor at Ephesus
    James R. Harrison 203

16. Honoring the Concord of the Ephesian Demos
    James R. Harrison 211

17. Dishonoring the Honored: The Problem of Recycling Public Monuments
    James R. Harrison 231

18. The Problem of *invidia* at Ephesus: Handling Big Egos at the Big End of Town
    James R. Harrison 243

Economic Issues

19. Maintaining the Market Supply of Wheat for Rome: Revelation 6:6 and 18:11–13
    James R. Harrison 259

20. Getting a Rise out of the Ephesian Bakers
    Bradley J. Bitner 271

Building Activity and Local Sites

21. The Kaystros River and the Silting of the Ephesian Harbor: How Viable Is William Ramsay's Interpretation of Revelation 2:5?
    James R. Harrison 283

22. The "Fullness" of Ephesians 1:23 and 3:19
    Phillip T. Ort 293

Graffiti

23. The Wall Scribblers of Terrace House 2, Unit 6
    James R. Harrison 321

24. The New Testament and the Serious Side of Toilet Humor
    James R. Harrison 333

25. Finding the Right Spot to Take a Leak
    James R. Harrison 347

Appendix 1: Contents of *NewDocs* 11B 357
Appendix 2: Translations of and Commentaries on Ephesian
    Inscriptions in *NewDocs* 1–10 359
Contributors...361
Ancient Sources Index...365
Modern Authors Index..392
Word Index...398
Subject Index..400

Abbreviations

Ancient Works

1QH	Hodayot
1QS	Serek Hayahad
2 Tars.	Dio Chrysostom, *Tarsica altera (Or. 34)*
Ab urbe cond.	Livy, *Ab urbe condita*
Acts John	Acts of John
Aen.	Vergil, *Aeneid*
Agr.	Cicero, *De lege agraria*
A.J.	Josephus, *Antiquitates judaicae*
Alc.	Plutarch, *Alcibiades*
Alex.	Lucian, *Alexander (Pseudomantis)*; Plutarch, *Alexander*
Anab.	Arrian, *Anabasis*
Ann.	Tacitus, *Annales*
Ant.	Plutarch, *Antonius*
Arch.	Vitruvius, *De architectura*
Ars	Horace, *Ars poetica*
Att.	Cicero, *Epistulae ad Atticum*
Aug.	Suetonius, *Divus Augustus*
Bell. civ.	Caesar, *Bellum civile*; Appian, *Bella civilia*
Bib. hist.	Diodorus Siculus, *Bibliotheca historica*
B.J.	Josephus, *Bellum judaicum*
Cal.	Suetonius, *Gaius Caligula*
Cam.	Plutarch, *Camillus*
Cat.	Cicero, *In Catilinam*; Plutarch, *In Catilinam*
Cel. Phryg.	Dio Chrysostom, *Celaenis Phrygiae (Or. 35)*
Claud.	Suetonius, *Divus Claudius*
Clu.	Cicero, *Pro Cluentio*
Conf.	Philo, *De confusione linguarum*

Conj. praec.	Plutarch, *Conjugalia praecepta*
Con. Liv.	Ovid, *Consolatio ad Liviam*
Contemp.	Philo, *De vita contemplative*
Contr.	Seneca the Elder, *Controversiae*
Deipn.	Athenaeus, *Deipnosophistae*
Descr.	Pausanias, *Graeciae descriptio*
Did. apost.	Didascalia apostolorum
Diss.	Maximus of Tyre, *Dissertation*
Eleg.	Tibullus, *Elegies*
Ep.	Lucillius, *Epigrams*; Martial, *Epigrams*; Pliny the Younger, *Epistulae*; Seneca, *Epistulae morales*
Ep. Apoll.	Philostratus, *Epistle Apollonii*
Eph.	Xenophon, *Ephesiaca*
Epit.	Livy, *Epitome*
Ethn.	Stephanus of Byzantium, *Ethnica*
Fact. et dict.	Valerius Maximus, *Factorum et dictorum memorabilium libri IX*
Fast.	Ovid, *Fasti*
Fast. Caer.	Fasti *Caeretani*
Fast. Praen.	Fasti *Praenestini*
Flacc.	Philo, *In Flaccum*
F.W.	Appian, *Foreign Wars*
Geogr.	Strabo, *Geographica*
Har. resp.	Cicero, *De haruspicum responso*
Haer.	Irenaeus, *Adversus haereses*
Hell.	Xenophon, *Hellenica*
Herm. Mand.	Shepherd of Hermas, Mandate(s)
Herm. Sim.	Shepherd of Hermas, Similitude
Hist.	Herodotus, *Historiae*; Polybius, *Historiae*; Tacitus, *Historiae*; Thucydides, *Historia belli Peloponnesiaci*
Hist. Aug.	Scriptores historia Augustae
Hist. Rom.	Dio Cassius, *Historiae romanae*; Velleius Paterculus, *Historiae romanae*
Hom. Hymn. Ven.	Homeric Hymn to Venus
In cont.	Dio Chrysostom, *In contione* (*Or.* 48)
Inst.	Quintilian, *Institutio oratoria*
Jul.	Suetonius, *Divus Julius*
Leg.	Philo, *Legum allegoriae*

Legat.	Philo, *Legatio ad Gaium*
Leok.	Lykourgos, *Kata Leokrates*
Leuc. Clit.	Achilles Tatius, *Leucippe et Clitophon*
Lucil.	Seneca, *Ad Lucilium*
LXX	Septuagint
Lys.	Plutarch, *Lysander*
Marcell.	Cicero, *Pro Marcello*
Mem.	Xenophon, *Memorabilia*
Metam.	Apuleius, *Metamorphoses*; Ovid, *Metamorphoses*
Migr.	Philo, *De migratione Abrahami*
M.W.	Appian, *Mithridatic Wars*
Mur.	Cicero, *Pro Murena*
Nat.	Pliny, *Naturalis historia*
Noct. att.	Aulus Gellius, *Noctes atticae*
Oct.	Minucius Felix, *Octavius*
Oec.	Xenophon, *Oeconomicus*
Off.	Hierocles, *De officiis*
Onir.	Artemidorus, *Onirocritica*
Or.	Aelius Aristides, *Oration*; Dio Chrysostom, Musonius Rufus, *Oration*
Phar.	Lucan, *Pharsalia*
Phil.	Cicero, *Orationes philippicae*
Plant.	Philo, *De plantatione*
Pomp.	Plutarch, *Pompeius*
Por.	Xenophon, *Poroi*
Praep. ev.	Eusebius, *Praeparatio evangelica Preparation*
Quaest. conv.	Plutarch, *Quaestionum convivialium libri IX*
Reg.	Nepos, *De regibus*
Rep.	Cicero, *De republica*
Rer. gest.	Ammianus Marcellinus, *Rerum gestarum libri XXXI*
Res gest. divi Aug.	Res gestae divi Augusti
Rhod.	Dio Chrysostom, *Rhodiaca (Or. 31)*
Rosc. Amer.	Cicero, *Pro Sexto Roscio Amerino*
Sat.	Horace, *Satirae*; Juvenal, *Satirae*; Persius, *Satirae*
Satyr.	Petronius, *Satyricon*
Sent.	Paulus, *Sententiae*
Sept. sap. conv.	Plutarch, *Septem sapientium convivium*
Sept. mirac.	Philo of Byzantium, *De septem miraculis*

Silv.	Statius, *Silvae*
Spec.	Philo, *De specialibus legibus*
Stoic. rep.	Plutarch, *De Stoicorum repugnantiis*
Superst.	Plutarch, *De superstition*
Symp.	Lucian, *Symposium*
t.	Tosefta
Ti. C. Gracch.	Plutarch, *Tiberius et Caius Gracchus*
Theog.	Hesiod, *Theogony*
Tox.	Lucian, *Toxaris*
Tumult.	Dio Chrysostom, *De tummultu*
Var. hist.	Aelian, *Varia historia*
Verr.	Cicero, *In Verrem*
Vesp.	Aristophanes, *Vespae*
Vit.	Diogenes Laertius, *Vitae philosophorum*
Vit. Apoll.	Philostratus, *Vita Apolloni*
Vit. aere al.	Plutarch, *De vitando aere alieno*
Vit. soph.	Philostratus, *Vitae sophistarum*

Modern Editions, Journals, and Series

AAWW	*Anzeiger der Österreichischen Akademie der Wissenschaften in Wien, philosophisch-historischen Klasse*
ABD	Freedman, David Noel, ed. 1992. *Anchor Bible Dictionary.* 6 vols. New York: Doubleday.
ABSA	*Annual of the British School at Athens*
ActAnt	*Acta Antiqua Academiae Scientiarum Hungaricae*
AE	*Année épigraphique*
AJA	*American Journal of Archaeology*
AJEC	Ancient Judaism and Early Christianity
AM	*Athenische Mitteilungen*
AnBib	*Analecta Biblica*
ANRW	Temporini, Hildegard, and Wolfgang Haase, eds. 1972–. *Aufstieg und Niedergang der römischen Welt: Geschichte und Kultur Roms im Spiegel der neueren Forschung.* Part 2, *Principat.* Berlin: de Gruyter.
AnSt	*Anatolian Studies*
ANTC	Abingdon New Testament Commentaries

AUSS	*Andrews University Seminary Studies*
AYB	Anchor Yale Bible
b.	Babylonian Talmud
BAGD	Bauer, Walter, William F. Arndt, F. Wilbur Gingrich, and Frederick W. Danker. 1979. *Greek-English Lexicon of the New Testament and Other Early Christian Literature.* 2nd ed. Chicago: University of Chicago Press.
BASOR	*Bulletin of the American Schools of Oriental Research*
BBRSup	Bulletin for Biblical Research Supplements
BCH	Bulletin de correspondance hellénique
BDAG	Danker, Frederick W., Walter Bauer, William F. Arndt, and F. Wilbur Gingrich. 2000. *Greek-English Lexicon of the New Testament and Other Early Christian Literature.* 3rd ed. Chicago: University of Chicago Press.
BE	*Bulletin épigraphique*
BECNT	Baker Exegetical Commentary on the New Testament
Ber.	Berakhot
Bib	*Biblica*
BNP	Cancik, Hubert, ed. 2002–2011. *Brill's New Pauly: Encyclopaedia of the Ancient World.* 22 vols. Leiden: Brill.
BR	*Biblical Research*
BS	Mazar, Benjamin, Moshe Schwabe, and Baruch Lifshitz. 1973–1976. *Beth She'arim.* 3 vols. Jerusalem: Israel Exploration Society.
BSac	*Bibliotheca Sacra*
BTB	*Biblical Theology Bulletin*
BTS	Biblical Tools and Studies
BZNW	*Beihefte zur Zeitschrift für die neutestamentliche Wissenschaft*
CBQ	*Catholic Biblical Quarterly*
CBQMS	Catholic Biblical Quarterly Monograph Series
CHANE	Culture and History of the Ancient Near East
CIG	Boeckh, August, ed. 1828–1877. *Corpus Inscriptionum Graecarum.* 4 vols. Hildesheim: Olms.

CIIP	Cotton, Hannah M., et al. 2010–. *Corpus Inscriptionum Iudaeae/Palaestinae*. Berlin: De Gruyter.
CIJ	Frey, Jean-Baptiste. 1936–1952. *Corpus inscriptionum Judaicarum*. 2 vols. Rome: Pontifical Institute of Christian Archaeology.
CIL	Mommsen, Th., ed. 1863–. *Corpus inscriptionum Latinarum*. Berlin: Reimerum.
CJ	*Classical Journal*
ConBNT	Coniectanea Biblica: New Testament Series
CP	*Classical Philology*
CQ	*Classical Quarterly*
DocsGaius	Smallwood, E. Mary. 1967. *Documents Illustrating the Principates of Gaius, Claudius, and Nero*. London: Cambridge University Press.
DocsNerva	Smallwood, E. Mary. 1966. *Documents Illustrating the Principates of Nerva, Trajan and Hadrian*. Cambridge: Cambridge University Press.
DNP	Cancik, Hubert, and Helmuth Schneider. *Der neue Pauly: Enzyklop.die der Antike*. Stuttgart: Metzler, 1996–.
EA	*Epigraphica Anatolica*
EC	*Early Christianity*
ESV	English Standard Version
FD 3.4	Colin, G., et al., eds. 1930–1976. *La terrasse du temple et la zone nord du sanctuarie*. Vol. 3.4 of *Fouilles de Delphes*. Paris: de Boccard.
FGrHist	Jacoby, Felix, ed. 1954–1964. *Die Fragmente der griechischen Historiker*. Leiden: Brill.
FiE	Forschungen in Ephesos
Führer Selçuk	Bammer, Anton, Robert Fleischer, and Dieter Knibbe, eds. 1974. *Führer durch das Archäologische Museum Selçuk-Ephesos*. Vienna: Österreichisches Archäologisches Institit.
GR	Taeuber's graffiti/drawings/paintings
GIBM	Newton, C. T., Edward Lee Hicks, and Gustav Hirschfeld. 1874–1916. *The Collection of Greek Inscriptions in the British Museum*. 5 vols. Oxford: Clarendon.
GRBS	*Greek, Roman, and Byzantine Studies*

HesperiaSup	Hesperia: Journal of the American School of Classical Studies at Athens Supplement Series
Historia	*Historia: Zeitschrift für Alte Geschichte*
HSCP	Harvard Studies in Classical Philology
HTR	Harvard Theological Review
HTS	Harvard Theological Studies
HUT	Hermeneutische Untersuchungen zur Theologie
IAphrodisias 2007	Reynolds, Joyce Marie, Charlotte Roueché, and Gabriele Bodard, eds. *Inscriptions of Aphrodisias*. 2007. http://insaph.kcl.ac.uk/iaph2007.
IAsia Mixed	Kearsley, R. A., with Trevor V. Evans. *Greeks and Romans in Imperial Asia: Mixed Language Inscriptions and Linguistic Evidence for Cultural Interaction until the End of AD III*. IGSK 59. Bonn: Habelt, 2001.
ICC	International Critical Commentary
ICos	Segre, M., ed. 1993–2007. *Iscrizioni di Cos*. Rome: L'Erma di Bretschneider.
ICrete	Guarducci, Margarita. 1935–1950. *Inscriptiones Creticae*. 4 vols. Rome: La Libreria dello Stato.
IDelta	Bernand, André. 1970. *Les confins libyques*. Vol. 1 of *Le Delta égyptien d'après les textes grecs*. Cairo: Institut français d'archéologie orientale.
IDidyma	Rehm, R., ed. 1958. *Die Inschriften*. Vol. 2 of *Didyma*. Berlin: Mann.
IEgypte prose	Bernand, André. 1992. *La prose sur pierre dans l'Égypte hellénistique et romaine*. 2 vols. Paris: Editions du Centre national de la recherche scientifique.
IEph	Wankel, Hermann, et al., eds. 1979–1984. *Die Inschriften von Ephesos*. 8 vols. Bonn: Habelt.
IErythrai	Engelmann, H., and R. Merkelbach. *Die Inschriften von Erythrai und Klazomenai*. 2 vols. Bonn: Habelt.
IEstremo Oriente	Rossi, Filippo Canali De. 2004. *Iscrizioni delle Estremo Oriente Greco: Un repertorio*. IGSK 65. Bonn: Habelt.
IG	Inscriptiones Graecae

IG Porto	Sacco, Giulia. 1984. *Iscrizioni greche d'Italia: Porto*. Rome: Edizioni di storia e letteratura.
IGRR	Inscriptiones graecae ad res romanas pertinentes
IGSK	Inschriften griechischer Städte aus Kleinasien
IIasos	Blümel, W. 1985. *Die Inschriften von Iasos*. 2 vols. Bonn: Habelt.
IJO	Noy, David, et al., eds. 2004. *Inscriptiones Judaicae Orientis*. 3 vols. Tübingen: Mohr Siebeck.
IK	Inschriften griechischer Städte aus Kleinasien
IKeramos	Varinlioğlu, E. 1986. *Die Inschriften von Keramos*. IGSK 30. Bonn: Habelt.
IKL	Taeuber's small inscriptions
IKnidos	Blümel, W., ed. 1991–1992. *Die Inschriften von Knidos*. 2 vols. Bonn: Habelt.
IKret.	Guarducci, Margherita, ed. *Inscriptiones Creticae*. 4 vols. Rome 1935–1950.
IKyzikos	Schwertheim, E., ed. 1980–1983. *Die Inschriften von Kyzikos und Umgebung*. Bonn: Habelt.
ILS	Dessau, Hermann. 1906. *Inscriptiones Latinae Selectae*. Berolini: Weidman.
IMagnesia	Kern, Otto. 1900. *Die Inschriften von Magnesia am Maeander*. Berlin: Spemann.
IMT Kyz Kapu Dağ	Barth, Matthias, and Josef Stauber, eds. 1993. *Inschriften Mysia und Troas. 'Mysia, 'Kyzikene, Kapu Dağ'*. Munich: University of Munich.
IMT LApollon/Milet	Barth, Matthias, and Josef Stauber, eds. 1996. *Inschriften Mysia und Troas*. Leopold Wenger Institut. Munich: University of Munich.
IPergamon	Boehringer, Erich, et al. 1890–1969. *Altertümer von Pergamon*. Berlin: de Gruyter.
IPergamon Asklepieion	Habicht, Christian. 1969. *Die Inschriften des Asklepieions*. Vol. 8.3 of *Altertümer von Pergamon*. Berlin: de Gruyter.
IPerge	Şahin, Sencer. 1999, 2004. *Die Inschriften von Perge*. 2 vols. IGSK 54, 61. Bonn: Habelt.
IPessinous	Strubbe, J. H. M. 2005. *The Inscriptions of Pessinous*. IGSK 66. Bonn: Habelt.
IPhilippes	Brélaz, Cédric. 2014. *Corpus des inscriptions*

	grecques et latines de Philippes. Athens: Ecole Française d'Athênes.
IPriene	von Gaertringen, F. Hiller. 1906. *Inschriften von Priene.* Berlin.: de Gruyter.
IPrusa	Corsten, Th. 1991–1993. *Die Inschriften von Prusa ad Olympum.* IGSK 39–40. 2 vols. Bonn: Habelt.
IRhodes Peraia	Blümel, W. 1991. *Die Inschriften der rhodischen Peraia.* IGSK 38. Bonn: Habelt.
ISardis 1	Buckler, W. H., and David M. Robinson. 1932. *Greek and Latin Inscriptions.* Vol. 7 of *Sardis.* Leiden: Brill.
ISmyrn	Petzl, G. 1982–1990. *Die Inschriften von Smyrna.* 2 vols. Bonn: Habelt.
IST	Taeuber's stone inscriptions
IStratonikeia	Şahin, M. Ç. 1981–2010. *Die Inschriften von Stratonikeia.* IGSK 21–22. 2 vols. Bonn: Habelt.
IThèbes Syène	Bernand, André. 1989. *De Thèbes à Syène.* Paris: Editions du Centre national de la recherche scientifique.
JAC	*Jahrbuch für Antike und Christentum*
JACSup	Supplments to *Jahrbuch für Antike und Christentum*
JB	Jerusalem Bible
JBL	*Journal of Biblical Literature*
JBRec	*Journal of the Bible and Its Reception*
JGRChJ	*Journal of Greco-Roman Christianity and Judaism*
JHI	*Journal of the History of Ideas*
JHS	*Journal of Hellenic Studies*
JJS	*Journal of Jewish Studies*
JNSL	*Journal of Northwest Semitic Languages*
JÖAI	*Jahreshefte des Österreichischen archäologischen Instituts*
JRS	*Journal of Roman Studies*
JRS Monograph	Journal of Roman Studies Monograph Series
JSJ	*Journal for the Study of Judaism*
JSNT	*Journal for the Study of the New Testament*
JSNTSup	Journal for the Study of the New Testament Supplement Series
Klio	*Klio: Beiträge zur Alten Geschichte*

LBW	Le Bas, Philippe, and W. H. Waddington. 1870. *Inscriptions grecques et latines.* Vol. 3 of *Voyage archéologique en Grèce et en Asie Mineure, fait par ordre du gouvernement français pendant les années 1843 et 1844.* Paris: Firmin-Didot.
LGPN	Fraser, P. M., et al., eds. 1987 –. *A Lexicon of Greek Personal Names.* Oxford: Oxford University Press.
LNTS	The Library of New Testament Studies
LSAM	Sokolowski, Franciszek. 1955. *Lois sacrées de l'Asie Mineure.* Paris: Boccard.
LSJ	Liddell, Henry George, Robert Scott, and Henry Stuart Jones. 1996. *A Greek-English Lexicon.* 9th ed. with revised supplement. Oxford: Clarendon.
MAAR	*Memoirs of the American Academy in Rome*
MAMA	Calder, W. M., et al. 1928–1993. *Monumenta Asiae Minoris Antiqua.* 11 vols. London: Manchester University Press.
MDAI(A)	Mitteilungen des deutschen Archäologischen Instituts [Athen.AbL]
MGWJ	*Monatsschrift für Geschichte und Wissenschaft des Judentums*
MM	Moulton, James H., and George Milligan. 1995. *Vocabulary of the Greek Testament.* Grand Rapids: Baker.
MnemosyneSup	Mnemosyne Supplementum
Mionnet	Mionnet, T. 1806–1837. *Description de Médailles antiques grecques et romaines.* 15 vols. Paris: Testu.
NASB	New American Standard Bible
NBCB	New Cambridge Bible Commentary
NEA	*Near Eastern Archaeology*
Neot	*Neotestamentica*
NewDocs	Horsley, Greg H. R., and Stephen Llewelyn. 1981–. *New Documents Illustrating Early Christianity.* North Ryde, NSW: The Ancient History Documentary Research Centre, Macquarie University.
NICNT	New International Commentary on the New Testament

NIGTC	New International Greek Testament Commentary
NIV	New International Version
NovT	*Novum Testamentum*
NovTSup	Supplements to Novum Testamentum
NRSV	New Revised Standard Version
NTOA	Novum Testamentum et Orbis Antiquus
NTS	*New Testament Studies*
OCD	Hornblower, Simon, and Antony Spawforth, eds. *Oxford Classical Dictionary*. 4th ed. Oxford: Oxford University Press, 2012.
OGIS	Dittenberger, Wilhelm. 1903–1905. *Orientis graeci inscriptiones selectae*. 2 vols. Leipzig: Hirzel.
OTS	Old Testament Studies
P.Amh.	Grenfell, B. P., and A. S. Hunt, eds. 1900–1901. *The Amherst Papyri, Being an Account of the Greek Papyri in the Collection of the Right Hon. Lord Amherst of Hackney, F.S.A. at Didlington Hall, Norfolk*. London: Frowde.
P.Dura	Welles, C. B., R. O. Fink, and J. F. Gilliam. 1959. *The Parchments and Papyri*. Final Report 5.1 of *The Excavations at Dura-Europos conducted by Yale University and the French Academy of Inscriptions and Letters*. New Haven: Yale University Press.
P.Mich. 1	Edgar, C. C. 1931. *Zenon Papyri*. Vol. 1 of *Michigan Papyri*. Cairo: Impr. de l'Institut francais d'archeologie orientale.
P.Mich. 6	Youtie, Herbert Chayyim, and Orsamus Merrill Pearl. 1944. *Papyri and Ostraca from Karanis*. Vol. 2 of *Michigan Papyri*. Ann Arbor: University of Michigan Press.
P.Oslo 3	Eitrem, S., and Leiv Amundsen. 1936. *Papyri Osloenses*. Vol. 3. N.p.: Oslo.
P.Oxy.	Grenfell, Bernard P., et al., eds. *The Oxyrhynchus Papyri*. London: Egypt Exploration Fund, 1898–.
PDM	*Papyri Demoticae Magicae*. Demotic texts in PGM corpus as collated in Hans Betz, Dieter, ed. 1996. *The Greek Magical Papyri in Translation, including the Demotic Spells*. Chicago: University of Chicago Press.

PGM	Preisendanz, Karl, ed. 1973–1974. *Papyri Graecae Magicae: Die griechischen Zauberpapyri*. 2nd ed. Stuttgart: Teubner.
PHI	Packhard Humanities Institute Greek Inscriptions
PIR	Edmundus Groag, et al., eds. 1933–2015. *Prosopographia Imperii Romani*. 2nd ed. Berlin: de Gruyter.
PNTC	Pelican New Testament Commentaries
PSB	*Princeton Seminary Bulletin*
PSI	*Papiri della Società Italiana*
RAr	*Revue archéologique*
RAC	*Reallexikon für Antike und Christentum*
RDGE	Sherk, R. K. 1969. *Roman Documents from the Greek East: Senatus Consulta and Epistulae to the Age of Augustus*. Baltimore: John Hopkins Press.
RE	Wissowa, Georg, et al. 1893–1980. *Pauly's Realencyclopädie der classischen Altertumswissenschaft*. Stuttgart: Druckenmüller.
REA	*Revue des études anciennes*
REG	*Revue des études grecques*
RevExp	*Review and Expositor*
RevPhil	*Revue de philologie*
RGRW	Religions in the Graeco-Roman World
RhM	*Rheinisches Museum für Philologie*
RIC 1	Mattingly, Harold, Edward Allen Sydenham, Carol Humphrey Vivian Sutherland, and Robert A. G. Carson. 1984. *Augustus to Vitellius (31 BC–AD 69)*. Vol. 1 of *The Roman Imperial Coinage*. 2nd ed. London: Spink & Son.
RIC 2	Mattingly, Harold, Edward Allen Sydenham, Ian Carradice, and Theodore Vern Buttrey. 1926. *Vespasian to Hadrian (AD 96–138)*. Vol. 2 of *The Roman Imperial Coinage*. London: Spink & Son.
RIDA	*Revue internationale du droit d'auteur*
RPC	Burnett, Andrew, et al., eds. 1992–. *Roman Provincial Coinage*. London: British Museum Press; Paris: Bibliothèque Nationale.
RPh	*Revue de philologie, de littérature et d'histoire anciennes*

RSV	Revised Standard Version
SBAW	*Sitzungsberichte der Akademie der Wissenschaften*
SBLDS	Society of Biblical Literature Dissertation Series
SBLMS	Society of Biblical Literature Monograph Series
SE	Alpers, Michael, and Helmut Halfmann, eds. 1995. *Supplementum Ephesium*. Hamburg: Deutsche Forschungsgemeinschaft.
SEG	Supplementum epigraphicum graecum
SIG	Dittenberger, Wilhelm, ed. 1915–1924. *Sylloge Inscriptionum Graecarum*. 4 vols. 3rd ed. Leipzig: Hirzel.
SNGCop	Breitenstein, Niels, and Willy Schwabacher. 1942–1979. *Sylloge Nummorum Graecorum, Copenhagen, The Royal Collection of Coins and Medals, Danish National Museum*. Copenhagen: Munksgaard.
SNGvA	von Aulock, Hans. 1957–1967. *Sylloge Nummorum Graecorum, Deutschland*. Berlin: Mann.
SNTSMS	Society for New Testament Studies Monograph Series
SR	*Studies in Religion*
Staatsverträge	Bengston, Hermann, et al., ed. 1960–2020. *Die Staatsverträge des Altertums*. 4 vols. Munich: Beck.
SUNT	Studien zur Umwelt des Neuen Testaments
TAM	Kalinka, Ernst, et al. 1901–2007. *Tituli Asiae Minoris*. Wein: Akademie.
TAPA	*Transactions of the American Philological Association*
TDNT	Kittel, Gerhard, and Gerhard Friedrich, eds. 1964–1976. *Theological Dictionary of the New Testament*. Translated by Geoffrey W. Bromiley. 10 vols. Grand Rapids: Eerdmans.
TLZ	*Theologische Literaturzeitung*
TSAJ	Texte und Studien zum antiken Judentum
TynBul	*Tyndale Bulletin*
VC	*Vigiliae Christianae*
VT	*Vetus Testamentum*
WBC	Word Biblical Commentary

WGRWSup	Writings of the Greco-Roman World Supplement Series
WUNT	Wissenschaftliche Untersuchungen zum Neuen Testament
YCS	Yale Classical Studies
ZECNT	Zondervan Exegetical Commentary on the New Testament
ZAW	*Zeitschrift für Alttestamentliche Wissenschaft*
ZNW	*Zeitschrift für die neutestamentliche Wissenschaft*
ZPE	*Zeitschrift für Papyrologie und Epigraphik*

Overview of the New Series

The Focus of *NewDocs* 11–17

Under the chief-editorship of Greg Horsley (vols. 1–5) and Stephen Llewelyn (vols. 6–10), each pentad of *New Documents Illustrating Early Christianity* presented translations of and commentaries on new papyri, inscriptions, and ostraca. These were selected by the editors from the new publications of the documentary material within a nominated time frame. Volumes 1–5, edited by Horsley, were philological in approach, culminating in the defining essay of the series in volume 5 where the myth of Septuagintal Greek was demythologized once and for all. Volumes 6–10, edited by Stephen Llewelyn, focused more on the social and administrative institutions, with a view to casting light on exegetical issues in the New Testament and its historical background. The series, written by Australian scholars associated with The Ancient History Documentary Research Centre of Macquarie University, rapidly acquired an international reputation for its illuminating contribution towards classical, New Testament, and Jewish studies.

Volumes 11–17 of *New Documents Illustrating Early Christianity* will concentrate on the epigraphic evidence of the Mediterranean cities that were the center of the early Christian mission in the first century CE and beyond. Rather than being solely a production of Australian scholars, the new series also draws upon an international team of scholars for each volume who have expertise in the epigraphy of each urban center. At any time, two volumes are being worked upon concurrently, with a view to finishing off the seven-volume series within a decade.

The material evidence relevant to the history and culture of each city—archaeology, iconography, and numismatics—is now more prominently brought into play in the scholarly discussions of the local epigraphy and its relation to the New Testament documents. The aim of the new series is to equip New Testament exegetes in situating more accurately the texts they are analyzing in their historical, political, civic, religious, cultural, and social context, as well as to make its own unique contribution to scholarship on urban antiquity.

NewDocs 11–17 remains a production of the Faculty of Arts, Department of History and Archaeology, at Macquarie University, Sydney, Australia.

The Structure and Progression of *NewDocs* 11–17

The structure of each volume, which will comprise two books (part A and part B), consists of

- an introduction to the history the city/cities being discussed and their epigraphy (part A);
- a section of (minimally) twenty-five translated inscriptions, with original texts and accompanying commentary (part A);
- a section of thematic essays, drawing on the local epigraphic evidence, relating to the religious, political, civic, social, cultural, and economic life of each city (part B);
- a section of exegetical essays, drawing on the local epigraphic evidence, discussing the New Testament documents relevant to each city (part B).

The progression of Mediterranean cities to be investigated in volumes 11–17 is as follows:

- 11: Ephesus;
- 12: Colossae, Laodicea, and Hierapolis;
- 13: Philippi;
- 14: Rome, Ostia, and Puteoli;
- 15: Thessalonica;
- 16: Ancyra, Pessinous, Pisidian Antioch, and the Galatian cities; and
- 17: Corinth, Cenchreae, and Isthmia.

Upon the completion of volume 17, the entire series of *New Documents Illustrating Early Christianity* will have reached its culmination. No further volumes are planned beyond these.

Methodological Issues Arising from a Study of Urban Epigraphy

In narrowing the focus of *NewDocs* 11–17 to a corpus of inscriptions from specific New Testament cities in the western and eastern Mediterranean basin, the new series abandons the focus of the previous pentads on newly published or reedited inscriptions, papyri, and ostraca from antiquity generally. Notwithstanding, recently published and reedited inscriptions of the cities from select publications will be included in volumes 11–17 (e.g., vol. 11A: Harrison, "The Wall Scribblers of Terrace House 2, Unit 6"; vol. 11B: Llewelyn and Robinson, "Epigram for a Young Slave [SEG 59.1318]"). Further, the philological and sociohistorical emphases of the two previous pentads will also be retained throughout in the various discussions of the documentary materials.

But by focusing on well-established and previously published epigraphic collections of the Mediterranean cities, readers may well wonder what is actually *new* about *New Documents Illustrating Early Christianity*, volumes 11–17. First, the series, in contrast to the two former pentads, adopts a new locality-based, corpus-concentrated, historically-focused, and materially-integrated (i.e., documentary, iconographic, numismatic, and archaeological) approach to each city. Second, as noted, newly published documents relevant to the relevant city/cities will still be incorporated in each volume. Third, there is a new exegetical emphasis to each volume, with several essays being allocated to precise textual engagements with New Testament pericopes and texts. In the current volume, for example, there are new exegetical and epigraphic engagements with the New Testament writings that either address the church generally or mention believers living in Ephesus (i.e., the Epistle to the Ephesians, Acts 19:1–41; Acts 20:17–38; Rev 2:1–7, and the Pastoral Epistles). In the case of Ephesus, we are especially well placed because the Ephesian epigraphic corpus is the largest Greek collection of inscriptions published. Horsley (1992, 121) estimated in 1992 that the Ephesian corpus comprised some 3,750 inscriptions, but undoubtedly this number has long since been exceeded.[1] For previous translations and commentaries on Ephesian inscriptions in *NewDocs* 1–10, see appendix 2 at the end of the book. Last, there are new commentaries in this volume on particular Ephesian inscriptions that

---

1. Knibbe and Iplikcioglu (1984, 10) estimated in 1982 that the number of inscriptions that had come to light in Ephesus since the beginning of systematic excavations have exceeded the five thousand mark.

have not garnered much academic attention beforehand, given the size of the epigraphic corpus of the city (e.g., Harrison, "Blessings of Harmonia"; Harrison, "Honoring the Concord of the Ephesian Demos").

However, because our approach is necessarily confined to the epigraphic corpora of the Mediterranean cities, we also face the methodological limitations posed by the epigraphic genre itself. Dieter Knibbe and Bülent Iplikcioglu (1984, 10) capture well the strengths and limitations of epigraphic evidence:

> They are to a certain extent eye-witnesses of historical moments, large ones, as well as smaller and the smallest ones. They report just as objectively the speech of an emperor or a decree by the council and the people of Ephesos, as they do the funeral of an unknown child. Their disadvantage is that they are merely flashes in the large framework of events, and that even their sum total does not provide a coherent historical picture.

Thus the ensuing historical overview of the development of Ephesus from the first millennium BCE to the Flavian period in the second century CE is absolutely crucial for a proper understanding of the selection of inscriptions translated and discussed in this volume.

Finally, despite the contemporaneity of the inscriptions with the events reported, we have to remember that certain groups from antiquity were invariably omitted from the purview of the inscriptions. Steven J. Friesen (2003, 150) highlights the "emancipatory rhetoric" that is required if we are to redirect our historical gaze to include various "overlooked" groups and individuals of antiquity:

> We tend to read the inscription and perhaps even consider the statue atop the inscribed base without thinking about its ancient urban context. An emancipatory rhetoric challenges us to lower our gaze from the statue, to glance around the base, and to consider those whose labour and lives are implied by the monument but whose voices have been silenced by the dominion of wealth, class, and gender. An emancipatory rhetoric forces us to think about the masons who quarried the stone for a pittance, the day labourers who moved the finished product into place in order to keep their relatives from starvation, and the wo/men who struggled to sustain their families on such meagre earnings.[2]

---

2. On Friesen's use of *wo/man*, borrowed from Elisabeth Schüssler Fiorenza, see Friesen 2003, 149. On marble quarrying at Ephesus, including the problems caused to

The advantage of a study of the intersection of the Graeco-Roman urban epigraphy with the New Testament documents is that the latter corpus intentionally redirects our vision, to borrow Paul's words, from the powerful, wise, and strong to the nothings of this world (1 Cor 1:28; cf. 11:22). In sum, we gain methodologically from a close contextual study of the New Testament unexpected perspectives regarding the lives of the marginalized in antiquity, routinely ignored by the status-obsessed inscribers of epigraphy.[3]

This volume of *NewDocs* is dedicated to Dr. Paul W. Barnett, Chairman of the Committee for *New Documents Illustrating Early Christianity*. Paul served as chairman from 1981 until his resignation on 22 February 2022, though he will continue as a committee member into the future. During his forty years of service as chairman, Paul has seen the transition of three *NewDocs* editors, each of whom he has encouraged in their production of each volume of the series. His commitment to the highest quality scholarship on Second Temple Judaism, the Graeco-Roman world, and the New Testament has meant that his academic advice and astute wisdom on the many issues faced by the committee over the years has been invaluable. Last, since Paul's first honoring in *NewDocs* 9 (2002) for his contribution as the *NewDocs* chairman and for his own productivity as a scholar in New Testament historical studies, a steady stream of new monographs in the discipline has continued to appear from him to this day.

Finally, some of the English translations of the Ephesian inscriptions in this volume are adapted from an unpublished course reader prepared for the Macquarie University Ancient History Department course unit, Cities of the Roman East: Ephesus and Aphrodisias, more than two decades ago. The course reader was compiled in 1999 through the (then) Ancient History Documentary Research Centre at Macquarie and reached its completion for undergraduate and postgraduate teaching in the year 2000.

---

the harbor by marble-sawing on the harbor-quay of the city, see Long 2012, 174–212. See the discussion of IEph 1a.23 in Harrison, "The Kaystros River and the Silting of the Ephesian Harbor," in this volume. Additionally, see Bowden, 2020.

3. In this volume, no judgment is made regarding whether Ephesians is a Pauline or pseudonymous epistle. Both possibilities are left open. The interest is more in how the language of the epistle, whoever its author might be, intersects with the Ephesian epigraphic corpus. The authors contributing to the volume adopt their own approach to the issue. For a succinct summary of the issues, see Trebilco 2022, 161–87.

Bibliography

Bowden, Anna M. V. 2020. *Revelation and the Marble Economy of Roman Ephesus: A People's History Approach.* Lanham, MD: Lexington/Fortress Academic.

Friesen, Steven J. 2003. "High Priestesses of Asia and Emancipatory Interpretation." Pages 136–50 in *Walk in the Ways of Wisdom: Essays in Honour of Elisabeth Schüssler Fiorenza.* Edited by Shelley Matthews, Cynthia Briggs Kittredge, and Melanie Johnson-DeBaufre. Harrisburg, PA: Trinity Press International.

Horsley, G. H. R. 1992. "The Inscriptions of Ephesos and the New Testament." *NovT* 34:105–68.

Knibbe, Dieter, and Bülent Iplikcioglu. 1984. *Ephesos in Spiegel seiner Inschriften.* Vienna: Schindler.

Long, Leah Emilia. 2012. "Urbanism, Art, and Economy: The Marble Quarrying Industries of Aphrodisias and Roman Asia Minor." PhD diss., University of Michigan.

Trebilco, Paul. 2022. "Reading Ephesians in Ephesos: A Letter to Pauline *and* Johannine Christ Followers?" Pages 161–87 in *Ephesos as a Religious Center under the Principate.* Edited by Allen Black, Christine M. Thomas, and Trevor W. Thompson. WUNT 488. Tübingen: Mohr Siebeck.

Introduction: Ephesus in Documentary Perspective

James R. Harrison

1. Ephesus from Its Origins to the Flavian Era: The Epigraphic, Literary, and Archaeological Evidence

1.1. Ephesus: From Androklos to Alexander the Great (323 BCE)

The name Ephesus was most likely the Hellenized form of the Anatolian name Apasa, used of the settlement by the mid-second millennium BCE.[1] In first-millennium BCE Hittite writings, Apasa referred to the main place of inhabitation or capital in "*Arzawa*-land." The latter term designated "a buffer zone between the Hittite Empire and the Mycenaean settlements on the coast" of Asia Minor (Scherrer 2000, 14). By that time the area was already inhabited by a Mediterranean people who were later called Carians and Leleges by the migrating Greeks (Pausanias, *Descr.* 7.2.6–9; see also 7.4.2–3). However, upon the dissolution of Mycenaean civilization in 1200 BCE when the Sea Peoples invaded from the north, the colonization movement from mainland Greece saw settlements established along the western coast of Asia Minor. Upon the arrival of the Greeks in the bay of Ephesus (Herodotus, *Hist.* 1.142; Vitruvius, *Arch.* 4.1.4), they decided to settle in the northern base of modern Panayir Dagh or ancient Mount Pion (Strabo, *Geogr.* 640). This first site of Ephesus had a natural harbor at the delta of the Kaystros river. This first period of Ephesian settlement,

---

1. The identification has not been undisputed. Originally, endorsing the identification, see Garstand and Gurney 1959, 88. Contra, see Bammer 1986–1987, 23–28, who suggests instead an unexplored site of Illecatepe, south of Kusadasi. On recent scholarly confidence that the initial identification of Apasa with Ephesus is correct, see Rykwert 1999, 446–47 n. 28. See especially Hawkin's (1998, 1, 10, 24, 22–25) work on the Karabel inscription, reaffirming the identification of Miletos with Millawanda/Milawata and of Ephesus as Apasa.

focused upon the old Ionian city, lasted from 1000 to 550 BCE.[2] Twelve cities were colonized in Asia Minor during the Greek migration movement overseas.[3] The Pan-Ionic League was established, with Ephesus assuming the privileged position, in Strabo's memorable turn of phrase (*Geogr.* 633), of being "the royal seat of the Ionians." On Ephesus and the Greek colonization movement, see Dominguez 1999. For the literary sources on Ephesus, Murphy-O'Connor 2008.

According to the foundation legend of Ephesus (Athenaeus, *Deipn.* 8.361d–e; Strabo, *Geogr.* 14.1.3–4; 14.1.21; Pausanias, *Descr.* 7.2.8–9; Ephoros, *FGrHist* 70 F 126), Androklos, son of the Athenian King Kodros (ca. 1089–1066 BCE), founded the city after fleeing from Greece, his escape probably being occasioned by the Dorian invasions. Upon arriving at Ephesus at the behest of an oracle, Androklos established a settlement there, expelling the local pre-Hellenic populations of the Lydians, Carians, and Leleges. The vital importance of this foundation myth is demonstrated by the production of reliefs and sculptures of the founder (at five Ephesian processional sites), numismatic legends (also accompanied by founder iconography), and the mention of the founder in several important inscriptions. This rich deposit of mythological evidence first appears in the Hellenistic Age and continued well into the late Roman Imperial period. For discussion, see Harrison, "Androklos, Founder of Ephesus," in this volume. For Androklos's heroon, see Scherrer 2000, 128. On paleogeographic issues regarding the identification of the site of Androklos's colony, see Kraft et al. 2007, 123–31. The descendants of Androklos, known as the Basilids, continued to rule at Ephesus, but the city, like other Greek city-states of the time, transitioned from monarchy to oligarchy and then to tyranny (e.g., Melas II, 580–570 BCE [Herodotus, *Hist.* 1.74]; Pindar or Pindaros, 570–550 BCE [Aelian, *Var. hist.* 3.26]).

A very important development in Ephesian sacral identity occurred during the Ionian period of settlement. The old indigenous female fertility deity of the region—a local variant of the Anatolian mother goddess Cybele—was identified with Artemis, goddess of the hunt, by the Greek immigrants and was incorporated into their pantheon, establishing a holy district where the later Artemision would eventually stand. On the mythi-

---

2. For discussion, see Knibbe and Iplikcioglu 1984, 13–15; Scherrer 2000, 14–17; Hueber, Erdemgil, and Büyükkolanci 1997, 30–33.

3. The cities, in addition to Ephesus, were Miletus, Myus, Lebedus, Colophon, Priene, Teos, Erythrae, Phocaea, Clazomenae, Chios, and Samos.

cal association of the Amazons with the foundation of the Artemision, see Strabo, *Geogr.* 11.5.3–4. The fame of Ephesian Artemis was soon established internationally, her power being demonstrated by the epiphany of the goddess to the Phocaeans (Strabo, *Geogr.* 4.1.4) and, to cite a much later imperial age example, by acts of soteriological deliverance from sorcery in second-century CE Sardis (*NewDocs* 10, §8 [165 CE]). See Graf 1992; Harrison 2012a.

On the Artemision generally, see Scherrer 2000, 126; Wiplinger and Wlach 1996, 20–21, 93–95, 107–9, 146–50; Knibbe and Iplikcioglu 1984, 40–45; Immendörfer 2017, 123–44. See also Immendörfer, "Ephesian Artemis and Her City," in *NewDocs* 11B. On the early Artemision, see Kerschner 2017; Kraft et al. 2007, 123–35. On the imperial Artemision, see Zabrana 2020. On the imperial worship of Artemis, see Auffarth 2017. On the Artemis cult generally, see Rogers 1991; Oster 1987; Horsley 1987; Kearsley 1992a; 1992b; Knibbe 1995. On indigenous and imperial cults generally at Ephesus, see Oster 1990; Friesen 1995; Walters 1995.

The second period of Ephesian settlement (550–300 BCE), centered upon the Greek city with strong Asiatic influences (i.e., the archaic-classical state), extended from the hegemony of Croesus to the commencement of the rule of Lysimachus (306 BCE), the Thracian king and one of Alexander's generals (306 BCE).[4] During this period time, the population would eventually inhabit the region near the Artemision south west of Ayasoluk in a new unfortified city, but, as we will see below, this occurred well after the construction of the Artemision. In the middle of the sixth century BCE, Ephesus came under the domination of the proverbially rich and powerful Lydian king Croesus after his siege of the city, though it was not actually captured due to a clever stratagem of the Ephesians (Herodotus, *Hist.* 1.26; Aelian, *Var. hist.* 3.26). Croesus erected the first temple to Ephesian Artemis (Vitruvius, *Arch.* 7.pref.16), the original building having been destroyed by a flood in the seventh century BCE (Pausanias, *Descr.* 7.7–8). Chersiphron was employed as its architect in ca. 570 BCE (Strabo, *Geogr.* 14.22–23; Pliny, *Nat.* 36.95–97), planning it according to the Ionic style. Furthermore, Croesus included Ephesus in his extravagant offerings to the cities of Hellas (Herodotus, *Hist.* 1.92) and unified the people within the city. On the history and archaeology of Croesus's campaign against Ephesus, see Leloux 2018.

---

4. Knibbe and Iplikcioglu 1984, 15–16; Scherrer 2000, 17–21; Hueber, Erdemgil, and Büyükkolanci 1997, 34–46.

Several important features of Ephesian life at this time are worth noting. First, our earliest Ephesian inscription (IEph 1a.1 [sixth century BCE]) comes from this period, providing us the oldest epigraphic record of an Ephesian sanctuary. The gifts of gold and silver mentioned in the document probably relate to the reconstruction of a sanctuary by Croesus (Reinach 1909, s.v. "Éphèse"), though it is not identified. Second, another important influence at the beginning of this period was the cosmology of the Ephesian philosopher Heraclitus (535–475 BCE), which set in motion a rich intellectual culture in the city that would contribute to the western philosophical tradition (Diogenes Laertius, *Vit.* 9.1–3). Third, the newly constructed Artemision of Croesus was located in the valley on the north side of the Marnas and Selinus Rivers, as opposed to the northern base of modern Panayir Dagh (ancient Mount Pion) where the original Ionian settlers resided. This eventually led to the first change of site of Ephesus when the inhabitants moved from down the hill to the valley where the Artemision was situated. Nevertheless, this did not happen until much later, probably ca. 409 BCE (Murphy-O'Connor 2008, 18–19).

The reign of Croesus, however, did not last long, the ruler being defeated by the Persian King Cyrus in 546 BCE in the battle of Halys. As a consequence, Ephesus came under Persian rule until the liberation of Greece from the Persian invasion of mainland Greece at the battles of Salamis (480 BCE) and Plataea (479 BCE). The initial attachment of Ephesus to the maritime Delian League of Greek city-states under the leadership of Athens—note Themistocles's visit to Ephesus in 471 BCE (Thucydides, *Hist.* 1.136.3)—would normally have extended to support for the Athenian cause during the protracted Peloponnesian War (431–404 BCE). But Ephesus later sided with Sparta, the war's ultimate victor, providing an important place of anchorage for the Spartan general Lysander (Diodorus Siculus, *Bib. hist.* 13.103.3–4). Indeed, Ephesus was listed among the allies of Lysander at the battle of Aegespotami (405 BCE: Pausanias, *Descr.* 10.9.9) where the Spartans defeated the Athenian fleet.

Upon the defeat of Athens and its allies by Sparta in the Peloponnesian War—the Spartan admiral Lysander having visited Ephesus in 405 BCE (Diodorus Siculus, *Bib. hist.* 13.103.3–4)—Ephesus continued its political attachment to Sparta. The Spartan King Agesilaus later visited the city in 396 BCE (Xenephon, *Hell.* 3.4.3–8; Plutarch, *Lys.* 3.2–3) and trained his troops there in the following year (Xenephon, *Hell.* 3.4.3, 3.4.16–17). The reason for Agesilaus's mobilization of his troops was that Sparta had begun its military engagement against the new coalition of Thebes, Athens, and

Argos in the Corinthian War (395–387 BCE), an alliance of Greek states which was supported by the Achaemenid (i.e., Persian) Empire. However, upon significant Athenian successes towards the end of the Corinthian War (Pausanias, *Descr.* 2.17.4; Plutarch, *Lys.* 5.1; *Alc.* 36.5–6), the Persian king became increasingly concerned by the specter of renewed Athenian imperialism and decided instead to side with Sparta. Upon the establishment in 387 BCE of the so-called King's Peace (the Peace of Antalcidas), Persia resumed control of Ionian Asia Minor, declaring all other Greek states autonomous in order to forestall the emergence of any further leagues and coalitions and commissioning Sparta to be the guardian of the peace. Thus Ionian Ephesus remained under Persian control until the advent of Alexander the Great, the Macedonian general and king. Alexander invaded Asia Minor in reprisal for the two Persian invasions of Greece (492–490, 480–479 BCE), conquering the Persians in 334 BCE at the battle of Granicus. The victorious Alexander made an offer to the Ephesians to rebuild the temple of Artemis (Arrian, *Anab.* 1.17), which had been recently burnt down by an arsonist called Herostratus in 356 BCE (Strabo, *Geogr.* 14.1.22; Plutarch, *Alex.* 3.5–6; Aulus Gellius, *Noct. att.* 2.6.18; Valerius Maximus, *Fact. et dict.* 8.14, ext. 5). However, Alexander's offer was diplomatically declined by the Ephesians (Strabo, *Geogr.* 14.1.22).[5] The temple was subsequently reconstructed after 323 BCE on an even grander scale. Pliny the Elder describes the temple as having 127 columns, each 60 feet in height, having been adorned with sculptural reliefs and carved by the famous sculptor Scopas (*Nat.* 36.21). For a brief history of the building of the Artemision, see Strabo, *Geogr.* 14.22–23. On its status as one of the seven wonders of the world, see Philo of Byzantium (*Sept. mirac.* 7 [second century BCE]; cf. Pausanias, *Descr.* 4.31.8; Herodotus, *Hist.* 2.148). Regarding its use as a bank, see Dio Chrysostom, *Cel. Phryg.* 35.54.

In an important sidelight to this period, an inscription (IEph 1a.2 [second half of the fourth century BCE]) highlights the sensitivities associated with the worship of Artemis in a legal case where death sentences were ordered for religious outrages perpetrated in Sardis. Apparently, some inhabitants of the city had insulted a sacred embassy, consisting

---

5. Scherrer (2000, 17) comments that Herostratus "was probably put up to it by the priesthood with the aim of relacing the old Croesus building which was slowly sinking in the ground water. The cautious Ephesians fearing for their independence and that of their shrine refused Alexander's offer to rebuild one temple with the polite excuse that it would be unseemly for the one god to donate a temple to another god."

of priests and ambassadors, who had been dispatched from Ephesus to Sardis in order to present "robes to Artemis in accordance with ancestral custom." For discussion, Sokolowski 1965.

1.2. Ephesus: From the Early Hellenistic Age to the Triumph of Augustus (31 BCE)

The struggle for power among Alexander's generals and "successors" (*diadochoi*) resulted in the establishment of the Seleucid dynasty when Lysimachus became king of Thrace in 306 BCE, ruling Macedon, Thrace, and Asia Minor.[6] The alertness of Ephesus to the delicate politics and shifting alliances as power transitioned from Alexander to his generals is seen in the Ephesian cultivation of key Macedonian luminaries, including some of their generals, who were passing through the region at the time. This large corpus of seventy-seven Hellenistic citizenship decrees from Ephesus was originally inscribed at the site of the Artemision (IEph 4.1408–1413, 1417–1445; 5.1447–1476; 6.2002–2016), emphasizing thereby its fundamental importance. The purpose of the allocation of the Ephesian citizenship grants to powerful Macedonian players was clear: to negotiate the democratic independence of Ephesus and the sanctity of its Artemision, both before and after the time of Alexander's death in 323 BCE.

On this period, see Harrison, "The Citizenship Decrees of Hellenistic Ephesus," in *NewDocs* 11B. Ephesus would continue to exercise a clever balancing act until the 280's, oscillating "between tyranny, oligarchy, and democracy," while "carefully honouring partisans and apparatchiks of each Successor regime at appropriate moments" (Davies 2011, 193). This political adeptness on the part of Ephesus—apart from the serious mistake of supporting the revolt of Mithridates VI in 88 BCE, which precipitated subsequently the savage Roman revenge at the hands of Sulla in 84 BCE—continued right down to their careful balancing of the competing interests of the Roman triumvirs Antony and Octavian (the future Augustus) in the unstable period of the late republican 30s.

In 300 BCE, King Lysimachus founded a new city Arsinoë, named after his wife, next to the small town founded by Croesus at the Artemision. This Hellenistic city corresponds to the ruins of Ephesus today,

---

6. On Hellenistic Ephesus, see Scherrer 2000, 17–21; Hueber, Erdemgil, and Büyükkolanci 1997, 39–46.

located at the western base of Mount Pion and in the narrow valley south of Mount Pion and northwest of Mount Koressos. The new city, now the second change of site for ancient Ephesus, was designed in a grid pattern of streets that met at right angles. It was enclosed by massive fortification walls erected by Lysimachus, reaching 10 meters in height and extending 9.6 kilometers in length. The inscription IEph 1a.3 (290 BCE) sets out specifications for the wall, including its towers, route, quarries, and road/water transportation for the stones. See, too, the edict of the proconsul M. Herennius Picens from the Augustan period noting the disappearance of the cross-wall "because of some vicissitude of fate or the war or because of the carelessness of [those in charge]" (IEph 5.1521). On the city of Lysimachus, see Kraft et al. 2007, 135–39, who propose that "Lysimachus was probably quite far-sighted and an excellent town planner" (135). Peter Scherrer (2000, 18) suggests that there were two practical reasons for Lysimachus building of the city: (1) the replacement of the old silted-up harbor in the old city of Croesus at the foot of Panayir Dagh and (2) the periodic flooding of the Artemision due to the rising water table. Either way, the prestige of the royal house of the Thracian king as hegemon of Asia Minor was greatly enhanced by such a construction.[7] To ensure the viability and longevity of the city, Lysimachus also forced the small nearby communities of Colophon, Teos, and Lebedos to move into the city in a *synoikism* ("a joining together": Pausanias, *Descr.* 1.9.7; 7.3.4–5).

However, in 281 BCE, a Seleucid-Ptolemaic coalition—ironically "an alliance of his colleagues" (Knibbe and Iplikcioglu 1984, 15)—defeated and killed Lysimachus at the battle of Corupendium (Nepos, *Reg.* 21.3.2). The identity of his city, Arsinoë, did not survive his demise as ruler. Finally, to the same period belongs a long and intricate debt law (IEph 1a.4 [297/296 BCE]), which Guy MacLean Rogers suggests (2012, 55) "may well be connected to assaults by Lysamachos upon Ephesian estates during 'the common war' between Demetrios and Lysamachos." For further discussion, see Lund 1992, 84–85.

After the dissolution of Lysimachus's hegemony over Ephesus, the city became part of the Seleucid Empire until the death of King Antiochus

---

7. By contrast, Knibbe and Iplikcioglu (1984, 15) suggest the following: "The reason for Lysimachus' decision to re-settle the city was to restore its link with the sea, which it had lost long ago because of the silting up of the bay. Perhaps he also wished to loosen the city's close bonds with the Artemision, which had burnt down in the year 356 BC and which had been rebuilt to be even larger and more resplendent."

II Theos in 246 BCE, whereupon the city fell under the control of Ptolemaic Egypt for several decades. But the Seleucid King Antiochus III again wrested Ephesus away from the Ptolemaic dynasty at the beginning of the second century BCE, only to be defeated soon after by the Romans at Magnesia (190 BCE). According to the stipulations of the Peace of Apamea (188 BCE), Antiochus III ceded all control of Asia Minor north of the Taurus Mountains (Polybius, *Hist.* 21.48). The rulers of the Attalid kingdom of Pergamum, whose king, Eumenes II, had sided with the Romans against the Seleucids, became loyal client-kings of Rome. Consequently, the Attalids of Pergamum were rewarded with huge tracts of western Asia Minor, including Ephesus. The last Attalid king, Attalus III, bequeathed his entire kingdom to Rome in his will in 129 BCE, thereby leading to the establishment of the Roman Province of Asia (Strabo, *Geogr.* 13.4.2; Livy, *Epit.* 58).

During this period, several inscriptions provide interesting sidelights into the second century BCE Ephesus. First, an honorific decree eulogizing the gymnasiarch Diodorus (IEph 1a.6 [second century BCE]) affords us keen insight into the *paideia* experienced by the young elite males at the gymnasium of Ephesus. See Harrison, "Sponsors of *Paideia*," in *NewDocs* 11B. Second, further insight into *paideia* can be gleaned from the effusive letter of Attalus II (IEph 2.202) praising the Ephesian tutor of his brother's son. However, the name of the tutor, Aristo[---], is only partially preserved. For discussion, see Saunders 1998. Third, an Ephesian decree (IEph 1a.5 [end of second century BCE]) reveals that the island of Astypalaia offered effective resistance to pirates, rescuing Ephesian citizens from the very considerable threat posed by these stateless outlaws. For discussion, see Souza 1999, 100–101; 2008, 85.

Upon Rome's assumption of provincial rule in Asia, her governors reaffirmed the preexisting arrangements of (1) the sacrosanctity of Ephesian temple lands, (2) the tax-free status of old cities like Ephesus as *civitates liberae et immunes*, and (3) the freedom of Ephesian government. However, the exploitative role of the Roman tax farmers precipitated the invasion of Asia Minor by Mithridates VI Eupator of Pontus in 89 BCE. Because Rome was preoccupied with the unrest among her Italian allies over the privileges of the Roman citizenship during the period of the Social War (91–87 BCE), this was the perfect time for Mithridates to revolt. The Ephesians greeted Mithridates favorably upon his arrival in the city (88 BCE), overthrowing all the Roman statues erected in the city because of the widespread frustration felt in Asia towards the avaricious Roman tax-collectors, bankers and merchants (Appian, *F.W.* 3.21). Even more remarkably, the Ephesians violated the sanctity of their Artemision by murdering blameless Romans who had sought asylum in its precincts (Appian, *M.W.* 12.4.23). However, when Athens was captured by the Roman general, L. Cornelius Sulla, in 86 BCE, Ephesus quickly changed sides to Rome. But this dramatic shift in alliance did not save Ephesus from Rome's fury later on. When Sulla entered Ephesus in 84 BCE, he killed those who had sided with Mithridates in revolting against Rome, imposed on the Ephesian citizenry taxes for five years to be paid all at once (including war costs), and, finally, deprived the city of its freedom by imposing regular Roman taxes to be collected by the *publicani* (Appian, *F.W.* 9.61–62). Moreover, the short-term agreement that the Romans had negotiated with Mithridates did not last long. Mithridates relaunched his invasion of Asia Minor, Cappodocia and Pontus, but he was eventually defeated by the later Roman triumvir, Pompey, during the Third Mithridatic War (74–63 BCE).

By the time of the civil war in the late Roman republic, Ephesus had adeptly reconciled itself to the fluctuations of political power occurring at Rome and had already become indebted to Julius Caesar. After the battle of Pharsalus (48 BCE [Caesar, *Bell. civ.* 3.105.2]), Ephesus was visited by Caesar, who kept the Artemision on two occasions from being plundered by Metellus Scipio and by a renegade partisan of Pompey called T. Ampius (Caesar, *Bell. civ.* 3.33.1–2; 3.105.1–2). Consequently, an inscription from Ephesus in that year eulogizes Julius Caesar (IEph 2.251) as "descended from Ares and Aphrodite, a god made manifest and common Savior of humanity." After the assassination of Julius Caesar in 44 BCE, Ephesus came under the control of the Second Triumvirate at Rome (43–32 BCE), comprising the triumvirs Mark Antony, Marcus Aemilius Lepidus, and Octavian, the future ruler Augustus. During the triumviral years Mark Antony visited Ephesus on two occasions (41, 34/33 BCE), in the former case being accosted as Dionysos "Giver of Joy and Beneficent," in the latter case accompanied by his consort Cleopatra (Plutarch, *Ant.* 24.3; 56.1). The Ephesian acknowledgement of the triumvirs at this time is demonstrated by a bronze coin minted at Ephesus, which shows Antony, Octavian, and Lepidus on the obverse, with the reverse displaying the statue of Artemis (*RPC* 1.2572). Furthermore, upon the senatorial decree endorsing the apotheosis of Caesar in 42 BCE, a Roman decree was erected at Ephesus (41 BCE?) regarding the cult of Divus Julius (IEph 7.2.4324).

Four important inscriptions belong to the first century BCE, one being linked to a famous public honorific monument in the city of Ephesus.

First, in an extensive inscription (IEph1a.7 [98/97 or 94/93]) predating the outbreak of the Mithridatic war, the proconsul of Asia in 94–93 BCE, Quintus Mucius Scaevola, establishes a treaty between Ephesus and Sardis, articulating the responsibilities for both parties. Here we see how Rome could intervene in its provinces to ensure stability of relations between the city-states located therein.

Second, in IEph 1a.8 (86/85 BCE), we encounter two decrees regarding the war against Mithridates. The first decree states the loyalty of Ephesus to Rome and sets forth the decision of the demos to declare war against Mithridates, whereas the second decree articulates the measures required to strengthen Ephesian readiness for war, opening up the citizenship in this time of emergency to all free residents. What is intriguing is the dramatic shift in attitude to Mithridates from the original welcome given to him earlier at Ephesus in 88 BCE. Now, barely two years later (86/85 BCE), Mithridates is roundly dismissed as deceitful and intimidating in what is clearly an epigraphic rewriting of history at the Ephesian end:

> Mithridates the king of Cappadocia transgressed the treaties with Rome and collecting forces attempted to become master of territory in no way belonging to him, and having occupied beforehand the cities lying before us by deceit he also conquered our city having terrified (it) by the size of his forces and the unexpectedness of his attack.[8]

Third, a letter of Octavius to Ephesus (Reynolds 1982, §12 [36 BCE]) requests the Ephesians to remove a golden Eros—acquired by Ephesus from war loot—that the Ephesians had offered to Artemis in the Artemision. Such a dedication was totally inappropriate in Octavian's view because his father had originally dedicated the Eros as an offering to Aphrodite in Aphrodisias, as opposed to dedicating it to Artemis at Ephesus. Here we are witnessing another instance of the dishonorable use of honorific statues, a phenomenon which appears elsewhere in the Ephesian epigraphic corpus (IEph 1a.25.1–28). See Harrison, "Dishonoring the Honored" and "The Problem of *Invidia*," in this volume.

---

8. Note, however, the perceptive comment of Davies (2011, 200) who considers that the Ephesians in IEph 1a.8 are "emphasising the city's loyalty to Rome in their preamble while simultaneously adopting most of the populist agenda which Mithridates VI of Pontus had been promulgating."

Last, a Latin inscription (IEph 2.403 [third quarter of the first century BCE]) is found on the western side frieze of an honorific monument, honoring C. Memmius, the grandson of Sulla, the dictator and general of Rome: "To Gaius Memmius, son of Gaius Memmius, grandson of Sulla Felix, (paid for this monument) from his own money." The status of Memmius and the reason for the erection of the monument is not mentioned, though it is likely that he was the *consul suffectus* in 34 BCE at Rome (*RE* 15.618, no. 10; Olson 2013, 113). This tower-like structure, reminiscent of Hellenistic tombs and monuments, had four levels. The monument was located prominently at the eastern end of the Embolos (Kuretes Street) in Ephesus.[9] First, there was a high podium base, surmounted by a three-stepped crepidoma, upon which the entire structure stood. Second, an impression of a triumphal arch at the first story was cleverly conveyed by the niches on its three main facades. Here were placed reliefs of dancing Caryatids, which supported the arches of the niches. Third, on the second story, the reliefs of three standing male togate figures on plaques "have been interpreted as members of Memmius' family and personifications of his characteristic virtues" (Scherrer 2000, 86). The three figures have been putatively identified as Sulla, his son-in-law, and his grandson Memmius. Mallios Yorgos (2002, 3), however, has challenged this construct, arguing that two of the figures "probably depicted mythological/heroic figures." For discussion of the Memmius monument reliefs, see Alzinger 1971, 101–7; for the reliefs, see 100, plates 90–91; 103, plates 92–93; Scherrer 2000, 96; Yorgos 2002. Fourth, a pyramidal roof stood on a richly decorated cylindrical tympanum.

This very public honoring of a grandson of Sulla had considerable symbolic significance when one remembers the Ephesian overturning of Roman statues in Ephesus and the slaughter of innocent Romans in the Artemision in 88 BCE. Ephesus had paid a heavy penalty for their anti-Roman activities subsequently at the hands of Sulla in 84 BCE. The new realities of Roman power in Asia now demanded from Ephesus a permanent reorientation in honorific protocols and an astute accommodation to Roman rule in the province. For what reason and by whom was the Memmius monument erected? And what was the reason for a hated enemy (Sulla) being mentioned so prominently at Ephesus in the late first century BCE? The

---

9. Scherrer (2000, 86) notes regarding the Memmius monument: "Its re-erection as an architectural pastiche is more a modern interpretation than an illustration of an ancient edifice."

suggestion of Yorgos (2002, 5, translation slightly adapted) has cogency: "The hypothesis that the monument, a work of Roman architectural conception, designed by an Italian architect, was funded by Italian inhabitants of the town who referred to C. Memmius and his ancestor C. Sulla with gratitude, emphasizing their particular status as conquerors in the province of Asia, cannot be far from the truth." Additionally, Schowalter (2022, 141) attributes the erection of the monument to the considerable civic status that Memmius himself had acquired: "One would expect that Sulla's demands for retribution from the city would certainly not be remembered fondly, but somehow his grandson had gained status in the city that merited or at least allowed for the erection of his monument." On the outfitting of the Memmius monument with a fountain on the west side of the building in the Augustan period and the link between the provision of this water and the Memmius family as civic heroes, see Weiss 2011, 91–97.

Finally, Augustus triumphed over Antony and Cleopatra at the battle of Actium in 31 BCE, establishing the unrivaled ascendancy of the Julian house over the old republican noble houses, many members of which had been killed during the civil war. A seismic shift in power relations had occurred that would reshape politics in the ancient world for centuries to come. An ancestral law, summarized in a third-century CE inscription (IEph 1a.10.13–15), captures well the shift in attitude of the Ephesians to their Roman overlords. Upon the daily animal sacrifices to the gods, the worshipers "are to sing the paeans at the sacrifices, at the processions and at the night festivals which must be held according to the ancestral practices and at which it is necessary to pray on behalf of the sacred senate and the people of Rome and the people of Ephesus."

1.3 Ephesus: From Julio-Claudian to Flavian Rule

Preface

This section will discuss the epigraphic evidence relating to (1) Ephesian engagement with the rulers and family members of the Julio-Claudian and Flavian houses, (2) the various letters of the Roman rulers to the Ephesians, and (3) the development of city facilities and building structures under imperial patronage or via dedications to the ruler by other benefactors during the period.

The arrival of the first Christians (Acts 18:24–20:1; 1 Cor 15:32; 16:8; Eph 1:1; 1 Tim 1:3; 2 Tim 1:18; 4:12; Rev 2:1–7; Acts John 37–54) and the ultimate triumph of their heirs at Ephesus is therefore bypassed. For discussion, see C. Arnold 1992; Strelan 1996; Trebilco 2004; Witetschek 2008; Immendörfer 2017; Tellbe 2009; Karaman 2018; Georges 2017, 223–357; Baugh 1990. On Ephesus and the believers living there in late antiquity, see Foss 1979; Pülz 2020; Koester 1995. On the triumph of Christianity, see Scherrer 2000, 32–33; Knibbe and Iplikcioglu 1984, 49–52. On imperial Ephesus, see Scherrer 1995; 2000, 21–32; White 1995; Hueber, Erdemgil, and Büyükkolanci 1997, 54–91. On late antique Christian epigraphy at Ephesus, see Harrison, "The Life of Christians in Late Antique Ephesus," in *NewDocs* 11B.

Also omitted is the celebrated arrival of Apollonius of Tyana at Ephesus (Philostratus, *Vit. Apoll.* 4.1), his upbraiding of the Ephesian citizenry for their soft living (4.2), his prediction of a plague at Ephesus (4.4), his address of the Ephesians on the death of Domitian (8.26), the fictional letters of Apollonius to Ephesus (*Ep. Apoll.* 32), and his death at Ephesus (*Vit. Apoll.* 8.30). On philosophers at Ephesus, see Harrison 2018, 50–52 n.169.

Further, our sharp focus on the Julio-Claudian and Flavian rulers excludes any discussion of Ephesian cultic religion, civic life, elite benefaction, social relations, and popular culture in the imperial era. Nevertheless, many of these emphases appear in the commentaries of this volume. They are more extensively treated in the thematic and exegetical essays of *NewDocs* 11B, the table of contents of which may be consulted in appendix B of this book. Last, an extensive discussion of these issues is found in Harrison 2018; cf. also Knibbe and Iplikcioglu 1984, 29–45.

The officialdom of Ephesus has been well explored elsewhere. On the asiarchs, see Kearsley 1986; 1987; 1990; Friesen 1999; Witetschek 2009. On the *grammateus*, see Harrison, "An Incomparable Secretary," in this volume. On the *curetes*, see Hoag 2013, 124–27. On the priestesses of Artemis, see Harrison 2012b; Rogers, "Some Priestesses of Artemis of Ephesos," in *NewDocs* 11B. On the *neopoios*, see Harrison 2012d. For additional discussion, see Knibbe and Iplikcioglu 1984, 22–23. On civic administration generally in Asia Minor, see Dmitriev 2005. Notwithstanding, there still remain many Ephesian officials to be more fully researched. On the base of the social pyramid, the slave, and, conversely, high status freedmen, see Harrison 2018, 29–42.

Agonistic culture, festivals, and processional culture in Ephesus has been investigated extensively elsewhere and need not be pursued here. On gladiatorial contests, see Grossschmidt, Ganz, and Müzesi 2002; Robert 1940, §§198–222; on Asia more generally, Carter 1999, 194–207. On athletic culture, see Brunet 1998; 2003. On festivals, see J. Arnold 1972. On processional culture, Portefaix 1993: Rogers 1991. Generally, see Harrison 2018, 42–49.

The ancient economy of Ephesus has also gained scholarly traction in recent years, as well as of the Roman province of Asia more generally. On the political and economic role of the local sanctuary, see Dignas 2002. On the Roman taxation system in Asia, see Cottier et al. 2009. On benefaction in Asia Minor, see Zuiderhock 2009. More generally, see Levick 2004; Mitchell and Katsari 2005. On the social viability of Revelation's stinging critique of the man-made idolatry associated with the marble trade (Rev 9:20), including the call for the withdrawal from all cultural participation (18:4), see Bowden 2020. On the marble trade in Asia, see Long 2012. On IEph 1a.23 in this regard, see Harrison, "The Kaystros River and the Silting of the Ephesian Harbor," in this volume. Attention should also be paid to the market prices of ordinary goods revealed in the Ephesian graffiti: see Harrison, "Wall Scribblers of Terrace House 2, Unit 6," in this volume.

Finally, the history of the archaeological excavations at Ephesus and the villages of the Kaystros valley, including especially its consequences for the collation of the modern epigraphic and numismatic corpus of the city, is explored in Harrison 2015, 24–29; Horsley 1992; Knibbe and Iplikcioglu 1984, 19–21. For the archaeology and epigraphy of the villages and cities in the Kaystros valley, see Meriç 2009; Ricl 2020. For a discussion of the epigraphy of the Ephesian villages, see Harrison 2024.

What, then, does the Ephesian epigraphy reveal about the interactions between Ephesus and the Julio-Claudian and Flavian rulers during the New Testament period? For the renovations made to buildings and the establishment of new structures in Ephesus during the period, with references to the Ephesian epigraphic corpus, see Bammer 1988, 156–57. For a catalogue of building-associated inscriptions from early imperial Ephesus, see Kalinowski 1996, 213–28. For a discussion of the imperial context of Ephesians, see Winzenburg 2022.

The Reign of Augustus (31 BCE–14 CE)

A wide variety of inscriptions honoring Augustus and his family are found at Ephesus. An imperial decree, found in a house above the Nymphaeum Traiani, sets out the stipulations regarding the cultic honoring of the dead Augustus and his house (IEph 4.1393.3 ["to the memory of the god Augustus"]) by means of sacrifices and drink-offerings. Also a dedication, erected by the imperial freedmen Mazaios and Mithridates (IEph 7.1.3006 [3 BCE]) at the south side of the southeastern triple gateway of the Agora, is offered to Augustus, Livia, Agrippa, and Julia. A Latin and Greek inscription, found in various locations of Ephesus, honors the family of Germanicus: Drusus Iulius Caesar, Nero Iulius Caesar, and Agrippina, the wife of Germanicus (IEph 2.256 [13 BCE / 23 CE]; cf. the decree of the Demetriastai honoring the sons of Drusus the Younger [IEph 7.2.4337 [19/20 CE]). An association of *neoi* from the gymnasium honor the "god Augustus, son of a god" (IEph 2.252), while a Latin inscription has also been found on a base in honor of Lucius Caesar (IEph 7.1.3007 [7 BCE / 2 CE]). In 11 CE, a temenos of Divus Julius and Dea Roma is dedicated to Artemis, Augustus, Tiberius, and the city of Ephesus (IEph 2.404). Finally, several inscriptions reveal the epistolary interactions of Augustus and his family members with the *gerousia* of Ephesus regarding the endorsement of their privileges. For example, Octavian: *JÖAI* 62:119, no. 11a.1–6 (48/47–27 BCE); 113, no.1.1–6 (48/47–27 BCE); 114, no. 2–7.7–16 (29 BCE). For example, M. Agrippa: *JÖAI* 62:115, no. 6.48–50 (17–14 BCE). For full discussion and translations of the inscriptions, see Bailey 2006.

Upon the victory of Augustus at Actium in 31 BCE, Ephesus became the residence for the Proconsul of Asia in 29 BCE, taking over the role of capital of Asia that the city of Pergamon had formerly held. The role of the Ephesian boule, the traditional Ephesian cults, and the imperial cult now seamlessly intersected in the civic life of the city. An increase in public building through the agency of the local elites and other upwardly mobile aspirants occurred, as these luminaries sought to acquire civic status in heated public competition for precedence. Two pertinent examples are the erection of the triple gateway of Mazaeus and Mithridates (IEph 7.1.3006 [4–3 BCE]), noted above, and the *stoa basilikê* of Gaius Sextilius Pollio (IEph 2.404), dedicated to Augustus. On the prominence of the leading family of the Vedii at Roman Ephesus, well known epigraphically for more than a century in the city, see Kalinowski 2021. Note especially the remarkable roll-call of family honor recounted in an inscription honoring a young priestess of Artemis, the daughter of Vedius Servilius Gaius (IEph 7.1.3072).

However, several inscriptions point to the improvement of city amenities through the munificence of Augustus himself. Several civic benefactions involve the Artemision and its environs. On a stela of white marble, built into the encirclement wall of the Artemision, there is reference to new measurements of the ways and canals in the possession of the temple of Artemis (IEph 5.1523–1524 [6/5 BCE]). Additionally, there is mention of the restoration of the sacred processional way of Artemis by means of Augustus's beneficence (SEG 41.971 [22–21 BCE]), the restoration of the boundaries of Artemis's land (*ZPE* 120:83, no. 1 [late first century BCE]), and the building of the encirclement wall of the Artemision (IEph 5.1522 [5 BCE]), which was subsequently repaired in the same year (IEph 5.1523). Furthermore, the aqueduct bearing the name "aqua Iulia" was built (IEph 2.401; cf. 2.414), along with the aqueduct named "aqua Throessitica" (IEph 2.402 [4–14 CE]). In the latter case, both Augustus and his adoptive son, Tiberius, are the donors. For discussion, see Weiss 2011, 83–85. On the processional way, see Thür 1995. On Augustan beneficence at Ephesus, see Harrison 2012c.

The Reign of Tiberius (14–37 CE)

In addition to an honorary inscription for Germanicus Caesar (IEph 2.255A [4/19 CE]), there is also a dedication of a statue for the health of Tiberius and the permanence of the Roman hegemony (IEph 2.510–514A). See Harrison, "Long Live Rome!," in this volume. As was the case with Augustus, there are several epistolary interactions of Tiberius and his family members with the *gerousia* of Ephesus affirming their ongoing privileges. For example, *JÖAI* 62:114, no. 3.17–27 (12/13 CE). For example, Germanicus: *JÖAI* 62:115, no. 4.26a–37 (18 CE). For example, Gaius or Germanicus: *JÖAI* 62:115, no. 5.38–47 (4 CE or 18 CE). From this time onward, the letters relating to the ratification of the privilege of the *gerousia* were sent by the Roman proconsul as opposed to the Roman ruler. Last, after the serious earthquake in Ephesus in 23 CE, devastating Hellenistic private houses on the lower Bubuldag slope, various rebuilding programs commenced: Terrace Houses 1 and 2 (Harrison, "The Wall Scribblers of Terrace House 2, Unit 6," in this volume; Ladstätter 2013) and the new Tetragonos Agora, finally finished in the Neronian era (IEph.7.1.3003 [54/55 CE]). For discussion, see Scherrer 1995, 7–8.

The Reign of Caligula (37–41 CE)

Our epigraphic evidence from Ephesus regarding Caligula is especially thin. An inscription from "the cities of Asia and the peoples and nations," found in the Byzantine aqueduct (IEph 2.251 [37–41 CE]), honors Gaius Caligula with these words: "the manifest god from Ares and Aphrodite and (the) common savior of humanity." Gaius is further honored on a statue base (IEph 3.684). In terms of city amenities, Suetonius (*Cal.* 21) informs us that Gaius had intended to finish the temple to Didymaean Apolllo at Ephesus.

The Reign of Claudius (41–54 CE)

An assembly (*conventus*) of Roman citizen negotiators in Asia (IEph 7.1.3019 [43/44 CE]) honors Claudius. Such Italian assemblies are well known from the literary and epigraphic record from the second century BCE through to the fourth century CE. They convened to practice their religion, socialize, and conduct business, and, in the process, they often became the nucleus for forming new colonies and municipia civium Romanorum ("towns of Roman citizens"). There is also a dedication to Claudius from the heirs of the will of Tiberius (IEph 2.259B [41/54 CE]). Last, in an important inscription found in the theater of Ephesus, the proconsul of Asia, Paullus Fabius Persicus, enacts a decree banning the corrupt sale of priesthoods in the imperial cult (IEph 1a.17–18 [44 CE]). For discussion, see Soon, "Economic Conflagration of the Sacred Cult and Early Christian Preservation of Sacred Funds," in this volume.

The Reign of Nero (54–68 CE)

There is a dedication in Latin and Greek to Artemis Ephesia, Divus Claudius, Nero, Agrippina, and the demos of Ephesus by a dedicator—whose name is missing due to the damage to the stone—and his wife Claudia Metrodora on an architrave of the wall of Agora (IEph.7.1.3003 [54/55 CE]).[10] A similar dedication to Artemis Ephesia and Nero (IEph 2.411 [54/68 CE]) has been made by Stertinius Orpex in a foundation endowment, discovered in a building inscription from the west front of the stadium. Of considerable importance is the inscription, dedicated to Nero and to Julia Agrippina Augusta, his mother (IEph 1a.20 [54–59 CE]), listing the material and monetary contributions made for the erection of the toll house of the fishermen and fishmongers in the harbor of Ephesus.

---

10. Note the observation of van Tilborg (1996, 184): "After Nero, the first dedication to a member of the imperial family is in the time of Domitian and again it is the wife who receives the honour."

For discussion, see Horsley 1989; *pace*, Friesen 2022; Ascough, "Associating with Ephesian Associations," in *NewDocs* 11B.

The stadium was restructured and refurbished to its present monumental shape by C. Stertinius Orpex and his wife Stertina Murena (IEph 2.411; 7.2.4123). Last, another dedication to Nero has been discovered at an aqueduct in Ephesus (IEph 2.260 [59/60 CE]), as well as an inscription where Nero's name is partially erased in *damnatio memoriae* (IEph 2.410; similarly, 2.411). On honor and dishonor, see in this volume: Harrison, "The Problem of *Invidia*"; Harrison, "A Seafarer's Reward"; Harrison, "Dishonoring the Honored"; Bitner, "Noble and Well Born"; Soon, "They Love to Have the Place of Honor."

The Reign of Vespasian (69–79 CE)

Remarkably, the vast majority of honorific references to Vespasian in the Ephesian epigraphic corpus are inscribed interpolations of the name of Domitian, which had been erased from the inscription in a *damnatio memoriae* (IEph 2.232A, 2.233–235, 2.238, 2.241, 2.249, 5.1498, 6.2048). There are, however, fleeting references to the "neokorate temple of the god Vespasian" (IEph 3.710B, 3.710C), the "god Vespasian" (IEph 7.2.5102), and "an honor of Imperator Caesar Vespasian" (IEph 3.701). On neokorate Ephesus, see Friesen 1993 and, more generally, Burrell 2004.

The Reign of Titus (79–81 CE)

In IEph 2.412 (79/81 CE), we encounter another dedication for the health of the Roman ruler Titus and the permanence of the Roman hegemony, employing the same phraseology as the dedication to Tiberius noted above (IEph 2.255A [4/19 CE]). On this occasion, the restoration of a wall of the Augusteum is being celebrated. A dedicatory inscription to Titus in Latin and Greek, found reused between the fishing-duty house and the Byzantine town hall, had been originally erected by Eutaktos, the procurator of Asia and Lycia (IEph 2.262 [80 CE]). Last, the wall between the Augusteum and the Artemision, erected in the time of Augustus, was repaired under Titus (IEph 2.412). Sjef van Tilborg (1996, 176) highlights the public thanksgiving associated with this repair: "It is celebrated with a feast. The expenses for the dance are paid for by the legate Pomponius Bassus from the income of the temple of Artemis."

The Reign of Domitian (81–96 CE)

Found on the northern side of Kuretes Street at the Nyphaeum Traiani, an honorary inscription to Domitia Longina Augusta, the wife of Domitian, had been erected by the demos of Ephesus (IEph 2.260A [81/96 CE]). There is a letter from Lucius Pompeius Apollonios to the proconsul Lucius Mestrius Florus concerning a festival in Ephesus for Demeter Karpophoros and Thesmophoros and the *Divi Augusti* (IEph 2.213 [83/84 CE]). See Harrison, "The Fruitfulness of Demeter and the Fruitfulness of Believers," in this volume. There is a dedication originally made to Domitian—but rededicated anew to Vespasian after the erasure of Domitian's name from the stone in a *damnatio memoriae*—by the demos of Teos (IEph 2.239 [88/91 CE]). See Harrison 2016. Located in the big mosque on the west side of Ephesus is a dedication to Artemis Ephesia and Domitian (IEph 2.418 [89/96]). A road builder has also honored Domitian in the city (IEph 2.263; 263 A+B; similarly, Augustus [IEph 2.459] and Claudius [IEph 7.1.3163]).

There is epigraphic reference to the improvement of city amenities under Domitian. On a stone found in Nymphaeum Traiani in Kuretes Street (reused in the front wall of a splendid wash basin), there is a dedication to Domitian by the demos of Ephesus concerning the bringing of the waters of the Marnas and Klaseas rivers to the city (IEph 2.415 [92/93 CE]; see also 2.416, 419, 419A). This reinvigorates the famous fountain built by Sextilius Pollio. A nymphaeum in honor of Domitian is built (IEph 2.413, 419). There is a building inscription in Latin and Greek in honor of the roads constructed by Domitian in Asia (IEph 2.263B [86/96 CE]). The Embolos (i.e., Kuretes Street), the longest and widest street in the city, was paved for the first time (IEph 7.1.3008 (94/95 CE) and was finally finished at the end of Hadrian's age or the beginning of Trajan's (Scherrer 1995, 10). The *skênê* and the northern wing of the theater were expanded (IEph 6.2034–2035). Last, on two fragments of an arch in the Varius baths (i.e., the Scholastica baths) located in Kuretes Street, Domitian's old buildings were restored in order to confirm the grandeur of the new temple of Domitian (IEph 2.499 [86/96 CE]). For discussion of "Domitian Square" in the city, see Schowalter 2022.

Last, of particular interest, there are presently fifteen extant boundary stones of the estates belonging to Ephesian Artemis. The landed property belonging to Artemis, Marjiana Ricl (2020, 4) estimates, was one third of the region. In a boundary stone inscription from the Kaystros River Valley erected during the Domitianic era, in which the ruler's name was once again subsequently erased, we read: "In accordance with the ordinance of Imperator Caesar [[Domitianus]] Augustus [[Germanicus]] boundary stone of the sacred estate of Ar[temis, erected when the governor Poplius Nonius Asprenas Caesius was present in the area]" (§46). The seamless collaboration between Domitian's proconsul of Asia and the representatives of Ephesian Artemis is telling. For a sacred boundary marker of Artemis erected in the reign of Trajan in the Kaystros valley, see §58. On the land-holdings of Ephesian Artemis, see Davies, 2011, 180.

The Reign of Nerva (96–98 CE)

Given the brevity of Nerva's reign, our evidence is minimal and unenlightening. The god Nerva is honored at the nymphaeum of Trajan (IEph 2.420). In an inscription found in the ruins of the harbor complex (IEph 4.1124), Tib. Kl. Artemiodorus is given a statue because of his victory at Olympia, which the athlete dedicates to Artemis, Nerva, and the demos of Ephesos. There are also several other brief dedications to Nerva, the occasion of which we know virtually nothing (*JÖAI* 55:109–10, no. 4155; IEph 2.264, 264A; 4.1124).

The Reign of Trajan (98–117 CE)

There are various epigraphic dedications to Trajan, including a statue (IEph 5.1500 [115 CE]) and a dedication at the Baths of Varius made out to Artemis Ephesia, Trajan, and demos of Ephesus by Marcus Iulius [...] erianus (IEph 2.421 [102/117 CE]). A new aqueduct of 210 stadia was furnished by Aristion and his wife Julia Lydia Laterane (IEph 2.424, 424A). "Workshops" (ἐργαστή[ρια]) were built and dedicated to Trajan (IEph 2.421). Ischyrion, an Alexandrian, oversaw the construction of beautiful new buildings, in honor of Trajan, in order to adorn further the stoa of the Agora (IEph 7.1.3005). The bequest of C. Vibius Salutaris (IEph 1a.27 [104 CE]), found in the wall of the southern analemma of the Theater of Ephesus, illustrates the elaborate processional culture at the city during the reign of Trajan. See Rogers 1991. One of the crowning architectural and intellectual monuments at Ephesus, the Library of Celsus, was built in 117 CE (IEph 7.2. 5101–5113). On the Library of Celsus, see Harrison, "Sponsors of *Paideia*," in *New Docs* 11B; Hueber, Erdemgil, and Büyükkolanci 1997, 77–81. A wide variety of sculptural monuments are also donated during this period (IAsia Mixed §§158–161). Last, Trajan, like Augustus before him, restored the processional sacred way of Artemis (IAsia Mixed §162).

The Reign of Hadrian (117–138 CE)

During the reign of Hadrian, the diverse rituals of imperial honorific culture are widely evident, including (unusually) the imperial honoring of and request for a favor for freedmen from their city. There is a record of the *epheboi* singing in the theater during a visit of the Hadrian to the city (IEph 4.1145 [129 CE]). In another inscription for an unnamed recipient, the *hymnodes* of the temple of *theos* Hadrian are mentioned (IEph I3.742, undated). On the temple of Hadrian, see Hueber, Erdemgil, and Büyükkolanci 1997, 89. In the proconsulate of Q. Roscius Murena Pompeius Falco, a statue was erected in honor of Hadrian (IEph 2.276) by gold-bearing priests and winners of the games. The halls of Verulanus were covered in honor of Hadrian (IEph 2.430). On an altar there is an honorary inscription for Hadrian offered by the *mystai* of Dionysos (IEph 2.275 [119/129 CE]), as well as another dedicated by the *chrysophoroi* of Artemis (IEph 2.276 [123/124 CE]). The boule and the demos thank Hadrian (IEph 2.274 [129 CE]) and an avalanche of dedications honor Hadrian as "Zeus Olympios" (IEph 2.267–273). Further, honorific inscriptions are devoted to the wife of Hadrian, *thea* ("divine") Sabina Augusta (IEph 2.280 [124/125 CE]) and "for Hera Sabina, Sebasta" (IEph 7.1.3411; SEG 36.1212). Tib. Kl. Piso Diophantes asks for and receives a high priesthood of the temple of the god Hadrian (IEph 2.428). Publius Quintilius Valens Varius and his family honor Artemis Ephesia, Hadrian, and the demos of Ephesus at the temple of Hadrian (IEph 2.429). On Hadrian's creation of the international cultural Panhellenion, in which he figured as a divinised hero, see Spawforth 2003.

Several letters of Hadrian are preserved. First, Hadrian's letter to the gerousia, dated 27 September 120 CE (IEph 5.1486), addresses the usurpation of the gerousia's money by corrupt agents who were supposedly acting on behalf of the gerousia in retrieving the property of its debtors. Two letters of recommendation from Hadrian ask the Ephesian people to show favor towards freedman seafarers who had faithfully served the ruler (IEph 5.1487–1488 [128/129 CE]). See Harrison, "A Seafarer's Reward," in this volume. For further letters of Hadrian regarding various individuals, see IEph 5.1487, 1488. On Hadrianic building activity, see Scherrer 1995, 13.

2. Conclusion

From the Hellenistic Age onward, Ephesus was an astute political player on the international stage, carefully handling the many transitions in power from Alexander's successors onwards, including the hegemony of Lysimachus, the Ptolemaic and Seleucid dynasties, the rule of the Attalid kings, and the competing Roman generals until the eventual triumph of Octavian in 31 BCE. For discussion, see Davies 2011, 193–94, 199–201. The key diplomatic mistake that Ephesus made in this period was her support of the revolt of Mithridates VI in 88 BCE, killing Roman citizens in the Artemision and overturning Roman statues throughout the city—a mistake for which Ephesus dearly paid after Sulla wreaked revenge upon the city in 84 BCE. However, although in the early years of the first century BCE, the resistance of Ephesus to Rome's presence in Asia had been pronounced, the city's fraught relationship between Rome changed entirely for the better with the advent of the Augustan age of grace and the total triumph of the Julian family over all other political and military competitors at Rome. Stability of political rule in the capital meant that Ephesus could accommodate easily to the Roman rulers, projecting herself as an eager and faithful client of the Julio-Claudian and Flavian houses in provincial Asia.

During the Julio-Claudian and Flavian periods, coinciding with the time of the production of the New Testament documents, the Ephesian inscriptions reveal several important trends about the relationship between the imperial rulers and Ephesus, the city in which the proconsul of Asia resided. There is a strong mutuality of relationship between the Roman rulers and Ephesus: the ruler and his proconsul acted beneficently by sponsoring amenities in city, while the Ephesian *demos* responded reciprocally with appropriate honors for the ruler and his family. Indeed, the Julio-Claudian and Flavian rulers established a long tradition of regularly sponsoring various ameliorations of the water resources of Ephesus as a sign of their *fides* to its citizens. The Ephesian elites also acted beneficently in the city, while strategically advancing their personal status before the watching Roman dignitaries in the province in honoring the Roman ruler and his house. The public shame of dishonor was reserved for two Roman rulers (Nero, Domitian) in the form of the *damnatio memoriae*, with Domitian's erased name being replaced by the popular Vespasian.

The city sought and acquired neokorate status, which it vaunted. The eulogistic protocols of the imperial cult were carefully carried out on official occasions by the *epheboi* and *hymnodes* singing the praises of the visiting ruler. The Ephesians twice affirmed epigraphically the permanency of the Roman hegemony. Notwithstanding, the indigenous gods were never supplanted by the Roman rulers in the protocols of the imperial cult: Artemis and Demeter were always honored ahead of the Roman ruler and his family. The central identity of Ephesus as the city of Artemis remained uncompromised. This was the historical stage upon which the first Christians would eventually appear, placing the majesty of Artemis herself at risk throughout Asia by their dishonoring message about the idolatry of "man-made" gods (Acts 18:26b–27).

Bibliography

Alzinger, W. 1971. "Kunstgeschichtliche Stellung." Pages 81–107 in *Das Momument des C. Memmius*. Forschungen in Ephesos 7. Vienna: IM Selbstverlag des Österreichischen Archäologischen Instituts in Wien.

Arnold, Clinton E. 1992. *Ephesians, Power and Magic: The Concept of Power in Ephesians in Light of Its Historical Setting*. Repr. Grand Rapids: Baker.

Arnold, Jane Ringwood. 1972. "Festivals of Ephesus." *AJA* 76.1:17–22.

Auffarth, Christoph. 2017. "'Groß ist die Artemis von Ephesos!' Der Artemiskult im kaiserzeitlichen Ephesos." Pages 77–100 in *Ephesos: Der antike Metropole im Spannungsfeld von Religion und Bildung*. Edited by Tobias Georges. Civitatem Orbis Mediterranei Studia 2. Tübingen: Mohr Siebeck.

Bailey, Colin. 2006. "The *Gerousia* of Ephesus." PhD diss., University of British Columbia, Vancouver.

Bammer, Anton. 1986–1987. "Ephesos in der Bronzezeit." *JÖAI* 57:14–38.

———. 1988. *Ephesos: Stadt an Fluß und Meer*. Graz: Academische Druck- u. Verlagsanstalt.

Baugh, Steven Michael. 1990. "Paul and Ephesus: The Apostle among His Contemporaries." PhD diss., University of California, Irvine.

Bowden, Anna M. V. 2020. *Revelation and the Marble Economy of Roman Ephesus: A People's History Approach*. Lanham, MD: Lexington/Fortress Academic.

Brunet, Stephen Andrew. 1998. "Greek Athletes in the Roman World: The Evidence from Ephesos." PhD. diss. University of Texas, Austin.

———. 2003. "Olympic Hopefuls from Ephesos." *Journal of Sport History* 30:219–35.

Burrell, Barbara. 2004. *Neokoroi: Greek Cities and Roman Emperors*. Cincinnati Classical Studies 2/9. Leiden: Brill.

Carter, Michael J. D. 1999. "The Presentation of Gladiatorial Spectacles in the Greek East: Roman Culture and Greek Identity." PhD diss., McMaster University.

Cottier, M., M. H. Crawford, C. V. Crowther, J.-L. Ferrary, B. M. Levick, O. Salomies, and M. Wörrle, eds. 2009. *The Customs Law of Asia*. Oxford Studies in Ancient Documents. Oxford: Oxford University Press.

Davies, John K. 2011. "The Well-Balanced Polis: Ephesos." Pages 177–201 in *The Economies of Hellenistic Societies, Third to First Centuries BC*. Edited by Zosia Archibald, John K. Davies, and Vincent Gabrielsen. Oxford: Oxford University Press.

Dignas, Beate. 2002. *Economy of the Sacred in Hellenistic and Roman Asia Minor*. Oxford: Oxford University Press.

Dmitriev, Sviatoslav. 2005. *City Government in Hellenistic and Roman Asia Minor*. Oxford: Oxford University Press.

Dominguez, Adolfo J. 1999. "Ephesos and Greek Colonisation." Pages 75–80 in *100 Jahre österreichische Forschungen in Ephesos: Akten des Symposions, Wein 1995*. Edited by Herwig Friesinger and Fritz Krinzinger. Vienna: Verlag der Österreichischen Akademie der Wissenschaften.

Foss, Clive. 1979. *Ephesus after Antiquity: A Late Antique, Byzantine, and Turkish City*. Cambridge University Press.

Friesen, Steven J. 1993. *Twice Neokoros: Ephesus, Asia and the Cult of the Flavian Imperial Family*. RGRW 116. Leiden: Brill.

———. 1995. "The Cult of the Roman Emperors in Ephesos: Temple Wardens, City Titles, and the Interpretation of John." Pages 229–50 in *Ephesos, Metropolis of Asia: An Interdisciplinary Approach to Its Archaeology, Religion, and Culture*. Edited by Helmut Koester. HTS 41. Valley Forge: Trinity Press International.

———. 1999. "Asiarchs." *ZPE* 126:275–90.

———. 2022. "The Customs House Inscription from Ephesos: Exchange, Surplus, Ideology, and the Divine." Pages 115–38 in *Ephesos as a Religious Center under the Principate*. Edited by Allen Black, Christine M. Thomas, and Trevor W. Thompson. WUNT 488. Tübingen: Mohr Siebeck.

Garstand, John, and O. R. Gurney. 1959. *The Geography of the Hittite Empire*. BIAA Occasional Monograph Series 5. London: British Institute at Ankara.

Georges, Tobias. 2017. *Ephesos: Der antike Metropole im Spannungsfeld von Religion und Bildung*. Civitatem Orbis Mediterranei Studia 2. Tübingen: Mohr Siebeck.

Graf, F. 1992. "An Oracle against Pestilence from a Western Anotolian Town." *ZPE* 92:267–79.

Grossschmidt, Karl, Fabian Ganz, and Efes Müzesi, eds. 2002. *Gladiatoren in Ephesos: Tod am Nachmittag: Eine Ausstellung im Ephesos Museum*. Vienna: Österreichisches Archäologisches Institut.

Harrison, James R. 2012a. "Artemis Triumphs Over a Sorcerer's Evil Art." *New Docs* 10:37–47.

———. 2012b. "Family Honour of a Priestess of Artemis." *New Docs* 10:31–36.

———. 2012c. "The 'Grace' of Augustus Paves a Street at Ephesus." *NewDocs* 10:61–66.

———. 2012d. "A 'Worthy' *neopoios* Thanks Artemis." *NewDocs* 10:48–54.

———. 2015. "The First Urban Churches: Introduction." Pages 1–40 in *Methodological Considerations*. Vol. 1 of *The First Urban Churches*. Edited by James R. Harrison and L. L. Welborn. WGRWSup 7. Atlanta: SBL Press.

———. 2016. "The Erasure of Honour: Paul and the Politics of Dishonour." *TynBul* 66.2:161–84.

———. 2018. "An Epigraphic Portrait of Ephesus and Its Villages." Pages 1–67 in *Ephesus*. Vol. 3 of *The First Urban Churches*. Edited by James R. Harrison and L. L. Welborn. WGRWSup 9. Atlanta: SBL Press.

———. 2024. "Village Life in the Kaystros River Valley of Ephesus." Pages 223–39 in *The Village in Antiquity and the Rise of Early Christianity*. Edited by Alan H. Cadwallader, James R. Harrison, Angela Standhartinger, and L. L. Welborn. London: T&T Clark.

Hawkins, J. D. 1998. "Tarkasnawa King of Mira, 'Tarkondemos', Bokazkoy Sealings amd Karabel." *AnSt* 48:1–31.

Hoag, Gary G. 2013. "The Teaching on Riches in 1 Timothy in Light of Ephesiaca by Xenophon of Ephesus." PhD diss., University of Bristol and Trinity College, Bristol.

Horsley, G. H. R. 1989. "A Fishing Cartel in First-Century Ephesos." *New Docs* 5:95–114.

———. 1987. "Giving Thanks to Artemis." *NewDocs* 4:127–29.

———. 1992. "The Inscriptions of Ephesos and the New Testament." *NovT* 34.2:105–68.

Hueber, Friedmund, Selahattin Erdemgil, and Mustaga Büyükkolanci. 1997. *Ephesos: Gebaute Geschichte*. Mainz am Rhin: von Zabern.
Immendörfer, Michael. 2017. *Ephesians and Artemis: The Cult of the Great Goddess of Ephesus as the Epistle's Context*. WUNT 2/436. Tübingen: Mohr Siebeck.
Kalinowski, Angela V. 1996. "Patterns of Patronage: The Politics and Ideology of Public Building in the Eastern Roman Empire (31 BCE–600 CE)." PhD diss., University of Toronto, Toronto.
———. 2021. *Memory, Family, and Community in Roman Ephesos*. Cambridge: Cambridge University Press.
Karaman, Elif Hilal. 2018. *Ephesian Women in Greco-Roman and Early Christian Perspective*. WUNT 2/474. Tübingen: Mohr Siebeck.
Kearsley, R. A. 1986. "Asiarchs, *Archiereis*, and the *Archiereiai* of Asia." *GRBS* 27:183–92.
———. 1987. "Some Asiarchs in Ephesos." *NewDocs* 4:46–55.
———. 1990. "Asiarchs, *Archiereis*, and the *Archiereiai* of Asia: New Evidence from Amorium in Phrygia." *EA* 16:69–80.
———. 1992a. "Ephesus: *Neokoros* of Artemis." *NewDocs* 6:203–5
———. 1992b. "The Mysteries of Artemis at Ephesos." *NewDocs* 6:196–202.
Kerschner, Michael. 2017. "Das Artemision von Ephesos in geometrischer und archaischer Zeit: Die Anfänge des Heiligtums und sein Aufstieg zu einem Kultzentrum von überregionaler Bedeutung." Pages 4–75 in *Ephesos: Der antike Metropole im Spannungsfeld von Religion und Bildung*. Edited by Tobias Georges. Civitatem Orbis Mediterranei Studia 2. Tübingen: Mohr Siebeck.
Knibbe, Dieter. 1995. "*Via Sacra Ephesiaca*: New Aspects of the Cult of Artemis Ephesia." Pages 141–55 in *Ephesos, Metropolis of Asia: An Interdisciplinary Approach to Its Archaeology, Religion, and Culture*. Edited by Helmut Koester. HTS 41. Valley Forge, PA: Trinity Press International.
Knibbe, Dieter, and Bülent Iplikcioglu. 1984. *Ephesos in Spiegel seiner Inschriften*. Vienna: Schindler.
Koester, Helmut. 1995. "Ephesus in Early Christian Literature." Pages 119–40 in *Ephesos, Metropolis of Asia: An Interdisciplinary Approach to Its Archaeology, Religion, and Culture*. Edited by Helmut Koester. HTS 41. Valley Forge, PA: Trinity Press International.
Kraft, J. C., Helmut Brückner, Ilhan Kayan, and Helmut Engelmann. 2007. "The Geographies of Ancient Ephesus and the Artemision in Anatolia." *Geoarchaeology* 22:121–49.

Ladstätter, Sabine. 2013. *Terrace House 2 in Ephesos: An Archaeological Guide.* Istanbul: Homer Kitabevi.
Leloux, Kevin. 2018. "The Campaign of Croesus against Ephesus: Historical and Archaeological Considerations." *Polemos* 21.2:47–63.
Levick, Barbara. 2004. "The Roman Economy: Trade in Asia Minor and the Niche Market." *Greece & Rome* 51:180–98.
Long, Leah Emilia. 2012. "Urbanism, Art, and Economy: The Marble Quarrying Industries of Aphrodisias and Roman Asia Minor." PhD diss., University of Michigan.
Lund, H. S. 1992. *Lysimachus: A Study in Early Hellenistic Kingship.* London: Routledge.
Meriç, Recep. 2009. *Das Hinterland von Ephesos: Archäologisch-topographische Forschungen im Kaystros-Tal.* Vienna: Österreichisches Archäologisches Institut.
Mitchell, Stephen, and Constantina Katsari. 2005. *Patterns in the Economy of Asia Minor.* Swansea: Classical Press of Wales.
Murphy-O'Connor, Jerome. 2008. *St. Paul's Ephesus: Texts and Archaeology.* Collegeville, MN: Liturgical Press.
Olson, Emily Victoria. 2013. "Contextualizing Roman Honorific Monuments: Statue Groups of the Imperial Family from Olympia, Ephesus, and Leptis Magna." PhD diss., University of North Carolina, Chapel Hill.
Oster, R. 1987. "Holy Days in Honour of Artemis." *New Docs* 4:74–82.
———. 1990. "Ephesus as a Religious Center under the Principate I." *ANRW* 18.3:1662–1728.
Portefaix, Lilian. 1993. "Ancient Ephesus: Processions as Media of Religious and Secular Propaganda." Pages 195–210 in *The Problem of Ritual: Based on Papers Read at the Symposium on Religious Rites Held at Åbo, Finland, on the 13th–16th of August 1991.* Edited by T. Ahlbäck. Scripta Instituti Donneriani Aboensis 15. Åbo: Donner Institute.
Pülz, Andreas. 2020. "Selected Evidence of Christian Residents in Late Antique Ephesus." Pages 75-89 in *Religion in Ephesos Reconsidered: Archaeology of Spaces, Structures, and Objects.* Edited by Daniel Schowalter, Sabine Ladstätter, Steven Friesen, and Christine Thomas. NovTSup 177. Leiden: Brill.
Reinach, Adolphe. 1909. "Bulletin épigraphique (suite et fin)." *REG* 22.98–99:306–35.
Reynolds, Joyce. 1982. *Aphrodisias and Rome.* JRS Monographs 1. London: Society for the Promotion of Roman Studies.

Ricl, Marijana. 2020. *New Inscriptions from the Kaystros River (Küçük Menderes) Valley.* Beograd: Novi Sad.

Robert, Louis. 1940. *Les gladiateurs dans l'Orient grec.* Paris: Champion.

Rogers, Guy MacLean. 1991. *The Sacred Identity of Ephesos: Foundation Myths of a Roman City.* London: Routledge.

———. 2012. *The Mysteries of Artemis of Ephesos: Cult, Polis, and Change in the Graeco-Roman World.* Synkrisis. New Haven: Yale University Press.

Rykwert, Joseph. 1999. *The Dancing Column: On Order in Architecture.* Cambridge: MIT Press.

Saunders, R. 1998. "Attalus, Paul and PAIDEIA: The Contribution of *I. Eph.* 202 to Pauline Studies." Pages 175–83 in *Early Christianity, Late Antiquity, and Beyond.* Vol. 2 of *Ancient History in a Modern University.* Edited by T. W. Hillard et al. Grand Rapids: Eerdmans.

Scherrer, Peter, ed. 1995. "The City of Ephesus from the Roman Period to Late Antiquity." Pages 1–25 in *Ephesos, Metropolis of Asia: An Interdisciplinary Approach to Its Archaeology, Religion, and Culture.* Edited by Helmut Koester. HTS 41. Valley Forge, PA: Trinity Press International.

———. 2000. *Ephesus: A New Guide.* Istanbul: Ege Yayinlan.

Schowalter, Daniel. 2022. "Ephesos under the Flavians: The Domitianplatz as a Market of Local and Imperial Identity." Pages 139–57 in *Ephesos as a Religious Center under the Principate.* Edited by Allen Black, Christine M. Thomas, and Trevor W. Thompson. WUNT 488. Tübingen: Mohr Siebeck.

Sokolowski, F. 1965. "A New Testimony on the Cult of Artemis of Ephesus." *HTR* 58:427–31.

Souza, Philip de. 1999. *Piracy in the Graeco-Roman World.* Cambridge: Cambridge University Press.

———. 2008. "Rome's Contribution to the Development of Piracy." *MAAR* 6:71–96.

Spawforth, Anthony A. J. 2003. "Panhellenion, Attic." *OCD*, 1105–106.

Strelan, Rick. 1996. *Paul, Artemis, and the Jews in Ephesus.* BZNW 80. Berlin: de Gruyter.

Tellbe, Mikael. 2009. *Christ-Believers in Ephesus: A Textual Analysis of Early Christian Identity Formation in a Local Perspective.* WUNT 242. Tübingen: Mohr Siebeck.

Thür, Hilke. 1995. "The Processional Way in Ephesos as a Place of Cult and Burial." Pages 157–99 in *Ephesos, Metropolis of Asia: An Interdis-*

ciplinary Approach to Its Archaeology, Religion, and Culture. Edited by Helmut Koester. HTS 41. Valley Forge, PA: Trinity Press International.

Tilborg, Sjef van. 1996. *Reading John in Ephesus.* NovTSup 83. Leiden: Brill.

Trebilco, Paul. 2004. *The Early Christians in Ephesus from Paul to Ignatius.* Grand Rapids: Eerdmans.

Walters, James C. 1995. "Egyptian Religions in Ephesos." Pages 281–309 in *Ephesos, Metropolis of Asia: An Interdisciplinary Approach to Its Archaeology, Religion, and Culture.* Edited by Helmut Koester. HTS 41. Valley Forge, PA: Trinity Press International.

Weiss, Cecelia Feldman. 2011. "Living Fluidly: Uses and Meanings of Water in Asia Minor (Second Century BCE–Second Century CE)." PhD diss. Brown University.

White, L. Michael. 1995. "Urban Development and Social Change in Imperial Ephesus." Pages 27–79 in *Ephesos, Metropolis of Asia: An Interdisciplinary Approach to Its Archaeology, Religion, and Culture.* Edited by Helmut Koester. HTS 41. Valley Forge, PA: Trinity Press International.

Winzenburg, Justin. 2022. *Ephesians and Empire: An Evaluation of the Epistle's Subversion of Roman Imperial Ideology.* WUNT 2/573. Tübingen: Mohr Siebeck.

Wiplinger, Gilbert, and Gudrun Wlach. 1996. *Ephesus: One Hundred Years of Austrian Research.* Edited by Claudia Luxon. Vienna: Österreichisches Archäologisches Institut.

Witetschek, Stephan. 2008. *Ephesische Enthüllungen 1: Frühe Christen in einer antiken Grossstadt Zugleich ein Beitrag zur Frage nach den Kontexten der Johannes Apokalypse.* BTS 6. Leuven: Peeters.

———. 2009. "Artemis and Asiarchs: Some Remarks on Ephesian Local Colour in Acts 19." *Bib* 90:335–55.

Yorgos, Mallios. 2002. "Ephesus (Antiquity), Monument of Memmius." *Encyclopaedia of the Hellenic World, Asia Minor.* https://tinyurl.com/bdfhk3ne.

Zabrana, Lilli. 2020. "The Artemision in the Roman Era: New Results of Research within the Sanctuary of Artemis." Pages 158–70 in *Religion in Ephesos Reconsidered: Archaeology of Spaces, Structures, and Objects.* Edited by Daniel Schowalter, Sabine Ladstätter, Steven Friesen, and Christine Thomas. NovTSup 177. Leiden: Brill.

Zuiderhock, Arjan. 2009. *The Politics of Munificence in the Roman Empire: Citizens, Elites and Benefactors in Asia Minor.* Cambridge: Cambridge University Press.

Translations and Commentaries

The Gods

1. The Inviolate *temenos* of Artemis

Bradley J. Bitner

IEph 5.1520

GIBM 3.2.520 (*editio princeps*); FiE 1:280, no. 26; *SIG* 989; *LSAM* 85.
Provenance unknown. Date: second century BCE–first century CE.

1   τὸ τέμενος τῆς Ἀ[ρτέμιδος ἄσυλον]   The *temenos* of Artemis (is) inviolate:
    πᾶν ὅσον ἔσω π[εριβόλου· ὅς δ' ἄν]   everything as much as (is) inside the
                                          enclosure; whoever
    παραβαίνηι, αὐτὸς [αὐτὸν αἰτιάσεται]   transgresses (this provision), he will
                                          be his own accuser.

This inscription, treated in passing in Judge 1979, §78 is of general interest for the reconstruction of sacred space, cultic, and civic practices in Ephesus. More specifically, its potential relevance for the interpretation of the "wall of division" in Eph 2:14 has recently been discussed.

1. Date and Text

The editors of IEph give a date of second century BCE (following *GIBM* 3.2). Rigsby (1996, 388) inclines toward a date earlier than 129 BCE on the basis of the script but notes the high level of uncertainty. The difficulty in dating the inscription precisely is due to several factors: first, the stone was not discovered in situ (it was found reused in a "brick wall"; more precise findspot unknown); second, the boundaries of *asylia* and also of the *temenos* around the Artemis temple complex ebbed and flowed over time (see Strabo, *Geogr.* 14.1.23); and third, other Ephesian inscriptions provide evidence for building work on and within the perimeter during the time of Augustus (Rigsby 1996, 391; cf. Oster 1979, §19; Rogers 2012, 116–18). In addition, there are inscribed lines on the reverse of the same stone bearing our text; there, ten incomplete lines represent the sixth of seventeen section fragments apparently dating from the late Republican era and comprising a subscription list that presumably ran along the inner face of the *peribolos* wall (see IEph 5.1687). For these reasons we offer the date range of second century BCE–(early) first century CE above.

As for the text itself, the restoration is quite secure given parallels elsewhere. In line 1, the less common, synonymous φύκτιμον ("place of refuge") might possibly be restored instead of ἄσυλον, but the sense would be the same (Rigsby 1996, 168); see *FD* 3.4:372.5 (third century BCE) on the temple of Apollo at Delphi: ἄσυλον καὶ φύκτιμον. Frequently attested is the *protasis* of lines 2–3 ὅς δ' ἂν παραβαίνηι (following closely on περιβόλου), with similar variations on the verb of transgression. For threats of penalty in Ephesian funerary inscriptions, see IEph 6.2211, ὅς δ' ἂν κεινήσῃ; IEph 6.2216C, [ὅς δ' ἂν τολμήσει]; IEph 6.2326, ὅς δ' ἂν εἰσενέν[κῃ. See also the penalty *protasis* of the famous warning from Herod's temple in Jerusalem (of which there are two copies: *CIIP* 1.2, copy one, ll. 4–5, περιβόλου. ὅς δ' ἂν ληφθῇ). Elsewhere, only on Cos is the verb παραβαίνω closely linked with the transgression of a temple's ἀσυλία.[1] As for line 3, Louis Robert (1970, 415–17) noted several examples, from a variety of contexts (e.g., olive groves, public baths, temples), of the rather formulaic restoration (ἐ)αὐτὸν αἰτιάσεται. The use in our inscription of the nominative αὐτός, however, appears unparalleled and is perhaps emphatic because explicit. Depending on the context, the final threat clause in such texts may have legal (or quasi-legal) connotations or may merely be "vaguely menacing" (Robert 1970, 416; cf. IEph 1.520 ὅς ἂν ὧδε οὐρήσει, αὐτὸ[ν α]ἰτιάσεται; whoever urinates here is responsible for himself). On urination in the inscriptions, see Harrison, "Finding the Right Spot to Take a Leak," in this volume.

2. The τέμενος of the Artemesion and Other Ephesian τεμένη

Before turning to the question of whether this inscription provides an interpretive context for Eph 2:14, it is necessary to contextualize it within its Ephesian setting. τέμενος (nom. plural: τεμένη) is a term used, especially in relation to Hellenistic temples such as the Artemision, to denote the sacred area comprising a temple, an altar, and other related architectural structures or spaces; it is an area often delimited by boundary stones (ὅροι) or a perim-

---

1. For conceptual shades and terminology of refuge and inviolability, including in the LXX and Josephus, see Rigsby 1996, 30–39.

1. The Inviolate *temenos* of Artemis

eter wall (περίβολος; *BNP* 14, s.v. "*temenos*"; Berquist 1967, 5–7). Although most τεμένη marked out a kind of sacred inviolability, certain temples were granted the extraordinary legal right of *asylia*: these were places of (supposedly) inviolable refuge for suppliants, ambassadors from other *poleis*, for traveling athletes and competitors, fugitives, and others (Rigsby 1996, 142). The *asylia* of Artemis's temple at Ephesus was a well-known, even paradigmatic, case in the Hellenistic world (Cicero, *Verr.* 2.1.33.85; Achilles Tatius, *Leuc. Clit.* 7.13.3; 8.2.2; Plutarch, *Vit. aere al.* 3 [828D]; Dio Chrysostom, *Rhod.* 31.54). It was appealed to as a kind of model in the *senatus consultum de Aphrodisiensibus* of 39 BCE (Reynolds 1982, §8). Tacitus (*Ann.* 3.60–63) recounts that the Ephesian embassy led the way during the early first-century senatorial review of requests by the Greek *poleis* for the confirmation of rights and privileges (including *asylia*) in 22/3 CE.

Our inscription, together with Strabo, *Geogr.* 14.1.23, IEph 5.1522–24, and recent clarifying archaeological work near the Artemision, enables us to grasp the relimitation of the *temenos*, the area of inviolability, and the reconstruction of the *peribolos* (in or around 6/5 BCE) and other closely related structures. We offer below the text and translation of several inscriptions closely related to IEph 5.1520. IEph 5.1522 describes the (re)construction of the *peribolos* wall around the Artemision and the Augusteum (Sebasteion), both within the *temenos*. IEph 5.1523–24 (largely the same text with minor variation) relates the reestablishment for the Artemision of other Augustan construction projects, namely, roads and a watercourse, by the erection of sacred boundary markers (*stelai*). Together these inscriptions form part of the evidence for (1) the redistricting of the *temenos* of Artemis in the Augustan era and (2) the larger Augustan project of reconstituting the cultic and political interface between the Artemision and the city of Ephesos, and between Artemis, *Roma*, and *Divus Augustus*.

IEph 5.1522

Wood 1877, app. 1: "Inscriptions from the Peribolus Wall" (*editio princeps*); *GIBM* 3.2.522; *ILS* 97. Block of the *peribolos* wall found in situ. Another stone with the same text but different line breaks is *CIL* 3.6070, 7118. Date: 6/5 BCE.

1	Imp(erator)· Caesar· Divi· f(ilius)· Aug(ustus)· co(n)s(ul)· XII· tr(ibunicia)· pot(estate)·XVIII· pontifex	The Emperor Caesar Augustus, son of a god, consul for the twefth time, in the 18th year of his tribunician power, great high
	maximus· ex· reditu· Dianae· fanum· et· Augusteum· muro	priest from the revenues of Diana both the temple (of Diana) and the Augusteum
	muniendum· curavit· C(aio)· Asinio· [Gallo pro co(n)s(ule),] curatore	he saw to the building of the wall, when Gaius Asinius Gallus was proconsul, by the care of
	Sex(to)· Lartidio· leg(ato)	Sextus Lartidius the legate.
5	Αὐτοκράτωρ Καῖσαρ θεοῦ υἱὸς Σεβαστὸς ὕπατος τὸ ιβ΄·, δημαρχικῆς ἐξουσίας τὸ ιη΄	The emperor Caesar Augustus son of a god, consul for the twelfth time, in the 18th year of his tribunician power,
	[ἐκ] τῶν ἱερῶν τῆς θεοῦ προσόδων τὸν νεὼ (=ναὸν) καὶ τὸ Σεβαστῆον τιχισθῆναι προενοήθηι	from the revenues of the temple of the goddess provided so that the temple and the Sebasteion might be walled about
	[ἐπὶ ἀνθυπάτου Γαΐου Ἀσινίου Γάλλου], ἐπιμελῇᾳ Σέξστου Λαρτιδίου πρεσβευτοῦ.	during the proconsulship of Gaius Asinius Gallus, by the care of Sextus Lartidius the ambassador.

IEph 5.1523

Wood 1877, app. 1: "Inscription from the Peribolus Wall 2" (*editio princeps*); *GIBM* 3.2.523; Robert 1946, 138 n. 2. Stela of white marble found in situ built into the *peribolos* of the Artemision. Date: 6/5 BCE.

1	Αὐτοκράτωρ Καῖσαρ θεοῦ υἱὸς Σεβαστός, ὕπατος τὸ ιβ΄, δημαρχικῆς ἐξουσίας τὸ ιη΄,	The emperor Caesar Augustus son of a god, consul for the twelfth time, with the tribunician power for the eighteenth time,
5	στήλας ἱερὰς τῶν ὁδῶν καὶ ῥίθρων Ἀρτέμιδι ἀποκατέστησεν, [ἐπὶ ἀνθυπάτου] [Γαΐου Ἀσινίου Γάλλου]	the sacred boundary pillars of the roads and watercourses he reestablished for Artemis, during the proconsulship of Gaius Asinius Gallus
10	ἐπιμελῇᾳ Σέξτου Λαρτιδίου πρεσ-	by the care of Sextus Lartidius the

βευτοῦ.	ambassador.
τὸ ῥεῖθρον ἔχει πλά-	The watercourse is
τους πήχεις ιε'.	15 cubits wide.

IEph 5.1524

Wood 1877, app. 1: "Inscription from the Peribolus Wall 2" (*editio princeps*); *GIBM* 3.2.523; Robert 1946, 138 n. 2. Stela of white marble found in situ built into the *peribolos* of the Artemision. Date: 6/5 BCE.

1	Αὐτοκράτωρ Καῖσαρ	The emperor Caesar
	θεοῦ υἱὸς Σεβαστός,	Augustus son of a god,
	ὕπατος τὸ ιβ', δημαρ-	consul for the twelfth time, with the
	χικῆς ἐξουσίας τὸ ιη',	tribunician power for the eighteenth time,
5	στήλας ἱερὰς τῶν	the sacred boundary pillars of the
	ὁδῶν καὶ ῥίθρων Ἀρ-	roads and watercourses
	τέμιδι ἀποκατέστη-	he reestablished for Artemis,
	σεν, [ἐπὶ ἀνθυπάτου]	during the proconsulship
	[Γαΐου Ἀσινίου Γάλλου]	of Gaius Asinius Gallus
10	ἐπιμελῆι Σέξστου	by the care of Sextus
	Λαρτιδίου πρεσβευτοῦ ·	Lartidius the ambassador.
	[ἡ] ὁδὸς ἔχει σὺν τῶι	The road together with the
	[ῥ]είθρῳ τοῦ ποταμοῦ	watercourse of the river is
	πήχεις λ'.	30 cubits (wide).

At the lexical level, note the use of ἀποκαθίστημι (IEph 5.1523.7; IEph 5.1524.7–8) plus the dative for "reestablish" in a political-cultic context (see BDAG, s.v. "ἀποκαθίστημι" 1). Compare Acts 1:6 (κύριε, εἰ ἐν τῷ χρόνῳ τούτῳ ἀποκαθιστάνεις τὴν βασιλείαν τῷ Ἰσραήλ; and ἀποκατάστασις in Acts 3:21). See also Matt 17:11 (Ἠλίας μὲν ἔρχεται καὶ ἀποκαταστήσει πάντα; with Mark 9:12).

At the cultic and political level, what we glimpse here is a reconstituted and evolving Augustan *politeia* in Ephesos. IEph 7.3501–3516 also attest the restoration of boundaries and the shifting area of the *temenos* (again ἀποκαθίστημι/*restitutio* in 3501; ἀποκατάστασις in 3513), from the time of Augustus through at least that of Domitian and Trajan (Rogers 1991, 85). IEph 5.1522–24 above, however, attest the redrawing of the boundaries between the Artemision and the polis in the late first century BCE by means of a wall and stelae. But there is a growing permeability insofar as the worship of Artemis, Augustus (and other Julio-Claudian successors), and Roma penetrated both the cultic space of the *temenos* and the civic space of the polis. On the one hand, there was renewed separation in economic and (to a degree) political terms. Nevertheless, there was also a dynamic and emergent ideological synthesis. Understanding this will help us as we consider proposals for the possible relevance of IEph 5.1520 for interpreting Eph 2:14.

Although we know that Augustus rebuilt a wall around the Artemision, we do not know its precise placement, extent, dimensions, or total function. We do know, however, that by resiting the *peribolos* and the area of *asylum*, Augustus was apparently trimming Artemis's legal skirt after Antony had expanded the *asylum* area in 41 BCE. What Augustus accomplished in part was to distinguish freshly between the spaces (and authorities) related to the Artemision and to the polis of Ephesus. Simultaneously, building projects within the *peribolos* of the Artemision and in other parts of the city were interweaving civic and cultic loyalty both to Artemis and Augustus in sophisticated ways (Rogers 2012, 115–18). Once these boundaries were redefined and these cults related, the Kouretes, chief among the groups of attendants in the celebration of the mysteries of Artemis, were relocated to the prytaneion in the polis, thereby marking "a major turning point in the creation of a new structure and organization of authority within Ephesos" (IEph 4.1001; Rogers 2012, 9, 119–21). On *asylum* at Ephesus more generally, see Stevenson 2022.

Two recent studies, by Lilli Zabrana (2020) and François Kirbihler (2020), of structures and practices within the Artemision and also in the upper agora of Roman Ephesos, give us a sense of the architectural and ritual layers associated with multiple Ephesian *temenē* of the Augustan era. Zabrana summarized the total picture of "the densely built-up sacred precinct" surrounding the temple of Artemis. Her detailed work, focused especially on the Odeion but clarifying the archaeology of the temple precinct, should inform any future New Testament or early Christian studies considering the Artemision. Here we mention only a few pertinent features of her summary.

In some scholarship, there persists a false image of the Artemision: a *periobolos* demarcating a *temenos* containing only a massive, solitary temple with an altar. But Zabrana—drawing together the epigraphical evidence, archaeological field work, and the early archival reports (some previously unpublished) of John Turtle Wood—urges scholars to envision an evolving "complex of buildings that correspond to the multidimensional character of this ancient, extra-urban sanctuary in the Roman period" (158). Referring to our text, Zabrana notes, "The sanctuary of Artemis had the right of asylum and provided refuge to those seeking protection in an area that was separated by a wall from the rest of the sacred district, but very likely near the temple.... Accommodations for recognized refugees as well as for priests and permanent staff can be assumed" (159).[2] Her updated depiction of the scale plan of the Artemision (163, fig 9.1) allows us to perceive the relations among and the distances between the temple, the Augusteum, the Odeion, a building for accommodating priests, and other structures. All of these were over four hundred meters from the *peribolos* wall corner marked by Wood in 1869 when he uncovered IEph 5.1522, 1523, and 1524 detailed above (Zabrana 2020, 162–63). Zabrana also mentions evidence for "a gymnasium ... as well as a Hestia shrine" within the Artemision (160). She concludes by noting that, although only features of the temple itself and foundations of the Odeion remain visible today, the combined evidence points to a cluster of "official, public buildings (including the Odeion and Augusteum) to the south and southeast of the temple," while to the north and northeast is evidence for "accommodations for priests, cult specific employees, as well as shelter for persons officially granted asylum in this area." The Odeion (formerly thought to be a "tribune) was likely "used as a venue for artistic competitions ... during the [festival of] Artemisia" (166).

None of this tells us precisely where our *temenos-asylia* inscription (IEph 5.1520) was originally located, nor where the entrance(s) to the temple complex through the *peribolos* wall were located (see Rogers 2012, 117–18). But it does grant us a sense of scale that frames the embodied religious and political practices occurring within the cultic space and recommends caution in appealing to this inscription for interpretive assistance with Eph 2:14. With these structures and personnel in mind, brief mention should also be made of the many statues and images within the temple precinct. Not only were there images of Artemis, and presumably also of the *Augusti* and others as mentioned above, but as time went on other notables had statues erected within the *temenos*. This is evident from the following excerpt from a second century epigrammatic dedication celebrating the many statues (particularly that of Cn. Claudius Severus) in the *temenos* of the Artemision.

---

2. See also her major study, Zabrana 2018.

IEph 5.1539

Wood 1877, app. 3: "Inscription from the Site of the Temple of Diana 7" (*editio princeps*); additional postscript: app. 8: "Inscription from the City and Suburbs"; GIBM 3.2.539; Kaibel 1878, 888a; *JÖAI* 40:13-15; SEG 13.505. Provenance unknown. Date: 163-169 CE.

15 [τοιῶ]γδ̓', ἄνδρες "Ιωνες, ἀγάλματα καλὸν ὁρᾶσθαι [ἑσταότ' Ἀ]ρτέμ[ιδος πλου]σίωι ἐν τεμένει.	But for you, O men of Ionia, a beautiful thing (it is) to view statues set up in the ample *temenos* of Artemis

In addition to the work of Zabrana that helps us visualize the complexity and activity within the *temenos*, in a second relevant study, Kirbihler (2020) summarizes what is known of ruler cults, including imperial cults, at Ephesos throughout the Hellenistic and Roman period. Two features in particular of his work are helpful in our consideration of the *temenos* inscription. First, Kirbihler describes evidence that points to veneration of the Caesars within the *temenos* of the Artemision during the triumvirate and the early imperial period. It is likely that a cult of Roma and Caesar as *Divus Iulius* was located in the temple complex after 48 BCE. Subsequently, Augustus as well as others of the Julio-Claudian dynasty (including Germanicus and Tiberius) were honored with cult alongside Artemis within the ambit of the *peribolos*. The Augusteum (IEph 5.1522 [6/5 BCE]) provided one key site of imperial worship within the Artemision in this period (Kirbihler 2020, 199-203). Additionally, Kirbihler points to other *temenē* in Roman Ephesos within which Augustus (and Artemis) were rendered cult. The overall interpretation of the so-called Upper Agora continues to be debated and archaeological work is ongoing. But we know that the area, a major feature as one entered by the Magnesian Gate and passed along the north-eastern flank of Bülbüdağ, underwent "a lengthy formative process" during and beyond the Augustan period as a *locus* of imperial cult (Steuernagel 2020, 93-107).

Another *temenos*, dedicated in the Upper Agora of the polis, was for *Dea Roma*. Here there was possibly also cult to both Artemis and Augustus (see Kirbihler 2020, 202-3; Raja 2012, 68).

1. The Inviolate *temenos* of Artemis

IEph 3.902

JÖAI 50:15–20, no. 6 (*editio princeps*). See also *AE* 1975.799; *SEG* 26.1243; *SEG* 30.1306; *SEG* 36.1020. Provenance unknown. Date: after 20/19 BCE (late first century BCE–early first century CE).

1	Ἀπολλώνιος Ἡρακλείδου τοῦ (Ἡρακλείδου) Πασσαλᾶς, ὅς καὶ προενοήθη τῆς καθιδρύσεως τοῦ Σεβαστοῦ καὶ τῆς καθιερώσεως	Apollonios Passalas, son of (Herakleides), son of Herkleides, who also provided for the foundation-festival of Augustus
5	τοῦ τεμένους·	and for the dedication of the *temenos*

This list of *hieres*, likely of the cult of the goddess Roma, describes the dedication of a *temenos* in the Upper Agora. Here, there were temples of *Dea Roma* and *Divus Iulius*, built ca. 29 BCE, near the *bouleterion* and *prytaneion*. Also nearby was a shrine of Hestia. Altogether, this was "the religious and political center of the upper city" (Rogers 1991, 88; Engelmann 1993, 284).

In summary, there were multiple *temenē* in Ephesos in the Julio-Claudian era and the cults of Artemis, Augustus, Roma, Hestia, and others were observed in various ways in these different sacred precincts. The precise area of the *temenos* of the Artemesion shifted over time and, though its attendant privilege of *asylla* remained important, the cultic and political landscape of Ephesos from the Augustan era onwards was refashioned in ways that did not disregard but did complicate the significance of the line drawn by the *peribolos* wall.

3. The "Dividing Wall of Partition" in Ephesians 2:14

The meaning of τὸ μεσότοιχον τοῦ φραγμοῦ λύσας, τὴν ἔχθραν ἐν τῇ σαρκὶ αὐτοῦ in Eph 2:14 has perhaps most frequently been interpreted, if in relation to cultic space at all, with reference to the inscribed balustrade of Herod's temple at Jerusalem (*CIIP* 1.2, above; cf. Llewelyn and van Beek 2012). This was a well-known wall intended to maintain separation between Jews and gentiles on the Temple Mount (Abbott 1897, 61). Not all have been persuaded either that Paul (or the author of Ephesians) had this in mind or that, even if so, its relevance to his argument in Eph 2:11–18 would have been grasped by those to whom he wrote. Other scholars, emphasizing the unlikelihood that such a Jerusalem-based illustration would have much traction with Ephesian believers and other auditors in Asia Minor, have proposed different interpretations of the μεσότοιχος of 2:14 (e.g., cosmic division between earthly and heavenly, the Torah as a "fence"; see Best 1998, 253–57). But recently some have proposed that the *peribolos* referred to in IEph 5.1520 provides a possible (if not primary) context for interpreting Eph 2:14. (For μεσότοιχος as a structural wall in temple and domestic contexts, see, e.g., Josephus, *A.J.* 8.67, 70–71; P.Amh. 2.98.8–9; P.Dura. 19.11–14; IDidyma 25A.13–14).

Michael Immendörfer (2017, 238–41) appeals to "the wall enclosing the altar in the Artemision" and lists various features and associations that the language of Eph 2:14 may have evoked in relation to the *peribolos* and the *temenos* and altar it enclosed. He appeals to a variety of considerations, among which are the "geographic and cultic proximity" of the *peribolos* in contrast to the distant Jerusalem balustrade, that various Ephesian inscriptions use similar terminology to μεσότοιχος (though he admits μέσος and τοῖχος appear separately), and that the wall delimiting the *temenos* of the Artemision was a "separation symbol" in a similar way to what is signaled by the μεσότοιχος of Eph 2:14. But, ultimately, Immendörfer retreats from the theory that the *peribolos* of the Artemision could be the primary context for interpretation. He does so on the basis of theological and contextual reasons. Chiefly, he points to the emphasis on *enmity* between Jews and gentiles in the context of Eph 2:14, which he argues is not the same as the quality of "separation, exclusion, and preference" symbolized by the *peribolos*. Ultimately, Immendörfer suggests there *may* be an evocative general echo of cultic separation for auditors of Ephesians who were familiar with the Artemision. But given the evidence adduced above and the composite picture we have of the physical and cultic-civic setting of the Artemision in the Julio-Claudian period and beyond, it must be questioned whether separation and exclusion were of primary significance for the *periobolos* wall and the *temenos* of the Artemision (or other Ephesian *temenē*) and, further, whether there is even a general echo of this when we come to the text of Eph 2:14.

More recently still, H. C. McMurry (2019) has suggested that the *peribolos* wall may in fact aid in the interpretation of Eph 2:14. He goes beyond Immendörfer to argue that "this wall of the temple of Artemis symbolized cultural and ethnic division as well as the Ephesians' devotion to Artemis" (68). Paul, therefore, may have "contextualized this image," adapting it metaphorically in a way which signified division and separation "much in the same way as the balustrade in the Jerusalem temple did" (135). In light of the picture outlined by the epigraphical and archaeological evidence above, however, there does not seem to be a strong case for interpreting either the *peribolos* wall and the *temenos* of the Artemision as a symbol of cultural or ethnic division in Ephesos. One may presume, as McMurry does, that Jews may have refrained from entering the cultic space demarcated by the *periobolos* (or indeed into other *temenē* in the Upper Agora or elsewhere), but this remains an assumption without direct evidence. And because separation (ἀπηλλοτριωμένοι τῆς πολιτείας τοῦ Ἰσραηλ, 2:12), estrangement (ξένοι τῶν διαθηκῶν τῆς ἐπαγγελίας, 2:12), and enmity (τὴν ἐχθραν, 2:14, in apposition to μεσότοιχον) are the clear, thematic focal points of Eph 2:11–18, there does not appear to be any strong reason to link IEph 5.1520 to its interpretation.

Bibliography

Abbott, T. K. 1897. *Epistles to the Ephesians and to the Colossians*. ICC. Edinburgh: T&T Clark.

Benndorf, Otto, ed. 1906. *Forschungen in Ephesos*. FiE 1. Vienna: Hölder.

Berquist, Birgitta. 1967. *The Archaic Greek Temenos: A Study of Structure and Function*. Lund: Gleerup.

Best, Ernest. 1998. *A Critical and Exegetical Commentary on Ephesians*. ICC. London: T&T Clark.

Engelmann, Helmut. 1993. "Zum Kaiserkult in Ephesos." *ZPE* 97:279–89.

Immendörfer, Michael. 2017. *Ephesians and Artemis: The Cult of the Great Goddess of Ephesus as the Epistle's Context*. WUNT 2/436. Tübingen: Mohr Siebeck.

Judge, E. A. 1979. "παρουσία." *NewDocs* 4:167–69.

Kaibel, Georg. 1878. *Epigrammata Graeca ex lapidibus conlecta*. Berlin: Reimer.

Kirbihler, François. 2020. "Ruler Cults and Imperial Cults at Ephesos: First Century BCE to Third Century CE." Pages 195–210 *Religion in Ephesos Reconsidered: Archaeology of Spaces, Structures, and Objects*. Edited by Daniel Schowalter, Sabine Ladstätter, Steven Friesen, and Christine Thomas. NovTSup 177. Leiden: Brill.

Llewelyn, S. R., and D. van Beek. 2012. "The Temple Warning." *NewDocs* 10:136–40.

McMurry, H. C. 2019. "The Temple of God and the Temple of Artemis:

Exploring the Building/Temple Image in Ephesians." PhD diss.; Southwestern Baptist Theological Seminary.

Oster, R. 1979. "Holy Days in Honour of Artemis." *NewDocs* 4:74–82.

Raja, Rubina. 2012. *Urban Development and Regional Identity in the Eastern Roman Provinces, 50 BC–AD 250: Aphrodisias, Ephesos, Athens, Gerasa*. Chicago: University of Chicago Press.

Reynolds, Joyce. 1982. *Aphrodisias and Rome*. JRS Monographs 1. London: Society for the Promotion of Roman Studies.

Rigsby, Kent J. 1996. *Asylia: Territorial Inviolability in the Hellenistic World*. Berkeley: University of California Press.

Robert, Louis. 1946. *Hellenica: Recueil d'épigraphie, de numismatique et d'antiquités grecques*. Vol. 2. Paris: Librarie d'Amérique et d'Orient.

———. 1970. *Études anatoliennes: Recherches sur les inscriptions grecques de l'Asie mineure*. Repr., Amsterdam: Hakkert.

Rogers, Guy MacLean. 1991. *The Sacred Identity of Ephesos: Foundation Myths of a Roman City*. London: Routledge.

———. 2012. *The Mysteries of Artemis of Ephesos: Cult, Polis, and Change in the Graeco-Roman World*. Synkrisis. New Haven: Yale University Press.

Steuernagel, Dirk. 2020. "The Upper Agora at Ephesos: an Imperial Forum?" Pages 93–107 in *Religion in Ephesos Reconsidered: Archaeology of Spaces, Structures, and Objects*. Edited by Daniel Schowalter, Sabine Ladstätter, Steven Friesen, and Christine Thomas. NovTSup 177. Leiden: Brill.

Stevenson, Gregory. 2022. "'Do Not Harm the Suppliant.' Inviolability and Asylum at Ephesos and in the Book of Revelation." Pages 189–204 in *Ephesos as a Religious Center under the Principate*. Edited by Allen Black, Christine M. Thomas, and Trevor W. Thompson. WUNT 488. Tübingen: Mohr Siebeck.

Wood, John Turtle. 1877. *Discoveries at Ephesus*. London: Longmans, Green.

Zabrana, Lilli. 2018. *Das Odeion im Artemision von Ephesos*. FiE 12.6. Vienna: Österreichischen Akademie der Wissenschaften.

———. 2020. "The Artemision in the Roman Era: New Results of Research within the Sanctuary of Artemis." Pages 158–70 in *Religion in Ephesos Reconsidered: Archaeology of Spaces, Structures, and Objects*. Edited by Daniel Schowalter, Sabine Ladstätter, Steven Friesen, and Christine Thomas. NovTSup 177. Leiden: Brill.

2. The Fruitfulness of Demeter and the Fruitfulness of Believers

James R. Harrison

IEph 2.213

Riemann 1877, 289, no. 72; *SIG* 820; McCrum & Woodhead, Docs. 193; Ascough, Harland, and Kloppenborg 2012, §163. This letter of an Ephesian association of Demeter concerning the mysteries was discovered on a marble base. The Greek text has come down to us from Cyriacus of Ancona, a recorder of Greek and Roman antiquities, especially the inscriptions at various sites. He first saw our association letter in a Byzantine fort. Date: 88/89 CE.

	Λουκίῳ Μεστρίῳ Φλώρῳ ἀνθυπάτῳ παρὰ	To Lucius Mestius Florus, proconsul from
2	Λουκίου Πομπηίου Ἀπολλωνίου Ἐφεσίου·	Lucius Pompeius Apollonius of Ephesus:
	μυστήρια καὶ θυσίαι, κύριε, καθ' ἕκαστον	"Mysteries and sacrifices, lord, each
4	ἐνιαυτὸν ἐπιτελοῦνται ἐν Ἐφέσῳ Δήμητρι	year are completed in Ephesus to Demeter
	Καρποφόρῳ καὶ Θεσμοφόρῳ καὶ θεοῖς	Karpophoros and Thesmophoros and to (the) gods
6	Σεβαστοῖς ὑπὸ μυστῶν μετὰ πολλῆς ἁγνείας καὶ νομίμων ἐθῶν σὺν ταῖς	Augustan by initiates with much purity and lawful customs, (along) with the
8	ἱερίαις ἀπὸ πλείστων ἐτῶν συντετηρημένα	priestesses, (which) from most years have been closely watched
	ἀπὸ βασιλέων καὶ Σεβαστῶν καὶ τῶν	by kings and Augusti and
10	κατ' ἐνιαυτὸν ἀνθυπάτων, καθὼς αἱ παρακείμεναι ἐπιστολαὶ αὐτῶν περιέχουσιν·	annual proconsuls, as their appended letters contain:

12 ὅθεν, ἐπειγόντων καὶ ἐπὶ σοῦ τῶν μυστηρίων,	wherefore, since the mysteries also weigh down upon you,
ἀναγκαίως, κύριε, ἐντυγχάνουσί σοι δι'	(it is) of necessity, lord, (that) through
14 ἐμοῦ οἱ ὠφείλοντες τὰ μυστήρια ἐπιτελεῖν,	my (mediation) (those) obligated to complete the mysteries (should) petition you,
ἵνα ἐπιγνοὺς αὐτῶν τὰ δίκαια [-----]	in order that acknowledging their rights [—]"

1. Honorific Epithets for Association Deities: Claims to Prestige and Legitimation

The epithets of association deities expressed the heated rivalries for status between local associations and their city-states, pointed to the prestigious genealogical and geographical localities of the deities, and functioned as descriptors of the deity's powers and identity. The prestige conveyed by a deity's epithet was also reinforced by the architectural expressions of association prestige, the memorialization of foundation stories, and the citation of documentation demonstrating either the antiquity or the purity of the god's cult.

In our association inscription above, the epithets of Ephesian Demeter, Karpophoros ("Fruit Bringer") and Thesmophoros ("Law Bringer"), are significant for the status and identity of the goddess (IEph 2.213.4–5). First, the epithet Thesmophoros, from which the Thesmophoria festival perhaps originated, is best understood as the ancient rules and secret rituals revealed by the goddess to humanity regarding grain cultivation and the mysteries (Stallsmith 2008, passim).

More importantly for our New Testament context, the epithet Karpophoros arises from Demeter's Olympian status as the fertility goddess of agriculture, grain, and bread. In addition to Ephesus, the goddess was worshiped as Karpophoros in other cities and villages. For epigraphic examples of her worship, see IPessinous 22 (Galatia [imperial era]); Heberdey and Wilhelm 1896, 16, 44 (Cilicia and Isauria [imperial era]); SEG 51.1029 (Mytilene [first century CE]); Herrmann 1998:495–508 (Sardis [50 CE]); Hepding 1910, 442, no. 25 (Pergamon); TAM 5.2.1335, 1336 (?) (Dareiou Kome). For discussion of Demeter and other deities as *karpophoroi*, see Hermann 2016 and Wallensten 2014.

Remarkably, Karpohoros is only one of a plethora of epithets eulogizing the goddess for her fertility. Allaire Stallsmith (2008, 116–17) helpfully lists the multiple epithets of Demeter pertaining to her fecundity:

> She is *Amallophoros* (bringer of sheaves), *Anesidora* (bringer up of gifts), *Chloe* (the green shoot), *Drepanephoros* (sickle bearer), *Epogmios* (of the furrow), *Eukarpos* (of good crops), *Haloas* (of the threshing floor), *Himalis* (of abundance), *Ioulo* (of barley), *Karpophoros* (bringer of crops), *Likmaia* (the winnower), *Malophoros* (fruit bearer), *Megalartos* (of the big loaf), *Megalomazos* (of the big porridge), *Ompnia* (of grain), *Polysoros* (rich in grain-heaps), *Pyrphoros* (torch-bearing), *Sito* (grainy), and *Soritis* (of the grain-heap).

Significantly for the Ephesian context, the worship of Demeter as Karpophoros is mentioned in several further inscriptions. A summary of old sacred law concerning sacrifices legislates (IEph 1a.10.27–29 [third century CE]) that "the *prytanis* is to be required to pay for the adornment of the (statue), which stands in the prytaneion, of Fruitful (Karpophoros) Demeter to whom the temple belongs." In an honorific decree of the Demetriastai for the sons of Drusus the Younger (IEph 7.2.4337 [19–20 CE]), Livia, Augustus's wife and Tiberius's mother, is referred to as "Augusta Demeter Karpophoros." Finally, there is a dedication to Plouton, Kore, and Demeter Karpophoros (IEph 5.1228).

We turn to the various tactics by which associations established their superiority over their local cultic rivals, tactics which are additional to the honorific epithets assigned to their sponsoring deities. Several pertinent strategies can be identified. First, in our association inscription above, the "great purity and lawful customs" of the Ephesian Demetriasts, associated with their annual celebration of the mysteries (IEph 2.213.8–11), are secured by the protection of their rites over a long period of time, supported in this instance by the precedents of official documentation spanning the Hellenistic ("kings") and imperial periods ("Augusti"; "proconsuls").

Second, the acquisition of prestige over other local Ephesian associations was effected architecturally by the expansion of the facilities of the fishery toll office in Ephesus, achieved through the material and monetary donations of the fishermen and fish dealers (IEph 1a.20 [54–59 CE]; cf. Horsley 1989). A large slab, prominently displayed in the harbor area and inscribed on both sides, lists the Roman and non-Roman donors who had contributed to building the toll booth. This included their monetary contributions, ranging from the building materials to donations of twelve–fifty denarii, as well as the structure's bricks and tiles, columns, paving for the colonnade, and adjacent altars. Apart from the "glory" that accrued to the association from this important civic structure, deflected glory was also acquired by the toll booth's prestigious dedication to Nero, Julia Agrippina (his mother), and Octavia (his wife) (IEph 1a.20.sideA.1–5).

Third, an extensive dream revelation regarding the foundation of a Thessalonian association of Sarapis establishes the prestige and legitimation of the new household cult. In the process of conveying the dream revelation, the malice of a political rival towards the household association founder is also overcome (Ascough, Harland, and Kloppenborg 2012, §52 [= IG 10.2.1.68 (first–second century CE)]; cf. Sokolowski 1974; Rollens 2018; note Artemidorus, *Onir.* 5.82).

Fourth, Dionysos is given the epithet "Leader" (Kathegemon) at Hierapolis (Ascough, Harland, and Kloppenborg 2012, §148 [SEG 41.1202 (second century CE)]) and at Pergamum in regard to "the divine mysteries" conducted there (§115 [IPergamon 2.485 (first century CE)]). The Attalids of Pergamum, however, were the first dynasty to claim the patronage of Dionysos as their divine ancestor, with the Dionysiac artists acting as her priests and the cult being associated with the theater (Kileci and Can 2020, 302). The cult had commenced by the time of Attalus 1 (SEG 39.1334 [230–220 BCE]), was maintained by the ensuing Attalid royalty (Welles 1974, §§65–67), and was still present at Pergamum in imperial times (SEG 37.1020). Beate Dignas (2012, 134) poses the intriguing question whether political rivalry with the Ptolemies, who also traced their decent to Heracles and Dionysos, caused the Attalids to adopt Dionysos as their "Leader." The antiquity of the Dionysos Kathegemon cult, inaugurated at the commencement of the Attalid dynasty in Asia Minor, ensured its strong ties to a specific geographical locality and provided its legitimation as the patron deity of the Attalid royalty.

In sum, the appearance of the epithet of *karpophoros* in our association inscription identifies the identity and powers of the goddess, gratefully honored for her beneficence, but it also reflects the wider agonistic culture of the associations where deep-seated rivalries for civic status were present. Given this strong emphasis on the fruitfulness of Demeter at Ephesus and elsewhere more generally, what would Greco-Roman auditors of Paul have made of his use of fruitfulness imagery in describing the newness of the believer's life? What was distinctive about the apostle's approach?

2. The Fruitfulness of the Believer's Life in the New Age: Pauline Perspectives

At the outset, several preliminary lexical observations are warranted. The adjective καρποφόρος is listed in LSJ. In the case of New Testament lexicons, the stem καρπός is bypassed by Ceslas Spicq (1994). *TDNT* does not provide an entry for καρποφόος. By contrast, both BAGD and Moulton and Milligan 1997 have an entry for καρποφόρος. BAGD notes the word's appearance in the papyri (PSI 171, 40) and inscriptions but cites no epigraphic examples. Only Moulton and Milligan 1997 note the link of καρποφόρος to the Demeter cult, citing an inscriptional example (*SIG* 655 [83 CE]).

καρποφόρος only appears in the New Testament once (Acts 14:17). There it refers to the seasons bearing fruit (καιρούς καρποφόρους), but, in contrast to the Demeter inscriptions, the agent of this fecundity is the "living God" who is impartially beneficent to humanity (Acts 14:15–18; cf. Deut 5:6; Josh 3:10; Jer 10:10; 23:36; Dan 6:26). The refusal of Paul and Barnabas to accept the idolatrous sacrifices of the priest of Zeus at Lystra, offered in response to their miracles in the city (Acts 14:8–10), reinforces that it is the living God of Israel being spoken about. Eckhard J. Schnabel (2012, 611) comments regarding Acts 14:17: "In the context of Lycaonian and Greek traditions, Paul argues that it is the living God, the creator of the universe, who grants fertility, not the local fertility gods who came to be associated with Zeus, worshiped as a weather god and given epithets that communicated the conviction that he provided the harvest and fruit on which human beings depend." Darrell Bock (2007, 497) posits that there "may be a polemical and contextualised response to the idea of Zeus being *kalakagathios*, or 'the one who does good and is fruitful', a description of Zeus that has been uncovered in Phrygia and Pisidia." See also Keener 2013, 2168–72 for a comprehensive coverage of the literary evidence relating to the agricultural testimony in Acts 14:17.

It might be wondered whether a discussion of the intersection of καρποφόρος of the Demeter cult with Paul's use of καρπός and cognates is relevant for New Testament exegetes and historians, given the absence of καρποφόρος in the Pauline corpus. However, the use of the epithet καρποφόρος for Demeter was part of the general religious world-view of Paul's Greco-Roman audiences. Therefore, a discussion of the intersection of fruitfulness terminology opens up sympathetically for us the belief systems of antiquity and the ideological surprises that Paul's exposition of his gospel must have occasioned for his new believers. Prior to their conversion, some of the first believers may have been Demeter worshipers, either participating in the civic sacrifices honoring the goddess for successful harvests or being members of local associations where Demeter's patronage was acknowledged. Furthermore, the Lukan Paul does refer to καρποφόρος in its Greco-Roman religious context. So it is entirely possible that the appearance of καρπός in Paul's epistles may have been occasioned to some extent by the prosperity theology of the local fertility cults. Paul, it could be argued, decided to highlight the believer's experience of walking fruitfully with God, underscoring the mediation of Christ and the indwelling of his Spirit. In other words, the apostle operates at a general ideological level as opposed to conducting a precise polemic by using καρποφόρος, as was the case in Acts 14:17. On agricultural imagery in Paul, see Collins 2008, 166–69.

All occurrences of καρπός and its cognates (καρποφορέω, ἄκαρπος) in Paul's epistles are metaphorical. To be sure, καρπός designates the benefaction of the Jerusalem collection (Rom 15:28) and the expectation that the apostles, like farmers reaping the fruits of their crops, could expect payment in reciprocation for their service (1 Cor 9:7; 2 Tim 2:6; cf. Phil 4:17 *infra*). But this is not related in any way to the harvest-specific beneficence of the Demeter cult. Even more generally, in Philippians Paul's fruitful apostolic ministry includes his gospel ministry per se, with no reference to remuneration. There it is designated as a "fruit of labor," still eagerly pursued by the apostle while God in his grace continued to extend his life in his service (Phil 1:22). Similarly, in Rom 1:13, Paul's missionary work among the gentiles is a fruitful harvest that, hopefully, will include his future visit to the believers at Rome.

Elsewhere in Paul's epistles, καρπός terminology denotes the inbreaking of the new life in Christ for the believer. In sharp contrast to the Demeter inscriptions, where the καρποφόρος epithet is universally positive, Paul can employ fruitfulness terminology negatively, contrasting the spiritual fruit (καρπός) leading to sin and death (Rom 6:21) with the spiritual fruit leading to sanctification and eternal life (Rom 6:22). Salvific fruitfulness is the result of believers being baptized into the death and resurrection of Christ (Rom 6:1–10), with believers placed under the reign of grace and experiencing the newness of Christ's resurrection life and Spirit (6:11b, 13b, 14–15; cf. 7:6; 8:4b–5). Elsewhere the apostle uses the cognate ἄκαρπος in Eph 5:11 to denote the "fruitless deeds of darkness" (cf. Titus 3:14: "in order that they may not be unproductive").

2. The Fruitfulness of Demeter and the Fruitfulness of Believers

While these salutary warnings to believers are underscored by Paul's negative use of καρπός and ἄκαρπος, noted above, the ethical and noetic implications of the believer's life in Christ are given sharp definition by the positive καρπός terminology employed in Eph 5:9. There the new identity of believers as "children of light" is ethically characterized as "the fruit of the light in all goodness and righteousness and truth." The same ethical and noetic dimensions emerge in instances where Paul employs the verb καρποφορέω. Believers, through their incorporation into the death of Christ, are to bear fruit for God (Rom 7:4), as opposed to bearing fruit for death through a slavery to the sinful passions (Rom 7:5). The epistle to the Colossians similarly highlights the ethical and noetic aspects of the gospel's increasing fruitfulness throughout the world (1:6): it is evidenced by believers "bearing fruit in every good work" and "growing in the knowledge of God" (1:10).

Last, the apostle spotlights the mediatory, doxological, pneumatic, and eschatological dimensions of the fruitful life extended to believers in Christ. The believer is filled with "the fruit of righteousness," the experience of which is mediated though Jesus Christ (Phil 1:11; cf. 3:7–10, esp. v. 10) and redounds "to the glory and praise of God" (1:11; cf. 2:11b). At a pneumatic level, the fruit of the Spirit (Gal 5:22) represent a "list of virtues covering a broad range of Christian life, collectively and individually" (Fee 1994, 445). Each virtue expresses the wide-ranging activity of the Spirit that is the hallmark of the new age as opposed to the desires of the flesh, the product of slavery to the Law in the old age (443–54). An eschatological perspective is brought to bear in regards to the spiritual fruit emanating from the Philippians' monetary gift to their apostle (Phil 4:17; cf. 4:10–19; cf. more generally, Ogereau 2014). Markus Bockmuehl (1997, 265; cf. Holloway 2017, 189) draws out the eschatological implications thus: "Quite plausibly this 'fruit' should be understood in eschatological terms … as relating to the future reckoning on the 'day of Jesus Christ' (1:6; 2:16), when in fact the Philippian gift will not only accrue to their own account, but they themselves will be Paul's 'joy and crown' (4:1; cf. 2:16)."

In conclusion, the fruitfulness of the believer's life is a novelty when considered against the backdrop of the widespread καρποφόρος terminology of the Demeter cult. Nothing really approximates the comprehensive divine transformation offered in the Christ associations, overcoming for their members the legacy of an enslaving past, empowering vulnerable and faltering believers in the present, honoring the weak and marginalized over against the contemporary competition for precedence among the associations, and securing the eschatological destiny of the faithful in the future. Whatever similarities there may be communally with the local cultic associations, including those of the Ephesian Demetriasts, these distinctive dimensions of early Christian experience should be acknowledged (Harrison 2019).

Bibliography

Ascough, Richard S., Philip A. Harland, and John S. Kloppenborg, eds. 2012. *Associations in the Greco-Roman World: A Source Book*. Waco, TX: Baylor University Press.
Bockmuehl, Markus. 1997. *The Epistle to the Philippians*. BNTC. Peabody, MA: Hendrickson.
Bock, Darrell L. 2007. *Acts*. BECNT. Grand Rapids: Baker Academic.
Collins, Raymond F. 2008. *The Power of Images in Paul*. Collegeville, MN: Liturgical Press.
Dignas, Beate. 2012. "Rituals and Construction of Identity in Attalid Pergamon." Pages 120–43 in *Historical and Religious Memory in the Ancient World*. Edited by Beate Dignas and R. R. R. Smith. Oxford: Oxford University Press.
Fee, Gordon D. 1994. *God's Empowering Presence: The Holy Spirit in the Letters of Paul*. Peabody, MA: Hendrickson.
Harrison, James R. 2019. "Paul's House Churches and the Cultic Associations." Pages 297–329 in *Paul and the Ancient Celebrity Circuit: The Cross and Moral Transformation*. WUNT 430. Tübingen: Mohr Siebeck.
Heberdey, Rudolf, and Adolf Wilhelm. 1896. *Reisen in Kilikien*. Denkschriften der Kaiserlichen Akademie der Wissenschaften in Wien, philosophisch-historische Klasse 44.6. Vienna: Carl Gerold's Son.
Hepding, H. 1910. "Die Arbeiten zu Pergamon 1908–1909. II: Die Inschriften." *AM* 35:401–93.
Herrmann, Peter H. G. 1998. "Demeter Karpophoros in Sardeis." *REA* 100:495–508.
———. 2016. "Demeter Karpophoros in Sardeis." Pages 199–212 in *Kleinasien im Spiegel epigraphischer Zeugnisse*. Edited by Peter Hermann and Wolfgang Blümel. Berlin: De Gruyter.
Holloway, Paul A. 2017. *Philippians: A Commentary*. Hermeneia. Minneapolis: Fortress.

Horsley, G. H. R. 1989. "A Fishing Cartel in First-Century Ephesus." *NewDocs* 5:95–114.

Keener, Craig S. 2013. *3:1–14*:28. Vol. 2 of *Acts: An Exegetical Commentary*. Grand Rapids: Baker Academic.

Kileci, Senkal, and Birol Can. 2020. "A New Honorific Inscription from Blaundos: Tiberius Claudius Lucius, the Priest of Dionysos Kathegemon." *Adalya* 23:297–309.

McCrum, Michael, and A. G. Woodhead. *Select Documents of the Principates of the Flavian Emperors, A.D. 68–96*. Cambridge: Cambridge University Press, 1961.

Moulton, James H., and George Milligan. 1997. *The Vocabulary of the Greek Testament*. Repr. Peabody, MA: Hendrickson.

Ogereau, Julien M. 2014. *Paul's Koinonia with the Philippians: A Socio-historical Investigation of a Pauline Economic Partnership*. WUNT 2/377. Tübingen: Mohr Siebeck.

Riemann, Othon. 1877. "Inscriptions grecques provenant du receuil de Cyriaque d'Ancône. I. Manuscrit 996 de la bibliothèque Riccardienne à Florence." *BCH* 1:286–94.

Rollens, Sarah E. 2018. "The God Came to Me in a Dream: Epiphanies in Voluntary Associations as a Context for Paul's Vision of Christ." *HTR* 111:41–65.

Schnabel, Eckhard J. 2012. *Acts*. ZECNT 5.5. Grand Rapids: Zondervan.

Sokolowski, Franciszek. 1974. "Propagation of the Cult of Sarapis and Isis in Greece." *GRBS* 15.4:441–48.

Spicq, Ceslas. 1994. *Theological Lexicon of the New Testament*. Translated and edited by James D. Ernest. 3 vols. Peabody, MA: Hendrickson.

Stallsmith, Allaire. 2008. "The Name of Demeter Thesmophoros." *GRBS* 48.5:115–31.

Wallensten, Jenny. 2014. "Karpophoroi Deities and the Attic Cult of Ge: Notes on IG II² 4758." *Opuscula* 7:193–203.

Welles, C. Bradford. 1974. *Royal Correspondence in the Imperial Period: A Study in Greek Epigraphy*. Chicago: Ares.

3. The Blessings of Harmonia: A Happy Married Life

James R. Harrison

IEph 5.1539

Wood 1877, app. 3, "Inscription from the Site of the Temple of Diana," no. 7 and postscript; Wood 1877, app. 8, Inscription from the City and Suburbs, nos. 43–44; *GIBM* 3.2.539; Kaibel 1878, 888a; *JÖAI* 40:13–15; *SEG* 13.505. The inscription, a base for a statue, was inscribed on two related but not matching fragments, which were found in the sanctuary of Artemis. Date: between 163–169 CE (Jones 1972, 482); according to Ronald Syme (1968, 102), the inscription "should be earlier than L. Verus' death in the winter of 168/9" because the text refers to the "emperors" (ll. 5–6).

	- - - - -	[… For Severus]
	ὑπατικόν,	of consular rank,
2	ποντίφικα, ~ κ[ατὰ φύσιν]	pontifex, (the) [natural] father
	Οὐμμιδίου Κο[δράτου]	of Ummidius Qu[adratus],
4	πατέρα, κηδε[στὴν δὲ]	[and] related by marr[iage]
	τῶν θειοτ[άτων αὐτο-]	to the most [holy empe]-
6	κρατ[όρων - - -]	rors [—]
	[—] vacat	… vacat
	[— τὸν ἑα]υ-	[his ow]n
8	[τοῦ] προστ[άτη]ν	guar[dia]n
	παντοίης ἀ[ρετ]ῆ[ς σ]ταθμήν, ῥ[υσί]π-	[a p]aradigm of all kinds of v[irt]u[e],
	τολιν ἄνδρα	a man who s[ave]d the city,
10	ἔξοχον Ἑ[λ]λήνων, πρόκριτον Αὐσο-	honored among the G[r]eeks,
	νίων	princeps of the Italians,
	κλεινοῦ Κοδράτοιο φίλον πατέρ', ὧι	the dear father of the renowned
	βασίλειον	Quadratus, for whom
12	Ἁρμονίη θάλαμον πῆξατ' ἐπ'	Harmonia built a royal chamber for a
	εὐγαμίηι,	happy married life,

Ἁδριανὸς Μούσαισι μέλων ἀνέθηκε Σεουῆρον	Hadrianus, well-known to the Muses, has erected
14 εἰκὼ χαλκείην οὕνεκα προστασίης.	a bronze statue on account of his leadership.
[τοιῶ]νδ', ἄνδρες ῎Ιωνες, ἀγάλματα καλὸν ὁρᾶσθαι	Men of Ionia, (it is) good to see statues [of su]ch men
16 [ἑσταότ' Ἀ]ρτέμ[ιδος πλου]σίωι ἐν τεμένει.	[standing] in the [amp]le grove of [A]rt[emis].

In this honorific inscription, a person called Hadrianus (ll. 13-14) renders honor to the consul Cn. Claudius Severus (PIR C1024), the natural father of Ummidius Quadratus (ll. 2-4). Severus is related by marriage to the Roman rulers (ll. 4-6). The main historical figures, the erector of the inscription and its honorand, are well documented in history. Cn. Claudius Severus (l. 12) married Annia Galeria Aureli Faustina, the eldest daughter of the emperor Marcus Aurelius (*PIR* A0714, cited Pflaum 1960, 29), who was born in 146 CE (Hist. Aug. 1.6.6). The early *cursus honorum* of Severus is set out in an honorific inscription from the city Pompeiopolis in Paphlagonia (Doublet 1889, §14 [IGRR 3.134]), his native city. Son of a consular father (ll. 1-2), the career of Severus began with two priestly posts, including *archiereus* of Augustus (l. 4), progressing to military tribune of *legio III Cyrenaïca* (ll. 6-7) and *quaestor* designate of Caesar (ll. 8-9). This powerful senatorial family of Asia, to which Severus belonged (Pfluam 1960, 29), possessed considerable wealth. This is indicated by the accolade in the Ephesian inscription ("who saved the city," IEph 5.1539.9), as well as by an extended honorific phrase in the Paphlagonian inscription (Doublet 1889, §14.9-13: "*patronus* and savior and benefactor and founder of his native city"). The indebtedness that Hadrianus owes to Severus is underscored by the fact that he summons all the men of Ionia, not just the citizens of Ephesus, to witness the social good of honoring such men with statues in the sanctuary of Artemis.

Hadrianus of Tyre is the famous sophist from Tyre (PIR H4). The commencement of Hadrianus's early career is uncertain, but Philostratus claims that he was trained by Athens (*Vit. soph.* 2.10.1), only to appear subsequently in Rome where he attended the lectures of Galen upon anatomy before he commenced his career as a sophist (Jones 1972, 480-81). There, at the same lectures, he met Severus, who later became his patron, evidenced by the statue that Hadrianus set up to him in the grove of Artemis, with the base of our inscription eulogizing him as προστάτης (IEph 5.1539.8).

Hadrianus's first chair as a sophist was at Ephesus, subsequently being appointed to the chair at Athens (Philostratus, *Vit. soph.* 2.10.4) and eventually holding the chair at Rome after successfully declaiming before the emperor. It is beyond the scope of our commentary to discuss his enmity with Lucian (Jones 1972). For the two extant declamations of Hadrianus, see Amato 2009, as well as discussion of Guast 2019.

However, as important as the Ephesian elites and the orators of the Second Sophistic at Ephesus are, the main focus of our discussion of IEph 5.1539 is an overlooked but important religious and social sidelight of antiquity: the blessing of marriage by the goddess Harmonia (l. 12) and the gods more generally.[1] The ancient literary and documentary sources frequently comment on how the gods establish a harmonious household as the wife submits to the divine order and to the *paterfamilias*. Maximus of Tyre speaks of divine reason regulating sexual love in marriage:

> This is the sacred institution of the gods who preside over nuptials, over kindred, and the procreation of children … the human race … is gifted by (the) Divinity with reason, as that which is equivalent to every other possession. To this (the) Divinity also subjected amatory appetite, as a horse to the bridle, as a bow to the archer, as a ship to the helm, as an instrument to the artificer. (*Diss.* 10)

Plutarch (*Conj. praec.* 18 [140D]) says that a married woman should recognize and only worship her husband's household gods, steering away from strange cults and foreign superstitions. Perictione's *On the Harmony of Women* underscores the importance of correct worship on the wife's part (Plant 2004, §16), as does the *laudatio "Turiae"* ("reverence [for the gods] without superstition": Horsley 1983).

As noted in an Ephesian context (IEph 5.1539.9–12), the inscription of the consul Severus speaks of the goddess Harmonia, daughter of Aphrodite and Ares (Hesiod, *Theog.* 937), blessing his marriage with happiness. As her name implies, the goddess presided over marital harmony, defusing outbreaks of strife and discord by soothing over any tensions between husband and wife. According to the inscription, Severus was

---

1. The remainder of this essay draws upon, in adapted and expanded form, Harrison 2008, 174–77.

a paradigm of all kinds of virtue, a man who saved the city, honoured among the Greeks, princeps of the Italans, the dear father of the renowned Quadratus, for whom Harmonia built a royal chamber for a happy married life.

Significantly, in the case of the visual evidence, the gods are depicted as having a special role in enhancing the beauty of the bride for her marriage day. This motif appears on Athenian vase paintings where Eros outfits the bride with special allure, bringing an alabastron, necklace, and cosmetic chest in order to adorn her. Harmonia, not unexpectedly, plays her own role in depicting the bride's beauty in Athenian visual art. Robert F. Sutton (1997–1998, 32, 46 n. 37) describes the bride Harmonia being attended and adorned cosmetically by the gods in a striking example from an Athenian vase: "One of the finest images of the bridal toilette appears on the eponymous epinetron of the Eretria Painter, where the bride Harmonia, seated in the center, is attended by her mother Aphrodite, assisted by Eros and Himeros, Hebe, Peitho, and Kore (Love, Desire, Youth, Persuasion, and the Maiden)."

Returning to the evidence of the popular philosophers, Hierocles (*Off.* 4.502; see Malherbe 1986, 100–104) provides a late Stoic perspective on the divine ordering of the household:

> The beauty of a household consists in the yoking together of a husband and wife who are united to each other by fate, are consecrated to the gods who preside over weddings, births, and houses, agree with each other and have all things in common, including their bodies, or their souls, and who exercise appropriate rule over the household and servants, take care in the rearing of their children, and pay an attention to the necessities of life which is neither intense nor slack, but moderate and fitting.[2]

Finally, Xenophon (*Oec.* 7.18–19) addresses the wife regarding the divine intent of marriage in this manner:

---

2. Musonius Rufus (*Or.* 14.9–17) posits that the deity created both sexes with "a strong desire for association and union with the other." Coupled with Musonius's Stoic monotheism, however, is the traditional polytheistic superintendence of marriage by the "great gods" (Hera, Eros, and Aphrodite: *Or.* 14.20–32).

3. The Blessings of Harmonia: A Happy Married Life

Wife, the gods seems to have shown much discernment in yoking together female and male, as we call them, so that the couple might constitute a partnership that is most beneficial to both of them. First of all, so that the various species of living creatures may not become extinct, this pair sleeps together for the purpose of procreation. Then this pairing provides offspring to support the partners in their own age, at least in the case of human beings.[3]

New Testament scholars need to be reminded of the religious dimension of marriage in antiquity, if the aforementioned evidence is representative. On this, see the excellent discussion of Balch 1981, 88–90. The husband's hierarchical rule over his wife extended to cultic affairs, touching their sexual life and procreation of children as much as the division of labor within the household.[4] If Paul (or the pseudonymous author) recycled materials from Colossians for his letter to the Ephesians (Dunn 1996, 36–37; Best 1997, 190), he expands upon the household codes, infusing the idea of the mutual submission of husband and wife (Eph 5:21, 22, 24, 25, 33) with a theology of the Spirit (5:18b),[5] the cross (5:24b, 25–27, 29b; cf. Mark 10:35–45), the lordship of Christ over the church (5:23–24, 25–27, 30, 32; cf. 18b–20), and the creation narrative (5:31 [cf. Gen 2:24]). Submission for each partner is motivated by reverence for Christ (Eph 5:21b). The wife submits to the husband as unto Christ (5:22) and the husband loves and serves the wife as Christ unto her (5:25). On submission in Colossians and Ephesians, see Gehring 2004, 234–35, 238, 244.

Did Paul (or pseudonymous author) feel that his teaching in Colossians had not gone far enough, given his strong emphasis on unity and mutuality elsewhere (Rom 10:12; Gal 3:28; 1 Cor 7:1–5; 11:11–12; 12:13; Col 3:11)? His teaching in Ephesians represents a theological revision of the Colossian household codes (cf. Zamfir 2013, passim), which, though relevant to their social setting, had not unfolded sufficiently the redemp-

---

3. Note the divine design of women for indoor work and men for outdoor work (Xenephon, *Oec.* 7.22). D. C. Verner (1981, 66), referring to an inscription (*OGIS* 308 [second century BCE]; cf. Polybius, *Hist.* 22.20), points to the piety and concord of Queen Apollonius Eusebes in her family life.

4. Note Goesler's (1999, 103) comment: "Harmony between the married couple reaches its highest form in agreement about religious matters."

5. On the dependence of the plural participle ὑποτασσόμενοι (Eph 5:21) upon the plural imperative πληροῦσθε ἐν πνεύματι (5:18b), see Hoehner 2003, 720; Gehring 2004, 244.

tive significance of Christ's death for household relations. Paul would have been aware that the Neopythagorean theology of harmony, hierarchical in the ancient literature,[6] expressed the divine ideal for marriage in antiquity. Even the late Stoicism of Hierocles, though more consensual in its model of household relations ("who ... agree with each other and have all things in common," *Off.* 4.502), consecrates marriage to the gods. Paul's theological response in Eph 5:18–33 provided the household with a redemptive, christological, and ecclesiastical framework that would potentially transform the hierarchical relationship between the *paterfamilias* and his wife. Paul enhances the church's unity (Eph 2:11–3:13; 4:1–6) in the household code (Eph 5:21–6.9), with a view to challenging a Roman world, which not only was intolerant of foreign cults, including early Christianity, but also which, in the case of Epicurus, had rejected the relevance of the divine world to household relations and, indeed, the very institution of marriage itself (Hoehner 2003, 727; Roskam 2020). Furthermore, the apostle was pinpricking the ethical curriculum of the eastern Mediterranean gymnasia in its hierarchical and androcentric view of household relations by his pneumatic and Christocentric understanding of mutual submission between husband and wife (cf. the ethical maxim of the Delphic canon: "Rule your wife" [IKyzikos 2.2.2, no. 3]; Harrison 2019, 135–71). But, significantly for our discussion of IEph 5.1539, Paul was also demoting the Greco-Roman gods from their privileged position as guardians of the household and its social relations, securing marriage instead in the inexhaustible and mutually affirming relationships constantly at show between the Father, Son, and Spirit.

Bibliography

Amato, E. 2009. *Severus sophista Alexandrinus: Progymnasmata quae exstant omnia*. Berlin: de Gruyter.
Balch, D. L. 1981. *Let Wives Be Submissive: The Domestic Code in I Peter*. SBLMS 26. Chico, CA: Scholars Press.

---

6. Goesler (1999, 101) observes: "Everything proceeds in harmonious unison and by mutual agreement between the married couple—but the husband is always the leader and the one who makes the decisions." For a fine inscriptional example of harmony between the husband (Euphrosynus) and wife (Epigone), see Hands 1968, §D13.

Best, Ernest. 1997. "The Haustafel in Ephesians (Eph 5:22–8.9)." Pages 189–203 in *Essays on Ephesians*. Edinburgh: T&T Clark.

Doublet, Georges. 1889. "Inscriptions de Paphlagonie." *BCH* 13:293–319.

Dunn, J. D. G. 1996. *The Epistles to the Colossians and to Philemon*. Grand Rapids: Eerdmans.

Gehring, R. W. 2004. *House Church and Mission: The Importance of Household Structures in Early Christianity*. Peabody: Hendrickson.

Goesler, L. 1999. "*Advice to the Bride and Groom*: Plutarch Gives a Detailed Account of His Views on Marriage." Pages 97–115 in *Plutarch's* Advice to the Bride and Groom *and* A Consolation to His Wife: *English Translation, Commentary, Interpretative Essays, and Bibliography*. Edited by Sarah B. Pomeroy. New York: Oxford University Press.

Guast, W. 2019. "Greek Declamation beyond Philostratus' Second Sophistic." *JHS* 139:1–34.

Hands, A. R. 1968. *Charities and Social Aid in Greece and Rome*. London: Thames & Hudson.

Harrison, James R. 2008. "Paul and the Gymnasiarchs: Two Approaches to Pastoral Formation in Antiquity." Pages 141–78 in *Paul: Jew, Greek, and Roman*. Pauline Studies 5. Leiden: Brill.

———. 2019. *Paul and the Ancient Celebrity Circuit: The Cross and Moral Transformation*. WUNT 430. Tübingen: Mohr Siebeck.

Hoehner, H. W. 2003. *Ephesians: An Exegetical Commentary*. Grand Rapids: Eerdmans.

Horsley, G. H. R. 1983. "A More Than Perfect Wife." *NewDocs* 3:33–36.

Jones, C. P. 1972. "Two Enemies of Lucian." *GRBS* 13:475–87.

Kaibel, Georg. 1878. *Epigrammata Graeca ex lapidibus conlecta*. Berlin: Reimer.

Malherbe, Abraham J. 1986. *Moral Exhortation: A Greco-Roman Sourcebook*. Philadelphia: Westminster.

Pflaum, Hans-Georg. *Les carrières procuratoriennes équestres sous le Haut-Empire romain*. Paris: Geuthner, 1960.

Plant, I. M. 2004. *Women Writers of Ancient Greece and Rome: An Anthology*. London: Equinox.

Roskam, Geert. 2020. "Epicurus on Marriage." Pages 119–41 in *The Discourse of Marriage in the Greco-Roman World*. Edited by Jeffrey Beneker and Georgia Tsouvala. Madison: University of Wisconsin Press.

Sutton, Robert F., Jr. 1997–1998. "Nuptial Eros: The Visual Discourse of Marriage in Classical Athens." *The Journal of the Walters Art Gallery* 55–56:27–48.

Syme, Ronald. 1968. "The Ummidii." *Historia* 17:72–105.

Verner, David C. 1981. *The Household of God: The Social World of the Pastoral Epistles*. SBLDS 71. Chico, CA: Scholars Press.

Wood, John Turtle. 1877. *Discoveries at Ephesus*. London: Longmans, Green.

Zamfir, Korrina. 2013. *Men and Women in the Household of God: A Contextual Approach to Roles and Ministries in the Pastoral Epistles*. NTOA/SUNT 103. Göttingen: Vandenhoek & Ruprecht.

4. Epiphanic Protocols and the Pastoral Epistles

Bradley J. Bitner

IEph 1a.24B.8-23

GIBM 3.2.482 (*editio princeps*); CIG 2954 (part); LBW 137 and 140; SIG 867b; *LSAM* 31; SEG 15.696. Decree of the Ephesian *boule* and *demos* designating the month of Artemision holy. Right facing side of a statue base found at Ephesus. Date: 162/164 CE.

[ἐπειδὴ ἡ π]ροεστῶσα τῆς πόλεως ἡμῶν θεὸς Ἄρτε[μις]	Since the leader of our city, the goddess Artemis,
[οὐ μόνον] ἐν τῇ ἑαυτῆς πατρίδι τειμᾶται, ἣν ἁ[πασῶν]	is honored not only in her own native city, which of all
10 [τῶν πόλεων] ἐνδοξοτέραν διὰ τῆς ἰδίας θειότητ[ος πεποίη]-	cities she has made more eminent, through her own divinity,
[κεν, ἀ]λλὰ καὶ παρὰ [Ἕλλησίν τε κ]αὶ [β]αρβάρ[ο]ις, ὥ[στε παν]-ταχοῦ ἀνεῖσθαι αὐτῆς ἱερά τε κα[ὶ τεμένη, ναοὺς δὲ]	but even among Greeks and also barbarians, with the result that everywhere her shrines and sacred precincts have sprung up, and temples
αὐτῇ τε εἰδρύσθαι καὶ βωμοὺς αὐτῇ ἀνακεῖσθαι διὰ	for her have been established and altars to her have been dedicated on account of
τὰς ὑπ' αὐτῆς γεινομένας ἐναργεῖς ἐπιφανείας,	the epiphanies rendered self-evident by her,
15 καὶ τοῦτο δὲ μέγιστον τοῦ περὶ αὐτὴν σεβασ-	And this also is the greatest proof of reverence with respect to her,
μοῦ ἐστιν τεκμήριον, τὸ ἐπώνυμον αὐτῆς	that a month should be named after her,
εἶναι μῆνα καλούμενον παρ' ἡ[μ]ῖν μὲν Ἀρτεμισ[ι]-	(a month) called *Artemision* among us,
ῶνα, παρὰ δὲ Μακεδόσιν καὶ τοῖς λοιποῖς ἔθνεσιν	but among the Macedonians and the rest of the Greek

τοῖς Ἑλληνικοῖς καὶ ταῖς ἐν αὐταῖς πόλεσιν	nations and by the cities among them
20 Ἀρτεμίσιον, ἐν ᾧ μηνὶ πανηγύρεις τε καὶ ἱερο-	Artemisios, in which month festivals and
μηνίαι ἐπιτελοῦνται, διαφερόντως δὲ ἐν [τῇ]	cessation from public business are celebrated, and especially in
ἡμετέρᾳ πόλει τῇ τροφῷ τῆς ἰδίας θεοῦ τῆς Ἐφ[εσί]-	our own city, the nurse of its own Ephesian
ας, ...	goddess ...

1. Epiphany, Artemis, and Ephesus

This is an excerpt from a well-known inscription dealing with festival days of Artemis. It highlights the foundational role of the goddess's epiphanies in Ephesian civic life. It also affords us a glimpse of epiphanic protocols and their efficacy in Ephesus and the Greco-Roman world. Some aspects of this text received helpful commentary in Oster 1979, §19. In recent decades, however, research on Greco-Roman epiphanies has progressed. Likewise, scholarship on the significance of epiphany for interpreting the Pastoral Epistles has advanced, often with only somewhat cursory reference to the Ephesian epigraphical material. The aim of this commentary is, first, to reexamine the Ephesian epigraphical evidence for epiphany; second, to set this within the context of Greco-Roman epiphanic conventions; and finally, to indicate potential insights for understanding the so-called epiphany Christology of the Pastoral Epistles. We begin with the decree above.

The decree is part of a longer text that is dated to ca. 162–164 CE. It was unearthed and recorded in the eighteenth century by F. Hessel and H. van der Horst (found "almost entirely underground on the *xenodochian* [i.e., hostel] road to the aqueduct of Ephesus"; see the commentary on IEph 24). The inscription was later joined to two related texts, each from a different facing side of the same statue base. The text from which the excerpt here is taken is designated "B" by the editors of IEph 1a; it was inscribed on the right side of the block as one faced the statue. It records a decision of the Ephesian *boulē* and *demos* that extended the celebrations and cessation of business in honor of Artemis for the entire month of Artemision (March–April). IEph 1a.24.A, which was inscribed on the left face of the statue base, preserves an edict of the *proconsul* C. Popillius Carus Pedo. In it he confirms this proposal, referring as he does so to precedent set by his proconsular predecessors, his own reverence for Artemis (τὴν εὐσέβειας τῆς θεοῦ, IEph 1a.24A.11), and his regard for the honor of the most illustrious city of the Ephesians (τὴν τῆς λαμπροτάτης Ἐφεσίων πόλεως τειημήν, IEph 1a.24A.12-13). The front face of the statue base, IEph 1a24C, was inscribed with a text honoring Titus Aelius Marcianus Priscus, an Ephesian *agonothetēs* who was "leader of the festival" (προεστῶτος τῆς πανηγύρεως, IEph 1a.24A.16-17) when the decree calling for expanding the festal holiday was put forward. The statue atop the base would have been a representation of Priscus and the whole monument was designed and erected by his relative L. Faenius Faustus (IEph 1a.24C.16-18). Although the ἱερομηνίαι of IEph 1a.24B.20-21 might be understood as "sacrifices belonging to the sacred month," it is better translated as "cessation of public business," especially in connection with ἐκεχειρίας in IEph 1a.24C.8. In support of this, see Kalinowski 2021, 102-5. The festival honoring the goddess for her epiphanies was in effect a month-long administrative and judicial sabbath, but simultaneously it would surely have been an economic boon for the city. For the larger significance of the decree within the late second century Ephesian civic economy and political life, see Rogers 2012, 222-24.

The decree in IEph 1a.24B above preserves lexical choices and syntax that warrant our attention because they enable us to understand the social, political, and theological role that the epiphanies of Artemis played in Ephesus. The ἐπειδή clause beginning in line 8 presents the first reason for the extension of the Artemis festival: she is honored not only in Ephesus but also far more widely "even among Greeks and also barbarians." The means by which she has made her home city more eminent is "through her own divinity" (διὰ τῆς ἰδίας θειότητος πεποίηκεν, ll. 10-11). That is, a widespread knowledge of her divine nature led many to honor her *and* to glorify Ephesus by association (τῇ ἑαυτῆς πατρίδι τειμᾶται, ἣν ἁπασῶν τῶν πόλεων ἐνδοξοτέραν, ll. 9-10). A further result of the knowledge of her divinity is evidenced in the result clause of lines 11-13, which describes the widespread foundation of shrines and temples to Artemis and dedication of altars to her (ὥστε πανταχοῦ ἀνεῖσθαι αὐτῆς ἱερά τε καὶ τεμένη, ναοὺς δὲ αὐτῇ τε εἰδρύσθαι καὶ βωμοὺς αὐτῇ ἀνακεῖσθαι).

What follows next in the decree firmly grounds all of these realities—knowledge of divinity, honor, civic glory, and temple cult—in the epiphanies of Artemis (διά + accusative, ll. 13-14). The basis for Artemis-glory and Ephesian-glory is "the epiphanies rendered self-evident by her" (διὰ τὰς ὑπ' αὐτῆς γεινομένας ἐναργεῖς ἐπιφανείας, ll. 13-14). For the phrase διὰ τάς + ἐπιφανείας in collocation, see IG 12.4.1.166.A.7-8 and B29-30

(Cos and Calymna [200–150 BCE]; Decree of Knidians inviting the Koans to participate in games in honor of Artemis Hyakinthotrophos = ICos ED 77); ICrete 29.3.A.20–21 (Crete [late second century BCE]; Chaniotis 1996, no. 17); IKnidos 1.220.7–8 (ca. 200 BCE); IPergamon 1.248.49–50 (Mysia, Pergamon [135/4 BCE]). This clause similarly provides the basis for honoring Artemis in the form of festivals and cult in other civic decrees (especially IIasos 613 = SEG 45.1508, which is a *lex sacra* from Bargylia in Caria, second–first century BCE, on which, see Müller and Prost 2013). That is, there is a formulaic nature to this language, especially by the first and second centuries CE; this is language that alludes to a larger epiphanic script that would have been widely understood (to be discussed below). The decree then proceeds to another "proof" (τεκμήριον, l. 16) of widespread reverence for Artemis's epiphanic glory: she has her own festival named after her, one which is even celebrated throughout the Greek world (ll. 15–21). Thus, the decree goes on to argue (ll. 23–34), it is fitting to set aside the entire month Artemision as sacred and dedicated to the goddess.

2. Ἐνάργεια and Epiphanic Protocols

We should note the precise language in line 14 describing the epiphanies that are so central to the glory and appeal of Artemis. They are epiphanies that are rendered self-evident (γεινομένας ἐναργεῖς ἐπιφανείας). The term ἐνάργεια connotes that which is evident or manifest. Almost always this refers to a visible appearance of a god/dess. R. Oster (1979, 80) focused on how this appeal to the epiphanies of Artemis as ἐναργεῖς might have functioned in an apologetic context in Ephesus. He rightly noted that cities could appeal with such language to divine manifestations in a defensive or competitive mode. It is also true that many times a festival was dedicated to celebrating a victory made possible by a divine epiphany (see Garbrah 1986). But the terminology should also be associated with a longer and broader tradition of epiphanic narrative and theology. In fact, ἐνάργεια is part of the lexicon of "the formulaics of epiphany." The term signals "that which is founded in immediate sensory experience and thus needs no demonstration, but rather serves as the basis for all argument and inference" (Mackey 2006, 12–13).

A visible manifestation of a goddess such as Artemis was understood to occur within a larger, scripted narrative. Robert Cioffi (2014, 3–4) has coined the phrase "epiphanic protocols" to speak of a tripartite process often observed in the literary sources: first, the god/dess reveals herself

4. Epiphanic Protocols and the Pastoral Epistles

(often expressed with φαίνεσθαι); second, mortals perceive this appearance (often ὁράω in the aorist); and, finally, there is recognition and understanding (usually γινώσκω). In these narratives, the efficacy of divine epiphanies was manifold, its functions potentially overlapping: "Epiphanic gods can hinder or prevent; they can provide aid or advice to mortals; and they can establish new rituals" (4–5). Epiphanies could offer explanation or legitimization for circumstances or function as tools of crisis management (Petridou 2015, 10–16). Visible manifestations might be in response to hymnic invocation or might inspire and authorize poetry, hymnody, or an aretological narrative that focused on specific and salient divine attributes (V. Platt 2011, 60–62; Cioffi 2014, 5). While the inscriptions did not record full narratives like the literary sources did, there was a kind of compression, understood reference, and strategic ambiguity in the way the epigraphical sources appealed to these epiphanic protocols (on "distancing technique … in epigraphic narratives of epiphanies," see Cioffi 2014, 34–35). In light of our text, and its implications (below) for the Pastoral Episltes, Verity Platt's (2011, 50) insight into the inscribing of epiphanies is worth quoting at length:

> In order to document and publicise divine appearances in material form, Hellenistic cities and sanctuaries needed a concise, formulaic term that would capture the force and import of the divine agency they hoped to direct for strategic ends.… Beyond this the term is conveniently ambiguous: although it suggests a visual experience of deity, *epiphaneia* gives a minimum of detail. It leaves open the possibility of single or multiple viewers, and is applied to a broad range of supernatural incursions into the everyday, from fully anthropomorphic visitations to extreme meteorological conditions. The epigraphic use of *epiphaneia* thus leaves anything beyond the manifest nature of the event to the imagination of the reader, allowing the text to concentrate on the epiphany's immediate significance for the community—whether the safety and status of a city or sanctuary, or the vowing of appropriate honours for the deity in question. Most importantly, the substantive noun allows the fact of epiphany to be engraved concisely in stone, reifying and perpetuating divine presence while providing an accessible language within which to imagine such events in the future. Epiphany thus provided a means of transforming the elusive, ephemeral nature of epiphany into a verbal and physical *sēma* (sign) of divine favour.

By the time of our inscription, these epiphanic protocols and the compressed and formulaic epigraphical lexicon in which they were expressed at a civic level were firmly in place. And the manifestations of Artemis were monumentalized as a verbal sign commemorating and perpetuating the possibility of the visible epiphanies to which they referred and highlighting the potential of epiphanic effects for the community. "References to multiple manifestations [in civic inscriptions] reinforce this relationship between epiphany and state security by suggesting that divine salvation is a constant potential" (Platt 2011, 158; see also Petridou 2016). We will return to this verbal fixing of dynamic epiphanies and their efficacy shortly when we turn to the Pastoral Epistles.

3. Epiphanies in Ephesus and Environs

Other references to the epiphanies of Artemis at Ephesus include the following:

SEG 34.1170

JÖAI 55:139–40, no. 4363 (*editio princeps*). Fragment concerning appearances of goddess Artemis. Found near the church of St. John. No date.

Ω	
Γ ΟΝ	
ΙΟ ΗΣ	??
4 ἐπιφανείας ποιῆσαι	to make (perform?) epiphanies
τῆς θεᾶς Ἀρτέ[μιδος]	of the goddess Artemis

This fragmentary text, though difficult to contextualize, preserves the phrase ἐπιφανείας ποιῆσαι, which is rare in the inscriptions but which fits well within the language of epiphanic protocols described above.

IEph 1a.27D.384–87

Wood 1877, app. 6, "Inscriptions from the Great Theatre," no. 1.6.1–40 (*editio princeps*); *GIBM* 3.2.481; Oliver 1941, no. 3.370–413. Letter of *legatus pro praetore* Publius Afranius Flavianus approving the benefaction of Gaius Vibius Salutaris. Found at Ephesos. Date: 104 CE.

… εἴ]ς τε τειμὴν καὶ εὐσέβ[ειαν τῇ]	… for the honor and the reverence of
ς ἐπι-	the most

4. Epiphanic Protocols and the Pastoral Epistles

385 φανεσ[τάτης θεᾶς] Ἀρτέμιδος καὶ τοῦ   manifest goddess Artemis and the
οἴκου τῶν αὐτοκρατό-   house of the emperors
ρ[ω]ν δ[ωρεαῖς καὶ χρη]μάτων   by gifts and dedication of money,
ἀφιερώσει τὰ νῦν φιλοτειμου-   which things now he has
μένου ...   lavished ...

In this excerpt from the famous Salutaris foundation inscription (see Rogers 1991), we see two important things. First, Artemis is referred to with the superlative epithet, already formulaic by at least the end of the first century, ἐπιφανεστάτης ("most manifest"; cf. IEph 1a.17.70; IEph 1a.27C.344–45 [also 104 CE]: ἐπιφανεστάτης καὶ μεγίστης θεᾶς Ἀρτέμιδος). By the turn of the third century, the epithet was applied by extension to the lords of the Severan house (IEph 2.296.8–10 [205 CE]: διὰ τῆς ἑαυτὸν προνοίας τῆς ἐναργεστάτης ἐπιφανεστάτης τε οἱ κύριοι ἡμῶν Σεουῆρος ...). Indeed, the *simplex* had long been used of Hellenistic rulers and was applied early to the Caesars (in IEph 2.251.6 [48 BCE] Julius Caesar is θεὸς ἐπιφανής). This has led some toward an antiimperial reading of the epiphany Christology of the Pastoral Epistles (see discussion below of Gill 2008). A second feature to note in the Salutaris inscription's use of this epiphanic epithet is the way it contributes to the intertwining of honor and reverence for Artemis, Ephesus, and the imperial house.

IEph 5.1898 + *JÖAI* 55:146, no. 4407 (part)

SEG 34.1106; Engelmann 1986, 34; SEG 36.1023. Honorary inscription for athlete Attalos on base. Roman; found at Ephesos. No date.

[ἀγ]αθῇ τύχῃ·   To Good Fortune.
[—Ἀ]τταλος ἀκροβάτης   Attalos the athlete
[τῆς ἐπιφα]νεστάτης θεᾶς Ἀρτέμιδος   belonging to the most manifest goddess Artemis
[—Ἐ]φέσιος, πύκτης.   Ephesia, the boxer.

Here we simply note that others of lesser status than emperors—in this case an athlete—might advertise honor derived from association with the Ephesian goddess, her epiphanies, and the city.

JÖAI 59:181–82, no. 14

Honorific inscription (fragmentary) for an unknown (*prytanis*?); inscribed on a pillar. Ephesus. Undated.
[—]

0	[ἐκτελέσασαν τὰ μυσ]-	they completed all
	τήρια [πάντα]	the mysteries
	[κ]αὶ φιλ[οτείμως ὅλον]	and ambitiously the
	τὸν ἐνια[υτὸν],	whole year (long),
	πληροῦσ[αν]	they fulfilled
5	μὲν τὴν ἐψ[ηφισμένην —]	the proposed
	κοσμοῦσα[ν —].Η[—]	beautifications(?)
	τειμῆς λα[μπ]ρο[—]	of the honor illustrious(?)
	καὶ τὴν τοῦ γένο[υς ἐπι]-	and the epiphany of the
	φάνειαν.	*genos*.

IEph 3.987 + Add p. 23

JÖAI 45:87–89, no. 14 (*editio princeps*). (Cf. the parallel text in IEph 3.988 for the sister Vipsania Polla.) Honorary inscription for Vipsania Olympias, priestess of Artemis, by *boule* and *demos*. Found at Ephesos. Date: first century BCE–first century CE.

Excerpt from lines 9–18

	… ἱερατεύ-	… they carried out the
10	[σασαν] τῆς Ἀρτέμιδος	priesthood of Artemis
	[ἱεροπρε]πῶς τά τε μυσ-	sacredly administering the
	[τήρια κ]αὶ τὰς θυσίας	mysteries and the sacrifices
	[ἀξίως] ἐπιτελέσασαν	worthily they completed
	[καὶ κ]αταστέψασαν	and they decked with garlands
15	[τόν τ]ε ναὸν καὶ τὰ πε-	the temple and all the things
	[ρὶ αὐτ]ὸν πάντα ἐν ταῖς	pertaining to it in the
	[ἐπιφαν]εστάταις τῆς θε-	days of the most manifest
	[οῦ ἡμέρ]αις …	goddess …

In the two texts above, we are reminded that the epiphanies of Artemis were closely associated with the celebration of her mysteries and the cult surrounding her famous temple in Ephesus. On this, see Rogers 2012 and Rogers, "Some Priestesses of Artemis of Ephesos," in *NewDocs* 11B.

Of course, Artemis was not the only deity in and around Ephesus to manifest her presence and power in epiphany. And not all epiphanies were salvific; a divine manifestation could also bring judgment. In the following text, we see the goddess Hygeia honored at Ephesus for her epiphany (see also Petridou 2015, 172–79).

IEph 4.1212

JÖAI 52:48, no. 85 (*editio princeps*). Dedication to Hygeia. Found at Ephesos. No date.

1	ἐπιφανεῖ	She shows forth in epiphany
	θεᾷ Ὑγείᾳ.	To the goddess Hygeia.

At the village of nearby Notion (ca. 15km from Ephesus), Apollo Klarios was also honored for his epiphanies (SEG 33.973.6 [late second century BCE]: τὰς ἐπιφανείας). The following text from Pergamon honors a new Asklepios by thanking him for his salvific epiphany (see also IErythrai 223 for a similar dedication at Erythrai).

IPergamon 2.296

Pergamon. Roman?

[— — — — — — — — Ἀσκλη]-	... to Asklepios
πιῶι, ἐπιφαν[εῖ γενομένωι]	he shows forth his epiphany by becoming
σωτῆρι, χαριστ[ή]ρ[ιον].	savior, a thanksgiving-stela.

One more text to mention is a confession inscription. It narrates the story of a punishment visited upon a woman called Apphia by means of an epiphany of the moon god Men. The god's epiphany, by which he manifests his justice, is sudden and violent: "in this manner the god showed forth his epiphany ... and tore Apphia ... the virgin" (οὕτως τε ἐπιφανεὶς ὁ θεὸς ... Ἀπφίαν ... οὖσαν παρθένον διέρηξε, Petzl 1994, 59.11–14; for debate over whether Men's epiphany killed Apphia or took her virginity, see Chaniotis 2004, 20–21). But in any case, we see in this text, in a region not far from Ephesus, an example of divine manifestation as double-edged: the justice of the god is upheld even as justice is meted out upon a wrongdoer by means of epiphanic punishment. This adds an important corrective to summaries of epiphany in New Testament scholarship that focus solely on the salvific aspect of epiphany.

In summary, what we see from the epigraphic evidence from Ephesus (especially captured in IEph 1a.24B above) and its environs is the following pattern:

1. The god/dess exercises her divine agency by means of
2. a self-evident epiphany that manifests salient attributes
3. either to save or bring justice and judgment (or both),
4. with the result that a temple is built and cult established; all of this leads to
5. a civic festival being celebrated as
6. an expression of piety that brings
7. honor to the god/dess, glory to the city and to various associated figures,
8. all of which is verbally fixed on an inscribed monument in order to
9. serve a variety of ends (e.g., explain, legitimate, manage crisis, warn, give hope).

In other words, the efficacy of epiphany is powerful and variegated. Epiphany operates in these inscriptions within a theological and sociopolitical logic whereby "individuals and communities used the epiphanic schema to make claims on exclusive religious knowledge and practice" (Petridou 2015, 10–11). In this schema, and notwithstanding the compressed and strategic verbal expression of the epiphanic narratives in the inscriptions, the appeal to the ἐνάργεια ("visible, self-evident manifestation") of divine appearance serves to ground multiple claims. When we turn to the Pastoral Epistles, we will see some similarity but also difference with these epiphanic protocols.

4. The So-Called Epiphany Christology of the Pastoral Epistles

4.1. Representative Issues in Scholarship

There is good reason to set the evidence represented here in relation to the texts of the Pastoral Epistles, especially given their association with Ephesus (Trebilco 2004, 205–36). This is even more the case because the language and concepts associated with epiphany appear with relative frequency in the Pastoral Epistles and help to frame the Christology of those epistles.

4. Epiphanic Protocols and the Pastoral Epistles

While this is not the place for a full history of scholarship on the so-called epiphany Christology of the Pastoral Epistles, it is worth noting a renewed and steady stream of studies since the mid-late 1990s, which includes Lau 1996; Läger 1996; Bassler 1996b; Stettler 1998; Bassler 2002; Mitchell 2004; Trebilco 2004, 355–61; van Houwelingen 2019; Manomi 2019 (most of these works include full bibliography of earlier scholarship). Among these studies, there is a general consensus that epiphany is a key theme or controlling framework in the Pastoral Epistles, particularly in terms of the Christology and discourse of Titus and 2 Timothy. Lau 1996, Mitchell 2004, Towner 2006, and Gill 2008, and especially Bassler 1996a, 1996b, and 2002 are quite helpful for summarizing key interpretive issues and directing us to the focal texts in the Pastoral Epistles.

Andrew Lau (1996, 15) began his study by noting that we must understand what epiphanies *are* and are *for* before we can discern their function in the Pastoral Epistles. Yet in working this out, he appeals only in the most cursory fashion to IEph 2.251 (48 BCE, above) and three very late (late third/early fourth centuries) references to ἐπιφανεστάτης and ἐπιφανής each an epithet for human figures (IEph 7.2.3603, 3604, 3825). This is somewhat understandable as Lau does not emphasize the Greek inscriptions. He focuses instead on the Jewish intertestamental adaptation of the way epiphany language worked in Hellenistic sources. Lau (1996, 224–25) ultimately makes a case for seeing the theophanies of the Maccabean literature (esp. 2 Macc 3:30; 12:22; 14:15; 15:34; and various Old Testament/LXX texts, e.g., Gen 35:70; Deut 33:2; Ps 117:27; Jer 36[29]:14; Zeph 2:11) as the putative background and key to the way epiphany functions in the Pastoral Epistles. For Lau, the payoff is a perceived continuity of epiphany across the LXX tradition and the Pastoral Epistles whereby in the latter there are a variety of ways epiphanic language is applied to the first and second comings of Christ.

Margaret Mitchell (2004, 184–85) notes that Lau's philological approach to the issue was at the time a culmination of a fruitful line of investigation which had been "amassing … the widest possible range of sources which employ the term ἐπιφάνεια and cognates—most valuably the inscriptions." But, she argues, this lexically-driven method risks missing important data and theological-political patterns. She proposes instead a focus on the "epiphanic logic" of how a "mediated divine presence" was exploited in creative ways in New Testament texts, especially by the apostle Paul, whom she names an "epiphanic envoy" (186–87). Paul presented himself in various texts (e.g., Gal 1:12–16; 2:19–20; 3:1; 4:14; 6:17) as a kind of embodied epiphany of Jesus Christ. He styles himself "as a one-man multi-media presentation of the gospel of Christ crucified … [wherein] message and messenger were indivisibly united in re-presenting to the audience an aural-visual icon of Christ crucified" (Mitchell 2004, 187–89). In the Pastoral Epistles, we witness "paradoxically, an attempt to fix the dynamic epiphanic medium" presented in other Pauline epistles (199). By drawing on the lexicon *and* logic of epiphany, the author of the Pastoral Epistles does not merely speak of a first and second coming. Rather, the "revelatory event is neither singular nor dual, past nor future, because it is not confined to any static moment … [ἐπιφάνεια] in the Pastorals includes … the entire history of its mediated revelation through the Pauline proclamation … the epistolary epiphany of the Pauline proclamation … *now* mediates the full spectrum of divine disclosure—from before recorded history on into the future" (Mitchell 2004, 200–201; see also Donelson 1986, 81–85; 132–37). A final note in Mitchell's (2004, 201) essay is striking considering the monumentalization of epiphanic protocols highlighted above: "The epiphanic media of the early Christian cult," she concludes, "were to be neither τόπος nor tomb, but apostolic envoys and then texts." Although Mitchell does not pursue a full application of her insights to the epiphany Christology of the Pastoral Epistles, we should bear her approach in mind especially once the evidence above is taken into account.

Philip Towner (2006, 418) is a good representative of the view that epiphany language, often associated with salvation terminology, is calibrated "to engage the dominant religious-political discourse." This, in Ephesus and Asia Minor, he argues, would overwhelmingly have been the imperial cult and the Augustan house. The epiphany Christology of 1 Timothy is therefore designed to prompt "a rethinking of common cultural categories as it tells of God's story in Hellenistic christological dress … [and] present a christological complement to the vivid counter-Imperial claims expressed in the striking multitiered description of God to come" (418–19). In sum, for "Timothy and the Ephesian church, 'epiphany' Christology reconceptualizes the relation between eschatology and ethics" (419). Although he disagrees as to the dominant Jewish background of the epiphanic language, Towner comes quite close to Lau in summarizing the function in 1 Timothy and the Pastoral Epistles: "Paul conceives of the whole epoch bounded by the two epiphanies and characterized by his mission as subject to God's eschatological 'clock'" (420). Malcolm Gill (2008) has argued along similar lines, with particular reference to 1 Tim 2:1–7. His antiimperial reading of the epiphanic language presents Paul as capitalizing "upon the concept of 'epiphany' ... common to his readers" and applying this "to Christ ... [by] calling his readers to obedience in light of the impending appearance, not of an emperor but, of the true sovereign Jesus Christ" (98–99). Towner and Gill are to be commended for insisting that the epiphanic language of the Pastoral Epistles must have not only important Old Testament/Jewish antecedents but also Greco-Roman political-theological implications. But their terminological focus on (primarily) the imperial titulature of ἐπιφανεστάτης and ἐπιφανής does not allow them fully to take into consideration the "epiphanic logic" or "protocols" evinced by texts testifying to the centrality of Artemis and her manifest epiphanies in Ephesian civic life and religion.

Jouette Bassler has given sustained thought to the patterns and meaning of epiphany in the Pastoral Epistles. Her view of the so-called epiphany Christology has evolved over time. In her Thompson lecture, Bassler (1996b, 311) argued that the "epiphany Christology of [the Pastoral Epistles] functions as the foundation of a pervasive epiphanic pattern that touches almost the whole of the letters' contents." Several aspects of her essay are noteworthy. First, she asserts that Christ, in the Pastoral Epistles, is the "vehicle" rather than the "content" of epiphany. In addition, Bassler contends that the language of epiphany communicates not simply a "static picture of a curtain going up twice to reveal tableaux of the divine reality"; rather; there is "a live drama." In fact, developing an earlier insight of Hans Windisch (1935, 213–38), Bassler sees that the saving intervention alluded to by the epiphany discourse of the Pastoral Epistles maps the first and final "christological epiphanies" as two poles of a spectrum "filled with a whole series of epiphanic moments," including, particularly, "Christian proclamation and teaching" (315).

Bassler is attentive not only to epiphanic language but also to the literary-discourse *function(s)* of epiphany as she analyzes and categorizes the relevant passages. For Bassler, Jesus's first epiphany encompasses more than the entire incarnational arc of his life and saving death. It emphasizes, for example, in 2 Tim 1:9–10, "Christ's role as revealer" and the "revelatory aspect" of God's saving will in the Christ event (Bassler 1996b, 318–20). This first epiphany category thus shades quickly into another: interim epiphanies or epiphanic moments in the now-age. Here, "proclamation is an epiphanic event," those who proclaim the gospel "become themselves agents of epiphany," and the letters of the Pastoral Epistles themselves take their place among "quotidian" epiphanies that mediate in various ways the salvific power of the Christ event (2 Tim 1:9b–10; Tit 1:2–3; 2:11; 3:4;

1 Tim 1:12, 15–16; 2:5–7; Bassler 1996b, 321–24; recall Mitchell's "epiphanic media" above). For Bassler, the final epiphany points to the *parousia* (1 Tim 6:14; Tit 2:13; 2 Tim 4:8) and serves as an eschatological-ethical motivation (Bassler 1996b, 317; or, more precisely, to delineate the "duration of the charge to Timothy" [205]).

In a subsequent essay, Bassler (2002, 194–95) questioned the late-1990s consensus in which she had participated, namely, that there is a foundational and fully "integrated epiphany pattern" underlying the Christology of all three Pastoral Epistles. She emphasizes the need to investigate the discourse-theological function of epiphany with even more attention to its contribution to each of the individual Pastoral Epistles. And she warns against assuming a unified, presupposed "epiphany Christology" (196). Nevertheless, Bassler continues to affirm the presence in the Pastoral Epistles of "a continuum of epiphanies that reveal, actuate, and perpetuate God's plan and motivate compliance with it." These epiphanies include (prominently) proclamation (207). She concludes that whereas 1 Timothy "simply [uses] epiphany language," 2 Timothy evinces "a highly developed … epiphany Christology." And Titus shows perhaps the most "complex" pattern, what she terms a "mosaic of epiphany concepts" (208–14). Overall, Bassler's close attention to the particular discourse-theological function of epiphany in each epistle leads her to develop more fully important insights found elsewhere in the interpretive tradition (especially those of, for example, Windisch 1935, Donelson 1986, and Mitchell 2004). Crucially, Bassler's sensitive reading of this "gradual emergence of an epiphany Christology" across the Pastoral Epistles suggests important points of contact with the efficacy of epiphany we have seen embedded in the inscriptions.

With insights from Bassler and others in mind, I conclude with reflections on how the epiphanic protocols of the epigraphical evidence might fruitfully aid New Testament scholars in interpreting the efficacy of epiphany Christology in the Pastoral Epistles. There is more to consider than space allows, but I offer a few lines for further investigation.

4.2. Κήρυγμα versus Ἐνάργημα in 1 Tim 3:16

Although Bassler is correct that an epiphany pattern is less obvious in 1 Timothy, there is nevertheless a clear epiphanic narrative, one that charts the coordinates of a continuum that is filled out with further detail in Titus and 2 Timothy. This emerges in the faithful saying of 1 Tim 1:15: "Christ

4. Epiphanic Protocols and the Pastoral Epistles 79

Jesus came into the world to save sinners" (the verb is ἔρχομαι rather than ἐπιφαίνω vel sim; but note the complementary infinitive σῶσαι). First Tim 6:14, which together with 1:15–16 frames the epistle and which uses explicit epiphanic language (μέχρι τῆς ἐπιφανείας τοῦ κυρίου ἡμῶν Ἰησοῦ Χριστοῦ), offers confirmation that we should read the earlier passage, too, as implying epiphany (Donelson 1986, 82, 152–53; Lau 1996, 226). Indisputably, in the center of this two epiphanies continuum (perhaps at the center of the epistle itself, in structural terms) lies a doctrinal confession with some of the very epiphanic protocols described and glimpsed in the epigraphical script above. The text of 1 Tim 3:16 follows, with cola divided and labeled for reference (for discussion of form with bibliography, see Bassler 1996a, 74–77; Stettler 1998, 80–85):

A   καὶ ὁμολογουμένως μέγα ἐστὶν τὸ τῆς εὐσεβείας μυστήριον·
B   ὃς ἐφανερώθη ἐν σαρκί,
C   ἐδικαιώθη ἐν πνεύματι,
D   ὤφθη ἀγγέλοις,
E   ἐκηρύχθη ἐν ἔθνεσιν,
F   ἐπιστεύθη ἐν κόσμῳ,
G   ἀνελήμφθη ἐν δόξῃ

Note first the formulaic epiphanic verbs in cola B and D (ἐφανερώθη, ὤφθη; recall Cioffi 2014, 4–5). But rather than the standard verb of recognition (e.g., γινώσκω), and in line with the lexicon of Pauline faith-response, we see ἐπιστεύθη in colon F. In other words, there is in this confession a variation on the pattern *revelation–appearance–recognition* that characterized epiphany narratives and was latent in the epigraphical references. Without entering into important debates concerning the arrangement and meaning of this text, I simply want to point out that at—or near—the structural and conceptual center of the confession stands colon E, with the verb ἐκηρύχθη (ἐν ἔθνεσιν). In the context of 1 Timothy (cf. 1:15–16, πιστὸς ὁ λόγος … ἵνα … ἐνδείξηται … πρὸς ὑποτύπωσιν; 2:5–7, τὸ μαρτύριον … εἰς ὃ ἐτέθην ἐγὼ κῆρυξ καὶ ἀπόστολος … διδάσκαλος ἐθνῶν), this would seem to underline the kerygmatic efficacy of Christ's epiphany, proclaimed among the nations. That is to say, the focus in this compressed confession in its discourse context is on κήρυγμα (proclamation) rather than ἐνάργημα (visible manifestation). What is prominent is the importance (and efficacious glory-power?) of proclaiming, hearing, and trusting the received gospel message rather than on seeking or seeing a manifestly self-evident vision of Christ. This interpretation complements that offered by Bassler (2002, 199–204) and Mitchell (2004, 200–201).

Two further points may be worth pursuing: First, if, as in the epigraphic pattern above, epiphany resulted in the establishment of temple and cult, then the epiphanic design of 1 Tim 3:16 may include 3:14–15 as well. In those immediately preceding verses, many have rightly noted how the church is portrayed both with Hellenistic sanctuary terminology and with strong echoes of the Old Testament/Jewish temple background (οἶκος θεοῦ ... ἐκκλησία θεοῦ ζῶντος, στύλος καὶ ἑδραίωμα τῆς ἀληθείας; Stettler 1998, 80–109; Collins 2012, 99–105). Second, if the inscribing of compressed epiphanic narratives (such as IEph 1a.24B) served to explain, legitimate, warn, stir up hope, et cetera as Platt (2011) insisted, then there may be a verbal compression, intended with similar effect, inscribed here at the center of 1 Timothy. Perhaps the Christ-epiphany confessed in 1 Tim 3:16 is more than a bare use of epiphany language, especially if its kerygmatic-revelatory form and power anchors the discourse, and more broadly supports the purpose of 1 Timothy, and does so in accord with the efficacy of epiphany in places like Ephesus.

4.3. Epiphany, Victory, and Life Through the Gospel in 2 Tim 1:8–12

In 2 Timothy, where the epiphany pattern is more obviously present, Paul urges Timothy not to be ashamed of his μαρτύριον (1:8; cf. 1 Tim 2:6) about the Lord. This testimonial of grace is anchored in the incarnation of Christ (1:9–10; χάριν ... φανερωθεῖσαν δὲ νῦν διὰ τῆς ἐπιφανείας τοῦ σωτῆρος ἡμῶν Ἰησοῦ Χριστοῦ). And just as the theophany or epiphany of a god/dess recorded in the inscriptions might involve salvation brought about by conquering an enemy that threatened the city, there is a degree of similarity in the result of epiphany here. Divine power revealed in the gospel *saves* (1:8–9; τῷ εὐαγγελίῳ κατὰ δύναμιν θεοῦ τοῦ σώσαντος ἡμᾶς) and does so with a double benefit. In part, salvation is shown forth in Christ himself who abolished death (1:10; καταργήσαντος μὲν τὸν θάνατον). But the epiphanic power that irrupted epiphanically in the Christ's person and work continues to operate effectively through the gospel (1:10; διὰ τοῦ εὐαγγελίου; cf. 1:8). Christ's salvific power, then, is further manifested as it produces life and incorruptibility by means of *proclamation* (1:10; φωτίσαντος δὲ ζωὴν καὶ ἀφθαρσίαν). As in 1 Timothy, yet even more insistently, the emphasis of epiphanic discourse in 2 Timothy is on the power of the gospel proclamation to achieve—first through Paul, then through Timothy (1:8–12), and finally through other faithful proclaimers (2:1-2)—a variegated victory and efficacy (cf. 4:1-8; Bassler 2002, 204-8).

4.4. Epiphanic Pedagogy in Titus 2:11-14

Titus bursts with epiphany, from its opening promise of the hope of eternal life (1:2) made manifest by means of proclamation (1:3; ἐφανέρωσεν … ἐν κηρύγματι) through to a final, important soteriological passage (3:4-7). At the center of this "mosaic of epiphany concepts" (Bassler 2002, 209-12) stands 2:11-14, a text which knits together the fabric of the whole discourse and in which the full epiphanic continuum is compressed. Many read the epiphany in 2:11 as pointing to the incarnation or the entire Christ-event (Ἐπεφάνη … ἡ χάρις τοῦ θεοῦ σωτήριος πᾶσιν ἀνθρώποις; e.g., van Houwelingen 2019, 97). But this is an unwarranted restriction. It quickly becomes clear in the clauses that follow that this manifestation of divine, saving grace is one that has continued and continuous efficacy. This is expressed in somewhat surprising terms as an epiphany that *instructs* (2:12; παιδεύουσα ἡμᾶς). The kerygmatic content of this grace-epiphany is characterized in full and specific christological terms in the final relative clause (2:14; ὅς ἔδωκεν ἑαυτόν). But the focus throughout is on the interim pedagogical efficacy of epiphany. Revealed grace *trains* believers for the purpose of pious living (2:12; παιδεύουσα ἡμᾶς … ἵνα … δικαίως καὶ εὐσεβῶς ζήσωμεν). This manner of life is to be characterized negatively by a denial of impiety (2:12l ἀρνησάμενοι τὴν ἀσέβειαν) and positively by an eager fastening upon a horizon of hope that will arrive as a further and fuller epiphany of salvific glory (2:13; προσδεχόμενοι τὴν μακαρίαν ἐλπίδα καὶ ἐπιφάνειαν τῆς δόξης). The γάρ of 2:11 demonstrates at the very least that this epiphanic pedagogy of grace in Christ grounds the community instructions in 2:1-10. But in light of the epiphanic protocols above there is good reason to reexamine just how crucial 2:11-14 may be as a nexus of the entire epistle's discourse, not least with reference to the salient divine attributes of grace (χάρις, 2:11) and glory (δόξα, 2:13).

Bibliography

Bassler, Jouette M. 1996a. *1 Timothy, 2 Timothy, Titus*. ANTC. Nashville: Abingdon.

———. 1996b. "A Plethora of Epiphanies: Christology in the Pastoral Letters." *PSB* 17:310-25.

———. 2002. "Epiphany Christology in the Pastoral Letters: Another Look." Pages 194–214 in *Pauline Conversations in Context: Essays in Honor of Calvin J. Roetzel*. Edited by Calvin J. Anderson, P. Harl Sellew, and Claudia Setzer. JSNTSup 221. London: Sheffield Academic.

Chaniotis, Angelos. 1996. *Die Verträge zwischen kretische Poleis in der hellenistischen Zeit*. Stuttgart: Steiner.

———. 2004. "Under the Watchful Eyes of the Gods: Divine Justice in Hellenistic and Roman Asia Minor." Pages 1–43 in *The Greco-Roman East: Politics, Culture, Society*. Yale Classical Studies 31. Cambridge: Cambridge University Press.

Cioffi, Robert L. 2014. "Seeing Gods: Epiphany and Narrative in the Greek Novels." *Ancient Narrative* 11:1–42.

Collins, Raymond F. 2012. *1 and 2 Timothy and Titus: A Commentary*. Louisville: Westminster John Knox.

Donelson, Lewis R. 1986. *Pseudepigraphy and Ethical Argument in the Pastoral Epistles*. HUT 22. Tübingen: Mohr Siebeck.

Engelmann, H. 1986. "Notizen zum Repertorium ephesischer Inschriften." *EA* 8:33–35.

Garbrah, K. 1986. "On the θεοφάνεια in Chios and the Epiphany of Gods in War." *ZPE* 65:207–10.

Gill, Malcolm. 2008. *Jesus as Mediator: Politics and Polemic in 1 Timothy 2:1–7*. New York: Lang.

Houwelingen, Rob van. 2019. "The Meaning of ἐπιφάνεια in the Pastoral Epistles." *Journal for the Study of Paul and His Letters* 9:89–108.

Kalinowski, Angela V. 2021. *Memory, Family, and Community in Roman Ephesos*. Cambridge: Cambridge University Press.

Läger, Karoline. 1996. *Die Christologie der Pastoralbriefe*. HTS 12. Münster: Lit.

Lau, Andrew Y. 1996. *Manifest in Flesh: The Epiphany Christology of the Pastoral Epistles*. WUNT 2/86. Tübingen: Mohr Siebeck.

Mackey, Jacob L. 2006. "Saving the Appearances: The Phenomenology of Epiphany in Atomist Theology." Princeton/Stanford Working Papers in Classics, no. 050601. May.

Manomi, Dogara Ishaya. 2019. "Salvific, Ethical, and Consummative 'Appearances' in the Pastoral Epistles? A Response to Rob van Houwelingen." *Journal for the Study of Paul and His Letters* 9:109–117.

Mitchell, Margaret M. 2004. "Epiphanic Evolutions in Earliest Christianity." *Illinois Classical Studies* 29:183–204.

Müller, C., and F. Prost. 2013. "Un décret du *koinon* des Ionian trouvé à Claros." *Chiron* 43:93–126.
Oliver, James H. 1941. *The Sacred Gerousia*. Athens: The American School of Classical Studies at Athens.
Oster, R. 1979. "Holy Days in Honour of Artemis." *NewDocs* 4:74–82.
Petridou, Georgia. 2015. *Divine Epiphany in Greek Literature and Culture*. Oxford: Oxford University Press.
———. 2016. "Amorphous Epiphanies and Divine Bilingualism: Crossing Physical and Cultural Borders on the Battlefield." Pages 155–72 in *Borders: Terminologies, Ideologies, and Performances*. Edited by Annette Weissendrieder. Tübingen: Mohr Siebeck.
Petzl, Georg. 1994. "Die Beichtinschriften westkleinasiens." *EA* 22:1–174.
Platt, Verity. 2011. *Facing the Gods: Epiphany and Representation in Graeco-Roman Art, Literature and Religion*. Cambridge: Cambridge University Press.
Rogers, Guy MacLean. 1991. *The Sacred Identity of Ephesos: Foundation Myths of a Roman City*. London: Routledge.
———. 2012. *The Mysteries of Artemis of Ephesos: Cult, Polis, and Change in the Graeco-Roman World*. Synkrisis. New Haven: Yale University Press.
Stettler, Hanna. 1998. *Die Christologie der Pastoralbriefe*. WUNT 2/105. Tübingen: Mohr Siebeck.
Towner, Philip H. 2006. *The Letters to Timothy and Titus*. NICNT. Grand Rapids: Eerdmans.
Trebilco, Paul. 2004. *The Early Christians in Ephesus from Paul to Ignatius*. Grand Rapids: Eerdmans.
Windisch, Hans. 1935. "Zur Christologie der Pastoralbriefe." *ZNW* 34:213–38.
Wood, John Turtle. 1877. *Discoveries at Ephesus*. London: Longmans, Green.

Androklos, the Founder of Ephesus

5. Androklos, Founder of Ephesus

James R. Harrison

A significant change in the processional route of Ephesian Artemis, the Via Sacra, had occurred by the imperial era. The old Archaic and Classical route, which had incorporated beautiful seaside vistas, was replaced by a new landlocked, territorial alternative, necessitated by the re-siting of the city in the Hellenistic age (281 BCE) due to the silting of the Ephesian harbor (see "The Kaytros River and the Silting of the Ephesian Harbor" in this volume). The later second-century procession of the statues through Ephesus, funded by a bequest of C. Vibius Salutaris, reinforced for Ephesian citizens the realities of Roman control and power in provincial Asia Minor (IEph 1a.27). For discussion, see Rogers 1991. Nevertheless, this new route was intimately connected to the traditional Ephesian foundation myths. Along the processional way of Artemis were three sites (Heroon of Androklos, the temple of Hadrian, the Nymphaeum of Trajan) associated in various ways from the second century BCE to the second century CE with the founder (κτίστης) of Ephesus, Androklos. Indeed, among the many statues belonging to Salutaris's procession was a statue of Androklos himself (IEph 1a.27.183 [104 CE]: "and a silver image [of Androklos(?)]"), although the Greek text is restored.[1] Here we are witnessing the continuing impact of and centrality for Ephesus of its foundation mythology long after the establishment of the city. For full discussion of the role of Androklos in Ephesian mythology from Hellenistic to late antiquity Ephesus, see Mortensen 2015, 110–27. But before we can appreciate the significance of the epigraphic evidence relating to

---

1. The restoration is virtually assured by the fact that since three sites honoring Androklos have been carefully incorporated into the processional itinerary of Vibius Salutaris at Ephesus, it is impossible to conceive that the statue of Androklos was somehow omitted from the procession, even if the procession was dominated by images of Artemis. See Ng 2007, 220 n. 74 for a strong rebuttal of such scepticism.

Androklos, it needs to be contextualized by a detailed examination of the literary, archaeological, and numismatic evidence regarding the founder of Ephesus.

1. Androklos: The Literary, Archaeological, and Numismatic Evidence

The literary sources about the foundation story of the city and the role of Androklos as founder (Athenaeus, *Deipn.* 8.361d-e; Strabo, *Geogr.* 14.1.3-4; 14.1.21; Pausanias, *Descr.* 7.2.8-9; Ephoros, *FGrHist* 70 F 126 [= *Stephanus of Byzantium, Ethn.* 68, s.v. "Benna"]) pose their unique set of problems. The fusion of founder traditions which later came into being in Ephesian mythology is well known. Adroklos, the son of the legendary King Kodros of Athens (ca. 1089–1066 BCE), was forced to flee from Greece (due to the Dorian invasions?) and sailed to Anatolia with his followers. He was told in a Delphic oracle that he would found a new city through portents given by a fish and a wild boar. After a long journey, the Greeks finally beached their boats in the Kaystros bay. There the fishermen prepared their meal by grilling fish near the Hypelaios Spring. But a fish with a piece of burning coal attached to it jumped from the fire into the dry brushwood. This provoked a boar, startled by the ensuing brush fire, to flee. Androklos pursued the boar and killed it at the site where the later temple of Athena stood (Strabo, *Geogr.* 14.1.3-4, 21). This led Androklos to establish a settlement at the site of Ephesus, expelling the local pre-Hellenic populations of the Lydians, Carians, and Leleges after his arrival.

However, Scherrer (2014, 114–15) argues that the entire myth is a political creation, being

> most likely ... an invention of the fifth century BC, when the city of Ephesus was temporarily yet strongly influenced by Athens and part of the Attic-Delian League.... This is clearly a version of the myth influenced, or totally made up, by democratic politicians with ties to Athens.

Moreover, there are important differences between our sources regarding various aspects of the foundation myth. Both Strabo and Pausanias, writing in the late second–early third centuries CE, attribute the founding of Ephesus to Androklos. By contrast, Athenaeus, drawing upon the early *Annals of Ephesus* by Kreophlos (fifth century BCE), provides a more elaborate account of the founding of Ephesus in terms of the portents but totally excludes any reference to Androklos. By comparison, Strabo

(*Geogr.* 14.1.21) provides a leaner account but identifies the sites of the settlement as being around the Athenaion and the Hypelaios Spring. For the differences, see Feldman 2019, 147–48.[2]

Whatever the truth regarding the invention of the Androklos myth and irrespective of the subsequent amalgamation of the myth's diverse elements into one metanarrative, the continuing importance of the founding myth at Ephesus was demonstrated by its appearance in the archaeological, numismatic, and epigraphic record spanning the Hellenistic Age and the later Roman imperial period. What does the archaeological and numismatic evidence reveal? We will concentrate on the relief and sculptural evidence from the Heroon and Fountain of Androklos, the temple of Hadrian, the Nymphaeum of Trajan, and the baths of Vedius in the gymnasium complex. The sites included in the procession of statues during and immediately after the time of the Salutaris bequest (104 CE) would have been the Heroon and fountain of Androklos (Hellenistic Age), the Nymphaeum of Trajan (98–117 CE), and the temple of Hadrian (117–138 CE). The baths of Vedius belong to the later period of Antoninus Pius (138–161 CE), to whom they were dedicated, but they also became another site in Ephesus for the honoring of Androklos.

First, the Heroon and fountain of Androklos was located at the three-way intersection of the Embolos (the ancient name for Curetes Street), Marble Street, and the Sacred Way. For the plan, ruins, and reconstruction of the Heroon, see Thür 1995b, 188–90, figs. 1–4. The Heroon was strategically placed near the Triados gate where civic processions departed for the birthplace of the twin gods, Artemis and Leto, who were born according to Ephesian tradition in the sacred grove outside of the city walls at Ortygia (Strabo, *Geogr.* 14.1.20). Thür dates the tomb dedicated to Androklos to the second century BCE, having a *terminus ante quem* of 80 BCE. The limestone ashlar masonry of the tomb conveniently functioned as the back

---

2. Weiss (2011, 82–83), drawing upon the Thür's examination of the archaeological remains, argues that Androklos's Heroon was a fountain from its earliest phases. This has real symbolic consequences, as Weiss correctly notes: "Its form combining an honorific monument with a hypaethral water basin, however, was unusual among other contemporary monuments in western Asia Minor. Water figured into the Ephesian foundation myth and Androklos' ability to develop fresh water sources was part of his characterization as a *ktistes*, or founder. This connection between civic founder or patron and water was one that was capitalized upon and resonated in subsequent honorific monuments throughout the Ephesian cityscape."

wall of a fountain, perhaps marking (or at least alluding to) the site where Androklos founded the city (the Hypelaios Spring). The Heroon commemorated a time of (limited) political freedom for Ephesus—before the full Roman expansion into the Greek East and Asia Minor—when the Greek cities on western coastal Asia Minor gained temporary autonomy upon the bestowal of the Attalid kingdom's territory to Rome in the second century BCE. For discussion, see Thür 1995a, passim; 1995b, 175–77; Weiss 2011, 78–83; Ng 2007, 184–89; Scherrer 2000, 126; Harrison, "Introduction: Ephesus in Documentary Perspective," in this volume.

Crucially, a six-panel relief, depicting battle scenes on a broken pediment from the second storey of the Heroon, shows on one panel a figure which has been identified as Androklos. For the relief, see Thür 1995b, 199, plate 2. Wearing a short chiton and belt, the figure is seated on a rearing horse with his short chlamys fluttering behind him, his right arm raised backwards in a position indicating that he was about to throw something (a lance or javelin?). What he was aiming at, however, is no longer recoverable due to damage of the panel.

Second, on the continuous frieze from the temple of Hadrian, located on Curetes Street, is an almost identical representation of Androklos on a rearing horse, but in this case he is preparing to hurl a spear at a wild boar, placed off to the upper right of the frieze. Beneath the animal is the figure of a fallen warrior who holds an oval shield for protection, having dropped abjectly to one knee. For the relief, see Thür 1995b, 200, plate 3. Ng (2007, 195–96) sums up the significance of the Hadrianic frieze most effectively:

> There can be no doubt that this boar hunt was a reference to the Ionian foundation legend of the city, since much of the rest of the Frieze from the Temple of Hadrian is concerned with other aspects of the early history of Ephesus, and includes details such as a depiction of the Hypelaios spring by which the campers were cooking the fish that was also part of the oracular prophesy.

What, then, was the (now unidentifiable) object against which the rider on the rearing horse was preparing to throw his spear in the panel relief of the Heroon of Androklos? On the basis of the later numismatic evidence, Thur (1995a, 70) refers to a coin of Marcus Aurelius that shows a very similar pose of Androklos on a horse with the boar fleeing below in the foreground. See also the Ephesian coin of Macrinus (217–218 CE) depicting the naked Androklos attacking a boar with a spear (Mionnet 3.369; *SNGCop* 438), with the legend ΕΦΕΣΙΩΝ ΑΝΔΡΟΚΛΟΣ ("Androklos of the Ephesians"). Further, the Ephesian coin of Gallienus (253–268 CE) portrays the naked Androklos, with a boar skin slung over his shoulder, walking to the right with his spear in hand. While this numismatic evidence is anachronistic, having been issued long after the Hellenistic age, the consistency of motifs referring the foundation story makes it likely that the damaged section of the relief panel of the Heroon of Androklos also depicted the founder's slaying of the boar.[3] In conclusion, the traditional Ionic warrior image of Androklos (Pausanias, *Desc.* 7.2.6–9) has been redefined in the temple of Hadrian for a new understanding that fitted the providential and peaceful ordering of history by Artemis and the Roman ruler.[4]

Third, the Nymphaeum of Trajan, located in the southwest of Curetes Street, exhibited a colossal, partly nude statue of the Roman ruler, a statue of his adoptive father Nerva, and a statue of a youthful hunter, identified with Androklos, with a statue of Apollo standing opposite—another clear allusion to the Delphic origins of the foundation myth. See Ng 2007, 209; for the statue, see Rathmayr 2010, 28 and fig. 11. Nor must we forget the substantial deflected glory that accrued to the benefactor Claudius Aristion, who was an asiarch (IEph 2.427), high priest of the city and temple warden of the imperial cult (IEph 2.234; 2.235; 2.237; 2.239; 2.241; 2.424A; 2.425A; 2.461; 2.508; 3.638; 7.2.4105; 7.2.5113). He was one of two benefactors who funded the Nymphaeum (IEph 2.424 [102/114 CE]) and various other projects (IEph 2.425; 7.1.3217a, b). In sum, we are seeing here the intersection of imperial and elite Ephesian benefactors, who draw upon the foundational myths of Ephesus and the rerouted processional way of Artemis in order to enhance the social and political impact of their patronage.

Fourth, in the northeast of the city, in the aediculated hall of the baths of Vedius was found another large statue of a youthful figure (196 cm), identified as Androklos by "the nearby find of a dog's paw resting on tufts of boar bristles—another obvious reference to the mythical boar hunt" (Ng 2007, 214). Guy MacLean Rogers (1991, 107) proposes that the sculp-

---

3. For the coin images, see Jochen1 et al. 2021.

4. Ng (2007, 208) writes: "By choosing another identity for Androklos, one that emphasized his participation in a divinely preordained hunt, the program at the Nymphaeum of Trajan turned away from a foundation legacy of conflict and towards one of peaceful fulfillment of prophecy, implying that Roman rule and the cooperation of elites was similarly preordained."

ture was placed there in the middle of the second century CE, based on its dedication to Antoninus Pius (IEph 5.1491 [149/50 CE]), but Angela Kalinowski (2002, 121), on the basis of the wall plaque found in the gymnasium (IEph 2.439), correctly dates the dedication precisely to 144/5 CE. The baths of Vedius, belonging to the larger gymnasium complex, would have been one of the sites where oil was dispensed to the athletes of the day of Androklos (see IEph 3.644, below: Ng 2007, 215–16).[5] The benefactor of the gymnasium, Vedius Papianus Antoninus, was also acclaimed, like Androklos, to be the founder of the city (see also Messalinus, IEph 6.2044, below).[6] Thus, as noted, the Ephesian elites have acquired substantial personal honor by their benefaction of projects associated with the legendary founder of the city.

Finally, Androklos appears on the *homonoia* coin issues, which promoted the concord between Greek city-states. For discussion of *homonoia* and its numismatic use, see Harrison, "Honoring the Concord of the Ephesian Demos," in this volume. On a coin from Sardis, the city's *homonoia* with Ephesus is depicted. The hero Tylos of Sardis holds in his right hand the cult statue of Kore of Sardis, while Androklos of Ephesus faces him in his armor, lance in his left hand and chlamys over his shoulder (reign of Geta [209–211 CE]: Franke and Nollé 1997, §1840). On other *homonoia* coins, Androklos, with the statuette of Artemis Ephesia in his right hand (§12), sits before Tyche of Aphrodisias, whereas on a coin from Alexandria Adroklos, cradling a long scepter in his left arm, faces Alexander the Great (§544). Additionally, see the *homonoia* coins of Magnesia on the Menander (§§1278, 1279) and Pergamum (§§1561, 1562).

In sum, whereas in the Hellenistic age the Androklos founder tradition was employed to confirm the short-lived autonomy of Ephesus when

---

5. The statue of Androklos was found in 1927 in the Vedius Gymnasiun in Ephesus and is now in the Izmir Archaeological Museum (Inv. no. 45 [Roman period, 131–161 CE, ca. 150 CE]). See John n.d., for a picture of a fragmentary marble statue of Androklos with his dog hunting a wild boar. The head of the statue was probably a portrait of Antinoos, the favorite of Hadrian (Rogers 1991, 107). Note, too, the reference to ἐν τῷ Ἀνδρωκλ[…] in SEG 34.1107.9. The SEG editor postulates that "either the club building of the *paraphylakes* or the tomb of Androklos (Paus. 7.2.9)" is being referred to. Additionally, see Kalinowski (2021, 275–80) who discusses IEph 7.1.3079 and the Androkleidai "doing business in this place." The Ephesians themselves are called the Ἀνδροκλίδαι, the descendants of Androklos (IEph 5.1548; 7.1.3079).

6. The association inscription of the woolworkers honor Vedius Papianus Antoninus as "founder of the city of the Ephesians" (IEph 3.727).

it was finally freed from Attalid control in the second century BCE, in the later Roman Empire the Androklos tradition emphasizes the concord of Greek city-states under Roman provincial rule, and it is brought into sympathetic dialogue with the imperial cult as part of the local Ephesian honorific rituals (e.g., the temple of Hadrian Androklos panel reliefs). The pro-Roman Asian elites comfortably incorporate the local honoring of the founder figures and the mythological past within the wider Roman honorific system and their local urban building activities.

What distinctive contribution does the Ephesian epigraphy offer regarding the founder traditions of Androklos?

2. Androklos: The Epigraphic Evidence

IEph 4.1064

JÖAI 3:88 (*editio princeps*); Keil 1939, 119, no. 1; FiE 9.1, no. F3. Cuboid, white marble: 44 cm high, 159 cm wide, 40 cm deep, letters 2 cm high. Date: ca. 170 CE.

1	ὦ τῆς ἀρίστης Ἀνδροκλείου καὶ σοφῆς δαῖμον πόληος, Ἑστί' ἀειπάρθενε,	O goddess of the best and wise city of (the founder) Androklos, ever virgin Hestia,
	σύ τ', ὦ θεῶν μέγιστον οὔνομ' Ἄρτεμι,	and you, O greatest name of the gods, Artemis,
	τῇ Τυλλίᾳ γείνοισθ' ἀρωγοὶ πανταχοῦ,	may you be everywhere helpers to Tullia,
5	ἀνθ' ὧν προθύμως ἐπρυτάνευσ' ὑμῶν ἄδην,	because she has readily been a prytanis of you (in the city),
	τὸν πλοῦτον εἰς πᾶν πρᾶγμ' ἀναλοῦσ' ἀφθόνως.	by using her wealth bounteously for every fit cause.

In the inscription above, a young female prytanis, named Tullia, prays to the goddesses Artemis and Hestia and asks their help, confident that she will be heard because of the considerable wealth she has expended in her civic role in the famous city of Androklos. This is the first of two prayers of Tullia in the Ephesian epigraphic corpus. The second (IEph 4.1063) is a prayer to Hestia for children in reward for her performance as a cult official. She claims before Hestia to have "perfected your house immaculately" and to have displayed as a prytanis "immaculate chastity" and "cleverness" before all people (IEph 4.1063).

Several features of IEph 4.1064 are especially noteworthy. First, Hestia is the goddess of the "best and wise city," Ephesus. The phrase is arresting, not only emphasizing Ephesus's precedence ("best") among the Ionian cities but also the city's "wisdom." Why wisdom? The context of our inscription provides the clue. Because Ephesus was founded by Androklos after he had heeded the oracle of Delphi, the epithet "wisdom" probably alludes to the foundation myth of a city established upon oracular wisdom. Note, however, that one of the four personified statues at the Ephesian Library of Celsus is inscribed Σοφία Κέλσου (IEph 7.2.5108), there attributing the virtue to the library's benefactor (cf. Harrison, "Sponsors of Paideia," in *NewDocs* 11B).

Second, in what sense are Artemis and Hestia helpers of Tullia? Since Tullia's civic beneficence is clearly the grounds for her confident prayer to the goddesses and expectation of reciprocated favor, R. Merkelbach (1980, 87) has viably suggested that Hestia, as the bestower of blessings and riches, would replace the part of Tullia's wealth (or the wealth of her parents) that she had expended in service of the city during her year in office as a prytanis. However, as noted, the reference is dual in its mention of divine help, so the same role must also be assigned to Artemis, the tutelary deity of Ephesus. Moreover, the unity of the goddesses in blessing the cult officials of the Ephesian Prytaneion (below) is striking, though the precedence of Artemis in an Ephesian context is clearly asserted ("the greatest of the gods"). Nevertheless, it is fascinating that Hestia, as Merkelbach (1980, 86) rightly observes, is invoked as the goddess of Ephesus.

Third, the reference to Hestia as "ever virgin" is explained by the Homeric myth about the goddess. Upon being courted by Poseidon and Apollo, Hestia rejected their proposals and swore to remain a virgin (Hom. Hymn Ven. 21–32). Becoming the center of the family, the city, and the cosmos, Hestia was worshiped at Ephesus, with the Ephesian officials, the *prytaneis* and *kouretes*, supervising her cult (Kajava 2005, 5). On the *prytaneis*, see Rogers 2022. At the Ephesian Prytaneion, the sacred flame was kept eternally lit in dedication to her as the Greek goddess of the hearth and fire. There are sixteen Ephesian inscriptions honoring Hestia (IEph 5.1059, 1060, 1065, 1066, 1067, 1069, 1070, 1070A, 1071, 1072, 1073, 1077, 1078, 1079; FiE 10.1, no. N4; *JÖAI* 55:126, no. 4272). Most of the inscriptions are thanksgivings to Hestia and the gods, some of whom are occasionally named. Male and female cult officials (πρύτανις, ἑστιοῦχος, καλαθηφόρος) in the Prytaneion are mentioned in IEph 4.1060, 4.1066, 4.1070, 4.1072. Last, Hestia is also eulogized in cosmic dimensions in an Ephesian epigram (IEph 4.1062). After praising Hestia for giving the gods their meals and keeping the fatherland's fire continuously burning (IEph 4.1062.2–3), the epigram explodes in exuberant language that magnifies her communion with the heavens and her eternal sustenance of the universe: "Dearest Goddess, Blood of the Universe, Eternal Fire, Goddess, you maintain the fire on the hearth altar that comes from heaven" (ll. 4–5).

IEph 2.501.1

JÖAI 3:88 (*editio princeps*); Keil 1939, 119, no. 1. Statue base found in the rubble on the street in front of the Great Theater at Ephesus. Date: ca. 170 CE.

Left side of the base	
Ἄνδροκλον	Androklos,
2 τὸν τῆς πόλεως	of the city
κτίστην	(the) founder,
4 οἱ περὶ Αὐρ(ήλιον) Νεικόστρατον τὸν	the guards, under the (guiding presence) of Aur(elios) Nikostratos,
καὶ Εὐπάλιν Εὐπαλίου φιλο-	(whose name is) also Eupalis, son of Eupalios,
6 σέβαστον παραφύλακες	loyal to the Emperor,
ἀνενεώσαντο.	have restored.

In this inscription, we learn that guards have restored the statue of the city's founder, Androklos, under the guidance of Aurelius Nikostratos. The circumstances of the statue's restoration are unknown: was it deliberately or accidentally damaged or interfered with in some fashion? We know nothing further about Nikostratos, but his loyalty to the imperial ruler is strategically emphasized in the inscription. Here, we are witnessing the ease and versatility with which the Romans engaged the ancestral myths of the provincial cities of Asia Minor, maintaining diplomatic links with the Asian urban elites by means of their local clients such as Aurelius Nikostratos. The Ephesians, reciprocally, are faithful to their own founder traditions, honoring those like the guards who help to maintain them, while also astutely cultivating their imperially connected residents or citizens who contribute to the city's welfare.

What precisely was the role of the παραφύλακες at Ephesus? Several inscriptions provide slender clues. First, it seems to be a specific Ephesian magistracy or possibly a voluntary beneficent office assumed on behalf of the city by the elites as occasion demanded. It is mentioned alongside important Ephesian public offices: *prytanis* (IEph 3.612A, 3.661); *strategos* (general: IEph 3.661, 3.838; *JÖAI* 55:121-22, no. 4238); *neopoios* (IEph 3.612A, 3.661; *JÖAI* 55:121-22, no. 4238); *dekaprotos* (chief municipal authority: IEph 3.802); *limenarches* (harbor master: IEph 3.802); *eirenarchos* (police magistrate: IEph 3.612A, 3.802); *boularchos* (president of the senate: *JÖAI* 55:121-22, no. 4238); *grammateus* (secretary: IEph 3.661); and *agoranomos* (clerk of the market: IEph 3.612A). The παραφύλακες clearly belong to the Ephesian elites.

Second, the bequest of Caius Vibius Salutaris (IEph 1a.27.48, 96, 209 [104 CE]) specifies that the fifteen statues representing the city of Ephesus should be carried out from the temple of Artemis to the theater along the processional route and then brought back to the temple, the entire process being supervised by the guards (φύλακες), two *neopoioi*, and the beadle. See Rogers 1991, passim; Portefaix 1993, passim. Thus, in the case of IEph 1a.27, the guards are exercising oversight of the sacred images of the city. Consequently, regarding IEph 2.501.1, we might legitimately speculate that the παραφύλακες exercised a similar supervisory role in caring for the sacred images within the temples and public squares of Ephesus, protecting them from impiety, desecration, and accidental damage and also, as public benefactors, contributing to their restoration as required.

IEph 6.2044

Kaibel 1050a; *RhM* 34:212, no. 1050a; *JÖAI* 11:77, no. 2; FiE 2, no. 44; *RPh* 27:49-51; Grégoire 1922, no. 100; Bakhuizen van den Brink 1923, 82, no. 1; Robert 1948, 62, 87-89, 117; *Teatri Classici* 4:222, no. 20. Date: late fourth century CE. For the date, see Malcus 1967, 130-31.

τὴν βριαρὴν ἁψῖδα, τὸ καρτερὸν ἔρμα θεάτρου,	Look at the massive tier, the strong support of (the) theater,
δέρκεο καὶ θαύμαζε τὸν ἄξιον οἰκιστῆρα	and admire the worthy (new) founder
τηλεφανοῦς Ἐφέσου, προφερέστερον Ἀνδρόκλοιο	of conspicuous Ephesus, (who is) more excellent than Androklos,
Μεσσαλῖνον, μεγάλης Ἀσίης μέγαν ἰθυντῆρα.	Messalinus, (the) great ruler of (the) great (province) of Asia.

Note on the translation: Louis Robert (1948, 87-89) brings IEph 6.2044 into dialogue with another epigram (IEph 6.2043) eulogizing the proconsul of Asia, Messalinus (fourth century CE). The occasion of IEph 6.2043 was the repair of the surrounding wall of the theater, establishing thereby the context for our inscription above. The epigram celebrates the illustrious deeds of Messalinus (IEph 6.2043.2: Μεσσαλινοῦ κλεινοῖς ἔργμασιν) by which, as the subsequent relative pronoun (οἷς) indicates, the proconsul "saved the huge circle of the theater (οἷς θεάτρου κύκλου περιώσιον ἐξεσάωμεν) (IEph 6:2043.3)." Robert (1948, 88) argues that the "architectural term," θεάτρου κύκλου περιώσιον, corresponds to τὸ καρτερὸν ἕρμα θεάτρου in IEph 6.2044.1, which Robert translates as "the solid support of the theater." By contrast, Elisabeth Rathmayr (2010, 24) translates the phrase as "the strong retaining walls of the theater." Either option is possible. The first phrase, τὴν βριαρὴν ἀψῖδα (IEph 6.2044.1), not commented on by Robert, is translated by Rathmayr (2010, 24) as "the massive semicircle." However, there is no LSJ evidence for the nuance of "semi-circle" for ἀψίς (pace, κύκλος, IEph 6.2043.3). Therefore, I have opted for the translation "tier" (ἀψῖδα), appropriate for the theatrical context, which is found in LSJ (s.v. "ἀψίς 5.c"), referring there to the uppermost "tier" of a theater (ἡ ἀνωτάτω ἀψίς θεάτρου).

Remarkably, the proconsul Messalinus is called the second founder of Ephesus because of his restoration of the theater. Not only is the rhetoric stratospheric in its eulogistic intent, but we are witnessing in this inscription another important development, noted before, in the founder traditions in the late empire at Ephesus. As Ng (2007, 191–92) observes, "the Hellenic foundation hero Androklos came to be framed as a predecessor to contemporary patrons, who wished to be regarded as new city 'founders' and as members of the broader Greco-Roman cultural world." On Vedius Papianus Antoninus also as the new founder of Ephesus, see IEph 3.727 (n. 5 above).

IEph 3.644

JÖAI 49:67–69, no. 7. Statue base, built into the Scholastica baths. Date: Undated.

πρώτης καὶ μεγί[σ-]	(As citizens) of (the) first and large
της μητροπόλεως τῆς	-est metropolis of
Ἀσίας καὶ δὶς νεωκόρου	Asia and of (the) twice *neokoros*
4 τῶν Σεβαστῶν Ἐφεσίων	of the Augusti, the city
πόλεως ἡ βουλὴ καὶ ὁ	of the Ephesians, the council and the

	δῆμος ἐτείμησαν	people honored
	Τιβέριον Κλαύδιον	Tiberius Claudius
8	Μαρκιανόν,	Marcianus
	παραφυλάξαντα φιλοτεί-	who served as a guard eag-
	μως καὶ ἐλαιοθετήσαντα	erly and donated oil
	ἐν πᾶσιν τοῖς γυμνασίοις	in all the gymnasia
12	τῇ τοῦ Ἀνδρόκλου ἡμέρᾳ·	on the day of Androklos;
	τὴν τειμὴν ἀναστήσαντος	(on that occasion) the honor was established
	Αἰλίου Μηνοφίλου τοῦ φίλου	by his friend Aelius Menophilus,
	αὐτοῦ καθὼς ἐν τῇ βουλῇ ὑπέ-	in the council (meeting) as he pro-
16	σχετο.	mised.

Once again the link between the role of "guard" (παραφυλάξαντα) and public benefaction is securely established through the mention of Marcianus providing the gymnasium oil supplies. Further, traditional benefaction rhetoric is employed adverbially of Marcianus's role as a guard (φιλοτείμως), reinforcing the strong likelihood that the public office of guard was a civic benefaction carried out by the urban elites on behalf of the city. Significantly, the foundation myth of Androklos had been officially incorporated into the civic calendar of the city, providing benefactors not only the opportunity of acquiring personal and ancestral honor through their beneficence but also of demonstrating *pietas* towards the mythological origins of the city by regularly maintaining the memory of its founder. As important as the imperial calendar was for Greeks inhabiting the province of Roman Asia (e.g., the birthday of Augustus, *OGIS* 458: Priene, [9 BCE]), the calendric memorialization of Ephesus's foundation was equally strategic for the civic identity of the city.

3. The Epistle to the Ephesians and the Androklos Founder Traditions

Paul was aware of the importance of traditional founder figures in contextualizing his theology in the epistle to the Romans in its first-century imperial context (see Harrison 2020, passim). Over against the Roman mythological foundation stories of Romulus and Aeneas, which had found their culmination in the advent of Augustus as the new Romulus and Aeneas, Paul universalized the story of human origins and its founder figure by retelling the story of Gen 3 in light of its soteriological and messianic fulfilment in Christ (Rom 1:2–4; 5:12–21; 10:4; 16:25–27). Adam, who had inaugurated the reign of sin and death (Rom 5:14, 5:15a, 16a, 17a,18a, 19a, 20a)—already present before the arrival of the Mosaic law's enslaving and condemnatory power (5:13; 7:7-13)—was supplanted by the overflowing reign of grace in the crucified and risen Christ (5:15b, 16b, 17b,18b, 19b, 20b, 21b). Christ triumphed over the debilitating effects of the disobedience of humanity's founder figure upon humankind, transferring to his fallen dependents God's justifying righteousness through his atoning death (Rom 5:18b-19b; 2 Cor 5:21). Moreover, in a further universalizing narrative based around the Jewish founder figure, Paul depicted the uncircumcised Abraham as equally the father of Jews and gentiles through his paradigmatic dependence on justifying faith without works (Rom 4:1-25).

But how does Paul address the founder narrative of Androklos at Ephesus in the epistle to the Ephesians? Indeed, is the Ephesian founder tradition any concern to the apostle at all? It is certainly unwise to assume that we have historical omniscience regarding Paul's intentions in this regard, given the richness of Paul's theological response on many fronts in the epistle and, relatedly, the complexity of Ephesus as a city. But, nevertheless, we can point minimally to various intersections with the founder narrative of Ephesus that would have resonated with astute Ephesian auditors.

First, in the processional hymn of Eph 1:3-14, where Paul traverses the ages from our pretemporal election to our future inheritance, the apostle continually reverts to our incorporation in our founder figure, Christ. For the explosion of the "in Christ" terminology, see "in him" (ἐν αὐτῷ), "in Christ" (ἐν Χριστῷ/ἐν τῷ Χριστῷ), "in whom" (ἐν ᾧ), and "in the beloved one" (ἐν τῷ ἠγαπημένῳ), a total of eleven occurrences (Eph 1:3b, 4a, 6b, 7a, 9b, 10b, 10c, 11a, 12b, 13a, 13b). In light of the Androklos traditions above, Paul's interminably long Greek sentence (vv. 3-14) proceeds relentlessly by unleashing three participial clauses that emphasize the manifold blessings of Christ, the soteriological founder, to sinners and their predestination in the merciful Father. For full discussion, see Harrison, "Ephesian Cultic Officials," in *NewDocs* 11B.

Second, this sweeping soteriological perspective is reinforced at an ecclesiological and christological level in Eph 2:19-22. The church is built upon the foundation (ἐπὶ τῷ θεμελίῳ) of the apostles and the prophets, with Christ as the cornerstone (ἀκρογωνιαίου αὐτοῦ Χριστοῦ) and believers being built into a holy temple in the Lord (ἐν κυρίῳ) in whom God dwells (εἰς κατοικητήριον τοῦ θεοῦ). The procession of the statues through the city past the three sacred sites of the city founder Androklos, including the temple of Hadrian, is totally bypassed in terms the corporate identity of Ephesian believers. Precisely because Christ is their cornerstone and they have been incorporated into his apostolic and prophetic church (cf. Eph 3:5; 4:11), Ephesian believers have become the living temple of God. This implied contrast with Ephesian civic identity is made even more explicit in the transition of Ephesian believers from being strangers and aliens (ξένοι καὶ πάροικοι) to being "fellow-citizens [συμπολῖται] of the saints and members of the household of God [οἰκεῖοι τοῦ θεοῦ]." Rather than being Ἀνδροκλίδαι (IEph 5.1548; 7.1.3079: see n. 4 above)—the status of all citizens of Ephesus—Ephesian believers now have an alternative citizenship that vastly surpasses its Ephesian counterpart because of the prestigious family status conferred and the eternal privilege of divine access. This reconfiguration of the identity of Ephesian believers punctured the pretension of a city which vaunted itself as "the best and wise city of Androklos" (IEph 4.1064), "conspicuous Ephesus" (IEph 6.2044), and "(the) first and largest metropolis of Asia and (the) twice *neokoros* of the Augusti" (IEph 3.644).

Third, we argued that the use of σοφῆς in the phrase "the best and wise city of Androklos" (IEph 4.1064) alluded to the fact that Ephesus was established on the oracular wisdom of Delphi revealed in the founder story of Androklos. In the case of Ephesian believers, they experience the work of the Spirit who imparts to them wisdom and revelation (πνεῦμα σοφίας καὶ ἀποκαλύψεως: Eph 1:17),[7] enabling them to know through an enlightened heart their eschatological hope and glorious inheritance. While the eschatological focus is spotlighted in Eph 1:17, in 5:15 the present implications of the Spirit-generated wisdom of believers is drawn out graphically for their discipleship: they are to walk μὴ ὡς ἄσοφοι ἀλλ᾽ ὡς σοφοί. The so-called oracular wisdom of the city of Ephesus is of no avail because true wisdom now has a new residence: it is found in the body of Christ through which the "multi-faceted wisdom of God" (Eph 3:10: ἡ πολυποίκιλος σοφία τοῦ θεοῦ) is heralded.

Last, a final but important sidelight. Hestia's transfer of the heavenly fire to earth is another passing sideshow of no significance, as is her alleged cosmological significance. Believers are already raised with Christ and sit

---

7. On πνεῦμα as referring to the Holy Spirit and not to the human spirit (Eph 1:17), see Best 1998, 163.

with him in the heavenlies (Eph 1:18; 2:6). There is only one cosmological narrative. Heaven and earth will experience its cosmic *anekephalaiōsis* in Christ (ἀνακεφαλαιώσασθαι τὰ πάντα ἐν τῷ Χριστῷ: Eph 1:10), which is accomplished for the blessing of his redeemed people (3:8–18), and, above all, for the magnification of God's glory in the coming ages (1:6, 12, 14, 17, 18; 3:13, 16; 21; cf. 2:7). For discussion, see Caragounis 1977, 143–46.

Bibliography

Aurenhammer, Maria. 1990. *Die Skulpturen von Ephesos: Bildwerke aus Stein; Idealplastik 1*. FiE 10.1. Vienna: Akademie.

Bakhuizen van den Brink, Jan Nicolaas. 1923. *De oud-christelijke monumenten van Ephesus: epigraphische studie*. The Hague: Die Nederlandsche Boek- en Steendrukkerij.

Best, Ernest. 1998. *A Critical and Exegetical Commentary on Ephesians*. ICC. London: T&T Clark.

Caragounis, C. C. 1977. *The Ephesian* Mysterion: *Meaning and Content*. ConBNT 6. Lund: Gleerup.

Feldman, Cecelia A. 2019. "Created at the Water's Edge: Poetics and Politics in Greek Foundation Myths." Pages 145–57 in *Ancient Waterlands*. Edited by Betsey A. Robinson, Sophie Bouffier, and Fumado Otega. Archéologies Méditerranéennes. Marseilles Université: Presses Universitaires de Provence.

Franke, Peter Robert, and Margret Karola Nollé. 1997. *Katalog*. Vol. 1 of *Die Homonoia-Münzen Kleinasiens und der thrakischen Randgebiete*. Saarbrücker Studien zur Archäologie und Alten Geschichte 10. Saarbrücken: Saarbrücker Druckerei und Verlag.

Grégoire, Henri. 1922. *Recueil des inscriptions grecques-chrétiennes d'Asie mineure*. Vol. 1. Paris: LeRoux.

Harrison, James R. 2020. *Reading Romans with Roman Eyes: Studies on the Social Perspective of Paul*. Paul in Critical Contexts. Lanham: Lexington/Fortress.

Jochen1 et al. 2021. "Androklos and the Ephesian Boar." CoinTalk. http://tinyurl.com/SBL9031.

John, David. n.d. "Androklos Frieze Temple of Hadrian Ephesus." My Favourite Planet. http://tinyurl.com/SBL9031b.

Kaibel, Georg. 1879. "Supplementum epigrammatum Graecorum ex lapidibus conlectorum." *RhM* 34:181–213.

Kalinowski, Angela V. 2002. "The Vedii Antonini: Aspects of Patronage and Benefaction in Second-Century Ephesos." *Phoenix* 56:109–49.

———. 2021. *Memory, Family, and Community in Roman Ephesos*. Cambridge: Cambridge University Press.

Kajava, Mika. 2005. "Hestia: Hearth, Goddess and Cult." *HSCP* 102:1–20.

Keil, Josef. 1939. "Kulte im Prtaneion von Ephesos." Pages 199–128 in *Anatolian Studies Presented to William Hepburn Buckler*. Edited by W. M. Cadler and Josef Keil. London: Machester University Press.

Knibbe, Dieter. 1981. *Der Staatsmarkt: Die Inschriften des Prytaneions; Die Kureteninschriften und sonstige religiöse Texte*. FiE 9.1. Vienna: Akademie.

Malcus, B. 1967. "Die Prokonsuln von Asien von Diokletian bis etian bis Theodosius II." *Opuscula Atheniensia* 7:91–154.

Merkelbach, R. 1980. "Der Kult der Hestia im Prytaneion der griechischen Städte." *ZPE* 37:77–92.

Mortensen, Eva. 2015. "*Ktistes*: Mythical Founder Hero and Honorary Title for New Heroes." Pages 213–37 in *Tradition: Transmission of Culture in the Ancient World*. Edited by Jane Fejfer, Mette Moltesen, and Annette Rajhte. Acta Hyperborea 14. University of Copenhagen: Museum Tusculanum Press.

Ng, Diana Yi-man. 2007. "Manipulation of Memory: Public Buildings and Decorative Programs in Roman Cities of Asia Minor." PhD diss., University of Michigan.

Portefaix, Lilian. 1993. "Ancient Ephesus: Processions as Media of Religious and Secular Propaganda." Pages 195–210 in *The Problem of Ritual: Based on Papers Read at the Symposium on Religious Rites Held at Åbo, Finland, on the 13th–16th of August 1991*. Edited by T. Ahlbäck. Scripta Instituti Donneriani Aboensis 15. Åbo: Donner Institute.

Rathmayr, Elisabeth. 2010. "Die Präsenz des Ktistes Androklos." *AAWW* 145.1:19–60.

Robert, Louis. 1948. "Épigrammes du Bas-Empire." *Hellenica* 4:5–151.

Rogers, Guy MacLean. 1991. *The Sacred Identity of Ephesos: Foundation Myths of a Roman City*. London: Routledge.

———. 2022. "Some Prytaneis of Ephesos." Pages 95–114 in *Ephesos as a Religious Center under the Principate*. Edited by Allen Black, Christine M. Thomas, and Trevor W. Thompson. WUNT 488. Tübingen: Mohr Siebeck.

Scherrer, Peter. 2014. "Hunting the Boar—The Fiction of a Local Past in Foundation Myths of Hellenistic and Roman Cities." Pages 113–19 in

Attitudes Towards the Past in Antiquity: Creating Identities; Proceedings of an International Conference Held at Stockholm University, 15–17 May 2009. Edited by Brita Alroth and Charlotte Scheffer. Acta Universitatis Stockholmiensis: Stockholm Studies in Classical Archaeology 14. Stockholm: Stockholm University.

———. 2000. *Ephesus: A New Guide.* Istanbul: Ege Yayinlan.

Thür, Hilke. 1995a. "Der mythische Ktistes Androklos von Ephesos und (s)ein Heroon am Embolos." *JÖAI* 64:63–103.

———. 1995b. "The Processional Way in Ephesos as a Place of Cult and Burial." Pages 157–99 in *Ephesos, Metropolis of Asia: An Interdisciplinary Approach to Its Archaeology, Religion, and Culture.* Edited by Helmut Koester. HTS 41. Valley Forge: Trinity Press International.

Weiss, Cecelia Feldman. 2011. "Livingly Fluidly: Uses and Meanings of Water in Asia Minor (Second Century BCE–Second Century CE)." PhD diss. Brown University, Providence.

Rome and Its Rulers

6. Long Live Rome!

James R. Harrison

IEph 2.599

The first edition was published in IEph 2. Copy from Werner Jobst. Graffito from one of the Ephesian terrace houses. Undated.

Ῥώμα ἡ παμβασίλεια, τὸ σὸν κράτος οὔποτ' ὀλεῖται.	Rome, queen of all, your power will never end.

Written by an unknown visitor at one of the Ephesian terrace houses in antiquity, this graffito spotlights one of the most important themes of imperial propaganda during the empire: the eternal power and rule of the city of Rome.[1] The evidence for this motif is abundant in the Roman literary, documentary, and numismatic evidence. At the outset, it should be noted that IEph 2.599 is not the only place in the Ephesian epigraphic corpus where the eternal power of Rome is mentioned. In a building inscription recording the restoration of the wall of the Augusteum, a dedication is made to the health of the emperor Titus and the "permanence [διαμονή] of the supremacy [ἡγεμονία, Latin equivalent: *imperium*] of the Romans" (IEph 2.412.3–4). Normally, one would have expected the use of αἰώνιος with διαμονή in this context because it is the most common terminological pairing in the Greek epigraphic corpus where αἰώνιος appears. When one looks at the use of the language of "eternity" (αἰώνιος) in the inscriptions of Ionia—to confine our examination of the evidence to the region in which Ephesus was located—there are many examples of this pairing. Composers of the Ionian inscriptions routinely chose the adjective αἰωνίος

---

1. The editor of IEph 2 does not specify which Ephesian terrace house contains the graffito. See also the dedication of a statue for the health (ὑγιείας) of Tiberius and the permanence of the Roman hegemony (διαμονῆς τῆς Ῥωμαίων ἡγεμονίας) (IEph 2.510–514A). Similarly, the inscription to Titus, IEph 2.412 (79/81 CE).

("eternal") to preface the noun διαμονή ("permanence"), thereby highlighting the everlasting nature of Roman rule.[2]

Four examples of the Ionian usage of αἰώνιος terminology will suffice, the final one being an exception to its normal association with διαμονῇ. At Smyrna in Mysia, a sacrifice and prayer is made for Hadrian "[on behalf of his eternal permanen]ce ([αἰωνίου διαμον]ῆς) and of the uncontest[ed supremacy of the Romans]" (ISmyrn 594.12-13 [124 CE]). At Kyzikene, another prayer is made "on behalf the eternal permanence [αἰωνίου διαμονῆς] of Gaius Caesar" (IMT Kyz Kapu Dağ 1439[37 CE]). An altar inscription from Rhodian Peraia (IRhodes Peraia 514), in honor of Marcus Aurelius and Lucius Verus (163/164 CE), makes a dedication "on behalf of the victory, health, and the eternal permanence [αἰωνίου διαμονῆς] of our lord imperators." Last, Antonia Tryphaena, a Pontus princess and Roman-client queen of Thrace, continually showed piety towards "the eternal house [αἰωνίον οἶκον] of Tiberius Augustus Caesar, (descended) from the great gods, and his undying supremacy [τὴν ἀθά(νατον ἡ)γεμονίαν αὐτοῦ]" (IMT Kyz Kapu Dağ 1431.3-4 [41-54 CE]). In the Julio-Claudian to the Flavian eras, therefore, the Roman rulers increasingly proclaimed the eternity and indestructibility of Rome and her goddess Roma in their political propaganda. The basis for their unquestioned confidence was plain for all to see. A meticulous maintenance of the traditional cults ensured the *pax deorum*; the Roman armies protected the borders of empire from barbarian incursion and, within Rome's territory, preserved the safety of her citizens from internal rebellion by disaffected subjects; the provincial governors and loyal client-kings ensured the stability of Rome's control of the provinces; and, last, the slave economy, the imposition of tribute upon the conquered nations, far-flung trade networks, and large *latifundia* maintained the continuing prosperity of Rome.

---

2. For other inscriptions mentioning the "eternal permanency" (αἰώνιος διαμονή) of the Roman rulers, see REG 19.100-102, no. 14 (Aphrodisias); Reynolds 1982, no. 48 (Aphrodisias [222-235 CE]); IEph 1a.26 (180-192 CE); IRhod. Peraia 514 (Caria, Rhodian Peraia [163-164 CE]); IMT LApollon/Milet 2196 (reign of Trajan). The language of eternity is also applied to social virtues, positions, honors, and the human worship of the gods: e.g., "eternal concord" ([αἰ]ωνίου ὁμονοίας; Reynolds 1982, no. 1), "eternal gymnasiarchy" (IEph 5.1500 [115-16 CE), "eternal stephanephoria" (i.e., the wearing of a wreath of victory; TAM 5.2.1345); "towards the eternal supremacy [τῆν αἰώνιον διαμονήν] of the piety of the gods" (IStratonikeia 1101).

The notion of the eternal city was also widely known in the Roman literature. The list of sources employing the phrase, cited below, is by no means exhaustive: Cicero, *Verr.* 2.4.69; *Rep.* 3.34 (frag. 2); *Att.* 9.10.3; *Marcell.* 22; Livy, *Ab urbe cond.* 5.7.9.2; 28.28.11; Ovid, *Fast.* 3.72, 421; Tibullus, *Eleg.* 2.5.23; Vergil, *Aen.* 1.278; Valerius Maximus, *Fact. et dict.* 5.3.1; 5.15.73; Pliny (the Elder), *Nat.* 2.18.2; 5.15.73; Tacitus, *Hist.* 1.84; *Ann.* 3.6; 14.6.1; 28.1.1; 29.6.17. The Latin inscriptions, too, regularly mention *Roma aeterna*: (1) *AE* 1983.443 a/b; (2) *ILS* 6751 (= *CIL* 5.6691); (3) *ILS* 3636 (= *CIL* 3.1422); (4) *ILS* 3926 (= *CIL* 8.1427); (5) *ILS* 3927 (= *CIL* 10.10); (6) *AE* 1985.726; (7) *AE* 1991.1644; *ILS* 3181 (= *CIL* 8.6965). For the Roman literary and Latin documentary references cited above, see Isaac 1998, an article in Hebrew. For further discussion of the eternal city, see Moore 1894; Pratt 1965; Whitlark 2012, 172–73. For ancient sources on Roman rule to the ends of the earth and its relevance for the book of Revelation, see Yeates 2017. On Roman rule as being "eternal" (e.g., Virgil, *Aen.* 1.278–279; Velleius Paterculus, *Hist. Rom.* 2.103), a perspective additional to but complementary with the *urbs aeterna* motif, see Harrison 2011, 317–19; Whitlark 2012, 173–74. For an imperial-critical reading of Ephesians, see Winzenburg 2022.

Furthermore, the numismatic evidence shows a decisive turn in adopting the motif from Hadrian onward. But it is worth noting at the outset that Vespasian's issue of a dupondius (*RIC* 2 §309) from the Illyricum mint (69–70 CE) anticipates the later coinage of Hadrian: on the reverse, Rome is presented sitting on a cuirass on the left, holding a Victory and *parazonium* (i.e., dagger, small sword), with the accompanying legend of ROMA PERPETVA ("everlasting Roma"). Though the language of "eternity" is not used, the meaning is synonymous. ROMA AETERNA ("eternal Rome") is found on two coins (dupondius, sestertius) of Hadrian (*RIC* 2 §§263, 774). The dupondius (*RIC* 2 §263) shows Roma seated to the left on a cuirass, holding the heads of the Sun and Moon, as well as a spear, behind a shield. The second coin (*RIC* 2 §774) varies the seating of Roma (positioned on a curule chair in this instance) and holding a Victory which carries a shield and spear. The Hadrianic coin issues employ cosmic, military, and triumphal motifs to illustrate the nature of and reasons for the eternity of Roman rule. On Roma in the Greek East, see Mellor 1975.

Several developments had contributed to the eternity of the city of Rome progressively becoming an article of faith for everyday Romans, beginning in the reign of Augustus and finding its full expression in the Flavian dynasty (Pratt 1965, 27). First, the linkage of the goddess Roma to Augustus was pivotal in this regard. Temples to Roma and Augustus were established throughout the empire. The sites of these may be traced in Taylor 1931, app. 3. To cite one striking example, the *sole* addition that was made to the iconic fifth and fourth century BCE buildings on the Athenian acropolis was a temple to Roma and Augustus: "The [Athenian] people [dedicated the temple] to the goddess Roma and Caesar Augustus" (IG 2.2.3173). For discussion, see Illou 2021. But, in the case of Ephesus, the identification of a temple to Roma and Augustus in the city has attracted disagreement among archaeologists, though Cassius Dio confirms the existence of the temple in the city (*Hist. rom.* 51.20.6). The double-cella temple next to the Prytaneion was thought by Peter Scherrer (1990, 98–101) to be a temple of Artemis and Augustus, whereas Wilhelm Alzinger (1974, 55–57) argues that the foundations are for a temple of Roma and Augustus. The Ephesian epigraphic evidence is equivocal on the matter, because IEph 3.902, consisting of a list of priest names, is only hypothetically suggested by the IEph 3 editor to be a Dea Roma cult inscription. No explicit identification of the cult occurs in the text, in contrast to the Athenian Acropolis inscription above. Instead IEph 3.902 speaks only "of the foundation-festival of Augustus and of the foundation-festival of the precincts of the temple."

Second, Martin P. Charlesworth (1936) has argued that the increasing importance of *Providentia*, whether issuing from the gods or the emperor, in the inscriptions and coins was designed to secure the *aeternitas* of the Roman people and state. By the time of Hadrian, the *aeternitas* of the emperor was well established (Bru 2011). From then onwards, *Roma aeterna* flourishes until the time of Ammianus Marcellinus (e.g., *Rer. gest.* 14.6.1; 15.7.1, 7, 10; 16.10.14) when *urbs aeterna* becomes the dominant phrase in use.

Third, Charlesworth (1936) draws attention to how Augustus associated his public image with the eternal goddess Vesta, who presided over the hearth, home, and family. The significance of Vesta and her virgins was not lost upon Augustus in the Res Gestae: the priests and Vestal virgins performed an annual sacrifice for his return from Parthia on 12 October 19 BCE (Res gest. divi Aug. 11), and they performed another annual sacrifice for his return from Spain and Gaul in 13 BCE (12:2). As Alison Cooley (2009, 152) observes, the Vestal virgins "appeared only at the most important occasions." There are no numismatic issues carrying images of Vesta in the Julio-Claudian period, but Ovid is particularly instructive in helping us see the connection of Vesta with Augustus' rule.

In *Fast.* 3.421–422, Ovid says that over Vesta's eternal fire "the divinity of Caesar, no less eternal, does preside: the pledges of empire you see side by side." The link is even clearer in *Fast.* 4.949–454. There the gods are said to inhabit Augustus's house on the Palatine, one of whom includes the tutelary deity of Augustus, Apollo (i.e., Phoebus). The temple of Apollo was located nearby to the left of Augustus's house. Augustus had also built a chapel of Vesta in his house, which was dedicated on the 28 April 12 BCE (Ovid, *Fast.* 4.951; *Metam.* 15.864; Fast. Caer. Fast. Praen. at IV.Kal.Mai, *CIL* 1.2, p. 213, 236, cited by Platner 1929, 557). Ovid brings the interconnection between these sacred spaces to a resounding crescendo by demonstrating that the house of Augustus had become the new sacred dwelling for Vesta and Phoebus, as well as the princeps himself:

> Vesta has been received in the home of her kinsman: so have the Fathers righteously decreed. Phoebus owns part of the house; another part has been given up to Vesta; what remains is occupied by Caesar himself. Long live the laurels of the Palatine! Long live the house wreathed with the oaken boughs! A single house holds three eternal gods.

By the time of the Flavian dynasty, there is an explosion in images of Vesta upon the imperial coinage (see *RIC* 2, s.v. index 3, "Vesta, head of, veiled"; index 4, "VESTA"). A few examples from the Flavian period will establish the point. This trend commences with Vespasian (*RIC* 2 §§40, 59, 60, 69, etc.) and progresses through to Titus (*RIC* 2 §57), Domitian (*RIC* 2 §231) Trajan (*RIC* 2 §737) and Hadrian (*RIC* 2 §§397, 410), and beyond. Charlesworth (1936, 127) helpfully sums up the progressive elevation of Vesta in the propaganda of the Roman rulers from the time of Augustus onwards to its culmination in the Flavian period: "On the coinage of the Flavians Vesta appears more frequently than any other god or goddess, and we have seen how Vesta and the Capitol stood for symbols of eternity to the Roman mind." The divine eternity that was transferred to the Roman ruler was inevitably transferred to the city in which he lived.

Is there any evidence for a critique of the conception of the eternal city in antiquity? We will confine our examination to the rabbinic evidence and the Epistle to the Hebrews. For Greco-Roman criticism of the consumptive drive of the voracious Roman Empire, see Harrison 2020, 234–36. For Jewish critiques of Rome and its empire, see Harrison 2011, 303–5. For the city in the book of Revelation, see Reapple 2001; Futral 2002; Yeates 2017.

First, the exposition of Rabbi Shila of 1 Chr 29:11a ("Yours, Lord, is the greatness and the power and the glory and the majesty and the splendor") is interpreted in b. Ber. 58a in this manner (cited Zalcman 1997, 312):

> (Quoting 1 Chronicles 29:11a)
> This refers to the fall of Rome, as it says:
> "their lifeblood bespattered My garments" (Isa 63.3).

Zalcman notes that the Hebrew word for "splendor" (1 Chr 29:11a) may also mean "everlastingness," highlighting the possibility that Shila's critique not only had in view Roman power but also Rome as the *aeterna urbs*.

Second, turning to the Epistle to the Hebrews, the writer states in 13:14: "Here we have no lasting city [μένουσαν πόλιν], but we are looking for the city to come [τὴν μέλλουσαν]." This is the city which has been divinely prepared for believers (Heb 11:16b: ἡτοίμασεν γὰρ αὐτοῖς πόλιν). Their citizenship in the city of the living God (12:22a: πόλει θεοῦ ζῶντος) had been secured by their names having already been written in heaven (12:23a: ἀπογεγραμμένων ἐν οὐρανοῖς), that is, in the heavenly Jerusalem (12:22a: Ἰερουσαλὲμ ἐπουρανίῳ). Abraham, the patriarch of the covenantal promises, had been continuously looking forward to this "city with foundations [θεμελίους ἔχουσαν πόλιν], whose architect and builder was God" (11:10).

These texts in Hebrews resonate with rich Jewish salvation-history motifs (Ramantswana 2013), emphasizing the fact that Mount Zion is the only unshakeable destination for believers (Heb 12:22a, 25–29), as opposed to the terror and death characterizing the giving of the Mosaic law at Mount Sinai (12:18–21). According to the Old Testament, God's resting place was both in the earthly Jerusalem (Ps 132:13–14; cf. Sir 36:13) and in the heavens (Isa 66:1), but this had now been relocated to the heavenly city of Jerusalem, the unseen city that would only be revealed in the days of the Messiah (4 Ezra 7:26–30; Thiessen 2007, 363 n. 40). These are now fully realized in Christ, the messianic Son and in his soteriological work as the heavenly high priest (Heb 1:1–4; 2:17–18; 3:1–6; 4:14–15; 5:5–9; 6:19–20; 7:23–10:18). The old covenant, therefore, is obsolete and outdated, including the city of Jerusalem and its temple, both of which would soon disappear (see Heb 8:13).

The question arises whether this critique of the present earthly Jerusalem and its temple (Heb 9:9–10; 10:11), including its replacement by the heavenly Jerusalem, is primarily directed at a Jewish or a Greco-Roman audience. This is a false antithesis, needless to say. But, to cite example from the Jewish side, C. van der Waal (1971, 90), referring to Heb 13:14, claims that we see here "a certain polemic against the synagogue in the term 'permanent city.'" But it is difficult to see how contemporary auditors would have made a conceptual link between Jerusalem as a city and an ancient association (the synagogue): the parallelism is not strong enough. In the case of Rome, however, it is hard to deny that an implicit criticism is being made of the eternal city, given the spread of evidence for the motif predating 70 CE noted above, even if the heavy concentration of the evidence is found in the Flavian period. Jason Whitlark (2022) has done Hebrews scholarship a service in demonstrating how the author's figured speech, appropriated from contemporary rhetoric by the author, allowed the elliptical reference in Heb 13:14 to allude covertly to a critique of the eternal city of Rome, without exposing his readers to the charge of engaging in anti-imperial sentiments.

But for readers of Hebrews in the Flavian period, especially those at Rome, there would have been an additional polemical edge in the message of Hebrews. The arch of Titus, erected on the Via Sacra outside the forum in 81 CE, and his second triumphal arch, positioned originally at the entrance to Rome's chariot-racing stadium (i.e., the Circus Maximus),[3] commemorated Vespasian's victory over the Jews at Jerusalem in 70 CE. It is beyond the scope of this commentary to discuss the iconography of Titus's arch at the Via Sacra. See DesRosiers 2019; Brandfon 2015. But it is important to realize, as Jodi Magness (2008) has argued, that the Flavian rulers would have believed that they had vanquished the God of Israel, triumphantly displaying the spoils of YHWH's temple in the Templum Pacis and rendering its spoils permanently in the iconography of the Via Sacra frieze. A triumphal attitude on the part of the Romans is not only graphically portrayed in the iconography of the Via Sacra arch, but it also stretches well beyond the normal limits of Roman boasting in the inscription found of the Circus Maximus arch, cited below (*CIL* 6.944):

The Senate and People of Rome [dedicate this arch] to the Emperor Titus Caesar Vespasian Augustus, son of the deified Vespasian, *pontifex*

---

3. On the announcement in 2015 of the discovery of the foundation of Titus's second triumphal arch at the Circus Maximus—i.e., large blocks of Carrara marble comprising more than three hundred fragments—see Anonymous 2021.

maximus, holding the tribunician power for the tenth year, acclaimed *imperator* seventeen times, consul eight times, father of his country, their imperator, because with the guidance and plans of his father, and under his auspices, he subdued the people of Judea and destroyed the city of Jerusalem, which all generals, kings and peoples before him had either failed to do or even to attempt.

The total destruction of the Jerusalem is spotlighted, and, remarkably, this is claimed to be unprecedented, ignoring entirely the destruction of Jerusalem and the first temple by the Babylonians in 587 BCE and the second temple's profanation and attendant massacre of the Jews by the Syrian ruler Antiochus Epiphanes in 167 BCE. The message of Hebrews about the participation of believers in an alternative heavenly Jerusalem, which had already been inaugurated by a crucified messianic pretender in Judea, claimed by his followers to be an alternative Son of God and heavenly high priest over against the current earthly Flavian ruler, would be provocative at the very least. But even more remarkably, Hebrews pinpricks the triumphal ideology of Rome by emphasizing that the shame of the cross preceded the joy of the resurrected and ascended Christ (Heb 12:2). So, similarly, Christ's disciples would face the same life of suffering, dispossession, and dishonor as they served their heavenly Lord (10:32–35). Ellen Aitken (2016, 207) sets out the collision between the Flavian dynasty and the early Christian view of the city of Jerusalem most effectively:

> The entire cityscape of the center of Rome was renovated by the Flavians to monumentalize their Judean victory as the legitimation of their reign. Within the logic of Roman religion, what the Flavians achieved through these activities was a symbolic acquisition of the Jerusalem temple, "reproducing" it in the city space of Rome.... The response of Hebrews is to undertake its own reproduction and reassembling of the tabernacle—in heavenly dimensions, as the true tabernacle in an eternal city.

This ideological, political, and religious collision would continue into the centuries well beyond the Flavian period. In the fifth century CE, Rutilius Namatianus's vision of the undiminished glory of eternal city of Rome in *De reditu suo* would be countered by Augustine in his *The City of God*.

Bibliography

Aitken, Ellen B. 2016. "The Body of Jesus Outside the Eternal City: Mapping Ritual Space in the Epistle to the Hebrews." Pages 194–209 in *Hebrews in Contexts*. Edited by Gabriella Gelardini and Harold W. Attridge. AJEC 91. Leiden: Brill.

Alzinger, Wilhelm. 1974. *Augusteische Architektur in Ephesos*. Sonderschriften des Österreichischen Archaologischen Institutes 16. Vienna: Oesterr. Archaeologisches Inst. im Selbstverl.

Anonymous. 2021. "Pieces of Triumphal Arch of Titus in Circus Maximus." The History Blog. http://tinyurl.com/SBL9031c.

Brandfon, Fredric. 2015. "The Arch of Titus in the Roman Forum: A Case Study of Vandalism and History." *Change over Time* 5.1:6–27.

Bru, Hadrien. 2011. "L'empereur et l'éternité." Pages 175–84 in *Le pouvoir impérial dans les provinces syriennes: représentations et célébrations d'Auguste à Constantin (31 av. J.-C.-337 ap. J.-C.)*. CHANE 49. Leiden: Brill.

Charlesworth, Martin P. 1936. "Providentia and Aeternitas." *HTR* 29.2:107–32.

Cooley, Alison E. 2009. *Res Gestae Divi Augusti: Text, Translation, and Commentary*. Cambridge: Cambridge University Press.

DesRosiers, Nathaniel. 2019. "Another Temple, Another Vessel: Josephus, the Arch of Titus, and Roman Triumphal Propaganda." *NEA* 82.3:140–47.

Futral, James R., Jr. 2002. "The Rhetorical Function of City as a Sociological Symbol in the Book of Revelation." PhD diss., New Orleans Baptist Theological Seminary.

Harrison, James R. 2011. *Paul and the Imperial Authorities at Thessalonica and Rome: A Study in the Conflict of Ideology*. WUNT 273. Tübingen: Mohr Siebeck.

———. 2020. *Reading Romans with Roman Eyes: Studies on the Social Perspective of Paul*. Paul in Critical Contexts. Lanham, MD: Lexington/Fortress.

Illou, Nefeli. 2021. "The Temple of Roma and Augustus on the Athenian Acropolis: A Symbol of Roman Power?" The Post Hole. http://tinyurl.com/SBL9031d.

Isaac, Benjamin. 1998. "Eternal Rome/(Roma Aeterna)" [Hebrew]. *Historia* 2:19–31.

Magness, Jodi. 2008. "The Arch of Titus at Rome and the Fate of the God of Israel." *JJS* 59.2:201–17.
Mellor, Ronald. 1975. *THEA ROME: The Goddess Roma in the Greek World*. Gottingen: Vandenhoeck & Ruprecht.
Moore, G. F. 1894. "On Urbs Aeterna and Urbs Sacra." *TAPA* 25:34–60.
Platner, Samuel B. 1929. *A Topographical Dictionary of Rome*. Revised by Thomas Ashby. Oxford: Oxford University Press.
Pratt, Kenneth J. 1965. "Rome as Eternal." *JHI* 26.1:25–44.
Ramantswana, H. 2013. "Mount Sinai and Mount Zion: Discontinuity and Continuity in the Book of Hebrews." *In die Skriflig/In Luce Verbi* 47.1:1–9.
Reapple, Eva M. 2001. "The Metaphor of the City in the Book of Revelation: A 'Textual' Image and Incentive for Imagination." PhD diss., University of Saint Andrews.
Reynolds, Joyce. 1982. *Aphrodisias and Rome*. JRS Monographs 1. London: Society for the Promotion of Roman Studies.
Scherrer, Peter. 1990. "Augustus, die Mission des Vedius Pollio und die Artemis Ephesia." *Jahreshefte des österreichischen archäologischen Instituts* 60:87–101.
Taylor, Lily Ross. 1931. *The Divinity of the Roman Empire*. Middletown, CT: American Philological Association.
Thiessen, Matthew. 2007. "Hebrews and the End of the Exodus." *NovT* 49:353–69.
Waal, C. van der. 1971. "'The People of God' in the Epistle to the Hebrews." *Neot* 5:83–92.
Whitlark, Jason A. 2012. "'Here We Do Not Have a City That Remains': A Figured Critique of Roman Imperial Propaganda in Hebrews 13:4." *JBL* 131:161–79.
Winzenburg, Justin. 2022. *Ephesians and Empire: An Evaluation of the Epistle's Subversion of Roman Imperial Ideology*. WUNT 2/573. Tübingen: Mohr Siebeck.
Yeates, Paul H. 2017. "Competing Cosmologies in Early Christianity: Cosmology in the Book of Revelation, Roman Imperial Ideology, and in the Province of Asia." PhD diss., Macquarie University.
Zalcman, Lawrence. 1997. "The Eternal City: Rome or Jerusalem?" *JJS* 48:312–13.

7. Hadrian Coenthroned with Dionysos: Perspectives from Ephesians and Revelation

James R. Harrison

IEph 2.275

JÖAI 50Supp:75–77, no. 6 (*editio princeps*); *AE* 1975.800; *SEG* 26.1272; sketchbook of Knibbe 3736. This honorific association inscription on an altar was erected for Hadrian by the *mystai* of Dionysos. It was found in a location in Selçuk on the eastern edge of the Artemision. Date: 119/129 CE.

	Αὐτοκράτορα Καίσαρα	Imperator Caesar,
2	θεοῦ Τραιανοῦ Παρθικοῦ	of (the) god Trajan Parthicus
	υἱόν, θεοῦ Νέρουα υἱωνόν,	(the) grandson, of (the) god Nerva (the) son,
4	[Τ]ραιανὸν Ἀδριανὸν Σε-	Trajan Hadrian Au-
	[β]αστόν, ἀρχιερέα μέγιστον, δη-	gustus, greatest high priest, (possessing) tr-
6	[μ]αρχικῆς ἐξουσίας, ὕπατον	ibunician power, consul
	τὸ γ', οἱ πρὸ πόλεως μύσται σύ[ν-]	three (times), the initiates before the city (honor the) co-
8	θρονον τῷ Διονύσῳ, ἱερεύοντ[ος]	enthroned with Dionysos, at the time of the priesthood
	Κλ(αυδίου) Ῥωμύλου,	of Claudius Romulus, when the
	ἱεροφαντοῦντος	revealer of sacred objects
10	Κλ(αυδίου) Εὐβίου, ἐπιμελητοῦ	(was) Claudius Eubios and the
	Ἀντωνίου	supervisor (was) Antonius
	Δρόσου· ἀναθέντος τὴν τειμὴν	Drosos: (this) honor was erected
12	ἐκ τῶν ἰδίων Θεοδότου τοῦ-	from the resources of (Theodotus)
	(Θεοδότου) Προκλ[ί-]	(the son) of Theodotos Procl-
	ωνος μυσταγωγοῦ μετὰ τῶν τέκν[ων]	ion, the initiation leader, (along) with his children

14 Πρόκλου ὑμνῳδοῦ καὶ Ἀθηνοδώρου   Proklos (the) hymn-singer and Athenodoros.

The translation above, somewhat stilted because of its replication of the order of the Greek text, reveals that the Roman ruler Hadrian was coenthroned with the god Dionysos in an association decree of the *mystae* of Ephesus. The word "coenthroned" (σύ[ν]θρονον) in lines 7–8 is infrequently used in the Greek epigraphic corpus, with only twenty-five occurrences revealed in a search of the Packhard Humanities Institute Greek Epigraphy programme (PHI). However, several of these inscriptions are directly relevant to our inscription and one, in particular, revealingly so because it is early in the New Testament period.

First, in an inscription honoring a priestess from Pergamum (IPergamon 2.497 [37–39 CE]), one of Germanicus's daughters, Julia Livilla, sister of Caligula, is listed among the cult deities worshiped at the city. Although Julia Livilla's cult would have had only a brief exposure at Pergamum, given her brother's fate as Roman ruler, she is nevertheless presented as coenthroned alongside the goddess Athena Polias (Stafford 2013, 31; Angelova 2015, 96): "The council and the people honored Otakilias Phaustina, daughter of Otakilios Phaustos, (who is) the priestess of Athena Nikephoros and Polias and Julia enthroned with her [συνθρόνου], (the) new Nikephoros, daughter of Germanicus Caesar" (IPergamon 2.497.1–6).

Second, in an inscription from Attica (IG 2.1076 [195–198 CE]), Julia Domna, the wife of the Roman ruler Septimius Severus, is honored. Sacrifices are offered "to J[ulia Sebaste the savior of the Athenians]" (ll. 15–16). The archon is summoned to do something in the temple of Athena Polias (the Erechtheion)—that is, presumably erect an honorific statue of Julia Domna (Stafford 2013, 31 [electronic copy])—"in order that she might be enthroned with the god (goddess?) (συνθρόν[ος ᾖ τῇ θεῷ])" (ll. 19–20). As Arthur Darby Nock (1930, 35) observes, "Here we notice the sharing of the temple of Athena, and, what is perhaps unique, the explicit provision for the sharing of a sacrifice ... it is an expression of gratitude." On Julia Domna generally, see Langford 2013.

Third, Antinous, the Bithynian Greek youth and paramour of Hadrian, is honored thus in Portus in Latium (IG Porto 6 [130–ca. 138 CE]): "To Antinous enthroned [συνθρόνῳ] with the gods in Egypt." Fourth, another Greek inscription from Rome also speaks of Antinous in similar manner: "To Antinous, enthroned with the gods of Egypt. M. Oulpios [Marcus Ulpius] Apollonius, prophet" (Meyer 1991, 172–73).

In sum, the extant epigraphic evidence regarding coenthronement is clear: the Roman ruler, his family members, and favorites were enthroned alongside the indigenous deities of cities in the Roman Empire from the time Caligula through to the reign of Septimius Severus and probably beyond. For discussion of Hadrian, see Burnett 2021, 107–8. For the imperial throne sharing of Julia Domna and Julia Livilla, see respectively 108–9 and 105–7.

Returning to our Ephesian inscription, the Roman ruler is not presented as supplanting the indigenous deities. The compound verb σύ[ν]θρονον underscores the mutual cultic honoring of the Ephesian indigenous deity and the Roman ruler Hadrian, with no sense of rivalry or demotion of status evinced in either case. Indeed, Hadrian is presented implicitly as the "new Dionysos" at Ephesus in our association inscription (cf. Commodus as νέον Διόνυσον in IEph 2.293 [180–192 CE]). Moreover, he is explicitly so designated by the thymelic synod in other cities of the Roman empire: for example, Sardis (ISard 1.13 [νέον Διόνυσον]; Ancyra (Bosch 1967, 130, 166: [νέ]ον Διόνυσον), and Aphrodisias (I.Aphrodisias 2007.12.27: νέον Διόνυσον). For non-thymelic occurrences of the same, see Athens (TAM 5.3.1456a: [θὲον νέον Διόνυ[σον]) and Chios (SEG 15.530 [νέον Διόνυσον]). These thymelic synods were ecumenical (i.e., international) associations of artists scattered throughout the Roman Empire. Thus, when the thymelic synods honored Hadrian as the "new Dionysos" in the cities above, a connection between the Dionysiac cult, the imperial rulers and the world of the theater was established (Fauconnier 2020). For discussion of the integration of the imperial cult with the Ephesian indigenous deities, see Harrison, "Ephesian Cultic Officials, Their Benefactors, and the Quest for Civic Virtue," in *NewDocs* 11B.

Notwithstanding, the association visual evidence also reveals additional perspectives. The reliefs of association inscriptions reinforce the primacy of the indigenous deities, showing Cybele enthroned above an inscription at Prusa by Olympos (IPrusa 50 [second century CE). Further, at Kyzikos (IMT Kyz Kapu Dağ 1539 [first century BCE]), Cybele is also depicted as enthroned with Apollo (?), both deities being placed above an altar where a slave makes an offering. We conclude, then, that mutuality in honorific rituals occurs where the Roman ruler is introduced into the eulogistic mix, but, when he is not present, the local indigenous deities command the stage visually. Romanization, it seems, had its limits.

A final comment on IEph 2.275 is pertinent at this stage. The reference to the "hymn-singer" in line 14 (Πρόκλου ὑμνῳδοῦ) is significant.

Associations of "hymn singers" (Friesen 2001, 104–13; Harland 2003, 93–95), which were dedicated to the praise of the imperial gods, arose in several locations in Asia Minor, namely, Pergamum (Ascough, Harland, and Kloppenborg 2012, §§117, 120), Ephesus (*supra* and *infra*), and Smyrna (Ascough, Harland, and Kloppenborg 2012, §198). One further Ephesian example will suffice to illustrate how these associations acquired substantial prestige and status by honoring the Roman ruler. On column 1 of an Ephesian association inscription (IEph 7.2.3801 = Ascough, Harland, and Kloppenborg 2012, §160 [41–54 CE]) is reproduced a (now fragmentary) letter from Claudius to the hymn singers, which acknowledges (what seems to be) their honorific decree praising him. Here we see how enthusiastically the hymn singers memorialize for perpetuity the very considerable social prestige of receiving in the province of Asia a personal response from the Julio-Claudian ruler at Rome. Column 2 replicates a resolution of the provincial assembly of Asia, setting forth its gratitude for the vital role that all the hymn singers from Asia, including Ephesus, played in celebrating the birthday of divine Augustus and his household. The prestige accrued by the synod of the *hymnodoi* through their participation in the imperial celebrations is highlighted in the resolution:

> The hymn singers from all Asia, coming together in Pergamon for the most sacred birthday of Augustus Tiberius Caesar, god, accomplish a magnificent work for the glory of the synod (εἰς τὴν [τῆς συνόδου δόξ]αν), singing hymns to the Augustan household, accomplishing sacrifices to the household gods, leading festivals and banquets.

What, then, would Flavian readers of the epistle to the Ephesians have made of Eph 1:20–21 and 2:6, given the enthronement of Hadrian alongside other local indigenous deities? It affords us sympathetic insight into why Paul has depicted the risen and ascended Christ as seated (καθίσας) at God's right hand in the heavenly places, exalted above all rule, authority, power, and dominion (Eph 1:20–21). Remarkably, believers have also been seated (συνεκάθισεν) in this present age with God in the heavenly places in Christ Jesus (Eph 2:6; cf. Mark 10:35–39). Caution is apposite here regarding the boundaries of what Paul is saying. Ernest Best (1998, 220) rightly comments that "it is not said that believers are exalted to the right hand of God as was Christ. Their position in the heavenlies is not then identical with his." But they do accompany Christ in his heavenly triumph and enthronement, participating in advance of the eschaton in his glory as Lord of all. So it is possible that Flavian auditors of Eph 1:20–21 and 2:6 understood their superior status as believers in Christ over against the honorific coenthroning of Hadrian with Dionysos in our Ephesian association, including, from another perspective within the Greco-Roman hermeneutical grid, Christ's triumph over the magical principalities and powers (Acts 19:19–20; see also Arnold 1992).

Most Ephesian commentators, however, confine their discussion to the Jewish angelic context of principalities and powers in Eph 1:20–21 (e.g., Lincoln 1990; Schnackenburg 1991; Hoehner 2003). Best (1998, 177–78) mentions the Hellenistic context, while Margaret Y. MacDonald (2000, 220) refers to the arguments of Clinton E. Arnold, noted above. But, for some reason (terminological?), the imperial context is entirely sidelined by commentators. But, as noted, the coenthroning of imperial family members with indigenous gods at Pergamum had already occurred by 37–39 CE: so Paul's original audience was probably aware of such enthroning rituals for the ruler. Furthermore, in terms of the indigenous deities, this exalted status for believers in Eph 2:6 also stands in contrast to the worshiping slave depicted below the goddesses Cybele and Apollo in the Kyzikos relief (*supra*). Indeed, at Ephesus only the Roman ruler was accorded the prestigious position of sitting enthroned alongside the indigenous deities in association inscriptions. Ephesian auditors could hardly have missed Paul's point about their extraordinary privilege in their Jewish, Hellenistic, and Roman contexts.

Last, while it is true that there is a mimicry of Roman imperial court ceremonial in Rev 4–5 (Aune 1983), the glorious theophanic depiction of "the one sitting on the throne" (Rev 4:2; 5:7) and his lamb at the center of the throne (5:6; 7:17) leads inexorably to the triumphant throne scene in the new creation (21:5; see Gallusz 2014). Interestingly from a Greco-Roman viewpoint, the mention of "the throne of God and of the lamb" alongside each other in Rev 22:1, 3 may not have been as conceptually challenging for John's Asian auditors, who were familiar with indigenous gods and imperial rulers being coenthroned in their rule over humanity. What would have been confronting, however, was the preposterous claim that this glorious risen and reigning Christ was the same disgraced and crucified criminal dispatched by the Roman prefect Pontius Pilate in the imperial backwater of Palestine in the early thirties. Indeed, John's portrayal of the vulnerability of the worthy lamb ("looking as if it had been slain"; Rev 5:6a), who unleashes the catastrophic seven seals (6:2,

4, 5, 7–8, 9, 12–14; 8:1) amid stratospheric accolades in heavenly throne room (Rev 5:6b–14; 7:9–17), reveals the deep paradox and ambiguity at the core of early Christian claims about Christ.

Furthermore, it is worth remembering that fifteen hymns or hymn fragments are found in Revelation (4:8; 4:9–11; 5:9–10; 5:12; 5:13; 7:10; 7:11–12; 11:15; 11:16–18; 12:10–12; 15:2–4; 16:5–7; 19:1–4; 19:5; 19:6–8). Adolf Deissmann (1910, 346) had famously suggested that there is "polemical parallelism" between the cult of the emperor and the cult of Christ, where "solemn concepts of the Imperial cult sounded … the same or similar." It is possible that this explosion of hymns in Revelation represents John's liturgical equivalent of the hymn singers honoring the imperial gods throughout Asia Minor. These *hymnodoi* were certainly known at three of the cities addressed in the oracles of Rev 2–3 (Ephesus, Smyrna, Philadelphia, *supra*). Paul Barnett (1989, 114–15) makes a similar observation regarding the five thousand equestrians, called *Augustiani*, who continuously acclaimed Nero at Rome: "Day and night they kept up a thunder of applause, and applied to the emperor's the voice and epithets of deities" (Tacitus, *Ann.* 14.15). Thus the *hymnodoi* in Asia Minor and Neronian *Augustiani* in Rome viably form the religious and social backdrop to the overflow of liturgy in praise of God and his Christ throughout Revelation.

Bibliography

Angelova, Diliana M. 2015. *Sacred Founders: Women, Men, and Gods in the Discourse of Imperial Founding, Rome through Early Byzantium.* Oakland: University of California Press.

Arnold, Clinton E. 1992. *Ephesians, Power and Magic: The Concept of Power in Ephesians in Light of Its Historical Setting.* Repr., Grand Rapids: Baker.

Ascough, Richard S., Philip A. Harland, and John S. Kloppenborg, eds. 2012. *Associations in the Greco-Roman World: A Source Book.* Waco, TX: Baylor University Press.

Aune, David E. 1983. "The Influence of Roman Imperial Court Ceremonial on the Apocalypse of John." *BR* 38:5–26.

Barnett, Paul. 1989. "Polemical Parallelism: Some Further Reflections on the Apocalypse." *JSNT* 35:111–20.

Best, Ernest. 1998. *A Critical and Exegetical Commentary on Ephesians.* ICC. London: T&T Clark.

Bosch, E. 1967. *Quellen zur Geschichte der Stadt Ankara im Altertum.* Ankara: Türk Tarih Kurumu Basımevi.
Burnett, D. Clint. 2021. *Christ's Enthronement at God's Right Hand and Its Greco-Roman Cultural Context.* BZNW 242. Berlin: De Gruyter.
Deissmann, Adolf. 1910. *Light from the Ancient East Illustrated by Recently Discovered Texts of the Graeco-Roman World.* New York: Hodder & Stoughton.
Fauconnier, Bram. 2020. "The Emperor and the Ecumenical Synods of Competitors." *Latomus* 79:647–60.
Friesen, Steven J. *Imperial Cults and the Apocalypse of John: Reading Revelation in the Ruins.* Oxford: Oxford University Press, 2001.
Gallusz, Laszlo. 2014. *The Throne Motif in the Book of Revelation.* LNTS 487. London: T&T Clark.
Harland, Philip A. 2003. "Imperial Cults within Local Cultural Life: Associations in Roman Asia." *Ancient History Bulletin* 17:47–69.
Hoehner, H. W. 2003. *Ephesians: An Exegetical Commentary.* Grand Rapids: Eerdmans.
Langford, Julie. 2013. *Maternal Megalomania: Julia Domna and the Imperial Politics of Motherhood.* Baltimore: John Hopkins University Press.
Lincoln, Andrew T. 1990. *Ephesians.* WBC 42. Dallas: Word.
MacDonald, Margaret Y. 2000. *Colossians and Ephesians.* Sacrina Pagina 17. Collegeville, MN: Liturgical Press.
Meyer, Hugo. 1991. *Antinoos: Die archäologischen Denkmäler unter Einbeziehung des numismatischen und epigraphischen Materials sowie der literarischen Nachrichten, Ein Beitrag zur Kunst- und Kulturgeschichte der hadrianisch-frühantoninischen Zeit.* Munich: Fink.
Nock, Arthur Darby. 1930. "Σύνναιος Θεός." *HSCP* 31:1–62.
Schnackenburg, Rudolf. 1991. *The Epistle to the Ephesians: A Commentary.* Edinburgh: T&T Clark.
Stafford, Emma. 2013. "The People to the Goddess Livia." *Kernos* 26:205–38.

8. The Economic Conflagration of the Sacred Cult and Early Christian Preservation of Sacred Funds

Isaac T. Soon

IEph 1a.18b.0–20; 1a.18c.0–13

JÖAI 23:280–86 (part); SEG 4.516; Dörner 1935, *passim*; *DocsGaius* 380; Cébeillac 1972, no. 14; IEph 18 and add. p. 1. The selections translated below (IEph 1a.18b.0–20 and IEph 1a.18.c.0–13) are two of four cuboids made of bluish marble, but the four are not connected to each other. Originally, they came from a pillar and were later made into another pillar. On the left side are the *agoranomos* ("market overseer") inscriptions. Found during excavations at Ephesus in 1926 near the "Wood" Basilica. Dimensions for cuboid IEph 1a.18b: height, 56.7 cm; width, 73 cm; thickness, 70 cm; letter height, 1.9 cm. Dimensions for cuboid IEph 1a.18c: height, 60m; width, 74.2; thickness left, 72.9; thickness right, 73.7 cm; letter height, 1.6 cm. Date: 44 CE.

18b.0–20

[πολλαὶ γὰρ θεῖαι οἰκίαι ἢ διὰ πυρὸς διεφθαρμέναι ἢ διὰ] συμπτώσεως ἀμόρφως εἰσὶν κατερριμμέναι, τό	[for many divine buildings having either been destroyed by fire or by] collapsing lie in shapeless ruins, and the
2 τε τῆς Ἀρτέμιδος αὐτῆς ἱερόν, ὃ τῆς ἐπαρχείας	temple of Artemis herself, which for the province
ὅλης ἐστὶν κόσμος καὶ {ὃ} διὰ τὸ τοῦ ἔργου μέγεθος	as a whole is an ornament both from the size of the work
4 καὶ διὰ τὴν τοῦ περὶ τὴν θεὸν σεβασμοῦ ἀρχαιότητ‹α›	and from the antiquity of the god's cult
καὶ διὰ τὴν τῶν προσόδων ἀφθονίαν τῶν ὑπὸ τοῦ	and from the unstinting flow of the revenues that by

6 Σεβαστοῦ ἀποκατασταθεισῶν τῇ θεᾷ, στέρεται	Augustus have been restored to the goddess, is stripped
τῶν ἰδίων χρημάτων, ἃ καὶ εἰς ἐπιμέλειαν καὶ εἰς	of its own resources, which both for the care and for the
8 κόσμον τῶν ἀναθημάτων ἐξαρκεῖν ἐδύ<νατο>· περισπᾶ-	ornament of the offerings might have sufficed. For they are
ται γὰρ εἰς τὴν ἄδικον ἐπιθυμίαν τῶν οὕτως τοῦ κοι-	directed to the unjust desires of those who only over the com-
10 νοῦ προϊσταμένων, ὡς ἑαυτοῖς λυσιτελεῖν νομίζου-	mon interest take the lead insofar as they expect to benefit themselves.
σιν· ὁσάκις τε γὰρ ἂν ἀπὸ Ῥώμης ἱλαρωτέρα ἔλθῃ	For whenever there arrives from Rome a happy
12 ἀγγελία, ταύτῃ πρὸς τὸν ἴδιον ἀποχρῶνται πορισ-	announcement, they abuse it for their own pro-
μὸν τό τε σχῆμα τῆς θείας οἰκίας προκάλυμμα	fit and, the routine of the divine building as a pretext
14 ποιούμενοι τὰς ἱερωσύνας ὥσπερ ἐν ἀπαρτεί-	taking, the priesthoods as though at an aucti-
ᾳ πιπράσκουσιν καὶ ἐκ παντὸς γένους ἐπὶ τὴν	on they sell and from every class for the
16 ὠνὴν αὐτῶν συνκ<α>λοῦσιν ἀνθρώπους, εἶτα οὐκ ἐγλέ-	sale of them they invite people, and then they do not sel-
γονται τοὺς ἐπιτηδειοτάτους, ὧν ταῖς κεφαλαῖς	ect the most suited people upon whose heads
18 ὁ πρέπων ἐπιτεθήσεται στέφανος· προσόδους	the proper crown will be set. And the revenues
[τε ὁρ]ίζουσιν τοῖς ἱερωμένοις, ὅσας ἂν οἱ λαμβάνον-	they allocate amongst those consecrated, at whatever rate those accepting
20 [τες θε]λήσωσιν, ἵνα ὡς πλεῖστον αὐτοὶ νοσφίζωντα. (block layer of unknown height missing)	[them de]sire, with a view to their embezzling as much as possible.

18c.0–13

[οὐ γὰρ χρὴ τοὺς τὰς ἱερωσύνας ὠνοῦντας τοιαῦτα ὑ-]	For it is not necessary for those purchasing the priesthoods to undertake

8. The Economic Conflagration of the Sacred Cult

πομένειν ἀναλώ[ματα, ὅπως ἀξιωθή]σεται τῆς	such expenses in order that he, who is always most suitable for it,
2 παρὰ τοῦ δήμου [τειμῆς ἀεὶ ὁ εἰς αὐτ]ὴν ἐπιτηδειό-	will be deemed worthy of the honor from the people.
τατος· ὑπέρμε[γα δὲ πόλεως χρέος διὰ τ]οῦ ἐπικρίμα-	And it is fitting to curtail a great debt
4 τος τούτου πε[ρικόπτειν προσῆκο]ν· ἐπεὶ τὴν ἀ-	of the city through this decree. Since I know that the
πόδοσιν τῶν χρη[μάτων δυσχερέ]α τῆι πόλει ἢ	payment of money is annoying to the city or
6 παντελῶς ἀδύνατον ο[ἶδα, ἐὰν ἀπ]αριθμεῖν νῦν	altogether impossible, if it must now pay back
ἀνανκάζηται, ἃ παρὰ τῶν ὠνησαμένων ἔλαβεν	what it received from the purchasers,
8 οὐδὲν πλέον παρέχεσθαι τοῖς ἱερεῦσιν τὴν πόλιν	it is my pleasure that the city provide nothing more to the priests
ἀρέσκει ἢ ἑκατοστὴν τῆς δεδομένης τότε τειμῆς	than a one hundredth of the price paid at that time
10 κατὰ τὴν Οὐηδίου Πωλλίωνος διάταξιν τὴν καὶ ὑπὸ	in accord with the constitution of Vedius Pollio which has also
τοῦ θεοῦ Σεβαστοῦ συνφυλαχθεῖσαν· διδόναι δέ τι	been confirmed by the divine Augustus. It is not my pleasure that
12 τῇ βουλῇ τοὺς ἱερεῖς ἢ πάλιν ἐν μέρει παρ' αὐτῆς λαμ-	priests give anything to the Senate or again in part receive
βάνειν οὐκ ἀρέσκει μοι. (Another nine lines of Greek follow.)	(anything) from it.

This excerpt of a larger inscription issued by the Roman proconsul Paullus Fabius Persicus to Ephesus deals with the worrisome mishandling of temple resources by Ephesian civic magistrates. Persicus's directive relates the current draining of Artemisian sacred funds with the destruction of divine buildings affected by fire or ruin (IEph 18b.0–1). While Dignas (2002, 149) argues that Persicus references the state of temples throughout the province of Asia, given the situation with sacred funds, I am inclined to read it as a comparison of the natural ways that ancient temples are usually destroyed in opposition to the situation in Ephesus, the willful and cognizant deterioration of Artemis's temple through economic neglect and corruption. Civic magistrates are auctioning off priesthood positions and, as a part of the deal, allowing the highest bidders to claim an unlimited portion of the revenues that are received by the temple. The selling of priesthoods was not unusual in Asia Minor, as fourth-century BCE records from Erythrae and Chios show (see Dignas 2002, 251–71, esp. 252–53). These records recorded the name of the priest, the deity, the price paid, a tax, and a guarantor. On the priesthood in Ephesus see Bremmer 2008. Whereas in these sales the money became revenue for the temple cult, in the case of the Ephesians, the money from the auction of positions appears to be going into the pockets of civic officials. The motivation for citizens to bid for positions in the temple cult is the allure of unlimited access to incoming revenue (Dignas 2002, 268). Persicus puts an end to the compounding system of embezzlement by paying back 1/100th of what the priests bid for their positions and discontinuing the sale of temple positions as well as any access to temple revenue. Apparently, the problem that the Ephesians face was not a novel issue as earlier measures were taken by Vedius Pollio (mentioned in IEph 18c.10) under the reign of Augustus. See Berdowski 2017–2018, 99–100.

Flavius Josephus describes the Second Temple catching fire both due to Jewish inhabitants and the Romans (*B.J.* 6.164–167, 346). As catastrophic the destruction of the Jerusalem temple was by the armies of Titus in the summer of 70 CE to the Jewish people, the burning of temples was not an infrequent occurrence in the ancient world. For examples, see Canter 1932. The notion of burning temples was not foreign to the Ephesians either, since it was well-known that a certain man (apparently named Herostratus) had decided to set fire to the first Ephesian temple in 356 BCE for glory (see Valerius Maximus, *Fact. et dict.* 8.14.ext.5). Josephus's account of the Jews setting fire to their own temple aligns with Persicus's metaphoric use of the destruction of sacred precincts as an analogy for economic conflagration happening among the Ephesian cult in 44 CE.

Financial corruption and a concern for the proper distribution of funds is not absent from New Testament texts. Various passages that deal with economic distribution within a cultic setting correspond with the different perspectives illuminated by the inscriptions above: that of (1) those who are trying to preserve resources (e.g., Persicus), (2) those who are embezzling resources (e.g., civic magistrates), and (3) and those who are mishandling resources (e.g., civic priests).

The most well-known case of embezzlement in the New Testament is perhaps the story of Ananias and Sapphira in Acts 5:1–11. The couple sell a piece of land but kept back some of the money for themselves. In the eyes of Peter and the apostles, the gift was already under the ownership of the Holy Spirit and God (5:3, 4, 9), and for Ananias and Sapphira to hold something back was akin to theft from the community, much like the priests who kept whatever amount of the revenues from the Artemesion above.

Paul the apostle attempts to relieve financial pressure from the congregations in Judea by way of the so-called Jerusalem collection (1 Cor 16:1–4; 2 Cor 8:1–9:15; Gal 2:10; Rom 15:25–31). The gift, collected from Macedonia, Achaia, and Asia Minor is an attempt to bring a balanced ledger (or in Paul's words, "equality" [ἰσότης]; 2 Cor 8:14) between the gentile assemblies and the Jewish ones. Here Paul is not so much concerned with corruption but with the proper distribution of funds—although his endorsement of Titus and the other brothers in 2 Cor 8–9 as trustworthy collectors of this gift stands as a guarantee of sorts that the funds are not be extorted but gathered (see 2 Cor 9:5). In this situation, Paul must convince the Corinthians that he is not taking the money for himself but that it is well and truly going on to the Jerusalem community (see 2 Cor 12:17–18). Such a notion is not without basis since, in the Acts of the Apostles, after Paul is imprisoned in Caesarea, he was called upon repeatedly to speak with the then procurator (governor) of Palestine, Antonius Felix who was hoping to receive a bribe from him (Acts 24:26), possibly from the collection. The text confirms nothing, but Paul appears to keep his promise regarding the funds.

The economic stability of the early Christian churches, linked through households, was of importance to the pastor who wrote 1 Timothy. As John Barclay (2020) has recently argued, the situation described in 1 Tim 5:9–16 concerns not young widows but young women who had the option to get married (and thus provide economic stability for herself and the wider Christian community) but chose to stay celibate (χῆραι). This excess of women who needed economic support jeopardized the care of widows who had no other means or options available to them and their children for support. The pastor advises these young celibate women to get married and have children (5:14). Of interest to us, however, is the pastor's description of the women going from house to house being idle (5:13, ἅμα δὲ καὶ ἀργαὶ μανθάνουσιν περιερχόμεναι τὰς οἰκίας). Although he mentions the tendency for such women to gossip, the idea that young celibate women were going from house to house may mean more than simply on house visitations. The pastor's emphasis on not burdening the church (5:16) suggests the possibility that some of the young women are not just visiting houses but moving from place to place being sustained by different ecclesial households. Alternatively, even if they are merely visiting houses (what Martin Dibelius and Hans Conzelmann [1972, 75] call "pastoral house calls"), they are merely being idle (ἀργαί) and neglecting the χῆραι duties of washing feet, helping the afflicted, and doing good works (5:10). In this situation the sacred funds devoted for true widows are being consumed not by household leaders but by members themselves, in this case, the young widows. The pastor, like Persicus, attempts to conserve funds for their proper use. Although this is not the same kind of cultic embezzlement as those done by the civic magistrates and priests above, there is an economic analogy that may be drawn between the proper use of sacred funds for the community and the misuse of those funds by individual members. By committing themselves in celibacy to their "first πίστις" (5:12), that is, Christ, the young χῆραι are "paying" a great spiritual cost and expecting reimbursement from the Christian community through economic support. The pastor halts their dependence upon the Christian community both because the resources can be better served for widows in need and because they start out with the intention to be celibate but later wish to marry anyway (5:11). The use of household resources to support such women goes to waste, when they should have been directed to older widows well-advanced in age who likely had fewer years of life left.

Bibliography

Barclay, John. 2020. "Household Networks and Early Christian Economics: A Fresh Study of 1 Timothy 5.3–16." *NTS* 66:268–87.

Berdowski, Piotr. 2017–2018. "Ex amicus divi augusti: P. Vedius Pollio." *Palamedes* 12:93–140.

Bremmer, Jan. 2008. "Priestly Personnel of the Ephesian Artemision: Anatolian, Persian, Greek, and Roman Aspects." Pages 37–53 in *Practitioners of the Divine: Greek Priests and Religious Figures from Homer to Heliodorus*. Edited by Beate Dignas and Kai Trampedach. Hellenic Studies 30. Washington, DC: Center for Hellenic Studies.

Canter, H. V. 1932. "Conflagrations in Ancient Rome." *CJ* 27.4:270–88.

Dibelius, Martin, and Hans Conzelmann. 1972. *The Pastoral Epistles: A Commentary on the Pastoral Epistles*. Hermeneia. Philadelphia: Fortress.

Dignas, Beate. 2002. *Economy of the Sacred in Hellenistic and Roman Asia Minor*. Oxford: Oxford University Press.

Dörner, Friedrich Karl. 1935. *Der Erlass des Statthalters von Asia*. Greifswald: Adler.

Cébeillac-Gervasoni, Mireille. 1972. *Les "Quaestores principis et candidate" aux Ier et IIème siècles de l'Empire*. Milan: Cisalpino.

The Ephesian Elites

9. Noble and Well-Born

Bradley J. Bitner

IEph 5.1540

Wood 1877, app. 3, "Inscriptions from the Site of the Temple of Diana," no. 14 (*editio princeps*); *GIBM* 3.2.540; *ILS* 8833; Wilhelm 1928, 227–28. The inscription was found in a wall on the site of the temple of Artemis. Date: first–third century CE.

1	Ἀττίδιον <Τ>οῦσκον[1]	Attidius Tuscus
	πραίτορα	praetor
	καὶ πρεσβευτὴν	and legate
	γενερῶσον καὶ	noble and
5	εὐγενέστατον	most well born
	Στερτίνιος Μάξιμος	Stertinius Maximus
	Εὐτύχης, ἱππικὸ[ς]	Eutyches, a Roman
	Ῥωμαίων,	of equestrian rank,
	θύτης τῶν ἑξήκοντα,	*haruspex* belonging to the college of LX,
10	σκρείβας λιβράριος	quaestorian
	κουαιστώριος,	*scriba librarius*,
	τὸν ἴδιον πάτρωνα.	[honored] his own patron.

Attidius Tuscus is praised on this stela as being noble (γενερῶσος, l. 4) and most well-born (εὐγενέστατος, l. 5). The first epithet, not in LSJ, is a rarely attested loanword from the Latin *generosus*: of noble birth, of good family or stock (IAsia Mixed §117; on γενερῶσος, Kearsley and Evans point to Drew-Bear 1972, 190). The second term is a superlative; its use here fits the first sense in BDAG, s.v. "εὐγενής" (pertaining to being of high status, *well-born, high-born*). The parable of Jesus in Luke 19:12 shows that

---

1. Inscribed ΙΟΥΣΚΟΝ but correctly restored to ΤΟΥΣΚΟΝ (IEph 5.1540; cf. Wood 1877, app. 3, "Inscriptions from the Site of the Temple of Diana," no. 14).

everyone recognized the wealth and status involved in being "well-born" (a certain εὐγενής man went into a far country to receive for himself a kingdom and then return). But our superlative in this text might be added to the comparative example (εὐγενέστερος) in BDAG (a fourth century CE text is cited after the headword; there is no superlative listed in MM, s.v. "εὐγενής").

Comparative and superlative forms are used elsewhere of local elites and leading citizens, for example, IG 5.2.269 (Εὐφρόσυνος Τίτου, πολίτης ... τὴν δὲ ψυχὴν εὐγενεστέραν τῆς φύσεως πλατύνας, Arkadia, Mantinea [10 BCE–10 CE]); IG 5.1.530 (Μᾶρκον Αὐρήλιον Πανκρατίδαν Ἑλλανίκου τὸν εὐγενέστατον πολίτην, Lakonike, Sparta [161–92]); *MAMA* 6.119 (Ἀμμίας Χα[ρ]μίδο[υ] ... μίαν τῶν εὐγενεστάτων ἀπὸ προγόνων βουλευτῶν, Herakleia, Salbake [date?]). For papyrological uses of the adjective, see Arzt-Grabner et al. 2006, 106. Epigraphically, forms of this epithet are overwhelmingly attested in Asia Minor and the Peloponnese, and so the socioeconomic dynamics they signal may perhaps be especially relevant to New Testament cities such as Ephesus and Corinth. Such dynamics come into sharper focus as we consider the named persons in our inscription and the few figures at Ephesus to whom the *simplex* (εὐγενής) is attributed.

The honorand, Attidius Tuscus (*PIR* A.1345) is not attested elsewhere but may be related to other Attidii who were second-century senators; his rank as *praetor* and legate is very high indeed (Chausson 2000, 866–68).[2] Stertinius Maximus Eutyches (missing from *LGPN* 5.1), who erected the stela for his patron, is an equestrian freedman who may be connected to another, earlier and high-ranking Stertinius in Ephesus. Gaius Stertinius Orpex was also a *scriba librarius* and was honored with a statue in recognition of the large sums he gave by foundations to the city of Ephesus (IEph 7.2.4123 after 23 [CE]; see Eck 1999, 15). Eutyches in our text, possibly descended from Orpex, was a *haruspex* or official soothsayer who belonged to the elite "order of the sixty" (l. 9; see Briquel 2014, 138). In this capacity Eutyches acted as a special adviser, most probably to the Senate or the emperor at Rome and perhaps also to his patron in the province of Asia Minor (Haack 2017, 365; but see Scheid, Cecere, and Grazia 1999, 136–38). Ours is the only Greek inscription referring to this college. Although *haruspices* at the civic level functioned as *apparitores* or

---

2. Dating of the figures attested in this inscription is difficult, with ranges from first–third centuries CE proposed; see Salomies 2007, 69.

assistants, it is unlikely that the high-flyer Eutyches was an *apparitor* of a middling social level (these civic *apparitores* and their relatively low rate of pay are mentioned in the Caesarian template for colonial constitutions, the *lex Ursonennsis* §62).³ By publicly honoring Tuscus as *his own* patron (τὸν ἴδιον πάτρωνα, l. 12), Eutyches augments—in the Ephesian context— his own status and ancestral connections with reference to the greater privilege and well-born pedigree of the former.

A further glimpse into what it meant to be well-born comes from three other Ephesian inscriptions that apply the epithet εὐγενής to local elites or semielites. IEph 1a.27 (104 CE) preserves the famous foundation of C. Vibius Salutaris who is "of most noble status" ([εὐγενέσ]τατος, l. 374; see Rogers 1991, esp. 16–19). In context, this is public testimony from the Ephesian magistrate Tib. Cl. Antipater Iulianus who names Salutaris his "most dear friend" ([ὁ] φίλτα[τος ἡμεῖν]) and praises him as of "being of the best character" (ἐκ τοῦ ἀξιώμ[ατος αὐτο]ῦ ὑπάρχ[ων]). Iulianus lays it on thick so that the Ephesians might recognize and appropriately honor Salutaris who, according to Rogers (1991, 18), exhibited "a strong desire for self-advertisement." The image of the late first-/early second-century figure of Salutaris—that of a wealthy Ephesian hungry for recognition—is a particularly instructive reminder: provincial nobility craved recognition. Another Ephesian, M. Pompeius Demeas Caecilianus (IEph 3.708 [date?]) is honored on a statue base as "a man of our forefathers, well-born and well-disposed concerning the fatherland" (ll. 6–7). The evidence of Caeclianus's nobility (possibly "mid-tier of the local elite") comes in the civic *cursus* that follows, a list of roles and benefits (ll. 7–9) he has worked for the city: he was sacred herald of Artemis, *irenarch*, *agoranomos*, and *grammateus* of the demos (Rogers 2012, 130–31). A final example of a well-born citizen is Pia Paula Aratiane (IEph 3.894, [third century CE?]), a priestess of Artemis honored by her husband (see Rogers, "Some Priestesses of Artemis of Ephesos," in *NewDocs* 11B). Across these figures, we see that at Ephesus the quality of εὐγένεια, combining nobility of birth and status, involved—for both men and women—significant wealth as well as family and patronal connections. Unsurprisingly, to be well-born was to be obligated to and associated with public service in a variety of civic roles,

---

3. On Eutyches as a *scriba librarius* and implications for social status and date, see Purcell 1983, 159.

liturgies, and sometimes cultic service; the well-born gave gifts that advertised and confirmed their nobility.

The picture of local wealth, privilege, civic, and cultic involvement that emerges here in the Ephesian inscriptions—and which is echoed particularly in the Peloponnese—provides further grist for debates concerning the social status and composition of the early Christian *ekklēsiai*. This is perhaps especially the case for Corinth, where Paul's rhetorical thrust in the phrase "not many of you were εὐγενεῖς" (1 Cor 1:26) must certainly imply *both* that at least a very few of those in the nascent assembly were in fact of notable wealth, lineage, and status in the provincial community *and* that the overwhelming majority were not, despite the social pretensions of many (Welborn 2016, 65–66; Nasrallah 2019, 111–13; Judge 1960, 59).

Bibliography

Arzt-Grabner, Peter, Michael Ernst, Ruth Elisabeth Kritzer, Amphilochios Papathomas, Franz Winter, Günther Schwab, and Andreas Bammer. 2006. *1 Korinther*. Papyrologische Kommentare zum neuen Testament 2. Göttingen: Vandenhoeck & Ruprecht.

Briquel, Dominique. 2014. "Gli aruspici nell'*Imperium romanum*: Nuove prospettive per l'etrusca disciplina." Pages 129–49 in *Sacerdos: Figure del sacro nella società romana; Atti del convegno internatzionale Cividale del Friuli, 26–28 settembre 2012*. Edited by Gianpaulo Urso. Pisa: Fondazione Niccolà Canussio.

Chausson, François. 2000. "De Didius Iulianus aux Numii Albini." *Mélanges de l'École française de Rome: Antiquité* 112:843–79.

Drew-Bear, Thomas. 1972. "Some Greek Words, Part II." *Glotta* 50:182–228.

Eck, Werner. 1999. "*Ordo equitum romanorum, ordo libertorum*. Freigelassene und ihre Nachkommen im römischen Ritterstand." Pages 5–29 in *L'ordre équestre: Histoire d'une aristocratie (IIe siècle av. J.-C.–IIIe siècle ap. J.-C.); Actes du colloque international de Bruxelles-Leuven, 5–7 octobre 1995*. Publications de l'École française de Rome 257. Rome: École Française de Rome.

Haack, Marie-Laurence. 2017. "Prophecy and Divination." Pages 357–67 in vol. 1 of *Etruscology*. Edited by Alessandro Nasso. Berlin: De Gruyter.

Judge, E. A. 1960. *The Social Pattern of Christian Groups in the First Century*. London: Tyndale Press.

Nasrallah, Laura Salah. 2019. *Archaeology and the Letters of Paul.* Oxford: Oxford University Press.
Purcell, Nicholas. 1983. "The *Apparitores*: A Study in Social Mobility." *Papers of the British School at Rome* 51:125–73.
Rogers, Guy MacLean. 1991. *The Sacred Identity of Ephesos: Foundation Myths of a Roman City.* London: Routledge.
———. 2012. *The Mysteries of Artemis of Ephesos: Cult, Polis, and Change in the Graeco-Roman World. Synkrisis.* New Haven: Yale University Press.
Salomies, Olli. 2007. "*Asinnii, Licinnii,* etc. in the East." *Arctos* 41:59–74.
Scheid, John, Granino Cecere, and Maria Grazia. 1999. "Les sacerdoces publics équestres." Pages 79–189 in *L'ordre équestre: Histoire d'une aristocratie (IIe siècle av. J.-C.–IIIe siècle ap. J.-C.); Actes du colloque international de Bruxelles-Leuven, 5–7 octobre 1995.* Publications de l'École française de Rome 257. Rome: École Française de Rome.
Welborn, L. L. 2016. "Inequality in Roman Corinth: Evidence from Diverse Sources Evaluated by a Neo-Ricardian Model." Pages 47–84 in *Roman Corinth.* Vol. 2 of *The First Urban Churches.* Edited by James R. Harrison and L. L. Welborn. Atlanta: SBL Press.
Wilhelm, Adolf. 1928. "Lateinische Wörter in griechischen Inschriften." *Wiener Studien* 46:227–33.
Wood, John Turtle. 1877. *Discoveries at Ephesus.* London: Longmans, Green.

10. An Incomparable Secretary: Acts 19:35 in Perspective

James R. Harrison

IEph 3.672

JÖAI 15:164–65; *AE* 1913.170. Base built into the wall at the Octagon. Date: 166 CE.

Τ(ίτον) Φλάουιον Δαμιανόν,	To Titus Flavius Damianus
γραμματεύσαντα ἐ[πι-]	who was secretary in an
φανῶς καὶ μετρήσαν[τα]	outstanding manner and paid for
4 μυριάδας μεδίμνων [εἴ-]	twenty myriads of medimni
κοσι καὶ χειλίους δια[κοσί-]	and one thousand two hundred medimni
ους μησὶν δεκατρισὶν [ὅ]-	during thirteen entire months
λοις καὶ ὑποδεξάμενο[ν ἐν]	and received in
8 τούτοις στρατόπεδα τὰ ἀπὸ τ[ῆς]	these (months) the army which returned from
κατὰ Πάρθων νείκης ὑποστ[ρέ-]	the victory over the Parthians
φοντα καὶ πανηγυριαρχήσ[αν-]	and was panegyriarch
τα κατὰ τὸ αὐτὸ τῶν μεγάλω[ν Ἐ-]	at the same time of the Great
12 φεσήων ἐκτενῶς καὶ ἔργον ὑπο-	Ephesia with conspicuous success and promised
σχόμενον ἐν τῷ αὐτῷ ἐνιαυτῷ οἶ-	in the same year (to pay for)
κον ἐν τῷ Οὐαρίῳ βαλανείῳ μ[ε-]	a room in the Varius Bath,
τὰ οἰκοδομῆς καὶ παντὸς κόσ-	both its construction and every
16 μου καὶ μυριάδας ποιήσαντα	embellishment and made a surplus
περισσὰς ἐκ τῶν προσόδων τῆς	from the revenue of
ἰδίας γραμματείας τῇ πόλει	his own secretaryship in the city
δεκαδύο καὶ ἑπτακισχείλια ὀ-	of twelve myriads and seven thousand
20 κτακόσια δεκαέξ.	eight hundred and sixteen (denarii).
ἀναστησάντων τὴν τειμὴν	Erected
παρ' αὐτῶν τῶν ἐν τῇ ἀγορᾷ	by those in the agora

ἀνδρὸς τοῦ κατὰ πάντα for the honor of a man in all
24 ἀσυνκρίτου things incomparable.

1. A Profile of the γραμματεύς: Situating Acts 19:35

In Greek city-states, the officers who wrote the laws, decrees, and other documents are variously designated in the inscriptions with formulaic language, normally beginning with the noun ὁ γραμματεύς ("secretary," "scribe") and accompanied by a descriptive or clarifying phrase. At Athens, for example, there were alternative designations for γραμματεύς such as ἀναγραφεύς ("recorder"), ἀντιγραφεύς ("checking-clerk," "copying-clerk"), συγγραμματεύς ("cogrammateus"), συγγραφεύς ("commissioner"), as well as the mention of subordinate officers ὑπογραμματεύς ("under-secretary"). But, in terms of the clarifying phrases added to ὁ γραμματεύς there is (1) ὁ γραμματεὺς τῆς βουλῆς ("secretary of the boule"), (2) ὁ γραμματεὺς κατὰ πρυτανείαν ("secretary of the prytaneian"), (3) ὁ γραμματεὺς περὶ τὸ βῆμα ("secretary in attendance" or "at the platform"), (4) ὁ γραμματεὺς τῆς βουλῆς καὶ τοῦ δήμου ("secretary of the boule and the demos"), (5) ὁ γραμματεὺς τῶν εἰσαγωγῶν ("secretary of the eisagogeis), (6) ὁ γραμματεὺς τῶν πρυτάνεων ("secretary of the prytaneis"), (7) ὁ γραμματεὺς ἐπὶ τὸ ἀππόρητον ("secretary for that which cannot be mentioned"), and (8) ὁ γραμματεὺς ἐπὶ τοὺς νόμους ("secretary for the laws"). For full epigraphic discussion of the Athenian secretarial offices, see Abbott 2012, 34–103. More generally on the grammateis, see Wilamowitz-Möllendorff 1879; Goodman 2006; Hartmann 2020. For scribal involvement in the production of Paul's letters, see Richards 1991; 2004; Blumell 2006. For a major discussion of the γραμματεύς at Ephesus, see Schulte 1994, unavailable to me. See the review of the Schulte's book by Guy MacLean Rogers (1997). Additionally, see Knibbe and Merkelbach 1979; Bailey 2006, 139–49.

What is remarkable is the range of secretarial activity at Athens, embracing a wide spread of the civic institutions and citizenry in Athenian life: specifically, the boule, demos, prytaneis, eisagogeis, secretaries of the treasury, secretaries of the archons, and secretaries of other polis-level bodies (e.g., clerk of the court, etc.). By contrast, in the case of Ephesus, there is comparatively a limited range of secretarial offices. There is mention in the Ephesian inscriptions of the following secretarial officials:

10. An Incomparable Secretary: Acts 19:35 in Perspective

1. ὁ γραμματεὺς τῆς βουλῆς ("secretary of the *boule*"): IEph 5.1380; 5.1506; 7.1.3131.
2. ὁ γραμματεὺς τοῦ δήμου ("secretary of the *demos*"): IEph 1a.24B; 1a.27A + add. p. 2; 1a.27E; 1a.27F; 2.211; 2.435 + add. p. 11; 2.446; 2.449; 3.614C; 3.619A; 3.619B; 3.674A; 3.874; 4.1024; 4.1061; 5.1380A; 5.1387; 5.1396; 5.1750; 6.2018; 6.2479; 7.1.3088; 7.1.3091; 7.1.3131; 7.2.4343; *JÖAI* 53:135, no. 144; *JÖAI* 55:129, no. 4293; *ZPE* 67:151–52.
3. ὁ γραμματεὺς τῇ πόλει ("secretary in the *polis*"): IEph 3.672; 7.1.308. This description is clearly locative, not indicating the precise civic institution (*boule, demos, gerousia*) to which the γραμματεύς is attached.
4. ὁ γραμματεὺς γερουσίας ("secretary of the *gerousia*"): IEph 1a.26; 1a.27B.231–34; 2.442; and, possibly, 3.972.1–28: a list of names found at the end of Arcadiane Street, of whom two are *grammateis*, but the list is questionably referring to members of the *gerousia*.[1]

Apart from ἀντιγραφεύς (IEph 3.971A; 5.1687 + add. p. 27), there are no alternative designations for the γραμματεύς at Ephesus, as there were at Athens. What is revealed epigraphically regarding the public life of Ephesus is a bicameral system, which consisted of two legislative chambers. There is (1) the council or the *boule*, comprising three hundred *bouletae* ("council members") who met in the *bouleuterion* ("council chamber," or the so-called Odeon, i.e., "concert hall"/small theater),[2] and (2) the people's assembly, whose meetings were conducted in the great theater (cf. Acts 19:29). As noted from the Ephesian epigraphic terminology above, each legislative chamber had its own secretary (ὁ γραμματεὺς τῆς βουλῆς, ὁ γραμματεὺς τοῦ δήμου). In the estimation of Dieter Knibbe and Bülent Iplikçioglu (1984, 22), ὁ γραμματεὺς τοῦ δήμου "was evidently the head of the city government." Regarding the Ephesian civic magistracies and the obligations for the community generally, see Knibbe and Iplikçioglu 1984, 22–23. On the *bouleuterion* (Odeon), see Scherrer 2000, 80–84. On the great theater, see Scherrer 2000, 158–61; Wiplinger and Wlach 1996, 26–28, 163–65.

---

1. Bailey (2006, 322) writes: "Of the seven named individuals, only two are identified as *grammateis*, let alone the *grammateis* of the *gerousia*."

2. Scherrer (2000, 82) posits that the *bouleuterion* functioned as both a "council chamber" and "concert hall"/small theater (Odeon).

New Testament scholars and modern English translations, in discussing the unnamed Ephesian γραμματεύς in Acts 19:35 (presumably, the γραμματεὺς τοῦ δήμου), refer to the office as "town clerk/city clerk" (ESV; JB; NASB; NIV; NRSV; RSV). The office at Ephesus, it is argued, embraced a range of duties of a more prestigious order than routine scribal activities: it was not just confined to the recording of laws and their public reading. Rather the officials presided over popular assemblies, intervening in irregular or illegal assemblies (e.g., Acts 19:35–41) and functioning effectively as magistrates of cities in Asia Minor, though, it is argued, with considerably greater status accorded at Ephesus. The prestigious rank and esteemed status of the office is indicated by the fact that on several Ephesian coins the names of Ephesian *grammateus* are rendered. To cite two examples, see *RPC* 1.2601, whose reverse has the following legend: ΓΡΑΜΜΑΤΕΥΣ ΑΡΙΣΤΙΩΝ, "grammateus Aristion." Additionally, see the reverse in Franke and Nollé 1997, 317, type 1: ΕΠΙ ΠΑΙΤΟΥ ΓΡΑΜΜΑΤΕΟΣ ΗΟΜΟΝΟΙΑ, ΚΥΖΙΚΟΣ, "Concord in the secretary(ship) of Paitos, Cyzicus."

We turn now to a brief coverage of the history of scholarship on Acts 19:35 from the 1960s onward regarding the role of the γραμματεύς at Ephesus. Colin J. Hemer (1989, 122) argues that the secretary was "the chief executive magistrate in Ephesus." In the view of A. N. Sherwin-White (1963, 86), the Ephesian official appears in conjunction with the *strategoi* ("generals") as the "senior partner," supplanting them in civic importance. The γραμματεύς, Ben Witherington III posits (1998, 597), "was charged with keeping records, being present when money was deposited in the temple, serving as a registrar ... (see Apollonius of Tyana, *Letters* 32)." Craig S. Keener (2014, 2927–28) argues that the Ephesian official belonged to the "same social stratum" as Paul's patrons, the *asiarchs* (Acts 19:31), liaising between "Ephesus's local government and the Roman proconsul, headquartered in the same city" (similarly, Bock 2007, 612). The ubiquitous references in the Ephesian inscriptions to the γραμματεύς being a *philosebastos* (IEph 3.614C, 5.1380, 6.2018) and *philokaisar* (IEph 2.446, 449) gives credence to Keener's observation. Eckhard J. Schnabel (2012, 309) writes that the γραμματεύς "supervises municipal building projects, coordinates the erection of statues, and facilitates consecrations to the emperor." Last, Paul Trebilco (1994, 351 nn. 262–63) points to the role of the γραμματεύς in money distributions in the Salutaris inscription (IEph 1a.27.222–223, 297–300, 488–492), also noting that in two instances the year is dated by the clerk's year in office (IEph1a.21.10–12; 1a.27.418).

10. An Incomparable Secretary: Acts 19:35 in Perspective

Especially helpful in charting the rise in social importance of the γραμματεύς from the first century CE onward is the valuable discussion of Dmitriev 2000, 412–14 (subsequently published as Dmitriev 2005). Among the many riches of Dmitriev's discussion, the following points are especially noteworthy, to some of which I have added my own observations.

- By the late first century CE, legislative proposals were prepared by the γραμματεύς of the *demos* and the city's five *strategoi* (IEph 1a.27A.5–8; 2.449; 3.614C; 4.1387.6–14), with the secretary writing down the decisions of the assembly (IEph 1a.27.5–8; 2.280; 2.300A; 2.449; 3.695.20–25; 3.793.8–12; 5.1489.17; 5.1499.9–13; 5.1500) and giving them their final form (IEph 1a.211.6–16; 4.1387.6–14; 6.2018).
- In convening the assembly, the γραμματεύς could initiate his own proposals and dismiss others (IEph 4.1383.1).
- An individual γραμματεύς held cojointly the high priesthood of Tiberius Caesar and the secretaryship (SEG 37.883.4; 39.1176H.5), with other secretaries also holding the prestigious position of *agonothetês* (IEph 2.261 [of the Augustan games]; cf. Harrison 2016) and, from the second century CE onward, the *asiarchia* (IEph 2.435; 3.801; 4.1066; 7.1.3055, 7.1.3058; 7.2.4343). Not mentioned by Dmitriev, but certainly worth highlighting, is the fact that there are cases of a γραμματεύς also holding the significant civic position of gymnasiarch (IEph 2.442; JÖAI 55:129, no. 4293: "secretary of the people and often gymnasiarch of his native land"). Furthermore, another γραμματεύς in 188/189 CE is described as "high priest of the temples in Ephesus" (IEph 3.619A, 3.619B).
- Late second-century CE honorifics such as "the first secretary of the people" (IEph 3.845; 7.1.3055, 7.1.3058, 7.1.3071) and "the only secretary of the people" (7.1.3002) indicate the intense competition among the Ephesian elites to acquire this office. We might expand upon Dmitriev's observations by noting that some *grammateis* also highlight in conventional rhetorical manner that they are holding the secretarial post for the second time (IEph 1a.27E.48; 1a.27F.435; 3.748.7).
- Overlooked by Dmitriev is the (limited) administrative role undertaken by the γραμματεύς in the economic management of some

of the city's institutions. In Salutaris's bequest, we hear about the annual donation of money to the *gerousia* (IEph 1a.27B.231–34): "In the same way he (i.e., Salutaris) will give to the γραμματεύς of the assembly of the *gerousia* each year from the aforementioned interest three hundred and eighty-two denarii and nine asses." Whether these financial responsibilities of the γραμματεύς were merely ad hoc or permanent in the civic life of the *gerousia* is difficult to determine (Bailey 2006, 147–48). Moreover, is the γραμματεύς merely the distributor of the funds available from Salutaris's lottery for the *gerousia*? Or is there some type of oversight and accountability allocated here to the γραμματεύς regarding how the bequest's interest was to be spent by the more than 390 *gerousia* members? We do not know. As Rogers (1991, 62) correctly observes, "Salutaris did not specify either in the main foundation or the addendum exactly how the members were to spend their one-denarius allotments." But even if Salutaris provided no instructions regarding the spending of the bequest's interest, the *gerousia* may have decided to implement its own set of procedures regarding the handling of the bequest money by its members.

- The multiple honors accruing to these secretaries by virtue of their lineage and personal achievement is well conveyed by the inscription of an anonymous Ephesian honored by a village from the Kaystros River valley (Ricl 2020, §47: second–third century CE): "[… descendant of …]chs and of a secretary of the people and of priestesses of our mistress Artemis, elected first general, her own panegyriarch and logistes for life, on account of his goodwill and zeal for the katoikia."[3] On the interesting question whether there was a *cursus honorum* ("course of honors") at Ephesus, see Kirbihler 2012.

In assessing the role of the γραμματεύς in mid-50s Ephesus, therefore, we should realize that the office attracted candidates of considerable power, status, and wealth well into the late second century CE. The Ephesian elites cooperated with the Roman rulers and the provincial proconsul resident

---

3. Note the multiple honors of Pop(lius) Vedius Antoninus (IEph 3.728): "*prytanis* and gymnasiarch and twice secretary of the people and asiarch and panegyriarch of the great Ephesia and Pasithia, who went as an ambassador both to the senate and the emperors." See Harrison, "Ambassador in Chains," in this volume.

in the city, seeking not only to acquire benefits for the city but also to procure prestige for themselves and their house. The office of γραμματεύς at Ephesus was a pivotal honorific prize in this regard. Our mid-second-century CE inscription, IEph 3.672, translated above, depicts a γραμματεύς of substantial social status and wealth, undoubtedly a person of greater civic eminence than the unnamed individual whom Paul encountered in Acts 19:35. Nevertheless, we should remember that by the early Julio-Claudian period other *grammateis* had held cojointly imperial priesthoods and fulfilled the important roles of *agonothetēs* and gymnasiarch in the city. The lame English translation of "town clerk/city clerk" in Acts 19:35, therefore, fails to capture the social significance and substantial prestige of the γραμματεύς in Julio-Claudian Ephesus, a prestige which continued to grow well into the late second century CE.

What, then, emerges from a study of IEph 3.672 in regard to Acts 19:35, despite the fact that our inscription was erected later in the latter half of the second century CE? First, we gain additional insight into the civic role of the γραμματεύς, who was in this instance the famous Ephesian sophist Titus Flavius Damianus. The secretary is capable, as is the case with wealthy individuals like Damianus, to act as a benefactor to the city in times of crisis and prosperity. We know from literary sources that Damianus financed public and private buildings, including a dining hall and *stoai* spanning the length of one *stadion* (Philostratus, *Vit. soph.* 2.23). In our inscription, Damianus is eulogized for his provision of grain for thirteen months (ll. 4–6) during the Antonine plague in ca. 165–168 CE. This pandemic was caught and spread by returning soldiers from the Near East, causing massive disruption to beneficence, military, and civic networks.

Second, as a benefactor, Damianus housed the Roman troops at Ephesus returning from the Parthian wars in 166 CE (ll. 8–9). Undoubtedly the sojourning Roman soldiers at Ephesus would have benefited greatly from Damianus's largesse, through which Damianus strategically endeared himself to the Roman authorities (Rietveld 1998, 734).

Third, an additional benefaction of a beautifully ornamented room (hall?) in the baths of Varius is eulogized (Rietveld 1998, 734–35). On the baths of Varius, see Scherrer 2000, 120.

Fourth, as a financial manager, Damianus produced a surplus of 7,816 denarii for the city during his secretaryship (ll. 16–20). Clearly a financial role for the γραμματεύς in second century CE Ephesus is envisaged here. Whether these types of responsibilities extended back to the first century CE is a moot point.

Fifth, Damianus organized as a *panegyriarch* one of the great events of the Ephesian calendar: namely, the Great Ephesia festival (ll. 10–12; cf. Arnold 1972).

Additional insight into Damianus's strategic self-understanding as an Ephesian benefactor is evidenced in the Latin and Greek honorific inscription which he set up to Junius Maximus (IEph 3.811). The Latin inscription eulogizes this Roman senator and military tribune for his victory over the Parthian enemies in the East. Important for our purposes is the very brief Greek addendum to the Latin inscription, which says: "Having restored the honor from his own resources, Titus Flavius Damianus, secretary of the demos and archon of the feasts of the mighty Ephesians" (IEph 3.811.20–27 = IAsia Mixed §128). The significance of the addendum, which splits the text into two languages, is that there exists "a Latin portion to honor respectfully the Roman military officer, and a Greek portion to exhibit proudly his (i.e. Damianus') good deed to his fellow citizens" (Gatzke 2013, 204). There is another important Ephesian inscription celebrating the career of Damianus (IEph 7.1.3082), but the significance of Damianus's role as a γραμματεύς and benefactor has been sufficiently established in our exposition of IEph 3.672 above. The family fame of Damianus's house would continue. Damianus, having married into the prestigious Vedii family of Ephesus (IAsia Mixed §103), saw his descendants reach the consulate (Philostratus, *Vit. soph.* 2.23; IEph 7.1.3082–3084; *AE* 2011.1319). In sum, the prestige attached to the office of γραμματεύς in the second century CE stretched back to the Julio-Claudian period in the first century CE. Translators of Acts 19:35 should reconsider how they might render more appropriately the misleading English translation of γραμματεύς as "town clerk/city clerk."[4]

Finally, we turn to the description of Damianus as "a man in all things incomparable [ἀσυνκρίτου]."[5] How does this arresting phrase intersect with the New Testament documents?

---

4. Note the helpful comment of Murphy-O'Connor (2008, 34): "'Secretary' in these contexts carries the connotation of the modern Secretary of State; this person was a senior official with real administrative power."

5. Whether in actuality Damianus was correctly called "incomparable" is contestable: some of his benefactions (e.g., building the hall in the baths of Varius and his role as *panegyriarch* in the Great Ephesia) are typical of Ephesian benefactors and magistrates of his day. But his very impressive provision of grain and his hosting of the Roman army for thirteen months during a pandemic represents benefaction of

2. The Incomparable Damianus and the Foolishness of Comparison (2 Cor 10:12)

The Greek word ἀσύνκριτος does not appear in the New Testament documents other than as the name Asyncritus (Rom 16:14). The omission is significant given the prominence of the word in the honorific inscriptions. ἀσύνκριτος appears in the epigraphy of Asia Minor, to cite but one eastern Mediterranean region alone, occurring four times at Ephesus (IEph 3.672, 678, 828; 7.1.3080) and twenty-five times elsewhere in the province. Here is a semantic domain that the New Testament writers studiously avoided.

But a cognate of the word appears in 2 Cor 10:12 (see also 1 Cor 2:13: συγκρίνοντες). There the apostle Paul rejects as incomprehensible (οὐ συνιᾶσιν) the self-classification and self-comparison (συγκρῖναι ἑαυτούς; συκρίνοντες ἑαυτοῖς) that was occurring among the self-commending apostolic rivals at Corinth (2 Cor 10:12). From this revealing comment of Paul, it is evident that the interloping rivals were striving to establish their own superior credentials and criteria of apostolicity over against himself as the apostolic founder of the Corinthian church, while also attempting to achieve their own internal pecking order of apostolic importance and precedence. Paul was well aware of the spiritual and social pitfalls of self-commendation, having engaged in heated competition and mutual comparison with his chief Pharisaic rivals before his conversion (Gal 1:14; Phil 3:4b; cf. Josephus, *Vita* 1–9, 80–83, 187–188). In that period Paul might have been conceivably designated ἀσύνκριτος in a Jewish context (or in his own estimation) because of his perfection in nomistic righteousness (Phil 3:6) and advancement in Judaism beyond many of his contemporaries (Gal 1:14a).

The issue was brought to a searing conclusion when the apostle radically disavowed any inflated boasting and meritorious self-comparison due to the humility now demanded by God's justifying grace in Christ and from his own experience of God's soteriological power in weakness (Phil 3:7–11; 2 Cor 11:14–12:10). Moreover, in dismantling the culture of self-comparison and self-commendation at Roman Corinth, Paul deliberately spoofs the grand-boasting style of the ancient orators and honorific epigraphy in order to shame his boastful opponents, employing the well-known

---

the highest order. One has to allow for a certain amount of terminological slippage in epigraphic rhetoric.

mnemonics of the honorific genre (i.e., catalogs, numbers, elements of *cursus honorum* progression), while highlighting his own abject failure to achieve perceived status in the eyes of his critics by boasting in carefully chosen vignettes of his social humiliation and personal weakness.

This radical disemboweling of the Greco-Roman boasting system—the latter exemplified by the epithet ἀσύνκριτος in IEph 3.672—is reinforced by the apostle's strategic turning against himself several well-known tropes from the Greco-Roman world, which he ironically claims for himself in his self-presentation: namely, various character roles of the mime shows, including above all the fool; an allusion to the award of the *corona muralis*; the motif of the cowardly benefactor; a catalog of boasts from a *cursus pudorum* ("course of shame") as opposed to a *cursus honorum* ("course of honors"). The use of these tropes further illustrates the apostle's perceived foolishness, weakness, and humiliation in his opponents' eyes, playing fatally into the hands of his critics. For discussion, see Harrison 2003, 335–40; 2004, 46–55; 2018; Hellerman 2005; Judge 2008, 706–708; Welborn 1999; 2005. But in reality these tropes reveal Paul's cruciform understanding of Christian existence, reflecting the soteriological narrative of Christ's own career, which transitioned from the social shame and divine forsakenness of the cross to his glorious divine vindication through the resurrection and ascension. See Harrison, "Dishonoring the Honored: The Problem of Recycling Public Monuments," in this volume.

Finally, while Paul's perspective is driven by the soteriological and eschatological fulfilment of history in Christ, we must not overlook a fundamental datum that Paul inherited from the Old Testament. The incomparability of God is heavily emphasized in a series of penetrating questions regarding to whom God might be likened (Exod 5:11; 2 Chr 2:6; Pss 35:10; 77:13; 89:8; 113:5–6; Isa 40:18; 44:7; 46:5; Jer 49:19; Mic 7:18; cf. Exod 9:14; Deut 32:39; 1 Sam 2:1–10; 2 Sam 22:32; Isa 40:9–31; Ps 86:8). For discussion, see Labuschagne 1966; Human 2004; Lugt 2016.

The question is answered in several fundamental ways.[6] First, God's status as the Creator of the universe eliminates any competition from the lifeless idols: the latter are merely scarecrows in a melon patch (Jer 10:1–5), unable to save (Isa 46:7; cf. 45:20), and were to be carried as burdens on weary beasts (46:1, 7). Second, the lordship of Israel's God over history

---

6. Additionally, six divine self-predications in Deutero-Isaiah ("I am Yahweh"; I am Yahweh your God"; "I am the first and I am the last"; "I am He"; "I am God"; "I am your God") answer the question regarding God's likeness. See Phillips 1971.

distinguishes him all the lifeless idols: God knows not only the past but also what is to come thereafter (Isa 41:22–23; 44:24–45:8). See Wilson 2016. As Labuschagne (1966, 114) writes,

> For Deutero-Isaiah this quality of Yahweh affords clear proof that He is utterly distinct from the gods and that He is the only true God (cf. also 44:6 and 41:23). Yahweh's ability to declare the future, which Deutero-Isaiah associates with His incomparability (cf. also Jer. 10:7), is consequent upon the fact that He has revealed Himself as the all-wise Controller of history. Yahweh not only regulates human history, but also determines what is yet to be. Here we meet the idea of Yahweh's intervention in history carried to its ultimate conclusions, the most outstanding attribute of the incomparable God spanning past, present and future.

Third, the incomparability of God becomes a springboard for the inauguration of a radical social reversal. In Ps 84, the enthroned and incomparable God of Israel, Lord of all the nations (vv. 4–6), exalts the poor and the widow, seating them with princes and placing them in happy homes (vv. 7–9). Does Paul's strong emphasis on his apostolic weakness, shame, and failure in the eyes of some find its paradoxical justification in light of God's ultimate vindication of the downtrodden, as depicted in the Psalms?

To what extent, then, is the Old Testament doctrine of divine incomparability a fundamental datum in Paul's thought, and how does it relate to the self-comparison animating the Greco-Roman boasting system? In addition to the citation of Old Testament incomparability traditions (Rom 11:33–35 [cf. Isa 40:13; Job 41:11]; cf. Eph 3:20–21), the apostle points to the invisible qualities of the God's eternal power and divine nature indelibly imprinted upon creation (Rom 1:20; cf. 1:25b: "who is forever praised"). Therefore, to worship human-made images (Rom 1:23, 25) is an expression of thinking characterized by foolishness (1:21b–22), a depraved mind seduced by sexual immorality (1:28b; cf. 1:24, 26–27), and the exchange of the truth about God for a lie (1:25a). Here Paul reflects the teaching of Deutero-Isaiah that idolatry is occasioned and countenanced by "a twisted, deceived, uncomprehending mind (Isa 44:18–20; 45:1–7)" (House 1998, 232). At the very core of the human problem, therefore, is the tendency toward self-idolatry: "They exchanged the truth about God for a lie and worshiped and served created things rather than the creator" (Rom 1:25). On the idolatry of the self (Ezek 28; cf. Gen 3), see Beale 2008, 135–40.

Amid a plethora of human vices, boastfulness remains a fundamental preoccupation of the human heart (Rom 1:30), with the result that it becomes culturally the driving force behind the self-advertisement undergirding the Greco-Roman quest for ancestral and personal glory. Undoubtedly, the Old Testament provided the backdrop for Paul's portrait of the debilitating effects of idolatry, especially regarding its prominent social expression of boasting in the self, blurring thereby the distinction between the incomparable God and dependent human beings. But ultimately Paul's searing critique of Greco-Roman and Jewish boasting, including the apostle's strategic reconfiguration of its focus to the praise of Christ and the Father, was founded upon the divine transformation wrought by his experience of Christ's justifying grace at Damascus. See Harrison 2003; 2018. In conclusion, the Old Testament datum that Paul inherited as a Jew regarding the incomparability of God only goes so far in explaining the radical nature of his critique of the opponent's self-commendation and self-comparison at Roman Corinth.

Bibliography

Abbott, Terry J. 2012. "The Ancient Greek Secretary: A Study of Secretaries in Athens and the Peloponnese." PhD diss., University of Manchester.
Arnold, Jane Ringwood. 1972. "Festivals of Ephesus." *AJA* 76:17–22.
Bailey, Colin. 2006. "The *Gerousia* of Ephesus." PhD diss., University of British Columbia, Vancouver.
Beale, G. K. 2008. *We Become What We Worship: A Biblical Theology of Idolatry.* Downers Grove, IL: IVP Academic; Nottingham: Apollos.
Blumell, Lincoln H. 2006. "Scribes and Ancient Letters: Implications for the Pauline Epistles." Pages 208–26 in *How the New Testament Came to Be: The Thirty-Fifth Annual Sidney B. Sperry Symposium*. Edited by Kent B. Jackson and Frank F. Judd Jr. Provo. UT: Religious Studies Center, Brigham Young University; Salt Lake City; Deseret Book.
Bock, Darrell L. 2007. *Acts*. BECNT. Grand Rapids: Baker Academic.
Dmitriev, Sviatoslav. 2000. "Local Administration in the Province of Asia: The Problem of Roman Influence." PhD diss., Harvard University.
———. 2005. *City Government in Hellenistic and Roman Asia Minor*. Oxford: Oxford University Press.
Franke, Peter Robert, and Margret Karola Nollé. 1997. *Katalog*. Vol. 1 of *Die Homonoia-Münzen Kleinasiens und der thrakischen Randgebiete*.

Saarbrücker Studien zur Archäologie und Alten Geschichte 10. Saarbrücken: Saarbrücker Druckerei und Verlag.

Gatzke, Andrea F. 2013. "Language and Identity in Roman Anatolia: A Study in the Use and Role of Latin in Asia Minor." PhD diss., Pennsylvania State University.

Goodman, Martin. 2006. "Texts, Scribes and Power in Roman Judaea." Pages 79–90 in *Judaism in the Roman World: Collected Essays*. AJEC 66. Leiden: Brill.

Harrison, James R. 2003. *Paul's Language of Grace in Its Graeco-Roman Context*. WUNT 2/172. Tübingen: Mohr Siebeck.

———. 2004. "In Quest of the Third Heaven: Paul and His Apocalyptic Imitators." *VC* 58:24–55.

———. 2016. "Paul and the *agōnothetai* at Corinth: Engaging the Civic Values of Antiquity." Pages 271–326 in *Roman Corinth*. Vol. 2 of *The First Urban Churches*. Edited by James R. Harrison and L. L. Welborn. WGRWSup 8. Atlanta: SBL Press.

———. 2018. "From Rome to the Colony of Philippi: Roman Boasting in Philippians 3:4–6 in Its Latin West and Philippian Epigraphic Context." Pages 307–70 in *Roman Philippi*. Vol. 4 of *The First Urban Churches*. Edited by James R. Harrison and L. L. Welborn. WGRWSup 13. Atlanta: SBL Press.

Hartmann, Benjamin. 2020. *The Scribes of Rome: A Cultural and Social History of the* Scribae. Cambridge: Cambridge University Press.

Hellerman, Joseph H. 2005. *Reconstructing Honor in Roman Philippi: Carmen Christi as Cursus Pudorum*. SNTSMS 132. Cambridge: Cambridge University Press.

Hemer, Colin J. 1989. *The Book of Acts in the Setting of Hellenistic History*. WUNT 49. Tübingen: Mohr Siebeck.

House, Paul R. 1998. *Old Testament Theology*. Downers Grove: Intervarsity Press.

Human, Dirk. 2004. "Yahweh, the Israelite High God Bends Down to Uplift the Downtrodden: Perspectives on the Incomparability of Yahweh in Psalm 113." *JNSL* 30:41–64.

Judge, E. A. 2008. "The Conflict of Educational Aims in the New Testament." Pages 693–708 in *The First Christians in the Roman World: Augustan and New Testament Essays*. Edited by James R. Harrison. WUNT 229. Tübingen: Mohr Siebeck.

Keener, Craig S. 2014. *15:1–23:35*. Vol. 3 of *Acts: An Exegetical Commentary*. Grand Rapids: Baker Academic.

Kirbihler, François. 2012. "Un cursus honorum à Ephèse? Quelques réflexions sur la succession des magistratures de la cité à l'époque romaine." Pages 67–107 in *Folia Graeca in honorem Edouard Will: Historica*. Edited by P. Goukowsky and C. Feyel. Vol. 2. Études anciennes 51. Nancy: A.D.R.A.

Knibbe, Dieter, and Bülent Iplikcioglu. 1984. *Ephesos in Spiegel seiner Inschriften*. Vienna: Schindler.

Knibbe, Dieter, and R. Merkelbach. 1979. "Der ephesische γραμματεὺς τοῦ δήμου." *ZPE* 33:124–25.

Labuschagne, C. J. 1966. *The Incomparability of Yahweh in the Old Testament*. Leiden: Brill.

Lugt, Pieter van der. 2016. "The Dynamics of the Incomparable God: Highlighted by the Immobility of an Idol; The Rhetorical Integrity of Isa. 40:12–26, 41:1–7 and 46:1–13." Pages 159–79 in *The Present State of Old Testament Studies in the Low Countries*. Edited by Klaas Spronk. OTS 69. Leiden: Brill.

Murphy-O'Connor, Jerome. 2008. *St. Paul's Ephesus: Texts and Archaeology*. Collegeville, MN: Michael Glazier; Liturgical Press.

Phillips, Morgan L. 1971. "Divine Self-Predication in Deutero-Isaiah." *BR* 16:32–51.

Richards, E. Randolf. 1991. *The Secretary in the Letters of Paul*. WUNT 2/42. Tübingen: Mohr Siebeck.

———. 2004. *Paul and First-Century Letter Writing: Secretaries, Composition and Collection*. Downers Grove, IL: Intervarsity Press; Leicester: Apollos.

Rietveld, James Dirk. 1998. "Illustrious Ephesus: Portrait of the City of Artemis in the Imperial Age." MA thesis, California State University.

Ricl, Marijana. 2020. *New Inscriptions from the Kaystros River (Küçük Menderes) Valley*. Beograd: Novi Sad.

Rogers, Guy MacLean. 1991. *The Sacred Identity of Ephesos: Foundation Myths of a Roman City*. London: Routledge.

———. 1997. Review of *Die Grammateis von Ephesos: Schreiberamt und Sozialstruktur in Einer Provinzhauptstadt des Römischen Kaiserreiches*, by C. Schulte. *JRS* 1997: 298–300.

Scherrer, Peter. 2000. *Ephesus: A New Guide*. Istanbul: Ege Yayinlan.

Schnabel, Eckhard J. 2012. *Acts*. ZECNT 5.5. Grand Rapids: Zondervan.

Schulte, C. 1994. *Die Grammateis von Ephesos: Schreiberamt und Sozialstruktur in Einer Provinzhauptstadt des Römischen Kaiserreiches*. Stuttgart: Steiner.

Sherwin-White, A. N. 1963. *Roman Society and Roman Law in the New Testament: The Sarum Lectures 1960–1961.* Oxford: Oxford University Press.

Trebilco, Paul. 1994. "Asia." Pages 292–362 in *Graeco-Roman Setting.* Vol. 2 of *The Book of Acts in Its First Century Setting.* Edited by David W. J. Gill and Conrad Gempf. Grand Rapids: Eerdmans; Carlisle: Paternoster.

Welborn, L. L. 1999. "The Runaway Paul." *HTR* 92.2:115–63.

———. 2005. *Paul, the Fool for Christ: A Study of 1 Corinthians 1–4 in the Comic-Philosophic Tradition.* London: T&T Clark.

Wilamowitz-Möllendorff, U. v. 1879. "ΓΡΑΜΜΑΤΕΥΣ ΤΗΣ ΠΟΛΕΩΣ." *Hermes* 14:148–52.

Wilson, Ian Douglas. 2016. "Yahweh's Consciousness: Isaiah 40-48 and Ancient Judean Historical Thought." *VT* 66:646–61.

Wiplinger, Gilbert, and Gudrun Wlach. 1996. *Ephesus: One Hundred Years of Austrian Research.* Edited by Claudia Luxon. Vienna: Österreichisches Archäologisches Institut.

Witherington, Ben, III. 1998. *The Acts of the Apostles: A Socio-rhetorical Commentary.* Grand Rapids: Eerdmans; Cambridge: Paternoster.

11. Pontius Pilate and the Ephesian "Friends of Caesar"

James R. Harrison

IEph 3.716

JÖAI 48:3–5, no. 1 (*editio princeps*); *AE* 1971.460. The inscription was found incised on a base, installed in a western niche of the northern gate agora, but its notification has come down to us via the sketchbook of Knibbe (no. 3451). The damaged section in line 4 has had two scholarly restorations proposed as far as the original ten letters: [παντί τρόπῳ] and [πάτρονα καὶ]. Certainty is unachievable. Date: 42/43 CE.

1	[ἡ βουλὴ καὶ ὁ δ]ῆμος ἐτείμησαν	[The Council and the p]eople honored
	[Γάιον Σαλλούσ]τιον Κρίσπον Πασσιῆ-	Gaius Sallus]tius Crispus Passie-
	[νον τὸν γενό]μενον ἀνθύπατον καὶ [ ] εὐεργέτην γενόμενον	[nus who was] proconsul and [—] benefactor
5	[τοῦ τε ἱεροῦ τ]ῆς Ἀρτέμιδος καὶ τοῦ δή-	[both of the temple o]f Artemis and of
	μου	the people
	[προνοησαμέν]ου Λευκί[ου] Κουσινίου Λευκί-	when Leuki[os] Kousinios, (son of) Leuki
	[ου υἱοῦ Οὐελεί]να φιλοκαίσαρος καὶ φιλο-	[os, of the (tribe) Oueli]na, friend of Caesar and friend
	[σεβάστου ἐπιτρό]που τῆς πόλεως.	[of Augustus, was admini]strator of the city,
10	[ἐπισκόπ]ου δὲ τὸ γ΄	and (municipal) [inspect]or (for) the third (time).

Gaius Sallus]tius Crispus Passienus, the honorand of this Ephesian inscription, was proconsul of Asia in 42/43 CE. Significantly, during his post as an elite Roman magistrate in Asia, Passienus acted as a benefactor to the Ephesian people and the temple of Ephesian Artemis. This demonstrates how Roman governors could strategically identify as benefactors of the deities of important local deities during their governance of their province, thereby securing the good will of a city and its gods. The approach of the proconsul Passienus stands in sharp contrast to provocative actions of the prefect Pontius Pilate toward his Jewish subjects in the Roman province of Judea (Harrison 2021). Notwithstanding, Pilate attempted to ingratiate himself with the merchants and seafarers of Caesarea and the populace of Jerusalem by, respectively, his construction of a lighthouse (*CIIP* 2.1277) and an aqueduct (Josephus, *B.J.* 2.175–177; *A.J.* 18.60–62; cf. Silver 2000). The construction of the monumental 2000 foot-long Stepped Street from the Siloam Pool to the Temple Mount, which has been identified as having been built by Pilate around 30 CE by virtue of the 101 coins found beneath street level, the most recent dating to 30/31 CE, is another example of how the Roman prefect projected an image of himself as a builder and benefactor at Jerusalem (Szanton et al. 2019).

The magistracy of *epitropos* ("administrator": IEph 1a.4, 25; 2.262; 3.856, 868; 5.1489, 1492; 6.2061.2, 2274c; SEG 36.1027; SEG 39.1178) is well known at Ephesus, whereas *episkopos* occurs once in our inscription ("inspector": IEph 3.716) and once more in a Christian inscription of the city (IEph 7.2.4128: ἀρχιεπισκό[που]). The two honorific epithets, φιλόκαισαρ ("loyal to Caesar," "friend of Caesar") and φιλοσέβαστος ("loyal to Augustus," "friend of Caesar"), are applied to Luekios Kousinios, the administrator and municipal inspector of Ephesus, with Kousinios self-importantly noting in the inscription that the post of *episkopos* was held for the third time. The mention of the Ephesian tribe Ouelina is quite rare in the Ephesian epigraphic corpus, occurring only once elsewhere in a funerary inscription (IEph 7.2.4119). This small piece of boastful rhetoric on the part of Kousinios is interesting. It enables us to see why Paul, according to contemporary rhetorical conventions (Judge 2008, 706–8), resorts to the use of numbers in his boasting catalogs (e.g., 2 Cor 11:24; 12:2b), though in the process he spoofs the whole genre of Greco-Roman self-eulogy by boasting in his weaknesses (2 Cor 11:16–12:10) (Harrison 2004, 46–55). Further, it also allows us to appreciate why Paul mentions his membership of the tribe of Benjamin (Phil 3:5), which not only had a favored place in the history of Israel but also had remained faithful to the tribe of Judah despite the abdication of the other ten tribes from the Davidic monarchy (1 Kgs 12:21) (Hansen 2009, 224).[1] Again, Paul is reflecting the rhetorical conventions of boasting in the Greco-Roman world, seen in the patterned numerical display of the honorand's achievements as a mnemonic (Judge 2008, 707), while simultaneously undermining the inflated rhetoric by means a cruciform construct of honor (Phil 3:7–11) (Harrison 2008).

The term φιλόκαισαρ has substantial interest for New Testament historians and Johannine exegetes. An independent tradition from the Gospel of John is worth noting in this regard for the insight that it throws upon the impact of the crowd upon Pilate.[2] The Jews threatened that Pilate would no longer be a "friend of Caesar" (φίλος τοῦ Καίσαρος) if the prefect did not accede to their wishes (19:12a).[3] What is the significance of the term in the Gospel of John? A similar title, "friend of the king," was the designation for loyal supporters of various kings during the Hellenistic Age (1 Macc 2:18; 3:18; 10.65; 3 Macc 6:23; Josephus, *A.J.* 12.298). As Adolf Deissmann (1978, 383) notes, φίλος τοῦ Καίσαρος ("friend of Caesar") and φίλος τοῦ Σεβαστοῦ ("friend of Augustus") emerged fully fledged in the imperial world from the "language of the court under the successors of Alexander."[4] Further, G. H. R. Horsley (1983, 87) comments that φιλόκαισαρ was "one of a cluster of epithets adopted, no doubt with official Roman approval, by individuals from the Greek East, particularly client kings, although by no means them alone." A few examples will suffice to establish the importance of *amici* ("friends") in the reigns of Augustus and Tiberius more generally, before we move onto a discussion of φιλόκαισαρ in the Jewish world and at Ephesus.

First, six proconsuls were selected by Augustus for portrait honors and various mentions on local coins in Africa and Asia after 7 BCE. They

---

1. Pilhofer (1995, 123–27) has argued that Philippian auditors would have drawn a rhetorical connection between Paul's birth into the "tribe of Benjamin" (Phil 3:5) and the prestigious Philippian tribe of Voltinia, regularly referred to in the epigraphy of Philippi.

2. Schnackenburg (1982, 262) posits that John did not find this tradition in his independent sources "but deduced the Jewish accusers' means of pressure from a general knowledge of the contemporary political situation."

3. The imperial context of John's Gospel, touching particularly on the kingship of Jesus, has been extensively studied: Reed 2005; Richey 2007; Justice 2008; Carter 2008; Ripley 2015; 2019; Kim 2018; Wright 2019.

4. For discussion of epigraphic samples across the eastern Mediterranean basin, see Horsley 1983, 87–88; see also Braund 1984, 105–8.

were "without exception *amici principis*, and every one of them was related to him" (Grant 1950, 53). Augustus also appointed C. Asinius Gallus, the proconsul of Asia in 5/4 BCE and his personal *amicus*, to investigate the murder of Euboulus in 6/5 BCE: "I commissioned my friend Asinius Gallus to examine under torture the slaves who were involved in the case" (IG 12.3.174) (Sherk 1966). Second, in the reign of Tiberius, *amicitia princeps* ("friendship of the *princeps*") continued to play an important role in the dynamics of Julio-Claudian rule. We see this preeminently in Tiberius's elevation of Sejanus, commander of the praetorian guard from 14–31 CE, as an *amicus principis* ("friend of the *princeps*"), linking him to the *domus Augusta* by the betrothal of his daughter to the son of Claudius (Grant 1950, 54). An *ara amicitiae* ("altar of friendship") was also set up, flanked by statues of Sejanus and Tiberius (Tacitus, *Ann.* 4.74). Indeed, as the otherwise unknown Marcus Terentius says regarding Sejanus as a conduit for imperial patronage, "I confess that not only was I the friend of Sejanus, but that I strove for his friendship, and that when I attained it, I rejoiced.... The closer a man's intimacy with Sejanus, the stronger his claim to the emperor's friendship" (Tacius, *Ann.* 6.8).[5] Several personal companions of Tiberius, present with him during his withdrawal to Capri, were also chosen as *amici* to be part of the ruler's *consilium* (i.e., state council) (Grant 1950, 54; Crook 1955; Millar 1977, 110–22). Additionally, coin issues with governors' portraits and names on them were also issued by Tiberius in 21 CE in Africa, following on from the Augustan precedent of 7 BCE, allowing local cities "to emphasize his reliance on *amici* as supporters of the dynasty" (Grant 1950, 50–59). Third, even local associations vaunted their friendship with the Julio-Claudian rulers. In

---

5. Stauffer (1949–1950) famously argued that Pilate was a client and *amicus* of Sejanus, but, upon Sejanus's execution by Tiberius for treason in 31 CE, the prefect was suddenly left politically exposed to the threats of the crowd (John 19:12a). However, there is no evidence for an *amicus* connection between Pilate and Sejanus in the Roman literary sources. The idea that Pilate was politically exposed before Tiberius upon the execution of his patron Sejanus at Rome is highly doubtful, given the fact that Pilate remained a trusted governor of Tiberius until 36 CE. Moreover, the so-called evidence for a shared anti-Semitism on the part of Sejanus and Pilate, based on the evidence of Philo (*Legat.* 299-305), is abstracted from its highly polemical rhetorical context in the *Legatio ad Gaium* and therefore does not take into account its deliberately exaggerated intent (McGing 1991, 430-33; Bond 1998, 26–48). Stauffer's thesis is now rightly abandoned, despite its influential status over such a long time. See the useful summary of the debate in Webb 2009, 722–23.

the early imperial era, for example, we hear of a priestess from Pergamon setting up an altar "for Asklepios Soter and for the association of friends of the Augusti" (φιλοσέβαστοι).[6] In sum, *amicitia* represented an important modus operandi in the relationship between Tiberius, Sejanus, his personal companions, and governors during the ruler's principate.

Turning now to the imperial language of friendship in a Judean context, Jews were also familiar with the potency of the honorific epithet φιλόκαισαρ ("loyal to Caesar," "friend of Caesar"). An inscription from a statue base found on the Acropolis of Athens referred to Herod the Great, an internationally known benefactor, as φιλόκαισαρ, eulogizing his virtue and good deeds (*OGIS* 427) (Rocca 2008, 44 n. 80). A similar but damaged honorific inscription from the Athenian agora also designates Herod as "a pious king and a friend of Caesar [φιλοκαίσαρα]" (SEG 12.150).[7] Later, Herod Agrippa I (37–41 CE), the client-king of Judea, also used the term on the reverse of his coins.[8] The importance of these imperial ties of friendship is also underscored by Philo (*Flacc.* 40), who speaks of the

---

6. For a translation, see Ascough, Harland, and Kloppenborg 2012, §120. Ernst Bammel (1952, 210 n. 2) comments that φιλόκαισαρ and φιλοσέβαστος are titles employed in honorific inscriptions for the high priests of the imperial cult in Asia. For example, see the late first-century/early second century CE Ephesian honorific inscription, which eulogizes its Ephesian honorand thus: "the [high priest] loyal to Caesar [φιλοκαίσαρα] both of Asia and [the city], the first man [of the city]" (SEG 46:1524). See also Donner 1961.

7. See Richardson 1996, 207–8. Horsley (1983, 88) cites the φιλόκαισαρ epigraphic evidence from Dittenberger (*OGIS* 419, 420, 424, 427) referring to Herod Agrippa I and II, as well as Agrippa I's nephew Herod Eusebes. However, Horsley (1983, 88–89) overlooks the two Herod the Great φιλόκαισαρ inscriptions discussed above, claiming that no such inscriptions were extant. This is incorrect, though Horsley readily accepts that there probably were examples from the reign of Herod the Great (just not extant in his view). First, Horsley accepts Dittenberger's attribution of *OGIS* 427 to Herod Eusebes, whereas Richardson (1996, 208) rightly dismisses the suggestion, arguing that the inscription honors instead Herod the Great: "The location in Athens, the usage 'king,' and the description of the person honored suggests Herod." Second, Horsley is unaware of SEG 12.150, another inscription of Herod the Great.

8. ΒΑΣΙΛΕΩΣ ΑΓΡΙΠΠΑ ΦΙΛΟΚΑΙΣΑΡ ("King Agrippa, friend of Caesar"): Hendin 1996, §552 (40/41 CE); ΑΓΡΙΠΠΑΣ ΦΙΛΟΚΑΙΣΑΡ ΒΑΣΙΛΕΥΣ ΜΕΓΑΣ ("Of Agrippa, friend of the great Caesar"): Hendin 1996, §554 (42/43 CE); ΟΡΚΑΙ ΒΑΣ ΑΓΡΙΠΠΑ ΠΒΣΕΒ ΚΑΙΣΑΡΑ Κ ΣΥΝΚΛΗΤΟΝ Κ ΔΗΜΟ ΡΩΜ ΦΙΛΙ Κ ΣΥΝΜΑΧ ΑΥΤΙΥ ("A vow and treaty of friendship and alliance between the great King Agrippa and Augustus Caesar [i.e., Claudius], the Senate and the People of Rome"): Hendin 1996, §557 (43/44 CE). Theophilos (2018, 39) lists twelve provincial coins (three from

social danger of insulting "a king and friend of Caesar." For full discussion of the Herodian epigraphy, see Wassell 2021, 238–41.

Moreover, if we allow for an Ephesian provenance of the Gospel of John (Carter 2008, 19–89; Keener 2003, 142–49), several φιλόκαισαρ inscriptions from Ephesus can also be drawn upon for consideration, though first-century CE examples are very few, with the vast majority of occurrences belonging to the second century CE onwards. In terms of the strictly first-century CE Ephesian examples, there are only four, including our text translated above. As noted, our 42/43 CE inscription honors a consul and benefactor, along with a reference to the *epitropos* ("administrator") of the city, who is described as φιλόκαισαρ and φιλοσέβαστος (IEph 3.716). The three other inscriptions are datable to 85/96 CE, the reign of Domitian, the likely time of the composition of the Gospel of John. The clerk (*grammateus*) of the city of Ephesus is designated φιλόκαισαρ in a dedication to Artemis Ephesia and Domitian (IEph 7.1.3008), as is the clerk of the city in another decree discussing how old buildings at Ephesus should be restored to the grandeur of Domitian's new temple (IEph 2.499). Finally, another clerk in an honorific inscription eulogizing a city benefactor (IEph 3.793) is ascribed the status of φιλόκαισαρ. What is intriguing about each of these first-century CE Ephesian inscriptions, contemporary with the composition of the Gospel of John, is that elite officials (*epitropos, grammateus*) of the city who are not the focus of the decree seize the opportunity to vaunt publicly their status as φιλόκαισαρ that they possess with the ruler at (undoubtedly) official level.[9] Thus this idle threat of the withdrawal of Caesar's friendship, which the crowd did not have the power to effect anyway, would have been a salutary reminder to any Roman prefect to act in ways that fostered Julio-Claudian interests by maintaining civic stability in the provinces, earning thereby the continuing approval of the Roman ruler and manifesting the fidelity and allegiance expected of an imperial client.[10] As Carson (1991, 607) comments, the threat would have

---

Judea, five from Philadelphia in Lydia, and four from Tripolis in Lydia) employing φιλόκαισαρ during the period 14–43 CE.

9. See Evans 1997. Upon a search of the papyrus archives of www.papyri.info, accessed 25 December 2020, there are no cases of φιλόκαισαρ employed in the papyri.

10. Theophilos (2018, 38) writes: "The semantic domain of included clients who were recipients of political favours or privilege from their patron. This political matrix indebted the client to a relationship of obligation, responsibility and commitment to their patron, in what could only be described as fidelity and allegiance."

reminded Pilate that bad reports had already been forwarded to Tiberius at the time of the military standards episode, forcing the prefect on that occasion to reverse his course of action. The threat of Tiberius's potential withdrawal of friendship at an unofficial level would have been well understood by the prefect even though there is no evidence that Pilate possessed the status of φιλόκαισαρ, unlike his Jewish and Ephesian compatriots who had been granted the honor formally.

Last, the papyrological evidence shows that there were imperial friends among the entourage of the Roman prefects in Egypt, in the same way that there had been first friends of the Ptolemaic king (Evans 1997, 188–90). Friendship, therefore, would have been an important modus operandi for Pilate in securing his power base in Judea, building upon bonds of reciprocity and obligation with elite players in a complex network of relationships. But, as noted, there is no evidence that Pilate had acquired the honorific φιλόκαισαρ from Tiberius or Sejanus.

Notwithstanding, the irony was that the Jews, to borrow John's terminology, did not need to remind Pilate about remaining a loyal friend of Caesar. It is true that the taunt of the Jews in John 19:12a focuses on the obligation of the prefect in a manner that might be mistakenly conceived as a political threat (Theophilos 2018, 41). But the prefect had already demonstrated that he was a loyal governor of Tiberius by building the Tibereium (i.e., an aqueduct) in Jerusalem in honor of the Roman ruler (Eck 2011, §1277; Lémonon 2007, 15–17, 23–33), commemorating the death of Livia (matron of the Julio-Claudian house and mother of Tiberius) with his 29/30 CE *quadrans* issue,[11] and suppressing any hint of civil unrest that had emerged in a troublesome province (Harrison 2021).

So what are the dynamics of Roman politics in this instance? Pilate, by means of his carefully stage-managed vacillations about executing Christ,[12] had whipped the frenzied crowd into affirming the priority of maintaining Tiberius's good will by crucifying messianic pretenders (John 19:12b). Even more remarkably, Pilate elicits from the chief priests a confession of the priority of Caesar's kingship over that of YHWH (John 19:15b). As

---

11. For discussion of Pilate's coinage, see Bond 1996, 1998, 20–23; Lémonon 2007, 94–98; Taylor 2006, 556–63; Jacobsen 2019.

12. Wright (2017, 217) concludes regarding Pilate's strategy: "His repeated statements that he finds 'no case' against Jesus come off as feints to release him, which provoke the Jewish authorities and reinforce their dependent status. Pilate does not think Jesus is innocent, and Pilate has no strong concern to release him."

much as Pilate works with his high priestly retainer to ensure a peaceable province by eliminating troublemakers,[13] he also humiliates the priests as a group before the altar of Rome in the process. In the case of the gospels, however, the comments of evangelists regarding Pilate's motivations are *evaluative*, assessing his character from the providential perspective of salvation history and the biblical understanding of fallen human nature. Through their strategic use of irony, the gospel writers depict the Roman strong man Pilate as weak, not realizing that his power was always derivative and ultimately elusive in its retention (Harrison 2021).

Bibliography

Ascough, Richard S., Philip A. Harland, and John S. Kloppenborg, eds. 2012. *Associations in the Greco-Roman World: A Source Book*. Waco, TX: Baylor University Press.

Bammel, Ernst. 1952. "Philos tou Kaisaros." *TLZ* 77.4:205–9.

Bond, Helen K. 1996. "The Coins of Pontius Pilate: Part of an Attempt to Provoke the People or Integrate Them into the Empire?" *JSJ* 27:241–62.

———. 1998. *Pontius Pilate in History and Interpretation*. SNTSMS 100. Cambridge: Cambridge University Press.

Braund, D. C. 1984. *Rome and the Friendly King: The Character of Client Kingship*. London: Croom Helm.

Carson, D. A. 1991. *The Gospel according to John*. Leicester: IVP.

Carter, Warren. 2003. *Pontius Pilate: Portraits of a Roman Governor*. Collegeville, MN: Michael Glazier; Liturgical Press.

———. 2008. *John and Empire: Initial Explorations*. New York: T&T Clark.

Crook, John A. 1955. *CONSILIVM PRINCIPIS: Imperial Councils and Counsellors from Augustus to Diocletian*. Cambridge: Cambridge University Press.

Deissmann, Adolf. 1978. *Light from the Ancient Near East: The New Testament Illustrated by Recently Discovered Texts from the Graeco-Roman World*. 2nd ed. Repr. Grand Rapids: Baker.

---

13. Carter (2003, 69–74) has suggested that Pilate's three questions (or interactions in the case of Luke) in the Synoptic Gospels with the assembled multitude regarding the fate of Christ (Matt 27:17 [repeated v. 21], 22, 23; Mark 15:9, 12–13, 14a; Luke 23:14, 20, 22) should be more understood as a case of Pilate polling the crowd. Pilate is adeptly gauging what levels of support Christ still mustered among the general populace after his recent triumphal entry into Jerusalem.

Donner, Herbert. 1961. "Der 'Freund des Königs.'" *ZAW* 32:269–77.
Eck, Walter. 2011. "Inscription Attesting the Restoration of a Lighthouse, Called Tiberieum, by the *praefectus* Iudaeae Pontius Pilatus." *CIIP* 1.2:228–30.
Evans, Katherine G. 1997. "Friendship in the Greek Documentary Papyri and Inscriptions: A Survey." Pages 181–202 in *Greco-Roman Perspectives on Friendship*. Edited by John T. Fitzgerald. RBS 34. Atlanta: Scholars Press.
Grant, Michael. 1950. *Aspects of the Principate of Tiberius: Historical Comments on the Colonial Coinage Issued Outside of Spain*. Numismatic Notes and Monographs 116. New York: The American Numismatic Society.
Hansen, G. Walter. 2009. *The Letter to the Philippians*. PNTC. Nottingham: Apollos.
Harrison, James R. 2004. "In Quest of the Third Heaven: Paul and His Apocalyptic Imitators." *VC* 58:24–55.
———. 2018. "From Rome to the Colony of Philippi: Roman Boasting in Philippians 3:4–6 in Its Latin West and Philippian Epigraphic Context." Pages 307–70 in *Roman Philippi*. Vol. 4 of *The First Urban Churches*. Edited by James R. Harrison and L. L. Welborn. WGRWSup 13. Atlanta: SBL Press.
———. 2021. "Reactions to Roman Officialdom to Jesus and His Followers in the Early First Century AD: A Case Study of Pontius Pilate." Pages 1–55 in vol. 2 of *The Impact of Jesus of Nazareth: Historical, Theological and Pastoral Perspectives*. Edited by Peter G. Bolt and James R. Harrison. Macquarie Park: SCD Press.
Hendin, David. 1996. *Guide to Biblical Coins*. 3rd ed. New York: Amphora.
Horsley, G. H. R. 1983. "Minor Philological Notes: 75. Φλκόαισαρ." *NewDocs* 3:87–89.
Jacobsen, David M. 2019. "Coins of the First-Century Governors of Judaea and Their Motifs." *Electra* 26:73–96.
Judge, E. A. 2008. "The Conflict of Educational Aims in the New Testament." Pages 693–708 in *The First Christians in the Roman World: Augustan and New Testament Essays*. Edited by James R. Harrison. WUNT 229. Tübingen: Mohr Siebeck.
Justice, David W. 2008. "Competing Visions: Kingship in the Gospels and in Roman Ideology." PhD diss., New Orleans Baptist Theological Seminary.

Keener, Craig S. 2003. *The Gospel of John: A Commentary.* 2 vols. Peabody, MA: Hendrickson.
Kim, Sehyun. 2018. *The Kingship of Jesus in the Gospel of John.* Eugene, OR: Pickwick.
Lémonon, Jean-Pierre. 2007. *Ponce Pilate.* Rev. ed. Paris: Les Éditions de L'Atelier.
McGing, Brian C. 1991. "Pontius Pilate and the Sources." *CBQ* 53:416–38.
Millar, Fergus. 1977. *The Emperor in the Roman World.* London: Duckworth.
Pilhofer, Peter. 1995. *Die erste christliche Gemeinde Europas.* Vol. 1 of *Philippi.* WUNT 87. Tübingen: Mohr Siebeck.
Reed, David. 2005. "Rethinking John's Social Setting: Hidden Script, Antilanguage, and the Negotiation of Empire." *BTB* 36:93–106.
Richardson, Peter. 1996. *Herod: King of the Jews and Friends of the Romans.* Columbia: University of South Carolina Press.
Richey, L. B. 2007. *Roman Imperial Ideology and the Gospel of John.* CBQMS 43. Washington, DC: Catholic Biblical Association of America.
Ripley, Jason J. 2015. "'Behold the Man?' Subverting Imperial Masculinity in the Gospel of John." *JBRec* 2.2:219–39.
———. 2019. "Glorious Death, Imperial Rome, and the Death of Jesus." *JGRChJ* 15:31–76.
Rocca, Samuel. 2008. *Herod's Judea: A Mediterranean State in the Classical World.* TSAJ 122. Tübingen: Mohr Siebeck.
Schnackenburg, Rudolf. 1982. *Commentary on Chapters 13–21.* Vol. 3 of *The Gospel according to St John.* Tunbridge Wells: Burns & Oates.
Sherk, Robert K. 1966. "C. Asinius Gallus and his Governorship of Asia." *GRBS* 7:57–62.
Silver, Kenneth K. A. 2000. "Pontius Pilate—An Aqueduct Builder?—Recent Findings and New Suggestions?" *Klio* 82:459–74.
Stauffer, Ethelbert. 1949–1950. "Zur Münzprägung und Judenpolitik des Pontius Pilatus." *Nouvelle Clio* 1–2:495–514.
Szanton, Nahshon, et al.. 2019. "Pontius Pilate in Jerusalem: The Monumental Street from the Siloam Pool to the Temple Mount." *Journal of the Institute of Archaeology of Tel Aviv University* 46:147–66.
Taylor, Joan E. 2006. "Pontius Pilate and the Imperial Cult in Judaea." *NTS* 52:555–82.
Theophilos, Michael P. 2018. "John 15:14 and the ΦΙΛ- Lexeme in Light of Numismatic Evidence: Friendship or Obedience?" *NTS* 64:33–43.

Wassell, Blake. 2021. *John 18:28–19:22 and the Paradox of Judgement.* WUNT 2/534. Tübingen: Mohr Siebeck.

Webb, Robert L. 2009. "The Roman Examination and Crucifixion of Jesus: Their Historicity and Implications." Pages 669–773 in *Key Events in the Life of the Historical Jesus: A Collaborative Exploration of Context and Coherence.* Edited by Darrell L. Bock and Robert L. Webb. Grand Rapids: Eerdmans.

Wright, Arthur M. 2017. "What Is Truth? The Complicated Characterization of Pontius Pilate in the Fourth Gospel." *RevExp* 114:211–19.

———. 2019. *The Governor and the King: Irony, Hidden Transcripts, and Negotiating Empire in the Fourth Gospel.* Eugene, OR: Pickwick.

12. Julius the Jewish *archiatros*: On Being the "Chief Physician" at Ephesus

James R. Harrison

The archaeological evidence for a Jewish presence at Ephesus is almost nonexistent in comparison to, for example, the Jewish synagogue, inscriptions, and shops at Sardis. Six pieces of archaeological evidence have been unearthed. A menorah, often overlooked in modern discussions (e.g., Scherrer 2000, 130–32; Strocka 2003, 33–43), has been carved into the steps leading up to the entrance of the Celsus library, incised by an unknown Jewish resident of the city sometime after the construction of the library (*IJO* 2.151; Knibbe 1998, 123 n. 296). A fragment of a marble block, possibly from the synagogue, has been found in the narthex of the domed church at Ephesus with the word τό θυσιαστήριον ("altar"), accompanied by an incised menorah to its right (IEph 7.2.4130 [*IJO* 2.31] [fourth century CE or later]). There is also (1) a glass flask painted with a menorah, ethrog, lulab, and shofar; (2) four lamps with menorahs; (3) a Jewish magical amulet with a menorah, but it was found in the area between Ephesus and Smyrna; and (4) another Jewish amulet, a carnelian gemstone, written in Greek on the obverse and in Hebrew on the reverse (Kraabel 1968, 56–57; Horsley 1992, 125; Trebilco 2004, 48 n. 224). Lines 6–8 of the Greek text of the gemstone render a Jewish invocation that is clearly reminiscent of Exod 3:14 LXX (ἐγώ εἰμι ὁ "Ων: "I am who I am"). The text of the amulet says: "(You) whom myriads of angels tend, O ever-living Adonaie, for You are the one who is [<ἀ>ίζων, Ἀδωναίε ὢν γὰρ εἶ]" (Kraabel 1968, 57; Keil 1940).[1] In sum, there are the visual symbols of Jewish presence here that one would routinely expect in any eastern Mediterranean city, as well as other features such as the Jewish practice of apotropaic magic

---

1. Horsley (1992, 125 n. 93) rightly points to the problem of provenance of the gem: "The item was purchased at Smyrna in 1912, and was claimed to be from Ephesos. Not included in *I.Eph*." This commentary is drawn from Harrison 2018, 24–29.

(Bohak 2008) and the use of Old Testament intertextual echoes in their texts. However, the archaeological evidence tells us nothing in detail about the Jews living at Ephesus other than providing us fleeting insights into their bilingualism, liturgy, piety, magical rituals, and biblical traditions.

Possibly the most helpful material evidence we have regarding the presence of the Jews in Ephesus comes from the public inscriptions, even though the documents are considerably later than the New Testament period and also generally very brief. Several Jewish inscriptions, in addition to the altar stone noted above, have been found (Baugh 1990, 81–86; Horsley 1987, §116; Trebilco 1991, 43–48; *IJO* 2.152–62). There is mention of

1. the (possibly) Jewish-named M. Aurelius Sambathius (*IJO* 2.34 [third century CE]) at a grave site,[2] a name given, some have argued, to Jews born on the Sabbath (Trebilco 2004, 47 n. 2);
2. a funerary monument to Julius the "official physician" or "chief physician" (ἀρχιατρός, IEph 5.1677 [*IJO* 2.32] [Antonine period]), the subject of our translation and commentary below;
3. the acclamation for the "ruler of the synagogue" (ἀρχισυνάγωγος) and the elders (I Eph 4.1251 [*IJO* 2.30] [fifth century CE]);
4. a gravestone for a priest (ἰαιρέος) named Marcus Mussius (IEph 5.1676 [*IJO* 2.33] [200 CE]).[3]

From this list of Jewish inscriptions at Ephesus, I have chosen to discuss the stela honoring Julius, the Jewish *archiatros* of Ephesus, along with his wife, noted above. The Greek text and the English translation of the honorific tombstone are set out below. Not only does the inscription point to the elite status of some Jews at Ephesus and to the prestigious role of the

---

2. Baugh (1990, 85) raises the possibility that Sambathios may have been "a Jewish convert to Christianity" on the basis of the appearance of a (Sa)mbathios—note, however, that the name is restored—in an Ephesian tomb with the Christian symbols of the cross and Alpha-Omega sign (IEph 6.2306k). For other Christian instances of the name, see Horsley 1987, §116. However, see Horsley's (1992, 126–27) critique of this position, noting that (1) in some papyri σάμβαθον refers to a container and not to the Sabbath, and (2) the cross and other Christian symbols could have been added subsequently to a Jewish inscription.

3. See also the letter of bishop Hypatios mentioning the Jews at Ephesus (*IJO* 2.35).

12. Julius the Jewish *archiatros*

archiatros there, but it also it throws light on Jewish acculturation and the contribution of Jews to the civic life of the city.

IEph 5.1677

Hicks 1890, 263, no. 677 (*editio princeps*); CIJ 2.745; Oehler 1909, 297, no. 55; IJO 2.32. The exact location of the inscription is unknown. The stela is made entirely of white marble. Lines 6–7 of the inscription were added later by another hand. Date: Hicks has assigned the style of the letters to the Antonine age.

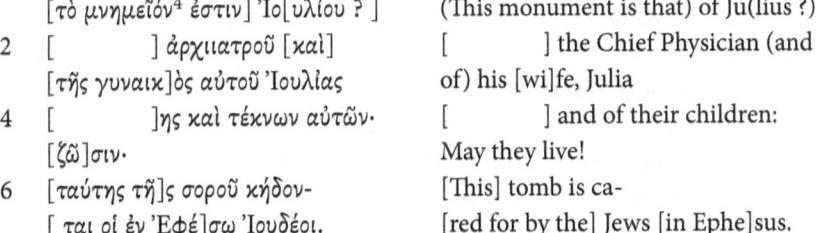

[τὸ μνημεῖόν⁴ ἐστιν] Ἰο[υλίου ?]	(This monument is that) of Ju(lius ?)
2 [ ] ἀρχιιατροῦ [καὶ]	[ ] the Chief Physician (and
[τῆς γυναικ]ὸς αὐτοῦ Ἰουλίας	of) his [wi]fe, Julia
4 [ ]ης καὶ τέκνων αὐτῶν·	[ ] and of their children:
[ζῶ]σιν·	May they live!
6 [ταύτης τῆ]ς σοροῦ κήδον-	[This] tomb is ca-
[ται οἱ ἐν Ἐφέ]σῳ Ἰουδέοι.	[red for by the] Jews [in Ephe]sus.

The role of the ἀρχιατρός was well known in antiquity. Ákos Zimonyi (2015) has argued that changes in meaning of ἀρχιατρός occurred during the Roman Empire. Whereas the term initially referred to a court physician, by the second century CE, it denoted a public physician—undoubtedly facilitated by the edict of Antoninus Pius (Nutton 1977)—but, according to the scholarly consensus, it was only in late antiquity that the term acquired its force as an honorific accolade. However, Zimonyi has challenged this construct, convincingly demonstrating that an inscription from Alexandria of C. Proculeius Themison, erected in 7 CE, is clearly honorific, thereby opening up the strong likelihood that the eulogistic use of the term was well established in the early imperial age:

> The assembly of physicians in Alexandria honours Gaius Proculeius Themison, *archiatros*, because of his benevolence [in the] 37th [year] of Caesar (Augustus), on [...] of the month Phaophi. (trans. Zimonyi 2015, 232).

---

4. Ameling (*IJO* 2.32) draws attention to Oehler's rejection of the restoration of τὸ ἡμῷον (l. 1) in favor of the current restoration of τὸ μνημεῖον (l. 1). Furthermore, Oehler has dismissed the spelling variations suggested by previous editors (ἀρχειατροῦ, ἀρχιατροῦ) for the current restoration of ἀρχιιατροῦ (l. 2).

In a further discussion of medical competitions in their Ephesian context, Zimonyi (2014, 365, 366) expands upon the meaning of ἀρχιατρός in its Ionian context. On the basis of the Ephesian epigraphy, he argues that at Ephesus ἀρχιατρός could organizationally "indicate the head of a medical school or a *collegium*" in addition to its flattering function as honorific denoting "a famous and skilled physician." It is difficult to decide which nuance of ἀρχιατρός might be in view here in an Ephesian context: public physician, head of a medical school (*collegium*) or a eulogistic accolade for his skill as a physician? In my opinion, the honorific use is less likely because the tombstone genre in Jewish contexts generally commemorates individuals more minimally than the grand style of Greco-Roman honorific rhetoric where a carefully selected *cursus honorum* testifies to the honorand's civic virtue. At the very least, Julius is a public physician and, perhaps even more remarkably (but much less likely, in my estimation), the head of a medical school or *collegium*. Either way, Julius has very substantial social status and public recognition as a Jew at Ephesus.

Concentrating now upon our inscription, the *nomen* of the wife of Julius, Julia (l. 3), is gentile, but her *praenomen* is missing. Ameling (*IJO* 2, p. 155) correctly states that, because the husband and wife are both Iulii, it invites legitimate speculation about how they acquired such civic rights, but in the absence of any other evidence we cannot come to a firm conclusion. If Julius is a Jew, as is highly likely,[5] we gain here keen insight into how well the Ephesian Jews had integrated as a people group into Ephesian civic life. S. M. Baugh (1990, 84) has observed that the sentiment ζῶσιν was a commonplace on non-Jewish Ephesian tombs (see Park 2000), demonstrating how the Jews "had assimilated many of the practices of their neighbours despite their existence as a distinct social group." By contrast, Baugh opines that the *hasidim* of Palestine would have refused such a convention (Baugh 1990, 84). But this imposes a Palestinian matrix upon the cultural context of diaspora Jews and, in the process, misunderstands the reason for Ephesian Jews choosing such a widespread funerary motif. So what is the religious ethos of our Ephesian inscription?

In the case of the Ephesian Jews such as Julius and Mussius (IEph 5.1676 [*IJO* 2.33]), the more open-ended ζῶσιν or ζῇ was probably adopted

---

5. The singular form ζῇ ("May he live!") is also used in the Ephesian inscription of the Jewish priest Marcus Mussius (IEph 5.1676 [*IJO* 2.33]). The care of Julius's tomb, along with the grave of Mussius, by the Jewish community would be highly unlikely if he were an unbelieving gentile.

because it could embrace the varied postmortem expectations within the Ephesian Jewish community (e.g., Sheol [Hades], immortality of the soul, bodily resurrection?).[6] The funerary expression would certainly not alienate their gentile neighbors, and it allowed flexibility regarding the public expression of the diverse beliefs of the Ephesian Jewish community about the afterlife. Moreover, ζῶσιν may have acquired additional force as a sentiment because of its perceived resonances with the redemptive activity of the Old Testament "living God" (Deut 5:6; Josh 3:10; Jer 10:10) over against the lifelessness of the gentile idols and their inability to save (Ps 115:3–7; Isa 41:21–24; 43:10–13; 44:6–23; 45:20; Jer 10:1–16). What mattered ultimately was that the Ephesian Jews would live with their living God, entrusting their final postmortem journey to him in a prayer wish (ζῶσιν). We must remember that because diaspora Jews were summoned to seek the welfare of the city (Jer 29:7), it was appropriate for some of them to be honored with the conventional Greco-Roman inscriptional moral accolades and coronal honors as a sign of their devotion to the wellbeing of the city (Lifshitz 1967, §§13, 33). So, in this case, the Ephesian Jews adopted a routine and inoffensive funerary sentiment to express implicitly their communal postmortem faith beliefs.

Little doubt Julius was a high-status Ephesian citizen, given that the city's inscriptions mention several other prominent individuals holding the office of ἀρχιατρός (IEph 3.622; 4.1161–67; 7.1.3239).[7] The status was underscored by the edict of a triumvir, which freed doctors from liability to taxes and liturgies (IEph 7.2.4101 [first century BCE]), freedom from liturgies being an honor traditionally accorded prominent benefactors.[8] Ephesian doctors could gain further kudos by competing in the city's two-day Asklepeian games, which involved "theoretical," "surgery," "problem-solving," and "surgical instruments" contests (IEph 4.1162).[9]

---

6. On Sheol/Hades, see *BS* 2.127, *CPJ* 1530A (van Der Horst 1991, 151–52, 156–57). On the soul, see *CPJ* 1530A, see van der Horst 1991, 156–57. On the resurrection, see *BS* 2.194: "Good luck with your resurrection!" (van der Horst 1991, 118).

7. On the status of Julius as "official doctor," note Trebilco 1991, 173–74: "Such officially recognised public physicians were paid by the city and their principal task was to give medical attention to citizens." There is little doubt, therefore, that Julius treated the general Ephesian community and not just his fellow Jews.

8. On ἀλειτούργητος ("free from the public services"), see Harrison 2017, 254. For Ephesian epigraphic examples of ἀλειτούργητος, see IEph 2.219; 3.946; 3.956A; 7.2.4337.

9. For a translation of this inscription, see Harland 2015.

Certainly, as this particular inscription shows, the chief-physicians of Ephesus were not only the director of the contests but also competitors in and winners of the games:

> [...] when Tiberius Claudius Demostratos Caelianus, the Asiarch, was priest of Asclepius, [...] was the leader of physicians, [...] director of contests for the great Asclepieia was Publius Vedius Rufinus (?) chief-physician (*archiatros*) for the fourth time. Here are the winners of the contests of physicians:
> Composition: Publius Vedius Rufinus the younger (?).
> Surgery: Publius Aelius Menandros, chief-physician.
> Problem: Publius Aelius Menandros, chief-physician.
> Instrument: Publius Aelius Menandros, chief-physician.
> To good fortune. Of the Ephesian physicians who meet in the Mouseion [...] our leader Asclepius [...] the sacrifices pleased [...] Polythallos (?) the younger was head of the gymnasium for the two days of the contests. (trans. Zimonyi 2014, 357–58, modifying Harland).

But to what extent did Julius maintain boundary markers between himself and the other Ephesian physicians? The latter sacrificed to "ancestor Asklepios and to the Sebastoi" (IEph 3.719) and, as noted, staged competitions in honor of Askelpios (IEph 4.1162) (Harland 2014, §129). As the ἀρχιατρός, Julius must have belonged to the "association [τὸ συνέδριον] of [physicians] from the Mousseion in [Eph]esus" (IEph 6.2304), presumably being on familiar terms with the "instructors in the Mousseion" (IEph 6.2065; 7.1.3068). Undoubtedly, he would have been exposed to the association's banqueting and cultic activities, having to negotiate not only issues of food purity but also the dedication of food to idols at its private celebrations. On rabbinic thought on idolatry and laws concerning gentile food, see Tomson 1990, 151–76. Moreover, how one skirted the idolatrous statues—ubiquitous in any Greco-Roman city, including the Ephesian Mousseion with (presumably) its statue of Asklepios—was an issue that consumed rabbinic debate in antiquity (Eliav 2008). For an Ephesian statue of Asklepios at the Selçuk Museum, see Topai 2010, 43. Did Julius absent himself from banquets and professional occasions involving idolatry, as occasion demanded, while going to other events that were less compromising? Or did he simply treat the idols as nonexistent powers with no ability to act punitively or to save and thus attended important occasions in freedom of conscience regarding idolatry? We simply do not know. But while there may have been differing views among the Ephesian Jews regarding the limits of their integration into Greco-Roman society, it would seem that Julius, as an ἀρχιατρός, was able to differentiate between the legitimate civic demands of his professional life, maintaining the Jewish boundary markers as required and expressing the corporate expression of his faith in the synagogal community of Ephesus and in his own family life. Certainly his fellow Jews who looked after his grave saw no problem with his faith commitment.

In terms of New Testament references to the Jews at Ephesus, we are confined to the references in the book of Acts to the Jewish synagogue (18:19; 19:8–9), itinerant (?) Jewish exorcists (19:13–16), the seven sons of Scaeva, the Jewish chief-priest (19:14: Ἰουδαίου ἀρχιερέως), and, more generally, the Jews incorporated with the Greeks in the city (19:17). On the Jewish community at Ephesus at the time of Paul's missionary visit, see Keener 2014, 2920–22. How much we can infer from this Antonine inscription regarding what the status of some elite Jews, assuming that there were several of social influence in Ephesus, might have been in the first-century CE city more widely is unknown and very risky methodologically.

Bibliography

Baugh, Steven Michael. 1990. "Paul and Ephesus: The Apostle among His Contemporaries." PhD diss., University of California, Irvine.

Bohak, Gideon. 2008. *Ancient Jewish Magic: A History*. Cambridge: Cambridge University Press.

Eliav, Yaron Z. 2008. "Roman Statues, Rabbis, and Greco-Roman Culture." Pages 99–116 in *Jewish Literatures and Cultures: Context and Intertext*. Edited by Anita Norich and Yaron Z. Eliav. Providence, RI: Brown Judaic Studies.

Harland, Philip A. 2014. *North Coast of the Black Sea, Asia Minor*. Vol. 2 of *Greco-Roman Associations: Texts, Translations and Commentary*. BZNW 204. Berlin: De Gruyter.

———. 2015. "Victors in Competitions of Physicians–Rufinus (138–161 CE)." Associations in the Greco-Roman World. http://tinyurl.com/SBL9031e.

Harrison, James R. 2017. *Paul's Language of Grace in Its Graeco-Roman Context*. WUNT 2/172. Tübingen: Mohr Siebeck.

———. 2018. "An Epigraphic Portrait of Ephesus and Its Villages." Pages

1–67 in *Ephesus*. Vol. 3 of *The First Urban Churches*. Edited by James R. Harrison and L. L. Welborn. WGRWSup 9. Atlanta: SBL Press.

Hicks, Edward Lee. 1890. *Priene, Iasos and Ephesos*. Part 3 of *The Collection of Ancient Greek inscriptions in the British Museum*. Oxford: Clarendon.

Horsley, G. H. R. 1987. "Jews at Ephesos." *NewDocs* 4:231–32.

———. 1992. "The Inscriptions of Ephesos and the New Testament." *NovT* 34:105–68.

Horst, Pieter W. van der. 1991. *Ancient Jewish Epitaphs: An Introductory Survey of a Millennium of Jewish Funerary Epigraphy (300 BCE–700 CE)*. Kampen: Kok Pharos.

Keener, Craig S. 2014. *15:1–23:35*. Vol. 3 of *Acts: An Exegetical Commentary*. Grand Rapids: Baker Academic.

Keil, Josef. 1940. "Ein rätselhaftes Amulett." *JÖAI* 32:79–84.

Knibbe, Dieter. 1998. *Ephesus: Geschichte einer bedeutenden antiken Stadt und Portrait einer modernen Großgrabung*. Frankfurt am Main: Lang.

Kraabel, Alf. T. 1968. "Judaism in Western Asia Minor under the Roman Empire, with a Preliminary Study of the Jewish Community at Sardis, Lydia." PhD diss., Harvard University.

Lifshitz, B. 1967. *Donateurs et fondateurs dans les synagogues juives: Répertoire des dédicaces grecques relatives à la construction et à la réflection des synagogues*. Paris: Gabalda.

Nutton, Vivian. 1977. "Archiatri and the Medical Profession in Antiquity." *Papers of the British School at Rome* 45:191–226.

Oehler, Johann. "Epigraphische Beiträge zur Geschichte des Judentums." *MGWJ* 53 (1909): 292–302.

Park, Joseph S. 2000. *Conceptions of Afterlife in Jewish Inscriptions, with Special Reference to Pauline Literature*. WUNT 2/121. Tübingen: Mohr Siebeck.

Scherrer, Peter. 2000. *Ephesus: A New Guide*. Istanbul: Ege Yayınları.

Strocka, Volker M. 2003. "The Celsus Library in Ephesus." Pages 22–43 in *Ancient Libraries in Anatolia: Libraries of Hattusha, Pergamon, Ephesus, Nysa*. Ankara: Middle East Technical University Library.

Tomson, Peter J. 1990. *Paul and the Jewish Law: Halakha in the Letters of the Apostle to the Gentiles*. Minneapolis: Fortress.

Topai, C. 2010. *Ephesus Museum Selçuk*. Translated by P. Rhode. Istanbul: BKG Press.

Trebilco, Paul. 1991. *Jewish Communities in Asia Minor*. SNTSMS 69. Cambridge: Cambridge University Press.

———. 2004. *The Early Christians in Ephesus from Paul to Ignatius*. Grand Rapids: Eerdmans.

Zimonyi, Ákos. 2014. "The Context of Medical Competitions in Ephesus." *ActAnt* 54:355–70.

———. 2015. "*Archiatres Id Est Medicus Sapientissimus*: Changes in the Meaning of the Term *Archiatros* in the Roman Empire." Pages 231–41 in *Sapiens Ubique Civis: Proceedings of International Conference on Classical Studies (Szeged, Hungary, 2013)*. Edited by Zoltán Farkas et al. Budapest: ELTE Eötvös József Collegium.

13. "Ambassador in Chains" (Eph 6:20): What Might Ephesian Auditors Have Heard?

James R. Harrison

Ambassadors were well-known figures in Greco-Roman antiquity (Adcock and Mosley 1975; Oller 1995; Bash 1997; Eilers 2009), especially in the Greek East prior to and during the imperial period (Snowdon 2010). Before the Roman hegemony, Hellenistic communities had traditionally chosen philosophers to act as ambassadors when important issues were at stake, including famous sophists such as Gorgias of Leontini, Hippias of Elis, and Prodicus, among others. In a Jewish context, the famous embassy of Philo, the philosopher-ambassador, to the entirely dismissive Gaius Caligula at Rome regarding the Roman ruler's disastrous plan to place his statue in the Jerusalem temple, recounted in *Legatio ad Gaium*, is another instance of the same phenomenon (Lyons 2011, 58–103). During the Hellenistic period, Rome carefully stage-managed these philosopher-ambassadors, with prominent Roman philhellenes promoting their visits as grand occasions (33).

As the Roman hegemony was increasingly established throughout the Greek East and good relations were facilitated through the visits of Greek ambassadors to Rome or to the local provincial seat of the Roman proconsul (Bowman 1987), reciprocity became the modus operandi in interstate relations, cemented by interstate benefactions and strong social relationships (*amicitia*, patronage). Records of official decisions were assiduously kept by the Roman bureaucrats, documenting Rome's interactions with other city states. These documents of the Roman state, the *senatus consulta*, after having contextualized the decree in the prescript, set out the motion decided, including the motivations for the resolution, the names of the ambassadors, and the speeches given (Snowdon 2010, 21–23). Petitions delivered by ambassadors were dealt with, including those, to cite just two examples, from Delphi and Rhodes (Lyons 2011, 145, 183), with decisions being made by the Senate or a Roman magistrate.[1]

Last, during the local games and festivals at the Greek cities that were held throughout the eastern Mediterranean basin, the city hosting the games sent out *theoroi* ("observers": i.e., sacred ambassadors) to the city states that it wanted to attend its games in order to proclaim the festival. In a cultural institution called the *theorodokia*, they were accorded great respect, being entertained and hosted by the elites of the other cities at their residences. In reciprocation, the cities that wanted to participate would have sent their own sacred embassy to the city hosting the games in order to represent themselves there. In this regard, Robert Parker (2004, 9) draws attention to an extant list of *theorodokoi* from Delphi that lists the 330 places, spanning Syria in the East and Sicily in the West, that the sacred ambassadors visited. From this vast list of cities would have come the individual state ambassadors who had reciprocated the initial invitation of Delphi. On the *theoroi*, see Dimitrova 2008. Ephesus would have been intimately familiar with all these types of ambassadorial interactions in their imperial and agonistic contexts, as the sixty-two occurrences of πρεσβεύω and cognates in the Ephesian epigraphic corpus amply demonstrate. In each inscription, Ephesus appropriately honors its ambassadorial elites. On the epigraphic and literary evidence regarding ambassadors, see Bash 1997, 55–80.

We will confine our investigation to three important Ephesian inscriptions below honoring ambassadors of the city. From there we will be well placed to consider how Paul's original auditors might have assessed the apostle's paradoxical self-designation as an "ambassador in chains" (Eph 6:20).

IEph 3.728

AAWW 94:18–20, no. 3 (*editio princeps*); *JÖAI* 44:257–63, no. 3; *AE* 1959.13; *SEG* 36.1019. Base, built into the pillars of the Scholastica baths. From the sketchbook of Miltner, no. 2740, 2743. Date: 166 CE/ca. 180.

---

1. Snowdon (2010, 196 n. 13) cites *RDGE* 4.5–10 as an example of this type of interaction: "the ambassadors of Ambracia and Athamana approached me so that I might give them a meeting with the senate." For references to ambassadors in the inscriptions and literary texts in the classical period, see Harding 1985, index 2, s.v. "Ambassadors/Envoys." In the Hellenistic Age, see Burstein 1985, index 2, s.v. "Ambassadors." For the hegemony of Rome in the Greek East, see Sherk 1984, index 4, s.v. "Envoys."

13. "Ambassador in Chains" (Eph 6:20)

τῆς πρώτης καὶ μεγίστης μητροπόλεως	The council and people of the city of the Ephesians
τῆς Ἀσίας καὶ δὶς νεωκόρου τῶν Σεβαστῶν	of the first and greatest metropolis
Ἐφεσίων πόλεως ἡ βουλὴ καὶ ὁ δῆμ[ος]	of Asia and twice temple-warden of the emperors
4 ἐτείμησεν	honored
Πο. Οὐήδιον Ἀντωνεῖνον, υὸν Πο.	Po(plius) Vedius Antoninus, the son of Po(plius)
Οὐηδίου Ἀντωνείνου, πρυτάνεως καὶ γυμνασ[ιάρχο]υ καὶ δὶς γραμματέως	Vedius Antoninus, prytanis and gymnasiarch and twice secretary
8 τοῦ δήμου [καὶ ἀ]σιάρχου καὶ πανη-	of the people and asiarch and panegyriarch
γυριάρχου τῶν μεγάλ[ω]ν Ἐφεσήων καὶ Πασιθέων, πρεσβεύσαντος	of the Great Ephesia and the Pasithia, who went as an ambassador
πρός τε τὴν σύγκλητον	both to the senate
12 καὶ τοὺς αὐτοκράτορας,	and the emperors,
καὶ αὐτὸν πρύτανιν καὶ	(who was) also himself prytanis and
γραμματέα καὶ ἀσιάρχην	secretary and asiarch
καὶ πανηγυρίαρχον τῶν	and panegyriarch of the
16 μεγάλων Ἐφεσήων καὶ	Great Ephesia and
ἀλυτάρχην τῶν Ὀλυμπίων,	alytarch of the Olympia,
πρεσβεύσαντα πρός τε τὴν	who went as an ambassador both to the
σύγκλητον καὶ τοὺς αὐτο-	senate and the emperors
20 κράτορας περὶ τῶν μεγίστων	concerning matters of greatest importance
καὶ ἀεὶ νικήσαντα γυμνα- σιαρχήσαντα δὲ καὶ ἐν ταῖς	and was always victorious, and who was also gymnasiarch during the
ἐπιδημίαις τοῦ μεγίστου	visits of the greatest
24 αὐτοκράτορος Λουκίου	emperor Lucius
Αὐρηλίου Οὐήρου ἀνεν- δεῶς πᾶσιν αἷς ἐπεδήμη- σεν ἡμέραις πολλοῖς καὶ	Aurelius Verus faultlessly, on all days he stayed, and who with many
28 μεγάλοις ἔργοις κεκοσ- μηκότα τὴν πόλιν καὶ	great projects adorned the city and

ἐν παντὶ καιρῷ προθύμως	at every opportunity actively
καὶ ἐκουσίως πεφιλοτειμη-	and voluntarily pursued
32 μένον.	honor.
τὸν ἀνδριάντα επέστησαν	Those concerned with (preparation of) the
οἱ ἐπὶ τὸ γεῦμα πραγμα-	meal erected this
τευόμενοι	statue.

This inscription is particularly interesting because the father (Poplius Vedius Antoninus) and the same-named son are both honored for their ambassadorial activities to the senate and the emperors. Here the plural "emperors" (l. 19) is used because the succession of Lucius Aurelius Verus to the emperorship, together with Marcus Aurelius (ll. 23–25), marked the first time that the Roman Empire was ruled by multiple emperors, which became the paradigm for successions in the later empire. The son demonstrates his persuasive power and impressive relational skills in continuously securing for the Ephesians the agreement of the Romans in "matters of greatest importance" (l. 20), effusively signified by the language of "victory" (ἀεὶ νικήσαντα). This carefully chosen language is interesting. While reciprocity is the modus operandi between Rome and the cities of the province of Asia, the Ephesians would have had no illusions about where the real weight of political and military power resided in the relationship, so such cleverly negotiated outcomes in their favor were thought of in agonistic terms as a victory over a powerful and determined opponent. The son also demonstrates "faultlessly" his diplomatic skills as gymnasiarch in welcoming Lucius Aurelius Verus on his visits to Ephesus (ll. 23–24), the one which we know about being Verus's marriage to Marcus's daughter, Annia Aurelia Galeria Lucilla, in 164 CE. A series of prestigious civic posts are held by both by father and son: *prytanis*, secretary, asiarch, panegyriarch, and gymnasiarch. On gymnasiarchs, see Harrison 2008. On asiarchs, see Kearsley 1987. The son replicates all the same posts as his father but also adds a new and prestigious attainment ("alytarch of the Olympia"), as well as acting generously as an Ephesian benefactor by adorning the city with substantial civic projects (ll. 27–29). Consequently, the inscription insightfully highlights how the son replicated and surpassed his ancestral honor (ll. 30–31).

Another attainment of considerable interest in the case of the father and the son is the role of panegyriarch ("president of a *panegyros*" [i.e., local festival]: ll. 8–9, 15–16) in the Great Ephesia and the Great Pasi-

13. "Ambassador in Chains" (Eph 6:20)

thia. The rare term "Pasithia"—"panegyriarch of the great Pasithia" (IEph 3.633, 923, 938), "panegyriarch of the ancestral Pasithia" (3.664b), "of the Pasithia" (4.1384)—seems to refer to games in Ephesus. The Ephesia and Artemisia were the oldest and most highly revered of the festivals in Ephesus, with the Ephesia being celebrated annually from the sixth and fifth century CE onwards. They became more popular than the Artemesia, as evidenced by their more frequent appearance in the epigraphic record (IEph 1.22.42; 3.627; 3.672; 3.727.9, 16; 3.811; 3.859a; 4.1080B; 4.1106.6-8; 4.1123; 4.1130.1, 4; 4.1132.15; 5.1152; 6.2067, 2072.26; 7.1.3014; 7.1.3056; 7.1.3072; 7.1.3080). Notwithstanding, the Artemesia, in contrast to the Ephesia, were celebrated more elaborately and fulsomely at Ephesus and, indeed, widely throughout the entire Greek world. All types of contests were held in the Ephesia, with there being an especially strong emphasis on the music programme (Arnold 1972, 17-18). It is therefore likely that the father and the son, as presidents of the Great Ephesia and the Great Pasithia, received and welcomed the ambassadors from other Greek cities during these important games and festivals at Ephesus. There is no doubt that this family of Ephesian ambassadors belonged to the social elites of Ephesus, associating with the imperial rulers and the luminaries of many Greek cities in the East of the Roman Empire.

IEph 3.802

SBAW 1956, no. 3; AE 1971.455; SEG 17.505. See BE 71:422; Picard 1957, 108-12 (incorrectly cited in IEph). Base, installed in a wall at the Scholastica baths, along the street to the East of the Celsus library. From the sketchbook of Keil, no. 1273. Date: 217/218 CE.

- - - -	[who served as ambassador]
ἐπὶ τὸν [κύ]ριον [ἡ]μῶ[ν]	to our lord
Αὐτοκράτορα	imperator
Μ(άρκον) [[Ὀπέλλιον]] Σεουῆρο[ν]	Marcus [Opellius] Severu[s]
4 [[. Μακρεῖνον]] Εὐσεβῆ Σεβαστὸ[ν]	[Macrinus] Pius Augustu[s]
καὶ τὸν ἱερώτατον Καίσαρα	and the most holy Caesar
[[Διαδουμενιανόν,]] υἱὸν το[ῦ]	[Diadumenianus], son of
Σεβαστοῦ,	Augustus,

8   περὶ τῶν πρωτείων καὶ τῶν λο[ι-]   concerned with the principal citizens and other
    πῶν δικαίων καὶ νεικήσαντα, πρεσ[βεύ-]   dignitaries and who won; and who served
    σαντα δὲ καὶ συνδικήσαντα ἐπὶ θεοὺς [Σε-]   also as ambassador and advocate to the divine
    ουῆρον καὶ Ἀντωνῖνον εἴς τε τὴν βασιλ[ίδα]   [Se]verus and Antoninus both to imper[ial]
12 Ῥώμην πλεονάκις καὶ εἰς Βρετανίαν κα[ὶ Γερ-]   Rome often and to Britain and upper
    μανίαν τὴν ἄνω, καὶ γενόμενον καὶ μέχ[ρι]   [Ger]many; and who traveled also as far as
    τοῦ Γρανίου Ἀπόλλωνος διὰ τὴν πατρ[ίδα]   (the temple) of Apollo Grannus for his native land
    [κα]ὶ ἐν Σιρμίῳ καὶ ἐν Νεικομηδείᾳ   [an]d in Sirmium, Nikomedeia
16 [κ]αὶ ἐν Ἀντιοχείᾳ, γενόμενον δ[ὲ]   and Antioch; and who traveled
    [κ]αὶ μέχρις Μεσοποταμίας πλεον[ά-]   also as far as Mesopotamia often
    κις διὰ συνδικίας, καὶ πάντα κατο[ρ-]   arising from advocacy; and who accomplished all (his posts)
    θώσαντα, στρατηγόν, παραφύ[λα-]   successfully having become general, guard,
20 κα, δεκάπρωτον, λιμενάρχ[ην],   decaprotos, harbor-master,
    εἰρήναρχον μόνον γενόμεν[ον]   sole police magistrate
    [τ]ῆς χώρας, συνδικήσαντα δὲ καὶ ὑπ[ὲρ]   of the countryside; and who also served as advocate on
    [το]ῦ κοινοῦ τῆς Ἀσίας ἔθνους κ[αὶ]   behalf of [th]e koinon of the people of Asia a[nd ...]
    - - - -

Marcus Opellius Severus Macrinus (ll. 3–4) ruled as emperor from April 217 to 8 June 218 CE. Fleeing from the siege of Antioch, he was subsequently executed in Cappadocia and replaced by the new emperor Elagabalus. His son and coregent, Diadumenianus (ll. 5–7), was captured before the execution of his father and was then killed. At the time, he was about ten years old. The unpopularity of the Roman ruler and his son is indicated by the subsequent erasure of both of their names from the epigraphic record, indicated in our inscription by the double brackets ([[...]], ll. 3–5). See Harrison 2016. If our restoration for line 1 is correct, then our unnamed ambassador—missing due to the damage incurred on the inscription—visited this Roman ruler and his coregent on behalf of

13. "Ambassador in Chains" (Eph 6:20)   185

Ephesus, airing the concerns of the principal citizens and other dignitaries of the city, and winning (νεικήσαντα, l. 9) by his personal persuasion and diplomacy the Roman rulers over to his position (cf. IEph 3.728.21: ἀεὶ νικήσαντα, "was always victorious").

Before this most recent round of diplomacy, our unknown honorand had previously acted as an ambassador and advocate to the divine emperors Septimius Severus (r. 193–211 CE) and Caracalla (r. 198–217 CE), who was formerly known as "Antoninus" (l. 11) and, being the elder son of Septimius Severus, he acted as coregent with his father. The geographical focus of these diplomatic missions was the Latin West (ll. 12–13). There were repeated ambassadorial visits (1) to Rome, (2) to Britain, coinciding with Septimius Severus's military campaigns in the far north of the country in 208 CE (Picard 1957, 109), (3) to upper Germany, and (4) to the Roman province of Pannonia, in which Sirmium was situated (i.e., modern Serbia). Moving from Europe into the Greek East, his travels took him from Nikomedia to Antioch and even extended to Mesopotamia (ll. 15–17), again, as C. Picard (1957, 109) notes, possibly coinciding with the expeditions of Caracalla (216–217 CE) and Macrinus there (217 CE). The time spent in Nikomedia may also have coincided with Caracalla's visit to Nikomedia, who spent the winters of 214 and 215 CE in the city.

What is remarkable about this list of ambassadorial and advocacy visits is their extraordinary geographical spread, extending from the far West of the Roman Empire to its far East. Consequently, Picard (1957, 109) memorably describes our honorand as "ce juriste globe-trotter." But equally as mesmerizing is the clever strategy employed: it is predicated upon the emperors' presence in many of the regions that he visited at the time (Rome, Britain, Nikomedia, Mesopotamia), with the result that diplomatic and advocacy connections could be made with high-ranking court and military officials and occasionally even with the emperor himself. Our honorand's personal prestige was thereby substantially enhanced. His social status as an advocate would also have been considerably heightened by his work on behalf of the koinon of Asia.

Of considerable interest is the honorand's visit to "(the temple) of Apollo Grannus for his native land." The difficulty is that we do not know to which site of Apollo Grannus, a Celtic deity, our inscription is referring. Was it:

- the Grannus Apollo temple at Bavarian Faimingen in Lauingen, Germany, to which Caracalla appealed when he was sick (Dio Cassius, *Hist. Rom.* 78.15.5–7), or
- the Latin named *Aquae Granni* ("the waters of Grannus") at Aix-la-Chapelle (modern Aachen) in Germany, a town famous for its hot springs and cures, or
- the sanctuary at Andesina (the modern city of Grand), the town of the Gallic Leuci, situated in the mountainous Vosges region of France?

Nor is the reason for visiting this site clear from the evidence of the inscription. Are we witnessing here the attraction of another visit of our ambassador to a site that had become associated with the imperial ruler's interest in its healing powers? Or was it, as Picard (1957, 109–12) proposes, simply a personal visit of the epigraphic honorand to the *Aquae Granni* for healing? If the latter option is correct, then the ambassador's voyage to Aix-la-Chapelle belonged to a much wider third-century CE phenomenon of various work trips and missions, undertaken far and wide and in every direction, for medical cures, as much as for official business (112). We simply do not know which option is correct, as intriguing as either possibility is. More could be said on the remarkable series of civic posts that our ambassador and advocate held (ll. 19–22). But next to the imposing travels of Titus Flavius Zeuxis of Hierapolis (Nasrallah 2017), we are witnessing here one of the most-traveled men in antiquity.

IEph 7.1.3066

FiE 1, no. 49 n. 3 (*editio princeps*); FiE 3, no. 66. A base center piece without profiles and made of bluish marble. It is walled in the hinterland of the agora south hall between the second and third chamber west of the south gate. Height 1.04m, width 0.60m. From the sketchbook of Heberdey, 882. Date: late first–early second century CE, though possibly the inscription is precisely datable to 105 CE on the basis of the prytany of Gaius Likinius Maximus Iulianus being in that year (IEph 4.1022).

ἡ βουλὴ κα[ὶ ὁ δῆμος]	The council and the people
2 ἐτείμησα[ν]	honored
Γ(άιον) Λικίνιον Μενάνδρου υἱὸ[ν]	Gaius Licinius

13. "Ambassador in Chains" (Eph 6:20)

4 Σεργία Μάξιμον Ἰουλιανὸν	(of) Memandros (of the tribe of) Sergia,
φιλοσέβαστον τὸν πρύτανιν	the *prytanis* loyal to the emperor,
6 καὶ ἱερέα Ῥώμης καὶ Ποπλίου Σερ- ουειλίου Ἰσαυρικοῦ, ἄνδρα λαμπρὸ[ν]	priest of Rome and of Poplius Servilius Isauricus, an illustrious man
8 καὶ φιλοτείμως γυμνασιαρχήσαντα,	and who also served emulously as a gymnasiarch,
νεοποιήσαντα, στρατηγήσαντα, πρεσ-	*neopoios* (lit: "temple-keeper"), general, (and) amba-
10 βεύσαντα πρὸς τὸν Σεβαστὸν καὶ ἐν ταῖς	ssador to the Augustus and who also in the
λοιπαῖς δὲ τῆς πατρίδος χρείαις εὔχρηστ[ον]	remaining needful affairs of the fatherland was serviceable,
12 γεγονότα, δόντα καὶ τὰ ὑπὲρ τῶν θεωρι[ῶν]	and who undertook numberless (visits) on behalf of the state-ambassadors
τῆς πρυτανείας C μ(ύρια) εἰς τὴν αἰώνιον γυ[μνα-]	of the presidency for the eternal office of the gymna-
14 σιαρχίαν καὶ ἐν τῆι πρυτανείᾳ εἰς τὴν τ[οῦ]	siarchy and in the presidency for the
λιμένος κατασκευὴν C, βφ΄, δόντα δὲ κ[αὶ]	state of the harbor, and also who gave (10,000 denarii)
16 εἰς τὴν κατασκευὴν τοῦ καινοῦ γυμνα[σί-]	for the state of the new gymnasi-
ου, ἑστιάσαντα δὲ καὶ ἐν τῷ τῆς πρυτανεία[ς]	um, and who also who entertained hospitably, both in the time of his prytany
18 χρόνῳ καὶ ἐν τῷ τῆς νεοποιείας τοὺς	and in the allotment of his (office as) *neopoios*,
πολείτας κλήρωι κατὰ φυλὴν καὶ διὰ	the citizens by tribe and who unassisted
20 τοῦ υἱοῦ Μενάνδρου γυμνασιαρχή-	(as) the son of Menandros served as a gymnasiarch
σαντα καὶ ἀγορανομήσαντα καὶ	and as an *agoranamos* ("clerk of the market") and
22 πρεσβεύσαντα.	as an ambassador.

Several points of historical interest are worth highlighting in this inscription. First, Iulianus is the "priest of Rome and of Poplius Servilius Isauricus" (ll. 6–7). Poplius Servilius Isauricus, a long-term friend of

Julius Caesar, was coconsul in 48 CE during the dictatorship of Caesar and then was subsequently proconsul of Asia, attaining a good reputation there when he returned to Pergamum "its ancestral laws and its unenslaved democracy" (*OGIS* 449 [46–44 BCE]). In a remarkable act of commemoration on the part of Ephesus, Isauricus was made an object of cultic worship alongside the goddess Roma, as our inscription indicates and another Ephesian inscription also confirms (IEph 702.7-8 [98/117 CE]). For discussion, see Friesen 1993, 9–10. This is not the only case of a republican luminary being extravagantly honored at Ephesus. Caius Memmius, the grandson of the Roman Dictator L. Cornelius Sulla, built a monument at the end of Embolos Street, directly below the Panayir hill in the third or the fourth quarter of the first-century BCE. There were two inscriptions of the grandson Memmius incised on the monument (IEph 2.403.1 and 2), each referring to the grandfather Sulla and the fact that the grandson had paid for the structure from his own money. The two-floor building, with a pyramidal roof, has sculptural decoration that includes three togate figures on the first floor: L. Cornelius Sulla, his son-in-law (the son of Pompeius Rufus), and his grandson Caius Memmius. But, as Peter Scherrer (2000, 96 §50) correctly notes, the monument, as it stands in Ephesus today, is only a reerected architectural pastiche, being "more a modern interpretation than an illustration of an ancient edifice." For a hypothetical reconstruction of the building, see IEph 2.132. For full discussion, see Yorgos 2002. What is interesting about this Ephesian commitment to famous republican figures is that the city honors both the *optimates* (Sulla) and *populares* traditions (Isauricus) of Roman politics, though in one instance it is more a matter of family honor, whereas the other is an astute nod to the effectiveness of Roman provincial rule in Asia Minor under the house of the Caesars.

Second, the arresting phrase, "the eternal office of the gymnasiarchy" (ll. 13–14), is also found in IEph 4.1143 and 5.1500, with a slight variation found in the former inscription ("who served as the gymnasiarch of the god of the eternal gymnasium," passim). The divine legitimation articulated in IEph 4.1143 explains the language of eternity being applied to the Ephesian gymnasium in the three inscriptions. Third, Louis Robert (1967, 33, cited in IEph 7.1:66), referring to IEph 2.462.4-6 ("with the 10,000 denarii of the prytany in it"; cf. 5.1722), argues that Iulianus made no use of the 10,000 sesterces that he had received for the purpose of funding spectacles during his prytany; instead, he used it for a foundation for the gymnasium, a conclusion reflected in our translation above.

In terms of the ambassadorial activities of Iulianus, he acts as an ambassador to the emperor ("the Augustus") on behalf of Ephesus and assumes the role of ambassador in many visits during his two presidencies, substituting for state-ambassadors who were (presumably) otherwise preoccupied with various civic affairs or other ambassadorial visits themselves. The status conferred by the many magistracies held by Iulianus, coupled with his generous role as civic benefactor within the city, would have given his role as ambassador not only the credibility of extensive civic experience but also the glory of ancestral honor and social prestige in the estimation of his fellow citizens.

In sum, given this backdrop of prestigious ambassadorial embassies on behalf of the city and accumulated ancestral honor, how would Ephesian auditors have responded to the Paul's self-designation as an "ambassador" (Eph 6:20: πρεσβεύω)? At one level, the transferred ambassadorial connection to Paul would not have been immediately obvious to the Ephesians. Paul lacks the ancestral wealth, social status, posts in the civic *cursus honorum*, and connectivity with the Ephesian elites (pace, Acts 19:31: τῶν Ἀσιαρχῶν) to make any credible claim to being an ambassador. To be sure, it is true to argue that it was a great insult to imprison an ambassador (though certainly not unprecedented), as Anthony Bash states (1997, 131–32). But Paul's assertion to be an ambassador would have foundered because his legitimation was based upon a messianic pretender crucified by Rome in a provincial backwater of the empire. This outlandish claim would not have convinced the Ephesian council and people who were loyal to the Roman ruler (φιλοσέβαστος: 1Eph 2.281), nor many other individuals, also designated φιλοσέβαστος, who had held significant posts in the *cursus honorum* at Ephesus.[2] Clearly, upon conversion, the vast reorientation required of new converts' assumptions about the nature of status and honor at Ephesus would have dramatic and personally challenging.

Turning now to the startling qualifier employed of Paul's ambassadorial status in Eph 6:20, ἐν ἁλύσει ("in chains"), Margaret Y. MacDonald

---

2. For a few examples of Ephesian magistracy holders designated φιλοσέβαστος, see (1) "asiarch and prytanis" (IEph 2.445), (2) secretary (IEph 4.1061), (3) gymnasiarch (IEph 4.1143), (4) an individual who held the posts of "hierokerux, agoranomos, strategos, and neopoios" (IEph 3.962), (5) "athlete and first general" (IEph 4.1113), (6) "hymnodos of the temple of divine Hadrian" (IEph 3.921), and (7) theologos (IEph 5.1935).

(2000, 347) perceptively comments that "it is important to keep in mind the wretched conditions of an ancient prison." For modern auditors, there is also the genuine danger of adopting a "'docetic' view of Paul's imprisonment, a view that sees Paul as basically uninfluenced by imprisonment" (Wansink 1993, 86). Ernest Best (1998, 609) points out the word used for Paul's prison confinement in Col 4:18 (μου τῶν δεσμῶν) denoted "the condition of restraint rather than its actual physical means" in Ephesians (ἐν ἁλύσει). In other words, as in Ephesians, Paul is accentuating the shock of his physical experience of imprisonment.

What would Ephesian auditors have understood by such an oxymoronic phrase, which, as we have seen from the documentary evidence above, exudes incongruity, irony, and paradox in its ambassadorial context (Muddiman, *Ephesians*, 296; MacDonald 2000, 347; Barth, *Ephesians*, 782; Lincoln 1990, 454; Hoehner 2003, 864)? Elsewhere the apostle Paul and the book of Acts does not shirk from mentioning the difficult physical conditions of imprisonments (2 Cor 11:23b: "far more imprisonments, with countless floggings, and often near death"; Col 4:18; Acts 16:23–24; 28:16, 20 [τὴν ἅλυσιν ταύτην περίκειμαι]) and arraignments (2 Cor 11:24–25a), including (metaphorically) the death assigned to the apostolic prisoners (1 Cor 4:9), as well as the enchainment of the other apostles (Acts 12:6–7: ἁλύσεσιν δυσίν). What do the ancient literary sources reveal about the conditions of imprisonment in antiquity, a topic most effectively addressed by Craig S. Wansink (1993, 91–86) and Brian Rapske (1994, 195–225; see also Rapske 1991)? What is said specifically about enchainment (Rapske 1994, 206–9; Wansink, 1993, 26, 28–29, 37–38, 41)? How does Paul construe theologically, socially, and pastorally his imprisonments?

Both Rapske and Wansink insightfully discuss the ancient evidence on enchainment in prison and custody more generally, upon which I selectively draw. The early Roman legislation of the Twelve Tables specified that debtors be bound with fetters of fifteen pounds' weight (Lex 12, table 2.3.3; cf. Livy, *Ab. urbe cond.* 32.36.18: "chains of not less than ten pounds' weight"). Prisoners wore a collar and were manacled by hand or with one or both legs chained day and night (Livy 32.26.18; Seneca the Elder, *Contr.* 1.6.2; Lucian, *Tox.* 29, 32, 33). Sometimes prisoners had chains placed around their necks (Ovid, *Con. Liv.* 273–274). Long imprisonment resulted in flesh being corroded by iron fetters on hands (Lucan, *Phar.* 72–73; Seneca the Elder, *Contr.* 1.6.2) and the resilience of prisoners was weakened by the weight, noise, and pain of their fetters (Philostratus, *Vit. Apoll.* 7.36; Seneca the Younger, *Ep.* 9.9; Juvenal, *Sat.* 6.560–561). Lucian's

13. "Ambassador in Chains" (Eph 6:20)   191

depiction of the imprisonment of Antiphilus, legs in stocks at night and collared and manacled during the day, is worth reproducing:

> Moreover, the stench of the room and its stifling air (since many were confined in the same place, cramped for room, and scarcely able to draw breath), the clash of iron, the scanty sleep—all these conditions were difficult and intolerable for such a man, unwonted to them and unschooled to a life so rigorous. (*Tox.* 29)

Similarly, Plutarch speaks graphically of the perpetual torment caused by chains when prisoners were awake:

> Sleep makes light the chains of prisoners, and the inflammations surrounding wounds, the savage gnawing of ulcers in the flesh, and the tormenting pains are removed from those who have fallen asleep. (*Superst.* 3 [165E])

Last, the significance of imprisonment in dreams is interpreted by Artemidorus in his *Oneirocritica*. There he says that a dream about being buried alive portended prison and fetters (2.50), whereas a dream about the descent into Hades signified that the dreamer would "be forcibly restrained by certain people and thrown into prison" (2.55). Here we gain a sense of the deep psychic shock engendered by imprisonment in antiquity and the fear with which it was viewed. The social disdain of imprisonment, too, is well captured in Blandus's comment about people reproaching him regarding his chains (Seneca the Elder, *Contr.* 9.1.7).

How then does Paul reconfigure this highly negative perception of enchainment in antiquity and establish his divine legitimacy as an ambassador? First, Paul moves the believers' focus away from the painful actualities of his imprisonment to his divinely imposed opportunity (Eph 6:20b: ὡς δεῖ με λαλῆσαι; cf. 1 Cor 9:16–18) for a forthright, free, and bold articulation of "the mystery of Christ" despite his enchainment (6:20b: ἐν αὐτῷ παρρησιάσωμαι: Lincoln 1990, 454–45). This hidden mystery is revealed as the apostolic proclamation of the "riches of Christ" to the gentiles (Eph 3:1 ["a prisoner for Christ Jesus for the sake of you gentiles"], cf. 3:8–9). Paul's ambassadorial announcement of the divine reconciliation of implacable enemies, Jews and gentiles, in the crucified Christ (Eph 3:14–20) is such a ground-changing social novelty that the apostle's enchainment is radically reevaluated. Paul's sufferings in prison, therefore, should not concern the Ephesians because, rather than being a matter of social disdain (as with Blandus above) or a discouragement for Ephesians, they are instead their "glory" (Eph 3:13b: δόξα ὑμῶν). The Ephesian participation in Paul's sufferings are not only theologically a prelude to eschatological glory (2 Cor 4:17; Rom 8:17–18), but also, paradoxically in Christ, they point to "the reputation or honour enjoyed by them as new creatures in Christ" in the present age, no matter their personal circumstances or (in the estimation of antiquity) the shame of their socially humiliated apostle in prison (Hoehner 2003, 470). The stratospheric civic honor of the elite Ephesian ambassadors is thereby sidelined. Second, we must not forget to whom the enchained Paul is ambassador: the glorious risen Lord of all who would conform the believers' mortal bodies to Christ's body of glory at the eschaton (Eph 1:15–23; 4:8–10; cf. Phil 2:9–11; 3:20–21). Third, this christological and eschatological perspective leads the apostle to a radical redefinition of human honor and success in the present age by virtue of the believer's incorporation in the soteriological career of the crucified, risen, ascended, and reigning Christ. For Paul, his apostolic experience as an ambassador of Christ simultaneously reflects in his pastoral ministry the career extremes of the dishonor and rejection of the crucified Christ and, concomitantly, the honor and vindication of the risen Christ: honor and dishonor, ill-repute and good repute, imposters yet true, unknown yet well-known, dying yet alive, punished yet not killed (2 Cor 6:8–9). Literally stripped of all his resources in prison, the impoverished apostle was making others rich (2 Cor 6:10b) through the divine reconciliation he offered the world as Christ's ambassador (5:19–20).

Bibliography

Adcock, Frank, and D. J. Mosley. 1975. *Diplomacy in Ancient Greece*. London: Thames & Hudson.
Arnold, Jane Ringwood. 1972. "Festivals of Ephesus." *AJA* 76:17–22.
Bash, Anthony. 1997. *Ambassadors for Christ: An Exploration of the Ambassadorial Language in the New Testament*. WUNT 2/92. Tübingen: Mohr Siebeck.
Benndorf, Otto, ed. 1906. *Die Viersäulenbau auf der Arkadianetrasse... Inscriftliche Zeugnisse über das Artemision*. FiE 1. Vienna: Heberdey.
Best, Ernest. 1998. *A Critical and Exegetical Commentary on Ephesians*. ICC. London: T&T Clark.
Bowman, Denvy A. 1987. "Roman Ambassadors in the Greek East: 196–146 BC." PhD diss., University of North Carolina at Chapel Hill.

Burstein, Stanley M, ed. and tr. 1985. *The Hellenistic Age from the Battle of Ipsos to the Death of Kleopatra VII*. Translated Documents of Greece and Rome 3. Cambridge: Cambridge University Press.

Dimitrova, Nora M. 2008. *Theoroi and Initiates in Samothrace: The Epigraphical Evidence*. HesperiaSup 37. Athens: American School of Classical Studies.

Eilers, Claude, ed. 2009. *Diplomats and Diplomacy in the Roman World*. MnemosyneSup 304. Leiden: Brill.

Friesen, Steven J. 1993. *Twice Neokoros: Ephesus, Asia and the Cult of the Flavian Imperial Family*. RGRW 116. Leiden: Brill.

Harding, Phillip, ed. and trans. 1985. *From the End of the Peloponnesian War to the Battle of Ipsus*. Translated Documents of Greece and Rome 2. Cambridge University Press.

Harrison, James R. 2008. "Paul and the Gymnasiarchs: Two Approaches to Pastoral Formation in Antiquity." Pages 141–78 in *Paul: Jew, Greek, and Roman*. Pauline Studies 5. Leiden: Brill.

———. 2016. "The Erasure of Honour: Paul and the Politics of Dishonour." *TynBull* 66:161–84.

Hoehner, H. W. 2003. *Ephesians: An Exegetical Commentary*. Grand Rapids: Eerdmans.

Kearlsey, R. A. 1987. "Some Asiarchs in Ephesos." *NewDocs* 4:46–55.

Lincoln, Andrew T. 1990. *Ephesians*. WBC 42. Dallas: Word.

Lyons, Evangeline Z. 2011. "Hellenic Philosophers as Ambassadors to the Roman Empire: Performance, Parrhesia, and Power." PhD diss., University of Michigan.

MacDonald, Margaret Y. 2000. *Colossians and Ephesians*. Sacrina Pagina 17. Collegeville, MN: Liturgical Press.

Meriç, Recep, et al. 1981. *Die Inschriften von Ephesos Teil VII.1: Nr. 3001–3500 (Repertorium)*. Bonn: Habelt.

Muddiman, John. 2001. *The Epistle to the* Ephesians. BNTC. London: Continuum.

Nasrallah, Laura S. 2017. "Imposing Travelers: An Inscription from Galatia and the Journeys of the Earliest Inscriptions." Pages 273–96 in *Journeys in the Roman East: Imagined and Real*. Edited by Maren Niehoff. Tübingen: Mohr Siebeck.

Oller, G. H. 1995. "Messengers and Ambassadors in Ancient Western Asia." Pages 1465–74 in vol. 3 of *Civilizations of the Ancient Near East*. Edited by Jack S. Sasson, et al. New York: Scribner's.

Parker, Robert. 2004. "New 'Panhellenic' Festivals in Hellenistic Greece." Pages 9–22 in *Mobility and Travel in the Mediterranean from Antiquity to the Middle Ages*. Edited by Renata Schlesier and Ulrike Zellman. Münster: LIT Verlag.

Picard, C. 1957. "D'Éphèse à la Gaule, et de Stobi (Macédoine) à Claros." *REG* 70:108–17.

Rapske, Brian. 1991. "The Importance of Helpers to the Imprisoned Paul in the Book of Acts." *TynBul* 41.2:3–30.

———. 1994. *Paul in Roman Custody*. Vol. 3 of *The Book of Acts in Its First Century Setting*. Grand Rapids: Eerdmans.

Reich, Emil. 1923. *Forschungen in Ephesos*. FiE 3. Vienna: Akademie.

Robert, Louis. 1967. "Sur des inscriptions d'Éphèse: Fêtes, athlètes, empereurs, épigrammes." *RevPhil* 41:7–84.

Scherrer, Peter. 2000. *Ephesus: A New Guide*. Istanbul: Ege Yayinlan.

Sherk, Robert K, ed. and trans. 1984. *Rome and the Greek East to the Death of Augustus*. Translated Documents of Greece and Rome 4. Cambridge: Cambridge University Press.

Snowdon, Michael. 2010. "Greek Freedom and Roman Hegemony: The Transaction of Roman Rule in the Greek East (201 BCE–14 CE)." PhD diss., McMaster University.

Wansink, Craig S. 1993. "'Imprisonment for the Gospel': The Apostle Paul and Roman Prisons." PhD diss., Yale University.

Yorgos, Mallios. 2002. "Ephesus (Antiquity), Monument of Memmius." *Encyclopaedia of the Hellenic World, Asia Minor*. https://tinyurl.com/bdfhk3ne.

The Centrality of Honor and Its Disruption

14. "They Love to Have the Place of Honor": Ephesian Priority Seating and Early Christian Honorific Culture

Isaac T. Soon

SEG 34.1688a–d

JÖAI 55:126–27 (=IKeramos 76.T7) (*editio princeps*); Jones 2008, 337. White marble seats, found on the street between the stadium or theater. Ephesus. Date: ca. 128 CE.

a. upper side: [—] τῆς Ἀσίας
b. upper side: [—] Ἀριστοκράτο[υς—]
c. upper side: [—ν]αῶν τῶν ἐν Ἐφέσῳ Οὐλπίου
d. upper side: [—] μιηταις τόπ[—]

front side: [—] Κεραμιητ[—]
front side: no inscription
front side: [—] τόπος ὁ δο[—]

front side: no inscription

Reconstruction:

Upper side: [Κερα]μιήταις τόπ[ος ὁ δοθεὶς ὑπὸ τοῦ ἀρχιερέως] τῆς Ἀσίας [ν]αῶν τῶν ἐν Ἐφέσῳ Οὐλπίου Ἀριστοκράτο[υς];
Front side: Κεραμιητ[αις] τόπος ὁ δο[θεὶς ὑπὸ τοῦ ἀρχιερέως τῆς Ἀσίας ναῶν τῶν ἐν Ἐφέσῳ Οὐλπίου Ἀριστοκράτους]

Upper side: To those from Keramus, a place that was given by the high priest of Asia of the temples that are in Ephesus, Ulpios Aristokratos.
Front side: To those from Keramus, a place that was given by the high priest of Asia of the temples that are in Ephesus, Ulpios Arisokratos.

IEph 6.2086a–b

RPh 41, no. 86a, b, c, no. 87a, b (*editio princeps*); Robert 1967, 73 Jones 2008, 337. Inscriptions from theater statue bases. Date: second–third century CE.

2086a [κρ]ατίστης Βο[υλῆς]	(Place of) those who hold positions on the senate[1]
2086b front side: [—] γερου[σίας]	(Place of?) those from the council of elders
2086b back side: [—βουλ]άρχου στρα(τήγου)	(Place of?) the *strategos*, leader of the council

These inscriptions inform us of the different ways that designated seating could be publicly assigned and acknowledged. Those from SEG 31.1168 are on the very seats themselves, while those from IEph 2086 were inscribed on statue bases from around the theater. Harrison (2018, 43) notes that the bases on which the latter were found were donated by C. Vibius Salutaris (see IEph 1a.27), whose dedication was on the front of the base while the rear end of the statue held the seating designations. Although the designations were not attached to the seats themselves, they acted like a kind of social seating map, reminding the public of the allocated arrangement for each section of the building. This method of designation reinforced the social hierarchy in places other than where privileged members of the elite sat. Additionally, contours of the hierarchy underlying privileged seating can be seen in SEG 31.1168, as places are granted by someone who occupies an official position and therefore has a higher status (e.g., the high priest of Asia, Ulpios Aristokratos; cf. IEph 3.618).

The ancients frequently used architectural space and placement within that space to generate, perpetuate, and maintain social hierarchy. As the inscriptions above and elsewhere show (e.g., in Aphrodisias and Hierapolis, see Jones 2008, 319–26, 344–45), Greek cities often employed designated and priority seating at the theater, often the front row of seats known as the *prohedria* (see also Xenophon, *Por.* 3.4). Seating arrangements were also applied to meals and banquets and great thought went into ensuring that there was proper order and that those who needed to be honored received their due (e.g., Plutarch, *Quaest. conv.* 1.2–3). The Romans followed Greek customs by deploying priority seating for members of the elite classes. Once when a senator was refused a seat at games in Puteoli, Augustus legislated that the first row of all public gatherings should be reserved for

---

1. Regarding IEph 6.2086a, the translation is literally "(Place of) the most illustrious council." However, Jones (2008, 337) notes that the adjective κράτιστος "is the Greek equivalent of *clarissimus*, the title accorded to those of senatorial rank." This is reflected in the translation above.

senators (Suetonius, *Aug.* 44), a practice continued by Claudius (Suetonius, *Claud.* 21) when senators were seated among the regular people. In some cases, it may have been that there were enough reserved seats for every single senator even if they wanted to come or not (Moore 1994–1995). Both Augustus and Claudius also separated those of equestrian rank from the rest of the people (see, for example, the numerous *epigrammata* about *equites* and their seating by Martial, *Ep.* 5.8, 14, 23, 25, 27 or Tacitus, *Ann.* 15.32). Adherence to social mores of seating was no mere triviality. Tacitus records the story of a certain Domitius Corbulo who brought to the Senate at the time a young noble, Lucius Sulla, who had not given up his seat at a gladiatorial game (*Ann.* 3.31). On Corbulo see Kavanagh 2004.

In Jewish contexts, there were chief seats in ancient Jewish synagogues (e.g., Luke 11:43; Matt 23:6). Of the Therapeutae, the sequestered Jewish community in the area of Alexandria, Philo reports that during their assemblies members sat according to age and men and women were separated from one another in different seating areas (*Contempl.* 30–33). On the separation of men and women in Jewish synagogues, see Spigel 2012. The community at Qumran prioritized the seating of the priests, followed by elders and the rest of the people according to their rank (1QS VI, 8–9, cf. 1QSa II, 13–22). The Tosefta records arranged seating at a basilica-synagogue in Alexandria where different tradespeople were seated together (t. Sukkah 4.4). Diasporic Jewish groups also had places reserved for them at theaters (see Baker 2005). Regardless of the context, whether it was a theater or stadium or symposium or synagogue, the same general principles of priority seating applied. Members of higher social ranks—senators, equites, priests, et cetera—would receive choice seating reflective of their position.

In the gospels, Jesus critiques the desire of both scribes and Pharisees to be publicly recognized and to be honored at banquets and synagogue meetings by having the best seats (Mark 23:6 // Matt 23:6 // Luke 20:46). In these passages, public honor is what is at stake. In the parable of the wedding banquet in Luke 14:7–11, however, honor is not portrayed negatively in itself, but it is the presumption of one's own honor that is problematic. It is better to sit in the lowest space and to be upgraded to the seat of honor than to sit in the best seats and to be demoted to a lower position. The Epistle of James addresses a different type of situation, the favoring of a rich person who comes into the believing assembly and is offered a spot to sit as opposed to the poor person who is made to stand or sit on the ground (Jas 2:1–5). As Nancy Jean Vyhmeister (1995, 280) argues, allocated seating here is possibly a reflection of the benefactor potential of each guest; the rich person has much to offer the congregation while the poor person does not. James reconfigures his audience's attitude toward the treatment of the less important, much like Paul's emphasis about how inferior members of the community deserve greater honor in 1 Corinthians (12:24). Although the gospels and James repudiate holders of high offices and the rich for presuming that seats of honor belong to them, such expectations were perfectly in line with ancient practices of priority seating as seen in the inscriptions above. Elite members were not the only ones who would have had to adjust. In assemblies like those whom James addresses, the poor would indeed be shocked to be able to sit in a seat of honor as ones who did not and could not contribute euergetistically.

Given the trajectory in Paul and the Epistle of James toward the elimination of partiality, one might be tempted to posit that the New Testament is unique in its emphasis on those who do not regularly deserve seats of honor in wider social and cultural circumstances. There are a few examples, however, of priority seating for the masses that are similar to the trajectory found in some New Testament passages. Although the community at Qumran clearly prioritized the seating of priests and elders as mentioned in the Serekh documents above (1QS, 1QSa), there were other passages among the scrolls that seem to envision priority seating for more than those who held higher offices. 4Q416, otherwise known as a part of a collection of apocalyptic sapiential works called Musar le-Mevin (Instruction for the Learner), for example, mentions the learner being seated among "the nobles" (4Q416 2 III, 9–11), a possible reference to being seating among angels (see also 4Q417 1 I, 16–18). Second-century seating inscriptions from Gerasa also illuminate an instance where the seemingly undeserved are given priority seating (see Retzleff and Mjely 2004, especially 40–41). While the front eastern *cunei* of the odeum had places for the *boule*, as was typical, and various seats were reserved for members of each tribe from the city throughout, the front western *cunei* surprisingly held places for members of a local linen association. Good seats at public events like the theater could be gained through guilds or professional associations (Retzleff and Mjely 2004, 40). How could members of such a low-paying trade afford the means to have seats on the very front row of the Odeum? Retzleff and Mjely suggest that "the inscription at the odeum of Gerasa suggests that the linen workers there gained some sort of official recognition subsequent to the formation of the original city tribes, from which they originally may have been excluded ... on the basis of their poverty" (41).

While texts from the early Jesus movement stigmatized the desire for seats of honor over and above the care and importance of all members of local assemblies, the New Testament technically never does away with priority seating altogether. What is transformed in passages from the Epistle of James or Paul's first correspondence with the Corinthians are the drawbacks of prioritizing those who would normally get priority seating—that is, the rich and the elite. Such texts never even suggest that having a seat of honor is inherently bad, only that one should be cautious in case it leads to the devaluation of members who appear less important or, worse, is merely gained in the pursuit of vanity (e.g., Matt 23:6).

The presence of priority seating in early Christian communities and assemblies continued long after the books of the New Testament were written. Early Christian texts from the second century onward like the Shepherd of Hermas (Herm. Sim. 3.9.7 [17.7]; Herm. Mand. 11.12 [43.9]), Irenaeus's *Against Heresies* (*Haer.* 4.26.3), and the Didascalia Apostolorum (Did. apost. 2.57–58) assume the presence of "seats of honor." In the Shepherd, what is of concern is not the seats of honor themselves but that the conduct of those who sit on such seats is in line with the best interests of the church, a theme echoing that of the New Testament. The eleventh chapter of the Mandates, for example, warn of a prophet who sits on a chair and deceives the faithful who sit on benches (Herm. Mand. 11.12 [43.9]). Irenaeus warns presbyters for whom the allure of holding a chief seat contaminates the integrity of their service to others (*Haer.* 4.26.3). The Didascalia is not concerned with doing away with designated seating. On the contrary, it provides a detailed seating arrangement. The text is pedantic concerning the placement of presbyters, bishops, laymen, and women. They must be positioned properly, facing the right direction for prayer (east). The elderly and the children and the married women with their children also had their places as well. Like the Epistle of James, the Didascalia also focuses on making sure that visiting members (orthodox or heterodox!), presbyters, bishops, city officials, or the poor have been given a valued place to sit—even so much as encouraging the bishop to give up his seat for a poor visitor, especially if it means he sit on the ground (Did. apost. 2.58.6). For an English translation of these passages from the Didascalia, see Stewart-Sykes 2009, 174–77. Despite the fact that this spatial order *could* be subverted by a surprise visitor to the congregation, the segregation of the whole assembly into groups still reinforced social hierarchy in early Christian communities. Although leaders were warned not to abuse this hierarchy, such structure was nevertheless viewed as important for the stability and harmony of early Christian gatherings. Given that designated seating was ubiquitous in the daily life of peoples throughout the Mediterranean, it is not surprising that early Christians maintained this practice in their own assemblies, albeit occasionally with more flexibility than their pagan neighbors.

Bibliography

Baker, Murray. 2005. "Who Was Sitting in the Theater at Miletos? An Epigraphical Application of a Novel Theory." *JSJ* 36:397–416.
Harrison, James R. 2018. "An Epigraphic Portrait of Ephesus and Its Villages." Pages 1–67 in *Ephesus*. Vol. 3 of *The First Urban Churches*. Edited by James R. Harrison and L. L. Welborn. WGRWSup 9. Atlanta: SBL Press.
Jones, Tamara. 2008. "Seating and Spectacle in the Graeco-Roman World." PhD diss., McMaster University.
Kavanagh, Bernard. 2004. "Elder Corbulo and the Seating Incident." *Historia* 53:379–84.
Moore, Timothy J. 1994–1995. "Seats and Social Status in the Plautine Theater." *CJ* 90:113–23.
Retzleff, Alexandra, and Abdel Majeed Mjely. 2004. "Seat Inscriptions in the Odeum at Gerasa (Jerash)." *BASOR* 334:37–48.
Spigel, Chad. 2012. "Reconsidering the Question of Separate Seating in Ancient Synagogues." *JSJ* 63:62–83.
Stewart-Sykes, Alistair. 2009. *The Didascalia Apostolorum*. Studia Traditionis Theologiae 1. Turnhout: Brepols.
Vyhmeister, Nancy Jean. 1995. "The Rich Man in James 2: Does Ancient Patronage Illumine the Text?" *AUSS* 33:265–83.

15. A Seafarer's Reward: The Imperial Allocation of Honor to Freedmen at Ephesus

James R. Harrison

IEph 5.1487

Wood, app. 5, "Inscriptions from the Odeum," no. 1; *GIBM* 487; Lafoscade 1902, no. 26; *SIG* 838; Abbott and Johnson 1926, 85; *DocsNerva* 72a; Lewis 1974, 26h; Oliver 1989, no. 82A; Drew-Bear and Richard 1994, 742–51; Guerber and Le Bouedec 2013, 9–10, no. 7. Inscribed on the marble cladding of the proscenium (part of the stage) of the bouleuterion (council chamber, town hall). Date: 128/129 CE.

1	Αὐ[το]κράτωρ Καῖσαρ θεοῦ Τ[ραιανοῦ]	Imperator Caesar, son of the divine T[raianus]
2	Παρθ[ι]κοῦ υἱός, θεοῦ Νέρ[ο]υα υ[ἱ]ων[ός,]	Parthicus, grandson of divine Nerva,
3	Τραια[ν]ὸς Ἁδριαν[ὸ]ς Σεβασ[τός, ἀρ]χιερεὺ[ς]	Traianus Hadrianus August[us, Pon]tifex
4	μέγισ[το]ς, δημαρχ[ικῆ]ς ἐξουσί[ας το ι]γ', ὕπατος τὸ γ',	Maximus, tribune for the third time, consul for the third time,
5	πατὴ[ρ πατ]ρίδος Ἐφ[εσί]ων τοῖς ἄ[ρ]χουσ[ι καὶ τῆι β]ουλῆι χαίρειν.	father of the [nat]ion, to the magistrates [and c]ouncil of the Ephesians, greetings.
6	Λ(ούκιος) Ἔ[ρ]αστος καὶ πολε[ί]της ὑ[μ]ῶν εἶναί φ[ησιν, κ]αὶ πολλ[ὰ ἔτη]	Lucius Erastus s[ays] that he is indeed a citizen of yours, and for many [years]
7	πλῖ καὶ τ[ὴ]ν θάλασ[σαν, καὶ ὅ]σα ἀπὸ τούτ[ου δυν]ατὸς [ἦν]	he has sailed the sea; (he says) that so far as he [was ab]le from this,
8	χρήσιμ[ο]ς γενέσ[θαι τῇ πατρ]ίδι, καὶ τοῦ ἔθν[ους] τρ[ὺς] ἡγε-	he became of service [to his native la]nd, and that he always transported (alternatively, "convoyed")

-203-

9 μόνας ἀεὶ δι[α]χομ[ίζειν·] ἐ[μ]οὶ δὲ δ[ὶς] ἤδη συ[νέπλευ]σεν,	the leaders of the people. T[wice] already he has [sailed] with me;
10 τὸ μὲν πρῶτον εἰς Ῥόδον ἀπὸ τῆς Ἐ[φέ]σου κο[μιζ]ομέ[νῳ,]	the first time when traveling to Rhodes from Ephesus,
11 νῦν δὲ ἀπ' Ἐλευσεῖνος πρὸς ὑμᾶς ἀφικ[ν]ουμέν[ῳ· εὔ]χετα[ι]	and now when coming from Eleusis to you. He prays
12 δὲ βουλευτὴς γενέσθαι· κἀγὼ τὴν μὲν [δοκι]μασία[ν ἐ]φ' ὑμεῖν	to become a counsellor. The examination I leave to you.
13 ποιοῦμαι· εἰ δὲ μηδὲν ἐνποδὼν [εἴη αὐτῷ, ἀλλὰ δόξαι τῆς τει]μῆς ἄξ[ι]ος,	On the other hand, should [there be] no impediment [to him but he seem] worthy [of the ho]nor,
14 τὸ ἀργύριον ὅσον διδόασιν οἱ βουλεύοντες [δώσω τῆς ἀρχαι]ρεσίας [ἕ]νεκα.	the money as much as the counsellor's pay [I will pay] for [his election.]
15 εὐτυχεῖτε.	Farewell.

Petitions to the Roman ruler from eastern Mediterranean communities were very common in antiquity, causing the ruler to respond to the issues raised by diplomats or local civic representatives to the issues raised. For example, the many honorific decrees and letters conferred in a single inscription upon Opramoas of Rhodiapolis, the Lycian benefactor, for his extraordinary philanthropic exploits express the local and provincial esteem in which he was held. A resolution of Lycian league appoints envoys to communicate to the Roman ruler Antoninus Pius the provincial goodwill toward Opramoas in the form of a decree and to convey a petition of Xanthos on his behalf (IGRR 3.739.26.55–76). In the inscription, fourteen letters from Antoninus Pius are subsequently cited, mediated via his provincial officials, providing the proof that the Lycian intervention had been favorably received at Rome and that the civic munificence of Opramoas had been officially honored (IGRR 3.739.37–42, 44, 46–51, 59), along with many other commendations from the Lycian league and various luminaries (IGRR 3.739.31–36, 43, 52–58, 60–69). See Danker 1982, §19. This stratospherically effusive example of how petitions were normally answered illustrates why our Ephesian inscription is highly unusual. Instead of responding to a petition, Hadrian directly asks a favor of the magistrates and the council of Ephesus. The inscription regarding Erastos is also unusual for another reason: it is identical to another inscriptional missive from Hadrian (IEph 5.1488) requesting exactly the same favor for Philokyrios. In view of their names, both men were most likely freemen, having joined the imperial fleet with their differing ships, proceeding from Rhodes to Ephesus and from Eleusis to Ephesus.

T. Drew-Bear and F. Richard (1994) argue that these freedmen, belonging to the houses of Ephesian elites, were not transporting Hadrian himself. Rather, the infinitive διακόμιζειν (IEph 5.1487.9) should carry its alternate and simpler meaning of "conveying," as opposed to "carrying over" (LSJ, s.v. "διακομίζω"). This sense is reinforced by συ[νέπλευ]σεν, present in the same line, which has the sense of accompanying by sea. Thus the ships of Erastos and Philokyrios were part of the imperial convoy accompanying Hadrian on two occasions, but who traveled in his own warship. One wonders how both men made contact with Hadrian as part of the much larger fleet, expressing their desires to become councilors at Ephesus. There is no sign that Hadrian was prompted by a petition from a civic group or influential citizen from Ephesus, resulting in a decree in favor of Erastos and Philokyrios (Kokkinia 2017, 381). Certainly a measure of entrepreneurial spirit was required on the part of both men in approaching Hadrian, but presumably their skillful seamanship and faithful service as captains had also impressed him. In contrast to his early imperial predecessors who only ventured outside of Italy for mainly military reasons, Hadrian, after dealing with an initial military crisis in Syria in 123 CE, undertook major tours in Africa and in the East (twice) until 132 CE for nonmilitary considerations, involving prolonged absences from Rome. Thus the opportunity of Hadrian to evaluate the skills of his accompanying sea captains close up would have been sufficient, given the extent and duration of his overseas journeys. See Chowen 1954; Birley 2003; Poignault 2015. Our two documents are also valuable because they add to the very limited documentary evidence we have regarding the traveling companions of Hadrian. Lucius Vitalis, to cite another rare example, abandoned his studies at Rome and accompanied Hadrian on one of his provincial tours (perhaps to Athens?) to study art (*CIL* 5.8991), only to die prematurely during the journey before arriving at his destination. See Chowen 1954, 124.

What do we discern from Hadrian's rhetoric of praise in IEph 5.1487? In Hadrian's letter of recommendation, we witness a delicately worded, carefully balanced weighing of the demands of honor on the part of the Roman ruler for his seafaring clients. However, he also demonstrates respect for the right of the councils of provincial cities to allocate honor to their own citizens without any outside interference, but nevertheless he offers the inducement of imperial benefaction to make the local Ephesian council's favorable decision easier (IEph 5.1487.11–14). Kokkinia (2017, 383) sums up the long-term social and political consequences thus:

> Given how commonly this category of imperial letters was monumentalised, it may seem that cities and individuals subscribed to Aelius Aristides' depiction of the Roman empire as a *polis*, and of the emperor as its most distinguished citizen, the most prominent benefactor, recipient, and source of honours. From that viewpoint, the emperor and his representatives in the empire-wide *polis* were being offered the highest honours, and were expected to offer the greatest benefits in return.

In sum, we have seen that in the early second-century CE provincial cities such as Ephesus negotiated the rhetoric of praise within the ambits, demands, and rewards associated with the imperial authorities. In the middle of the first century CE, Paul, by using the singular verb ποίει, enjoins an unspecified individual within the Roman house and tenement churches to do good (Rom 13:3b: τὸ ἀγαθὸν ποίει) before the watching imperial authorities (13:3a), with a view to earning the ruler's praise (13:4b: ἔπαινον). This use of the imperative is delivered in the wider context of Paul's general endorsement of Greco-Roman honorific rituals in Rom 13:7b (τῷ τὴν τιμὴν τὴν τιμήν). We are seeing here on Paul's part a careful rhetorical balancing of perspectives, in a manner similar to IEph 5.1487.11–14, even though Paul's viewpoint is entirely theocentric. Because of God's sovereign appointment of the imperial authorities (Rom 13:1–2a), the believer is summoned to be obedient to the God-appointed ruler (13:5), who, wielding the sword (13:4b), is a terror to the bad conduct of the disobedient (13:4b). But, in an honorific culture (Rom 13:7b), the very same imperial authorities—whom the apostle ironically strips of their exalted honorific status in the imperial propaganda, reducing them in Old Testament fashion to being God's servants (13:4a, 6b)—give praise to the one who does good. On the Old Testament background to Paul's argument, see Harrison 2011, 300–308. What, then, is driving Paul's rhetoric of praise in the context of mid-50s Neronian Rome?

Bruce W. Winter (1994, 25–40) has proposed in his benefaction hermeneutic for Rom 13:3b–4 and 1 Pet 2:14–15 that the good that the beneficent individual is summoned to do in Rom 13:4b is sponsoring public buildings, supplying grain, constructing roads, or embarking on civic diplomatic missions in Roman civil society. But the idea of Christian individuals acting as wealthy urban benefactors in the mid-first century CE is highly unlikely (Williams 2013). The early Christians did not come close to having the economic resources of an elite Ephesian or a Corinthian civic benefactor, for example. Those believers who had the resources to act as benefactors—that is, in comparison to the other economically challenged believers—were expected to do so within the wider ambits of the ministry of the house churches, not within the civic spaces of the self-promoting urban elites. Thus Winter pushes the traditional benefaction model too far in terms of what was feasible for believers living in *first*-century cities and in terms of what were their priorities in ministry.

The vast economic resources of the Ephesian elites preserved their social insularity as a group as they ostentatiously competed among themselves for precedence in civic benefaction. By contrast, the early Christian communities were interdependent and highly vulnerable to the seasonal fluctuations of economic privation and the exploitation of the powerful (e.g., Gal 2:9–10; 1 Cor 11:22; 2 Cor 8:1–5; cf. Acts 11:27–30; Jas 2:1–7; 5:1–6; 1 Tim 5:5; Heb 10:34). Hence Paul speaks practically about meeting the needs of the saints and extending hospitality toward strangers (Rom 12:13), including doing good to the enemy (12:20–21). He also warns believers against assuming the superior airs and competitiveness for honor displayed by the urban elites in their social relations (Rom 12:10b, 16). The wealthy within the Christian community, therefore, give out of their surplus so that there might be equality and a balanced reciprocity in resources among believers (1 Cor 16:2; 2 Cor 8:13–15). See Welborn 2012.

Perhaps Paul expected churches to establish networks of benefaction, as occasion demanded, spanning the eastern and western Mediterranean basin for specific ministry projects like the Jerusalem collection, but even this did not fit the elite models of urban benefaction that confined munificence to one's own citizens. The inter-urban, cross-provincial, and transethnic dimension of the Jerusalem collection offered a dynamic model of beneficence in the eastern Mediterranean that could be adopted when regional crises unexpectedly impoverished believers. Last, the Roman ruler's praise would possibly be won, Paul had hoped, because of the social cohesion that the early Christians sponsored through their impartial service of the needy, inside and outside of their communities. It would perhaps break down the stereotype of the *Christianoi* being "haters of humanity" (Tacitus, *Ann.* 14.44; *Hist.* 5.5; Minucius Felix, *Oct.* 9.5–6). For the above three paragraphs, see more fully Harrison 2016, 362–63.

Bibliography

Abbott, Frank F., and Allan C. Johnson. 1926. *Municipal Administration in the Roman Empire*. Princeton: Princeton University Press.

Birley, A. R. 2003. "Hadrian's Travels." Pages 425–41 in *The Representation and Perception of Roman Imperial Power*. Edited by Paul Erdkamp, O. Hekster, G. de Kleijn, Stephan T. A. M. Mols, and Lukas de Blois. Leiden: Brill.

Chowen, Richard H. 1954. "Traveling Companions of Hadrian." *CJ* 50.3:122–24.

Danker, Frederick W. 1982. *Benefactor: Epigraphic Study of a Graeco-Roman and New Testament Semantic Field*. St. Louis: Clayton.

Drew-Bear, T., and F. Richard. 1994. "Hadrien et Erastos, nauclère d'Éphèse." Pages 742–51 in *L'Afrique, la Gaule, la Religion à l'époque romaine: Mélanges à la mémoire de M. Le Glay*. Edited by Y. Le Bohec. Brussels: Latomus.

Guerber, Éric, and Gérard Le Bouedec. 2013. *Gens de mer: Ports et cités aux époques ancienne, médiévale et modern*. Rennes: Presses universitaires de Rennes.

Harrison, James R. 2011. *Paul and the Imperial Authorities at Thessalonica and Rome: A Study in the Conflict of Ideology*. WUNT 273. Tübingen: Mohr Siebeck.

———. 2016. "Sponsors of *Paideia*: Ephesian Benefactors, Civic Virtue and the New Testament." *EC* 7:346–67.

Kokkinia, Christina. 2017. "Martyriai: Civic Honours and Imperial Government." Pages 371–85 in *The Politics of Honour in the Greek Cities of the Roman Empire*. Edited by Anna Heller and Onno van Nijf. Leiden: Brill.

Lafoscade, Léon Jules. 1902. *De epistulis (aliisque titulis) imperatorum magistratuumque romanorum quas ab aetate Augusti usque ad Constantinum graece scriptas, lapides papyrive servaverunt*. Edebant fratres Le Bigot, Insulis.

Lewis, Naphtali. 1974. *The Roman Principate: 27 B.C.–285 A.D. Greek Historical Documents*. Toronto: Hakkert.

Oliver, James H. 1989. *Greek Constitutions of Early Roman Emperors from Inscriptions and Papyri*. Philadelphia: American Philosophical Society.

Poignault, Rémy. 2015. "Les voyages de l'empereur Hadrien: des sources antiques à Mémoires d'Hadrien." Pages 89–103 in *Nouveaux horizons sur l'espace antique et modern*. Edited by Marie-Ange Julia. Bordeaux: Ausonius Éditions.

Welborn, L. L. 2012. "'That There Might Be Equality': The Contexts and Consequences of a Pauline Ideal." *NTS* 57:73–90.

Williams, T. B. 2013. "Benefiting the Community through Good Works? The Economic Feasibility of Civic Benefaction in 1 Peter." *JGRChJ* 9:147–95.

Winter, Bruce W. 1994. *Seek the Welfare of the City: Christians as Benefactors and Citizens*. Grand Rapids: Eerdmans.

Wood, John Turtle. 1877. *Discoveries at Ephesus*. London: Longmans, Green.

16. Honoring the Concord of the Ephesian Demos

James R. Harrison

IEph 6.2052

FiE 2, no. 52 (*editio princeps*). This white marble square base, simply profiled, was found at the mouth of the cross passage from the stage corridor in a room behind the stage building. This room, used by the actors either for dressing or another auxiliary purpose, was located under the Roman *logeion* pavement. The pavement—that is, the front of the Roman stage occupied by the speakers or actors—was 2.7 meters higher than the previous Hellenistic orchestra, the traditional site for staging plays. For Vitruvius's definition of the *logeion*, see *Arch.* 5.7.2. See IEph 6.2039 (= *OGIS* 510: mid-second century CE) for a detailed description of the repair of the Ephesian theater in the Antonine period (Csapo and Slater 1995, §121). Date: 132/214 CE, according to Donald McCabe (PHI Ephesos 1893).

[ἡ φιλοσέβ]αστος Ἐφεσίων [βουλὴ]	The Augustus-loving council of the Ephesians (honor)
2 [τὸ]ν δὶς ν[ε]οκόρον Ἐφεσίων δῆμο[ν]	the twice neokorate people of the Ephesians
ἀρετῆς ἕνεκα καὶ ὁμονοίας,	on account of (its) virtue and concord,
4 ἐπιμεληθέντος τῆς ἀναστάσεως τοῦ	(the person) having taken care of the erection of the
[ἀ]νδριάντος [.] Οὐλπίου Στράτωνος	statue [.] (being) Oulpios Straton.

The benefactor who provided the statue of the Ephesian demos at the Ephesian theater, Oulpios Straton, is known from other Ephesian inscriptions because of his prestigious priestly family descendants. He was (1) the father of Oulpios Moudrianos (IEph 3.989.3–4) and (2) the grandfather of Oulpia Euodia Moudiane, a priestess of Artemis (IEph 3.989.1–2), and also (3) the grandfather of Oulpia Strato, the *kosmeteira* ("adorner") of the goddess (IEph 3.989.8-9). The latter word was the official title of young girls who dressed the statue of Artemis (IEph 3.892, 980, 983-984, 989; 7.1.3034). On the role of the Ephesian priestess and *kosmeteira*, see Harrison 2012. Whether the council approached Oulpios Straton, an elite dignitary of Ephesus, to be the benefactor who consequently funded the statue and the inscribing of its base, or whether, as a member of the *boule* of the Ephesians, he offered his services voluntarily, is impossible to determine.

It is intriguing that ὁμόνοια ("sameness of mind," "agreement in sentiments," "unity") is not used in the New Testament despite what potentially seems a promising semantic range emphasizing harmony, concord, and unity (Judge 1982, 106). What made the New Testament writers shy away from a word that could have been enlisted in the rhetoric of unity and reconciliation? In order to understand how ὁμόνοια and its Latin equivalent *concordia* ("harmony," "peace," "concord," "union," "amity") functioned in the first and early second century CE, we will explore three themes: (1) the cult of the goddess Homonoia at Ephesus; (2) ὁμόνοια and *concordia* in their imperial context; and (3) ὁμόνοια in its epigraphic ethical context. From there, we will be able to discern more clearly why New Testament writers like Paul did not appropriate the word as a theological resource.

1. The Goddess Homonoia at Ephesus

Apart from a fragmentary reference to the virtue of ὁμόνοια in IEph 2.1479, supplementary to IEph 6.2052, only three other occurrences of *homonoia* appear in the Ephesian corpus, each referring the goddess Homomoia (Thérialt 1996, 5-70, esp. 61-62). First, there is mention of a priest of the cult of Homonoia ("Preimigenes [priest] of Homonoia"), demonstrating that the cult was well attested in Ephesus (IEph 5.1600 [180-192 CE]).

Second, in the bequest of C. Vibius Salutaris, an image of the goddess Homonoia is said to be standing in the first sector of the theater of Ephesus (IEph 1a.27.440 [104 CE]). G. Thérialt (1996, 61; see also Rogers 1992, 226-27) concludes in regards to the strategic placement of the image that "it seems that the Ephesians, in the second century of our era, tried to encourage the members of the council and the assembly to meet in harmony and calm by installing monuments in the meeting places consecrated to Homonoia." This is the case with our ὁμονοία inscription and its statue, found under the Roman *logeion* pavement behind the stage building. The civic ethic of ὁμονοία characterizing the Ephesian boule operates in a city where the goddess Homonoia is regularly honored in the city's public places and, as we will see, in religious and imperial processions.

Third, a fortnightly procession of thirty-one statues and images, representing imperial family members and various divinities, was undertaken each fortnight following a prescribed route through the city of Ephesus. This extravaganza was funded by the extraordinarily generous bequest of the Ephesian benefactor, C. Vibius Salutaris (Rogers 1991; Kokkinia 2017–2018). Significantly, an image of Homonoia was carried in the procession, and, upon reaching its point of arrival, it was placed at the regular assembly (IEph 1a.27.470–477): "Equally a silver image of Sebaste Homonoia Chrysophoros, weight of six pounds, with the silver plating of its base, dedicated to Artemis, and to whoever the priests who bear the gold, and the sacred victors of the city shall be placed at every assembly above the block, where the sacred victors sit."

In sum, this Ephesian procession of a vast array of images of divinities, along with the statues of members of the Antonine household, underscored the vitality and continuing importance of the *pax Romana* in the eastern provinces in the early second century CE. The divine concord associated with the Roman Empire had long ago been celebrated in an inscription from Halicarnassus (2 BCE) where Augustus was eulogized as the chosen instrument of Providence bringing social stability: "there is peace on land and at sea; cities are in bloom with good order, harmony [ὁμονοίαι], and prosperity; every good thing is at its zenith and point of maturity; there is a culmination of auspicious hopes for the future, and there is the present cheerfulness of men who have been filled" (*GIBM* 4.1.894.8–12). The same rhetoric appears in Aelius Aristides's Roman oration (*Or.* 26 [fl. 117–181 CE]) in which the concord of the Roman Empire is similarly idealized. Aristides's oration develops in a Flavian context some of the implications of Aristides's three treatises on ὁμόνοια (*Or.* 23–25), each addressed respectively to the citizens of Asia and the Rhodians (Kinlaw 2013, 203–30).

2. Homonoia, Concordia, and Twice Neokorate Ephesus

In the case of the city of Rome, Concordia, the Roman equivalent of the Greek goddess Homonoia, had long been worshiped in the city from the early republic. In 367 BCE, Marcus Camillus erected a temple to Concordia in the forum to celebrate the accord between patricians and plebeians (Plutarch, *Cam.* 42; Momigliano 1942; see also Skard 1932; Richard 1963;

Keil 2013; Akar 2013). The temple was restored in 121 BCE to affirm the renewed harmony between the Senate and the populares after the social dislocation caused by Tiberius and Gaius Gracchus (Appian, *Bell. civ.* 1.26; Plutarch, *Ti. C. Gracch.* 17.6).

However, Cicero shifted away from the traditional Roman understanding of *concordia* (the harmony of the republic) to new expressions of the ideal in the face of social disintegration and the threats posed to his own political career. In 63 BCE, Cicero suggested the establishment of a *concordia ordinum* (*Att.* 1.18.3)—an alliance between the senate and equites—with a view to maintaining the liberty and stability of the republic (*Clu.* 152; *Agr.* 3.4). Only concord between the senate and the equites could stave off the threats to traditional noble rule posed by the rebellion of Cataline (*Mur.* 1, 78; *Cat.* 4.15), the eventual split between the senate and the equites (*Att.* 1.17.8–10), and by the emergence of the anti-senatorial First Triumvirate (60–53 BCE).

After Cicero's exile from Rome in 58 BCE, the orator abandoned the alliance between the senate and the equites for an alliance of all loyal citizens of any rank who would support the cause of the republic over against the populares (*Har. resp.* 60–61; *Rep.* 1.49; 2.69). Cicero sums up this consensus of all good men under "the more inclusive concept of *concordia civium* or *concordia civitatis*" (Temelini 2002, 7; cf. Lobur 2008). Inevitably, this led Cicero to oppose Antony in 44 BCE, whom Cicero styled a threat to the republican consensus and harmony (*consensum et concordium*: *Phil.* 4.14; cf. 8.8). Cicero, however, paid the cost for his stance with his life the next year.

By the time of the Augustan principate, the cult of Concordia was beginning to be integrated into the Julio-Claudian cult. Livia, the wife of Augustus, erected a shrine to Concordia (Ovid, *Fast.* 6.637–640) in the Porticus Liviae, which the Roman ruler had built in her honor at Rome (Dio Cassius, *Hist. Rom.* 54.23.6). No archaeological remains of its existence have been found (Flory 1984, 309–10). However, the full Julio-Claudian numismatic appropriation of the motif of Concordia only emerged late in the Julio-Claudian period and during the civil wars (67–69 CE) when the goddess Concordia begins to appear regularly on coin reverses. The seated goddess Concordia is variously depicted (sitting on a throne or low-backed chair, with feet upon a stool, or before a lighted altar) and holds diverse objects in each hand (patera, corn ears, olive branch, branches, scepter, standards surmounted by small boar, cornucopia). Regarding Concordia on the Latin West coinage, see Noreña 2011, 132–35.

The coin legends are as follows: CONCORDIA AUGUSTA (*RIC* 1, §48); CONCORD (*RIC* 1, §91); CONCORD AUG SC (*RIC* 1, §§339, 380–384); CONCORDIA (*RIC* 1, §§132, 134); CONCORDIA AUGUSTI SC (*RIC* 1, §§126, 161–162); CONCORDIA PR (*RIC* 1, §§66, 72–73, 89–91); CONCORDIA PRAETORIAORVM (*RIC* 1, §§118, 120; §19); CONCORDIA PROVINCIA (*RIC* 1, §125); CONCORDIA PROVINCIARVM (*RIC* 1, §§35, 49, 104–108, 180–183). A few of the aforementioned legends are worth highlighting. CONCORDIA AUGUSTA represents Poppaea, Nero's wife, who appears as Concordia. Marital harmony within the imperial family is thereby emphasized, a motif replicated in other coin issues (Maier 2018, 96 n. 100). CONCORDIA PROVINCIA/ PROVINCIARVM belongs to the year 69 CE, the year of the four emperors. Galba was asserting the true source of his legitimacy and support as the Roman ruler: namely, the provinces of Gaul and Spain. In a counterblast to this numismatic propaganda, Vitellius responds that he had the support of the praetorian guard (CONCORDIA PRAETORIAORVM). In this tense atmosphere of claim and counter-claim, each claimant for the rule of the Roman Empire in 69 CE disengages with the Neronian past and establishes his own unique claim to Concordia, differentiating his power base from his predecessor (Ellithorpe 2017, 94–98).

In the Flavian period, the numismatic iconography of the goddess Concordia largely remains the same, but there are slight variations to the Julio-Claudian coin issues, including the veiled head of Concordia being rendered alone in one instance. In the coin issues of the seated goddess, a statue of Spes ("Hope") is placed under her elbow or stands behind her. Additionally, she sacrifices out of a patera over an altar. In an innovation, Concordia is presented as standing, occasionally leaning on a column.

Many of the same legends reappear (*RIC* 2, "index IV," pp. 321–33): CONCOR AUG SC; CONCORD; CONCORD AUG SC; CONCORDIA; CONCORDIA AVGVS; CONCORDIA AVGVST; CONCORDIA AUGVSTA (with Domitia on the obverse: *RIC* 2 §§215–215b); CONCORDIA AUGVSTI. There are innovations such as CONCDIAE (*RIC* 2:386: see asterisked footnote), showing Hadrian and Sabina clasping hands. Once again, the motif of marital harmony within the imperial family, noted above, reappears. CONCORDIA DAC or DACICO are variations on Concordia seated on a throne (*RIC* 2:405 n.), accompanied by Spes standing on a low column: it represents Hadrian's public propaganda regarding the hoped-for outcome of his two wars against the Parthians in Dacia (101–102, 105–106 CE). CONCORDIA EXERCITVVM ("Agreement of the armies": *RIC* 2 §§2, 14, 26) and CONCORDIA EXERCITVVM S C (*RIC* 2 §§69, 79, 95) reveal clasped hands, holding a legionary eagle, and in some cases, resting on a prow. In this instance, the amicable relations of Nerva with the Senate and the army is highlighted, with added reference to the navy where the prow appears (*RIC* 2 §§3, 15, 27, 53–54, 70, 80–81, 96–97). CONCORDIA SENATVI S C ("Senatorial Accord": *RIC* 2 §418) shows Vespasian standing to the left, holding Victory, and being crowned by the Senate. Last, one coin of Hadrian's wife, Sabina, has no legend but presents Concordia seated behind a statue of Spes, holding a patera and with cornucopiae under her seat (*RIC* 2 §§390–393). In this unconventional personification of Sabina, the empress is represented by herself as the exemplum of domestic harmony, a striking tribute to her perceived public virtue.

In conclusion, the coins of Vespasian and Hadrian demonstrate that the period of military claim and counterclaim in 69 CE was over (Stevenson 2010). The peace of the Roman Empire had been secured by the Flavian military conquest of the barbarian Parthians in Dacia; the traditional household value of marital harmony is again being upheld in contrast to its devaluation under Nero (despite the personification of Domitia as Concordia); the Senate needs no longer fear a renewed outbreak of rogue generals with their personal armies fighting for the control of the empire, as had occurred after Nero's death, because of the new spirit of consensus that now existed between the Flavian rulers, the Senate, army, and navy.

Nevertheless, the scarcity of reference to the *virtue* of ὁμόνοια, as opposed to the goddess Homonia/Concordia, is surprising, given the vast size of Ephesian epigraphic corpus, as well as the frequency of reference to ὁμόνοια as a political virtue in the inscriptions from the other Greek regions and cities of the eastern Mediterranean basin (e.g., in a search of PHI, the region of Attica has twenty-three inscriptions; Cos and Calymna, fifteen inscriptions; Priene, seven inscriptions). This does not mean, however, that Ephesus was indifferent to ὁμόνοια as a virtue. The epithet of Ephesus being "twice neokorate" is important in this regard. Our inscription, as we will see, belongs to a period of inter-city tensions over precedence in Asia Minor and the Ephesian people are accordingly praised for their ὁμόνοια in this situation.

In the first century CE, the epithet *neokoros* was applied to cities that had dedicated a temple to the current emperor (Burrell 2004; Friesen 1993; Ricl 2011; Theophilos 2018). Pergamum in Mysia was first given the honor by Augustus in 29 BCE (Dio Cassius, *Hist. Rom.* 51.20.6–9;

Burrell 2004, 17–37), edging out Ephesus because it was believed to be totally devoted to the worship of Artemis (Tacitus, *Ann.* 4.55). The next to receive the title in 23 BCE was Ionian Smyrna under Tiberius (Tacitus, *Ann.* 4.55–56; Burrell 2004, 38–54) and then Ionian Miletus under Gaius in 40 CE (*DocsGaius* 127; Dio Cassius, *Hist. Rom.* 59.28; Burrell 2004, 55–58). Finally, Ionian Ephesus received the *neokoros* title under Nero (coin legend: *SNGvA* 7863; IEph 6.2034: "the *neokoros* city of the Augusti of the Ephesians"; cf. Burrell 2004, 59–85). One can readily imagine the intense competition between the three Ionian neokorate cities, Smyrna, Miletus, and Ephesus, for precedence in the region. Moreover, Pergamum (IPergamon 2.299; 3.10, 11, 23, 24, 57), Smyrna (ISmyrn 637, 646, 649, 655, 666) and Ephesus (IEph 2.300A, 2.304A, 3.799, 4.1065, 5.1900.3, 5.1902.3, 5.1906.2, 5.1908.3, 5.1910.1, 5.1910.2, 5.1923.4, 5.1929.2, 6.2039, 6.2040, 6.2054, 6.2055, 6.2056, 6.2066, 6.2532, 7.1.3052, 7.2.4336) also claimed to be the metropolis of Asia, jealously jockeying against each other for primacy in Asia Minor.

Pergamum was the first city to gain twice *neokoros* status under Trajan (ca. 102 CE): "The council and the people of the metropolis of Asia and first twice *neokoros* city of the Pergamum people" (IPergamon Asklepieion 20). Ephesus would only achieve the same status under Hadrian (twice *neokoros* coin legend: SNGvA 1884). An inscription from Athens, a statue base of Hadrian from the Olympieion, sets forth the new international status of Ephesus in Asia Minor, leaving no doubt about Ephesus's perceived superiority to Pergamum: "The *first and greatest* metropolis of Asia and twice neokoros city of the Ephesians" (IG 2.2.3297).

This heated competition for precedence and the potential for discord among the Asian cities helps us to see the wider significance of the Ephesian ὁμόνοια coinage in the Flavian period (Thraede 1994; Lotz 1999, 180–85; Kienast 1995; Theophilos 2018; Kampmann 1998). The jealousies and disputes between Pergamum, Ephesus, and Smyrna were proverbial (Dio Chrysostom, *2 Tars.* 34; *In cont.* 48; Aelius Aristides, *Or.* 23), and the rivalry among Ionian cities, noted above, was intense. In this fractious context, ὁμόνοια coinage was minted in the Roman province of Asia, displaying the symbols of two or more cities side by side, mostly the distinctive gods honored in these cities. In Roman Asia, more than seventy-eight cities expressed over 110 combinations of ὁμόνοια ("concord") declarations (Baukova 2016, 6). Ephesus itself issued or had issued on its behalf *homonoia* coins with at least twenty-three other cities. To be sure, some of these numismatic affirmations of *homonoia* and alliance may well reflect trade relationships or the ties established by the common mythological identity of the cities (e.g., Hierapolis's patron god Apollo was the brother of Ephesian Artemis: Lotz 1999, 181). But, more fundamentally, *homonoia* agreements, symbolized by the coinage issues, were important ways of defusing inter-city tensions. Thus *homonoia* coins between Ephesus and the cities of Pergamum (Franke and Nollé 1997, §§305-311: cf. Kampmann 1998), Smyrna (Franke and Nollé 1997, §§305-311: cf. Ersoy 2017, 105-6) and Miletus (Mionnet 3.170, 3.793) were issued, along with many other cities.

However, periodic flashpoints occurred, undermining the (provisional) concord established by the issues of *homonoia* coinage. In a letter of Antoninus Pius to the Ephesians (IEph 5.1487, repeated twice more in 5.1489A and 5.1490 [140-144 CE]), we observe the tensions that arose when mistakes (deliberate snubs?) in honorific rituals occurred. As noted, each city had claimed to be the metropolis of Asia. Ephesus wrote to Antoninus, possibly in 143 CE, complaining that Smyrna and Pergamum were omitting the proper honorific titles when referring to their city. In a conciliatory letter of response, Pius stipulates that each city had to give mutual recognition to each other by including all the appropriate titles in their diplomatic correspondence and (speculatively) official protocols when ambassadors arrived in each city:

> I approved the way the Pergamenes in their epistle to you employed the titles which I permitted your city to use, I think that the Smyrneans have omitted them accidentally in the decree concerning the joint sacrifice and that in the future they will comply willingly, if, that is, you too appear in your letters to them to be mentioning their city in the manner that is becoming and has been decided.

A *homonoia* issue (Franke and Nollé 1997, §§305-311) was subsequently minted by Ephesus celebrating the restoration of concord between each of the cities, although no coin issue was forthcoming from Pergamum and Smyrna. The reverse shows the cult statue of Artemis Ephesia in the middle facing the front, flanked by Smyrnaean Nemesis to the left and by Pergameme Asklepios to the right. The centrality of position of Artemis Ephesia on the coin symbolically asserts the preeminence of Ephesus over the cult gods of the other two cities. Moreover, the threefold rendering of Antoninus's letter in the city at different sites—that is, the bouleuterion, the harbor gymnasium, and a site now unknown to us—was a not-too-subtle epigraphic acclamation of Ephesus's triumph over its rivals. The so-called *concordia* established was little more than diplomatic parlance.

The establishment of Julio-Claudian and Flavian concord throughout the empire, along with its outworking in the *homonoia* coinage of the Greek cities in Roman Asia, is an ambiguous, rivalry ridden, status conscious, and (ultimately) fragile construct. We gain glimmerings here why the apostle Paul would have had deep reservations about appealing terminologically to ὁμονοία as a leitmotif for his own theological understanding of unity and reconciliation in Christ.

3. The Epigraphic Significance of *homonoia* Phrases: A Study of Semantic Domains

The Greek equivalent of *concordia*, ὁμόνοια, was considered the greatest blessing to Hellenistic cities, in which senators and the best men were united and factions were dispelled (Xenophon, *Mem.* 4.4.16; Lysias 18.17). Interstate rivalries were ameliorated by fostering ὁμόνοια ("political concord"), as the legends and iconography of coins from the cities of Asia Minor, discussed above, demonstrate. The motif was employed by historians (Polybius, Appian, Dionysius of Harlicarnassus) and orators (Antiphon, Dio Chrysostom, Aelius Aristides) (see Welborn 1993, 5–6 n. 10; 1997, 1–75). What has not been sufficiently investigated are the semantic domains in which ὁμόνοια occurs in epigraphic contexts: What ethical import did the word have, if any? What was the relationship between the boule and the demos in the promotion of *homonoia* in the eastern Mediterranean basin?

An important perspective that emerges from the inscriptions is that the word ὁμόνοια often occurs in phrases commencing with εἰς/ἐπί/ὑπέρ, followed by civic welfare formulations that are expressed as doublets, triplets, or quadruplets. The aim of the phrases is to state succinctly, in stereotypical manner, the projected civil outcomes, either decreed (δεδόχθαι) for the demos by the elites or enacted on their behalf (ὑπέρ) by the benefactors and dignitaries of the city. Furthermore, phrases commencing with μετά/μεθ' illustrate the manner in which provisions of the decree or benefactor are to be carried out. As minute as these phrases are in the overall inscription, they reveal in miniature the civic ideal of a harmonious city in the eastern Mediterranean basin. Sometimes ὁμόνοια appears alone ("to establish the citizens in concord" [εἰς ὁμόνοιαν] IG 12.3.172; cf. 12.5.870; ISmyr 50, 579I), but normally the construction has multiple elements. Samples of the phrases, with their accompanying doublet, triplet, or quadruplet formulations, are set out below.

Doublets

- "for [εἰς] the growth and concord [ὁμόνοιαν] of the (citizens) of Lesbos" (IG 12sup.136)
- "with a view to [ἐπί] the safety and concord [ὁμονοίᾳ] of the citizens" (Staatsverträge 3.539.2 [Miletos])
- "choosing beforehand the people of Priene for [εἰς] concord [ὁμόνοιαν] and good will" (IPriene 8)
- "for [εἰς] beneficence and [concord] [ὁμονοίαι]" (IPergamon 2.256)
- "safety of the people and concord [ὁμονοίας]" (IPerge 236)
- "he sacrificed oxen from his own means for everyone, praying to the gods on behalf of [ὑπέρ] the safety and concord of the people" (MDAI[A] 32:278, no. 11)
- "and to Pluto and all the gods and everyone (else) on behalf of [ὑπέρ] the concord [ὁμονοίας] and safety of both the people and King Ariarathos" (ICos ED 5)
- "by those accomplishing something with a view to [ἐπί] good conduct and concord [ὁμονοίαι]" (IPergamon 2.256).

Triplets

- "for [εἰς] the safety and health and concord [ὁμονοίαι] of the craftsmen and the Magnesian people" (IMagnesia 54)
- Sometimes a triplet is introduced by a participial clause, as opposed to a phrase prefaced with preposition: "and of those increasing the just (attributes) of kindliness and friendship and concord [ὁμονοίας]" (SEG 12:511).

Quadruplets

- "for [εἰς] the good fortune and health and safety and concord [ὁμόνοιαν] of the Kamarinaioi and the Koioi" (IG 11.4.1.223)
- "for [εἰς] these (people) was peace, good order, prosperity and concord [ὁμονοία]" (IG 12.5.906).

μετά/μεθ' phrases

- "with all concord [(ὁ)μον(οία)ς] and justice" (IDidyma 486)
- "with peace and also (with) all concord [ὁμονοίας]" (IKret. 3.4.9).

Here we see that that ὁμόνοια belongs to a wide domain of words that, in the configurations above, revolve around the general welfare of the city. But, significantly, ὁμόνοια is a crucial value that consistently occurs across the semantic domains outlined above. Divine concord is the inevitable result within the city when appropriate cultic piety is demonstrated by elite benefactors towards the city's gods (MDAI[A] 32:278, no. 11; IPreine 113). Furthermore, when the council and aristocratic elites are functioning harmoniously for the sake of its inhabitants, concord should be the social experience of the citizenry and the local associations (e.g., IMagnesia 54, above).

An inscription from Perge in Pamphylia is interesting for its similarities and differences to our Ephesian inscription above (IEph 6.2052). The inscription says: "The council (erected this monument) on behalf of [ὑπέρ] the safety [σωτηρίας] of the people and concord [ὁμονοίας]" (IPerge 236 [first–second century CE]). Here, the elite members of Perge council erect the monument *on behalf of the σωτηρία* of the people of the city. But, significantly, neither concord nor any other virtue is ascribed in honor of the people of Perge, in sharp contrast to our Ephesian inscription. Indeed, ὁμόνοια functions in the Perge boule inscription more as a general wish for the city, a rhetorical flourish at the end of the inscription. In other words, the people bring *nothing ethically* to the life of the city in terms of ὁμόνοια. So our inscription from Ephesus is unusual in that the elite Ephesian council honors *the people* of the city on account of (ἕνεκα) their ἀρετή and ὁμόνοια. Most other inscriptions make it plain that the elites establish ὁμόνοια in the city. This is well exemplified in an honorific inscription from Thracian Perinthos, which praises its high-profile recipient as "the most illustrious and unsullied leader, M. Oulpios Senekio Satourninos, the patron [προστάτην] of the concord [ὁμονοίας] of the city" (IMT Kyz Kapu Dağ 1449).

Why, then, did the Ephesian council decide to honor the people of Ephesus for its virtue and concord with an inscription and statue in a prominent public place? There is no direct contextual evidence that throws any light on the reason in the case of this inscription, but we can posit a possible explanation on the basis of the wider literary and Ephesian epigraphic evidence. It is clear that civic riots (Kelly 2007), corruption among the elites, and ravages of *invidia* ("jealousy"; see Konstan and Rutter 2003) periodically broke out among the associations and elites of Ephesus. The evidence is telling, including (1) the silversmiths' association riot at the theater during Paul's visit to the city (Acts 19:23–41), (2) the riots associated with the baker's association (IEph 2.215 [200 CE]), (3) Claudius's concern over the embezzlement of funds raised by the illegal sale of imperial priesthoods to the highest bidder (IEph 1a.18b.11–22 [44 CE]), and (4) the outbreak of *invidia* among the elites over a prominent civic benefactor, addressed in Antoninus Pius's letter to the Ephesians (IEph 5.1491 [145 CE]). These tensions, by no means atypical, could undermine the concord of any city-state, let alone Ephesus. So the Ephesian council astutely praised the people for their unity of purpose and concord at this period of the Antonine era, with a view to securing its continuance well into the future. This tactic represents a sophisticated form of social and political manipulation, needless to say, where the hierarchical control of the elites is reinforced by accentuating the benefits of conformity to existing social structures on the part of those who belong to the lower echelons of the social pyramid.

I conclude with three final observations from the epigraphic evidence touching on the ethical, political, and religious implications of ὁμόνοια. First, a clear instance where ὁμόνοια is given sharp ethical focus is found in one of the injunctions from the Dephic canon where the elite ephebes of the gymnasium at Aï-Kanoum at Bactria are individually exhorted to "pursue consensus" (ὁμόνοιαν δίωκε; IEstremo Oriente 383; see also Harrison 2019, 173–216). Second, in a 287 BCE decree from Cos, the council decides to sacrifice an ox with gilded horns to Pythian Apollo on behalf of the safety of the Greeks. The council makes a vow that good things would occur for the people of Cos and that public affairs would be administered with concord (μεθ' ὁμονοίας) in their democracy (ἐν δαμοκρατίαι; SIG 398 [287 BCE]). Thus, in this Hellenistic age inscription at least, ὁμόνοια is closely associated with democracy, as opposed to oligarchy, in the cities of the Greeks. Last, in a treaty-oath between three Greek cities (Reynolds 1982, §1 [late second–first century BCE]), we see the close connection between the goddess Homonoia—associated here with Zeus Philios and Dea Roma—and the ὁμόνοια sponsored between the Greek cities and Rome, who is the ultimate arbiter of peace in Asia Minor (Reynolds 1982, §8). Importantly, the language of eternity is attached to ὁμόνοια alone, thereby signaling its centrality among the semantic domains associated with civic welfare in political and diplomatic discourse:

> To Zeus Philios, Concord ['Ομονοίαι] and Dea Roma; (dedicated by) the Peoples of Plarasa/Aphrodisias, of Cibyra and of Tabae who have taken oaths over newly-burnt offerings and made blood-offerings for their natural alliance, eternal concord [ὁμονοίας (ἀι)ωνίου], and brotherhood with each other.

4. Why Is *homonoia* Absent from New Testament Discourse?

It is curious that the word ὁμόνοια is absent from 1 Corinthians, which so extensively deals with Corinthian discord throughout the epistle (1 Cor 1:10; 12:25). Four New Testament scholars have argued that *homonoia* discourse, as employed in Greco-Roman rhetoric, has rhetorically shaped Paul's response to the Corinthian divisions in the body of Christ, as well as his rhetoric in Ephesians (assuming Pauline authorship of the epistle).

Margaret M. Mitchell has argued that 1 Corinthians is a unified deliberative letter that urges concord in the face of Corinthian factionalism (1 Cor 1:10; σχίσμα). In response to the divisiveness undermining unity in Christ, Paul employs a series of topoi found in Greco-Roman deliberative rhetoric: namely, (1) an appeal to advantage (Mitchell 1991, 25–39; see 1 Cor 6:12; 7:35; 10:33; 12:7); (2) the citation of exempla (Mitchell 1991, 39–60; see 1 Cor 4:16; 11:1); (3) the motif of factionalism (Mitchell 1991, 65–80; see 1 Cor 1:10; 11:18; 12:25); (4) terminology derived from ancient politics (Mitchell 1991, 68–99; see 1 Cor 1:11, 13; 3:3, 4); and (5) the motif of concord (Mitchell 1991, 60–64, 99–11; see 1 Cor 3:9–17). In so doing, the apostle sought to persuade the Corinthians regarding the foolishness of their schisms over leadership (1 Cor 1:11–4:21) and, citing example-by-relentless example, to convict them of the destructiveness of their self-seeking behavior in multiple areas of church life (1 Cor 5–15). As Mitchell (1991, 297) sums up, Paul's argument, "centred in the προθέσις in 1:10, can be well be understood, both in terms of its content and compositional structure, by comparison with other Greco-Roman discourses which urge unity on divided groups." On discord in the Pastorals against the backdrop of ὁμόνοια, see Maier 2018, 173–79.

Dale B. Martin (1995, 47), after analyzing the ideology of *homonoia* in the ancient rhetoricians, proposes that "1 Corinthians is a *homonoia* letter." Martin insightfully writes:

> Paul's appropriation of the rhetoric of unity is surprising and quite at odds with the dominant goal of *homonoia* speeches, which is to solidify the social hierarchy by averting lower-class challenges to the so-called natural status structures that prevail in society. Paul is well acquainted with the rhetoric of concord, but in 1 Corinthians he turns it against its usual role as a prop for upper-class ideology. (47)

This social tour de force was accomplished by Paul advocating "what upper class ideology feared the most: the disruption of the stable hierarchy of the political and cosmic body" (68). Instead the apostle advocated a radical reversal of status for the sake of unity (69–136).

L. L. Welborn (1997, 1–42) has argued that it is not a theological controversy but rather an internal power struggle among the Corinthian house churches that motivates Paul's response in 1 Cor 1–4 to the internal schisms of 1 Cor 1:12. Each expression of these divisions was characterized by the partisan party politics of antiquity. The divisions were shaped by social and economic inequality (1 Cor 11:17–34), the inflated importance given to rhetoric by the ancients (1:17–2:5), and the stated possession of superior knowledge on the part of the elites (2:6–3:3). What is apparent from Paul's rhetorical response in 1 Cor 1–4 is that it has much "in common with speeches on concord (περὶ ὁμονοίας) by ancient politicians and rhetoricians" (Welborn 1997, 7). Welborn (1997, 65–75) argues that Paul's appeal in 1 Cor 4:6 (μὴ ὑπὲρ ἃ γέγραπται) was to dissuade the Corinthians from faction and to promote concord. Paul, however, was intent on turning his converts away from politics, reminding them that their fate "did not rest on the precepts of statecraft, but upon the word of the cross" (Welborn 1997, 40).

Last, John Paul Lotz (1999, 176–85), after investigating the *homonoia* coinage of the Greek city states, argues that Christ's heavenly supremacy in Eph 1:21, which is described as far above "every title than can be given," is to be understood against the rivalries of the Asian cities for titles (*neokoros, metropolis*). The precarious bonds of *homonoia* stood at odds with Christ's eternal reign, breaking down "the dividing wall of hostility" in order to create unity (Eph 2:14).

The great virtue of the scholarly approaches above is that they situate Paul's rhetoric within the wider concerns of rhetoricians and Greek city-states regarding concord in the first-century CE. What is not answered, however, is why Paul—and every other New Testament writer for that matter—studiously avoids ὁμόνοια terminology, the leitmotif of political and civic unity in the eastern Mediterranean basin. Mitchell (1991, 76–77) is correct, on the basis of Iamblichus's *Epistle Concerning Concord* (Diels 1959–1960, 2.356), in saying that that Paul's phrase in 1 Cor 1:10 ("in the same mind"; ἐν τῷ αὐτῷ νοΐ) functions as a synonym for ὁμόνοια. But why substitute this phrase, the very rarity of which is admitted by Mitchell (1991, 76), for the ubiquitous ὁμόνοια? The issue is even more puzzling when we consider Paul's interaction with other motifs belonging to concord discourse in Greco-Roman deliberative rhetoric. What was so problematic about ὁμόνοια as a terminological choice? The focus of my answer will be on the writings of the apostle Paul. The irony, however, was that Christians in the late empire extensively relied on the tropes of *homonoia* rhetoric, despite Paul's disavowal of its central term (Ralph 2019; Breytenbach 2003).

Several suggestions can be made as to why Paul avoided ὁμόνοια terminology. First, it is important to realize that ὁμόνοια united the Greek city-states in Asia Minor. There is a strong ethnic focus here, even if we also include Rome's adoption of the Greek goddess Homonoia in the form of Concordia. I suspect that the apostle felt that ὁμόνοια did not embrace the universal openness to all cultures and ethnicities that was the defining characteristic of God's extension of unconditional and impartial grace to the redeemed (Rom 10:12; 15:5–7; 1 Cor 12:13; Gal 3:28; Col 3:11; Eph 2:14–22; 4:2–6).

Second, the fact that ὁμόνοια had been hypostasized into a goddess (Homonoia) was also highly problematic for the monotheism of the apostle. To be sure, the three divine Charites were related to the cycle of *charis* expressed in gift-giving rituals (Blanton 2017, 16–17), and Paul does not shy away from grace language. But Paul studiously avoids the plural form of χάρις so that there could be no confusion between the χάρις of the Father and Christ and the reciprocity rituals inaugurated by the Charites (Harrison 2003, 285–86). In the case of ὁμόνοια, Paul bypassed the word entirely because of the potential confusion with the goddess.

Third, ὁμόνοια, apart from its sole occurrence in the Delphic canon, had no substantive ethical import. It describes the settled state of political affairs within a city (between the council and the people in our inscription) or the peaceable relations between city-states. The vast bulk of its accompanying terminology (peace, good-fortune, health, safety, friendship) highlights this state of concord and any potential ethical terms (justice, kindness, kindness), very rarely used in the *homonoia* inscriptions, are also to be understood within the framework of a *settled* state of political affairs.

There is nothing here of the Pauline understanding of actively maintaining and enhancing the concord already established in Christ or that it is undergirded by the continuous indwelling of the Spirit. By contrast, believers are called to ethical action in order to maintain divine unity within the body of Christ (Rom 12:16; 14:19; 1 Cor 1:10; 2 Cor 13:11; Col 3:13–14; Phil 2:2; Eph 4:3). Where there is a relationship between Homonoia and ὁμόνοια in the inscriptions, it functions either as an honorific acknowledgement of the goddesses of cities involved in the treaty-oath (Reynolds 1982, §1, above) or as a cultic ritual designed to appease the god/goddess so that concord might ensue (MDAI[A] 32:278, 11; *SIG* 398). There is no idea of overflowing divine grace empowering ethical transformation corporately (Rom 7:6; 8:3–4, 11–13; Gal 5:16–26).

Fourth, Martin is correct in saying that ὁμόνοια rituals were designed to bolster the status quo of the elite ruling class, whereas Paul's gospel inverts hierarchical relations and the pinpricks the Greco-Roman quest for the acquisition of status (see Harrison 2019, passim). The rationale for this was the self-humbling of the crucified and resurrected Christ (2 Cor 13:4; Phil 2:5–11). In this regard, as Welborn has reminded us, the word of the cross, as opposed to an appeal to ὁμόνοια, was the real dynamic behind Paul's inversion of the status rituals associated with ancient politics in the Corinthian house churches. Moreover, God's choice of the nothings of this world overthrew all human pretension and boasting (1 Cor 1:28–29). Furthermore, I have argued that our honorific inscription (IEph 6.2052) is a cynical manipulation of the people by the Ephesian council to keep the somewhat unruly Ephesian people under control, while exempting the elites from any accountability for the excesses in their own behavior. Moreover, the indebtedness evinced in the inscription to the elite citizen Oulpios Straton by the Ephesian council for his beneficence emphasizes the centrality of the traditional hierarchies of wealth and honor at Ephesus. Lotz is also correct in his observation that all earthly hierarchies, with their petty and self-centered rivalries over titles, are subordinated to the ascended and reigning risen Christ whose heavenly authority is superior to every earthly title. A political critique with enormous social consequences has been launched by the apostle.

Fifth, the ὁμόνοια agreements were fragile constructs and had to be continuously renewed by city states. Sadly, the self-centered behavior of the Corinthian believers had similarly torn apart the unity of the body of Christ, demonstrating that believers were affected by the same rivalries, power struggles, and jealousies that afflicted the Greek elites in the eastern

Mediterranean cities. Indeed, by the end of 2 Corinthians, Paul laments whether his converts had even begun to address properly the divisive behavioral issues that he had raised with them in his previous letters. Airing the possibility of an impending third apostolic visit to Corinth, Paul reveals a deep-seated anxiety: "I fear that there may perhaps be strife [ἔρις], jealousy, anger, factions [ἐριθεῖαι], slander, gossip, conceit and commotions." On ἔρις in Greco-Roman literature, see Mitchell 1991, 81–82. But, in Paul's view, the ultimate solution to factionalism did not reside in human hands. Certainly believers were to think the same thing and be at peace with each other, but this was because the God of love and peace had promised to be with them (2 Cor 13:11). Unity in Christ and communal life in the Spirit (1 Cor 12:12–13), therefore, would overcome human fallibility and weakness, beginning in this age (2 Cor 3:18) and culminating in the age to come (Rom 8:29–30). But, above all, in the future kingdom the greatest expression of full Christian maturity is love, surpassing even the highpoints of faith and hope (1 Cor 13:13). This is the central reason why Paul studiously avoided *homonoia* terminologically: it was a totally inferior virtue, a human construct loosely affiliated with a civic deity, whereas divine love was the driving force behind the incarnation and crucifixion, transforming all human relationships from the apex to the base of the social pyramid.

Bibliography

Akar, Philippe. 2013. *Concordia: Un idéal de la clase dirigeante romaine à la fin de la République*. Histoire ancienne et médiévale 122. Paris: Publications de la Sorbonne.

Blanton, Thomas R. 2017. *A Spiritual Economy: Gift Exchange in the Letters of Paul of Tarsus*. New Haven: Yale University Press.

Baukova, A. 2016. "Roman Province of Asia through the Prism of Urban History." *The World of the Orient* 1:5–10.

Breytenbach, Cilliers. 2003. "Civic Concord and Cosmic Harmony: Sources of Metaphoric Mapping in 1 Clement 20:3." Pages 259–73 in *Early Christianity and Classical Culture: Comparative Studies in Honor of Abraham J. Malherbe*. Edited by John T. Fitzgerald, Thomas H. Olbricht, and L. Michael White. Leiden: Brill.

Burrell, Barbara. 2004. *Neokoroi: Greek Cities and Roman Emperors*. Cincinnati Classical Studies 2/9. Leiden: Brill.

Csapo, Eric, and William J. Slater. 1995. *The Context of Ancient Drama*. Ann Arbor: University of Michigan Press.

Diels, Hermann. 1959–1960. *Die Fragmente der Vorsokratiker, griechisch und Deutsch.* Vol. 2. Berlin: Weidmann.

Ellithorpe, Corey J. 2017. *Circulating Imperial Ideology: Coins as Propaganda in the Roman World.* PhD diss., University of North Carolina, Chapel Hill.

Ersoy, Akın. 2017. "Smyrna and Related Cities in the Light of Finds." Pages 101–16 in *Smyrna/Izmir: Excavations and Research II.* Antik Smyrna Kazısı Yayın Çalışmaları 10. Edited by Burak Yolaçan, Gözde Şakar, and Akın Ersoy. Istanbul: Yayinlari.

Flory, Marleen Boudreau. 1984. "Sic Exempla Parantur: Livia's Shrine to *Concordia* and the *Porticus Liviae.*" *Historia* 33:309–33.

Franke, Peter Robert, and Margret Karola Nollé. 1997. *Katalog.* Vol. 1 of *Die Homonoia-Münzen Kleinasiens und der thrakischen Randgebiete.* Saarbrücker Studien zur Archäologie und Alten Geschichte 10. Saarbrücken: Saarbrücker Druckerei und Verlag.

Friesen, Steven J. 1993. *Twice Neokoros: Ephesus, Asia and the Cult of the Flavian Imperial Family.* RGRW 116. Leiden: Brill.

Harrison, James R. 2003. *Paul's Language of Grace in Its Graeco-Roman Context.* WUNT 2/172. Tübingen: Mohr Siebeck.

———. 2012. "Family Honour of a Priestess of Artemis." *NewDocs* 10:31–36.

———. 2019. *Paul and the Ancient Celebrity Circuit: The Cross and Moral Transformation.* WUNT 430. Tübingen: Mohr Siebeck.

Judge, E. A. 1982. "Moral Terms in the Eulogistic Tradition." *NewDocs* 2:105–6.

Kampmann, U. 1998. "Homonoia Politics in Asia Minor: The Example of Pergamon." Pages 373–92 in *Pergamon, Citadel of the Gods: Archaeological Record, Literary Description, and Religious Development.* Edited by H. Koester. HTS 46. Harrisburg, PA: Trinity Press International.

Keil, Matthew Adam. 2013. "CONCORDIA as an Historiographical Principle in Sallust and Augustine." PhD diss. Fordham University, New York.

Kelly, Benjamin. 2007. "Riot Control and Imperial Ideology in the Roman Empire." *Phoenix* 61:150–76.

Kienast, Dietmar. 1995. "Zu den Homonoia-Vereinbarungen in der römischen Kaizerzeit." *ZPE* 109:267–82.

Kinlaw, Joshua A. 2013. "*HOMONOIA* in the Roman Empire." PhD diss., The City University of New York, New York.

Kokkinia, Christina. 2017–2018. "A Roman Financier's Version of Euergetism: C. Vibius Salutaris and Ephesos." *Tekmeria* 14:215–52.
Konstan, David, and N. Keith Rutter. 2003. *Envy, Spite and Jealousy: The Rivalrous Emotions in Ancient Greece.* Edinburgh Leventis Studies. Edinburgh. Edinburgh University Press.
Lobur, John Alexander. 2008. *Consensus, Concordia, and the Formation of Roman Imperial Ideology.* Studies in Classics. London: Routledge.
Lotz, John Paul. 1999. "The Homonoia Coins of Asia Minor and. Ephesians 1:21." *TynBul* 50.2: 173–88.
Maier, Harry O. 2018. *Picturing Paul in Empire: Imperial Image, Text and Persuasion in Colossians, Ephesians and the Pastoral Epistles.* London: T&T Clark.
Martin, Dale B. 1995. *The Corinthian Body.* New Haven: Yale University Press.
Mitchell, Margaret M. 1991. *Paul and the* Rhetoric of Reconciliation: *An Exegetical Investigation of the Language and Composition of 1 Corinthians.* Louisville: Westminster John Knox.
Momigliano, A. 1942. "Camillus and Concord." *CQ* 36:111–20.
Noreña, Carlos F. 2011. *Imperial Ideals in the Roman West: Representation, Circulation, Power.* Cambridge: Cambridge University Press.
Ralph, Allison K. 2019. "The Functions of *Homonoia* in the Rhetoric of Constantius II: Persuasion, Justification of Coercion, Propaganda." *Rhetorica* 37:215–41.
Reynolds, Joyce. 1982. *Aphrodisias and Rome.* JRS Monographs 1. London: Society for the Promotion of Roman Studies.
Richard, Jean-Claude. 1963. "Pax, Concordia et la religion officielle de Janus à la fin de la République romaine." *Mélanges d'archéologie et d'histoire* 75:303–86.
Ricl, Marijana. 2011. "Neokoroi in the Greek World." *Belgrade Historical Review* 2:7–26.
Rogers, Guy MacLean. 1991. *The Sacred Identity of Ephesos: Foundation Myths of a Roman City.* London: Routledge.
———. 1992. "The Assembly of Imperial Ephesos." *ZPE* 94:224–28.
Skard, E. 1932. *Zwei religiös-politische Begriffe: Euergetes-Concordia.* Oslo: Avhandlinger ulgittav Det Norske Videnskaps-Akademi i.
Stevenson, T. R. 2010. "Personifications on the Coinage of Vespasian (AD 69–79)." *Acta Classica* 53:181–205.
Temelini, Mark A. 2002. "Cicero's *CONCORDIA*: The Promotion of a

Political Concept in the Late Roman Republic." PhD diss., McGill University, Montreal.

Theophilos, Michael P. 2018. "Ephesus and the Numismatic Background to νεωκόρος." Pages 299–331 in Ephesus. Vol. 3 of *The First Urban Churches*. Edited by James R. Harrison and L. L. Welborn. WGRWSup 9. Atlanta: SBL Press.

Thériault, G. 1996. *Le culte d'Homonoia dans les cités grecques*. Collection de la maison de l'Orient méditerranéen 26, épigraphique et historique 3. Lyon: Maison de l'Orient méditerranéen.

Thraede, Klaus. 1994. "Homonoia (Eintracht)." *RAC* 16:176–289.

Welborn, L. L. 1993. "The Pursuit of Concord: A Political Ideal in Early Christianity." PhD diss., Vanderbilt University, Nashville.

———. 1997. *Politics and Rhetoric in the Corinthian Epistles*. Macon, GA: Mercer University Press.

17. Dishonoring the Honored: The Problem of Recycling Public Monuments

James R. Harrison

IEph 1a.25.1-28

GIBM 3.2.1890, no. 497 (part) (*edito princeps*); *JÖAI* 1Supp:78-79 (part); *RAr* 32:466 (part); *OGIS* 508 (part); FiE 2, no. 23; Oliver 1941, 11; Oberleitner and Lessing 1978, 118-20, no. 172. The Greek text was inscribed on five blocks of white marble from one wall. Regarding their discovery, blocks a, b, c, and e were found during the excavations of 1897 and 1898, whereas block d was discovered earlier in the theater at Ephesus by J. T. Wood. Blocks a, b, c, and e are now exhibited in the Ephesus museum of the Kunsthistorisches Museum in Vienna. Block d is exhibited at the British Museum in London. R. Heberdey argues, however, that the blocks most likely originate from the wall of the *gerousia* meeting house. The section translated below renders lines 1-24 of the inscription, which is in its entirety is sixty-one lines long. Lines 41-61 are so fragmentary that the editor of IEph 1 (pp. 158-59) did not consider that section of the inscription worthy of a German translation. Date: 162-163 CE.

	αὐτοκράτωρ Καῖσαρ Μᾶρκος Αὐρήλιος Ἀντωνεῖνος	Emperor Caesar Marcus Aurelius Antoninus
	Σεβαστὸς καὶ αὐτοκράτωρ Καῖσαρ Λεύκιος Αὐρήλιος Οὐῆρος	Augustus and Emperor Caesar Lucius Aurelius Verus
	Σεβαστὸς Ἀρμενιακὸς Οὐλπίῳ Εὐρυκλεῖ	Augustus Armeniacus to Ulpius Eurycles,
4	χαίρειν.	greetings.
	ὅτι μὲν ὑπ' ἀνθυπάτων δοθέντα σε τῇ γερουσίᾳ τῶν Ἐφεσίων	Since you have been appointed by the *proconsul*ar governors as curator of the Senate of the Ephesians,

λογιστὴν ἐκείνοις ἔδει, περὶ ὧν
ἠπόρεις, ἀναφέρειν, αὐτός τε εὐγνω-

μόνως ἐδήλωσας ἐπιστάμενος, καὶ
ἡμεῖς διὰ τοῦτο ἐπεμνήσθημεν,

8 ὡς μὴ ῥᾳδίως ἀνάγεσθαί τινας τῷ
παραδείγματι. ὃ δὲ πρῶτον ἡμῖν
ἐκοίνωσας,

τὸ περὶ τῶν ἀργυρῶν εἰκόνων, πρᾶγμα
ὡς ἀληθῶς τῆς ἡμετέρας συνχωρήσε-

[ως] προσδεόμενο<ν>, δῆλόν ἐστί
σοι καὶ τὴν εἰς τὰς ἄλλας ἐρωτήσεις
ἀφορμὴν συμβε-

[βλη]μένον. τὰς οὖν εἰκόνας τῶν
αὐτοκρατόρων, ἃς ἀποκεῖσθαι λέγεις
ἐν τῷ συνε-

12 [δρί]ῳ τούτῳ, παλαιάς, ἑνὶ μὲν λόγῳ
πάσας δοκιμάζομεν φυλαχθῆναι τοῖς
ὀνόμασιν, ἐφ᾽ ο-

[ἷς] γέγονεν αὐτῶν ἑκάστη, εἰς δὲ
ἡμετέρους χαρακτῆρας μηδέν τι τῆς
ὕλης ἐκείνης

[μ]εταφέρειν· οἳ γὰρ [ο]ὔ[τ'] ἄλλως
[εἰς τ]ὰς ἡμε[τέ]ρας τιμάς ἐσμεν [π]
ρόχειρο[ι, πολὺ] δή τ[ι ἧ]τ[τον ἂν]
[ἄλλας εἰς ἡμᾶς μετ]αβα[λλο]μένας
ἀνασχοίμεθα· ἀλλ᾽ ὅσαι μ[ὲν αὐτῶν
....ca. 12....]

16 [.....ca. 15......] ἔχουσι τὰς
μορφάς, κἂν ὅσον γνωρίζε[σθαι τῶν
προσώπων τοὺς χα-]

[ρακτῆρας, ταύτας κα]ὶ σοὶ παρέστη
λελογισμένως, ὅτι τοῖς αὐτ[οῖς δεῖ
φυλαχθῆναι ὀνό-]

[μασιν, ἐφ᾽ οἷς γεγόνασιν·] περὶ δὲ
τῶν οὕτως ἄγαν συντεθραυ[σμένων,
ὡς ἀναφέρεις, καὶ]

you must refer to them the matters concerning which you were in doubt. You yourself with

prudent awareness have stated that policy and for this reason we have mentioned the matter,

that some may not be lightly influenced by the precedent. What you first communicated to us,

(namely,) the matter concerning the silver images which truly needs our consent,

it is clear, has given occasion also to you for the other questions.

Now as for the ancient statues of the emperors that you say are stored in the council

hall, to put it briefly, we decree that all shall be preserved with the names of those emperors for

whom they were made and that none of that material whatever shall be transformed for our images,

for we are not at other times eager for our own honors and still less

shall we endure that the honors of others be converted to us. But as many of the statues ...

which have features insofar as the characteristic outlines can be recognized,

these, as it seemed to you after consideration, ought to be preserved under the same names

as those for whom they were made. But for images so excessively corroded, as you report, and

17. Dishonoring the Honored

[οὐδεμίαν μορφὴν ἔτ]ι̣ φαίνειν δυναμένων τάχα μὲν ἂν καὶ [τούτων ἐκ τῶν ἐπὶ τοῖς βά]-	no longer able to represent features, perhaps capable of identification in part from inscriptions on their bases
20 [θροις ἐπιγραφῶν, τ]άχα δ' ἂν καὶ ἐκ βιβλίων, εἴ τινα ἔστι τῷ [συνεδρίῳ τούτῳ ..ca. 8...]	or from records preserved in the council hall, ...
[.....ca. 14....., τὰ ὀνό]ματα συνπορισθείη, ὥστε τοῖ[ς προγεγονόσι μᾶλλον τὴν]	the names may be supplied, so that honor may rather be revived for our predecessors
[τει]μὴν ἀνανεωθῆναι [ἤπερ διὰ τ]ῆς ἀναχων[εύσεως ἐξαφανισθῆναι τῶν] εἰκόνων. τῇ δὲ χωνεύσει πρῶτον μέν σε παρὰ τυχ[..........24– 26..........]	than vanish completely with the melting down of the images. In the event of re-smelting you first must ...
24 ταλαμβάνῃ τοῦ μέτρου τῆς λογιστείας· ἀλλ' ἐπειδ[ὴ ....26–28...........]	take account of the weight for the record office. But since ...
ὑπῆρξω καὶ τὸ συγχωρηθῆναι διεπράξω παρ' ἡμῶ[ν ....25–27...........]	you began and secured permission from us ...
πραχθῆναι, ἔπειτα καὶ ἄλλους πρὸς τὸ μάλιστα ἀνεσ[........20– 22........, οὓς ἂν]	to be done, and then others ... whomsoever
ὁ κράτιστος ἀνθύπατος εἴτε ἐξ αὐτῆς τῆ[ς γερουσίας ε[ἴτε ἐξ ἁπάντων τῶν πολει-]	the excellent *proconsul* may approve either from the Senate itself or else from the whole body of
28 τῶν δοκιμάσῃ. (The remainder of the Greek text in line 28 is omitted here.)	citizens. (The remainder of the Greek text in line 28 is not translated.)

The delicate issue of the preservation of the ancient honorific statues of the imperial rulers, which had been originally erected with an indefinite future in view as far as their preservation, had increasingly become a problem at Ephesus due to the ravages of time. The progressive corrosion of the silver images of previous Roman rulers had posed in the mind of some the important question whether these honorific images should be melted down and resmelted for new honorands. Currently, such images were being stored in the council hall (ll. 11–12). The curator of the Senate, Ulpius Eurycles, had aired the ticklish issue in 162–163 CE with the Roman rulers Marcus Aurelius Antoninus and Caesar Lucius Aurelius Verus, perhaps informing them that some unidentified individuals (the Ephesian senators and civic elites?) had suggested that the badly corroded statues could be resmelted and reerected in honor of the two current rulers of Rome. Probably these Ephesian luminaries naively thought that this would be another strategic way in which the Senate of Ephesus might cultivate further favor with the current Roman rulers. Ulpius himself may have been initially uncertain regarding the way in which to proceed regarding imperial honorific policy ("the matters in which you were in doubt," l. 6) and had therefore approached the rulers with several clarificatory questions (l. 10) before he made a final decision. In the view of the Roman rulers, Ulpius had shown "prudent awareness" in broaching the issue (l. 7).

However, it is equally possible that Ulpius, before raising the problem with the Roman rulers, had ventured his personal opinion to the Ephesian senators and civic elites that the honorific statues of previous Roman rulers should not be interfered with, lest the protocols of honorific culture were violated, but he had made a promise to his fellow-citizens to seek the final adjudication of the Roman rulers on the matter ("which truly needs our consent," l. 9). However we might reconstruct of the initial avenues of communication of Ulpius on the issue—given the considerable difficulties in reconstituting the specifics of the prior discourse with the Roman rulers owing to the cryptic nature of the introductory comments (ll. 5–10)—lines 1–28 of our inscription represent the official response of the Roman rulers to his proposal or enquiry, as case may be. The epigraphic communication of Marcus Antoninus and Lucius Verus was designed to provide a firm precedent for the undefined "some" of line 8, who were most likely proposing the resmelting of the silver statues. Three policies regarding the recycling of imperial statues are articulated in the inscription.

First, all those statues stored in the council hall whose characteristic outlines could still be discerned should be preserved, with no change being made to their honorific dedications. The eternity of imperial honor is clearly underscored here. The well-intended but inappropriate suggestion of some Ephesian senators and elites that the honors of others could be transformed into new honors for Marcus Antoninus and Lucius Verus is roundly rejected (ll. 12–13). The personal opinion on the issue of the two Roman rulers is very bluntly put so that there can be no equivocation: "we are not at other times eager for our own honors and still less shall we endure that the honors of others be converted to us" (ll. 14–15).

Second, where corrosion has robbed the statues of their essential features, rendering them unrecognizable, the statues should nonetheless be preserved. This was especially the case where the identifying inscriptions on the statue bases were still clearly visible or where the records in the archives of the council hall allowed identification of the original honorand. Again, the imperishable nature of honor is spotlighted: the intention of the imperial decision is that "that honor may rather be revived for our predecessors than vanish completely with the melting down of the images" (ll. 21–23).

Third, it is conceded that there may be occasion for the resmelting of corroded statues, but no other details of the precise circumstances when this might occur are provided other than the injunction that the weight should be accounted for the record office (ll. 23–24). By means of this stipulation, the potential danger of the corrupt under-reporting of the true value of the melted silver is nipped in the bud. Where the permission of the Roman rulers has been secured, the policy can be implemented in consultation with the provincial proconsul, the Ephesian Senate, and the demos of the city (ll. 24–28). Nevertheless, the sensitive negotiations with the rulers and the provincial proconsul required in such cases are confidential. On the economic implications of recycling statues in late antiquity, see Baker 2020. On Romans and the recycling habit more generally, see Duckworth and Wilson 2020. For the dishonor of the people of Ephesus dedicating a gold statue of Eros—originally dedicated by Octavian's father to Aphrodite—inappropriately in the temple of Artemis at Ephesus, see Reynolds 1982, §12 (36 BCE). For brief discussion, see Harrison, "Ephesus in Documentary Perspective" in this volume.

This debate about the recycling of honorific statues was not new in antiquity. Dio Chrysostom (40–110) CE, who belonged to a prominent family famous for its benefactions to Prusa—the city in which his family lived—was highly sensitive to the importance of δόξα in the world of honor.[1] On the issue of honor in Dio Chrysostom, see Moxnes 1994, 203–30. This is particularly evident in the Rhodian oration, where Dio is addressing the problem of the recycling of old statues with new inscriptions at Rhodes for the honoring of the city's crop of new benefactors (*Rhod.* 8, 9, 12). Peter Stewart (2003, 79 n. 4) cites the following sources as further instances of the recycling of statues in antiquity: Cicero, *Att.* 6.1.26; Plutarch, *Ant.* 60; Pausanias, *Descr.* 2.17.3; Philo, *Legat.* 134–136. For further inscriptional examples of recycling, see Shear 2007. On honorific statues at Ephesus and Isthmia, see Harrison 2019, 277–79.

---

1. The following four paragraphs are drawn from Harrison 2010, 170–74.

In the Rhodian oration, a positive evaluation of the lasting contribution that glory contributes to civic life emerges. Throughout the oration Dio makes the point that the duplicitous actions of the citizens of Rhodes violated the reciprocation of honor that animated the ancient benefaction system. When gratitude is properly allocated to benefactors, it spawns worthy favors for the recipients (*Rhod.* 7). The Rhodians, however, are robbing benefactors—past and present (*Rhod.* 12)—of their honor (*Rhod.* 8–9). Their actions in removing the original honorific inscriptions accompanying the public statues not only deprives the original benefactors of honor but also dishonors them by blighting their illustrious career with the *damnatio memoriae* reserved for tyrants and the treasonous (*Rhod.* 27–31). Moreover, in acting with mockery towards the benefactors of the past, the Rhodians fill their current benefactors with suspicion regarding the longevity and genuineness of their proposed honors. In the face of such dishonorable ingratitude on the part of the Rhodians and their denial of honorable benefactors of rightful recompense (*Rhod.* 36–37, 65), there is only one conclusion to be drawn:

> Therefore, the man who courts the person who is present, but slights his former friend, and having forgotten the service this friend has rendered, places the highest importance on the hoped-for benefit from the other—do you not know the term that is applied to him? Is such a man not called a toady elsewhere? Is he not considered ignoble, a man not to be trusted? (*Rhod.* 33)

Dio concludes that the Rhodians, living under the hegemony of Rome, had no new opportunities to establish world leadership other than to show themselves better than the rest of the world by properly honoring their benefactors (*Rhod.* 161–162). On Dio Chrysostom and Rome, see Moxnes 1994, 207–20.

An interesting sidelight to the Rhodian oration is the way that Dio resorts to the language of glory throughout the speech to drive home the ingratitude of the Rhodians towards their benefactors. The sacrifices for the city made by the benefactors of the past demands that their name be heralded and that they also receive "some other honor" (δόξαν τινά) (*Rhod.* 16). Fortune provides cities with men who advanced to "glory" (εἰς δόξαν) and power precisely because they were jealous of honor and regarded their fame as more precious than life itself (*Rhod.* 20). Thus the proper honoring of such men is the debt they were owed by their ancestors and consequently they are "the glory of the city" (ἡ δόξα τῆς πόλεως) in the present (*Rhod.* 62). Even in the case of the uninscribed statues of demigods, "their glory [ἡ δόξα] has remained and time has guarded their fame" (*Rhod.* 92). As far as the reciprocation of the beneficence of mortals, honorific statues are erected because of the benefactor's "distinguished achievement" (διὰ τό δόξαι) and his nobility (*Rhod.* 94). Thus the Rhodians should keep their eyes on "their own reputation" (τὴν ἑαυτῶν δόξαν) and the proud position of their city (*Rhod.* 126). They are to avoid the mistake of other Greek cities who have blotted out their "ancient glory" (τὴν παλαιὰν δόξαν) or those individuals who have destroyed "the glory of their own family" (τὴν ὅλην δόξαν) (*Rhod.* 158–159).

Furthermore, Nero, in contrast to the Rhodians, did not remove any of the statues of Rhodes from their sites. This stood in sharp contrast to Nero's policy elsewhere of taking public objects from other cities for the embellishment of the Roman sacred places (*Rhod.* 149–151). The great number of Rhodian statues, Dio wryly comments, brought the Rhodianas "renown of another sort" (δόξαν ὑμῖν ἑτέραν), namely, the respect and friendship of the ruler (*Rhod.* 149). As Dio quips, "So then, when the Romans and Nero guarded your possessions so scrupulously and esteemed them inviolate, shall you yourselves fail to protect them?" (*Rhod.* 150).

On the erasure of honor in antiquity and its relevance for the context of the apostle Paul, see Harrison 2016. On the issue of *damnatio memoriae* and the erasure of honor, see Varner 2004; Flower 2006. How, then, does the Paul in his epistles handle the debilitating blight of dishonor, as articulated by Dio Chrysostom in the Rhodian oration and by the imperial rulers in the Ephesian inscription above? We will first examine the apostle's dishonor terminology (ἀτιμία, ἄτιμος, ἀτιμάζω) and then briefly consider the Ephesian epigraphic context of δόξα and its relevance for the Epistle to the Ephesians. Readers who desire a more thorough exploration of the motifs of shame and honor in the apostle's thought should consult Jewett 2003; Finney 2012; Harrison 2019.

At the outset, in the Epistle to the Romans, the chief consideration of dishonor enunciated by Paul does not involve the imperial authorities (Rom 13:1–7; cf. Harrison 2011, 271–323), as does our Ephesian inscription. Instead the apostle highlights the foolishness (Rom 1:22), dishonor, and ingratitude of human beings (Rom 1:21–22: see v. 22: οὐχ ὡς θεὸν ἐδόξασαν ἢ ηὐχαρίστησαν) toward the divine Creator and Benefactor of the universe. They suppress the divine truth (Rom 1:25) by erecting idolatrous statues for cultic worship fashioned in the image of human beings (including the imperial rulers, 1 Cor 8:5–6), animals, and reptiles (1:22). Note the stance of the Lukan Paul towards images as reported by the Ephesian silversmiths in Acts 19:26–27. For discussion of the Corinthian imperial context and 1 Cor 8:5–6, see Winter 2015, 269–86; 2015; Fantin 2011, 225–23; contra, Burnett 2024, 222–23. On idolatry, see Barton 2007; Beale 2008, 202–15. Significantly, the inglorious dishonoring of God (Rom 1:21, 23a) resulted in the sexual dishonoring of human bodies through their sexual immorality (Rom 1:24, 26). While Paul reflects aspects of ancient benefaction culture in his insistence upon the reciprocation of honor and gratitude for divine munificence in Rom 1:22 (Harrison 2003, 214–19), his teaching draws heavily upon the LXX in verses 21–25 (Ps 106:20; Jer 2:11; Hos 4:7). Furthermore, the ethical link made by the apostle between idolatry and sexual immorality in Rom 1:24 reflects the Pentateuchal, historical, and prophetic denunciations of the association between both activities in the Old Testament (1 Cor 10:8–9 [Num 25:1–3; Judg 2:17]; see also Exod 32:6; Deut 23:17; 1 Kgs 14:24; 2 Kgs 23:7; Isa 57:3–8; Jer 2:20; 3:6 [2 Macc 6:4–5]; Amos 2:7; Hos 4:13–14). Indeed, God's deliberate "giving over" of idolaters in his judgement (παρέδωκεν, 2x) to the sexual dishonoring of their bodies (Rom 1:24, ἀτιμάζεσθαι; 1:26, ἀτιμίας) is heavily underscored by Paul, revealing thereby the strong Jewish dimensions of his thought on the issue. Human beings are to honor God *morally* as opposed to appeasing the god/gods by dedicating idolatrous honorific statues. The same ethical point is made by Paul in a Jewish context as well. One should honor God morally by obedience to the Mosaic law, as opposed to dishonoring God by boasting in the possession of the law while at the same time breaking its injunctions (Rom 2:23, τὸν θεὸν ἀτιμάζεις).

Last, a final use of the language of dishonor occurs in Rom 9:21. There Paul employs the widespread metaphor of God as potter (e.g., Job 10:9; Isa 45:9; Jer 18:7–10; Wis 15:7; Sir 27:5; 38:29–30; 1QS XI, 22; 1QH III, 23–24; see also 2 Tim 2:20) in order to spotlight the sovereign freedom of God's electing grace. From the *same* clay, Paul states, God makes *different* objects for "honorable" (εἰς τιμήν) and "dishonorable" purposes (εἰς ἀτιμίαν). This familiar metaphor allows the apostle to expand upon his theodicy regarding the fate of disobedient Israel (Rom 9:1–6, 30–33; 10:1–3; 10:16–11:7, 11–12, 29–32). In the immediate context, Paul focuses upon the fate of the objects of mercy prepared beforehand for glory (Rom 9:23) and the objects of wrath prepared for destruction (9:22) before unfolding the respective destinies of historical Israel, remnant Israel, and the elect gentiles in God's providential plan. In this apocalyptic and prophetic unveiling of salvation history, which had culminated in Christ as the Lord of all nations (Rom 1:2-5; 8:28-30; 10:4; 15:7-12; 16:25-27), the contemporary honoring of the imperial rulers and their clients was in reality a passing sideshow.

The remaining occurrences of Paul's language of dishonor appear in the Corinthian epistles. Here, we see that Paul's concern for honor and dishonor moves well beyond the restricted social orbit of the Ephesian elites and the imperial rulers, who were exclusively preoccupied with the enduring honor of the house of the Caesars, their family members, and their provincial clients. As we have seen, the apostle has dismissed the myopic quest for statuary honor, divine and human, in antiquity as an idolatrous expression of human rebellion against the Creator and Benefactor of the universe. What further distinctive elements regarding dishonor in the believer's life emerge in the Corinthian epistles?

First, in sharp contrast to the elite perspectives of the Roman rulers and their Ephesian clients, Paul, like the author of James (2:6, ὑμεῖς δὲ ἠτιμάσατε τὸν πτωχόν), does not countenance the dishonoring of the poor in the body of Christ (1 Cor 11:22, καταφρονεῖτε καὶ καταισχύνετε τοὺς μὴ ἔχοντες). Admittedly Paul's terminology is different in this case, but the sentiment is still the same. For discussion, see Welborn 2016a, 2016b. Second, Paul totally reconfigures the elitist and hierarchical construct of honor in social relations by ensuring that the dishonorable and shameful members in the body of Christ, who were neither especially gifted nor publicly valued, are honored above all the other gifted members in the *ekklesia* (1 Cor 12:23, ἀτιμότεροι). Third, Paul paradoxically depicts his apostolic ministry as a simultaneous experience of honor and shame (1 Cor 4:10, ὑμεῖς ἔνδοχοι, ἡμεῖς δὲ ἄτιμοι; 2 Cor 6:8, διὰ δόξης καὶ ἀτιμίας). Significantly, in the case of 1 Cor 4:10, Paul is either drawing upon the imagery of the criminals facing capital punishment in the last event of the day's gladiatorial program, or he is referring to the physical abuse and demeaning insults inflicted upon the morons and fools of the mime shows. For discussion, see Harrison 2019, 294-94; Welborn 2005, 246-47. In sum, Paul's apostolic ministry, therefore, not only reflects Christ's own soteriological experience of cruciform shame (1 Cor 1:18-31) but also the honorific vindication of his resurrection at the Father's behest (Phil 2:9-11). This Christocentric nexus between honor and dishonor is transferred seamlessly to the believer's daily experience of dying and rising in Christ (2 Cor 4:10-12). See Harrison 2019, 79-107.

Two final examples of dishonor terminology in 1 Corinthians remain. Paul, in a discussion of the appropriate attire practices in worship meetings, appeals rhetorically to natural (i.e., cultural?) norms about male hair-styles at Corinth (1 Cor 11:14, ἀτιμία). Last, the apostle highlights the dishonor of the mortal bodies of humans ruled by Sin and Death (1 Cor 15:43, σπείρεται ἐν ἀτιμίᾳ) in comparison to the believer's glorious resurrection body of the future.

In conclusion, Paul's understanding of the relation between honor and dishonor in the believer's life had strong counter-cultural elements that must have been confronting to the elites at Ephesus, perhaps provoking some of them to reevaluate their obsession with honorific status, but, more likely, causing them to reject his message outright, given its deeply cruciform imprint. See Gorman 2001. Furthermore, Paul's reconfiguration of glory (δόξα) terminology in the Epistle to Ephesians would have collided with Ephesian conceptions of glory, which, as we have seen from Dio Chrysostom's Rhodian oration above, was a prominent term of honorific discourse in antiquity. At Ephesus, δόξα was indissolubly tied to Artemis (IEph 2.212.2; cf. Acts 19:23–40), imperial rule (IEph 5.1480.14–15), and civic honor (IEph 1a.6.23; 1487.13; 5.1488.15). For Paul, however, glory resided in the salvific grace of the Father (Eph 1:6, 12), the revelatory work of his empowering Spirit (1:17; 3:16), and the eschatological inheritance of the saints (1:18), each of which occasioned the believer's exuberant praise of the Father's glory (1:14; 3:21). But the jarring impact of cruciformity in the believer's life again comes to the fore in Paul's discourse on glory in the Epistle to the Ephesians: the apostle's sufferings on behalf of the Ephesian believers are also their glory (Eph 3:13, δόξα ὑμῶν). Thus, as was the case with ἀτιμία and its cognates in Paul's epistles, the same cruciform paradox of the apostle's suffering on behalf of his gospel attends the revelation of divine δόξα in the lives of his converts.

Bibliography

Barker, Simon J. 2020. "Reuse of Statuary and the Recycling Habit of Late Antiquity: An Economic Perspective." Pages 105–89 in *Recycling and Reuse in the Roman Economy*. Edited by Chloë N. Duckworth and Andrew Wilson. Oxford Studies in the Roman Economy. Oxford: Oxford University Press.

Barton, Stephen C., ed. 2007. *Idolatry: False Worship in the Bible, Early Judaism and Christianity*. London: T&T Clark.

Beale, G. K. 2008. *We Become What We Worship: A Biblical Theology of Idolatry*. Downers Grove, IL: IVP Academic; Nottongham: Apollos.

Burnett, D. Clint. 2024. *Paul and Imperial Divine Honors: Christ, Caesar, and the Gospel*. Grand Rapids: Eerdmans.

Duckworth, C. N., and A. Wilson, eds. 2020. *The Romans as Recyclers: Recycling and Reuse in the Roman Economy*. Oxford: Oxford University Press.

Fantin, Joseph D. 2011. *The Lord of the Entire World: Lord Jesus, a Challenge to Lord Caesar?* New Testament Monographs 31. Sheffield: Sheffield Phoenix.

Finney, Mark T. 2012. *Honour and Conflict in the Ancient World: 1 Corinthians in Its Greco-Roman Social Setting*. LNTS 460. London: Bloomsbury.

Flower, H. I. 2006. *The Art of Forgetting: Disgrace and Oblivion in Roman Political Culture*. Chapel Hill: University of North Carolina Press.

Gorman. Michael J. 2001. *Cruciformity: Paul's Narrative Spirituality of the Cross*. Grand Rapids: Eerdmans.

Harrison, James R. 2003. *Paul's Language of Grace in Its Graeco-Roman Context*. WUNT 2/172. Tübingen: Mohr Siebeck.

———. 2010. "The Brothers as the 'Glory of Christ' (2 Cor 8:23): Paul's *Doxa* Terminology in Its Ancient Benefaction Context." *NovT* 52:156–88.

———. 2011. *Paul and the Imperial Authorities at Thessalonica and Rome: A Study in the Conflict of Ideology*. WUNT 273. Tübingen: Mohr Siebeck.

———. 2016. "The Erasure of Honour: Paul and the Politics of Dishonour." *TynBull* 66:161–84.

———. 2019. *Paul and the Ancient Celebrity Circuit: The Cross and Moral Transformation*. WUNT 430. Tübingen: Mohr Siebeck.

Jewett, R. 2003. "Paul, Shame and Honor." Pages 551–74 in *Paul in the Greco-Roman World*. Edited by J. P. Sampley. Harrisburg, PA: Trinity Press International.

Moxnes, Halvor. 1994. "The Quest for Honor and the Unity of Community in Romans 12 and in the Orations of Dio Chrysostom." Pages 203–30 in *Paul in His Hellenistic Context*. Edited by Troels Engberg-Pedersen. Edinburgh: T&T Clark.

Oberleitner, Wolfgang, and Erich Lessing. 1978. *Funde aus Ephesos und Samothrake*. Vienna: Kunsthistorisches Museum.

Oliver, James H. 1941. *The Sacred Gerousia*. Athens: American School of Classical Studies at Athens.

Reynolds, Joyce. 1982. *Aphrodisias and Rome*. JRS Monographs 1. London: Society for the Promotion of Roman Studies.

Shear, J. L. 2007. "Reusing Statues, Rewriting Inscriptions and Bestowing Honours in Roman Athens." Pages 221–47 in *Art and Inscriptions in the Ancient World*. Edited by Z. Newby and R. Leader-Newby. Cambridge: Cambridge University Press.

Stewart, Peter. 2003. *Statues in Roman Society: Representation and Response*. Oxford Studies in Ancient Culture and Representation. Oxford: Oxford University Press.

Varner, E. R. 2004. *Mutilation and Transformation: Damnatio Memoriae and Roman Imperial Portraiture*. Leiden: Brill.

Welborn, L. L. 2005. *Paul, the Fool for Christ: A Study of 1 Corinthians 1–4 in the Comic-Philosophic Tradition*. London: T&T Clark.

———. 2016a. "Inequality in Roman Corinth: Evidence from Diverse Sources Evaluated by a Neo-Ricardian Model." Pages 47–84 in *Roman Corinth*. Vol. 2 of *The First Urban Churches*. Edited by James R. Harrison and L. L. Welborn. WGRWSup 7. Atlanta: SBL Press.

———. 2016b. "The Polis and the Poor: Reconstructing Social Relations from Different Genres of Evidence." Pages 189–243 in *Roman Corinth*. Vol. 2 of *The First Urban Churches*. Edited by James R. Harrison and L. L. Welborn. WGRWSup 7. Atlanta: SBL Press.

Winter. Bruce W. 2001. *After Paul Left Corinth: The Influence of Secular Ethics and Social Change*. Grand Rapids: Eerdmans.

———. 2015. *Divine Honours for the Caesars: The First Christian's Responses*. Grand Rapids: Eerdmans.

18. The Problem of *invidia* at Ephesus: Handling Big Egos at the Big End of Town

James R. Harrison

IEph 5.1491

Waddington 1867, 210; Wood 1877, app. 5, "Inscriptions from the Odium," no. 3; *GIBM* 3.2.491; Lafoscade 1902, no. 54; *SIG* 850; Abbott and Johnson 1926; Lewis 1974, 89, no. 26i. From the marble wall covering of the *proscenium* (stage) of the *bouleuterion* (council chamber, town hall). Date: 145 CE.

	[Αὐτοκράτω]ρ Καῖσ[α]ρ θε[οῦ Ἀδ]ρι[ανο]ῦ	[Imperato]r Caes[ar] [Titus] Aeliu[s Had]ri[anu]s [Antoninus Augu]stu[s],
2	[υἱός, θεοῦ Τραι]ανο[ῦ Παρθ]ικο[ῦ υἱω]νός,	[son of the deified Traianu]s, [grandson of the deified Trai]anu[s Parth]icu[s],
	[θεοῦ Νέρουα ἔ]κγον[ος Τίτος] Αἴλιο[ς Ἀδρι]ανὸς	great [g]rand[son of the deified Nerva], [*pontifex maximus*], (possessing)
4	[Ἀντωνεῖνος Σεβα]στό[ς, ἀρχιερεὺ]ς μ[έγιστος, δη]μαρ-	[tr]ibu[ni]c[ian power] for the eighth time, two times (acclaimed) i[*mperator*], [four times] consul, [fa]-
	[χι]κ[ῆς ἐξουσίας] τὸ η′, α[ὐτοκράτωρ τ]ὸ β′, ὕπατος τ[ὸ δ′, πα-]	ther of his [c]ountry, to the [chi]ef magistrates and th[e] council and
6	τὴρ π[ατρίδος Ἐφεσ] ίων τοῖς [ἄρ] χουσι καὶ τ[ῇ] βουλῇ καὶ	[the people of Ephes]us, [g]reetin[gs]. [T]he liberality which V[ediu]s Antoninus lavishly contrib[utes]
	[τῶι δήμωι χ]αίρε[ιν· τ]ὴν φιλοτιμίαν ἣν φιλοτιμε[ῖται]	[toward yo]u I have learned not so muc[h] from
8	[πρὸς ὑμ]ᾶς Ο[ὐήδιο]ς Ἀντωνεῖνος ἔμαθον οὐχ οὕτω[ς] ἐκ	you[r lett]ers as from (the personal communication) of [hi]mself. For wish-

-243-

τῶν ὑμετέρω[ν γραμ]μάτων ὡς ἐκ τῶν   ing to gain help from me [for the]
[ἐκ]είνου· βουλόμε-   decoration of
10 νος γὰρ παρ' ἐμοῦ τυχεῖν βοηθείας   the (civic) works which he promised
[εἰς τὸ]ν κόσμον τῶν   to you, he made k[nown (to me) how
                                                 many a]nd how big
ἔργων ὧν ὑμεῖν ἐπηνγείλατο   buildings he bestows to the ci[ty; but
ἐδήλ[ωσεν ὅσα κ]αὶ ἡλίκα οἰ-   yo]u do not genuinely
12 κοδομήματα προστίθησιν τῇ πόλ[ει·   accept him; and (consequently) I also
ἀλλ' ὑμ]εῖς οὐ[κ] ὀρ-   gr[anted t]o him [. . .]
θῶς ἀποδέχεσθε αὐτόν· κἀγὼ καὶ   what he aske[d] and I fully accept that
συ[νεχώρησα α]ὐτῷ [...]ς   he—[not] in the manner of [many]
14 ἃ ᾐτήσατ[ο] καὶ ἀπεδεξάμην ὅτι [οὐ]   administrators of public affairs, who,
τὸν π[ολλῶν τῶ]ν πο-   f[o]r the sake of being [imm]ediatel[y
                                                 popu]lar,
λειτευομένων τρόπον, οἳ τοῦ [παρ]   sp[e]nd for spectacle[s a]nd distribu-
αχρῆμ[α ?εὐδοκιμ]εῖν χά-   tions and the [prizes of games]
16 [ρ]ιν εἰς θέα[ς κ]αὶ διανομὰς καὶ τὰ   (their) [munifice]nce, but (instead)
τῶ[ν ἀγώνων θέματα ? δαπαν]ῶ[σιν   through (his civic benefaction) he
?]   [hopes] in regard to the [future]—
[τὴ]ν φι[λοτιμ]ίαν, ἀλλὰ δι' οὗ πρὸς   pref[ers] [to m]ake the city [more a]
τὸ [μέλλον ἐλπίζει ? σ]εμνο-   ugust. (This) [letter] the most excel-
                                                 lent
18 [τέραν ποιή]σειν τὴν πόλιν   proc[onsul] [Claudius Ju]lianus [sen]
προήρη[ται. τὰ γράμματα ἔπε]μψεν   t. [Farewell]l,[1]
[Κλ(αύδιος) Ἰου]λιανὸς ὁ κράτιστος   [Imperato]r Caes[ar] [Titus] Aeliu[s
ἀνθύ[πατος. εὐτυχεῖτ]ε   Had]ri[anu]s [Antoninus Augu]
                                                 stu[s].

In this letter from Antoninus Pius to the archons, council, and people of Ephesus (IEph 5.1491 [145 CE]), we see the operation of *invidia* graphically portrayed.[2] The letter, which commends the generosity of the Ephesian benefactor, Vedius Antoninus, reveals the dark underside of the benefaction system where the Ephesian elites competed for social precedence. The letter addresses a breakdown in honorific rituals. Apparently, after consulting with the boule regarding the building of a new structure

---

1. For a translation and full exposition of the letter, see Kalinowski 1996, 102–27; now expanded in Kalinowski 2021, 305–12.

2. The following nine paragraphs, slightly adapted and expanded, come from Harrison 2018, 19–22. Used by permission.

at Ephesus, Vedius Papianus Antoninus had written to Antoninus Pius regarding the embellishment of the public work, but the Ephesians had clearly not written to the Roman ruler regarding the fact that the project was underway and that they were supportive of the project and its mooted decoration. Antoninus Pius takes this as a case of the Ephesians not properly appreciating their benefactor—a damning assessment of the Ephesian elites from the perspective of Greco-Roman reciprocity system. Several questions emerge. What building was Vedius intending to embellish and why? Why did he approach Antoninus Pius regarding the issue? Why had the Ephesians been so churlish about his plans? And what was the result of this exchange for Vedius Antoninus? What differentiates Vedius from other Ephesian benefactors?

First, the inscription gives us no indication which building at Ephesus is in mind, but most likely it is the Vedius bath-gymnasium complex in the north of the city (IEph 2.431), which was dedicated in 146–148 CE after the correspondence with Antoninus Pius. For full discussion, see Kalinowski 1996, 110–16. On the Vedius bath-gymnasium complex, see Steskal and Torre 2008. Angela V. Kalinowski (1996, 116) argues that Vedius was probably targeting as clients "the powerful mercantile and manufacturing classes in Ephesus that operated in the stoa of Servilius and probably lived near the gymnasium and the Koressos gate." The evidence for this is the general proximity of the Vedius bath-gymnasium to the trade booths of the various associations (including the bath attendants [IEph 6.2078]). Additionally, there were reserved seats in the latrines of the gymnasium complex for a whole variety of trade associations (IEph 2.454a, b, c, d, e, f). For a translation, see Ascough 2012, §172. Even more important are the honors accorded Vedius by the Ephesian associations. See here the discussion of Kalinowski 1996, 117–19.

The strong reciprocal bond between Vedius and the trade associations is evident in the association inscription of the woolworkers who honor him as "founder of the city of the Ephesians" (IEph 3.727). A statue was set up for Vedius by the association of the wine tasters in the Scholastika baths by the Ephesian council and the people, detailing the full *cursus honorum* of his magistracies and benefactions on behalf of the city (IEph 3.728 [162–162 CE]). For a translation, see Ascough 2012, §170. On the issue of whether the Ephesian inscriptions had a proper *cursus honorum*, see Kirbihler 2012. The temple builders also call him their founder and benefactor (IEph 7.1.3075) and the teachers near the Mousseion honor him (IEph 6.2065). The support base of the mercantile and manufacturing groups of city not only provided Vedius with alternative pathways of honor via the local associations, but also it boosted his civic profile among influential sections of the city, enabling him to broker local trades and financial contacts, including the bankers (IEph 2.454a), that could prove useful for his future building projects, as well as the current bath-gymnasium complex.

Second, the reason for approaching Antoninus Pius was, as Kalinowski (1996, 120–22) argues, to provide the Roman ruler with the opportunity of decorating the gymnasium with a hall devoted to the imperial cult, including the erection of statues of the Roman ruler, his family, and, perhaps, Vedius himself.[3] This likelihood is reinforced by the fact that Antoninus Pius "granted him all that he asked." The deflected glory to Vedius in such a project would have been inestimable.

Third, there is little doubt that the *invidia* of Vedius's rivals explains their recalcitrance in writing to the Roman ruler about the progress of the bath-gymnasium complex. Several pieces of evidence confirm this. In the highly effusive imperial letter of Constantius II, honoring the benefactor Flavius Philippus (IEph 1a.41.17–22 [344 CE]), we read of the potential danger of excessive civic fame provoking the jealousy of others:

> Even when we too are silent his extraordinary deeds shine forth. In their light he stood out brilliantly as so great and gifted a man that with the grace of affection he rose above envy [*invidiam*]. For it could not happen that he provoked arrows of jealousy against himself who made it his purpose to be more pleasing to his emperor. And therefore if anyone envied [*invidit*] him because of his right actions, someone who nevertheless up to now could not be discovered—the poison of his character against the advantage of our republic he did not date to show.

Moreover, in the case of the Ephesian benefactor, Claudius Aristion, the destructive effects of the *invidia* of his fellow citizens were personally felt when he was arraigned before Trajan's court for treason. As Pliny (*Ep.* 6.31) elaborates,

---

3. Wiplinger and Wlach (1996, 46; see also p. 47, fig. 57) write of the Vedius gymnasium: "In the middle of the west side, a particularly magnificent furnished room, with rich two-storey tabernacle architecture, opens onto the palaestra. A shallow niche in the middle of the west side contains a base, upon which a statue of the Emperor could well have been placed, and the foundation of an altar—the room is therefore called the Emperor Hall."

Claudius Aristion pleaded his case. He was the leading citizen of the Ephesians, generous and one who sought popularity in a harmless way; for this reason he had aroused the envy [*invidia*] of people of a vastly different character who had suborned an informer against him. He accordingly was cleared of the charge and acquitted.

Last, to cite another Ephesian epigraphic example, the unknown Philip appropriated for his own honor much later one of Celsus's four personifications of virtue at Celsus's library (IEph 7.2.5110: "The good sense (or 'intention') of Philip" [Ἔννοια Φιλίππου]), by removing the honorific inscription of Celsus and replacing it with a new one of his own. For details, see Harrison 2016b, 353, reproduced in this volume.

Clearly, in each case above, the high status and prominent profile of Ephesian benefactors had rankled some of their contemporaries. This either elicited *invidia* or provoked accusations of treason on their part. Others who were aggrieved either appropriated or erased from the epigraphic record the virtue of the luminary where possible. On erasure, see Harrison 2016a. As we have seen, a similar fate had befallen Vedius at Ephesus, but he was eventually vindicated, with the Ephesians being forced to acknowledge before the Anoninus Pius that they had received benefactions from him: "You make known to me who already knows of it the generosity which Vedius Antoninus has vouchsafed you, he who has contributed also the gifts which he received from me toward the decoration of the city" (IEph 5.1492 [150 CE]) (trans. Kalinowski 1996).

It is worthwhile pondering what precisely differentiated Vedius from his powerful Ephesian rivals. As we have seen, Antoninus Pius perceptively commented that, in contrast to his contemporaries, who, for the "sake of immediate popularity expend their generosity on spectacles and distributions and the prizes of games" (ll. 15–16), Vedius did so "in a manner that looks to the future" (l. 17) (trans. Kalinowski 1996). Those contemporaries, who undoubtedly, like Vedius, had also contributed to public works in Ephesus, would have thought that they were investing in the future as well. But, in the case of the bath-gymnasium complex, Vedius courted the imperial favor and, even more remarkably, turned strategically to the trades and mercantile associations for the endorsement and strategic placement of his building project.[4] Few Ephesian citizens were

---

4. I am not suggesting that all Ephesians associations forged connections with the provincial imperial cult (e.g., IEph 1a.18d.4–24; 7.2.3801), acted as benefactors

able to enlist such wide-ranging sponsorship across the social echelons for a transformative building program in Ephesus. The contemporaries of Vedius seethed internally with *invidia* at how he had so comprehensively outcompeted them at their own game.

Even the literary evidence of ancient novels confirms this strong impression of the periodic outbreak of *invidia* at Ephesus evidenced in the epigraphic evidence. The *Ephesiaca* of Xenophon of Ephesus (fl. second century–third century CE: Reardon 1989, 125–69), a love-story about two young peoples from Ephesus (Tagiliabue 2017), is filled with episodes touching on the insidious evil of envy in human relationships, a vice on which Plutarch wrote a tract in his *Moralia* (*De invidia et odio*). The effects of the vice are clear: envy is aroused on the rejection of amorous advances, with the result that the rejected lover dishonors her paramour (*Eph.* 2.5.5; 2.11.1–9). Envy leads to bribery (3.2.5–8), murder (3.12.4–6), and jealousy among suitors who lust over the same woman (1.15.5–16.7; 2.13.5–8; 4.5.3–6). For the wider context of these examples, see Hoag 2015, 57. As Gary Hoag concludes, "The message of Xenephon of Ephesus to the wealthy in Ephesus would have been clear regarding envy: avoid its destructive power" (75).

What picture emerges about the operations of *invidia* among the elites in the papyrological evidence? A single example will suffice. However, on the evil eye and φθόνος ("envy," "jealousy") in P.Mich. 6.423–424, see Bryen and Wypustek 2009. In P.Mich. 1.23, the rivalry of people of (presumably) elite status in nominating Aristeides to be the commissary of corn are aired, despite the fact that Aristeides was not the right age for the post nor was even due for the liturgy:

> I have had the misfortune to be proposed by the citizens [ὑπὸ τοῦ πολιτῶν] as commissary of corn, though I am not yet of the right age nor due for that burden [τῆς λειτουργίας ταύτης], but I have been proposed by certain persons [τινές] out of jealousy [φθονερίαν]. I and my brother Theronides therefore have sent Dromon to explain these things to Apollonios, in order that he may help us and release me from that responsibility. You would do me a favor then by immediately admitting

---

(e.g., IEph 1a.20), possessed world-wide connections (e.g., the Dionysiac Artists: IEph 1a.22), or could exercise significant local sway (e.g., the silversmith riot: Acts 19:23–41; IEph 2.425; 2.547; 2.585; 2.586; 3.636; 6.2212; 6.2441; e.g., the bakers strike at Ephesus: IEph 2.215). The small guilds of the nut-sellers (IEph 6.2709) and the bed-builders (IEph 6.2213) would have been insignificant, among many others. See Harland 1996.

Dromon to Apollonius's presence and assisting him to have speech with Apollonios as soon as possible and seeing that he sends him back to us immediately after settling everything.

What are the motives of the civic elites in nominating the young Aristeides ahead of time to be the commissary of corn, and how does it relate to jealousy? The text gives us no explanation as to why it is a case of jealousy, so we enter here into the territory of speculation. Furthermore, we are assuming that the "certain persons" (τινές) mentioned are powerful local elites among the citizenry (ὑπὸ τοῦ πολιτῶν) mentioned in the papyrus. In my view, the young Aristeides came from a powerful aristocratic family, being in the future a strong political rival to other similarly placed young sons of the aristocratic civic elites: this is the origin of the jealousy on the part of the unspecified nominators. If Aristeides was elected to the position due to his family influence, the hope of the rival elites would be that he would fail lamentably in the post due to his youth and inexperience. Even if after holding the post for a brief time, he astutely withdrew before any significant political damage to his career occurred, such a withdrawal would create shame for himself and for his family: the reason for his hasty abdication could only be interpreted by his enemies as either political inexperience or lack of resilience in the face of challenges. Another possibility is that his opponents had hoped that Aristeides did not have sufficient financial means to carry out the liturgy effectively over an extended period of time and thereby bring dishonor to his family name. Or perhaps they discerned a character flaw that would be Aristeides's undoing if he was pressured into this position before his time. This cleverly devised strategy, instigated by some elite rivals within the city, emanated from their jealousy over a young well-positioned rival from a powerful family who might outcompete their own sons in public. To humiliate publicly such a contender would resolve the problem temporarily for their own sons, allowing them to thrive in the public *cursus honorum* ("course of honors") while Aristides languished in retrieving his lost reputation.

Finally, as an important aside, other areas of research into jealousy in antiquity might also be profitably investigated. The role of φθόνος and *invidia* in the Greek and Latin literature could be explored: for example, Isocrates (Said 2003), Cicero (Bragova 2018) and Ovid (Shiaele 2010). A geographical focus on a city and region, such as Athens in Attica, enables us to see the popular jealousy of the rich elites that was widely felt in antiquity, as well as the methods that Athens used in response to build social cohesion and equality and the manner in which the politics of envy was rhetorically manipulated in civic discourse (Fisher 2003; Sanders 2010; Cairns 2003). The essay collection of David Konstan and N. Keith Rutter (2003) helpfully situates φθόνος and *invidia* in the range of rivalry emotions, positive and negative, within the ancient world. Last, the role of *invidia* in the visual evidence helps us to see the importance of the apotropaic rituals designed to counter its blighting influence through the evil eye.[5]

What relevance does the Ephesian epigraphic and papyrological evidence on *invidia* among the elites have for the New Testament? The common denominator behind both episodes discussed above is the quest for honor, with its rivalries, through either the traditional pathways of civic beneficence or by posts in the local *cursus honorum*. The elites who succeed in the traditional pathways of honor accumulation inevitably attracted the jealousy of the general populace, a phenomenon discussed widely by ancient authors, or the *invidia* of rivals among their elite peers. The clearest instance of this in the New Testament is Mark 15:10, which speaks thus of Pilate's assessment of the motivations of the chief priests in handing over Jesus to him for arraignment: "For he realized that it was out of jealousy [διὰ φθόνου] that the chief priests had handed him over." Immediately, a series of important interpretative questions emerge. Against what interpretative grid should φθόνος be historically assessed in this instance? How would Pilate have known the motivations of the chief priests at this juncture? Are we able to speak decisively regarding the motivations of any actor in history without assuming "historical omniscience" (Martin 2015, 342–44), whether it is ourselves as modern historians or the New Testament writers themselves? Further, against what interpretative grid is Pilate himself making this judgement of the chief priests? How promising an interpretative grid for this verse is the quest for honor and its unravelling in jealous rivalries articulated in the Ephesian documentary evidence above?

In a major discussion of Mark 15:10, Anselm Hagedorn and Jerome Neyrey set out the evidence for rivalries against the backdrop of the social dynamic of the quest for honor and the arousal of envy. Not only do the authors provide a major analysis of envy in the Gospel of Mark (Hage-

---

5. For iconographic examples from Corinth and elsewhere, see Slane and Dickie 1983, 1993. For *invidia* inscriptions and mosaics in Africa, see Dunbabin 1989. For iconographic examples from Ostia, see 41; see also Dunbabin 1991, 35.

18. The Problem of invidia at Ephesus

dorn and Neyrey 1998, 43–54), but they also set this out comprehensively within the frameworks of sociological, socioeconomic, and psychological analysis, exploring the objects and strategies of envy, as well as the quest for φιλοτιμία, in the ancient literature (17–38). As immensely insightful as the analysis is, the authors do not set out the perceptions of honor from the *Roman* viewpoint of Pilate and the *Sadducean* perspective of the chief priests. There is a certain generic approach to the quest for honor on the part of Hagedorn and Neyrey that is insufficient for the historical particularity demanded by our text. When we penetrate behind the rhetoric of the Gospel of Mark on envy, what further insights emerge from the ancient evidence?

First, what are the lineaments of Roman honor in the case of Pontius Pilate? For full discussion, Harrison 2021. In terms of the ancestral honor of the Roman prefect Pontius Pilate, the family of the Pontii furnished celebrated Samnite generals during the republic and a consul under Tiberius. As a "Pilatus" ("javelin-armed"), the Roman prefect also had an equestrian military background, with one of his ancestors perhaps serving as a *primus pilus* ("First Spear"), the highest-ranking centurion in a legion (Smith 2018, 45). Thus, as an equestrian centurion and now as provincial prefect, Pilate was committed to the traditional quest for ancestral glory in the same way as the republican *nobiles* ("nobles") were (Harrison 2011, 201–25). The honorific dimensions of this is well illustrated by the equestrian inscriptions at Philippi (IPhilippes 2.47–71). Thus the motivation of the prefect Pilate, in governing the province of Judaea and periodically handling its dissidents, would have been to maintain and surpass his ancestral honor.

Second, the motivation of Pilate as a Roman prefect was also to maintain and enhance the honor of the Julian house by strategically eulogizing the ruler Tiberius. This was demonstrated by Pilate's construction of the Tiberium (*CIIP* 2.1277), a lighthouse erected in honor of the ruler at Caesarea Maritima, and the release of a coin commemorating the death (?) of Tiberius's mother (Julia Augusta=Livia) in 29 CE (ΙΟΥΛΙΑ ΚΑΙΣΑΡΟΣ; see Hendin 1996, §648). Pilates's honoring of Julian rule was further demonstrated by Pilate's more forceful imposition of Roman authority, in comparison to his prefect predecessors, upon agitators in the province (Josephus, *B.J.* 2.169–174; *A.J.* 18.55–59; *B.J.* 2.175–177; *A.J.* 18.60–62; Luke 13:1–2). This is also illustrated by Pilate's unprecedented use of Roman augury and sacrificial motifs upon his coinage in order to underscore the traditional gods' blessing of the Roman Empire, its sacrificial system, and its priesthood (Hendin 1996, §§648, 649, 649a, 650), including Tiberius as *pontifex maximus*. Thus, this is the ancestral, equestrian, and imperial context of Roman honor from which Pontius Pilate would have evaluated his role as governor and his own personal ambitions.

When we come to speak about the quest for honor on the part of the Sadducean chief priests we face a problem: all our information about the Sadducees derives from sources written by others as opposed to their own writings, and, indeed, many of these writings are highly hostile. However, we gain a strong sense of what ancestral honor for the hereditary Sadducean priesthood might have looked like for the priestly caste of Jerusalem from Josephus's extensive boasting in his Hasmonean priestly ancestors in his *Vita* 1–9. A brief selection follows (1–2, 7–9):

> My family is not an ignoble one, tracing its descent far back to priestly ancestors. Different races base their claim to nobility on various grounds; with us a connection with the priesthood is the hallmark of an illustrious line. Not only, however, were my ancestors priests, but they belong to the first of the twenty-four courses—a peculiar distinction—and to the most eminent of its constituent clans. Moreover, on my mother's side I am of royal blood; for the posterity of Asamonauus, from whom she sprang, for a very considerable period were kings, as well as high priests, of our nation.... Distinguished as he was by his noble birth, my father Matthias was even more esteemed for his upright character, being among the most notable men in Jerusalem, our greatest city. Brought up with Matthias, my own brother by both parents, I made great progress in my education, gaining a reputation for an excellent memory and understanding. While still a mere boy, about fourteen years old, I won universal applause for my love of literature; insomuch that the chief priests and the leading men of the city used constantly to come to me for precise information on some particular in our ordinances.

We see here by analogy how the relationship between Annas, father-in-law of Caiaphas, and his son-in-law would have been dictated by a mutual desire for the maintenance of the dominance of their high-priestly house,[6] as well as for

---

6. At this early stage, the high-priestly house of Annas is still all-dominant, though by the 50 and 60's other rival houses had emerged (Boethus, Kathros, Phiabi); see Bond 2004, 35. Bond concludes about the elevation of Caiaphas through the house of Annas: "The high priest with his sons and son-in-law formed a tightly knit Sadducean clan, a force to be reckoned with in Jerusalem circles. The old man would probably have made sure that Caiaphas was quickly promoted up the temple hierarchy: after all, the higher the position Caiaphas held, the more useful he was to Annas" (39).

the expansion of its honor by ensuring the purity of the temple and its worship. Moreover, by continuing to act as faithful clients of Rome, Annas and Caiaphas, belonging to Roman ruler's retainer class (Josephus, A.J. 20.251; Carter, 2003, 38–40), ensured the political prominence of their family.

Pontius Pilate, because of his own devotion to ancestral and imperial honor, would have understood well the motivations of the chief priests, albeit from a Roman honor perspective (Barton 2001). In sum, "when Pilate observed that it was 'out of envy' that Jesus was handed over, this refers to the pain felt by Jesus' rivals over his fame and prestige" (1998, 20). Envy of the honor of Christ, not merely conflicts or controversies, generated the personal decision of the chief priests to act decisively in arraigning Jesus (55–56). The fame, teaching, and activities of Jesus detracted from their own public and private honor. What then was so dishonoring about Jesus in the estimation of the chief priests, which generated a fire in their bones over their own lost honor?

Hagedorn and Neyrey (1998, 42–43) correctly highlight the widespread positive evaluation of Jesus by the public that targeted him as an object of Sadducean envy (Mark 1:28; 1:45; 2:1–2; 2:13; 3:7–8; 3:20; 4:1; 5:20, 21, 22–23, 27–28; 6:14, 32–34, 53–56; 7:24–25, 31; 8:1, 22, 27–30; 9:14–29; 10:1, 46–47; 11:18; 12:37). Further, the public authority of Jesus in his teaching (Mark 11:18; 12:34b) was demonstrated in humiliating fashion to the Sadducees when their cleverly created conundrum regarding the impossibility of the resurrection hope (12:18–27), based upon their acceptance of the Pentateuch as their sole scriptural authority, was destroyed by Jesus's appeal to the Pentateuch for the reality of the resurrection (12:26 [see Exod 3:6]). Last, however we interpret Jesus's intentions in provocatively cleansing the temple (Matt 21:12–17; Mark 11:12–18; Luke 19:45–48; John 2:13–22), his prediction of its immanent destruction (Matt 23:38; 24:1–2; Mark 13:1–2; Luke 19:41–44), and his announcement its replacement by a new temple/community (Matt 12:6; 17:24–27, esp. v. 26; Mark 14:38; John 2:18–22; 4:23–24), Jesus was undermining the raison d'être of the Sadducees and their power base. For discussion, see Ådna 2012; Snodgrass 2009. This not only aroused their fury but also provoked fear about their increasing loss of honor to this itinerant apocalyptic prophet and messianic pretender, whose fame and popularity continued its meteoric rise among the nonelites.

Bibliography

Abbott, Frank F., and Allan C. Johnson. 1926. *Municipal Administration in the Roman Empire*. Princeton: Princeton University Press.

Ådna, Jostein. 2012. "Jesus and the Temple." Pages 2635–75 in *The Historical Jesus*. Vol. 3 of *Handbook for the Study of the Historical Jesus*. Edited by Tom Holmén and Stanley E. Porter. Leiden: Brill.

Ascough, Richard S., Philip A. Harland, and John S. Kloppenborg, eds. 2012. *Associations in the Greco-Roman World: A Source Book*. Waco, TX: Baylor University Press.

Barton, Carlin A. 2001. *Roman Honor: The Fire in the Bones*. Berkeley: University of California Press.

Bond, Helen K. 2004. *Caiaphas: Friend of Rome and Judge of Jesus?* Louisville: Westminster John Knox.

Bragova, Arina. 2018. "Cicero on Vices." *Studia Antiqua et Archaeologica* 24:253–77.

Bryen, Ari Z., and Andrzej Wypustek. 2009. "Gemellus' Evil Eyes (*P.Mich.* VI 424–424)." *GRBS* 49:535–55.

Cairns, D. L. 2003. "The Politics of Envy: Envy and Equality in Ancient Greece." Pages 236–52 in *Envy, Spite and Jealousy: The Rivalrous Emotions in Ancient Greece*. Edited by David Konstan and N. Keith Rutter. Edinburgh Leventis Studies 2. Edinburgh: Edinburgh University Press.

Carter, Warren. 2003. *Pontius Pilate: Portraits of a Roman Governor*. Collegeville, MN: Liturgical Press.

Dunbabin, Katherine M. D. 1989. "Baiarum Grata Volupta: Pleasures and Dangers of the Baths." *Papers of the British School at Rome* 57:6–46.

———. 1991. "INBIDE CALCO TE … Trampling Upon the Envious." Pages 26–37 in *Tesserae: Festschrift für Josef Engeman*. JACSup 18. Münster: Aschendorff.

Fisher, Nick. 2003. "'Let Envy Be Absent': Envy, Liturgies and Reciprocity in Athens." Pages 181–215 in *Envy, Spite and Jealousy: The Rivalrous Emotions in Ancient Greece*. Edited by David Konstan and N. Keith Rutter. Edinburgh Leventis Studies 2. Edinburgh: Edinburgh University Press.

Hagedorn, Anselm C., and Jerome H. Neyrey. 1998. "'It Was Out of Envy That They Handed Jesus Over' (Mark 15:10): The Anatomy of Envy and the Gospel of Mark." *JSNT* 69:15–36.

Harland, P. A. 1996. "Honours and Worship: Emperors, Imperial Cults and Associations at Ephesus (First to Third Centuries CE)." *SR* 25.3:319–34.

Harrison, James R. 2011. *Paul and the Imperial Authorities at Thessalonica and Rome: A Study in the Conflict of Ideology.* WUNT 273. Tübingen: Mohr Siebeck.

———. 2016a. "The Erasure of Honour: Paul and the Politics of Dishonour." *TynBull* 66:161–84.

———. 2016b. "Sponsors of *Paideia*: Ephesian Benefactors, Civic Virtue and the New Testament." *EC* 7:346–67.

———. 2018. "An Epigraphic Portrait of Ephesus and Its Villages." Pages 1–67 in *Ephesus*. Vol. 3 of *The First Urban Churches*. Edited by James R. Harrison and L. L. Welborn. WGRWSup 9. Atlanta: SBL Press.

———. 2021. "Reactions to Roman Officialdom to Jesus and His Followers in the Early First Century AD: A Case Study of Pontius Pilate." Pages 1–55 in vol. 2 of *The Impact of Jesus of Nazareth: Historical, Theological and Pastoral Perspectives*. Edited by Peter G. Bolt and James R. Harrison. Macquarie Park: SCD Press.

Hendin, David. 1996. *Guide to Biblical Coins*. 3rd ed. New York: Amphora.

Hoag, Gary G. 2015. *Wealth in Ancient Ephesus and the First Letter to Ephesus: Fresh Insights from* Ephesiaca *by Xenephon of Ephesus*. BBRSup 11. Winona Lake, IN: Eisenbrauns.

Lafoscade, Léon Jules. 1902. *De epistulis (aliisque titulis) imperatorum magistratuumque romanorum quas ab aetate Augusti usque ad Constantinum graece scriptas, lapides papyrive servaverunt*. Edebant fratres Le Bigot, Insulis.

Lewis, Naphtali. 1974. *The Roman Principate: 27 B.C.–285 A.D. Greek Historical Documents*. Toronto: Hakkert.

Kalinowski, Angela V. 1996. "Patterns of Patronage: The Politics and Ideology of Public Building in the Eastern Roman Empire (31 BCE–600 CE)." PhD diss., University of Toronto.

———. 2021. *Memory, Family, and Community in Roman Ephesos*. Cambridge: Cambridge University Press.

Kirbihler, François. 2012. "Un cursus honorum à Éphèse? Quelques réflexions sur la succession des magistratures de la cité à l'époque romaine." Pages 67–107 in *Folia Graeca in honorem Edouard Will: Historica*. Edited by P. Goukowsky and C. Feyel. Vol. 2. Études anciennes 51. Nancy: A.D.R.A.

Konstan, David, and N. Keith Rutter. 2003. *Envy, Spite and Jealousy: The Rivalrous Emotions in Ancient Greece*. Edinburgh Leventis Studies. Edinburgh. Edinburgh University Press.

Martin, Dale. 2015. "Response to Downing and Fredericksen." *JSNT* 37.3:334–45.

Reardon, B. P. 1989. *Collected Ancient Greek Novels*. Berkeley: University of California Press.

Said, Suzanne. 2003. "Envy and Emulation in Isocrates." Pages 217–34 in *Envy, Spite and Jealousy: The Rivalrous Emotions in Ancient Greece*. Edited by David Konstan and N. Keith Rutter. Edinburgh Leventis Studies 2. Edinburgh: Edinburgh University Press.

Sanders, Edward M. 2010. "Envy and Jealousy in Classical Athens." PhD diss., University College London.

Shiaele, M. 2010. "Ovid's *Invidia* and the Literary Tradition." *Rosetta* 8.5:127–38.

Slane, Kathleen Warner, and M. W. Dickie. 1983. "*Invidia vipantur pectora*: The Iconography of *Pthonos/Invidia* in Graeco-Roman Art." *JAC* 26:7–137.

———. 1993. "A Knidian Phallic Vase from Corinth." *Hesperia* 62:483–505.

Smith, Mark D. 2018. *The Final Days of Jesus: The Thrill of Defeat, the Agony of Victory; A Classical Historian Explores Jesus' Arrest, Trial and Execution*. Cambridge: Lutterworth.

Snodgrass, Klyne R. 2009. "The Temple Incident." Pages 429–80 in *Key Events in the Life of the Historical Jesus: A Collaborative Exploration of Context and Coherence*. Edited by Darrell L. Bock and Robert L. Webb. Grand Rapids: Eerdmans.

Steskal, Martin, and Martino La Torre. 2008. *Das Vediusgymnasium in Ephesos: Archäologie und Baubefund*. FiE 14.1. Vienna: Verlag der österreichischen Akademie der Wissenschaften.

Tagliabue, Aldo. 2017. *Xenephon's Ephesiaca: A Paraliterary Love-Story from the Ancient World*. Ancient Narrative Supplements 22. Groningen: Barkhuis.

Waddington, William Henry. 1867. *Mémoire sur la chronologie de la vie du rhéteur Ælius Aristide*. Paris: Imprimerie impériale.

Wiplinger, Gilbert, and Gudrun Wlach. 1996. *Ephesus: One Hundred Years of Austrian Research*. Edited by Claudia Luxon. Vienna: Österreichisches Archäologisches Institut.

Wood, John Turtle. 1877. *Discoveries at Ephesus*. London: Longmans, Green.

Economic Issues

19. Maintaining the Market Supply of Wheat for Rome: Revelation 6:6 and 18:11–13

James R. Harrison

IEph 2.211

JÖAI 47:6–10 (*editio princeps*); AE 1968.478; BE 1968.465; Wörrle 1971, 325–40. Two fragments matching the break in the stone, found in the rubble of the east inner hall of the agora. From sketch book 3415 + 3415 (Knibbe). Date: Undated.

[— διὰ]	[—because of]
2 [τὸ] μέγεθ[ος τῆς λαμπροτάτης?]	[the] stature of your [most illustrious]
ὑμῶν πό[λεω]ς καὶ τὸ πλ[ῆθος]	c[it]y and the mu[ltitude]
4 τῶν οἰκούντων παρ' ὑμεῖ[ν· —]	of you[r] inhabitants [.—]
πρόδηλον δὲ ὅτι καὶ ὑμεῖς εὐγνω-	It is clear that you also
6 μόνως χ[ρ]ήσεσθε τῇ τοιαύτῃ συν-	will use charitably such permission when you
χωρήσει λογιζόμενοι, ὅτι ἀναγκαῖον	reason that it is [n]ecessary
8 πρῶτον τῇ βασιλευούσῃ πόλει	foremost that for the ruling city
ἄφθονον	
εἶναι τὸν π[ρ]ὸς τὴν ἀγορὰν	the wheat prepared fo[r] market
παρασκευα-	
10 ζόμενον [κ]αὶ ἀθροιζόμενον πανταχό-	[a]nd collected from everywhere be plent-
θεν πυρόν, ἔπειθ' οὕτως καὶ τὰς ἄλλας	iful, then likewise also that the other
12 πόλεις εὐπορεῖν τῶν ἐπιτηδείων.	cities abound in provisions.
εἰ μὲν οὖν ὁ Νεῖλος φαίνοιτο, ὥσπε[ρ]	If therefore the Nile should appear, just a[s]
14 εὐχόμε[θ]α, παρέχων ἡμεῖν τῆς ἀνό-	we pr[a]y, to grant us
δου τὸ σύνηθ<ε>ς μέτρον καὶ γεωρ-	the customary measure of rising and should
γο[ῖτο	
ΣΥΝΗΘΣΣ (on the stone)	

16	παρὰ Αἰγυπτίοις ἄφθονος ὁ πυρός,	wheat be plentifully cultivated by the Egyptians,
	καὶ ὑμ[ε]ῖς ἐν πρώτοις μετὰ τὴν πα-	you also among the first after the father-coun[try] ...
18	τρί[δα —]	[—because of]

This Ephesian inscription concludes with a prayer (εὐχόμε[θ]α) to the divine river Nile (ll. 13–16) for its customary beneficent "rising" (ll. 14–15) so that the planting of wheat might be successful and abundant (l. 15, ἄφθονος). This underscores the potential fragility of the economy of Rome, which was dependent upon strategic centers for its grain supplies (mostly durum wheat): Egypt, North Africa, Sicily, and Sardinia. Despite the smallness of the contribution of Sicily, its proximity to Rome was very important, especially when, just before the sailing season, the Roman grain supply ran low (Erdkamp 2005, 219). During the early empire, Sardinia and Sicily waned in their importance as suppliers of grain to Rome in contrast to Egypt and Africa (Bauckham 1983, 362, citing Josephus, *B.J.* 2.283, 386). On the grain supply of Rome generally, see Rickman 1980; Garnsey 1988, 218–43. On the grain provinces, see Erdkamp 2005, 206–57. On the importance of Egypt as a grain supplier, see Tacitus, *Hist.* 1.11; Suetonius, *Aug.* 18. On the grain trade between Greece and Egypt, see Roebuck 1950. The importation and distribution of the grain for the residents of Rome was known as the *cura annonae* ("care for the grain supply"), named in honor of the goddess Annona and sarcastically dismissed by Juvenal as "bread and circuses" (*Sat.* 10.78–81). On the *cura annonae*, see Jongman 1997.

What arrangements had been made at Rome, spanning the republican and imperial periods, for the distribution of the grain supply in the city upon its arrival from the overseas grain centers?

Grain at Rome: The Pathway to Ensuring Stability of Supply and Peace in the Social Order

In the early Roman republic (509–28 7BCE), the senatorial government of Rome had subsidized grain at reduced prices, the aediles being in charge of the market price. But, by 123 BCE, the *Lex Frumentaria* of Gaius Gracchus legislated that a fixed number of citizens receive a monthly dole ration of 5 *modii* of grain (33 kg), the grain having been bought at a low price from North Africa and Sardinia. This system continued until 58 BCE, when grain became free due to the *Lex Clodia frumentaria* (Cicero, *Rosc. Amer.* 25; Dio Cassius, *Hist. Rom.* 38.13). On the prior *leges frumentariae* (e.g., the *Lex Terentia et Cassia frumentaria*, the *Lex Gabinia*, among others), see Anonymous 1875. For discussion, see Cristofori 2002; Vervaet 2020. On the grain trade in the Hellenistic world, see Casson 1954.

In 57 BCE, the passing of the *Lex Cornelia et Caecilia* gave Pompey extraordinary powers to supervise the grain dole for five years (Cicero, *Att.* 4.1; Dio Cassius, *Hist. Rom.* 39.9; Plutarch, *Pomp.* 49). After the civil war and the assassination of Pompey in 49 BCE, Julius Caesar set out to reform the management of the *annona* (grain supply) in 44 BCE, which had become an increasingly difficult task (Suetonius, *Jul.* 38). He reduced the dole to a more manageable 150,000 recipients and appointed two new aediles (*aediles Cereales*) for the administration of the grain supply (Cassius Dio, *Hist. Rom.* 43.51). However, Julius Caesar's assassination in 44 BCE curtailed any further developments, including his plans for the development of the port at Ostia for the storage of grain and its dissemination to nearby Rome. This development at Ostia would be later commenced by Claudius and finished in its final details by the additions of Nero, now confirmed archaeologically. For numismatic evidence for the Claudian harbor at Rome's port of Ostia, developed so that the grain fleet could safely reside there, see *RIC* 1.178–183. For discussion of the visual evidence, see Weiss 2013; Cuyler 2014. For the archaeological evidence for the Neronian additions to the Claudian port at Ostia, see Keay and Millett 2005, 275–77, esp. 276–77. More generally, see Mattingly and Aldrete 2000. For the inscriptions and mosaics of the Ostian hall of the grain measurers—where grain was registered upon arrival and was stored in public warehouses (*horrea*) until it was transferred to river boats for transportation along the Tiber River from Ostia to Rome—see Van der Meer 2012, §23. In sum, the internal divisions of the late republic meant that the Senate could not effectively reorganize the *annona* or maintain its traditional control over the grain distribution, with the result that the triumvirs Pompey and Caesar temporarily filled the void, but their violent deaths brought their initially promising efforts to an end.

Augustus, upon taking upon himself the administration of the *annona* (22 BCE), appointed a prefect for the grain supply (*praefectus annonae*) in 10 CE (Dio Cassius, *Hist. Rom.* 55.26.2; 55.31.4). This official guaranteed a reliable grain supply, ensured the correct measurements and weights of grain, and made sure that grain was safely stored. Until the third century CE, the *praefectus annonae* and his staff maintained the grain supply for the Roman rulers, creating regulations for the market, judging any legal cases arising from corrupt practices and disputes, and arranging the trade of the Roman ruler's own personal grain supply. See Noreña 2011, 112–13. The creation of this office saved Rome from "the utter ruin of the state," the fear that Tiberius had voiced in a letter to the Senate (22 CE), should the Cura Annonae ever be neglected (Tacitus, *Ann.* 3.54.6–8). On Augustus's responses to crises involving grain shortages, see Res gest. divi Aug 5.5 and 15 (23 BCE; see also Dio Cassius, *Hist. Rom.* 55.26.3). For commentary, see Cooley 2009, 129, 171. More generally on the Augustan reforms of the grain supply, see Reinarcher 2014.

What do we know about the grain supply and the Nile River from the documentary evidence?

The Grain Supply at Egypt as a Gift of the Divine Nile: The Documentary Evidence

The epigraphic documentary evidence highlights the divine status of the Nile River. At the Elephantine Island (115 BCE), there is reference to the great god Nile (ὁ μέγας θεὸς Νεῖλος, IThèbes Syène 244 [*OGIS* 168]; IEgypte prose 2). In a dedication to the gods Sarapis and Isis, as well as king Ptolomaios and Queen Berenike, the Nile is the third god addressed (IDelta 235.5). In a bilingual inscription on the island of Philae (29 BCE) in honor of the Roman equites Caius Cornelius (*OGIS* 654), the text concludes with thanks-offerings (χαριστήρια; d[onum] d[edit]) "to the gods of the forefathers" and the Nile River. Finally, in an inscription honoring the prefect of Egypt, Tiberius Claudius Balbillus, at Bousirus (Memphis) in 55–59 CE (*OGIS* 666.7–11; IEgypte prose 55), the beneficence of the divine Nile is graphically described. Prior to the motion of the village dwellers near the pyramids to honor of the Roman magistrate, the beneficence of Balbillus is strategically placed alongside the overflowing generosity of the Nile:

> Because of this man's favors and benefactions Egypt is full of all good things, sees the gifts of the Nile growing greater year by year, and now enjoys even more the well-balanced rising of the god [i.e., the Nile].

From this epigraphic evidence, it is clear that the divine vitality of the Nile River ensured the grain supply of Rome.

In the case of the papyri, a similar picture emerges. Two papyri will establish the point. First, in P.Mich.inv.2920r (210/211 CE, Kerkesoucha,

Arsinoite nome, Egypt),[1] a petition is made to the Egyptian *epistrategos* by the landowners and public cultivators regarding their inability to complete a wattle weir: their complaint was that they had not been furnished the materials for it. What is interesting from the extract below—a side issue to the overall intent of the papyrus—is the strong realization that the favor of the sacred Nile is required if immanent sowing was to be undertaken successfully:

> Since the land runs the risk of going dry on this account and inflicting injury on the most sacred treasury in the matter of the dues paid for these (arourai), which come to not a few myriads (of artabai), at a time when the most sacred Nile has shown himself most favorable to us for a good issue, we request, if it seems best to your beneficent genius, that you order with your (characteristic) vigor that that work be done, <so that> we may be able blamelessly to maximize the imminent sowing—may it be for good!—and nothing be lost to the most sacred treasury.

Second, in P.Oslo 3.78 (unknown place, Arsinoiton polis?, Egypt: pre-May 31, 136 CE), the Roman ruler Hadrian grants variations in the payments of rent (i.e., a money tax) for the inhabitants of the Thebaid, given that the inundation of the Nile had been insufficient for the last two seasons. In the papyrus extract below, the cyclical view of lean and abundant years in Egypt is articulated with great clarity, depending totally on the inundation of the Nile. The implications are plain. The precariousness of the Egyptian harvests, a consequence of the periodic rises and falls of the Nile inundation, would not only have impacted upon the collection of Roman taxes in the province of Egypt, paid in kind by grain, but also put at risk the future availability of grain at Rome due to the shortfall from one of its most important overseas gain suppliers. The text says:

> Proclamation of the Emperor Caesar, son of the deified Traianus Pathicus, grandson of the deified Nerva, Traianus Hadrianus Augustus pontifex maximus, holder of the tribunician power for the twentieth time, imperator for the second time, consul thrice, father of his country: having been informed that even now, just as last year, the Nile has risen rather deficiently … < >, —even considering the fact that during the preceding years successively its rise was not only plentiful, but rather almost

---

1. See, in the digital collection Advanced Papyrological Information System (APIS UM), https://tinyurl.com/SBLPress9031a1.

higher than any time before, and that, flooding all over the country, it caused the produce of abundant and beautiful crops, still I have deemed it necessary to bestow a favor on the cultivators, although I hope—this be said with God!—that in years to come any possible deficiencies will be supplied by the Nile itself and the earth, according to the revolving (?) nature of things, changing from prosperous flow and abundancy to scarcity, and from scarcity to plenty.

In conclusion, the epigraphic and papyrological evidence underscores the divine beneficence of the Nile in providing abundant harvests and, concomitantly, the paucity of harvests when the annual rise and overflow of the Nile did not occur. The collection of the Roman grain supply would have been thereby affected, with the result that Roman taxation was considerably diminished. What, then, is the relevance of this background evidence to the city of Ephesus, and what does it reveal about the intention of the author of the inscription in regards to the grain supply?

Ephesus and the Grain Supply of Egypt: The Interconnectedness of Imperial Trade Markets

This letter from an unidentified Roman ruler (second–third century CE) is addressed to the Ephesians regarding grain shipments from Egypt and is perhaps written in response to complaints from the local grain dealers in the city (Casson 1980, 23–24). The abundance of these grain supplies was totally dependent upon the divine Nile's rising and, subsequently, upon the successful cultivation of the grain by the Egyptians—a process to which the ruler alludes in his prayer (IEph 2.211.13–16). The Roman ruler makes it plain to the Ephesians that the collected Egyptian harvest was always primarily destined for the consumption of Rome ("necessary foremost," ll. 7–8) because Egypt was one of the two largest provincial grain centers for the Roman people, the other being Africa. The *annona*, therefore, was a central strut in the imperial policy of maintaining the daily survival of the people at Rome and in ensuring long term the stability of the social order there.

Nevertheless, at the times of the Nile's abundance, Egyptian grain would be available on the free market. The grain dealers of the "most illustrious" Ephesus could expect that they would have informal access to the grain supplies as "would-be buyers" (Casson 1980, 24) and subsequently be able to sell provisions without any regulatory interference. The only proviso was that the Ephesian grain dealers sought permission in a considered manner from the Roman ruler or, more likely, from the *praefectus annonae* himself, or a lower official in the imperial bureaucracy locally. As Bauckham (1983, 362–63) observes, "The immense importance of the corn supply meant that the state increasingly supervised the system, but private merchants and shippers continued to run it." The same right presumably extended to other prestigious cities of the empire, provided that they also behaved in a consultative manner and prioritized the needs of Rome in the dissemination of produce. There is also perhaps a hint in the last two lines that there was some type of hierarchical order (ll. 17–18: "you also among the first after the father-coun[try]") regarding which cities could actually have grain dealers and with what precedence they could take up the right. In sum, in times of the overflow of grain supplies at Egypt, the grain traders of Ephesus could buy their grain from Egypt and sell it elsewhere with no imposition of imperial regulations other than fulfilling their supply obligations to Rome and acting consultatively beforehand with the imperial bureaucracy, except when the grain harvest at Egypt had collapsed or was too meager. On those occasions, Rome would monopolize all grain supplies for her own citizens.

Finally, the goddess Annona, who was the personification of the grain supply, became an integral part of the imperial propaganda. She was rendered in the iconography of the Julio-Claudian coinage (Nero), the coin issues of 69 CE (Vitellius), and the Flavian coinage (Titus, Domitian, Trajan, Hadrian), as well as in the numismatic issues of subsequent rulers later in the empire (Antoninus Pius, Septimius Severus, Severus Alexander). Moreover, Annona becomes part of the imperial cult of the virtues, being rendered as a theophany of the Roman ruler by his care for the Roman people through the provision of grain. See Noreña 2011, 111–22. The goddess Annona is also often accompanied in numismatic images by Ceres, the goddess of agriculture of agriculture, grain crops, and fertility.

On the numismatic Annona issue of Nero, see *RIC* 1, s.v. index 5: "ANNONA AVGVSTI CERES," §§98–99; "ANNONA AVGVSTI CERES S C," §§137–42, 372, 389–91, 430–31, 493–97, 566–72. On the numismatic Annona issue of Vitellius, see *RIC* 1, s.v. index 5: "ANNONA AVG," §§131, 144, 155, 166. On the Flavian coin issues, see *RIC* 2, s.v. index 3: "Annona"; index 4: "ANNONA AUG." For photos of the Annona coins of Nero, Vespasian, and Severus Alexander, see respectively Noreña 2011, 118 fig. 3.4, 115 fig. 3.1, and 116 fig. 3.2.

Shortages of Wheat:
The Economic and Imperial Context of the New Testament

The New Testament is realistic about the ever-present threat of famine in antiquity, with its inevitable shortfalls of grain, especially during the reign of Claudius (Acts 11:28; cf. Mark 13:8). For discussion of the ancient sources in regard to the Claudian famine (39–42 CE), see Bock 2007, 417–18; Keener 2013, 1856–58. Note, too, the limited famines during the reigns of Nero (Tacitus, *Ann.* 15.5, 18; Suetonius, *Nero* 45.1; Josephus, *A.J.* 20.9.2) and Vespasian (Dio Chrysostom, *Tumult.* 46.5–14). For discussion, see Smalley 2005, 154. On grain crises at Rome in the Julio-Claudian period, see Casson 1980, 24–25. The seriousness with which Rome secured its overseas grain supplies, demonstrated above, sets the crisis provoked by the Claudian famine in sharp relief, with the first believers responding to the needs of their impoverished brethren in Judea with the Antioch collection (Acts 11:27–30). For discussion of the Antioch collection, Joubert 2000, 91–93. Two brief vignettes from John's Apocalypse are important for the light they throw upon the economic impact of wheat availability in Asia Minor and, specifically, for the local focus of our study, Ionian Ephesus.

In Rev 6:6, the author of Revelation, having already established that there was one worthy to open the seals on the scroll (5:2, 5), unveils the third of the seven seals recounted in 6:1–8:1. These series of seals unveil for John's auditors the preliminary judgements that will usher in the culmination of world history, anticipating the full revelation of the eschaton, already underway but not to be decisively unleashed until the scroll is finally opened after the seventh seal. In Rev 6:6, the third of the "four horsemen of the apocalypse" (Rev 6:1–8), appears, holding a pair of scales. The terrible economic effects of famine, one of the results of war (6:1–4; cf. 4.7–8), is revealed by a heavenly voice: "A quart of wheat [χοῖνιξ σίτου] for a day's pay, and three quarts of barley [τρεῖς χοίνικες κριθῶν] for a day's pay, but do not damage the olive oil and wine!" We will concentrate on the components of wheat, the food mostly of the wealthy, and barley, the food of the poor (Osborne 2002, 280). This "slogan in the market place" (Smalley 2005, 153) sets the maximum price for staple foods but at highly inflated prices, "eight to sixteen times the average price in the Roman Empire at the time" (Beale 1999, 381; see Cicero, *Verr.* 3.81; for full economic discussion, see Aune 1998, 397).

The first believers would have felt the full impact of these inflationary trends on the market availability of staple foods: they were being economically persecuted at Smyrna and possibly even excluded from Domitian's upper market place at Ephesus (Rev 2:9; 13:16–17; Beale 1999, 381; Judge 2008, 425). Furthermore, as Klaus Wengst (1987, 224) has argued, "The general economic background to the phenomenon described in Rev. 6:6–8—a lack of basic foods, a surplus of wine and oil—is a result of the extension of *latifundia* which took place in the first century AD with the cultivation of wine and oil, which was more profitable than grain." The supply of grain, therefore, was increasingly less abundant in markets than in times past. Since the cities of Asia Minor were dependent on the importation of grain due to bad harvests (Magie 1950, 581–82), the situation would have been stark for people living in the Roman province during such times of economic crisis, especially in the case of the urban poor. This periodic scarcity of grain is confirmed by the offer of the unnamed Roman ruler in IEph 2.211 to ensure that the grain dealers of Ephesus, along with those of other cities, received the right to engage in the grain trade untrammeled by legislation, after the needs of Rome had been fully met. However, John's message is unequivocal. Political devotion to the imperial cult and the Roman ruler—who had economically marginalized believers at Smyrna and Ephesus, notwithstanding his numismatic image as a generous grain provider for his subjects—was not the solution to the problem of grain privation and the temptations of idolatry faced by Asian believers.

Finally, in Rev 18:11–13, the goods of the merchants, who had depended on idolatrous Rome (Babylon), are listed, including "fine flour and wheat [σῖτον]" (18:13a). Of particular interest is how slaves and "human souls" (ψυχὰς ἀνθρώπων) are also listed alongside cattle, sheep, horses, and chariots in the goods of the merchants (18:13b). Koester (2008, 796) sums up the attitude of the ancient merchants with these words: we see here "the problems inherent in a society that turns everything into commodities that can be sold to meet the insatiable demand of the ruling power." As Beale (1999, 910) concludes, "All the trade products in the list in vv. 12–13 are good in and of themselves, but the telltale mark of their sinful use is the reference to slaves at the end of their list."

Bibliography

Anonymous. 1875. "Frumentariae Leges." Pages 548–51 in *A Dictionary of Greek and Roman Antiquities*. Edited by William Smith. London: John Murray.

Aune, David. E. 1998. *Revelation 6–16*. WBC 52B. Grand Rapids: Zondervan.
Bauckham, Richard. 1983. *The Climax of Prophecy: Studies on the Book of Revelation*. Edinburgh: T&T Clark.
Beale, G. K. 1999. *The Book of Revelation: A Commentary on the Greek Text*. NIGTC. Grand Rapids: Eerdmans.
Bock, Darrell L. 2007. *Acts*. BECNT. Grand Rapids: Baker Academic.
Casson, Lionel. 1954. "The Grain Trade in the Hellenistic World." *TAPA* 8:168–87.
———. 1980. "The Rome of the State in Rome's Grain Trade." *MAAR* 36:21–23.
Cooley, Alison E. 2009. *Res Gestae Divi Augusti: Text, Translation, and Commentary*. Cambridge: Cambridge University Press.
Cristofori, Alessandro. 2002. "Grain Distribution in Late Republican Rome." Pages 141–53 in *The Welfare State: Past, Present and Future*. Edited by Henrik Jensen. Edizioni Plus. Pisa: Pisa University Press.
Cuyler, Mary Jane. 2014. "*Portus Augusti*: The Claudian Harbour on Sestertii of Nero." Pages 121–34 in *Art in the Round: New Approaches to Coin Iconography*. Edited by Nathan T. Elkins and Stefan Krmnicek. Tübingen: Tübinger Archäologische Forschungen.
Erdkamp, Paul. 2005. *The Grain Market in the Roman Empire: A Social, Political and Economic Study*. Cambridge: Cambridge University Press.
Garnsey, Peter. 1988. *Famine and Food Supply in the Graeco-Roman World: Responses to Risk and Crisis*. Cambridge: Cambridge University Press.
Jongman, W. M. 1997. "Cura annonae." *DNP* 3:233–36.
Joubert, Stephan. 2000. *Paul as Benefactor: Reciprocity, Strategy and Theological Reflection in Paul's Collection*. WUNT 2/214. Tübingen: Mohr Siebeck.
Judge, E. A. 2008. "The Mark of the Beast, Revelation 3:16." Pages 424–26 in *The First Christians in the Roman World: Augustan and New Testament Essays*. Edited by James R. Harrison. WUNT 229. Tübingen: Mohr Siebeck.
Keay, Simon J., and Martin Millett. 2005. "Integration and Discussion." Pages 269–96 in *Portus: An Archaeological Survey of the Port of Imperial Rome*. Edited by Simon J. Keay, Martin Millett, Lidia Paroli, and Kristian Strutt. London: British School at Rome.
Keener, Craig S. 2013. *3:1–14:28*. Vol. 2 of *Acts: An Exegetical Commentary*. Grand Rapids: Baker Academic.

Koester, Craig R. 2008. "Roman Slave Trade and the Critique of Babylon in Revelation 18." *CBQ* 70:766–86.

Mattingly, David J., and Greg S. Aldrete. 2000. "The Feeding of Imperial Rome: The Mechanics of the Food Supply System." Pages 142–65 in *Ancient Rome: The Archaeology of the Eternal City*. Edited by J. Coulston and Hazel Dodge. Oxford: Oxford University School of Archaeology.

Magie, David. 1950. *Text*. Vol. 1 of *Roman Rule in Asia Minor to the End of the Third Century after Christ*. Princeton: Princeton University Press.

Noreña, Carlos. F. 2011. *Imperial Ideals in the Roman West: Representation, Circulation, Power*. Cambridge: Cambridge University Press.

Osborne, Grant R. 2002. *Revelation*. BECNT. Grand Rapids: Baker Academic.

Reinarcher, Jan C. 2014. *Die Organisation der Getreideversorgung im Augusteischen Zeitalter: Augustus und seine "cura annonae."* Norderstedt: GRIN VerlagGmbH.

Rickman, Geoffrey. 1980. *The Corn Supply of Ancient Rome*. Oxford: Clarendon.

Roebuck, Carl. 1950. "The Grain Trade between Greece and Egypt." *CP* 45:236–47.

Smalley, Stephen S. 2005. *The Revelation to John: A Commentary on the Greek Text of the Apocalypse*. London: SPCK.

Van der Meer, L. Bourke. 2012. *Ostia Speaks: Inscriptions Buildings and Spaces in Rome's Main Port*. Leuven: Peeters.

Vervaet, Frederik Juliaan. 2020. "No Grain of Salt: Casting a New Light on Pompeius' *cura annonae*." *Hermes* 148:149–72.

Weiss, Naomi A. 2013. "The Visual Language of Nero's Harbor Sestertii." *MAAR* 58:65–81.

Wengst, Klaus. 1987. *Pax Romana and the Peace of Jesus Christ*. Philadelphia: Fortress.

Wörrle, Michael. 971. "Ägyptisches Getreide für Ephesos." *Chiron* 1:325–40.

20. Getting a Rise out of the Bakers

Bradley J. Bitner

IEph 2.215

Foucart 1883, 504–6, no. 10 (*editio princeps*); Waltzing (1899) no. 144; Buckler 1923, 30–33; Merkelbach 1978, 164–65; Arnaoutoglou 2002, 39–42; Harland 2014, 237–38; Perry 2015. Found at Magnesia Mai but may originate from Ephesus. Date: late second century CE.

1	[ca. 4 ...] δὲ καὶ κατὰ συνθήκην πα[... ca. 5...]άντων.[... ca. 8 ...] λιχ[... ca. 12 ...] ὥστε συμ-[βαί]νειν ἐνίοτε τὸν δῆμον ἰς ταραχὴν καὶ θορύβους ἐνπίπτιν διὰ τὴν σ[ύλ]-	... and according to an agreement ... as a result it happens that sometimes the *dēmos* falls into commotion and confusion on account of the meeting
	λογον καὶ ἀθρασίαν τῶν ἀρτοκόπων ἐπὶ τῇ ἀγορᾷ· στάσεων ἐφ' οἷς ἐχρῆν [αὐ]-	together and insolence of the bakers at the *agora*, (namely,) of the seditious meetings for which they ought already,
	τοὺς μεταπεμφθέντας ἤδη δίκην ὑποσχεῖν· ἐπεὶ δὲ τὸ τῇ πόλει συμφέ[ρον χρὴ]	after having been summoned, to have undergone a trial. But since one should rather prefer the benefit for the city
5	τῆς τούτων τιμωρίας μᾶλλον προτιμᾶν, ἀναγκαῖον ἡγησάμην διατάγ[ματι]	over the punishment of these men, I thought it necessary with an edict
	αὐτοὺς σωφρονίσαι· ὅθεν ἀπαγορεύω μήτε συνέρχεσθαι τοὺς ἀρτοκ[ό]-	to bring them back to their senses. For which reason I forbid the bakers either to assemble
	πους κατ' ἑταιρίαν μήτε προεστηκότας θρασύνεσθαι, πειθαρχεῖν δὲ π[άν]-	as if they were a faction or for the leaders to stir up trouble, but rather to obey
	τως τοῖς ὑπὲρ τοῦ κοινῇ συμφέροντος ἐπιτατομένοις καὶ τὴν ἀ[ναγ]-	completely the things commanded for the sake of the common welfare and

καίαν τοῦ ἄρτου ἐργασίαν ἀνενδεῆ παρέχειν τῇ πόλει· ὡς ἂν ἁλῷ τι[ς αὐ]-	to provide for the city the necessary production of bread without any lack. Whenever anyone
10 τῶν τὸ ἀπὸ τοῦδε ἢ συνιὼν παρὰ τὰ διηγορευμένα ἢ θορύβου τινὸς [καὶ στά]-	from among them is caught either in the act of meeting contrary to the things issued in this edict or taking the lead in any confusion
σεως ἐξάρχων, μεταπεμφθεὶς τῇ προσηκούσῃ τειμωρίᾳ κολασθή[σεται·]	and seditious meetings, after having been summoned, he will be punished with the appropriate punishment.
ἐὰν δέ τις τολμήσῃ τὴν πόλιν ἐνεδρεύων ἀποκρύψαι αὐτόν, δεκυείρ[οις ἐπὶ πο-	And if anyone dares, while plotting against the city, to hide himself, he will be branded with "by the decurions(?)"
δὸς προσσημιωθήσεται· καὶ ὁ τὸν τοιοῦτον δὲ ὑποδεξάμενος [τῇ] αὐτῇ τιμωρίᾳ ὑπεύθυνος γενήσεται.	on his foot. And the one who harbors such a person will become liable for the same punishment.
15 ἐπὶ πρυτάνεως Κλ(αυδίου) Μοδέστου, μηνὸς Κλαρεῶνος δ' ἰσ(ταμένου), βουλῆς	In the year of the *prytanis* of Claudius Modestus, on the fourth day from the beginning of the month Klareon, when a special meeting of the *boulē*
ἀγομέ[νης —]	was called,
ἄλλο μέρος· Μαρκελλεῖνος εἶπεν· τῆς δὲ ἀπονοίας τῶν ἐργαστηριαρχῶ[ν μέγι]-	Marcellinus said, "Now of the madness of the leaders of the workshops,
στον δεῖγμα χθὲς Ἑρμείας ὁ πρὸς τῇ ταμίᾳ ᾧ μετ[...... ca. 16 ......] αντη.	Hermias (gave) a perfect example yesterday, (Hermias) the one associated with the treasurer/y(?)[1] to whom ... [2]

Although this inscription was discovered at Magnesia ad Maeandrum (Foucart 1883), it has generally—because of the details of the dating formula (l. 15)—been attributed to Ephesus (from at least 1915; see Buckler 1923, 30 nn. 1 and 46 for reasons and history; some still demur: Trebilco 1994, 338–39). It was early labeled "an edict of a Roman governor ... on

---

1. IEph 2.215, n. 17: ταμίᾳ = ταμείᾳ, Merkelbach 1978.
2. For the possible restoration ἱεροφ]άντῃ, see IEph 1.5.18–19. For the *hierophant* as a cult attendant at Ephesus, especially in the mid- to late second century CE, see Rogers 2012, 148–49, 173–80.

the occasion of a baker's strike" (Reinach 1883, 41). The genre identification as an edict or proconsular decree was correct (διάταγμα, l. 5; see also ἀπαγορεύω, l. 6). But the characterizations of the cause of the tumult as a "strike" and of the group of bakers as a "union" (Buckler 1923, 31 n. 3) or an "association" (Waltzing 1895, 49–50) have proven more problematic. The relevance of the text to the uproar of the Ephesian silversmiths in Acts 19:23–20:1 has long been grasped (e.g., Abbott and Johnson 1926, 449–50). G. H. R. Horsley (1987, 9–10) remarked briefly on some terminological and conceptual connections to the New Testament. The most recent text, translation, and commentary of this inscription is found in Harland 2014, 237–38. Here, the complete text of IEph 2.215 (which reflects readings and restorations proposed by Merkelbach 1978) is given, along with an updated translation and the following comments.

In line 2, the *dēmos* has been stirred up "into commotion and confusion" (ἰς [=εἰς] ταραχὴν καὶ θορύβους). These terms for popular unrest or rioting are precisely those that frame the Lukan account of the Ephesian riot in Acts 19:23–20:1 (τάραχος, 19:21; θόρυβος, 20:1; see also στάσις in Acts 19:40 and l. 3 of our inscription). The cause of this uproar, and its origin, are provided in lines 2–3 but with less clarity than one might wish. The people fell into this confusion "on account of" the actions of the bakers (διά + acc.). These actions included "the meeting together" (σ[ύλ]λογον) and "insolence" (ἀθρασίαν) of the bakers—or at least some of them (see ll. 7, 18, and below). But two issues immediately require a decision: What is the most probable restoration of the first term? And how is it best translated? These questions have a direct bearing on our reconstruction of the scenario reflected in the inscription. First, the restoration σύλλογος is not universally reflected in editions and translations. This is because W. H. Buckler (1923, 31, 46 note on ll. 2–3) earlier offered the restoration σ[καιολ]όγον = *recklessness in evil speaking* (adopting a proposal made by W. M. Calder), although Buckler (1923, 31 n. 2) also mentioned a suggestion by Adolf Wilhelm: σ[μικρολ]όγον = *recklessness in complaints about trifles*. In IEph 2.215, the reading adopted by the editors is σ[ύλ]λογον; this is on the basis of R. Merkelbach (1978, 164–65) who draws an analogy with an illegal *coetum* in a similar context in Pliny, *Ep.* 10.93 (*turbas et illicitas coetus*). Although Jonathan S. Perry (2015, 186–91, 199–200) has recently reverted to Wilhelm's restoration (σμικρολόγος), which he thinks better emphasizes the *speech* of the instigators, this is an incredibly rare term. The far more commonly attested σύλλογος is to be preferred, and it fits with the following injunction against meeting (συνέρχεσθαι) in lines 6–11.

The second issue involves the appropriate translation of σύλλογος. Philip Harland (2014, 237–38) agrees with the restoration but either leaves the term untranslated or perhaps merges it with ἀθρασία, rendering the paired phrase only as "recklessness." A more accurate translation of σύλλογος as "the assembling together" is provided by Horsley (1987, 9–10). This is not only lexically preferable since the term on its own has a neutral connotation; it also brings out the unspecified nature and status of the meeting that led to the civic uproar (and perhaps depicts the group responsible with less precision than some have thought, on which, see below). Though σύλλογος does not occur in the New Testament, one might compare the use of the verb συναθροίζω ("gather together") in Acts 19:25.

Not only the cause but also the origin or locus of the unrest is indicated in line 3: it was "at (or in) the *agora*." If we accept that the inscription belongs to Ephesus, we should at least briefly consider the possible location of the public space referenced here. By the mid- to late second century, Ephesus had two well-established *agorai*: the Lower or *Tetragonos* agora, which served as a commercial market (see Scherrer and Trinkl 2006), and the Upper or so-called State *agora*, which, from about the time of Augustus, was flanked to the north by a *prytaneion* and *bouleuterion* and for which the total identity and function is still debated (see Steuernagel 2020). Acts 19:29 is even less clear on where the tumult instigated by the silversmiths originated before they "rushed together into the theater" (ὥρμησάν τε ὁμοθυμαδὸν εἰς τὸ θέατρον). The *Tetragonos agora* lies directly adjacent to the theater. Nearby runs Arkadiane street where a topos inscription (IEph 2.547) reserved two places for the ἀργυροκόποι. Moreover, Kouretes street, which connected the Lower to the Upper *agora*, was the site of another inscription acclaiming the silversmiths (IEph 2.586; see Harland 2014, 246–47). We have no such topos inscriptions for ἀρτοκόποι at Ephesus. But for graves, a *graffito*, and other references to bakers at Ephesus, Pisidian Antioch, Didyma, and elsewhere, see Harland 2014, 237.

If the origin of the tumult is impossible to pinpoint precisely, what about the nature of the group of bakers and the characterization of the commotion? Is this an organized group recognized by the city or the provincial authorities, that is, a "union" (Buckler 1923) or an "association" or *collegium* as it is usually called in the literature (e.g., Harland 2003, 238; 2014, 169–70)? Ilias Arnaoutoglou (2002, 40) notes the general "terminological vagueness" in ancient texts dealing with associations and links it here to the rhetorical approach of the provincial governor, doubting whether one can call this a baker's *guild* with certainty. John S.

Kloppenborg (2019, 32 and n.45) also points to the wide "variety of self-designations used by occupational guilds" and cautiously considers the bakers here to be such an association. The crafted rhetoric of this inscription is treated attentively by Perry (2015, 192–200). He prefers to speak of an "interruption of work" rather than a strike, and rather than identifying the group as a guild or association, he describes it as having "a complex internal organization" with leaders and would-be followers. Although we cannot be certain on the basis of the text of the inscription alone, it does seem likely that this would be an association. According to Harland (2003, 246), there are approximately sixty Ephesian inscriptions attesting some two dozen occupational guilds.

The recent study of Jared T. Benton (2020) adds importantly to our understanding of the plausible scenario reflected in our text. Benton gathers the Latin and Greek terms for bakers from the epigraphical evidence and notes the "core processes" of the production of bread by bakeries serving the cities in the Latin West and Greek East. For Ephesus, Benton registers IEph 6.2225, a sarcophagus for the baker Aurelius Hesychius who "describes himself as a member of the *gerousia*" (l. 143), and IEph 6.2226, a sarcophagus for the baker Aurelius Nikon that also refers to gladiatorial clubs. With respect to our inscription, Benton (2020, 142–43) judges that, although it probably deals with "a formal association," it is also possible that "bakers could have taken collective action … without the existence of a formal association." Furthermore, Benton points to the apparent case at Side (SEG 33.1165) of "multiple associations of bakers" within the same city, raising the possibility that a single guild might not necessarily represent all the bakers in a given city. Nevertheless, the danger to the stability and food supply of the city was such that it produced this response from the magistrate, a "remarkably transparent statement of the responsibility that Roman officials felt for provisioning the urban population" (Benton 2020, 145).

If Acts 19:23–20:1 attributes the silversmith's riot in part to the economic threat posed by Paul's gospel of Jesus, what might have sparked the bakers' meeting and the subsequent civic unrest? Two dynamics highlighted by Benton in relation to the craft of baking may prove helpful in considering the scenario depicted in our inscription. On the one hand, a text such as P.Oxy. 12.1454 (116 CE) preserves a contractual arrangement whereby some bakers agree to use grain supplied by the *agoranomos* to produce bread for the village. It is not difficult to imagine such arrangements and negotiations between bakers and magistrates becoming fraught, especially in a civic context such as Ephesus, perhaps even breaking down or leading to a situation like the one evidenced by our text. On the other hand, the conditions of labor and production bear considering. Even if we allow for hyperbole, as Benton does, some ancient sources depict what he calls the "horrific" conditions that could be associated with bakeries or workshops. Benton (2020, 129-30) notes several places where Plautus employs the trope of slaves who are "threatened with dispatch to the bakeries (*pistrina* = ἐργαστήρια) as punishment." Furthermore, Apuleius (*Metam*. 9.12) narrates the experience of Lucius who observes miserable, barely clothed figures toiling in a bakery, covered with flour as if with pale ash. Intriguingly, in light of the punishment threatened in our inscription, these wretched, shackled laborers are described as having "foreheads ... inscribed with brands [*frontes litterati*]" (Benton 2020, 121-23).

This brings us to the response in lines 5-14 of the inscription. First, a few notes on lexical and syntactical overlap with the New Testament texts. The magistrate says that the instigators ought already to have been summoned (μεταπεμφθέντας, l. 4) and tried; those who dare to stir up similar commotion in future will indeed be summoned (μεταπεμφθεὶς, l. 11) and punished, along with any who support them. For a similar use of summons in the New Testament, see μεταπέμπω in Acts 25:3. Although it is almost certainly right to conjecture that the edict was first drafted in Latin and then translated and inscribed in Greek, Merkelbach (1978, 165) correctly notes the phrase ἀναγκαῖον ἡγησάμην is "a standard expression" in such edicts. The phrase is followed by an aorist infinitive (σωφρονίσαι, l. 6) that expresses the intention and weight of the governor's edict: *to bring them back to their senses*. Paul employs the same phrase ἀναγκαῖον ἡγησάμην in in 2 Cor 9:5 (followed by the aor. inf. παρακαλέσαι) and Phil 2:25 (followed by the aor. inf. πέμψαι). At the lexical level, Horsley (1987, 10) noted the relevance of the meaning of σωφρονίζω here ("bring back to one's senses") in connection with its single New Testament occurrence in Titus 2:4. Unfortunately, however, BDAG (s.v. "σωφρονίζω") does not seem to have registered this in their revised definition and senses. BDAG's minor shortcoming here is also noted by Bruce W. Winter (2003, 155-59), who does not cite the governor's response to the bakers but who grasps correctly the lexical sense σωφρονίζω expressed in other sources and its import for the interpretation of Titus 2:4. The syntax of line 12, ἐνεδρεύων ἀποκρύψαι αὑτόν ("while plotting to hide/conceal himself"), resembles that found in Luke 11:54 where the Pharisees are said to be ἐνεδρεύοντες αὐτὸν θηρεῦσαί ("lying in wait to catch him").

As for the threatened punishment, it has been interpreted as branding (presumably with a hot iron) on the foot of a leader who stirs up further trouble or of someone who aids and abets such a one (ll. 13–15). The punishment, its purpose, and the precise part of the body, however, present interpretive challenges. The verb employed for branding, προσσημειόω (l. 13), is apparently a *hapax*. Although he does not deal with our inscription, C. P. Jones has demonstrated the difficulty of distinguishing branding from tattooing in many of our sources. He notes that penal tattooing of slaves and criminals, on the forehead, face, head, or hands, was common, whereas branding of humans was "exceptional" and "was used by the Greeks and Romans mainly on horses … and here the usual words [to express "brand"] were χαρακτήρ and καυτήριον (*nota*)" (Jones 1987, 140–41, 155). Indeed, in light of Jones's study, the *frontes litterati* of the slaves in Apuleius's bakery workshop mentioned by Benton are just as likely to have been *tattooed* foreheads. Buckler (1923, 46–47) entertained the possibility of tattooing in our inscription as well. But would a penal tattoo make any sense on the foot? Here we note the text [ἐπὶ πο]δὸς is plausibly restored but restored nonetheless (supplying eight letters at the end of l. 12 rather than the one to five letters restored at the conclusion of the other lines). Yet it is difficult to supply another body part with a genitive ending in -δος as a more plausible restoration. The brand, if such it was to be, would mark the offender with the word δεκυείροις (l. 12, *by/for/to the decurions*[?] = *a decemviris* according to Merkelbach 1978, 165). For what purpose, other than pain, was this brand to be applied? Buckler (1923, 46) restored the genitive δεκυειρίας and understood it as either "the property of the *decuria*" or, more imaginatively, "with the mark of the proconsul's *decuria* of lictors." In any of these scenarios, one might ask quite how this punishment fits the crime. Perry (2015, 190–91, 199) sees the offense as the agitator's political speech and wonders, too, how a punishment involving the foot is relevant.

More broadly, what is forbidden by the governor is of note and brings us back to the comparison with the account of the silversmiths in Acts 19. The governor forbids (1) that the bakers should meet *as if they were a* faction (συνέρχεσθαι … κατ' ἑταιρίαν, ll. 6–7, see also l. 10), (2) that their leaders should stir up trouble (προεστηκότας θρασύνεσθαι, l. 7, see also. ll. 10–11), and (3) that anyone should hide while themselves plotting or help and harbor a person engaged in these things (ll. 12–14). Arnaoutoglou (2002, 39) remarked on the dearth of interpretations of "the imposed sanction." His view was that this was no legal ban on associations in Ephesus or the region. Instead, it expresses "a provisional ban on gatherings" of "groups with embryonic, if not non-existent, internal organization," gatherings of the kind that might lead to unrest (41–42). Perry proposes that this is a rhetorically charged, strategic, political warning directed specifically to the leaders of the bakers. He argues that the "tone of the magistrate's decision, and the specific punishments he threatens to mete out, indicate that he has detected a complex internal organisation … and that he is as a result targeting the groups' officers" while simultaneously "appealing to the rank-and-file membership to distance themselves from their leaders" (Perry 2015, 193, 198–99).

This interpretation accounts well for certain features of the text, particularly the mention of "leaders" (προεστηκότας, l. 7) and "leaders of the workshops" (τῶν ἐργαστηριαρχῶν, l. 16). In fact, Buckler (1923, 32) referred to the luckless Hermias of line 17 as a "foreman" and suggested on that basis that he was not the owner of the bakery/workshop but an employee set over others (for an ἐργαστηριάρχης in judicial proceedings, see P.Oxy. 22.2340.6). We cannot say more—because of where the text breaks off—about Hermias's exact status, but Benton musters the evidence for the socioeconomic and supply chain dynamics of bakeries that provides a possible context. He points to "apprenticeships," violence, and abuse in the workshops and argues that "one's experience in the bakery was almost surely predicated on their status within the workgroup" (124). Thus, even though we cannot place Hermias more precisely among the leaders, we can appreciate his influence and grasp why the magistrate targets him and others like him. While there may not have been a well-defined association of bakers, there were leaders who had been and could again be instigators. Thus, it is not difficult to see similarities with the *grammateus*'s rebuke of Demetrius *and those with him* (Δημήτριος καὶ οἱ σὺν αὐτῷ τεχνῖται, Acts 19:38). Neither for the silversmiths in Luke's narrative nor for the bakers in IEph 2.215 was there any compelling "cause to justify this commotion" (Acts 19:40), at least not in the eyes of the magistrates.

Bibliography

Abbott, Frank Frost, and Allan Chester Johnson. 1926. *Municipal Administration in the Roman Empire*. Princeton: Princeton University Press.

Arnaoutoglou, Ilias N. 2002. "Roman Law and *collegia* in Asia Minor." *RIDA* 49:27–44.

Benton, Jared T. 2020. *The Bread Makers: The Social and Professional Lives of Bakers in the Western Roman Empire*. Cham: Palgrave Macmillan.

Buckler, W. H. 1923. "Labour Disputes in the Province of Asia." Pages 27–50 in *Anatolian Studies presented to Sir William Mitchell Ramsay*. Edited by W. H. Buckler and W. M. Calder. Manchester: Manchester University Press.

Foucart, Paul-François. 1883. "Inscriptions d'Asie Mineure: Philadelphie et Magnésie du Méandre." *BCH* 7:504–6.

Harland, Philip A. 2003. *Associations, Synagogues, and Congregations: Claiming a Place in Ancient Mediterranean Society*. Minneapolis: Fortress.

———. 2014. *North Coast of the Black Sea, Asia Minor*. Vol. 2 of *Greco-Roman Associations: Texts, Translations and Commentary*. BZNW 204. Berlin: De Gruyter.

Horsley, G. H. R. 1987. "The Silversmiths at Ephesos." *NewDocs* 4:1–10.

Jones, C. P. 1987. "Stigma: Tattooing and Branding in Graeco-Roman Antiquity." *JRS* 77:139–55.

Kloppenborg, John S. 2019. *Christ's Associations: Connecting and Belonging in the Ancient City*. New Haven: Yale University Press.

Merkelbach, R. 1978. "Ephesische Parerga (18): Der Bäkerstreik." *ZPE* 30:164–65.

Perry, Jonathan S. 2015. "'L'État intervint peu à peu': State Intervention in the Ephesian 'Baker's Strike.'" Pages 183–205 in *Private Associations and the Public Sphere*. Edited by V. Gabrielsen and C. A. Thomsen. Copenhagen: Royal Danish Academy of Sciences and Letters.

Reinach, S. 1883. *Manuel de philologie classique*. Paris: Hachette et Cie.

Rogers, Guy Maclean. 2012. *The Mysteries of Artemis of Ephesos: Cult, Polis, and Change in the Graeco-Roman World*. Synkrisis. New Haven: Yale University Press.

Scherrer P., and F. Trinkl. 2006. *Die Tetragonos Agora in Ephesos*. FiE 13.2. Vienna: Verlag der Österreichen Akademie der Wissenschaften.

Steuernagel, Dirk. 2020. "The Upper Agora at Ephesos: an Imperial Forum?" Pages 93–107 in *Religion in Ephesos Reconsidered: Archaeology of Spaces, Structures, and Objects*. Edited by Daniel Schowalter, Sabine Ladstätter, Steven Friesen, and Christine Thomas. NovTSup 177. Leiden: Brill.

Trebilco, Paul. 1994. "Asia." Pages 292–362 in *Graeco-Roman Setting*. Vol. 2 of *The Book of Acts in Its First Century Setting*. Edited by David W.

J. Gill and Conrad Gempf. Grand Rapids: Eerdmans; Carlisle: Paternoster.

Waltzing, J. P. 1899. *Étude historique sur les corporations professionnelles chez les Romains depuis les origins jusqu'à la chute de l'Empire d'Occident.* Vol. 3. Leuven: Peeters.

Winter, Bruce W. 2003. *Roman Wives, Roman Widows: The Appearance of New Women and the Pauline Communities.* Grand Rapids: Eerdmans.

Building Activity and Local Sites

21. The Kaystros River and the Silting of the Ephesian Harbor: How Viable Is William Ramsay's Interpretation of Revelation 2:5?

James R. Harrison

In the period spanning the first and the third centuries CE, four honorific inscriptions and an edict from Ephesus detail the measures undertaken to ensure the continuing health of the harbor of Ephesus and to render gratitude for the donations of benefactors made for construction work at the site. At the outset, the two earliest inscriptions, each roughly datable to ca. 105 CE (Kokkinia 2014, 184), record benefactions for construction work on the harbor. T. Flavius Montanus, the high priest of Asia, donates 75,000 denarii for the task (IEph 6.2061.2.14–15), whereas the prytanis C. Licinius Maximus Iulianus gives 2,500 denarii. Prior to this, the literary evidence also reveals that the proconsul Barea Soranus had experienced deteriorating relations with Nero by opening the port of Ephesus (Tacitus, *Ann.* 16.23).

A revealing honorific inscription, datable to 129 CE and cited below, honors Hadrian for the considerable privileges, economic and legal, that the Roman ruler had granted for the worship of Artemis in the city. Hadrian had also privileged Ephesus—the proconsular capital of western Asia Minor and the leading seaport and emporium of the region, linking Italy and Greece with the Aegean coastline in Asia Minor (Strabo, *Geogr.* 12.18.5; 14.1.24)—by supplying grain from Egypt to the city after the supplies of Rome had been fully met. See the commentary on IEph 2.211 ("Maintaining the Market Supply of Wheat for Rome: Revelation 6:6 and 18:11–13," in this volume). Important for our purposes is the reference to the harbor being kept navigable by the diversion of the waters of the Kaystros River, which had damaged the harbor. Unfortunately, the fragmentary text, cited in full below, breaks off exactly where the reason for the damage would have been articulated (διὰ τὸ [—]: l. 16), but we may reasonably guess that it was the traditional problem of silting.

IEph 2.274

Riemann 1877, 291, no. 78 (*editio princeps*); *SIG* 839; Abbott and Johnson 1926, 86; *DocsNerva* 494. Found at Ephesus. Date: 129 CE.

	Αὐτοκράτορα Καίσαρα θεοῦ	Imperator Caesar,
2	Τραιανοῦ Παρθικοῦ υἱόν, θεοῦ	son of divine Traianus Parthicus,
	Νέρουα υἱωνόν, Τραιανὸν Ἀδριανὸν	grandson of divine Nerva, Traianus Hadrianus
4	Σεβαστὸν καὶ Ὀλύμπιον, δημαρ-	Augustus and Olympius, tribune
	χικῆς ἐξουσίας τὸ <ι>γ′, ὕπατον	for the 13th time, consul
6	τὸ γ′, πατέρα πατρίδος	for the third time, father of the nation,
	ἡ βουλὴ καὶ ὁ δῆμος ὁ Ἐφεσίων	(is honored by) the council and people of Ephesus,
8	τὸν ἴδιον κτίστην καὶ σωτῆρα διὰ	its own founder and savior because of
	τὰς ἀνυπερβλήτους δωρεὰς Ἀρτέ-	his unsurpassed gifts to Artemis,
10	μιδι, διδόντα τῇ θεῷ τῶν κληρο-	granting to the goddess
	νομιῶν καὶ βεβληκότων τὰ δίκαια	the right to inherited and ownerless property
12	καὶ τοὺς νόμους αὐτῆς, σειτοπομπή[ας δὲ]	and her own laws, and providing supplies of grain
	ἀπ' Αἰγύπτου παρέχοντα καὶ τοὺς λιμένας	from Egypt and who ma[de] the harbors
14	πο[ιήσαν]τα πλωτούς, ἀποστρέψαντά τε	navigable, both diverting
	καὶ τὸν βλά[πτοντα τοὺς] λιμένας ποταμὸν	and … the river Kaustros, which dam[aged the] harbor
16	Κάϋστρον διὰ τὸ [- - -] (καὶ τὰ λοιπά)	because of the … (and the rest)

The effects of the silting of the Kaystros River at Ephesus are well known and need not overly detain us. Whether the Ephesian port's increasingly narrow mouth was ultimately attributable to the incompetence of the architects employed by King Attalus Philadelphus in the second half of the second century BCE (Strabo, *Geogr.* 14.1.24–25) or was more explained by the narrowness of the shoals at the river's mouth (Livy, *Ab urbe cond.* 37.14.6) depends on historical traditions that are probably no longer recoverable with any certitude (Kokkinia 2014, 183). Either way, the river posed a regular threat to the port of the city from the second century BCE onwards, necessitating the relocation of the city and the harbor farther to the west. As John C. Kraft et al. (2007, 140) conclude, "There was, in fact, very little that the Hellenistic and Roman engineers could do except to continue dredging and extend the mole westward in an attempt to protect shipping access of this metropolis on the Aegean coastline."

Notably, the Hadrianic inscription above (IEph 2.274) mentions several harbors (ll. 13, 15, τοὺς λιμένας; see Kraft et al. 2000, 199), indicating that the Kaystros River damaged not only the Great Harbor but all the harbors of the city. On the various harbors of Ephesus, see Oster 1992, 542–43.[1] Consequently, Hadrian diverted its waters, but contrary to Kraft et al. (2000, 199), there is no direct textual evidence in IEph 2.274 for their proposed restoration in lines 14–15: "He diverted the Cayster and let a large dam store up [the sediment]."

However, the evidence for the dam, upon which Kraft et al. draw for their restoration of IEph 2.274.14–15, is found in an honorific inscription published after the IEph series: that is, D. Knibbe, İplikçioğlu, and Engelmann 1993, 122, no. 12. The inscription, datable to 120 CE, says:

> To Ephesian Artemis and Imperator Hadrian Caesar Augustus, when Po. Rutilius Bassus was secretary. The city of the Ephesians had erected a dam of 60 feet on the right bank of the Manthites River according to the command of (Caesar) Augustus.

The damming of the Manthites River, one of five watercourses in the region of Ephesus, stopped the regular dredging of alluvial sand, which was brought in from the inland and which had progressively caused the silting problem in the harbor. Knibbe, İplikçioğlu, and Engelmann (1993, 123) observe that Hadrian's dam (1) forced the Manthites River to keep running, (2) protected the plain past the Artemision from floods, and (3) curtailed the extensive economic damage done in that region because of the flooding.

Another revealing inscription is the edict of the proconsul Lucius Anonoius Albus (IEph 1a.23), datable to 146/147 CE and cited below, which addresses the impeding of the far-flung imports ("from everywhere," l. 6) to Ephesus because of the harmful trade practices being practiced on the shorelines of the harbor. Here we learn that "the citizens of Ephe-

---

1. Oster (1992, 543) rightly questions the scholarly presumption of some that the silting caused by the Kaystros River precipitated an economic decline in first-century BCE Ephesus. Strabo (*Geogr.* 641) observes that Ephesus was the largest commercial center in Asia Minor west of the Taurus.

sus were causing their own environmental problems" (Kraft et al. 2007, 141). The wood and stone importers were placing their wood and stone on the shore, damaging the piers by the heavy weight and, in sawing the stone onshore, "were heaping the deep water ... with rock tailings which have been thrown in" (IEph 1a.23.18–19). Consequently, the current was restrained (IEph 1a.23.20), causing the silting up of the harbor over time. The punishments which the proconsul stipulates for those disobeying his new edict (IEph 1a.23.22–33) underscores the seriousness of the ecological problem that was gradually emerging over time at Ephesus.

For a translation and discussion of the decree, see Kokkinia 2014, passim. On marble quarrying at Ephesus, see Long 2012, 174–212. On the changes that the silting of the harbor made to the location of commercial activities of Ephesus, including the site of the artisanal workshops where some early believers may well have resided (see Acts 18:3; 19:23–47), see Thomas 2020.

IEph 1a.23

JÖAI 44:142–47 (*editio princeps*); SEG 19.684; Pleket 1964, 17; Führer Selçuk 98–100; *ZPE* 25:208–9; SEG 27.742; SEG 30.1311; IEph 1a.23 and add. p. 2. A stela made of yellowish marble that was intended to be inserted into a wall. There is a break across the stone. Height: 173 cm; width: 79 cm; thickness: 24 cm. It was found in 1956 on the northern edge of the early port of Ephesus. Date: 146/147 CE.

[ἀγαθῇ] τύχῃ·	For good fortune.
Λ(ούκιος) Ἀντώνιος Ἄλβος ἀνθύπατος	L. Antonius Albus, proconsul
λέγει·	says:
4 ἐπε[ὶ τῇ μεγίσ]τῃ μητροπόλει τῆς	Since for the greatest metropolis of
Ἀσίας [καὶ] μονονουχὶ καὶ τῷ κόσ-	Asia, and all but for the (whole) world,
μῳ [ἀναγκ]αῖόν ἐστιν τὸν ἀποδεχό-	it is necessary that the harbor,
μενον τοὺς πανταχ[όθ]εν εἰς αὐ-	which receives imports from everywhere to
8 τὴν καταγομένους λιμένα μὴ	it, not to be impeded,
ἐνποδίζεσθαι, μαθὼν τίνα τρόπον	I, having learned how
βλάπτ[ου]σι, ἀναγκαῖον ἡγησάμην	they are harming (it), thought it necessary

διατάγ[μ]ατι καὶ κωλῦσαι καὶ κατὰ ἀπει-	by edict to hinder (this) and against those
12 θούντων τ[ὴν] προσήκουσαν ζημίαν ὁρίσαι·	disobeying to define an appropriate punishment.
παραγγέλλω [οὖ]ν καὶ τοῖς τὰ ξύλα καὶ τοῖς	I announce therefore to those importing wood
τοὺς λίθους ἐνπορευομένοις μήτε τὰ ξύλα	and stone neither to put the wood
παρὰ τῇ ὄχθῃ τιθέναι μήτε τοὺς λίθους	nor to saw the stone on the shore.
16 πρίζειν· οἱ μὲν γὰρ τὰς κατασκευασθείσας ἐπὶ	Some damage the piers established for the
φυλακῇ τοῦ λιμένος πείλας τ[ῷ] βάρει τῶν φορτίων	protection of the harbor by the weight of burdens,
λυμαίνονται, οἱ δὲ ὑπὸ τῆς ἐνειεμ[έν]ης σμείρεως	others, heaping the deep water ...
[.....]τῃσεπει εἰσφερομένης τὸ βάθος [συ]νχωννύντες	with rock tailings which have been thrown in,
20 τὸν ῥοῦν ἀνείργουσιν, ἑκάτεροι δὲ ἀνόδευτον	restrain the current; each
τὴν ὄχθην ποιοῦσιν. ἐπεὶ οὖν ἐπιθεμέ[νο]υ μου	makes the shore impassable. Since then despite my command
οὐκ ἐ[γένε]το ἱκανὸς Μάρκελλος ὁ γραμματεὺς	Marcellus, the scribe, has been unable
ἐπισχεῖν αὐτῶν τὴν θρασύτητα, ἴστωσαν ὅτι	to check their audacity, let them know that
24 ἄν τις μὴ γνοὺς τὸ διάταγμα καταλημφθῇ τῶν	if anyone in ignorance of my edict is caught
ἀπειρημένων τι πράττων, εἰσοίσει <✳'>	doing any of the forbidden acts, he will pay ...
τῇ ἐπιφανεστάτῃ Ἐφεσίων πόλει, καὶ οὐ-	to the most illustrious city of the Ephesians and no
δὲν ἧττον αὐτὸς τῆς ἀπειθείας ἐμοὶ λόγον	less will he furnish an account of his disobedience to me.
28 ὑφέξει· τοῦ γὰρ μεγίστου αὐτοκράτορος περὶ	For since the greatest imperator
φυλακῆς τοῦ λιμένος πεφροντικότος	has given heed to the protection of the harbor
καὶ συνεχῶς περὶ τούτου ἐπεσταλκότος	and has continually written about this,

τοὺς διαφθείροντας αὐτὸν οὔκ ἐστιν δί-	it is not right for those who destroy it
32 καιον μόνον ἀργύριον καταβάλλοντας	by only paying money
ἀφεῖσθαι τῆς αἰτίας. vacat προτε-θήτω.	to be acquitted of the charge. Let it be displayed publicly.
γραμματεύοντος Τι(βερίου) Κλ(αυδίου) Πο-	Ti. Claudius Polydeukes
λυδεύκου Μαρκέλλου ἀσιάρχου.	Marcellus, the asiarch, being scribe.

Concluding our investigation of the epigraphic evidence regarding the Ephesian harbor, a third century CE association inscription of the Ephesian silversmiths (SEG 34 [1984] 1094; cf. Acts 19:23–47) honor's the enlargement of the harbor by the city's savior-benefactor, the proconsul Valerius Festus:

> To good fortune. The silversmiths of the first and greatest metropolis of the Ephesians in Asia—thrice temple-warden of the Augusti—set this up for Valerius Festus, the proconsul descended from proconsuls, founder of many works in Asia and in Ephesos after the passing of Antoninus, who enlarged (or "enhanced") the harbour of Croesus. He was their own savior and benefactor in everything. (trans. Harland).

What intersections with the New Testament documents does the literary and epigraphic evidence regarding the harbor of Ephesus in the early Roman Empire, discussed above, provide for social historians? No obvious terminological overlaps of any significance occur because there are only three fleeting references to *harbor* in the New Testament (Acts 27:8, 12 [2x]: λιμένας, λιμένος, λιμένα]), and none of these relates to Ephesus. However, William Ramsay (1904, 233–34, 245–46; cf. especially, Hemer 1986, 52–54) has famously argued that Ephesian auditors would have understood God's threat to remove the lampstand of the Ephesian church (Rev 2:5) against the background of the continuous danger of the silting of the Ephesian harbor by the Kaystros River and the various changes to the site of the city that occurred as a result. For a history of the changes of location of the Ephesian harbor from 1000 BCE onward, discussing the epigraphic, archaeological, and literary evidence, see Kraft et al. 2007, passim. Regarding this evidence, Ramsay (1904, 245–46) writes:

> The relation of land and sea has changed in quite unusual fashion: the broad level valley was once a great inlet of the sea, at the head of which

was the oldest Ephesus, beside the Temple of the Goddess, near where the modern village stands. But the sea receded and the land emerged from it. The city followed the sea, and changed from place to place to maintain its importance as the only harbour of the valley. All these facts were familiar to the Ephesians; they were recorded for us by Strabo, Pliny and Herodotus, but Ephesian belief and record are the foundation for the statements of these writers. A threat of removing the church from its place would be inevitably understood by the Ephesians as a denunciation of another change in site of the city, and must have been so intended by the writer. Ephesus and its Church should be taken up, and moved away to a new spot, where it might begin afresh on a new career with a better spirit. But it would still be Ephesus, as it had always hitherto been amid all the changes.

The case of Ramsay would have been strengthened by reference to the inscriptions discussed above. However, as intriguing as Ramsay's hypothesis is, considerable caution should be exercised before accepting it. First, as Colin J. Hemer (1986, 54) notes, the evidence is purely circumstantial, and, I would add, the hypothesis has to be imported into the text rather than arise out of its evidence. Second, there are no clear terminological links in the epigraphic evidence that would bolster the strength of Ramsay's suggestion: the minimal use of harbor language in the New Testament bypasses Ephesus, and the imagery in Rev 2:5 is that of lampstands. Third, none of the epigraphic evidence is contemporary with a putative Domitianic (or, if composed earlier, 69 CE) date for the book of Revelation. Fourth, the tenor of the epigraphic evidence is positive, apart from the edict's reference to the punishment of law-breakers (IEph 1a.23.22–33). Almost universally, our inscriptions adopt the eulogistic tone appropriate to the honorific genre in four out of the five epigraphic cases. We might speculate that the silting of the harbor was an ever-present psychic threat for the Ephesians, based on the clues provided in I Eph 1a.23 and 2.274, and that such a background *must* have been appropriated by Ephesian auditors hearing Rev 2:5 for the first time. But is this necessarily true? There is a certain overstatement in Ramsay's (1904, 245, emphasis added) quote: "A threat of removing the church from its place *would be inevitably understood* by the Ephesians as a denunciation of another change in site of the city, and *must have been intended* by the writer." Here Ramsay runs the risk of assuming historical omniscience regarding the thoughts of individuals and groups in antiquity. The Ephesians may well have been inured to a catastrophic interpretation of these ecological events, given the ease and regularity with which the Roman ruler, his officials, and the Ephesian elites intervened to address the issue of harbor silting and relocation; rather a quiet confidence regarding the future and a civic pride in the city's ability to overcome such serious challenges may well have been the general citizen consensus as opposed to the more apocalyptic scenario of Ramsay.² Fifth, the imagery should be primarily understood against the Jewish literature on lampstands—for example, 1 Kgs 11:36 (Aune 1997, 147); Zech 4:1–14; see also Isa 42:6–7; 49:6 (Beale 1999, 231)—and interpreted exegetically in that light. For additional lampstand references, see Exod 25:31–40; 27:20–21; Num 8:1–4; Lev 24:1–9; 1 Kgs 7:49; Jer 52:19; 1 Macc 1:21; 4:49–50; Josephus, *A.J.* 12.250; 14:72; 4 Ezra 10:22; cf. Rev 1:12, 13, 20; 2:1, 5: 11:4. For additional discussion on the background, see Aune 1997, 88–90. Sixth, Ramsay's suggestion interprets Rev 2:5 not as a threat of physical destruction but rather as a promise of being able to begin anew at another site. But this seems to underplay the strong accent on both the imminent *and* eschatological judgement present in the text (Osborne 2002, 118). Pace, see Hemer (1986, 55), who, while endorsing Ramsay's interpretation, says regarding κινήσω in Rev 2:5: "The danger was that the great harbour-city and its vigorous church would be moved back under the deadening power of the temple ... the old Anatolian theocracy would reassert itself." In sum, Ramsay's intriguing and novel suggestion only remains an outside possibility, circumstantial at best, and it should not be accorded exegetical priority over other equally viable interpretative suggestions.

Bibliography

Abbott, Frank Frost, and Allan Chester Johnson. 1926. *Municipal Administration in the Roman Empire*. Princeton: Princeton University Press.
Aune, David E. 1997. *Revelation 1–5*. WBC 52A. Grand Rapids: Zondervan.
Beale, G. K. 1999. *The Book of Revelation: A Commentary on the Greek Text*. NIGTC. Grand Rapids: Eerdmans.

---

2. Oster (1992, 543) writes: "Moreover, literary (Tacitus, *Ann.* 16.23) and epigraphic documents (*IvEph* 23, 274, 2061, 3066, 3071) testify to major efforts at keeping the harbour serviceable during and after the period of Paul's ministry there."

Harland, Philip A. 2015. "Honors by Silver-Melters for the Proconsul Valerius Festust (250–260 CE)." Associations in the Greco-Roman World. http://tinyurl.com/SBL9031f.

Hemer, Colin J. 1986. *The Letters to the Seven Churches of Asia in Their Local Setting*. JSNTSup 11. Sheffield: JSOT Press.

Knibbe, Dieter, Bülent İplikçioğlu, and Helmut Engelmann. 1993. "Neue Inschriften aus Ephesos XII." *JÖAI* 62:113–50.

Kokkinia, Christina. 2014. "Rome, Ephesos, and the Ephesian Harbor: A Case Study in Official Rhetoric." Pages 180–96 in *Infrastruktur und Herrschaftsorganisation im Imperium Romanum: Herrschaftsstrukturen und Herrschaftspraxis III Akten der Tagung in Zürich 19.–20. 10. 2012*. Edited by Anne Kolb. Berlin: De Gruyter.

Kraft, John C., Ilhan Kayan, Helmut Brückner, and George (Rip) Rapp Jr. 2000. "A Geologic Analysis of Ancient Landscapes and the Harbors of Ephesus and the Artemisions in Anatolia." *JÖAI* 69:175–232.

Kraft, John C., Helmut Brückner, Ilhan Kayan, and Helmut Engelmann. 2007. "The Geographies of Ancient Ephesus and the Artemision in Anatolia." *Geoarchaeology* 22:121–49.

Long, Leah Emilia. 2012. "Urbanism, Art, and Economy: The Marble Quarrying Industries of Aphrodisias and Roman Asia Minor." PhD diss., University of Michigan.

Osborne, Grant R. 2002. *Revelation*. BECNT. Grand Rapids: Baker Academic.

Oster, Richard J. 1992. "Ephesus (Place)." *ABD* 3:542–49.

Pleket, H. W. 1964. *Texts on the Economic History of the Greek World*. Leiden: Brill, 1964.

Ramsay, William M. 1904. *The Letters to the Seven Churches and Their Place in the Plan of the Apocalypse*. London: Hodder & Stoughton.

Riemann, Othon. 1877. "Inscriptions grecques provenant du receuil de Cyriaque d'Ancône. I. Manuscrit 996 de la bibliothèque Riccardienne à Florence." *BCH* 1:286–94.

Thomas, Christine M. 2020. "Invisible 'Christians' in the Ephesian Landscape: Using Geophysical Surveys to De-center Paul." Pages 171–91 in *Religion in Ephesos Reconsidered: Archaeology of Spaces, Structures, and Objects*. Edited by Daniel Schowalter, Sabine Ladstätter, Steven Friesen, and Christine Thomas. NovTSup 177. Leiden: Brill.

22. The "Fullness" of Ephesians 1:23 and 3:19

Phillip T. Ort

Louis Robert (1961) once warned that "two dangers lie in wait for the historian faced with interpreting inscriptions: not to use them, or to use them badly" (cited in McLean 2002, 1). This commentary proposes that an examination of the Athenian inscription IG 2.1.429 reveals a contextual use of the words πληρόω/μα that sheds exegetical light on Paul's meaning in Ephesians 1:23 and 3:19. To this end, this commentary will first survey the use of πληρόω/μα in the Ephesian epigraphic corpus to demonstrate the need for a broader epigraphic analysis. Second, this commentary will examine the text and history of IG 2.1.429 to show that πληρόω/μα can be used in an architectural context. Third, this commentary will explore how the architectural use of πληρόω/μα integrates with Paul's temple/body imagery in Ephesians and suggests that the architectural use of πληρόω/μα in Eph 1:23 and 3:19 further strengthens Paul's encouragement to the Ephesian believers living under the shadow of Artemis and her temple.

One of the few things that commentators on Ephesians agree on is that interpreting Paul's use of πληρόω/μα in 1:23 and 3:19 is difficult.[1] Unfortunately, while the Ephesian epigraphic corpus has proven essential in several studies, a study of πληρόω/μα encounters two difficulties.[2] First, the nominal form πλήρωμα does not occur in the Ephesian epigraphic corpus. Second, the verbal form of πληρόω only appears in twelve texts. Accordingly, the lack of illustrative evidence warrants a broader investiga-

---

1. This commentary assumes the Pauline authorship of Ephesians and defers to the case set forth by Hoehner 2002, 114–30. For arguments against Pauline authorship see Best 2001, 6–36 and Lincoln 1990, lix–lxxiii. For agreement on the difficulty of interpretation, see Best 2001, 183: "The difficulties of this verse have long been recognized."

2. See Harrison 2018b; Arnold 1989; Trebilco 2004; and Immendörfer 2017.

tion. A summary of the Ephesian texts follows with the inscriptions sorted by their senses as they appear in BDAG.

1. "To Fill"/"To be Filled"

SE 3808*3

Date: second century CE (?).

```
    [—] (vac.) ΝΑΤ[—]              [—] (space) [—]
5   [—] καὶ τοὺς ἐπὶ τ[—]          [—] and the (?) during [—]
    [— ἱέρ]ειαν τῆς Ἀρτέ[μιδος —]  [—] priestess of Arte[mis]
    [—]ν ἐπλήρωσαν [—]             [—] they fulfilled [—]
    [—] ναῶν τῆς Ἀσ[ίας —]         [—] of temples of As[ia]
    [— Τουενδι]ανοῦ Μάγ[νου —]     [— of Tuendi]anus Mag[nus]
```

The first inscription, although fragmentary, appears to draw a connection between a priestess of Artemis and some "filling" of the temples of Asia. While the precise import of this inscription is unclear, it appears to utilize the sense of "to fill" with reference to a substance filling an object.[3]

2. "To Bring to Completion"

IEph 1.46.7–11

Date: fifth–sixth century CE

8   μακάριος ὁ πιστεύσας [ἐ]ν ἐμοὶ μὴ   Blessed is the one who believes in me
    ἑωρακὼς με. γέγραπτε γὰρ περὶ ἐμοῦ·   not having seen me. For it is written
    "οἱ ἑωρακότες με μὴ πιστεύσουσιν ἐν   concerning me, "The ones who have
    ἐμοὶ καὶ οἱ ἑωρακότες μ[ε]   seen me shall not believe in me and
                                              the ones who have [not] seen me

---

3. BDAG, s.v. "πληρόω." Here entry 1a. pertains to the filling of objects while entry 1b. refers to the filling of persons. Accordingly, the usage in SE 3808*3 would appear to align with 1a; See also LSJ, "πληρόω," 1.1.

9	πιστεύσουσιν καὶ ζήσον[τ]ε." περὶ δὲ οὗ ἔγραψάς μοι ἐλθῖν πρός σε, δέον ἐ[στὶ]ν πάντα, δι' ἃ ἀπεστάλην, πληρῶ<σ>αι {τὰ πάντα} καὶ μετὰ τὸ πληρῶ[σαι]	shall believe and live." But concerning that which you wrote to me to come to you, it is necessary, on account of all things for which I was sent, to fulfill (all things) and, after fulfilling
10	τὰ πάντα ἀναλημφθῆναι πρὸς τὸν ἀποστίλαντά με· καὶ ἐπιδὰν ἀναλημφθῶ, ἀποστέλλω τινὰ τῶν μαθητῶ<ν> μου, ὅστις εἰάσεταί σου	all things, to be taken up to the one who sent me. And when I am taken up, I will send one of my disciples, who shall heal your
11	τὸ πάθος καὶ ζωήν σοι παράσχῃ καὶ τοῖς σὺν σοὶ <πᾶ>σιν καὶ τῇ πόλι τῇ σῇ <πρὸς τὸ> μηδένα τῶν ἐχθρῶν τῶν σῶν ἐξου<σί>αν ταύτης ἔχιν ἢ σχῖν ποτέ.	suffering and offer life to you and to all the ones with you and to your city so that none of your enemies might have power over it or shall have ever.

The second inscription contains an excerpt from the apocryphal work The Letters of Christ and Agbar, which claims to detail the conversion of Agbar, King of Edessa, to Christianity (see Elliott 1993, 538–42). The excerpt comes from Christ's response to Agbar's request: "Regarding what you wrote to me that I should come to you, I have completed here everything I was sent to do and, after I have accomplished it, to be taken up to him who sent me" (ll. 9a–10a, trans. Elliott). This inscription appears to utilize the sense of "completion."[4]

3. "To Fulfill"

Turning to the sense of "fulfill," a notable pattern emerges in those ten of the twelve Ephesian inscriptions that use πληρόω to refer to cultic officials who "fulfill" some office or obligation.[5] The inscriptions that follow have been organized into subgroups based on contextual referent and not a difference in sense. These labels are personal and are not intended to reflect a specific genre or technical classification.

---

4. BDAG, s.v. "πληρόω." Here both entries 3 and 5 indicate bringing something to completion and could reasonably be chosen. If the focus is on Christ's fulfilling his duty, then 4b. becomes the more specific category; see also LSJ, "πληρόω," 3.6.

5. BDAG, "πληρόω." Here the entries below align with entry 4b, since cultic offices or obligations appear to be view in each inscription. For a helpful introduction to cultic officials at Ephesus, see Harrison 2018a, 253–97.

3.1. "Fulfilling" the Mysteries and Liturgies

IEph 1a.43

Date: 372–78 CE.

25.2 Φῆστε τιμιώτατε καὶ προσφιλέστατε. ἡ ἐπαινετὴ ἐπειρία σου τοῦ ἡμετέρου θ[ε]σ-	... most honored and dearest Festus. Let your praiseworthy experience follow the
26 πίσματος ἀκολουθησάτω τῇ γνώμῃ καὶ πάντας τοὺς εἰς ταύτην τὴν τιμὴν ἐπιτρέχοντας πάσας πρότερον τὰς λιτουργίας τῇ ἑαυτοῦ πόλει ἀποπλη- ροῦν	decision of our decree and order all who pursue this honor beforehand to complete the liturgies for his own city,
27 προσταξάτω, πληρωθέντων δὲ τῶν λιτουργημάτων εἰς τὴν τιμὴν τὴν μίζονα, τουτέστιν ὅλης τῆς <ἐ>παρ- χίας, σπεύδουσιν αὐτοῖς ἄδιαν παρεχέτω δυναμένοις μ[ετὰ]	and when the liturgies have been completed, let it offer indemnity to them that hasten after the greater honor, (namely, that) of the whole province, who are able a[fter]...

The third inscription is a rescript in Latin and Greek of Valentinian, Valens, and Gratian addressed to Festus while he was governor of the province of Asia Minor (ca. 375–378 CE). The rescript was occasioned by a need to regulate the competition surrounding cultic offices at Ephesus as it appears that aspirants from other cities were vying to hold the more prestigious Ephesian offices (ll. 8–9). The petitioners are concerned that an inordinate focus on the Ephesian offices will result in the liturgies of smaller cities and towns being neglected (l. 25). Accordingly, the petitioners ask Festus to agree with their decree, which requires that all aspirants of the offices of *asiarch* or *alytarch* first fulfill the liturgies of their own city (ll. 25–27).

IEph 7.3072

Date: second–third century CE.

28 τὰς νομὰς πᾶσιν τοῖς συνεδρίοις παρα- σχοῦσαν καὶ πληρώσασαν τὰ μυστήρια	... the customary distributions to all the guilds they furnished and completed the mysteries

30 διὰ τοῦ πατρὸς Γαΐου τοῦ γένους ἀξίως	through her father Gaius worthily of her family.
ὁ πατὴρ τὴν ποθεινοτάτην	The father [honors] the most longed for
32 θυγατέρα	daughter.

The fourth inscription is an honorary inscription by Vedius Servilius Gaius set up on behalf of his daughter Vedia, a priestess of Artemis (on the Vedia and this inscription, see Rogers, "Some Priestesses of Artemis of Ephesos," in *NewDocs* 11B). Following a lengthy rehearsal of family honors, the inscription notes of Vedia that "the customary distributions to all the guilds she furnished and completed the mysteries through her father Gaius worthily of her family" (ll. 28–30).[6] Here the language of the inscription highlights the cost of pursuing public or cultic office as Vedia is credited with providing "the customary distributions to the guilds" and completing the "mysteries." Both functions would have required substantial wealth, and the inscription notes that the necessary monetary support was obtained "through her father Gaius."[7]

IEph 7.2.4330

Date: third century CE.

2 [γερουσιαστ]ής, μετέχών κ[αὶ τοῦ]	... [a member of the *gerous*]*ia*, [and (being) a member of the
[συνεδρίου τῶ]ν νεοποιῶν κ[ουρή-]	guild of Kouretes] (from which are drawn) the *neopoioi* (and)
4 [των χρυσοφόρω]ν, ἐσσηνεύσας τὰ[ς δύο]	[the *chrysophoro*]*i*, having served the [two
[ἐσσηνίας καὶ] ναοφυλακίας, π[ληρώ]-	terms of office and] as warden of the temple, [and also having
6 [σας δὲ καὶ τὰ] μυστήρια πάντ[α, ἑστιά]-	fulfilled all the] mysteries, [having
[σας τὰ συνέδρια] πάντα καὶ τοὺς [ἐξέ]-	entertained] all [the guilds] and the ...

---

6. A special thanks to James Harrison for the provision of a translation of IEph 7.3072.

7. For a treatment of the Vedia inscription, see Harrison 2018a, 269.

The fifth inscription is an honorary inscription for Annius Annulinus Perecennianus set up by the *neopoios* Zotikos Artemidorou. Among the items in the list of his achievements we find that he served in the two offices and as temple guard and also completed all of the mysteries (ll. 4–6).

3.2. "Fulfilling" an Office

IEph 3.956

Date: late second–early third century CE.

[— πληρώσας τ]ὰς δύ[ο]	[who fulfilled] the two
2 ἐσσηνείας ἐπὶ πρυτάνεως	terms of office during the *prytany* of
Κλ(αυδίας) Σεβήρας ὑπατικῆς, ἐπὶ ἱε-	Claudius Severus consul, during the
4 ρείας Φλ. Ἀτταλίδος, <ἱ>εροκήρυκος	priesthood of Fl(avius) Attalidus, and of the *hierokerux*
δὲ Εἰδομενέως Δημοκράτους Λ . [	Eidomeneus Demokratus L [

The sixth inscription is fragmentary and is missing its first half. Based on similarities to other Ephesian inscriptions, it is likely a thanksgiving by an unnamed *neopoios*, presumably to the goddess Artemis. The inscription can be roughly dated by the appearance of the *prytanis* Claudia Severa: "completed the two offices during the *prytanis* Claudia Severa" (ll. 2.1–3).

IEph 3.958

Date: second–third century CE.

[εὐχαριστῶ σοι, κυρία] Ἄρτ[εμι]	[I give thanks to you, lady] Art[emis],
[Τ(ίτος) Φλ(άουιος)? Λ]ούκιο[ς] ἐκ προγόν[ων]	T(itus) Fl(avius) Luciu[s] (being) from (my) ancestors
νεο[ποι]ὸς καὶ χρυσοφόρος, νε[οποιή-]	a *neo[poi]os* and *chrysophoros*, having
4 σας καὶ πληρώσας τὰς δύο ἐσ[σ]ην[ί-]	served as a *ne[opoi]os* and having fulfilled the two terms of office
ας καὶ κληρώσας τὰ συνέδρια πάντα	and having appointed all the guilds

The seventh inscription is a thanksgiving inscription to the goddess Artemis by Titus Flavious Loukios. The thanksgiving mentions the completion of the office of *neopoios* and *the two offices* along with other honors (ll. 3–5).

IEph 4.1059 (Ephesos 655)

Date: early third century CE[8]

[a.]	[ἡ πρύτανις εὐχαριστεῖ Ἑστίᾳ]	[The *prytanis* thanks Hestia]
[b.]	[Βουλαίᾳ καὶ πᾶσι τοῖς θεοῖς]	[Boulaia and all the gods]
1	[τοῖς ἐν] τῷ πρυ[τανείῳ ὅτι]	[who are in] the *prytaneion* [because]
	[εὐτυχῶ]ς ἐπλήρωσ[εν τὴν πρυ]-	[with good fortune] she fulfill[ed the *pry-*]
	[τανεία]ν μετὰ τῆς θρεψά[σης καὶ]	[*tany*] with her foster mother [and]
4	[τοῦ σ]υνβίου αὐτῆς κα[ὶ τῶν]	her husband and [of]
	[τέκνων] αὐτῶν	their [children.]

The eighth inscription contains a thanksgiving offered to the deity Hestia Boule on the occasion of successfully completing the *prytany* (ll. 2–3). The inscription also notes the involvement of the *prytanis*' husband and children, but their role is unclear (ll. 3–5). Priests and priestesses served in the Prytaneia, Claudia Trophima being one example (IEph 5.1012) in addition to the unnamed female honorand in the inscription above. Favonia Flacilla, who was both *prytanis* and *gymnasiarchos* (IEph 4.1065), is another example.

JÖAI 59:181–82, no. 14

Date: No date.

0	[ἐκτελέσασαν τὰ μυσ]-	[she having accomplished
	τήρια [πάντα]	all the mys]teries
	[κ]αὶ φιλ[οτείμως ὅλον]	gen[erously also for the whole]
	τὸν ἐνια[υτὸν],	yea[r],
	πληροῦσ[αν]	fulfill[ing]
5	μὲν τὴν ἐψ[ηφισμένην —]	the (?) de[cided by vote —]
	κοσμοῦσα[ν —].Η[—]	arrangin[g—] [—]

The ninth inscription, however, uses ἐκτελέσασαν to communicate the completion of the mysteries (ll. 0–1), while πληροῦσαν indicates the completion of a vote that resulted in an unspecified act of adornment

---

8. I added the bracketed [a.] and [b.] for ease of labeling.

(κοσμοῦσαν, ll. 5-6). Here the etymology of *kosmousan* suggests a relation to care of cultic property or adornments.[9] It is worth noting that subcategory 3.2, "fulfilling" an office, shares degrees of overlap with categories 3.1 and 3.3. In many instances, fulfilling an office would entail completing the mysteries/liturgies, making all necessary financial disbursements, et cetera. The distinction, however, lies between the office viewed as a whole and a particular duty or obligation.

3.3. "Fulfilling" That Which is "Customary" or "Right"

IEph 3.824

Date: No date.

5 [στρα]τηγόν, [τ]ὸν εὐσε[βῆ]	... [stra]tegos, the pious
[καὶ] φιλότειμ[ον] πρύτα-	[and] eager for distinction pryta[n-
[νιν, γυμ]νασ[ίαρχ]ον πάν-	is, gym]nas[iarc]h over all
[των τῶ]ν γυμ[νασ]ίων	the gym[nas]ia
[—]ησα[..4..]ον	--
10 [—]πλη[ρώσ]αντα	ful[fil]led
[τὰ συνέδ]ρια π[άν]τα	a[ll the counc]ils

The tenth inscription is an honorary inscription for an unnamed *strategos*. The honoree is described as "pious" ([τ]ὸν εὐσε[βῆ]) and as a "friend of honor" (φιλότειμ[ον], l. 6) who apparently served as a *prytanis* (ll. 6-7), was a *gymnasiarch* (ll. 7-8), and who "fulfilled the [customary distributions] to all the councils" (ll. 10-11). Here "customary distributions" (τὰς νομὰς) is supplied based upon similarity to IEph 3.990.5-6 and IEph 7.1.3072.28-29, which both use the phrase τὰς νομὰς πᾶσιν τοῖς συνεδρίοις to refer to the responsibility of a cultic official to oversee the disbursement of funds.

IEph 3.990

Date: No date.

[— τὴν ἱέρειαν]	[—the priestess]
1 [τ]ῆς ἁγιωτάτης Ἀρτέ[μι]-	of the most holy Arte[mi]s,

---

9. *LSJ*, s.v. "κοσμέω." *Kosmousan* may also be a reference to the office of *kosmēteria*. See Harrison 2018a, 269.

δος, τὴν ἐκ προγόν[ων]	who from (her) ancestors (entered civic life)
3 [ἐ]κ παρθενῶνος, συ[νγε]-	from the young woman's chamber, (being) a
[ν]ίδα ἀρχιερέων καὶ π[ρυτά]-	ki[nsm]an of high priests and p[ryta]neis,
5 [ν]εων, τὰς νομὰς π[ᾶσιν]	the distributions to all
[τ]οῖς συνεδρίοις π[ληρώ]-	the guilds she having f[ulf-
[σασαν —]	illed —]

The eleventh inscription is an honorary inscription for an unnamed priestess of Artemis who is noted to have "completed the customary distributions to all the guilds" (ll. 5–7). See IEph 3.990.5–6 and IEph 7.1.3072.28–29 on the aforementioned "customary distributions."

IEph 6.2061

Date: second century CE (103/116)

δ[όντα καὶ μ]ονομαχίας καὶ κυνήγια,	... [who also gave g]ladiatorial and beast shows,
κα[ταθέντα κ]αὶ τοῖς πολ[ε]ίταις τὸ	and se[t in order] the constitutions, the
12 ἄρισ[τ]ον [ἐκ]άστῳ δην(άρια) γ′, [τῇ] τε βο[υ]λῇ	luncheon for [ea]ch (he gave) three den[arii], and [to] the *boule*
καὶ τῇ γερουσίᾳ πληρώσαντα τὰ δίκαια	and to the *gerousia* rendered all the rights,
πάντα, ἀριθμήσαντα καὶ εἰς τὴν τοῦ	...

The twelfth inscription is an honorary inscription of the *boule* and *demos* of Ephesus concerning Titus Flavius Montanus a "priest of Asia." Here the inscription notes that the *boule* and the *gerousia* "rendered all the rights" concerning the honoree (ll. 12–14). Although the English translation above employs "rendered", the nuance of 'fulfilling' or "completing" all the rights remains. While these inscriptions shed light on civic honors, offices, mysteries, and liturgies in Ephesus, they do not shed light on Paul's use of πληρόω/μα in Eph 1:23 and 3:19. However, the Athenian inscription IG 2.1.429 contains unique architectural uses of the words πληρόω/μα that shed exegetical light on Paul's meaning in Eph 1:23 and 3:19.

4. IG 2.1.429—"Law on Rebuilding the Walls of Piraeus, with Appended Specifications"

AE 1900.91 (*editio princeps*); IG 2.244; Maier 1959–1961, 10; Schwenk 1985, 3; *BE* 1988.403; Richardson 2000, 601–15; Lambert 2012, 198–202. Inscribed law stela found near the remains of the theater of Dionysius in Mounichia. Grey marble with a smooth back and the present dimensions h. 0.80, w. 0.54, th. 0.125–0.13. The stone appears to have been reused with cutting marks on the bottom and right sides with traces of mortar on the right and top sides (Lambert 2012, 200). The findspot is the most likely place for the erection of the stela. Date: 337–336 BCE.

Column 1

46	[σ]υγγραφαὶ τοῦ τείχους τοῦ Μονιχ-	Specifications for the wall at Mounichia.
	[ί]ασι. οἱ μισθωσάμενοι τὰς τομὰς τῶ-	the contractors for the cutting of the
	ν λίθων ἐπὶ τὰ τείχη τεμοῦσιν πέτ-	stones for the walls will cut blocks
	ρας ὁπόθεν ἂν ἕκαστος μισθώσητα-	from where they are each contracted,
50	ι ὁμαλοῦς καὶ ὑγιοῦς καὶ πελεκή-	uniform and clean, and will hew them
	σουσιν ὀρθοὺς πανταχῆι καὶ εὐγων-	straight on all sides and right-angled
	ίους πρὸς τὰ μέτρα ἃ ἂν μισθώσητα-	according to the measurements to which
	ι ἕκαστος καὶ πρὸς τοὺς ἀναγραφέ-	each is contracted and the designs
	ας οὓς ἂν οἱ τὴν ἐργασίαν μισθωσά-	that the works contractors
55	μενοι κελεύωσιν, καὶ κομιοῦσι πρ-	specify; and they will transport
	ὸς τὸ ἔργον ἄγοντες ὁποίους ἂν κε-	to the work site first the stone
	λεύωσι πρώτους οἱ τὴν ἐργασίαν μ-	that the works contractors specify,
	[ι]σθωσάμενοι, καὶ καθαιρήσονται	and they will offload
	πρὸς τὸ ἔργον τὸ λίθον ἕκαστον ὁ-	by the work site each stone
60	ὗ ἂν οἱ τὴν ἐργασίαν μισθωσάμενο-	where the works contractors specify,
	ι κελεύωσιν, οὗ ἂν ἧι ζεύγει πρόσο-	where there is access for an ox-cart;
	δος· ἐὰν δέ τις τῶν λίθων ἔχει τι κρ-	and if any of the stones has an
	οιὸν μὴ μεῖζον ἢ ἡμιποδίου, ὃ μὴ ἔστ-	irregularity of not greater than half a foot,
	[αι φ]ανερὸν κειμένου τοῦ λίθου, ἔσ-	provided it is not apparent when the stone is laid,
65	[ται δό]κιμος. τέμνειν δὲ καὶ κομίζ-	it will be acceptable;

22. The "Fullness" of Ephesians 1:23 and 3:19

[ειν τοὺς λιθο]ὺς πρὸς τὸ ἔργον τοὺ- — and each day
[ς ἄνδρας ὡς ἂν ἕκ]αστος μισθώσητα- — [enough men] shall cut and transport
[ι ἱκανοὺς κατὰ τὴ]ν ἡμέραν ἑκάστη- — the stones to the worksite,
[ν ἐπιμελουμένους] ὅπως ἂν κομίζω- — as each is contracted, [to ensure] that
70 [νται οἱ λίθοι ἐν τ]οῖς χρόνοις τοῖ- — the stones are transported in the
[ς γεγραμμένοις, ἄρχε]ιν δὲ τοῦ κομ- — prescribed time; and the transport
[ίζειν τοὺς λίθους τὴν] δεκάτην ἡμ- — of the stones shall begin on the tenth
[έραν ἀφ' ἧς ἂν ἡμέρας παρα]λάβηι — day [after the day that the measure-
τὰ — ments?]
[μέτρα . . . . . . 14 . . . . . . γ]ένηται π- — have been received ... there may be
75 [. . . . . . .15. . . . . . .μισθως]αμενοι — have been received ... there may be
. . . . .21. . . . . .αμενοι — ... the contractors
[. . . . . .21. . . . . μ]αλακη — ... soft [stone]
. . . . .24. . . . . .η εν
. . . . 26. . . . .#[7]

Column 2

79 ποιῶν τὰ μέτωπα τῶν κλιμακτήρω[ν] — making the surfaces of the steps
80 λεῖα καὶ ὀρθά, καὶ ἐξαμησάμενο<ς> [τ]- — smooth and straight, and having scraped out
ὴν λατύπην τὴν ἐγκεχωμένην ἐκ τ[ō] στρογγύλο πύργο ἅπασαν, πληρώσ[α]- — all the heaped up chip fill from the round tower, and **having filled**
ς τὸμ πύργον λίθοις μὴ ἐλάττοσι[ν] ἢ δίποσιν, ἐὰμ μή που ἀνάγκη ἦι θε[ῖ]- — the tower with stones not less than two-feet, except for any place where
85 ναι ἐλάττω πρὸς τὸ χωρίον, τὸ δὲ [ὕψ]- — there may be a need to put smaller ones,
ος ἴσους τῶι στοίχωι τῶι ἔξωθ[εν, σ]- υντιθεὶς ἁρμόττοντας πρὸς [ἀλλή]- λους πανταχῆι, ποιῶν τοὺς ἁ[ρμοὺς] τοῦ πληρώματος τοῦτο ἀπότ[ους· λί]- — to same height as the external course, joining them together everywhere with clamps, making the [clamps] **of this filling** watertight;
90 θοις δὲ χρῆσθαι εἰς τὸ πλήρω[μα το]- — and they shall use for **the fill** the stones
ῖς ὑπάρχουσιν ἐν τῆι Μουνιχ[ίαι π]- — that are in the Mounichia,
λὴν ὁπόσοι ἂν ἐπισημανθῶσιν [χρή]- — except as many as have been identified
σιμοι ὄντες εἰς τὴν οἰκοδομ[ίαν τ]- — for use in the building of

ὧν νεωρίων, καὶ ἐπικόπτειν τ[ὰ πλη]-	the ship-sheds; and they shall cut **the fillings**
95 ρώματα ὀρθὰ κατὰ κεφαλὴν πρ[ὸς τὸ]-	true at the outer surface to align
ν τοῖχον τοῦ πύργου τὸν ἔξω ἐ[φ' ἑκά]-	with the external wall of the tower, in
στης τῆς ἐφόδου· ταῦτα οἱ μισ[θωσά]-	each course; and the contractors
μενοι ἀποδώσουσιν πεποιημ[ένα ἅ]-	will provide all these made
παντα ὀρθὰ καὶ ἁρμόττοντα πα[ντα]-	true and fitting on all sides
100 χῆι καὶ πρὸς τὴν ἔντορνον στρ[ογγ]-	and the round ones correctly turned,
ύλα καὶ τὰς προσαγωγὰς ὁμοία[ς κύ]-	the leading faces curved like a circle,
κλωι, ὅπως ἂν ἦι ὀρθὰ τὰ μεταπύ[ργι]-	so that the walls between the towers
α καὶ οἱ πύργοι ἁπανταχῆι καὶ α[ἱ κ]-	may be true, and the towers everywhere and
λίμακες, παρεχόμενοι αὐτοὶ αὑ[το]-	the stairways; and they shall provide
105 ῖς καὶ τοῖς λιθοτόμοις ἀναγρα[φέ]-	designs for themselves and the stonecutters
ας καὶ τἄλλα πάντα, ὧν ἂν δέωντα[ι ε]-	and everything else that may be needed
ἰς τὸ ἔργον· τοὺς λίθους τοὺς εἰ[ς τ]-	for the work; and each will himself
ὸ πλήρωμα τῶι πύργωι προσάξετ[αι]	bring all the stones that are needed
αὐτὸς αὑτῶι ἅπαντας, ὅσων ἂν δ[έητ]-	for **the fill** for the tower;
110 αι· ἀποδώσουσιν ταῦτα ἅπαν[τα πεπ]-	and they will supply all these things
οιημένα κατὰ τὰ γεγραμμέ[να ....]	made according to the written specifications...

The repairs detailed in the "appended specifications" bear witness to the remodeling campaign that commenced after the Athenian loss to Macedon at the battle of Chaironeia in 338 BCE. The Long Walls, constructed, repaired, and enhanced over four building phases from 462/1–mid 280s BCE (Conwell 2008, 54),[10] had once been "the most revolutionary development in the history of Greek strategy" (Hansen 2005, 26). However, Philip II's rapid advances in siege technology proved problematic and rendered the Athenian existing fortifications out of date.[11] The walls originally

---

10. See also Theocharaki 2020 and Fields 2006, who provide different timelines regarding the repairs of the Long Walls.

11. On this point Josiah Ober (1987, 569–604) has noted that, although the Macedonians had anti-personnel torsion catapults by ca. 340 BCE and siege catapults by

connected the Athenian *atsy* to the subject ports of Phaleron and Piraeus and served as the strategic culmination of Themistokles's naval strategy (Conwell 2008, 37).[12] However, by the time of IG 2.1.429, the Phaleric Wall had fallen out of use and the connection to Piraeus had been strengthened by an additional wall (Conwell 2008, 95). As for Ephesians, the use of πληρόω/μα in an architectural context in IG 2.1.429 warrants investigation as this usage may shed exegetical light on Paul's temple/body imagery in Eph 1:23 and 3:19.

Although various forms of συγγραφαί appear in inscriptions, IG 2.1.429 preserves a rare account of construction methods. This rarity is heightened by the fact that a πληρ- verb only cooccurs with συγγραφαί three times in the entire PHI Corpus. It is notable that each inscription comes from Athens and deals with construction or repairs completed during the last half of the fourth century BC. For example, IG 2.463 (307/6 BCE), which concerns the circuit walls of Athens, contains the instruction τοῦ τείχους ἀνα[πληρώσει πλινθ]-οις (l. 74) while IG 2.1668 (347/6 BCE) features συνπληρῶν (l. 71). However, IG 2.1.429 uniquely preserves *five* uses of πληρόω/μα when used in an architectural context (ll. 82, 89–90, 94–95, 108). For example, in lines 80–82, the contractors are directed to scrape out the rubble core of the round tower and subsequently fill it in with stones "not less than two feet ... to the same height as the external course" (ll. 82–84, 86). Furthermore, the contractors are directed to make the "clamps," or "joints," watertight (ll. 88–89) and to cut the stones "true

---

ca. 330 BCE, the Greek city states did not adequately prepare for siege engines which could destroy city walls. It is possible that the Athenians' reflection after the disastrous loss at Chaironeia (338 BCE) included a realization of the destructive power of Macedonian siege technology. Such a realization would explain the urgency and scope of the repairs detailed in IG 2.1.429 (337/6 BCE) and IG 2.463 (307/6 BCE). See also Nic Fields (2006, 9), who notes two ancient references to the urgent repairs following the battle of Chaironeia, which can be found in Lykourgos, *Leok.* 44, and Xenephon, *Hell.* 4.8.10. For a similar assessment, see also Theocharaki 2011, 120.

12. Themistokles's general strategy of naval superiority would be refined by Perikles and become known as the Perikleian strategy. The strategy required the Athenians: "1. To avoid engaging the more powerful army of the enemy; 2. To employ the Athenian navy rather than the army; 3. To carry out military action abroad; 4. To refrain from extending the Empire; 5. To maintain the allegiance of Athen's allies; 6. To rely on land, i.e. provisions, made accessible by Athenian sea power; 7. To abandon property outside the *atsy* in order to defends the sea lanes as well as Athens" (Conwell 2008, 81).

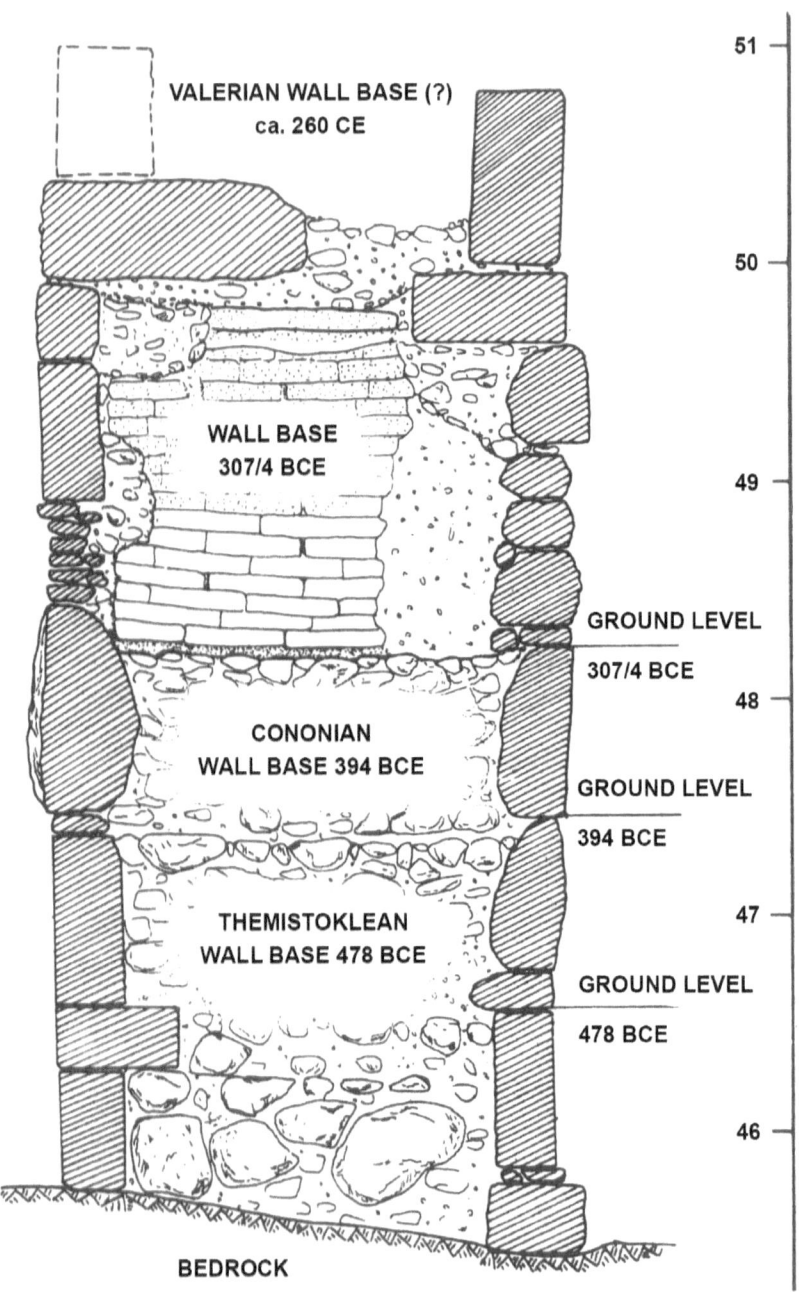

Cross-section of the Themistoklean wall at the Kerameikos, modeled after the drawing by Gottfried Gruben in Knigge 1951, 52, plate 51.

at the outer surface to align with the external wall of the tower" (ll. 94–95). However, the scope of the costly work described is difficult to appreciate without some knowledge of ancient construction practices.

The "heaped up chip fill" mentioned in line 81 refers to the rubble core of the round tower's walls, a common architectural technique in antiquity. In recent a monograph, Anna Theocharaki (2020, 148), helpfully reproduced Ursula Knigge's (1991, 52, pl. 51) cross-section of the Themistoklean wall at the Kerameikos, which illustrated the Athenian use of the rubble core and mud-brick masonry techniques.

In both techniques, the inner and outer courses of the wall would be erected and the hollow internal space would be filled in with a rubble core consisting of large stones, chip-fill, dirt, or a mud-brick filling into which headers and stretchers would intrude to link the three layers of the wall together (Theocharaki 2011, 146–47). Accordingly, the instructions to hollow out the rubble core (ll. 80–82) and replace it with solid stones "not less than two feet" (ll. 82–84) could indicate a costly transition from rubble core masonry to *emplekton* masonry (ll. 86, 88–89).[13] If such a transition was intended it would imply that πληρώσ[α]ς (ll. 82–83) refers to the process of "weaving" solid, interlocking layers of stone in courses. Subsequently, the "fill" or "fillings" (ll. 89–90, 108) would refer to solid worked blocks and not the material used for a rubble core.[14] However, this architectural distinction between rubble core masonry and *emplekton*

---

13. The precise meaning of *emplekton* masonry remains a matter of academic debate. After surveying the debate, this discussion accepts Poul Pedersen's recent contribution as a starting point. According to Pedersen (2019, 1–10), *emplekton* refers to structures made from worked blocks laid in a "woven" or interlocking pattern throughout the entire thickness of a structure. For a supporting view, see Dennis 1848. For contrary views, see Tomlinson 1961, 133–40 and Karlsson 1992. For ancient sources, see Vitruvius, *Arch.* 2.8.7 and Pliny, *Nat.* 36.51.171–172. See also Theocharaki 2011, 184.

14. Some scholars question whether the repairs detailed in IG 2.1.429 were ever completed. Theocharaki (2011, 120) writes that "the occurrence of this phase is not archeologically supported." See also Fields 2006, 20. Theocharaki (2011, 177) has also noted that from 347/6 BCE to 307/306 BCE that the "double-faced" and "all-stone" masonry techniques were used side by side. Her description of "double-faced" and "all-stone" masonry types appears to correspond to the rubble core and *emplekton* techniques identified in IG 2.1.429. The potential use of the *emplekton* technique is also supported by her assertion that IG 2.463 (307/6 BCE) provides instructions for all-stone construction (Theocharaki 2011, 179, 183). As for examples of *emplekton* masonry, Pederson (2019, 4–5) suggests that "we should look for [*emplekton*] where

masonry would not detract from Paul's argument since his architectural imagery treats the Ephesians as a corporate entity. In either case, these uses of πληρόω/μα in IG 2.1.429 align with the entries in *BDAG* that refer to an object filling another object.[15] Accordingly, IG 2.1.429 does not indicate a new sense of πληρόω/μα, but rather a unique contextual application.

However, despite the lack of epigraphic texts using πληρόω/μα to refer to rubble core masonry, this technique was not exclusive to the Athenians. Archaeological surveys have demonstrated the ubiquity of the technique across the Mediterranean for use in military and private structures. The Corinthian region features the fortifications at Stanotopi and Marsita (Caraher and Gregory 2006, 333–37) and the fortifications at Vayia (Caraher, Pettegrew, and James 2010, 391–405), while Euobeia features the collection of towers found on the Paximadi Penninsula (Seifried and Parkinson 2014, 277–313). Crossing the Mediterranean, the rubble core technique can be observed on the island of Andros (Koutsoukou and Kanellopoulos 1990, 155–74), in the Carian *Geländefestungen* (Konecny and Ruggendorfer 2014, 709–46), at Patara (Dündar and Rauh 2017, 509–81), and in Northern Syria (Clarke and Connor 1996–1997, 151–83).

Furthermore, rubble core masonry, and its later developments, were not limited to the fourth-third centuries BCE. Recent surveys have shown that the tower walls of the Magnesian Gate of Ephesus (ca. 100 BCE) made use of the rubble core technique (Sokolicek 2020, 109–10, fig. 6.1; see also Sokolicek 2009, 321–47; 2010, 359–82), while a first century Roman tribunal erected in the sacred precinct of the Artemision used the *opus caementitum* technique (Ladstätter 2010, 23–24).[16] Thus, while πληρόω/μα is likely not a technical term, the ubiquity of the rubble core technique invites the use of πληρόω/μα when referring to appropriate structures where archaeological evidence is found. In this case, the pervasiveness of rubble core masonry and the prominent local exam-

---

more substantial masonry is required, as in the foundations of temples, in terrace walls, in retaining walls and in fortifications."

15. *BDAG*, s.v. "πληρόω," 1a.; "πλήρμα," 1a.

16. This technique, called "Roman concrete," referred to a building process where the inner and outer courses of a wall would be erected and the concrete mixture would be poured into the hollow space between the walls. This Roman technique differed from Greek rubble core masonry in that the absence of headers and stretchers would result in three distinct vertical layers. See Pedersen 2019, 1–2 for a description of *opus caementitum*.

ples provides sufficient warrant for investigating the architectural use of πληρόω/μα at Ephesus even though this use is not attested in the local epigraphic corpus. In what follows, this commentary will suggest that Paul emphasized the Ephesians' union with Christ by using πληρόω/μα to refer to believers as the collective building materials that "fill up" the temple/body of Christ.

5. The "Fullness" of Christ's Temple/Body

Paul's presentation of the church as both the temple of God and the body of Christ in Ephesians has drawn considerable attention. Taken together, the temple and body metaphors form the pinnacle of Pauline ecclesiology, and Paul's combination of these images has provided fertile ground for theological interpretation. This commentary suggests that Paul used πληρόω/μα in Eph 1:23 and 3:19 as architectural imagery designed to frame his discussion of the temple/body of Christ in Eph 1–3.[17] In particular, Paul encouraged the Ephesian believers by highlighting their union with Christ while subtly setting the temple/body of Christ in implied opposition to another temple: the Artemision.[18] In short, Paul argued that "My God's temple is greater than your goddess's temple, so my God is greater than your goddess."

Recently, Howard McMurray made a case for Paul's theological polemic against Artemis and the Artemision. In his work, he noted that although exegetical attention had been given to temple imagery in Eph 2:20–22 the effect of Paul's rhetoric deserved further study (McMurray 2019, iv). He argued that

---

17. Note, however, that this commentary pertains only to Paul's usage of πληρόω/μα in Eph 1:23 and 3:19. The context of Paul's use of πληρόω/μα in Eph 4:10 and 5:18 does not indicate that the same architectural imagery was in view in those instances.

18. Although this commentary agrees with Howard McMurray (2019, 7 n.19, 16) that Paul's temple/body imagery should be understood with respect to the local Greco-Roman context at Ephesus and not the Jerusalem temple, this matter remains a subject of academic debate. For an opposing view, see Son 2001. While McMurray's argument illuminates the historical context, it should be noted that identifying the historical context as the Jerusalem temple would not diminish the case for an architectural use of πληρόω/μα. Rather, a change in historical context would only entail a change in interpretive application. For further interaction with McMurray's thesis, see Bitner "The Inviolate *temenos* of Artemis," in this volume.

> Paul intentionally contextualized the building/temple image in Ephesians to appeal to his audience's understanding and expectations of temple. By doing so, Paul challenged the power of Artemis and the influence of her temple, demonstrated Christ's authority, and instilled a sense of identity and unity among the believers in Ephesus pulled by the undertow of the temple of Artemis. (McMurray 2019, 12)

Central to his argument, was the pervasive dominance of Artemis as seen through the magnificence and influence of her temple. Some brief and suggestive examples from McMurray's work follow.

The Artemision dominated the geographic, spiritual, economic, and social landscape of ancient Ephesus. Geographically, the temple commanded the skyline of Ephesus with Jerome Murphy-O'Connor (2008, 106, 118) measuring its base at approximately 466 x 240 feet with an estimated height of 72 to 82 feet, making the Artemision the largest temple in the ancient world. Spiritually, the temple served as the symbol of Artemis's power (McMurray 2019, 74, 121–22). Not only was the goddess's name associated with safety itself (44–45), her perceived power resulted in her temple becoming an international refuge for asylum *par excellence* (72–73), while her name was frequently invoked for its power over malevolent spirits.[19] Economically, the temple functioned like a bank for the province of Asia even sometimes receiving deposits from other cities or monarchs.[20] Socially, Artemis was understood as the patroness of the city (IEph 1.25B.8–34) and was regarded as the Ephesian's primary benefactor (McMurray 2019, 45–46). Accordingly, Ephesus demonstrated the expected reciprocity by serving as the "νεωκόρος of Artemis" (50, 154–55). The Ephesians identification with Artemis was so prominent that Murphey-O'Connor (2008, 16) noted that "Artemis permeated the consciousness of the Ephesians to the point that it was a rock-bottom element in their collective and individual identities." Thus, McMurray's argument finds strong *prima facie* evidence in the historical setting of Ephesus and speaks to difficulties that gentile converts would have experienced. Abandoning Artemis meant forfeiting her benefits, so the gentile converts at Ephesus needed reassuring that they served a greater God, with a greater temple, and who was a greater benefactor who could provide greater benefits.

---

19. For application to Eph 1:23 and 3:19, see Arnold 1989, 70–102.
20. Aelius Aristides, *Or.* 23.24; Dio Chrysostom, *Rhod.* 31.54.

While the historical setting of Ephesus provided *prima facie* evidence for McMurray's argument, he sought to supply exegetical evidence by examining the building/temple imagery in Paul's letter (Eph 2:14; 2:20-22; 3:16-18; 4:1-16). However, while he cited sufficient evidence to justify his claim for a local Greco-Roman context, the simultaneous examination of building and temple imagery resulted in the mixing of architectural and cultic terms.[21] A subsequent investigation of architectural language using the *Lexicon of Ancient Architectural Terms* and other inscriptional sources revealed thirty words with architectural uses in Ephesians.[22] While McMurray's work provided a foundation for investigating architectural imagery, the refined results from *Lexicon of Ancient Architectural Terms* and inscriptional sources provide additional support for examining Paul's use of architectural imagery, in particular his use of πληρόω/μα.

In Eph 1:15-23, Paul prayed for the Ephesians that God would give them a "Spirit of wisdom and revelation" (1:17) so that they would know the "hope of his calling" (1:18) and "the immeasurable greatness of his

---

21. McMurray (2019, 78-124 and 125-171) organized his evidence into "explicit" (Eph 2:20-22) and "implicit" (Eph 2:14; 3:16-18; 4:1-16) categories of building/temple imagery. Explicit terms: ἐποικοδομέω (81-83); θεμέλιος (83-87); ἀκρογωνιαῖος (87-93); πᾶσα οἰκοδομή (93-95); συναρμολογέω (96-97); ναός (97-101); συνοικοδομέω (101-2); and τὸ κατοικητήριον (102-4). Implicit terms: μεσότοιχον (125-36); φραγμός (125-36); θεμελιόω (125, 144); πλοῦτος (137-42); πλάτος (143-54); μῆκος (143-54); ὕψος (143-54); βάθος (143-54); κατοικέω (143); οἰκοδομή (155-57); Psalm 68 with its temple context (157-66); and divine benefaction (166-70). It must be noted that McMurray counted οἰκοδομή as both explicit and implicit building/temple imagery.

22. See Orlandos and Traulous 1986: s.v. "ἀκρογωνιαῖος" (7); "ἁφή" (45); "βάθος" (47); "ἐνεργέω" (101); "ἐνέργεια" (see also ἐ"ργασία" [115]); "ἐποικοδομέω" (114); "ἔργον" (117); "θεμέλιος" (127); "θεμελιόω" (127-28); "κεφαλή" (152); "κραταιόω" (160); "κτίζω" (163); "λύω" (173); "μεσότοιχον" (176); "μέτρον" (178); "μῆκος" (178); "ναός" (182); "οἰκοδομή" (189); "πλάτος" (213); "πληρόω" (213); "πλήρωμα" (213); "ῥιζόω" (see also "ῥίζα" [228]); "συναρμολογέω" (241); "συνοικοδομέω" (242); "σῶμα" (244; see also "βάθος" [47]; "ὕψος" [261]); "ὕψος" (261); and "φραγμός" (263). The *Lexicon of Ancient Architectural Terms* was produced by The Archaeological Society at Athens in 1986, and no citations of this resource were discovered in the secondary literature consulted for this commentary. While this lexicon can provide fresh linguistic insights, it should be used in conjunction with other critical sources as well. I give special thanks to my friend Professor F. Alan Tomlinson for introducing me to this valuable resource. For the inscriptional sources, see σοφός: Shanor 1988, 463-64; ποιέω: LSJ, s.v. "ποιέω," A.I.1; IG 2.1.429.79, 88; ποίημα: IG 2.1.429.8.

power," which was displayed in raising Jesus Christ from the dead. After recounting Christ's exaltation and enthronement (Eph 1:20-22), Paul described the church through the two metaphors of "body" and "fullness" (Eph 1:23). In Eph 1:22-23, Paul developed the relationship between the head and church by placing σῶμα in apposition to ἐκκλησία.[23] In so doing, Paul communicated to the Ephesians that God has established Christ as the absolute authority over all things (Eph 1:20-22; see Ps 110:1). Here, Paul highlighted that Christ has ultimate authority over both the realm of evil spirits (Eph 1:21) and the church (Eph 1:22). However, while Paul portrayed Christ's relationship to the evil spirits as one of authority and subjection, Paul used the head/body imagery to highlight the nurturing aspect of Christ's relationship to the church (Eph 1:23; 5:25-32). He then developed the relationship between church and body by placing πλήρωμα in apposition to σῶμα, a relationship best explained by the architectural use of both terms. In IG 2.1.429, πλήρωμα referred to the "fill" or "filling" used in the rubble core or *emplekton* masonry techniques (ll. 80-82) and πληρόω referred to the action of "filling" the structure (ll. 82-83), while σῶμα could be used to refer to a building or structure.[24] By placing πλήρωμα in apposition to σῶμα in Eph 1:23, Paul presented the Ephesians collectively as the living stones used to build Christ's temple (1:23; 2:20-22; 3:18-19) and God as the wise master builder whose living temple far exceeds the Artemision in glory (1:19, 23; 3:20-21) (Shanor 1988, 463-64).[25]

---

23. For a discussion of the background of the head/body metaphor see Barth 1974, 183-99.

24. For examples of the rubble core technique see Caraher and Gregory 2006, 333-37; Seifried and Parkinson 2014, 277-313; Koutsoukou and Kanellopoulos 1990, 155-74; Konecny and Ruggendorfer 2014, 709-46; Dündar and Rauh 2017, 509-81; Clarke and Connor 1996-1997, 151-83. For examples of the *emplekton* technique, see Pedersen's (2019, 4-5) notes on the Servian Wall, the podium of the Capitoline temple of Jupiter, the foundation of the temple of Castor and Pollux, and the foundation-podium of the Parthenon as examples (see also *BDAG*, "πληρόω," 1a.; "πλήρμα," 1a.) See also *Orlandos* and Traulous 1986, s.v. "σῶμα" (244); "βάθος" (47): "ἤτοι μία τῶν τριῶν διαστάσεων τῶν σωμάτων, κατ᾿ ἀντιδιαστολὴν πρὸς τὸ μῆκος καὶ πλάτος"; and "ὕψος" (261): "ἡ ἀπὸ τῆς βάσεως μέχρι τῆς κορυφῆς σώματός τινος μετρουμένη ἀμόστασις (ἀντιθ. τῷ μῆκος, εὖρος)."

25. Seeing God as the master builder of his temple would also provide a polemical parallel to the legend of Artemis setting the lintel of her temple (McMurray 2019, 63-64). Here, Paul's metaphorical use of πλήρωμα is like a synecdoche in that a word

In Eph 3:14–21, Paul returned to his second prayer, which had been interrupted by his excursus on his apostolic ministry and the mystery of gentile inclusion (Eph 3:2–13).[26] His prayer included three primary petitions centered on God's empowering of believers (Eph 3:16, 18, 19) and culminated in a doxology (Eph 3:20–21). Notably, Paul's prayer included eleven words with architectural uses, which suggests that the architectural imagery provides an interpretive key for the passage.[27] In particular, an architectural interpretation solves the problem of the elliptical object in Eph 3:18 and the referent of πλήρωμα in 3:19. In this view, πλάτος, μῆκος, ὕψος, and βάθος refer to the dimensions of a building and not to God's wisdom, power, or love (Eph 3:18). As for Paul's use of πλήρωμα, the term is used collectively to refer to God's living temple (Eph 3:19; see also 1:23) and frames his discussion of gentile inclusion (Eph 2:14–22). These readings in turn reinforce one another as the arguments for one also support the other. When Paul prays that the Ephesians might "be *filled* to all the *fullness* of God" (Eph 3:19), he is asking that God would complete the work of "filling up" his temple by continuing to save sinners. Accordingly, in the doxology, God is praised as "the one who is able to *construct* far more abundantly" (Eph 3:20) and who will receive glory "*with respect to* the church" (Eph 3:21). Here, ποιέω could be rendered as "construct" owing to the influence of the other architectural terms in the context and the ἐν + dative as "with respect to" since Paul's imagery

---

which typically denotes the material used for a building is used to refer to the whole building. However, the collective nature of ἐκκλησία requires that the whole building is in view. This interpretation also helps to make sense of the often-discussed passive sense of πλήρωμα and the middle/passive participle πληρουμένου. See Best 2001, 188: "There is no easy exegesis of v. 23. All that can be said is that it is probably best to take both the participle and pleroma as passive and the clause as in apposition to σῶμα." If my interpretation is correct, Eph 1:23 would read "which is his body, the fullness of the one being filled completely in every way." Understanding the Ephesians as the temple in 1:23 also resonates with Harrison's benefactive reading of Eph 1:3–14 (Harrison 2018b, 3–7) and the practices for recording citizenship by inscribing names in the Artemision (Harrison 2018a, 290–91). On the mixed metaphor, see Harrill 2020, 223–46.

26. On the connection of 3:14–21 to 2:11–22, see McMurray 2019, 136–37; and Hoehner 2002, 472.

27. See Orlandos and Traulous 1986: s.v. "βάθος" (47); "ἐνεργέω" (101); "θεμελιόω" (127–28); "κραταιόω" (160); "μῆκος" (178); "πλάτος" (213); "πληρόω" (213); "πλήρωμα" (213); "ῥιζόω" (see also "ῥίζα," 228); "ὕψος" (261). See also, ποιέω: LSJ, s.v. "ποιέω," A.I.1; IG 2.1.429.79, 88.

pictures the public display of God's temple. If this interpretation is correct, then Paul brought his encouragement to a climax in Eph 3:14–21 by arguing that God's living temple, the church, has a better foundation (Eph 3:17), is built to far grander dimensions (Eph 3:18), by God who is able to construct beyond all imagination (Eph 3:20), and who will receive eternal glory from his temple which can never be destroyed (Eph 3:21).[28] Indeed, Paul's argument that "my God's temple is greater than your goddess's temple, so my God is greater than your goddess" would have provided encouragement and consolation to a young church struggling to survive at the cultic center of Asia Minor.

Bibliography

Arnold, Clinton E. 1989. *Ephesians, Power and Magic: The Concept of Power in Ephesians in Light of Its Historical Setting.* Cambridge: Cambridge University Press.

Barth, Markus. 1974. *Ephesians: Introduction, Translation, and Commentary on Chapters 1–3.* AB 34. New York: Doubleday.

Baugh, Steven Michael. 2016. *Ephesians.* Bellingham, WA: Lexham.

Best, Ernest. 2001. *Critical and Exegetical Commentary on Ephesians.* ICC. Edinburgh: T&T Clark.

Caraher, William R., David K. Pettegrew, and Sarah James. 2010. "Towers and Fortifications at Vayia in the Southeast Corinthia." *Hesperia* 79:385–415.

Caraher, William R., and Timothy R. Gregory. 2006. "Fortifications of Mount Oneion, Corinthia." *Hesperia* 75:327–56.

Clarke, Graeme W., and Peter J. Connor. 1996–1997. "Jebel Khalid in North Syria: The First Campaigns." *Mediterranean Archaeology* 9–10:151–83.

Conwell, David H. 2008. *Connecting a City to the Sea: The History of the Athenian Long Walls.* MnemosyneSup 293. Leiden: Brill.

Dennis, P. H. 1848. *The Cities and Cemeteries of Etruria.* 2 vols. London: John Murray.

Dündar, Erkan, and Nicholas K. Rauh. 2017. "The North Bastion on the Tepecik Acropolis at Patara: Dating 'Early Hellenistic' Fortification Walls in Southwestern Anatolia." *Hesperia* 86:509–81.

---

28. For another insightful perspective on Paul's presentation of the church as God's living temple that magnifies his glory, see Baugh 2016, 278–81.

Elliott, J. K. 1993. *The Apocryphal New Testament: A Collection of Apocryphal Christian Literature in an English Translation.* Oxford: Clarendon.
Fields, Nic. 2006. *Ancient Greek Fortifications: 500–300 BC.* New York: Osprey Publishing.
Hansen, V. D. 2005. *A War Like No Other.* New York: Harding.
Harrill, J. Albert. 2020. "Shaping Buildings into Stories: Architectural *Ekphrasis* and the Epistle to the Ephesians in Roman Literary Culture." Pages 223–46 in *Literature and Culture in the Roman Empire, 96–235.* Edited by Alice König, Rebecca Langlands, and James Uden. Cambridge: Cambridge University Press.
Harrison, James R. 2018a. "Ephesian Cultic Officials, Their Benefactors, and the Quest for Civic Virtue: Paul's Alternative Quest for Status in the Epistle to the Ephesians." Pages 253–98 in *Ephesus.* Vol. 3 of *The First Urban Churches.* Edited by James R. Harrison and L. L. Welborn. WGRWSup 9. Atlanta: SBL Press.
———. 2018b. "An Epigraphic Portrait of Ephesus and Its Villages." Pages 1–67 in *Ephesus.* Vol. 3 of *The First Urban Churches.* Edited by James R. Harrison and L. L. Welborn. WGRWSup 9. Atlanta: SBL Press.
Hoehner, Harold. 2002. *Ephesians: An Exegetical Commentary.* Grand Rapids, MI: Baker Academic.
Immendörfer, Michael. 2017. *Ephesians and Artemis: The Cult of the Great Goddess of Ephesus as the Epistle's Context.* WUNT 2/436. Tübingen: Mohr Siebeck.
Karlsson, L. 1992. *Fortification Towers and Masonry Techniques in the Hegemony of Syracuse, 405–211 BC.* Acta Instituti Romani Regni Sueciae 40. Stockholm: Åströms.
Knigge, Ursula. 1991. *The Athenian Kerameikos: History, Monuments, Excavations.* Athens: Krene.
Konecny, Andreas L., and Peter Ruggendorfer. 2014. "Alinda in Karia: The Fortifications." *Hesperia* 83:709–46.
Koutsoukou, Anthi, and Chysanthos Kanellopoulos. 1990. "Towers from North-West Andros." *ABSA* 85:155–74.
Ladstätter, Sabine. 2010. "II.5.1.2 Tribüne im Artemision." *JÖAI* 79:23–24.
Lambert, Stephen D. 2012. *Inscribed Athenian Laws and Decrees 352/1–322/1 BC: Epigraphical Essays.* Brill Studies in Greek and Roman Epigraphy 2. Leiden: Brill.
Lincoln, Andrew T. 1990. *Ephesians.* WBC 42. Dallas: Word.
Maier, Franz Georg. 1959–1961. *Griechische Mauerbauinschriften.* 2 vols. Heidelberg: Quelle & Meyer.

McLean, B. H. 2002. *An Introduction to Greek Epigraphy of the Hellenistic and Roman Periods from Alexander the Great down to the Reign of Constantine (323 B.C.–A.D. 337)*. Ann Arbor: University of Michigan Press.

McMurray, Howard. 2019. "The Temple of God and the Temple of Artemis: Exploring the Building/Temple Image in Ephesians." PhD diss., Southwestern Baptist Theological Seminary, Fort Worth, TX.

Murphey-O'Connor, Jerome. 2008. *St. Paul's Ephesus: Texts and Archeology*. Collegeville, MN: Liturgical Press.

Ober, Josiah. 1987. "Early Artillery Towers: Messenia, Boitotia, Attica, Megarid." *AJA* 91:569–604.

Orlandos, Anastasios K., and Iōannou N. Traulous. 1986. *Lexikón archaíon architektonikón óron*. Athens: Archaeology Society of Athens.

Pedersen, Poul. 2019. "*Emplekton*—The Art of Weaving Stones." Pages 1–10 in *Listening to the Stones: Essays on Architecture and Function in Ancient Greek Sanctuaries in Honour of Richard Alan Tomlinson*. Edited by Elena C. Partida and Barbara Schmidt-Dounas. Oxford: Archaeopress.

Richardson, M. 2000. "The Location of Inscribed Laws in Fourth-Century Athens: IG II2 244, on Rebuilding the Walls of the Peiraieus (337/7 BC)." Pages 601–15 in *Polis and Politics: Studies in Ancient Greek History Presented to Mogens Herman Hansen on His Sixtieth Birthday, August 20, 2000*. Edited by Pernille Flensted-Jensen, Thomas Heine Nielsen, and Lene Rubinstein. Copenhagen: Museum Tusculanum Press.

Robert, Louis. 1961. "Les épigraphies et l'épigraphie greque et romaine." Pages 453–97 in *L'Histoire et ses Méthodes: Encyclopédie de la Pleiade*. Edited by Charles Samaran. Paris: Gallimard.

Schwenk, Cynthia J. 1985. *Athens in the Age of Alexander. The Dated Laws and Decrees of "the Lykourgan era" 338–322 B.C.* Chicago: Ares.

Seifried, Rebecca M., and William A. Parkinson. 2014. "The Ancient Towers of the Paximadi Peninsula, Southern Euobia." *Hesperia* 83:277–313.

Shanor, Jay. 1988. "Paul as Master Builder: Construction Terms in First Corinthians." *NTS* 34:461–71.

Sokolicek, Alexander. 2009. "Zwischen Stadt und Land: neues zum Magnesischen Tor in Ephesos: Erste Ergebnisse." *JÖAI* 78:321–47.

———. 2010. "Chronologie und Nutzung des Magnesischen Tores von Ephesos." *JÖAI* 79:359–81.

———. 2020. "The Magnesian Gate of Ephesos." Pages 158–70 in *Religion in Ephesos Reconsidered: Archaeology of Spaces, Structures, and Objects.* Edited by Daniel Schowalter, Sabine Ladstätter, Steven Friesen, and Christine Thomas. NovTSup 177. Leiden: Brill.

Son, S. Aaron 2001. *Corporate Elements in Pauline Anthropology.* AnBib 148. Rome: Pontifical Biblical Institute.

Theocharaki, Anna. 2011. "The Ancient Circuit Walls of Athens: Its Changing Course and the Phases of Construction." *Hesperia* 80:71–156.

———. 2020. *The Ancient Circuit Walls of Athens.* Berlin: De Gruyter.

Tomlinson, R. A. 1961. "*Emplekton* Masonry and 'Greek Structura.'" *JHS* 81:133–40.

Trebilco, Paul. 2004. *The Early Christians in Ephesus from Paul to Ignatius.* Grand Rapids: Eerdmans.

Graffiti

23. The Wall Scribblers of Terrace House 2, Unit 6

James R. Harrison

The year 2012 was the fiftieth anniversary of the discovery in Ephesus of Terrace House 2. This 4,000-square-meter residential block, which upon excavation still retained its beautifully preserved walls, was located in the city center adjacent to Curetes Street and was divided into seven residential units. Situated on a steep slope with terracing, the residential complex had three units at the lowest level, two at the highest, and two final units in between (though this was originally a single unit). This complex represents a remarkable highpoint in wealthy Roman domestic culture in an eastern Mediterranean provincial context. Each unit was arranged around a large central courtyard (the atrium), being open to the light of the sky and fresh air. As the hub of internal circulation, the courtyard provided access to each unit, including the luxuriously decorated reception rooms and the convivial dining rooms. The remaining smaller and simpler rooms were bedrooms, kitchens, and (in some units) bathrooms and lavatories. The complex as it stands today was erected in the second quarter of the first century CE, but it was eventually destroyed around 270/280 CE by earthquake and subsequent fire.[1] For a very brief history of the excavation and the results of the excavation, see Wiplinger and Wlach 1996, 104–106.

Excavated by the Austrian Archaeological Institute from 1969–1986, Terrace House 2 has spawned a series of important publications leading up to and following on from the celebratory year of 2012: Zimmermann and Ladstätter 2011, 44–138; Ladstätter 2013; Thür and Rathmayr 2014; the two (undifferentiated) volumes of Rathmayr 2016; Ladstätter 2020; Rathmayr 2022.

---

1. Prior to the destruction in 270/280 CE, four phases of building occurred in Terrace House 2: Building Phase 1 (25–50 CE), Building Phase 2 (ca. 120 CE), Building Phase 3 (ca. 150 CE), Building Phase 4 (cs. 230 CE), Building Phase 4 (ca. 260 CE). See Ladststätter 2013, 75–110.

Crucially for our purposes, in the 2014 and 2016 publications cited above are found three chapters of Hans Taeuber (2014, 331–44; 2016b, 233–57; 2016a, 752–62), who authoritatively sets out, translates, and discusses the graffiti, inscriptions, paintings, and drawings from Terrace House 2. On the Ephesian graffiti more generally, see Harrison 2018, 49–56.[2] We will proceed publication-by-publication of Tauber in discussing the relevant evidence.

1. Taeuber, "Graffiti und Steininschriften" (2014)

1.1. Terrace House 2 Unit 6 Stone Inscriptions, the Ephesian Gods, Their Personnel and Cult

The apartment owner of Unit 6 Terrace 2 in the Phase 2 building phase (ca. 120 CE) was Gaius Flavius Furius Aptus, who is referred to directly in the stone inscriptions IST 1 and implicitly in IST 3, each epigrams bases carrying statues, as well as in GR 283 ("To Furius Aptus") and IKL 24 ("[Property] of another, not of the Aptus"). Tauber (2014, 143) also draws attention to another Terrace House 2 inscription (IST 3: Knibbe, İplikçioğlu, Engelmann, 1993, 133, no. 140.2; SEG 31.963). There, Aphrodite Kythere, as the overseer of seafaring, is invoked to "protect Gaius and Pericles, both in a foreign country also at home when you are a guest or host," the host in Taeuber's view being Furius Aptus. What do we learn about Furius Aptus that is significant in an Ephesian context?

---

2. Frustratingly, the two volumes of Rathmayr published in 2016 are not differentiated by volume number: that is, *Hanghaus 2 in Ephesos: Die Wohneinheit 7*, volume 1, and *Hanghaus 2 in Ephesos: Die Wohneinheit 7*, volume 2. This makes confusion in textual citation a genuine possibility if we do not proceed carefully. Readers also need to be aware of Taeuber's slightly differing German titles in the 2014 and two 2016 volumes so that they can check the correct volume for the original epigraphic texts, paintings, and drawings. In this commentary I cite the year of publication of the volume and the epigraphic number, ensuring thereby that there will be no mistake made in referencing. In discussing the primary sources, again so that there is no misunderstanding, I will proceed volume-by-volume. In each volume, Taeuber uses GR for references to graffiti/drawings/paintings, IKL for small inscriptions, and IST for stone inscriptions. I am indebted throughout to the German translations of Taeuber.

IST 1

JÖAI 53:112, no. 79 (*edito princeps*); IEph 4.1267. Chiseled upon on the central pillar of the rear parapet of the fountain. Date: built during Building Phase 2.

Διόνυσος "Ορειος Βάκχιος πρὸ πόλεως	Dionysus Oreios ("living on the mountains") Bakchios in front of the city,
οὗ ἱερᾶται Γάϊος Φλάβιος Φούριος Ἄπτος.	of whom Gaius Flavius Furius Aptus (is the) priest.

The sanctuary of Dionysus Oreios at the front of the city has C. Fl. Furius Aptus as its priest of Dionysos.[3] On Dionysos at Ephesus, see Oster 1990, 1673-76. There are abundant epigraphic references to the ancient Greek festival of Dionysos, the Dionysia, being held in the Hellenistic theater (IEph 5.1390, 1405, 1408, 1411, 1440, 1452, 1457, 1466; 6.2003, 2013). Antony had visited Ephesus as the new Dionysos to a rapturous response (Plutarch, *Ant.* 4, 24; Dio Cassius, *Hist Rom.* 48.39). The Ephesian epigraphic record refers to priests of Dionysos spanning the period from 25/24 BCE to the reign of Trajan (IEph 1a.9b.17 [3.902.6, 15; 4.1270.3–6; 7.1.3329.1–3]), as well as winter festivals in honor of Dionysos (3.661.20), a Baccheion where meetings were held (2.434.1–2), and an association of the Dionysiac mysteries in the time of Hadrian (2.275.7). Additionally, in Terrace House 6, there is also a statuette of Dionysos with the head broken off, and on the hem of the coat from the bottom to the top is the name of its slave manufacturer (IKL 23 [first century CE]: "Of Paramonos"). Thus Aptus was a priest in a cult that had a venerable tradition in Ephesus. On the mysteries of Ephesus, see G. Rogers 2012, 295–98. For discussion of C. Fl. Furius Arptus, named Python and a *neopoios* of Artemis during the Trajanic period, who was an ancestor of our Arptus discussed above, see Rathmyr (2022), along with the six epigraphic references cited (25 n. 25). For full discussion of the family tree of the Furii Arptii, who were of equestrian rank, see also Thür 20222, 42–44.

---

3. For eulogies and fragmentary letters of royal, imperial, and consular figures in Terrace House 6 graffiti, see Commodus (Taeuber 2014, GR 241), Hadrian (Taeuber 2014, GR 255: third consulate [119 CE]), Cn. Arrius Augur (Taeuber 2014, GR 284: consul [121 CE]); Lucius Verus (Taeuber 2016b, IST 10); Hadrian (Taeuber 2016b, IST 11, 12: "the savior and founder"); King Eumenes (Taeuber 2016b, IST 13 [188 BCE]).

In light of this backdrop, Cleon Rogers (1979) has argued that Paul's injunction not to be filled with wine but the Spirit is a polemic against the drunken practices associated with the worship of Dionysos. However, care must be taken that we do not assume that all cases of drunkenness at Ephesus are necessarily understood from this Dionysiac perspective: the centrality of alcohol to Roman civilization was well known. As Ray Laurence (2009, 112) observes, "drinking wine quite literally defined a person as a member of Roman society," and increasingly drinking on an empty stomach became a driving passion of the Romans in the capital (and, presumably, their provincial clients and imitators) in the early second century CE.

Finally, regarding religion in Terrace House 6 more generally, Aphrodite's role as protector of seafarers, noted above, is again highlighted by the mythological reference to her birth through the union of Zeus and Dione in another inscription (IST 2: Knıbbe, İPlıkçıoğlu, and Engelmann 1993, 132–33, no. 140.1; SEG 31.962), which describes her birth thus: "you are born with foam and from that you have risen to the sea." On Aphrodite at Ephesus, see Oster 1990, 1667–68.[4] On initiates of the Aphrodisian mysteries setting up an altar to Aphrodite Daitis, see IEph 4.1202.1–7. Other references to the gods and the cult occur in Terrace House 6 through the medium of diagrams. There is a drawing of Athena in profile, looking to the left, with a helmet on (GR 242) and possibly a knife (culter) used for sacrificial acts (GR 308). On the Christian *trisagion* formula (GR 298: "Holy, holy, holy, save Thomas!"), see the thematic essay of Harrison, "The Life of Christians in Late Antique Ephesus: An Epigraphic Portrait," in *NewDocs* 11B.

1.2. The Emotions, Adultery, and the Residents of Terrace House 6

Taeuber (2014, 331) has highlighted the role of emotion in graffiti from Terrace House 6. First, in GR 238, there is a curse against an adulteress:

---

4. Statuary and reliefs at Ephesus are plentiful: (1) a first century BCE torso of Aphrodite has been found in the Fountain of Pollio (Cansever 2010, 54); (2) a statue of Aphrodite in the Nymphaeum Traiani (59); (3) a statue of Aphrodite in the Gaius Laecanius Bassus Fountain (64); (4) a figurine of Aphrodite and Eros in Terrace House 1 (Cansever 2010, 78); (5) a relief of Aphrodite and Eros figures over the central arch of the Mazeus and Mithridates Gate (http://tinyurl.com/SBL9031h). See Aurenhammer 1995, 260–62.

"Calamity to the adulteress!" (Τὸ πῆμα μοιχ(ευ)τρίᾳ). Second, the love lament of GR 203 reveals the angst of soul of the lover facing the dissolution of a relationship: "If only the soul could let go! You didn't want to see an hour in which I made you sad; but I've done everything you want, given the little time left." This graffito has a peculiar humor as far as its site because, as Taeuber (2014, 331) observes, for the inscription to be written on the wall above the fish tank in Room 36a, "the disappointed lover must have stood in the water while writing (if the basin wasn't emptied)." On the emotions in antiquity, see Konstan 2008. For discussion of the emotions in the New Testament, see Barton 2011; 2015; Welborn 2001; 2011; Hockey 2019; Jew 2021.

The graffito GR 238 in especially interesting in a New Testament context because of its singling out of the woman adulteress, as opposed to the male adulterer, for unspecified disaster. One is reminded of the "floating fragment" in John's Gospel regarding the woman caught in adultery (7:53–8:11); there only the adulterous woman is presented before Jesus for accusation and subsequent stoning to death according to the Mosaic law. It has been argued that there existed a clear divergence in view between Jewish (Lev 20:10; Deut 22:22) and Roman law (Quintilian, *Inst.* 5.10.104–105; Seneca the Elder, *Contr.* 1.4) over whether an adulteress should be executed without, concomitantly, the same sentence being exacted upon the adulterer. Philips (2019) proposes that John 7:53–8:11 reflects this ideological and legal divide. On the later Roman jurists on adultery, see especially Papinianus, *On Adultery* 1–3; Paul, *Sent.* 2.26.1 8, 10–12, 14. For Augustus's legislation on marriage, see Frank 1975. On imperial adultery, see Langlands 2006, subject index, s.v. "Adultery." On adultery in the ancient novel, see Schwartz 2016.

2. Taueber, "Graffiti und Inschriften" (2016b)

Another common feature of Terrace House 6 graffiti is the appearance of the highly popular isopsephic (gematria) puzzles (GR 304, 310, 311, 312), which Taeuber (2016b, 233) postulates belonged to the social conversations occurring in the ancient symposia possibly held within the terrace house. In these puzzles, the name of the lover could be guessed by adding the numerical coding of the individual letters contained and encrypted therein: for example, GR 310: "And the one who loves her has the number 1995." Taeuber (2016b, 2016, 235) rightly comments that the puzzle is practically unsolvable for modern readers. Two examples (GR 311, 312), however, break out of the conventional enigmatic style by placing the solution right below in a second hand:

GR 311

Νῦν πάλι φιλῶ νὴ θεοῦς γθναῖκα ἧς ὁ ἀριθμὸς ωξέ {ΙΥΝ}ἐὰν ἧς Γόργος ὁ εὕρων, ὑπόγραψον. (2nd hand): Κλωδία.	Now again I love the woman, whose number is 865, among the gods. If you are Gorgos who finds out, write it under. (2nd hand): Klodia

For further examples of isopsephic (gematria) puzzles at Smyrna, see Burnett 2020, 157–58. More generally on numerical calculations in the inscriptions, see 148–58.

Although the genres and rhetorical intentions are vastly different, the book of Revelation adopts a similar coded use of numbers ("gematria riddle": Aune 1998, 770–73) for its readers in order to help them identity of the beast labeled as 666 (Rev 13:18; Burnett 2020, 140–62). These encoded puzzles, which also built upon a similar aggregate of letters, were also employed in popular anti-imperial rhetoric during the reign of Nero (Suetonius, *Nero* 39; cited by Robinson 1976, 235):

> Count the numerical values
> Of the letters in Nero's name
> And in "murdered his own mother":
> You will find out that their sum is the same.

Finally, several observations are apposite. First, as noted above, there is mention of the gods, one a conjuration of the sky god Uranus (GR 314: "by (you) Uranus!"), and the other a playful tongue-twister in the original Greek referring to Zeus (GR 328: "I give with Zeus's help through my own means").

Second, there is an (ironic) allusion to the dwelling of the Cynic philosopher Diogenes at Athens: "I'll grab (myself) a barrel where I'll sleep. I (? ---)" (GR 319). The Ephesian inscriptions and wall paintings show considerable interest in the Greek philosophers, highlighting Socrates the Athenian (IEph 2.560.1, 3) and Chilon the Spartan (IEph 2.560.2), one of the famous Seven Sages. As far as the wall paintings in Terrace House 2, Socrates is isolated as an important Greek figure for Ephesians (Ladstätter 2013, 82 fig. 47). In IEph 7.2.4340 and IEph 3.789, there is mention respectively of a "Platonic" and "eclectic" philosopher. Also φιλόσοφοι are frequently honored in the inscriptions at Ephesus (IEph 3.616, 3.789, 5.1958, 6.2066, 7.2.3901, 7.2.4340). The sophist Soterus, for example, is eulogized in IEph 5.1548 thus: "Twice did the Androclidae summon from Athens me Soterus, a sophist, first by decrees of the Council; and on me first as a reward for virtue in life and wisdom of speech they resolved by way of honor to bestow numberless gifts." In a dossier from 42 BCE, immunity is granted for professors, sophists, and doctors (SEG 56.1219: a revision of SEG 31.952). A delightful caricature of philosophers and their pseudo-wisdom is found in the latrine of residential unit 2 in Terrace House 2 (Ladstätter 2013, 185; Zimmermann and Ladstätter 2011, 87–88 figs. 136–137). As Zimmermann and Ladstätter (2011,88) explains, the philosophers not ruminating over esoteric or high truths but rather are "reminding the users of the latrine to hurry." On the physiognomy of identifying philosophers as a group in the wall paintings, see Zimmermann and Ladstätter 2011, 88. These types of divergent engagements with the philosophers in the Ephesian epigraphic corpus and in the visual evidence of Terrace House 2—some positive and others derisive—meant that Paul's dismissal of the wisdom of the "debaters of this age" in 1 Cor 1:20 (2 Cor 10:4–6) may have found on occasion some quasi-sympathetic auditors.

Third, arising out of the previous point, is the occurrence of a satirical thrust in the humor of some of the scribblings of Terrace House 2. There is a mocking tone adopted towards Agathemeros, who is possibly dismissed as effeminate and is certainly derided for his bizarre clothing (Taeuber, 2016b, 238): "Agathemeros, the non-warrior and with half a military coat" (GR 322). Similarly, the comic dismissal of the pony-tailed charioteer, the father of the honorand, is equally satirical: "Manes, son of the charioteer, the ponytail" (GR 324). In sum, we see here the ability of graffiti writers to spoof those they are lambasting, a rhetorical ability that Paul also has in abundance, except that he targets himself as the weak "fool" over against the inflated boasting of the rival "super-apostles" and the sophist-conditioned conventions and expectations of the Corinthians regarding his apostolate in 1 Cor 1–4 and 2 Cor 10–13. See Harrison 2004, 46–55; 2017; Welborn 1999; 2005.

Fourth, there is a frequent occurrence of accounts (GR 329, 369, 376), which leads Taeuber (2016b, 234) to speculate that Room 32e in Terrace House 2 possibly served as an office, among other functions. What is especially interesting is that these lists of household expenses from (admittedly wealthy) households stand in contrast to the expenses of wealthy benefactors recounted in the Ephesian honorific inscriptions: the graffiti deal with modest expenditure and staple objects of purchase. We gain here a clearer glimpse of everyday economic life at Ephesus. There are several samples of the lists of expenses found in the graffiti:

GR 329
    Soap
    10 denarii
    For Pol(y)bios
    4 (?) denarii sales tax (?) 11 denarii.

GR 370
Olive oil	2 denarii
Breads	2 denarii
Wine	2 denarii
Vegetables	9 assaria
Garum (sauce)	9 assaria
Vinegar	6 assaria
Lamp wick	2 assaria

Make 7 denarii 5 assaria (the total expense)

In GR 329, clues relating to the local economy are let slip, such as the sales tax, and, more extraordinarily in GR 370, "we have the conversion key between the denarii and the assaria for the first time in the sum calculation (possibly added by a second hand)" (Taeuber 2016b, 250). Another list of expenses (GR 357)—although all the items are not clearly identifiable—includes loaves, vegetables, barley (wood?), boiled rooster, Hepatos fish, garum sauce, entry into the thermal bath, an unspecified expense for the slave, and rings: the prices range from 12 to 4 assaria. Last, GR 369 lists the "warm meals" purchased from "take-away" cook-shops for Montanus, Romulus, and Aquitanius, each purchase set out in denarii and assaria.

What relevance does this strand of epigraphic evidence have for the New Testament? In Rev 6:6, the terrible economic effects of famine, precipitated by war, are announced by a heavenly voice: "A quart of wheat [χοῖνιξ σίτου] for a day's pay, and three quarts of barley [τρεῖς χοίνικες κριθῶν] for a day's pay, but do not damage the olive oil and wine!" For full discussion, see "Maintaining the Market Supply of Wheat for Rome," in this volume. In verse 6, the staple foods of the poor are being sold at inflated prices in a time of crisis. By contrast, the expenditure lists of Terrace House 6 reveal a time of extended social stability and provincial prosperity, setting the apocalyptic scenario of Rev 6 in even sharper relief in terms of the Asian believers' experience of protracted privation and desperation.

Perhaps the expenditure lists of Terrace House 6 afford us indirect insight into the unconscious social and material accommodations progressively made by the Ephesian church. Ephesian believers had lost their first love, even though many aspects of their ecclesial life and discipleship were still praiseworthy (Rev 2:1–8). The lure of everyday prosperity in the market place, the experience of quiet and untroubled lives in the household, and the desire for concord as citizens, as opposed to social confrontation (e.g., Acts 19:1–41), led the Ephesian believers progressively over time into a type of spiritual somnolence that blunted their full commitment to Christ. Terrace House 6 is the embodiment of these seductive but ultimately dangerous values for unwary believers.

3. Taeuber's "Graffiti" (2016a)

There is little of significance for the New Testament context in Taeuber's final collection of graffiti from Terrace House 6. There is (1) another instance of scatological humor (GRA 389: "We urinated here, may stink"), a phenomenon discussed in "Finding the Right Spot to Take a Leak," in this volume, and (2) a case of the popular adoption of the name of the philosopher Herakelitos at Ephesus (GR 405), pointing again to the importance of philosophers and their teaching at Ephesus, noted above.

4. Conclusion

We have only scratched the surface of the wealth of Taeuber's evidence from the diverse media in Terrace House 6. Much else could have discussed: for example, the designs on the marble wall paneling; the drawings in the house, including one of a lion's head (GR 210A [Taeuber 2014]); tradesman's notes (GR 271: "Above the door (panels to be attached)" [Taeuber 2014]); geometric patterns (GR 211, 212 [Taeuber 2014]); architectural drawings (GR 219 [Taeuber 2014]); stonemason's marks (GR 219 [Taeuber 2014]); fifteen depictions of gladiators (GR 374–375, 380–385 [Taeuber 2016b]); another animal drawing, in this case a horse (GR 351 [Taeuber 2016b]). While these types of evidence do not necessarily have any direct New Testament reference, though *pace* gladiators above, they give us a sense of the everyday in Ephesus and the shared humanity of the city's inhabitants that reaches out to us across the centuries. On gladiators and the New Testament writings, see Concannon 2014; Cadwallader 2015; Unwin 2017; Harrison 2022, 32–35.

Bibliography

Aurenhammer, Maria. 1995. "Sculptures of Gods and Heroes from Ephesus." Pages 251–80 in *Ephesos: Metropolis of Asia; An Interdisciplinary Approach to Its Archaeology, Religion, and Culture.* Edited by Helmut Koester. HTS 41. Valley Forge, PA: Trinity Press International.

Aune, David. E. 1998. *Revelation 6–16.* WBC 52B. Grand Rapids: Zondervan.

Barton, Stephen C. 2015. "Be Angry But Do Not Sin (Ephesians 4:26a): Sin and the Emotions with Special Reference to Anger." *Studies in Christian Ethics* 1:21–34.

———. 2011. "Eschatology and the Emotions in Early Christianity." *JBL* 130:571–91.

Burnett, D. Clint. 2020. *Studying the New Testament through Inscriptions: An Introduction.* Peabody, MA: Hendrickson Academic.

Cadwallader, Alan H. 2015. "Assessing the Potential of Archaeological Discoveries for the Interpretation of New Testament Texts: The Case of a Gladiatorial Relief from Colossae and the Letter to the Colossians." Pages 41–66 in *Methodological Foundations.* Vol. 1 of *The First Urban Churches.* Edited by James R. Harrison and L. L. Welborn. WGRWSup 7. Atlanta: SBL Press.

Cansever, Meltem. 2010. *Ephesus Museum: Guide.* Istanbul: BKG Press.

Concannon, Cavan W. 2014. "'Not for an Olive Wreath, but Our Lives': Gladiators, Athletes, and Early Christian Bodies." *JBL* 133:193–214.

Frank, Richard I. 1975. "Augustus' Legislation on Marriage and Children." *California Studies in Classical Antiquity* 8:41–54.

Harrison, James. R. 2004. "In Quest of the Third Heaven: Paul and His Apocalyptic Imitators." *VC* 58:24–55.

———. 2017. "'Laughter Is the Best Medicine': St Paul, Well-Being, and Roman Humour." Pages in 209–40 in *Well-Being, Personal Wholeness and the Social Fabric.* Edited by Doru Costache, Darren Cronshaw, and James R. Harrison. Cambridge: Cambridge Scholars Press.

———. 2018. "An Epigraphic Portrait of Ephesus and Its Villages." Pages 1–67 in *Ephesus.* Vol. 3 of *The First Urban Churches.* Edited by James R. Harrison and L. L. Welborn. WGRWSup 9. Atlanta: SBL Press.

———. 2022. "An Epigraphic Portrait of Thessalonica." Pages 1-62 in *Thessalonica*. Vol. 7 of *The First Urban Churches*. Edited by James R. Harrison and L. L. Welborn. Atlanta: SBL Press.
Hockey, Katherine M. 2019. *The Role of Emotion in 1 Peter*. SNTSMS 173. Cambridge: Cambridge University Press.
Jew, Ian Y. S. 2021. *Paul's Emotional Regime: The Social Function of Emotion in Philippians and I Thessalonians*. London: T&T Clark.
Knibbe, Dieter, Bülent İplikçioğlu, and Helmut Engelmann. 1993. "Neue Inschriften aus Ephesos XII." *JÖAI* 62:113–50.
Konstan, David. 2008. *The Emotions of the Ancient Greek: Studies in Aristotle and the Classical Literature*. Toronto: University of Toronto Press.
Ladstätter, Sabine. 2013. *Terrace House 2 in Ephesos: An Archaeological Guide*. Istanbul: Homer Kitabevi.
———, ed. 2020. *Eine frühkaiserzeitliche Grubenverfüllung aus dem Hanghaus 2 in Ephesos*. Österreichisches Archäologisches Institut 18. Vienna: Österreichisches Archäologisches Institut.
Langlands, Rebecca. 2006. *Sexual Morality in Ancient Rome*. Cambridge: Cambridge University Press.
Laurence, Ray. 2009. *Roman Passions: A History of Passion in Imperial Rome*. London: Continuum.
Oster, R. "Ephesus as a Religious Centre under the Principate, I." *ANRW* 2.18.3 (1990): 1661–726.
Philips, Thomas E. 2019. "A Woman Caught in Adultery? Or A Wandering Teacher Trapped Between Roman and Jewish Law? John 7:53 8:11 in Light of Quintilian and Seneca." Pages 71–87 in *Greco-Roman and Jewish Tributaries to the New Testament*. Edited by Christopher E. Crawford. Claremont, CA: Claremont Press.
Rathmayr, Elisabeth. 2016. *Hanghaus 2 in Ephesos: Die Wohneinheit 7; Textband*. FiE 8.10. Vienna: Österreichisches Archäologisches Institut.
———. 2022. "New Evidence for Imperial Cult in Dwelling Unit 7 in Terrace House 2 in Ephesos." Pages 9–35 in *Ephesos as a Religious Center under the Principate*. Edited by Allen Black, Christine M. Thomas, and Trevor W. Thompson. WUNT 488. Tübingen: Mohr Siebeck.
Robinson, John A. T. 1976. *Redating the New Testament*. London: SCM.
Rogers, Cleon L. 1979. "Dionysian Background of Ephesians 5:18." *BS* 136.543:249–57.
Rogers, Guy MacLean. 2012. *The Mysteries of Artemis of Ephesos: Cult, Polis, and Change in the Graeco-Roman World*. Synkrisis. New Haven: Yale University Press.

Schwartz, Saundra C. 2016. *From Bedroom to Courtroom: Law and Justice in the Greek Novel*. Ancient Narrative Supplementum 21. Groningen: Barkhuis and Groningen University Library.

Taeuber, Hans. 2014. "Graffiti und Steininschriften." Pages 331–44 in *Hanghaus 2 in Ephesos: Die Wohneinheit 6; Baubefund, Ausstattung, Funde; Textband 1*. Edited by Hilke Thür and Elisabeth Rathmayr. FiE 8.9. Vienna: Österreichisches Archäologisches Institut.

———. 2016a. "Graffiti." Pages 752–63 in *Hanghaus 2 in Ephesos: Die Wohneinheit 7; Textband*. Edited by Elisabeth Rathmayr. FiE 8.10. Vienna: Österreichisches Archäologisches Institut.

———. 2016b. "Graffiti und Inschriften." Pages 233–57 in *Hanghaus 2 in Ephesos: Die Wohneinheit 7; Textband*. Edited by Elisabeth Rathmayr. FiE 8.10. Vienna: Österreichisches Archäologisches Institut.

Thür, Hilke. 2022. "The House of C. Fl. Furius Arptus in Ephesos: Clubhouse of a Dionysiac Association?" Pages 37–67 in *Ephesos as a Religious Center under the Principate*. Edited by Allen Black, Christine M. Thomas, and Trevor W. Thompson. WUNT 488. Tübingen: Mohr Siebeck.

Thür, Hilke, and Elisabeth Rathmayr, eds. 2014. *Hanghaus 2 in Ephesos: Die Wohneinheit 6; Baubefund, Ausstattung, Funde; Textband 1*. FiE 8.9. Vienna: Österreichisches Archäologisches Institut.

Unwin, James R. 2017. "Subversive Spectacles: The Struggles and Deaths of Paul and Seneca." PhD diss., Macquarie University.

Welborn, L. L. 1999. "The Runaway Paul." *HTR* 92.2:115–63.

———. 2001. "Paul's Appeal to the Emotions in 2 Corinthians 1.1–2.13; 7.5–16." *JSNT* 23:31–60.

———. 2005. *Paul, the Fool for Christ: A Study of 1 Corinthians 1–4 in the Comic-Philosophic Tradition*. London: T&T Clark.

———. 2011. "Paul and Pain: Paul's Emotional Therapy in 2 Corinthians 1.1–2.13; 7.5–16 in the Context of Ancient Psychagogic Literature." *NTS* 57:547–70.

Wiplinger, Gilbert, and Gudrun Wlach. 1996. *Ephesus: One Hundred Years of Austrian Research*. Edited by Claudia Luxon. Vienna: Österreichisches Archäologisches Institut.

Zimmermann, Norbert, and Sabine Ladstätter, eds. 2011. *Wall Painting in Ephesos from the Hellenistic to the Byzantine Period*. Istanbul: Ege Yayinlari.

24. The New Testament and the Serious Side of Toilet Humor

James R. Harrison

In the three undamaged inscriptions below from Ephesus, we see the serious side of toilet graffiti.[1] One graffito is genuinely humorous in its intent but nevertheless raises implicitly the ticklish issue of host-guest relations in private banquets, whereas the other two articulate philosophical perspectives on life and death. Such diversity of motifs among the Ephesian latrine graffiti, found in two different sites of the city (the harbor gymnasium; Terrace House 2, apartment II), reminds us that latrine graffiti as an epigraphic genre do not always focus upon frivolous scatological humor (see Harrison 2017; Levin-Richardson 2015; generally, Beard 2014) but that it can be fruitfully explored for evidence on social relations and popular philosophical debates in antiquity.

There is a resonance here with the graffiti found at the Roman harbor port of Ostia relating to scatological humor. Several of the famous seven Greek sages (Solon, Thales, Chilon, Bias) are depicted seated in wall paintings at the Baths of the Seven Wise Men (Regio III, Insula X, 2: ca. 100 CE) with Latin texts above them,[2] dispensing pompous opinions on the refined art of defecation to twenty-four Romans, who are presented in the lower register seated in a latrine-like line. The defecation advice rhetorically imitates the pithy moral imperatives of the sages. Solon is said to have taught: "Solon rubbed his belly to defecate well," whereas "Thales recommended that those who defecate with difficulty should strain," and "the cunning Chilon taught how to flatulate unnoticed." By contrast, the twenty-four Romans offer practical advice in Latin on correct bowel movements

---

[1]. This commentary draws upon Harrison 2018, 49–56.

[2]. The wall paintings of the other three sages—Kleoboulos of Lindos, Periandros of Corinth, and Pittakos of Lesbos—have not survived (van der Meer 2012, 73).

(Bourke van der Meer 2012, 72–74, §23).³ "I'm making haste," one says; another recommends: "Push hard; you'll be finished more quickly." The disjunction between the abstract concerns of the philosophers and rhetoricians and the practicalities of real life is highlighted.

To what extent does this iconographic and epigraphic material provide us an interesting lens through which we can view Paul's dismissive attitude to the Greek wisdom espoused by the popular rhetoricians of Corinth because of his apostolic commitment to the foolishness of the cross (1 Cor 1:18–31: cf. 2 Cor 11:16–12:10; Litfin 1994; Winter 1997; Peterson 1998)? This is not the place to enter such a debate, but hopefully these examples of graffiti from Ostia establishes in advance the interpretive potential of our three Ephesian documents. In sum, these three Ephesian inscriptions provide us valuable comparanda for New Testament attitudes to social relations and popular philosophical debates in antiquity.

IEph 2.456.1

JÖAI 1:75, no. 1 (*editio princeps*); *JÖAI* 5:33–34, no. 1. Graffito epigram found in the later built-in latrine next to the marble hall of the harbor gymnasium, Ephesus, painted with black-blue paint on the stucco-wall. From the sketchbook of Heberdey. Undated.

λὰξ ποδὶ κινήσας καὶ πὺξ χερὶ μάκρον ἀείρας	Moving with your foot and long raising with the fist of your hand
κ(αὶ) βήξας κραδίνθεν, ὅλον δὲ τ[ὸ] σῶμα δονήσας	public a(nd) coughing from your heart, and shaking th[e] whole body
ἐξ ὀνύχων χέζων φρένα τέρπεο, μηδέ σε γαστὴρ	from the fingers' ends, (until) relieving (yourself) you cheered of joy, may your belly
μήποτε λυπήσειεν ἐμὸν ποτὶ δῶμα μολόντα.	never give you pain after you've come to my home.

We see here the potential social disaster for the host and the embarrassment for the guest that could be occasioned by food poisoning during hospitality in the host's home.⁴ The shame culture is implied in this instance rather

---

3. For the translated Latin texts and wall paintings, see https://tinyurl.com/SBL9031j.

4. I am indebted to Julien Ogereau (personal communication) for this insight and the translation.

than explicitly stated, because the bowel evacuation relieves the sufferer of the potential effects of any food poisoning. Mutual relief on the part of the guest and host is humorously underscored.[5] The frankness of this epigram in its mention of bowel movements and its muted shame culture is somewhat unusual. Normally, where critical attitudes are aired regarding a feast, they more focus on the unequal or inferior proportions assigned to the attendees because of their differing social status:

> Seeing that I am invited to dinner, and am no longer, as before, to be bought, why is not the same dinner given to me, as to you? You partake of oysters fattened in the Lucrine lake; I tear my lips in sucking at a limpet. Before you are placed splendid mushrooms; I help myself to such as are fit only for pigs. You are provided with a turbot; I with a sparulus. The golden turtle-dove fills your stomach with its over-fattened body; a magpie which died in its cage is set before me. Why do I dine without you, Ponticus, when I dine with you? Let it be of some profit to me that the sportula exists no longer; let us eat of the same dishes. (Martial, *Ep.* 3.60)

Of further interest is Ben-Sira's insightful exposé (Sir 29:21–28; see also 31:3–4) of the hostility implicit in benefaction rituals, engendered by the grudging hospitality of the benefactors, and by the ingratitude of their beneficiaries in a banqueting context:

> The chief thing for life is water, and bread, and clothing, and a house to cover shame. Better is the life of a poor man in a mean cottage, than delicate fare in another man's house. Be it little or much, hold yourself contented, for it is a miserable life to go from house to house: for where you are a stranger, you dare not open your mouth. You shall entertain, and feast, and have no thanks: moreover, you shall hear bitter words: Come, stranger, and furnish a table, and feed me of that you have ready. Give place, stranger, to an honorable man; my brother comes to be lodged, and I have need of my house. These things are grievous to a man of understanding; the upbraiding of houseroom, and the reproaching of the lender.[6]

---

5. The importance of carefully planned hospitality, in which the needs of guests are scrupulously catered for, is underscored by the appreciative graffito note recorded on the garden painting in the courtyard of residential unit of Terrace House 2 in Ephesus: "Attalianos, the boy, commemorated the beautiful hospitality" (Ladstätter 2013, 167).

6. For Philo's moralistic observations regarding the ingenuity of cooks and the spiritual dangers posed by their delicious food, see Philo, *Leg.* 3.48; 3.78; *Plant.* 38; *Migr.* 4; *Conf.* 20; *Spec.* 1.35.

Last, another instructive case regarding potential social conflicts at a dinner party is found in Horace, *Sat.* 2.8. There Nasadienus, the host, revels in the luxury of his exquisite fare served at his party, far surpassing more conventional meals. The host and his right-hand man, Nomentanus, highlight both the exotic origins of the food (ll. 6–7), its exquisite taste (ll. 8–9: "such things as whet a jaded palate"), and the danger of alcohol dulling "the subtle palette" (ll. 36–38). No aspect of the host's culinary triumph could escape the notice of his guests (l. 25: e.g., ll. 31–33) because of the detailed exposition given prior to each course of the banquet. However, the results did not meet the inflated gastronomic expectations of the host. To the host's absolute dismay and chagrin, a wall-hanging falls and lands upon the food (ll. 58–59), causing him to weep so inconsolably that Nomentanus had to intervene by rousing his host's spirits with a brief philosophical reflection on the whims of Fortune (ll. 61–63). Furthermore, the host's interminable commentary upon each course provoked rancor among the guests: "then we saw blackbirds with scorched breast and pigeons without rumps … sweet things, if our host had not gone on about their reasons and qualities" (ll. 90–92). The guests refused to eat further servings of the dinner, running away and humiliating their host (ll. 93–95).

Given the various scenarios for social humiliation outlined above, including the humorous tilt of our Ephesian epigram at dining rituals, it is not surprising that several basic protocols for meals had emerged in antiquity: (1) the proper assignment of guests' seats according to status (Plutarch, *Quaest. conv.* 1.2.1–3; *Sept. sap. conv.* 3 [148F–149F]; Pliny the Younger, *Ep.* 2.6.3); (2) the demonstration of appropriate decorum in peaceful and quiet behavior, including the avoidance of drunkenness (Danker 1982, §22 [*SIG* 1109]; Sir 13:9–11; 31:12–18, 25–31; Athenaeus, *Deipn.* 14.1; Plutarch, *Quaest. conv.* 7.6.3, 8.0.1, 4.0.1); and (3) the impropriety of guests arriving late (Lucian, *Symp.* 13; Plutarch, *Quaest. conv.* 12). For discussion of table etiquette, see Lee 2018, 94–108, from whose ancient source citations I have drawn above. Additionally, Smith 2003, 1–13; Taussig 2009, 23–32. How does the apostle Paul respond to such protocols? What protocols does Paul establish for private meals in a host's home—the situation of our inscription—and for the public love feasts and eucharistic celebrations within the body of Christ? For Paul, the real issue is the idolatrous connections of food on antiquity and conscience sensitivities within the body of Christ, not the personal embarrassment and potential social shame caused by bowel disorders, as is the case in our inscription.

In terms of a meal at an unbeliever's private home, Paul stipulates that the meal be eaten with thankfulness to God (1 Cor 10:30), both as an expression of the believer's freedom in Christ (10:29b) and as an acknowledgement of the goodness of God's creation (10:26). This would free believers from unwittingly shaming an unbelieving host at a private meal because of their refusal of sacrificial meat. Paul is explicit regarding the protocol about the food's potential idolatrous associations: "eat [ἐσθίετε] everything [πᾶν] put before you without raising questions of conscience" (1 Cor 10:27b; cf. Mark 7:19).[7] However, if another unspecified person present at the unbeliever's private home meal (ἐὰν δὲ τις ὑμῖν εἴπῃ) publicly airs scruples with the believer about eating sacrificial meat (1 Cor 10:28a), then a different protocol emerges. It is highly unlikely that the objector here is a Christian because the apostle would have identified the dissenting believer as having a weak conscience (1 Cor 8:12: τὴν συνείδησιν ἀσθενοῦσαν; cf. for ἀσθενής and cognates, see vv. 7b, 9b 10b, 11a; cf. Fitzmyer 2008, 401), whereas weakness terminology is absent here (10:29b: σθνείδησιν ... τὴν τοῦ ἑτέρου).[8] Why would an unbeliever raise the idolatry issue with a believer? It is possible that the objector might be Jewish, knowing that Christian believers were also monotheists in their faith (4 Macc 5.2; cf. Keener 2005, 90). Alternatively, the unbeliever might have wanted in a helpful manner to warn the believer about the perceived hypocrisy he would exhibit before the watching guests were he to proceed and eat the sacrificial meat (Ciampa and Rosner 2010, 493), or, in a more calculated move, he might have had malicious motives in publicly shaming the believer by forcing his hand before the host and guests on the issue. Either way, Paul's protocol is unequivocal: do not eat (1 Cor 10:28b: μὴ ἐσθίετε) so that the objector's conscience is respected by a compliant response rather than humiliated by a noncompliant response on the part of the believer. The overarching protocol here is the soteriological glory of God, seen in the believer's refusal to give offense to any ethnic and religious grouping by sensitively seeking their best so that they might be won to Christ (1 Cor 10:33: cf. 9:19–23). Paul's approach differs from the hierarchical and status-riddled protocols of ancient feasts, while still showing

---

7. See Gooch (1993, 105) on the difficulties for believers in avoiding food with a sacred history or the open use of food in religious rites before or during the meal.

8. Fee (1987, 484) comments that "Paul's hypothetical objector speaks from a pagan point of view by referring to 'sacrificial meat' (*hierothyton*) rather than the standard Jewish-Christian designation 'idol meat' (*eidōlothyton*)."

appropriate sensitivity to honor culture by not unnecessarily offending the unbelieving host and fellow guests.

As far as private meals of believers together, the priority is not to be a stumbling block to the weaker brother for whom Christ died (1 Cor 8:11–12). The priority of the Christian brother over the status rituals of ancient banqueting is spotlighted. In the case of Greco-Roman cultic banquets in temples (1 Cor 8:10b), Paul's recommendation is total abstention from the feasts on the part of believers due to the demonic influences undergirding sacrifices to the gods (10:14–22, esp. vv. 20–21), along with the dangers of sexual immorality (10:8; cf. 6:15b–18).

Finally, in terms of eucharistic meals, Paul highlights that some wealthy members of the body of Christ were violating basic Greco-Roman banquet protocols in becoming drunk at the Lord's supper (1 Cor 11:21). But, consonant with the same protocols (of which Paul is critical in this instance), they are acting in an ungodly manner by discriminating according to social status and wealth at meals (1 Cor 11:21; cf. v. 34): "For when the time comes to eat, each of you goes ahead with your own supper, and one goes hungry and another goes drunk." For Paul, such over-consumption of food—itself a visual marker of economic power (Fitzgerald 2017) and social positioning (1 Cor 11:20)—should be carried out instead by the wealthy in the privacy of their homes (1 Cor 11:22a), as opposed to indulging one's culinary appetites in public with contempt for those who have nothing. The result is that have-nots are socially humiliated through the exorbitance and self-centeredness of the wealthy (11:22b: Welborn 2016). Jettisoning the Greco-Roman protocol of arriving on time for meals, Paul instructs that believers are rather to wait for one another (1 Cor 11:33b: ἀλλήλους ἐκδέχεσθε) until the late have-nots have eventually arrived, so that there will be enough food at the Lord's supper for all to share in the communal hospitality (Garland 2003, 554–55).

Paul's strategy demonstrates considerable subtlety within the protocols of ancient banqueting, both in its private and public spheres. The apostle undermines its status rituals and hierarchicalism by virtue of his soteriological and equitable concern for all, including above all the weak and have nots for whom Christ had died. Yet the same protocols can also be invoked to shame the insensitive and dissolute behavior of the wealthy in the body of Christ, while also ensuring that the appropriate demands of the honor system are extended from the apex to the base of the social pyramid (Rom 12:9b, 16b; 13:7b; 1 Cor 12:21–26). On the Lord's supper at

Corinth and honorific practices in the local associations, see McRae 2011; Kloppenborg 2019, 209–44; Willis 1985; Cheung 1999.

IEph 2.456.2

JÖAI 1:75, no. 2 (*editio princeps*); *JÖAI* 5:33–34, no. 2. Graffito epigram found in the later built-in latrine next to the marble hall of the harbor gymnasium, Ephesus, painted with black-blue paint on the stucco-wall. From the sketchbook of Heberdey. Date: Undated.

ἂν μή γ' ἕλωμεν τὸν βίον τὸν δραπέτην	If we do not choose a fugitive life
πινῶντες ἢ τρυφῶντες ἢ λελουμένοι,	drinking or living in luxury or enfeebled,
ὀδύνην ἑαυτοῖς προξενοῦμεν πάντοτε	(then) we always manage distress by ourselves
ἀναξίους ὁρῶντες εὐτυχεστέρους.	(by) seeing unworthy things more successfully.

This graffito advocates a stoic approach to life, exhorting the disciplined control of the mind in face of life's sufferings, as opposed to numbing one's personal pain through unrestrained hedonism and reckless behavior. Such public philosophical musings were not unusual in the life of this famous Ionian city. Ephesian inscriptions and wall paintings show considerable interest in the Greek philosophers, highlighting Socrates the Athenian (IEph 2.560.1, 3) and Chilon the Spartan (IEph 2.560.2), one of the famous Seven Sages (see Harrison 2019, 173–216). In terms of wall paintings in Terrace House 2, Socrates is again isolated as an important Greek figure for Ephesians (Ladstätter 2013, 82 fig. 47). In IEph 7.2 4340 and IEph 3.789, there is mention respectively of a "Platonic" and "eclectic" philosopher. More generally, φιλόσοφοι are frequently honored in the inscriptions at Ephesus (IEph 3.616, 3.789, 5.1958, 6.2066, 7.2.3901, 7.2.4340). The sophist Soterus, for example, is eulogized in IEph 5.1548 in this manner: "Twice did the Androclidae summon from Athens me Soterus, a sophist, first by decrees of the Council; and on me first as a reward for virtue in life and wisdom of speech they resolved by way of honor to bestow numberless gifts." There is also a highly fragmentary inscription that is possibly a philosophical diatribe (SEG 33.960 [second century CE]). We read, too, in a dossier from 42 BCE that immunity is granted for professors, sophists, and doctors (SEG 56.1219, a revision of

SEG 31.952). Finally, a delightful caricature of philosophers and their pseudo-wisdom is found in the latrine of residential unit 2 in Terrace House 2 (Ladstätter 2013, 185; Zimmermann and Ladstätter 2011, 87–88 figs. 136–37). As Zimmermann and Ladstätter explain (2011, 88), "the scrawny men are not discussing high truths, but instead the right time, and are thus reminding the users of the latrine to hurry." On the physiognomy of identifying philosophers as a group in the wall paintings, see Zimmermann and Ladstätter 2011, 88. It is worth remembering that in Terrace House 2 the cultured Socrates is presented sympathetically elsewhere in a wall painting. Thus "the latrine paintings are therefore an example of self-conscious and selected irony, with which one wanted one wanted to distance oneself from the traditional keenness to display education and culture displayed elsewhere" (Zimmermann and Ladstätter 2011, 88).

In contrast to the Ephesian graffito writer, Paul sets forth the moral choice for believers in a more positive and focused way. In Paul's view, the "unworthy things," to borrow the epigram's language, are certainly to be "put off," but, as a significant counterpoint to the ethical message of the epigram, "worthy things" are to be "put on" instead (Col 3:5–14). Consequently, believers are to set their hearts on "the things above" as opposed to "earthly things" (3:2), counting themselves not only dead to sin but also alive to God's righteousness in Christ (Rom 6:11–14). They are to avoid acts of the sinful nature characteristic of those excluded from the Kingdom of God (5:19–21), choosing instead to keep in step with the Spirit (Gal 5:25b), who resides in the redeemed (5:25a; see also Rom 7:6; 8:4–5, 9b, 11b; 1 Cor 6:19; 12:3, 13). Above all, the fruit of the Spirit are to be the defining characteristic of their personal relationships and identity (Gal 5:22–23a; Rom 8:10, 13).

This Spirit-generated transformation, cruciform in its ethical imprint (1 Cor 5:7a–8; 6:19b–20; 8:9–12; 2 Cor 4:11–12; 5:15; 8:1–2, 9 [cf. 6:10b]; Eph 4:32), is given specific focus by virtue of the believer's conformity both to the image of God (Eph 4:24b; 5:2b; Col 3:10b) and Christ (Rom 8:29a; 2 Cor 3:18), as well as by their imitation of the exemplum of the Father (Eph 5:1) and the Son (Rom 15:1–2, 7; Phil 2:5–11; Col 3:13). The imitation is Christo-centric in its focus, so much so that the apostle can boldly exhort his converts: "Follow my example as I follow the example of Christ" (1 Cor 11:1; cf. 4:16; 1 Thess 1:6–7; Phil 3:17). In sum, believers are irrevocably caught up in their new existence in Christ, and there is no sense that they will "always manage distress" by themselves, as the epigram states. Rather

24. The New Testament and the Serious Side of Toilet Humor

the sufferings of believers, like the rest of their life, belong to the sufferings of Christ, their Lord and Redeemer (Rom 8:31–38; Phil 3:10b; Col 1:24).

IEph 2.561.1

AAWW 110:191 (*editio princeps*); FiE 8.1:88–89; *Gymnasium* 87:222; SEG 29, 1120. Inscription accompanying a caricature in a toilet. Found in Terrace House 2, apartment 2, latrine, Ephesus, over a thin man in front of a sundial. Date: Undated.

τὴν ὥραν ἢ τὸν θάνα-   (Choose) the right time or death.
του.

Another Ephesian latrine graffito evinces interest in popular philosophy by caricaturing one of its better-known motifs, though it draws upon a familiar trope of banquet poetry. But the topos is profaned by reducing its more serious sentiments to toilet humor. At face value, IEph 2.561.1 reads thus: "(Choose) the right time [ὥραν] or death [θάνατον]." What is the meaning of this puzzling graffito? V. M. Strocka (2010, 88–89; cited in IEph 2.561.1) argues that it refers to the defecatory process. The importance of timely digestion and defecation in everyday life is critical, otherwise, metaphorically speaking, the bodily results of delay or excess, both for those in the act of defecating and for those waiting to defecate, can be deadly in their effects.[9] But, as F. Preisshofen has observed (cited Stroka 2010, n. 293, referenced in IEph 2.561.1), the text is ambiguous, with ὥρα also meaning "the spring" or "prime of life," being effectively the equivalent of the phrase ἥβη ἄνθος ("[the] bloom of youth"). The connection between ὥρα, θάνατος, and banquet poetry becomes apparent in the poetic epigrams of Nicarchus (late first century CE).[10] Nicarchus spells out the desirability of maintain-

---

9. On the "right time" motif in the graffito of philosophers from Ephesian Terrace House 2, see our discussion above. Note, too, Zimmermann and Ladstätter 2011, 88 fig. 137 on the graffiti "three out of none" in the latrine of Residential Unit 2 as being another encouragement to the toilet user to hurry up.

10. On poets at banquets, see the contemporary of Nero, Lucillius, *Ep.* 11.10: "You know the rule of my little banquets. To-day, Aulus, I invite you under new convivial laws. No lyric poet shall sit there and recite, and you yourself shall neither trouble us nor be troubled with literary discussions" (trans. Paton). For examples of banquet poems, see Statius, *Silv.* 1.5 and Martial, *Ep.* 6.42. On Roman feasts, see Dunbabin 2003.

ing attendance at banquets notwithstanding the ravages of age and death's inevitable approach, while also affirming the desirable extension of the "bloom of youth."[11] Although toilet humor touches the base of the social pyramid as much as its apex, the clever ambiguity of this graffito points to a composer and audience familiar with the tropes of banquet poetry.

This graffito finds its closest New Testament resonance with Phil 1:19–26 in the polarized alternatives of life or death articulated in each document. In the case of the Ephesian graffito, the choice for the individual is either to live festively in the prime of life in the present age, no matter one's personal circumstances, or to accept the inevitability of death. Crucially, an individual's decision to engage in a fulfilled life on this side of death is entirely within a person's capacity after calm deliberation. The preferred alternative is not death but the right time of the bloom of youth, which is continuously extended into the present, while one's circumstances remains propitious and the individual's volition maintains its strength.

By contrast, the apostle Paul does not operate as an isolated individual but rather is a privileged heir among many other heirs, all of whom are united with Christ (Rom 6:5; 8:17). By means of his frequent use of σύν-verbal compounds, Paul establishes that he, along with other believers, has been crucified (Rom 6:6; Gal 2:20, buried (Rom 6:4) and raised with Christ (Rom 6:5, 7), suffering with him in the present age by being conformed to his death (Rom 8:17; Phil 3:10) and, after death, being glorified with him at the eschaton (Rom 8:17; Phil 3:20). Along with his fellow believers, the goal of Paul's goal is entirely directed towards Christ (Phil 1:21a: τὸ ζῆν Χριστός), both on this side of life and in the afterlife. Significantly, the afterlife is categorized as "much better" and "gain" (1:23b: μᾶλλον κρεῖσσον; 1:21b: κέρδος), the latter motif being well known in Greco-Roman literature (Palmer 1975, 208–17).

---

11. "Must I not die? What care I if I go to Hades with gouty legs or in training for a race? I shall have many to carry me; so let me become lame, if I wish. As far as that goes, as you see, I am quite easy, and never miss a banquet" (Nicarchus, *Anth. Gr.* 5.38). "Nicarete, who formerly was in the service of Athene's shuttle, and stretched out many a warp on the loom, made in honour of Cypris a bonfire in front of her house of her work-basket and bobbins and her other gear, crying, 'Away with you, starving work of wretched women, that have power to waste away the bloom of youth [νέον τήκειν ἄνθος].' Instead the girl chose garlands and the lyre, and a gay life spent in revel and festivity. 'Cypris,' she said, 'I will pay you tithe of all my gains. Give me work and take from it your due'" (Nicarchus, *Anth. Gr.* 6.285).

But, in sharp contrast to the Ephesian graffiti writer's decision to choose "the bloom of youth" in the present, Paul is genuinely perplexed as to which path to choose (Hansen 1994, 85). The apostle's rhetoric is entirely genuine here (Phil 1:22b: οὐ γνωρίζω); it is not a case of "feigned perplexity" fashioned after Isocrates's rhetoric (*De pace* 38–39), as Nathan N. Croy (2003, 529) has suggested. So how will the apostle choose between continued apostolic labor in Christ among the Philippians in the present (Phil 1:24b: "for the sake of you") or being with Christ in the afterlife upon his death (Phil 1:23)? Critically, the determination is not Paul's; rather, it is God's prerogative to determine what is necessary in ministry (Phil 1:24: ἀναγκαιότερον),[12] thereby convincing the apostle that he is to remain in his current ministry role to his churches and the gentile world more widely (1:25). Paul's selflessness in adversity, which is empowered by the Spirit of Jesus (Phil 1:19b), exhibits several similarities to Seneca's understanding of how the wise man should act in this age. However, in the case of Seneca, we gain no sense that the future gain beyond death is better by far (Phil 3:13–14, 20–21: Engberg-Pederson 2017).

Bibliography

Beard, Mary. 2014. *Laughter in Ancient Rome: On Joking, Tickling, and Cracking Up.* Berkeley: University of California Press.

Cheung, Alex T. 1999. *Idol Food in Corinth: Jewish Background and Pauline Legacy.* JSNTSup 176. Sheffield: Sheffield Academic.

Ciampa, Roy E., and Brian S. Rosner. 2010. *The First Letter to the Corinthians.* PNTC. Grand Rapids: Eerdmans.

Croy, Nathan N. 2003. "'To Die Is Gain' (Philippians 1:19–26): Does Paul Contemplate Suicide?" *JBL* 122:517–31.

Danker, Frederick W. 1982. *Benefactor: Epigraphic Study of a Graeco-Roman and New Testament Semantic Field.* Saint Louis: Clayton.

Dunbabin, K. M. 2003. *The Roman Banquet: Images of Conviviality.* Cambridge: Cambridge University Press.

Engberg-Pedersen, Troels. 2017. "Paul in Philippians and Seneca in *Epistle* 93 on Life after Death and Its Present Implications." Pages 267–84 in

---

12. Hawthorne (1983, 51) writes: "it is not Paul who, martyrlike, sacrifices his personal desire on the altar of service to others, and decides to keep on living, but God who chooses for him."

Paul and Seneca in Dialogue. Edited by Joey Dodson and David Briones. Leiden: Brill.

Fee, Gordon D. 1987. *The First Epistle to the Corinthians.* NICNT. Eerdmans: Grand Rapids.

Fitzgerald, John. 2017. "Food and Drink in the Greco-Roman World and in the Pauline Communities." Pages 205–44 in *Paul and Economics: A Handbook.* Edited by Thomas R. Blanton IV and Raymond Pickett. Minneapolis: Fortress.

Fitzmyer, Joseph A. 2008. *First Corinthians: A New Translation with Introduction and Commentary.* AYB 32. New Haven: Yale University Press.

Garland, D. E. 2003. *1 Corinthians.* BECNT. *1 Corinthians.* Grand Rapids: Baker Academic.

Gooch, Peter D. 1993. *Dangerous Food: 1 Corinthians 8–10 in Its Context.* Studies in Christianity and Judaism 5. Waterloo, ON: Wilfrid Laurier University Press.

Hansen, G. Walter. 1994. *Galatians.* IVP New Testament Commentary. Downers Grove, IL: InterVarsity Press.

Harrison, James R. 2019. *Paul and the Ancient Celebrity Circuit: The Cross and Moral Transformation.* WUNT 430. Tübingen: Mohr Siebeck.

———. 2017. "'Laughter Is the Best Medicine': St Paul, Well-Being, and Roman Humour." Pages in 209–40 in *Well-Being, Personal Wholeness and the Social Fabric.* Edited by Doru Costache, Darren Cronshaw, and James R. Harrison. Cambridge: Cambridge Scholars Press.

———. 2018. "An Epigraphic Portrait of Ephesus and Its Villages." Pages 1–67 in *Ephesus.* Vol. 3 of *The First Urban Churches.* Edited by James R. Harrison and L. L. Welborn. WGRWSup 9. Atlanta: SBL Press.

Hawthorne, Gerald F. 1983. *Philippians.* WBC 43. Waco, TX: Word.

Keener, Craig S. 2005. *1–2 Corinthians.* NCBC. Cambridge: Cambridge: Cambridge University Press.

Kloppenborg, John S. 2019. *Christ's Associations: Connecting and Belonging in the Ancient City.* New Haven: Yale University Press.

Ladstätter, Sabine. 2013. *Terrace House 2 in Ephesos: An Archaeological Guide.* Istanbul: Homer Kitabevi.

Lee, Jin Hwan. 2017. "Meal Practices in Associations: Reimagining Social Conflicts at the Corinthian Lord's Supper." PhD diss., University of St Michael's College.

Levin-Richardson, Sarah. 2015. "Bodily Waste and Boundaries in Pompeian Grafffiti." Pages 225–54 in *Ancient Obscenities: Their Nature and*

Use in the Ancient Greek and Roman Worlds. Ann Arbor: University of Michigan Press.

Litfin, Duane A. 1994. *St Paul's Theology of Proclamation: 1 Corinthians 1–4 and Greco-Roman Rhetoric.* SNTSMS 79. Cambridge: Cambridge University Press.

McRae, Rachael M. 2011. "Eating with Honour: The Corinthian Lord's Supper in Light of Voluntary Association Meal Practices." *JBL* 130:165–81.

Palmer, D. W. 1975. "'To Die Is Gain' (Philippians 1:21)." *NovT* 17.3:203–18.

Paton, W. R. 1916. *The Greek Anthology.* Vols. 1–5. LCL. London: Heinemann.

Peterson, Brian K. 1998. *Eloquence and the Proclamation of the Gospel in Corinth.* SBLDS 163. Atlanta: Scholars Press.

Smith, Dennis Edwin. 2003. *From Symposium to Eucharist: The Banquet in the Early Christian World.* Minneapolis: Fortress.

Stroka, V. M. 2010. *Forschungen in Ephesos: Die Wandermalerei der Hanghäuser in Ephesos,* FiE 8.1. Vienna: Österreichischen Akademie der Wissenschaften.

Taussig, Hal. 2009. *In the Beginning Was the Meal: Social Experimentation and Early Christian Identity.* Minneapolis: Augsburg Fortress.

Van der Meer, L. Bourke. 2012. *Ostia Speaks: Inscriptions Buildings and Spaces in Rome's Main Port.* Leuven: Peeters.

Welborn, L. L. 2016. "Inequality in Roman Corinth: Evidence from Diverse Sources Evaluated by a Neo-Ricardian Model." Pages 47–84 in *Roman Corinth.* Vol. 2 of *The First Urban Churches:* Edited by James R. Harrison and L. L. Welborn. WGRWSup 8. Atlanta: SBL Press.

Willis, Wendell Lee. 1985. *Idol Meat in Corinth: The Pauline Argument in 1 Corinthians 8–10.* SBLDS 68. Chico, CA: Scholars Press.

Winter, Bruce W. 1997. *Philo and Paul among the Sophists.* SNTSMS 96. Cambridge: Cambridge University Press.

Zimmermann, Norbert, and Sabine Ladstätter, eds. 2011. *Wall Painting in Ephesos from the Hellenistic to the Byzantine Period.* Istanbul: Ege Yayınlari.

25. Finding the Right Spot to Take a Leak

James R. Harrison

IEph 2.567

JÖAI 52:40, no. 54 (*editio princeps*). At the Mazaeus-Mithridates gate in the southern apsidal niche of the eastern passage of the gate. Sketchbook 1104 (Heberdey). Undated.

εἴ (Hekate image)[1]	If (Hekate image)
τις ἂν ὧδε	anyone here
οὐρήσι, ἡ Ἑκά-	shall urinate, Heka-
τη αὐτῷ κε-	te is an-
χώλωται[2]	gered by him.

IEph 2.568

FiE 3:25 (*editio princeps*); JÖAI 52:40, no. 55. From the agora. Undated.
ὅς ἂν ὧδε οὐρήσει, αὐτὸ[ν α]ἰτιάσεται
Whoever shall urinate here, a charge will be laid (against) him.

IEph 2.568A.1

From the Bouleuterion (former "Odeion"), eastern stairway. Sketchbook 1724 (Keil). Undated.

---

1. The Hekate image inscribed to the right of the first line on the stone shows the goddess standing on a pedestal, with both arms extended upwards and wearing a distinctive crown. For the image, see IEph 2, p. 235.
2. κεχώλωται = κεχόλωται. This perfect passive form χολόω (κεχόλωται: "has been angered") is treated here as having present tense force ("is angered").

κατ' ὄ ναρ³ In a dream
ἰς τὴν καμάραν μὴ οὔρει do not urinate in the *kamara*.

IEph 2.568A.2

Fragment of a base plate, Basilica, south side. Sketchbook 3522 (Knibbe). Undated.

κατ' ὄναρ In a dream
[ἰς τὴν κ]αμάραν μὴ οὔρε[ι] do not urinat[e] (in) [the k]*amara*.

IEph 2.569

Orthostat block (i.e., large stone set upright) from Domitian Street (between Domitian temple and the state market); very shallow, superficial writing. Sketchbook 3377 (Knibbe). Undated.

ὧδε οὐρήσαντι ἡ Ἄρτεμις By the one who unrinated here Artemis
κεχόλωται vacat is angered. (space)

These five graffiti, forbidding unknown miscreants from urinating in inappropriate spots in Ephesus (i.e., the Basilica, the Bouleuterion, Domitian Street, the agora, the Mazaeus-Mithridates gate), belong to the waking and sleeping worlds (κατ' ὄναρ) of the ancient Ephesians (see Pack 1955). Two of the graffiti are accompanied by divine threats from powerful deities, Artemis and Hekate, with the dire warning accentuated in one case by an incised image of Hekate herself. Note, too, the splendid first-century CE temple bas-relief, provenance uncertain, of Zeus throwing thunderbolts at a kneeling defecating man (Clarke 2007, 60–62). The fearsome reputation of Artemis was well known at Ephesus and more widely in Asia Minor (Acts 19:22–41; Harrison 2012a; Graf 1992), though, significantly, IEph 2.567 is the only place in the entire Ephesian corpus where Hekate is mentioned (Harrison 2012b). Thus the unusual invocation of Hekate, the goddess of boundaries who was associated with the forces of the underworld (i.e., magic, witchcraft, sorcery, necromancy, and ghosts), represents a formidable threat as a punitive deity for the Ephesians. Several Latin

---

3. The blockage of the letter flow in ὄναρ, indicated by the space in the Greek text above (ὄ ναρ), is due to stone damage at this point of the stela.

inscriptions also touch on the wrath of the gods towards defecating and urinating offenders (*CIL* 3.1966; 4.7716; 6.13740; see also Gillend 2008). For example, a graffito from the baths of Titus in Rome states: "Twelve gods and goddesses and Jupiter, the biggest and best, will be angry with whoever urinates or defecates here" (*CIL* 6.29848: Magness 2012, 82).

For literary references to defecators and urinators, see Plutarch, *Stoic. rep.* 22.2; Persius, *Sat.* 1.112–114; Suetonius, *Nero* 56; Aristophanes, *Vesp.* 393–394; Horace, *Sat.* 1.8.37–39; Petronius, *Satyr.* 71.8; Horace, *Ars* 470–472; Hist. Aug., Life of Caracalla, 5.7. On the scatological graffiti at Pompeii, see Levin-Richardson 2015, 228–37. See also Magness 2012; Gillend 2008. On Roman toilets, see Hobson 2009; Jansen, Koloski-Ostrow, and Moormann 2011. On ancient graffiti, see Keegan 2011. On the role of urine in Ephesian medical literature, see Rufus of Ephesus, *Treatise* 46 ("A Treatise on Urine"); *On Melancholy*, frags. 21, 53, 70, 75. See Abou-Aly 1992.

Why the graffiti writers have singled out these particular sites and, correspondingly, refrained from tagging other equally important locations and monuments in Ephesus—which presumably would also require protection from defecators and urinators—remains a mystery. We must not discount the sheer opportunism associated with graffiti in any culture, ancient or modern. Provided the text is highly visible in public, its fundamental aim has been accomplished in terms of scatological humor. As Sarah Levin-Richardson (2015, 228) notes regarding the graffiti in Pompeii, "Nearly 80 percent of the scatological graffiti were written in public view along streets, on civic structures, or in the front rooms of shops and taverns." Nevertheless, we should not assume that their public placement was inconsequential, even though our Ephesian graffiti provide no clues as to why they are situated where they are. In terms of clues, for example, no dialogue has been entered into by subsequent graffiti writers with the original Ephesian graffito (contra, e.g. Benefiel 2010, 65–67). Nor, to cite another example, is there any poetic dialogue between the inscriptions or dialogues between the inscriptions and their spatial context, as there is in the House of Maius Castricius in Pompeii (67–74). The sole intersection we have between text and its context is the dialogue between the text and the image of Hekate noted above (see also Benefiel 2010, 74–81). Most likely, as Jansen (2011, 170–72) concludes from the graffiti from Pompeii and Ephesus, these graffiti warned the viewer to act in a civilized manner.

However, the technical dream literature of antiquity perhaps affords us partial insight into the reasons for prohibition of urination in the case of our two κατ' ὄναρ graffiti (IEph 2.568A.1 and 2.568A.2). Why did this particular Ephesian graffito writer set his prohibition in a dream context, in sharp contrast to our three other graffiti writers in the city (IEph 2.567, 2.568, 2.569)? Artemidorus (*Onir.* 4.44), the second-century CE dream interpreter, cites a dream where a man lifted up his clothes and urinated upon the members of his local association, with the result that he was expelled from the group as unworthy because of his vile deed. Similarly, in another dream, a man urinates in the middle of the theater, showing contempt for the prevailing laws and the spectators. Seemingly contempt for public standards is at the core of the complaint. But such acts of public contempt have no social consequence for the elites. As Artemidorus wryly observes: "Nothing prevents magistrates, however, from dreaming that they scorn their subjects." Thus the civic (IEph 2.568) and divine punishment (IEph 2.567; 2.569) meted out to miscreants for their disdain towards the general public, exemplified by the vile act of public urination, has strict social boundaries: it only applies to the lower social echelons and not to the powerful elites who establish the laws. Would an Ephesian, trained in dream interpretation, have also understood this graffito as a salutary warning or oblique complaint about the elites and their scorn for their subjects in the public arena? Or are the Ephesian nonurination graffiti merely a warning against contemptuous public actions?

We can reasonably assume, therefore, that some Ephesians would have been as familiar with dream interpretation in antiquity, including the portentous significance of public urination, as other citizens of the city were conversant with the role of dream revelation in the magical papyri (Acts 19:19). On dream revelation in magic, see the (1) dream oracles (ὀνειραιτητόν): *PGM* 7.229-249; 7.250-254 [cf. 7.255-259]; 7.359-369; 7.703-726; 8.64-110 (including here a request for a "direct vision"); 12.190-192; 22b.27-31; 22b.32-35); and (2) the simple requests for dreams: *PGM* 12.144-152; *PDM* Sup 1-6. Experienced Ephesian dream interpreters, therefore, would have understood, if the tradition of Artemidorus is sufficiently representative, that the κατ' ὄναρ graffito on urination had in its sights the scornful attitudes of the elites towards their inferiors as much as the disdain of the lower social echelons for public conventions.

Other graffiti readers, however, may simply have regarded the κατ' ὄναρ graffito as a whimsical case of scatological humor poking fun at the portent mentality of the ancients (e.g., Lucian, *Alex.* 49; Oenomaus of Gadara: Eusebius, *Praep. ev.* 5.18-26; 6.7; see 5:25: "For at that time not only were the gods believed, but also cats and crows, and the delusions of dreams"). Last, whereas dream interpretation may throw indirect light on the more serious intent of IEph 2.568A and IEph 2.568A.1, the κατ' ὄναρ graffito remains challenging to understand because of the breadth of meaning attached to *kamara*, the projected urination site. What type of vaulted covered object is the graffito referring to? The options are varied (*LSJ*, s.v. "καμάρα"): a covered carriage, a vaulted chamber, a vaulted tomb, a vaulted sewer, and, undoubtedly, more besides.

In sum, in terms of our Ephesian graffiti, we are left with a variety of potential motivations for the inscribing of nonurination graffiti at Ephesus. We must not discount the secret notoriety attained by the graffiti writer in tagging such a highly visible place. Genuine outrage over those who dishonor public monuments by urination is another explanation, in the same way that the silversmith association considered Paul's preaching to be dishonoring to Artemis (Acts 19:27b). In the case of the two κατ' ὄναρ graffiti, the range of possibilities is more complex. It could just be another case of anger over the dishonoring of an important public place, as the dream interpretation of Artemidorus certainly highlights. But, appealing to the same oneirocritic evidence, it could equally be an oblique comment on the powerlessness of the lower social echelons in a hierarchical society, in sharp contrast to the Ephesian elites, who scorned their subjects. Alternatively, it may simply be a case of scatological humor, making fun of the portent mentality of antiquity. The latter option, however, is less likely, in my opinion: the powerful deities invoked must be taken seriously, one including the patron goddess of Ephesus. Moreover, the rarity of critiques like those of Lucian and Oenomaus of Gadara in antiquity emphasizes the seriousness with which the ancients took dream revelation. Thus we have to allow for the multivalence of the κατ' ὄναρ graffito, depending upon the interpretative grid of its auditors.

A final example of how nonurination inscriptions were integrated in an apotropaic context is especially worth highlighting. In Room 19 of the Esquiline Wing of Nero's Domus Aurea at Rome, the following graffito was inscribed in the middle of the south wall above a so-called *lararium*, an apotropaic painting of two serpents flanking an altar: "Twelve gods and Diana and Jupiter, the best and the greatest—may he face their wrath whoever urinates or defecates here" (*CIL* 6.29848b; Harton, 2018, 77, 80). The painting reflects the advice of Persius regarding unwarranted defecation (*Sat.* 1.112–114): "'Defecation prohibited here', you say. Paint up two snakes; 'Lads this place is off limits—piss outside'" (Harton 2018, 80). George Maurice Harton V (2018, 80–81) has persuasively argued that the strong temptation for slaves in this secluded service corridor of the Domus

Aurea, hidden from the watching eyes of the emperor and his officials, was to urinate or defecate. The act represented a silent protest against their master Nero or was an expression of their general frustration with hierarchical structures of Roman society. That someone, unknown to us, had painted two protective serpents on the wall, placing above it the graffito warning, ensured that the malevolent forces unleashed by the surreptitious action of slaves urinating and defecating would either not occur or cause any damage. Were these graffito writers also slave members of the *familia Caesaris*, but those who were grateful for the opportunity of upward mobility that its membership provided (P.Oxy 46 3312: Horsley 1983)?

What relevance do these Ephesian inscriptions, forbidding people to take a leak in civic places, have for the New Testament writings? First, there is no reference in the New Testament to prohibitions against public urination, so there is no explicit intersection between each tradition. But we have already made reference to the intense sensitivity of the Ephesians to the dishonoring of public monuments, exemplified by the bans on public urination, and the charge brought against Paul in Acts 19:27b regarding his belittling the greatness of Artemis through his preaching of Christ as Lord. In particular, the portent mentality of antiquity (Berger 1980; Lewis 1997)—evidenced in Julius Obsequens's epitomy of the portents of Livy and in the brontoscopic calendar of Nigidius Figulus (Solling 1978)—surfaces in the apocalyptic fare of Luke-Acts (Luke 17:24; 21:9-10, 25-27; 23:44-45; Acts 2:19a).

Two references to portents in Luke-Acts are especially important. The death of Jesus on the cross, which is accompanied by two portents, inaugurates Joel's Day of the Lord (Acts 2:18-19; see also 2:17: ἐν ταῖς ἐσχάτοις ἡμέραις; Luke 23:44-45; Allison 1985, 115-17). Luke's reference to the sacred stone, probably a meteorite, kept by the Ephesians in the temple of Artemis (Acts 19:35b: τοῦ διοπετοῦς) is also significant here. The megatheism promoted by the silversmiths of Ephesus (Acts 19:28, 34: Chaniotis 2010)—exemplified by the spectacular temple of Artemis, the statue of the goddess inside and her famous heavenly portent, assigning the city its *neokoros* status (19:35b)—is dismissed by Paul, according to his critics, as a man-made deity (19:26b; see also 7:48; 1 Kgs 7:27; Isa 66.1). In sum, Luke cleverly employs the traditional portents of Jewish apocalyptic to establish the eschatological significance of Jesus's death, while simultaneously undermining the portent mentality of ancient Ephesus. Paul, as a first-century Jew and Christ-follower, dismisses as idolatrous many of the public monuments which the Ephesians so cherished.

Second, given the clear reference to κατ' ὄναρ in two of our Ephesian inscriptions, it is worthwhile focusing on dream revelation in the book of Acts in order to establish what the Lukan understanding of the revelation of the divine will was in its ecclesial and social context. Apart from the single source reference derived from LXX Joel (ἐνύπνιον [Acts 2:17], Luke avoids any further usage of dream terminology in Luke-Acts (ἐνύπνιον; ὄναρ). Instead, he confines himself to "visions" (ὅραμα: Acts 9:10, 12; 10:3, 17, 19; 11:5; 12:9; 16:9–10; 18:9), choosing occasionally synonyms for stylistic variation (ὅρασις: Acts 2:17; ὀπτασία: Luke 1:22; 24:23; 26:19). The sole exception to this is "trance" (ἔκστασις: Acts 10:10; 11:15; 22:17). In restricting himself to a narrow strand of terminology, predominantly ὅραμα, one wonders if Luke is refusing to enter into the complex debates about dream theory and interpretation in antiquity, although he adopts some of the Greco-Roman techniques of dream narration in Acts (i.e., the double dream-vision report: Peter: Acts 10: 9–23; 11:4–17; Paul: 9:3–5, 15–16; 22:6–10, 14–16; 26:12– 18). On the latter, see Hanson 1980.

Further, M. M. B. Turner (2000, 82–139) has argued, over against Christopher Forbes's (1997, 51–52) constriction of prophecy to verbal inspiration, that the outpoured Pentecost Spirit brings prophetic revelation through visions (Acts 2:17b). Prophecy here includes *all* the revelatory phenomena mentioned in Acts 2:17–18, with the twofold καὶ προφεύσουσιν framing both verbal and vision/dream revelation under the motif of prophecy (vv. 17b, 18b). There are visions of far reaching theological and social import (Acts 10:10–23; 11:4–17), personal comfort (7:55–56; 18:9–10), and missionary initiative (Acts 9:10–16; 10:3–6; 16:9–10; 22:12–21; 26:12–23). On three occasions, the visions are closely linked to the revelatory work of the Spirit (Acts 7:55–56; 10:19; 16:7–9). We might also include under this wider category of nonverbal prophecy the various Spirit-inspired revelations in Acts (8:29, 39; 10:19; 11:12; 16:6–7; 20:22–23). The visions, therefore, provide a vibrant portrait of a pneumatically empowered, multi-ethnic, and theologically innovative church in its social relations, as its mission expanded throughout the eastern Mediterranean basin. Whereas the κατ' ὄναρ urination prohibition reinforced the social and cultural status quo at Ephesus, the prophetic work of dream revelation in the body of Christ at Ephesus established a new community, which, because of its distinctiveness of lifestyle and message, would in the perception of some eventually pose a threat to the social order (Acts 17:6–7).

Bibliography

Abou-Aly, Amal Mohamed Abdulla. 1992. "The Medical Writings of Rufus of Ephesus." PhD diss., University of London.

Allison, Jr., Dale C. 1985. *The End of the Ages Has Come: An Early Interpretation of the Passion and Resurrection of Jesus.* Philadelphia: Fortress.

Benefiel, Rebecca R. 2010. "Dialogues of Ancient Graffiti in the House of Maius Castricius in Pompeii." *AJA* 114:59–101.

Berger, Klaus. 1980. "Hellenistisch-heidnische Prodigien und die Vorzeichen in der jüdischen und christlichen Apokalyptik." *ANRW* 23.2:1428–69.

Chaniotis, Angelos. 2010. "Megatheism: The Search for the Almighty God and the Competition of Cults." Pages 112–40 in *One God: Pagan Monotheism in the Roman Empire.* Edited by Stephen Mitchell and Peter van Nuffelen. Cambridge: Cambridge University Press.

Clarke, John R. 2007. *Looking at Laughter: Humor, Power, and Transgression in Roman Visual Culture.* Berkeley: University of California Press.

Forbes, Christopher. 1997. *Prophecy and Inspired Speech in Early Christianity and Its Hellenistic Environment.* Peabody, MA: Hendrickson.

Gillend, Michael. 2008. "Commit No Nuisance." *Laudator Temporis Acti.* 5 October. https://tinyurl.com/SBL9031k.

Graf, F. 1992. "An Oracle against Pestilence from a Western Anotolian Town." *ZPE* 92:267–79.

Hanson, J. S. 1980. "Dreams and Visions in the Graeco-Roman World and Early Christianity." *ANRW* 23.2:1395–427.

Harrison, James R. 2012a. "Artemis Triumphs Over a Sorcerer's Evil Art." *NewDocs* 10:39–49.

———. 2012b. "Livia as Hekate." *NewDocs* 10:26–30.

Harton, George Maurice, V. 2018. "An Emperor for a Master: Slaves in the Palaces of Augustus and Nero." MA thesis, Austin, University of Texas.

Hobson, Barry. 2009. *Latrinae et foricae: Toilets in the Roman World.* London: Duckworth.

Horsley, G. H. R. 1983. "Joining the Household of Caesar." *NewDocs* 3:7–9.

Jansen, Gemma C. M. 2011. "Cultural Attitudes." Pages 165–74 in *Roman Toilets: Their Archaeology and Cultural History.* Edited by Gemma C. M. Jansen, Ann Olga Koloski-Ostrow, and Eric M. Moormann. Leuven: Peeters.

Jansen, Gemma C. M., Ann Olga Koloski-Ostrow, and Eric M. Moormann, eds. 2011. *Roman Toilets: Their Archaeology and Cultural History.* Leuven: Peeters.

Keegan, Peter. 2011. *Graffiti in Antiquity.* New York: Routledge.

Levin-Richardson, Sarah. 2015. "Bodily Waste and Boundaries in Pompeian Grafffiti." Pages 225–54 in *Ancient Obscenities: Their Nature and Use in the Ancient Greek and Roman Worlds.* Ann Arbor: University of Michigan Press.

Lewis, Naphtali. 1997. *The Interpretation of Dreams and Portents in Antiquity.* Mundelein: Bolchazy-Carducci.

Magness, Jodi. 2012. "What's the Poop on Ancient Toilets and Toilet Habits?" *NEA* 75.2:80–87.

Pack, Roger. 1955. "Artemidorus and His Waking World." *TAPA* 86:280–90.

Reisch, Emil. 1923. *Forschungen in Ephesos.* FiE 3. Vienna: Akademie.

Solling, P. 1978. "The Brontoscopic Calendar of Nigidius Figulus." *Ancient Society: Resources for Teachers* 8.1:47–64; 123–34.

Turner, M. M. B. 2000. *Power from on High: The Spirit in Israel's Restoration and Witness in Luke-Acts.* Sheffield: Sheffield Academic.

Appendix 1
Contents of *NewDocs* 11B

James R. Harrison, "An Overview"

Thematic Essays

1. Michael Immendorfer, "Ephesian Artemis and Her City"
2. Guy MacLean Rogers, "Some Priestesses of Artemis of Ephesos: An Epigraphic Profile"
3. Stephan Witetschek, "The Imperial Cult at Ephesos"
4. James R. Harrison, "Sponsors of *Paideia*: Ephesian Benefactors, Civic Virtue, and the New Testament"
5. R. A. Kearsley, "Women's Life in Public and Private: Ephesian Inscriptions in Their Greco-Roman Context"
6. Elif Hilal Karaman, "Widows, the Ephesian Inscriptions, and 1 Timothy 5"
7. Richard S. Ascough, "Associating with the Ephesian Associations"
8. Stephen Llewelyn and Will Robinson, "Epigram for a Young Slave"
9. James R. Harrison, "The Life of Christians in Late Antique Ephesus: An Epigraphic Portrait"

Exegetical Essays

10. Bradley J. Bitner, "Acclaiming Artemis in Ephesus: Political Theologies in Acts 19"
11. Bradley J. Bitner, "1 Timothy and the Confession Inscriptions of Asia Minor"
12. James R. Harrison, "Ephesian Cultic Officials, Their Benefactors, and the Quest for Civic Virtue: Paul's Alternative Quest for Status in Epigraphic Context"
13. James R. Harrison, "The Citizenship Decrees of Hellenistic Ephesus: Evaluating Paul's Alternative Citizenship in Epigraphic Context"

14. James R. Harrison, "Divine Grace (Eph 2:8–10) and the Construction of Virtue at Ephesus"

Appendix 2
Translations of and Commentaries on Ephesian Inscriptions in *NewDocs* 1–10

SEG 39 1189. Trans. Harrison, James R. 2012. "Family Honour of a Priestess of Artemis." *NewDocs* 10:31–38.

Graf, F. 1992. "An Oracle against Pestilence from a Western Anotolian Town." *ZPE* 92:267–79. Trans. Harrison, James R. 2012. "Artemis Triumphs Over a Sorcerer's Evil Art." *NewDocs* 10:39–47.

Harrison, James R. 2012. "A 'Worthy' *neopoios* Thanks Artemis." *NewDocs* 10:48–54.

IEph 2.459. Trans. Harrison, James R. 2012. "The 'Grace' of Augustus Paves a Street at Ephesus." *NewDocs* 10:61–66.

IEph 6.1980. Trans. Horsley, G. H. R. 1987. "The Silversmiths at Ephesos." *NewDocs* 4:7–10.

IEph 1a.27.220–246. Trans. Kearsley, R. A. 1987. "Some Asiarchs in Ephesos." *NewDocs* 4:46–55.

IEph. 1a.24. Trans. Oster, R. 1987. "Holy Days in Honour of Artemis." *NewDocs* 4:74–82.

JOÄI 52:50, nos. 92–93. Trans. Horsley, G. H. R. 1987. "Giving Thanks to Artemis." *NewDocs* 4:127–29.

IEph 1a.20; IEph 5.1503. Trans. Horsley, G. H. R. 1989. "A Fishing Cartel in First-Century Ephesos." *NewDocs* 5:95–114.

IEph 1a.47; IEph 4.1012, 1060, 1062, 1068. Trans. Kearsley, R. A. 1992. "The Mysteries of Artemis at Ephesos." *NewDocs* 6:196–202.

IEph 3.647. Trans. Kearsley, R. A. 1992. "Ephesus: *Neokoros* of Artemis." *NewDocs* 6:203–205.

Contributors

Richard S. Ascough is a Professor at the School of Religion at Queen's University in Kingston, Canada. He has written extensively on the formation early Christ groups and Greco-Roman religious culture, with particular attention to various types of associations. He has published widely in the field with more than fifty articles and essays and thirteen books, including *Christ Groups and Associations: Foundational Essays* (2022); *Early Christ Groups, Greco-Roman Associations: Organizational Models and Social Practices* (2022); and *Associations in the Greco-Roman World* (with John Kloppenborg and Philip Harland, 2012). He has also published *1 and 2 Thessalonians: Encountering the Christ Group at Thessalonike* (2014) and coedited *Ritual, Emotion, and Materiality in the Early Christian World* with Soham Al-Suadi and Richard E. DeMaris, 2022. He is the editor of the Studies in Christianity and Judaism (SCJ) series, published by McGill-Queen's University Press.

Bradley J. Bitner received his PhD in Ancient History with a focus on New Testament and Early Christianity from Macquarie University in 2013. He is Associate Professor of New Testament at Westminster Seminary California. His monograph *Paul's Political Strategy in 1 Corinthians 1–4: Constitution and Covenant* was published in 2015 by Cambridge University Press in the Society for New Testament Studies Monograph Series. He has also published book chapters in several edited volumes as well as articles in peer-reviewed journals such as *Novum Testamentum* and *Greek, Roman, and Byzantine Studies*.

James R. Harrison studied Ancient History at Macquarie University and graduated from the doctoral program in 1997. Professor Harrison is Distinguished Professor at the Sydney College of Divinity. His recent monographs include *Paul and the Imperial Authorities at Thessalonica and Rome* (Mohr Siebeck, 2011); *Paul and the Ancient Celebrity Circuit* (Mohr Siebeck, 2019); and *Reading Romans with Roman Eyes* (Fortress, 2020).

Along with several Australian and international coeditors, he is the chief editor of the series *New Documents Illustrating Early Christianity Volumes 11–17*. In conjunction with L. L. Welborn, he is coeditor of *The First Urban Churches* (9 vols. with SBL Press: vols. 1–7 have been published, 2015–2022). He is editor of E. A. Judge, *The Conflict of Cultures: The Legacy of Paul's Thought Today* (Cascade, 2020). With Alan Cadwallader, Angela Standhartinger, and L. L. Welborn, he is coeditor of *The Village in Antiquity and the Rise of Early Christianity* (T&T Clark, 2024). Last, with E. Randolph Richards, he is coeditor of *Inscriptions, Papyri, and Other Artifacts*, vol. 10 of *Ancient Literature for New Testament Study* (Zondervan, forthcoming 2024). He has published many book chapters and peer-reviewed articles in international presses and journals.

Michael Immendörfer studied Theology at the Theologisch-Missionswissenschaftliche Akademie in Germany and at the University of Wales, where he graduated from the doctoral program in 2016. He serves as the Academic Dean of the Martin Bucer Seminary Study Centre Stuttgart/Germany. He is the author of the monograph *Ephesians and Artemis. The Cult of the Great Goddess of Ephesus as the Epistle's Context* (Mohr Siebeck, 2017).

Elif Hilal Karaman studied Theology at Dokuz Eylül University, Izmir, Turkiye and graduated with her PhD in Religions and Theology at the University of Manchester, UK, in 2015. She is currently working as an Assistant Professor at Dokuz Eylül University, Faculty of Divinity, Department of History of Religions. Her monograph *Ephesian Women in Greco-Roman and Early Christian Perspective* was published with Mohr Siebeck in 2018. Her research focuses on early Christian women in the region of Asia Minor, on which she has written articles and conference papers.

R. (Rosalinde) A. Kearsley was a Senior Lecturer in the Department of Ancient History at Macquarie University and, in retirement, an Honorary Senior Research Fellow in the Department of History and Archaeology at Macquarie University. Her publications focus on the history and epigraphy of the Graeco-Roman cities of the Roman East, including the cultural context of early church groups there. She has also turned her attention to the history of Rome during the triumviral and Julio-Claudian periods. Kearsley's major epigraphic publication on Roman Asia Minor is *Greeks and Romans in Imperial Asia: Mixed Language Inscriptions and Linguistic Evidence for Cultural Interaction until the end of AD III* (IK 59, Bonn

2001). In addition to many book chapters in international presses, she has also published widely in peer-reviewed journals such as *Ancient West and East*; *Classical Quarterly*; *Greek, Roman and Byzantine Studies*; *Rheinisches Museum für Philologie*; and *Tyndale Bulletin*, among others.

Stephen Llewelyn, a Senior Research Fellow of the Department of History and Archaeology in Macquarie University (Sydney, Australia), taught in the Department of Ancient History for many years. His research interests include New Testament Studies, papyrology, Qumran and Second Temple Judaism, the Dead Sea Scrolls, and Greek and Hebrew languages. He was the chief editor of the second pentad of *New Documents Illustrating Early Christianity* (vols. 6–10: 1992–2012), replacing G. H. R. Horsley, the chief editor of the first pentad (vols. 1–5: 1981–1989). The vast majority of entries in *NewDocs* 6–10 were authored by Llewelyn. He has also published book chapters with various presses and in a wide variety of peer-reviewed journals: *Biblical Interpretation, Biblische Zeitschrift, Heythrop Journal, Journal for the Study of the Old Testament, Journal for the Study of Judaism, Journal of Biblical Literature, Journal of the Hebrew Scriptures, Novum Testamentum, Vetus Testamentum, Zeitschrift für Papyrologie und Epigraphik*.

Phillip T. Ort received an MDiv from Midwestern Baptist Theological Seminary, Kansas City and is currently working on a PhD at the same institution. He is executive assistant to the provost and assistant director of institutional research at Midwestern Baptist Theological Seminary. He is also the director of the Spurgeon Library at the seminary.

Will Robinson studied ancient history at Macquarie University (MA). He is an independent researcher based in London.

Guy MacLean Rogers studied Classics and Ancient History at the University of Pennsylvania and University College London. He received his PhD in Classics from Princeton University. He has taught Classics and Ancient History at Wellesley College since 1985, where he was chairman of the Department of History from 1997–2001. In 1997, he was a visiting fellow of All Souls College Oxford, and in 2003 he received the Perennial Wisdom Medal of the Monuments Conservancy of New York City. His most recent book, *For the Freedom of Zion: The Great Revolt of Jews Against Romans, 66–74 CE* (Yale University Press) was selected by Choice as one of the Outstanding Academic Titles of 2022.

Isaac T. Soon studied New Testament, early Christianity, and ancient Judaism at the University of Oxford and Durham University. Soon is Assistant Professor of Early Christianity at the University of British Columbia, Vancouver. His first book, *A Disabled Apostle: Impairment and Disability in the Letters of Paul*, is forthcoming with Oxford University Press. He has published peer-reviewed journal articles in the *Journal for the Study of the Pseudepigrapha*, *Early Christianity*, the *Journal for the Jesus Movement in Its Jewish Setting*, *Vigiliae Christianae*, *Novum Testamentum*, and *Religions*. He has forthcoming work in the *Journal of Biblical Literature* and the *Journal for the Study of Judaism*.

Stephan Witetschek studied Catholic Theology in Eichstätt, Augsburg, Rome and Munich and finished his Dr. theol. in 2007 at LMU Munich. His dissertation is published as *Ephesische Enthüllungen 1. Frühe Christen in einer antiken Großstadt; Zugleich ein Beitrag zur Frage nach den Kontexten der Johannesapokalypse* (Peeters, 2008). Having spent two years in a teaching position at the University of Cambridge, he completed his Habilitation again at LMU Munich, published as *Thomas und Johannes—Johannes und Thomas: Das Verhältnis der Logien des Thomasevangeliums zum Johannesevangelium* (Herder, 2015). After teaching appointments at the Universities of Freiburg and Tübingen, he has been a Heisenberg research fellow at LMU Munich since 2017 and leads the DFG-funded project "Memoria Apostolorum: Apostolische Gestalten in der christlichen Erinnerungskultur des 1.-3. Jahrhunderts," which expresses his research interest in the New Testament and second-century Christianities.

Ancient Sources Index

Hebrew Bible/Old Testament

Genesis
3   98, 151
2:24   61
35:70   75

Exodus
3:6   253
3:14   150
5:11   150
9:14   150
25:31   290
27:20–21   290
32:6   238

Leviticus
20:10   325
24:1–9   290

Numbers
25:1–3   238
8:1–4   290

Deuteronomy
5:6   51, 173
22:22   325
23:17   238
32:39   150
33:2   75

Joshua
3:10   51, 173

Judges
2:17   238

1 Samuel
2:1–10   150

2 Samuel
22:32   150

1 Kings
7:27   352
7:49   290
11:36   290
12:21   159
14:24   238

2 Kings
23:7   238

1 Chronicles
29:11   112

2 Chronicles
2:6   150

Ezra
7:26–30   112
10:22   290

Job
10:9   238
41:11   151

Psalms
35:10   150

Psalms (cont.)		36[29]:14	75
77:13	150	49:19	150
84	151	52:19	290
86:8	150		
89:8	150	Ezekiel	
106:20	238	28	151
110:1	312		
113:5–6	150	Daniel	
115:3–7	173	6:26	51
117:27	75		
132:13–14	112	Hosea	
		4:7	238
Isaiah		4:13–14	238
40:9–31	150		
40:13	151	Amos	
40:18	150	2:7	238
41:21–24	173		
41:22–23	151	Micah	
42:6–7	290	7:18	150
43:10–13	173		
44:6–23	173	Zephaniah	
44:7	150	2:11	75
44:18–20	151		
44:24–45:8	151	Deuterocanonical Books	
45:1–7	151		
45:9	238	Wisdom of Solomon	
45:20	150, 173	15:7	238
46:1	150		
46:5	150	Sirach	
46:7	150	13:9–11	336
49:6	290	25–31	336
57:3–8	238	27:5	238
63:3	112	29:21–28	335
66:1	112, 352	31:3–4	335
		31:12–18	336
Jeremiah		36:13	112
2:11	238	38:29–30	238
2:20	238		
10:1–5	150	1 Maccabees	
10:1–16	173	1:21	290
10:7	151	2:18	159
10:10	51, 173	3:18	159
18:7–10	238	4:49–50	290
23:36	51	10:65	159
29:7	173		

Ancient Sources Index

2 Maccabees
- 3:30 — 75
- 6:4–5 — 238
- 14:15 — 75
- 15:34 — 75
- 12:22 — 75

3 Maccabees
- 6:23 — 159

4 Maccabees
- 5.2 — 337

Dead Sea Scrolls

1QH
- III, 23–24 — 238

1QS
- VI, 8–9 — 199
- XI, 22 — 238

1QSa
- II, 13–22 — 199

4Q416
- 2 III, 9–11 — 200
- 1 I, 16–18 — 200

Ancient Jewish Writers

Josephus, *Antiquitates judaicae*
- 8.67 — 44
- 8.70–71 — 44
- 12.250 — 290
- 12.298 — 159
- 18.55–59 — 251
- 18.60–62 — 158, 251
- 20.9.2 — 266
- 20.251 — 253

Josephus, *Bellum judaicum*
- 2.169–174 — 251
- 2.175–177 — 128, 251
- 2.283 — 260
- 2.386 — 260
- 6.164–167 — 128
- 6.346 — 128

Josephus, *Vita*
- 1–2 — 252
- 1–9 — 149, 252
- 7–9 — 252
- 80–83 — 149
- 187–188 — 149

Philo, *De vita contemplative*
- 30–33 — 199

Philo, *In Flaccum*
- 40 — 161

Philo, *Legatio ad Gaium*
- 33 — 179
- 134–136 — 235

New Testament

Matthew
- 12:6 — 253
- 17:11 — 39
- 17:24–27 — 253
- 21:12–17 — 253
- 23:6 — 199, 201
- 23:38 — 253

Mark
- 1:28 — 253
- 1:45 — 253
- 2:1–2 — 253
- 2:13 — 253
- 3:7–8 — 253
- 3:20 — 253
- 4:1 — 253
- 5:20 — 253
- 5:21 — 253
- 5:22–23 — 253
- 5:27–28 — 253
- 6:14 — 253
- 6:32–34 — 253

Mark (cont.)		7:53–8:11	325
6:53–56	253	19:12	159, 163
7:19	337	19:15	163
7:24–25	253		
7:31	253	Acts	
8:1	253	1:6	39
8:22	253	2:17	353
8:27–30	253	2:17–18	353
9:12	39	2:18–19	352
9:14–29	253	3:21	39
10:1	253	5:1–11	128–129
10:35–39	120	5:3	129
10:35–45	61	5:4	129
10:46–47	253	5:9	129
11:12–18	253	7:55–56	353
11:18	253	8:29	353
12:18–27	253	8:39	353
12:26	253	9:10	353
12:34b	253	9:10–16	353
13:1–2	253	9:12	353
13:8	266	10:3	353
14:38	253	10:3–6	353
15:10	250–51	10:9–23	353
23:6	199	10:10	353
		10:10–23	353
Luke		10:17	353
1:22	353	10:19	353
11:43	199	11:4–17	353
11:54	276	11:5	353
13:1–2	251	11:12	353
14:7–11	199	11:15	353
17:24	352	11:27–30	207, 266
19:12	135–36	11:28	266
19:41–44	253	12:6–7	190
19:45–48	253	12:9	353
20:46	199	14:8–10	51
21:9–10	352	14:17	51–52
23:44–45	352	14:15–18	51
24:23	353	16:6–7	353
25–27	352	16:7–9	353
26:19	353	16:9–10	353
		16:23–24	190
John		17:6–7	353
2:13–22	253	18:3	286
2:18–22	253	18:9	353

18:9–10	353	1:23	151, 238
18:19	175	1:24	238
18:24–20:1	12–13	1:25	151, 237
18:26b–27	23	1:26	238
19	277	1:30	152
19:1–41	xxv, 329	2:23	238
19:8–9	175	4:1–25	99
19:19	350	5:12–21	98
19:19–20	121	5:13	99
19:22–41	348	5:14	99
19:23–40	240	5:15	99
19:23–41	222	5:16	99
19:23–47	286, 288	517	99
19:23–20:1	273, 275	5:18	99
19:25	274	518–19	99
19:26–27	238	5:19	99
19:27b	351–352	5:20	99
19:28	352	5:21	99
19:29	143, 274	6:1–10	52
19:31	144, 189	6:4	342
19:34	352	6:5	342
19:35	141–42, 144, 147, 148, 352	6:6	342
19:35–41	144	6:7	342
19:38	278	6:11	52
19:40	273, 278	6:11–14	340
20:17–38	xxv	6:13	52
22:12–21	353	6:14–15	52
22:17	353	6:21	52
20:22–23	353	6:22	52
24:26	129	7:4	53
25:3	276	7:5	53
26:12–23	353	7:6	52, 226, 340
27:8	288	7:7–13	99
27:12	288	8:3–4	226
28:16	190	8:4–5	52, 340
28:20	190	8:9	340
		8:10	340
Romans		8:11	340
1:2–4	98	8:11–13	226
1:2–5	239	8:13	340
1:13	52	8:17	342
1:20	151	8:17–18	192
1:21	238	8:28–30	239
1:21–22	237	8:29	340
1:22	237, 238	8:29–30	227

Romans (cont.)		1:28	xxvii
8:31–38	344	1:28–29	226
9:1–6	238	2:6–3:3	224
9:21	238	2:13	149
9:22	238	3:3	223
9:23	238	3:4	223
9:30–33	238	3:9–17	223
10:1–3	238	4:6	224
10:4	98, 239	4:9	190
10:12	61, 225	4:10	239
10:16–11:7	238	4:16	223, 340
11:11–12	238	5–15	223
11:29–32	238	5:7–8	340
11:33–35	151	6:12	223
12:9	338	6:15–18	338
12:10	207	6:19	340
12:13	207	6:19–20	340
12:16	207, 226, 338	7:1–5	61
13:1–2	206	7:35	223
13:1–7	237	8:5–6	238
13:3	206	8:9–12	340
13:3–4	206	8:10	338
13:4	206	8:11–12	338
13:7	206, 338	8:12	337
14:19	226	9:7	52
15:1–2	340	9:16–18	191
15:5–7	225	9:19–23	337
15:7	340	10:8–9	238, 338
15:7–12	239	10:14–22	338
15:25–31	129	10:26	337
15:28	52	10:27	337
16:14	149	10:28	337
16:25–27	98, 239	10:29	337
		10:30	337
1 Corinthians		10:33	223, 337
1–4	224, 327	11:1	223, 340
1:10	223, 225, 226	11:11–12	61
1:11	223	11:14	240
1:11–4:21	223	11:17–34	224
1:12	224	11:18	223
1:13	223	11:20	338
1:17–2:5	224	11:21	338
1:18–31	239, 334	11:22	xxvii, 207, 239, 338
1:20	327	11:33	338
1:26	138	11:34	338

12:3	340	13:4	226
12:7	223	13:11	226, 227
12:12–13	227		
12:13	62, 225	Galatians	
12:21–26	338	1:12–16	75
12:23	239	1:14	149
12:24	200	2:9–10	207
12:25	223	2:10	129
13	340	2:19–20	75
13:13	227	2:20	342
15:32	12	3:1	75
15:43	240	3:28	61, 225
16:1–4	129	4:14	75
16:2	207	5:16–26	226
16:8	12	5:22	53
		5:22–23	340
2 Corinthians		5:25	340
3:18	227, 340	6:17	75
4:10–12	239		
4:11–12	340	Ephesians	
4:17	192	1–3	309
5:15	340	1:1	12
5:19–20	192	1:3–14	99
5:21	99	1:6	240
6:8	239	1:10	101
6:8–9	192	1:12	240
6:10	192, 340	1:15–23	192, 311
8–9	129	1:17	100
8:1–2	340	1:18	101
8:1–5	207	1:19	312
8:1–9:15	129	1:20–21	120–1
8:9	340	1:20–23	312
8:13–15	207	1:21	224
8:14	129	1:23	293, 301, 305, 309,
9:5	129, 276	2:6	101, 120–21
10–13	327	2:11–3:13	62
10:4–6	327	2:14	35–36, 41, 43–45, 224, 311
10:12	149, 149–52	2:19–22	99, 225, 313
11:14–12:10	149	2:20–22	309, 311, 312
11:16–12:10	158, 334	3:1	191
11:23	190	3:2–13	313
11:24	158	3:5	99
11:24–25	190	3:8–9	191
12:2	158	3:10	100
12:17–18	129	3:13	192

Ephesians (cont.)		2:25	276
3:14–20	191	3:4	149
3:14–21	313–14	3:5	158
3:16	313	3:6	149
3:16–18	311	3:7–10	53
3:18	313	3:7–11	149, 159
3:18–19	312	3:10	341–42
3:19	293, 301, 305, 309, 313	3:13–14	343
3:20–21	312–13	3:17	340
4:1–6	62	3:20	342
4:1–16	311	3:20–21	192, 343
4:2–6	225	4:10–19	53
4:3	226	4:17	52, 53
4:8–10	192		
4:11	99	Colossians	
4:24	340	1:24	341
4:32	340	3:5–14	340
5:1	340	3:10	340
5:9	53	3:11	61, 225
5:11	52	3:13	226, 340
5:15	100	4:18	190
5:18–33	62		
5:21	61	1 Thessalonians	
5:21–6.9	62	1:6–7	340
5:22	61		
5:24	61	1 Timothy	
5:25	61	1:3	12
5:25–32	313	1:12	78
5:33	61	1:15	78–79
6:20	180, 189–90, 191	1:15–16	78–79
		2:1–7	76
Philippians		2:5–7	78
1:6	53	2:6	80
1:11	53	3:14–15	80
1:19	343	3:16	78–80
1:21	342	5:5	207
1:22	52, 343	5:9–16	129
1:23	343	6:14	78
1:24	343		
2:2	226	2 Timothy	
2:5–11	226, 340	1:8	80
2:9–11	192, 239	1:8–12	80–81
2:11	53	1:9–10	77
2:16	53	1:18	12–13
		1:19–26	342

2:6	52	1 Peter	
2:20	238	2:14–15	206
4:8	78		
4:12	12	Revelation	
		1:12	290
Titus		1:13	290
1:2	81	1:20	290
1:3	81	2–3	122
2:1–10	81	2:1	290
2:4	276	2:1–7	xxv, 12–13
2:11	81	2:1–8	329
2:11–14	81	2:5	288–90
2:12	81	2:9	267
2:13	81	4–5	121
2:14	81	4:2	121
3:4–7	81	4:8	122
3:14	52	4:9–11	122
		5:2	266
Hebrews		5:5	266
1:1–4	112	5:6	121
2:17–18	112	5:6–14	122
3:1–6	112	5:7	121
4:14–15	112	5:9–10	122
5:5–9	112	5:12	122
6:19–20	112	5:13	122
7:23–10:18	112	6	329
8:13	112	6:1–8:1	266
9:9–10	112	6:2	121–22
10:11	112	6:4	121–22
10:32–35	114	6:5	121–22
10:34	207	6:6	259–67, 283, 328
11:10	110	6:6–8	267
11:16	112	6:7–8	121–22
12:2	114	6:9	121–22
12:18–21	112	6:12–14	121–22
12:22	112	7:9–17	122
12:23	112	7:10	122
12:25–29	112	7:11–12	122
13:14	112–13	7:17	121
		8:1	121–22
James		9:20	14
2:1–5	199	11:4	290
2:1–7	207	11:15	122
2:6	239	11:16–18	122
		12:10–12	122

Revelation (cont.)		Greco-Roman Literature	
13:16–17	267		
13:18	326	Achilles Tatius, *Leucippe et Clitophon*	
15:2–4	122	7.13.3	37
16:5–7	122	8.2.2	37
18:4	14		
18:11–13	267, 283	Aelian, *Varia historia*	
19:1–4	122	3.26	2–3
19:5	122		
19:6–8	122	Aelius Aristides, *Oration*	
22:1	121	23	217
22:3	121	23–25	213
		26	213

Rabbinic Works

Ammianus Marcellinus, *Rerum gestarum libri XXXI*

t. Sukkah			
4.4	199	14.6.1	110
		15.7.1	110
		16.10.14	110

Early Christian Writings

Acts of John		Appian, *Bella civilia*	
37–54	12	1.26	214
Athenaeus, *Deipnosophistae*		Appian, *Foreign Wars*	
8.361d–e	2, 88	3.21	9
14.1	336	9.61–62	9
Didascalia apostolorum		Appian, *Mithridatic Wars*	
2.57–58	201	12.4.23	9
2.58.6	201		
		Apuleius, *Metamorphoses*	
Irenaeus, *Adversus haereses*		9.12	276
4.26.3	201		
		Aristophanes, *Vespae*	
Minucius Felix, *Octavius*		393–394	349
9.5–6	207		
		Arrian, *Anabasis*	
Shepherd of Hermas, Mandate(s)		1.17	5
11.12 [43.9]	201		
		Artemidorus, *Onirocritica*	
Shepherd of Hermas, Similitude		2.50	191
3.9.7 [17.7]	201	2.55	191
		4.44	350
		5.82	50

Ancient Sources Index

Athenaeus, *Deipnosophistae*
8.361d–e	2, 88
14.1	336

Aulus Gellius, *Noctes atticae*
2.6.18	5

Caesar, *Bellum civile*
3.33.1–2	9
3.105.1–2	9
3.105.2	9

Cicero, *In Catilinam*
4.15	214

Cicero, *De haruspicum responso*
60–61	214

Cicero, *De lege agraria*
3.4	214

Cicero, *De republica*
1.49	214
2.69	214
3.34 (frag. 2)	109

Cicero, *Epistulae ad Atticum*
1.17.8–10	214
1.18.3	214
4.1	261
6.1.26	235
9.10.3	109

Cicero, *In Verrem*
2.1.33.85	37
2.4.69	109
3.81	266

Cicero, *Orationes philippicae*
4.14	214
8.8	214

Cicero, *Pro Cluentio*
152	214

Cicero, *Pro Marcello*
22	109

Cicero, *Pro Murena*
1	214
78	214

Cicero, *Pro Sexto Roscio Amerino*
25	261

Dio Cassius, *Historiae romanae*
38.13	261
39.9	261
43.51	261
51.20.6	110
51.20.6–9	216–17
54.23.6	214
55.26.2	261
55.26.3	262
55.31.4	261
59.28	217
78.15.5–7	186

Dio Chrysostom, *Celaenis Phrygiae* (*Or.* 35)
35.54	5

Dio Chrysostom, *De tummultu*
46.5–14	266

Dio Chrysostom, *In contione* (*Or.* 48)
48	217

Dio Chrysostom, *Rhodiaca* (*Or.* 31)
7	236
8	235
8–9	236
9	235
12	235, 236
16	236
20	236
27–31	236
31.54	37
33	236
36–37	236

Dio Chrysostom, Rhodiaca (cont.)

62	237
65	236
92	237
94	237
126	237
149	237
150	237
149–151	237
158–159	237
161–162	236

Dio Chrysostom, Tarsica altera (Or. 34)

34	217

Diodorus Siculus, Bibliotheca historica

13.103.3–4	4

Diogenes Laertius, Vitae philosophorum

9.1–3	4

Ephoros, *FGrHist*

70 F 126	2, 88

Eusebius, *Praeparatio evangelica*

5.18–26	350
5.25	350
6.7	350

Hierocles, *De officiis*

4.502	60
4.502	62

Herodotus, *Historiae*

1.26	3
1.74	2
1.92	3
1.142	1
2.148	5

Hesiod, *Theogony*

937	59

Horace, *Ars poetica*

470–472	349

Horace, *Satirae*

1.8.37–39	349
2.8	336

Iamblichus, *Epistle Concerning Concord*

2.356	225

Isocrates, *De pace*

38–39	43

Juvenal, *Satirae*

6.560–561	190
10.78–81	260

Livy, *Ab urbe condita*

5.7.9.2	109
28.28.11	109
32.26.18	190
32.36.18	190
37.14.6	284

Livy, *Epitome*

58	8

Lucan, *Pharsalia*

72–73	190

Lucian, *Alexander (Pseudomantis)*

49	350

Lucian, *Symposium*

13	336

Lucian, *Toxaris*

29	190, 191
32	190
33	190

Lysias

18.17	219

Nepos, *De regibus*

21.3.2	7

Martial, *Epigrams*		Persius, *Satirae*	
3.60	335	1.112–114	349, 351
5.8	199		
14	199	Petronius, *Satyricon*	
23	199	71.8	349
25	199		
27	199	Philo of Byzantium, *De septem miraculis*	
		7	5
Maximus of Tyre, *Dissertation*			
10	59	Philostratus, *Epistle Apollonii*	
		32	13
Ovid, *Fasti*			
3.72	109	Philostratus, *Vita Apolloni*	
3.421	109	4.1	13
3.421–422	111	4.2	13
4.949–454	111	4.4	13
4.951	111	7.36	190
6.637–640	214	8.26	13
		8.30	13
Ovid, *Consolatio ad Liviam*			
273–74	190	Philostratus, *Vitae sophistarum*	
		2.10.1	58
Ovid, *Metamorphoses*		2.10.4	59
15.864	111	2.23	147, 148
Papinianus, *On Adultery*		Pliny, *Naturalis historia*	
1–3	325	36.95–97	3, 5, 109
Paulus, *Sententiae*		Pliny the Younger, *Epistulae*	
2.26.1–8	325	2.6.3	336
2.26.10–12	325	6.31	246–7
2.26.14	325		
		Plutarch, *Alcibiades*	
Pausanias, *Graeciae descriptio*		36.5–6	5
1.9.7	7		
2.17.3	235	Plutarch, *Alexander*	
2.17.4	5	3.5–6	5
4.31.8	5		
7.2.6–9	1	Plutarch, *Antonius*	
7.2.8–9	2, 88	4	323
7.3.4–5	7	24	323
7.7–8	3	24.3	9
10.9.9	4	56.1	9
		60	235

Plutarch, *Camillus*		11	110
42	213	15	262
Plutarch, *Conjugalia praecepta*		Rufus of Ephesus, *Treatise*	
18 [140D]	59	46	349
Plutarch, *De Stoicorum repugnantiis*		Rufus of Ephesus, *On Melancholy*	
2.22	349	frag. 21	349
		frag. 53	349
Plutarch, *De superstition*		frag. 70	349
3 [165E]	191	frag. 75	349
Plutarch, *De vitando aere alieno*		Scriptores historia Augustae	
3 [828D]	37	1.6.6	58
		5.7	349
Plutarch, *Lysander*			
3.2–3	4	Seneca the Elder, *Controversiae*	
5.1	5	1.4	325
		1.6.2	190
Plutarch, *Pompeius*		9.1.7	191
49	261		
		Seneca the Younger, *Epistulae morales*	
Plutarch, *Quaestionum convivialum libri IX*		9.9	190
1.2.1–3	336	Strabo, *Geographica*	
1.2–3	198	4.1.4	3
4.0.1	336	11.5.3–4	3
7.6.3	336	12.18.5	283
8.0.1	336	13.4.2	8
12	336	14.1.3–4	2, 88
		14.1.20	89
Plutarch, *Septem sapientium convivium*		14.1.21	2, 88–89
3 [148F–1449F]	336	14.1.22	5
		14.1.23	35, 37
Plutarch, *Tiberius et Caius Gracchus*		14.22–23	5
17.6	214	14.1.24	283
		14.1.24–25	284
Polybius, *Historiae*		633	2
21.48	8	640	1
Quintilian, *Institutio oratoria*		Suetonius, *Divus Augustus*	
5.10.104–105	325	18	260
		44	199
Res gestae divi Augusti			
5.5	262		

Ancient Sources Index 379

Suetonius, *Gaius Caligula*
21   17

Suetonius, *Divus Claudius*
21   199

Suetonius, *Divus Julius*
38   261

Suetonius, *Nero*
39   326
45.1   266
56   349

Tacitus, *Annales*
3.6   109
3.31   199
3.54.6–8   262
3.60–63   37
4.55   217
4.55–56   217
4.74   160
6.8   160
14.6.1   109
14.15   122
14.44   207
15.5   266
15.32   199
16.23   283
18   266
28.1.1   109
29.6.17   109

Tacitus, *Historiae*
1.11   260
1.84   109
5.5   207

Thucydides, *Historia belli peloponnesiaci*
1.136.3   4

Tibullus, *Elegies*
2.5.23   109

Valerius Maximus, *Factorum et dictorum memorabilium libri IX*
8.14, ext. 5   5, 128
5.3.1   109

Velleius Paterculus, *Historiae romanae*
2.103   109

Vergil, *Aeneid*
1.278   109
1.278–279   109

Vitruvius, *De architectura*
4.1.4   1
5.7.2   211
7.pref.16   3

Xenophon, *Ephesiaca*
1.15.5–16.7   248
2.5.5   248
2.11.1–9   248
2.13.5–8   248
3.2.5–8   248
3.12.4–6   248
4.5.3–6   248

Xenophon, *Hellenica*
3.4.3–8   4
3.4.16–17   4

Xenophon, *Memorabilia*
4.4.16   219

Xenophon, *Oeconomicus*
7.18–19   60

Xenophon, *Poroi*
3.4   198

Inscriptions and Papyri

AAWW
94:18–20, no. 3   180
110:191   341

AE		
1900.91		302
1913.170		141
1959.13		180
1968.478		259
1971.460		157
1971.455		183
1975.799		43
1975.800		117
1983.443 a/b		109
1985.726		109
1991.1644		109
2011.1319		148

Ascough Harland, Kloppenborg, *Associations in the Greco-Roman World*
§52	50
§63	47
§117	120
§120	120
§198	120
§148	50
§160	120
§170	245
§172	245

BE	
1988.403	302

CIG	
2954	65

CIIP	
1.2	43
1.2.4–5	36
2.1277	158, 251

CIL	
1.2	111
3.1422	109
3.1966	349
3.6070	37
3.7118	37
4.7716	349
5.6691	109
5.8991	205
6.944	113
6.13740	349
6.29848	349
6.29848b	351
8.1427	109
8.6965	109
10.10	109

Danker, *Benefactor*
§19	204
§22	336

DocsGaius
127	217
380	125

DocsNerva
72a	203
494	284

Eck, "Inscription Pontius Pilatus"
§1277	163

FD 3.4
372.5	36

FiE
1:280, no. 26	35
1, no. 49	186
2, no. 23	231
2, no. 44	96
2, no. 52	211
3:25	347
3, no. 66	186
8.1:88–89	341
9.1, no. F3	93
10.1, no. N4	94

Foucart, "Inscriptions d'Asie Mineure"
504–6, no. 10	271

Führer Selçuk
98–100	286

Ancient Sources Index

GIBM	
3.2.481	70
3.2.482	65
3.2.487	203
3.2.491	243
3.2.497	231
3.2.520	35
3.2.522	37
3.2.523	38
3.2.523	39
3.2.539	52, 57
3.2.540	135
4.1.894.8–12	213

GR	
203	325
210A	329
211	329
212	329
219	329
238	324–5
242	324
271	329
283	325
298	324
304	325
308	324
310	325
311	325–26
312	325–26
314	326
319	326
322	327
324	327
328	326
329	327, 328
351	329
357	328
369	327, 328
370	328
374–75	329
376	327
380–85	329
405	329

Grégoire, *Asie mineure*. vol. 1
1922, no. 100	96

Guerber and Le Bouedec, *Gens de mer*
7	203

IAsia Mixed	
103	148
117	135
128	148
158–161	21
162	21

ICos	
ED 5	220
ED 77	68

ICrete	
29.3.A.20–21	68

IDelta	
235.5	262

IDidyma	
25A.13–14	44
486	221

IEgypte prose	
2	262
55	262

IEph	
1a.2	5
1a.3	7
1a.4	7, 158
1a.5	8
1a.6	8
1a.7	10
1a.8	10
1a.9b.17	323
1a.10.13–15	12
1a.10.27–29	49
1a.17–18	17
1a.17.70	71
1a.18b	125

IEph (cont.)

1a.16b.11–22	222	1a.27E.48	145
1a.18b.0–20	125–26	1a.27F	143
1a.18c	125	1a.27F.435	145
1a18c.10	128	1a.37	20
1a.18c.0–13	125–27	1a.41.17–22	246
1a.20	17, 49–50	1a.43	296
1a.21.10–12	144	1a.211.6-16	145
1a.23	14, 240, 285–88	1a.1487.13	240
1a.23.18–19	286	1.22.42	183
1a.23.20	286	1.25B.8–34	310
1a.23.22–23	286, 289	1.46.7–11	294–95
1a.24.A	66–67	1.520	36
1a.24.A.11	67	2.132	188
1a.24.A.12–13	67	2.202	8
1a.24.A.16–17	67	2.211	143, 259–60, 267
1a.24B	67, 80, 143	2.211.13–16	264
1a.24B.20–21	67	2.212.2	240
1a24C	67	2.213	47
1a24C.8	67	2.213.4–5	48
1a24C.16–18	67	2.213.8–11	49
1a.24B.8–23	65	2.215	222, 271–73, 278
1a.24B	74	2.234	91
1a.25.1–28	10	2.235	91
1a.25	158	2.237	91
1a.25.1–28	231	2.239	91
1a.26	143	2.241	91
1a.27B.231–34	143	2.449	145
1a.27	87, 96, 137, 198	2.251	9, 16
1a27.48	96	2.252	15
1a.27.96	96	2.255A	16
1a.27.209	96	2.256	15
1a.27.222–223	144	2.259B	17
1a.27.183	87	2.260	18
1a.27.297–300	144	2.262	158
1a.27.418	144	2.232A	18
1a.27.440	212	2.233–235	18
1a.27.440–477	213	2.238	18
1a.27.488–492	144	2.239	19
1a.27A	143	2.241	18
1a.27A.5–8	145	2.418	19
1a.27B.231–34	146	2.249	18
1a.27C.344–45	71	2.251	75
1a.27D.384–87	70–71	2.251.6	71
1a.27E	143	2.255A	18
		2.260A	19

2.261	145	2.439	92
2.262	18	2.442	143, 145
2.263	19	2.446	143–44
2.263 A+B	19	2.547	274
2.263B	19	2,449	143–44
2.264	20	2.454a	245–46
2.264A	20	2.454b	245
2.267–273	21	2.454c	245
2.274	21, 284–85	2.454d	245
2.274.14–15	285	2.454e	245
2.275	21, 117–20	2.454f	245
2.276	21	2.456.1	334–35
2.280	21	2.456.2	339
2.293	119	2.461	91
2.296.8–10	71	2.462.4–6	188
2.300A	217	2.499	19, 162
2.304A	217	2.501.1	95–96
2.401	16	2.508	91
2.402	16	2.510–514	16
2.403	11	2.560.1	326, 339
2.403.1	188	2.560.2	326
2.403.2	188	2.560.3	326, 339
2.404	15	2.561.1	341
2.410	18	2.567	347–48, 350
2.411	17–18, 283	2.568	347, 350
2.412	18	2.568A	351
2.412.3–4	107	2.568A.1	347–48, 351
2.413	19	2.568A.2	348
2.414	16	2.569	348, 350
2.415	19	2.586	274
2.416	19	2.599	107
2.419	19	2.1479	212
2.419A	19	3.612A	96
2.420	20	3.614C	143, 144
2.421	20	3.616	339
2.424	20, 91	3.618	198
2.424A	20, 91	3.619A	143, 145
2.425	91	3.619B	143, 145
2.425A	91	3.622	173
2.427	91	3.627	183
2.428	21	3.633	183
2.429	21	3.644	92, 97–98, 100
2.430	21	3.638	91
2.431	245	3.661	96
2.435	143, 145	3.672	141–43, 147–50

IEph (cont.)

3.674	143	3.980	212
3.678	149	3.983–984	212
3.674A	143	3.987	72–3
3.664b	183	3.988	72
3.684	17	3.989.1–2	211
3.695.20–25	145	3.989.3–4	211
3.701	18	3.989.8–9	212
3.702.7–8	188	3.990.5–6	300
3.708	137	3.990	300–301
3.710B	18	4.1001	40
3.710C	18	4.1022	186
3.716	157–58, 162	4.1024	143
3.719	174	4.1059	299
3.727	97, 245	4.1061	143
3.728	245	4.1064	100
3.727.9	183	4.1065	217, 299
3.727.16	183	4.1080B	183
3.728	180–82	4.1106.6–8	183
3.728.21	185	4.1123	183
3.748.7	145	4.1130.1	183
3.789	326–27, 339	4.1130.4	183
3.793	162	4.1132.15	183
3.793.8–12	145	4.1124	20
3.799	217	4.1145	21
3.801	145	4.1161–7	173
3.802	96, 183–85	4.1162	174
3.811	148, 183	4.1202.1–7	324
3.811.20–27	148	4.1212	73
3.824	300	4.1267	323
3.828	149	4.1387.6–14	145
3.838	96	4.1393.3	14
3.845	145	4.1060	94
3.856	158	4.1062	95
3.859a	183	4.1062.2–3	95
3.868	158	4.1063	93
3.892	212	4.1064	93–94, 100
3.894	137	4.1066	94, 145
3.902	43, 110	4.1070	94
3.923	183	4.1072	94
3.938	183	4.1143	188
3.956	298	4.1162	173
3.958	298	4.1383.1	145
3.971A	143	4.1384	183
3.972.1–28	143	4.1408–1413	6
		4.1417–1445	6

5.1012	299	5.1539.9	58
5.1059	94	5.1539.9–12	59–60
5.1152	183	5.1540	135
5.1228	49	5.1548	100, 327, 339
5.1380	143–44	5.1600	212
5.1380A	143	5.1676	170, 172
5.1390	323	5.1677	170–71
5.1396	143	5.1687	36, 143
5.1405	323	5.1722	188
5.1408	323	5.1750	143
5.1411	323	5.1898	71
5.1447–1476	6	5.1900.3	217
5.1452	323	5.1902.3	217
5.1457	323	5.1906.2	217
5.1466	323	5.1908.3	217
5.1480.14–15	240	5.1910.1	217
5.1486	21	5.1910.2	217
5.1487	203, 205, 218	5.1923.4	217
5.1487.9	205	5.1929.2	217
5.1487.11–14	205–6	5.1958	327, 339
5.1487–1488	21	5.2387	143
5.1488	204	6.2002–2016	6
5.1488.15	240	6.2003	323
5.1489	158	6.2013	323
5.1489A	218	6.2018	143–45
5.1489.17	145	6.2034	217
5.1490	218	6.2034–2035	19
5.1491	222	6.2039	211, 217
5.1492	145, 247	6.2040	217
5.1499.9–13	145	6.2043	96–97
5.1491	92, 243-45	6.2043.2	97
5.1498	18	6.2043.3	97
5.1500	20, 145, 188	6.2044.1	97
5.1506	143	6.2044	92, 96–97, 100
5.1520	35, 37, 40–41, 44–45	6.2048	18
5.1521	7	6.2052	211–12, 221, 226
5.1522	16, 37–38, 41, 42	6.2054	217
5.1522–24	37, 39	6.2055	217
5.1523	16, 38–39, 41	6.2056	217
5.1523.7	39	6.2061.2.14–15	283
5.1523–1524	16, 37	6.2061	301–2
5.1524	39, 41	6.2066	217, 339
5.1524.7–8	39	6.2061.2	145
5.1539	42, 57–59, 62	6.2072.26	183
5.1539.8	58–59	6.2078	245

IEph (cont.)		7.2.3603	75
6.2211	36	7.2.3604	75
6.2216C	36	7.2.3801	120
6.2225	275	7.2.3825	75
6.2226	275	7.2.3901	327, 339
6.2274c	158	7.2.4101	173
6.2304	174	7.2.4105	91
6.2065	174, 245	7.2.4123	18, 136
6.2066	327	7.2.4128	158
6.2067	183	7.2.4130	169
6.2086	197–98	7.2.4119	158
6.2326	36	7.2.4324	9
6.2479	143	7.2.4330	297–98
6.2532	217	7.2.4336	217
7.1.3003	16–17	7.2.4337	15, 49
7.1.3008	143	7.2.4340	326–27, 339
7.1.3002	145	7.2.4343	143, 145
7.1.3005	20	7.2.5102	18
7.1.3006	15	7.2.5108	94
7.1.3007	15	7.2.5101–5113	20
7.1.3008	19, 162	7.2.5110	247
7.1.3014	183	7.2.5113	91
7.1.3019	17	7.3501–3516	39
7.1.3034	212	7.3072	296–297
7.1.3052	217		
7.1.3055	145	IErythrai	
7.1.3056	183	223	73
7.1.3058	145		
7.1.3066	186–88	IEstremo Oriente	
7.1.3068	174	383	222
7.1.3071	145		
7.1.3072	15	IG	
7.1.3072.28–29	300	2.1.429	293, 301–2, 305
7.1.3075	245	2.2.3173	110
7.1.3079	100	2.244	302
7.1.3080	149, 183	2.463	305
7.1.3082	148	2.1076	118
7.1.3082–3084	148	2.1688	305
7.1.3088	143	2.1.429	305, 308, 312
7.1.3131	143	5.1.530	136
7.1.3163	19	5.2.269	136
7.1.3217a	91	12.3.174	160
7.1.3217b	91	2.2.3297	217
7.1.3239	173	10.2.68	50
7.1.3411	21	11.4.1.223	220

12.3.172	219	*ILS*	
12.4.1.166.A.7–8	67	97	37
12.4.1.166.B29–30	67	3181	109
12.5.870	219	3636	109
12.5.906	220	3926	109
12sup.136	220	3927	109
		6751	109
IG Porto		8833	135
6	118		
		IMagnesia	
IGRR		54	220, 221
3.134	58		
3.739.26.55–76	204	IMT Kyz Kapu Dağ	
3.739.31–36	204	1431.3–4	108
3.739.37–42	204	1439	108
3.739.43	204	1449	221
3.739.44	204	1539	119
3.739.46–51	204		
3.739.52–58	204	IPergamon	
3.739.59	204	1.248.49–50	68
3.739.60–69	204	2.256	220
		2.296	73
IJO		2.299	217
2.30	170	2.485	50
2.31	169	2.497	118
2.32	170, 171	2.497.1–6	118
2.33	170, 172	3.10	271
2.34	170	3.11	271
2.151	169	3.23	271
2.152–62	170	3.24	271
		3.57	271
IKL			
23	323	IPergamon Asklepieion	
24	322	20	217
IKnidos		IPessinous	
1.220.7–8	68	22	48
IKret		IPhilippes	
3.4.9	221	2.47–71	251
IKyzikos		IPreine	
2.2.2, no. 3	62	113	221

ISmyrn		*OGIS*	
50	219	168	262
508	231	427	161
510	211	449	188
579I	219	458	98
594.12–13	108		
637	217	P.Amh.	
646	217	2.98.8–9	44
649	217		
654	262	*PDM* Sup	
655	217	1–6	350
666	217		
666.7–11	262	P.Dura	
		19.11–14	44
IST			
1	322, 323	*PGM*	
2	322, 324	7.229–49	350
3	322	7.250–4	350
		7.255–9	350
IThèbes Syène		7.539–69	350
244	262	7.703–26	350
		8.64–110	350
Kaibel, *Epigrammata Graeca*		12.144–152	350
888a	42, 57	12.190–2	350
1050a	96	22b.32–35	350
LBW		P.Mich 1	
137	65	23	248
140	65		
		P.Mich 6	
Lewis, N., *The Roman Principate*		6.423–424	248
26h	82		
89, no. 26i	243	P.Mich Inv	
		2920r	262–3
Lifshitz, B. *Donateurs ... synagogues juives*			
§13	173	P.Oslo 3	
§33	173	78	263
MAMA		P.Oxy. 12	
6.119	136	1454	275
NewDocs 10		P.Oxy. 22	
8	3	2340.6	278

Ancient Sources Index

P.Oxy. 46		39.1334	50
3312	352	39.1176	145
		39.1178	158
PSI		41.971	16
40	51	41.1202	50
171	51	45.1508	68
		51.1029	48
Reynolds, *Aphrodisias and Rome*		56.1219	327, 339–40,
1	222, 226	59.1318	xxv
8	37, 222		
12	10, 235	*SIG*	
		398	222, 226
SEG		655	51
4.516	125	820	47
12.150	161	838	203
12.511	220	839	284
13.505	42, 57	850	243
13.742	21	867b	65
15.530	119	989	35
15.696	65	1109	336
17.505	183		
19.684	286	*TAM*	
26.1243	43	5.2.1335	48
26.1272	117	5.2.1336	48
27.742	286	1456a	119
29.1120	341		
30.1306	43	Waltzing, *Étude historique*, vol. 3	
30.1311	286	no. 144	271
31.1168	198		
31.962	324	*ZPE*	
31.963	322	25:208–9	286
33.960	339	67:151–52	143
33.973	73	120:83, no. 1	16
33.1165	275		
34.1094	288	Modern Editions, Journals, and Series	
34.1170	70		
34.1106	71	*BNP*	
34.1688	197	14	37
36.1019	180		
36.1020	43	*JÖAI*	
36.1023	71	1:75, no. 1	334
36.1027	158	1:75, no. 2	339
36.1212	21	1Supp:78–79	231
37.883.4	145	3:88	93, 95
37.1020	50	11:77, no. 2	96

JÖAI (cont.)		Knibbe, *Ephesus*	
15:164–65	141–2	123 n.	296, 169
23:280–86	125		
40:13–15	42, 57	Knibbe, *Der Staatsmarkt: … Prytaneions*	
44:142–47	286	1981, no. F3	93, 95
44:257–63, no. 3	180		
47:6–10	259	Lafoscade, *De epistulis*	
48:3–5, no. 1	157	26	203
48:87–89, no. 14	72	54	243
49:67–69, no. 7	97–98		
50:15–20	43	*LSAM*	
50Supp:75–77, no. 6	117	31	65
52:40, no. 54	347	85	35
52:40, no. 55	347		
52:48, no. 85	73	MDAI(A)	
53:112, no. 79	323	32:278, no. 11	220–21, 226
53:135, no. 144	143		
55:33–34, no. 1	334–35	Oliver, *Greek Constitutions*	
55:33–34, no. 2	339	82A	203
55:109–10, no. 4155	20		
55:121–22, no. 4238	96	*PIR*	
55:126, no. 4272	94	A0714	58
55:126–27	197, 198	A1345	136
55:129, no. 4293	143, 145	C1024	58
55:139–40, no. 4363	70	H4	58
55:146, no. 4407	71		
59:181–82, no. 14	72, 299–300	*RAr*	
62:113, no.1.1–6	15	32:466	231
62:114, no. 2–7.7–16	15		
62:114, no. 3.17–27	16	*RE*	
62:115, no. 426a–37	16	15.618, no. 10	11
62:115, no. 5.38–47	16		
62:115, no. 6.48–50	15	Ricl, Marijana, *Kaystros River*	
62:119, no. 11a.1–6	15	§47	146
Kearsley, *Greeks and Romans*		Riemann, "Inscriptions … Cyriaque"	
103	148	289, no. 72	47
128	148	291, no. 78	284
158–161	21		
162	21	*RPC*	
		1.2572	9
Keil, "Kulte im Prytaneion von Ephesos"		1.2601	144
119, no. 1	93, 95		
		SE	
		3808*3	294

Van der Meer, *Ostia Speaks*
§23   261, 334

Coins

Hendin, *Guide to Biblical Coins*
§648   251, 251–52
§649   251–52
§649a   251–52
§650   251–52

Maier, *Picturing Paul in Empire*
96 n. 100   215

Mionnet
3.369   90
3.793   218
3.1730   218

RIC 1
Nero §153   215
The Civil Wars §§91, 118–120,
  132, 134   215
Galba §§35, 49, 104–108, 125–
  126, 339, 380–384   215
Vitellius §§66, 72, 89–91, 126,
  161–162   215

RIC 2
Vespasian §418   216
Titus §57   111
Nerva §§2, 3, 14, 15, 26, 27,
  54–55, 69, 70, 80–81, 95,
  96–97   216
Domitian §§215–215b, 231   111, 215
Trajan §737   111
Hadrian §§390–393, 397,
  410   111, 216

RPh
27:49–51   96
41, no. 86a   197
41, no. 86a, b   197
41, no. 86a, c   197
41, no. 87a, b   197

SNGCop
438   90

SNGvA
7863   217
1884   217

Modern Authors Index

Abbott, T. K. 43
Abbott, Terry J. 142
Abbott, Frank F. 203, 243, 273, 284
Abou-Aly, Amal Mohamed Abdulla 349
Adcock, Frank 179
Ådna, Jostein 253
Aitken, Ellen B. 114
Akar, Philippe 214
Aldrete, Greg S. 261
Allison, Jr., Dale C. 352
Alzinger, Wilhelm 11, 110
Amato, E. 59
Angelova, Diliana M. 118
Arnaoutoglou, Ilias N. 271, 274, 277–78
Arnold, Clinton E. 13, 121
Arnold, Jane R. 14, 148, 183
Arzt-Grabner, Peter 136,
Ascough, Richard S. 18
Auffarth, Christoph 3
Aune, David E. 121, 266, 290, 326
Bailey, Colin 15, 142, 146
Bammer, Anton 14
Barclay, John 129
Barnett, Paul W. xxvii, 122
Barton, Carlin A. 253
Barton, Stephen C. 238, 330
Bash, Anthony 179–80, 189,
Barth, Markus 190
Bassler, Jouette M. 75, 77–81
Bauckham, Richard 260, 265
Baugh, Steven M. 13, 170, 172
Baukova, A. 217
Beale, G. K. 151, 238, 266–67, 290
Beard, Mary 333
Beek, D. van 43

Benefiel, Rebecca R. 349
Benton, Jared T. 275–78
Berger, Klaus 352
Berquist, Birgitta 37
Best, Ernest 44, 61, 120–21, 190
Birley, A. R. 205
Bitner, Bradley J. 18
Blanton, Thomas R. 225
Bock, Darrell L. 51, 144, 266
Bockmuehl, Markus 53
Bohak, Gideon 170
Bosch, E. 119
Bowden, Anna M. V. 14
Bowman, Denvy A. 179
Bragova, Arina 254
Brandfon, Fredric 113
Bremmer, Jan 128
Breytenbach, Cilliers 225
Briquel, Dominique 138
Bru, Hadrien 110
Brunet, Stephen A. 13–14
Bryen, Ari Z. 248
Buckler, W. H. 271–74, 277–78
Burnett, D. Clint. 119, 238, 326
Burrell, Barbara 18, 216–17
Büyükkolanci, Mustaga 13, 20–21
Cadwallader, Alan H. 330
Cairns, D. L. 250
Can, Birol 50
Canter, H. V. 128
Caraher, William R. 308
Carson, D. A. 162–63
Carter, Michael J. D. 13
Carter, Warren 162, 253
Casson, Lionel 261, 264–66

Modern Authors Index

Cébeillac-Gervasoni, Mireille	125	Ersoy, Akın	218
Cecere, Granino	136	Evans, Katherine G.	163
Chaniotis, Angelos	68, 73, 352	Evans, Trevor V.	135
Charlesworth, Martin P.	110–11	Fauconnier, Bram	119
Chausson, François	136	Fee, Gordon D.	53
Chowen, Richard H.	205	Feldman, Cecelia A. 2019.	89
Ciampa, Roy E.	337	Fisher, Nick	250
Cioffi, Robert L.	68–69, 79	Flory, Marleen B.	214
Clarke, Graeme W.	308	Forbes, Christopher	353
Clarke, John R.	354	Foss, Clive	13
Collins, Raymond F.	52, 80	Foucart, Paul-François	272
Concannon, Cavan W.	330	Franke, Peter R.	92, 144, 218
Connor, Peter J.	308	Frank, Richard I.	325
Conwell, David H.	304–5	Friesen, Steven J.	xxvi, 3, 13, 18, 120, 188, 216
Conzelmann, Hans	130		
Cooley, Alison E.	110, 262	Futral, James R., Jr.	111
Cristofori, Alessandro	261	Ganz, Fabian	13
Crook, John A.	160	Garbrah, K.	68
Croy, Nathan N.	343	Garland, D. E.	338
Csapo, Eric	211	Garnsey, Peter	260
Cuyler, Mary Jane	261	Gatzke, Andrea F.	148
Davies, John K.	6, 20, 22	Gehring, R. W.	61
DesRosiers, Nathaniel	113	Georges, Tobias	13
Deissmann, Adolf	122	Gill, Malcolm.	71, 75–77
Dibelius, Martin	130	Gillend, Michael	349
Dignas, Beate	14, 50, 127–28	Goodman, Martin	142
Dimitrova, Nora M.	180	Gorman. Michael J.	240
Dmitriev, Sviatoslav	13, 145–46	Graf, Fritz	3, 348
Dominguez, Adolfo	2	Grant, Michael	160
Donelson, Lewis R.	76, 78–79	Grazia, Maria	136
Dörner, Friedrich K.	125	Gregory, Timothy R.	308
Doublet, Georges	58	Grossschmidt, Karl	13
Drew-Bear, Thomas	135, 203, 205	Haack, Marie-Laurence	136
Dündar, Erkan	314	Hagedorn, Anselm C.	250–51, 253
Dunn, J. D. G.	61	Hansen, G. Walter	159, 343
Eck, Werner	136	Hansen, V. D.	304
Eilers, Claude	179	Hanson, J. S.	353
Eliav, Yaron Z.	174	Harland, Philip A.	174, 271, 273–75, 288
Ellithorpe, Corey J.	215	Harrison, James R.	xxv–xxvi, 2–3, 6, 8, 10, 13–14, 16, 18–21, 36, 90, 92, 94, 99, 109, 111, 119, 150, 152, 182, 184, 198, 206–7, 212, 222, 235, 237, 239, 247, 251, 322, 324, 328, 330
Engelmann, Helmut	43, 71, 285, 322, 324		
Elliott, J. K.	295		
Engberg-Pedersen, Troels	343		
Erdemgil, Selahattin	13, 20–21	Hartmann, Benjamin	142
Erdkamp, Paul	260	Harton, George M. V.	351

Heberdey, Rudolf	48, 186, 231, 334, 339, 347	Kerschner, Michael	3
Hellerman, Joseph H.	150	Kienast, Dietmar	217
Hemer, Colin J.	144, 288–90	Kileci, Senkal,	50
Hepding, H.	48	Keegan, Peter	349
Herrmann, Peter H. G.	48	Keil, Josef	176
Hessel, F.	66	Keil, Matthew A.	228
Hoag, Gary G.	13, 248,	Kinlaw, Joshua A.	228
Hobson, Barry	349	Kirbihler, François	40, 42, 146, 246
Hockey, Katherine M.	325	Kloppenborg, John S.	274–75, 338–39
Hoehner, Harold W.	62, 121, 190, 192	Knibbe, Dieter	xxvi, 3, 7, 13–14, 93, 95, 117, 142–43, 157, 169, 259, 285, 322, 348
Holloway, Paul A.	53		
Horsley, Greg H. R.	xxiii, xxv, 3, 14, 18, 49, 59, 159, 169–70, 273–74, 276, 352, 363	Knigge, Ursula	307
		Koester, Craig R.	267
		Koester, Helmut	13
Horst, H. van der	66	Kokkinia, Christina	205–6, 213, 283–84, 286
Houwelingen, Rob van.	75, 81		
Hueber, Friedmund	13, 20–21	Koloski-Ostrow, Ann O.	349
Human, Dirk	150	Konecny, Andreas L.	308
Immendörfer, Michael	3, 13, 44	Konstan, David	222, 250, 325
Iplikcioglu, Bülent	xxvi, 3, 7, 13–14	Koutsoukou, Anthi,	308
Illou, Nefeli	110	Kraabel, Alf. T.	169
Isaac, Benjamin	109, 115	Kraft, John C.	2, 3, 7, 284–86, 288
James, Sarah	308	Labuschagne, C. J.	150–51
Jansen, Gemma C. M.	349	Ladstätter, Sabine	16, 308, 321, 326–27, 339–40
Jew, Ian Y. S.	331		
Johnson, Allan C.	203, 243, 273, 284	Lafoscade, Léon J.	243
Jones, C. 75	57–59, 277	Läger, Karoline	75
Jones, Tamara.	197–98	Lambert, Stephen D.	302
Jongman, W. M.	260	Langlands, Rebecca	325
Joubert, Stephan	266	Lau, Andrew Y.	75–76, 79
Judge, E. A.	35, 138, 150, 158–59, 212, 267	Laurence, Ray	324
		Lee, Jin Hwan	336
Kampmann, U.	217–18	Leloux, Kevin.	3
Kanellopoulos, Chysanthos	308	Lémonon, Jean-Pierre	163
Kalinowski, Angela V.	14–15, 67, 92, 245–47	Lessing, Erich	231
		Levick, Barbara	14
Karaman, Elif Hilal	13	Levin-Richardson, Sarah	333, 349
Katsari, Constantina	14	Lewis, Naphtali	352
Kavanagh, Bernard	199	Lincoln, Andrew T.	121, 190–91
Kearsley, Rosalinde A.	13, 135, 182	Litfin, Duane A.	334
Keay, Simon J.	261	Llewelyn, Stephen R.	xxiii, xxv, 43
Keener, Craig S.	51, 144, 162, 175, 266, 337	Lobur, John Alexander	214
		Long, Leah E.	14, 286
Kelly, Benjamin	222	Lotz, John Paul	217–18, 224, 226

Lugt, Pieter van der	150	Nock, Arthur Darby	118
Lund, Helen S.	7	Noreña, Carlos F.	214, 262, 265
Lyons, Evangeline Z.	179–80	Nollé, Margret K.	92, 144, 218
MacDonald, Margaret Y.	121, 189–90	Nutton, Vivian	176
Mackey, Jacob L.	68	Oberleitner, Wolfgang	231
Magness, Jodi	113, 349	Ogereau, Julien M.	53
Magie, David	267	Oliver, James H.	70, 231
Maier, Franz Georg	315	Oller, G. H.	179
Maier, Harry O.	223	Olson, Emily V.	11
Malherbe, Abraham J.	60	Osborne, Grant R.	266, 290
Manomi, Dogara I.	75	Oster, Richard J.	3, 35, 66, 68, 285, 323–24
Martin, Dale B.	223–24, 226, 250		
Mattingly, David J.	261	Pack, Roger	348
McCabe, Donald	211	Palmer, D. W.	342
McCrum, Michael	47	Park, Joseph S.	172
McLean, B. H.	293	Parker, Robert.	180
McMurry, H. C.	44–45	Parkinson, William A.	308
McMurray, Howard	309–11	Perry, Jonathan S.	271, 273, 275, 277–78
McRae, Rachael M.	339	Peterson, Brian K.	334
Meriç, Recep	14	Petridou, Georgia	69–70, 73–74
Merkelbach, R.	94, 142, 271, 273, 276–77	Pettegrew, David K.	308
		Petzl, Georg	73
Mitchell, Margaret M.	75–76, 78, 80, 223, 225, 227	Pflaum, Hans-Georg	58
		Philips, Thomas E.	325
Mitchell, Stephen	14	Picard, C.	183, 185–86
Millar, Fergus	160	Plant, I. M.	59
Millett, Martin	261	Platner, Samuel B.	111
Milligan, George	51	Platt, Verity.	69–70, 80
Mellor, Ronald	109	Pleket, H. W.	286
Meyer, Hugo	118	Poignault, Rémy	205
Mjely, Abdel Majeed	200	Portefaix, Lilian	14, 96
Momigliano, A.	213	Pratt, Kenneth J.	109
Moore, G. F.	109	Prost, F.	68
Moore, Timothy J.	199	Pülz, Andreas	13
Eric M. Moormann	349	Ralph, Allison K.	225
Mosley, D. J.	179	Ramantswana, H.	112
Moulton, James H.	51	Ramsay, William M.	283–90
Moxnes, Halvor	235–36	Rapske, Brian	190
Muddiman, John	190	Rathmayr, Elisabeth	91, 97, 321
Müller, C.	68	Raja, Rubina	42
Murphy-O'Connor, Jerome	2, 4, 310	Rauh, Nicholas K.	314
Müzesi, Efes	13	Reapple, Eva M.	111
Nasrallah, Laura Salah	138, 186	Reardon, B. P.	248
Neyrey, Jerome H.	250–51, 253	Reinach, Adolphe	4
Ng, Diana Yi-man.	90–92, 97	Reinach, S.	273

Reinarcher, Jan C.	262	Snowdon, Michael	179
Retzleff, Alexandra	200	Snodgrass, Klyne R.	253
Ricl, Marijana	14, 19–20, 216–17	Sokolicek, Alexander	308
Richard, F.	205	Sokolowski, Franciszek	6, 50
Richard, Jean-Claude	214	Soon, Isaac T.	17–18
Richardson, M.	302	Souza, Philip de.	8
Rickman, Geoffrey	260	Spawforth, Anthony A. J.	21
Rietveld, James Dirk.	147,	Spicq, Ceslas	51
Rigsby, Kent J.	35–37	Spigel, Chad	199
Robert, Louis 13, 36, 38–39, 96–97, 188, 197–98, 293		Stafford, Emma	118
		Stallsmith, Allaire	48, 49
Robinson, Will	xxv	Steskal, Martin	245
Rocca, Samuel	161	Stettler, Hanna	75, 79–80
Roebuck, Carl	260	Steuernagel, Dirk	42, 274,
Rogers, Cleon	324	Stevenson, Gregory	40
Rogers, Guy MacLean 3, 7, 13–14, 20, 35, 39–41, 43, 67, 71–72, 87, 91, 94, 96, 137, 142, 146, 212–13, 297, 323		Stewart-Sykes, Alistair	201
		Strelan, Rick	13
		Strocka, Volker M.	169, 341
Rollens, Sarah E.	50	Sutton, Robert F.	60
Roskam, Geert	62	Syme, Ronald	57
Rosner, Brian S.	337	Szanton, Nahshon	158,
Ruggendorfer, Peter	308	Tagiliabue, Aldo	248
Rutter, N. Keith	222, 250	Taeuber, Hans 322, 324–25, 327, 328–29	
Said, Suzanne	249	Taussig, Hal	336
Sanders, Edward M.	250	Taylor, Lily R.	110
Scheid, John	136	Tellbe, Mikael	13
Scherrer, Peter 1–3, 7, 11, 13, 16, 19, 21, 88, 90, 110, 143, 147, 169, 188, 274		Temelini, Mark A.	214
		Theocharaki, Anna	307
Schwartz, Saundra C.	325	Theophilos, Michael P.	163, 216–17
Shiaele, M.	249	Thérialt, G.	212
Schnabel, Eckhard J.	51, 144	Thiessen, Matthew.	112
Schnackenburg, Rudolf	121	Thomas, Christine M.	286
Schowalter, Daniel	12, 19	Thraede, Klaus	217
Schwenk, Cynthia J.	302	Thür, Hilke.	16, 89–90, 321, 323
Seifried, Rebecca M.	308	Tilborg, Sjef van	18
Shanor, Jay	312	Tomson, Peter J.	174
Sherk, Robert K.	160	Tomai, C.	174
Shear, J. L.	235	Towner, Philip H.	75–77
Sherwin-White, A. N.	144	Torre, Martino La	245
Silver, Kenneth K. A.	158	Trebilco, Paul 13, 74–75, 144, 169–70, 272	
Skard, E.	213		
Slater, William J.	211	Trinkl F.	274
Smalley, Stephen S.	266	Turner, M. M. B.	353
Smith, Dennis Edwin	345	Unwin, James R.	330
Smith, Mark D.	251	Van der Meer, L. Bourke	333–34

Vervaet, Frederik Juliaan	261
Vyhmeister, Nancy Jean	199–200
Waal, C. van der.	113
Waddington, William H.	243
Walters, James C.	3
Wallensten, Jenny	48
Wansink, Craig S.	190
Wassell, Blake	162
Weiss, Cecelia F.	12, 16, 90
Welborn, L. L.	138, 150, 207, 219, 224, 226, 239, 325, 327, 338
Welles, C. Bradford.	50
Waltzing, J. P.	273
Wengst, Klaus	267
White, L. Michael	13
Whitlark, Jason A.	109, 113
Wilamowitz-Möllendorff, U.	142
Wilhelm, Adolf	48, 135, 273
Williams, T. B.	206–7
Wilson, Ian Douglas	151, 235
Winter, Bruce W.	206–7, 238, 276, 334
Winzenburg, Justin	14, 109
Wiplinger, Gilbert	3, 143, 321
Witetschek, Stephan	13
Witherington, Ben, III.	144
Wlach, Gudrun	3, 143, 321
Wood, John T.	37–42, 57, 70, 135, 203, 231, 243
Woodhead, A. G.	47
Wörrle, Michael	259
Wypustek, Andrzej	248
Yeates, Paul H.	109, 111
Yorgos, Mallios	11, 12, 188
Zabrana, Lilli	3, 40–42
Zalcman, Lawrence	112
Zamfir, Korrina.	61
Zimmermann, Norbert	321, 327, 340
Zimonyi, Ákos	171–72, 174
Zuiderhock, Arjan	14

Word Index

Greek

ἄγαλμα	42, 58
ἁγνεία	47
ἀθρασία	271, 273-74
αἰώνιος	107-8, 187
ἀλειτούργητος	173
ἄλυσις	189-90
ἀντιγραφεύς	143
ἀπαγορεύω	271, 273
ἀποκαθίστημι	38-39, 126
ἀποκατάστασις	39
ἀργυροκόπος	274
ἀρτοκόπος	271, 274
ἀρετή	211, 221
ἀρχιατρός	170-75
ἀρχιεπίσκοπος	158
ἀρχιερεύς	117, 175, 197, 243, 301
ἀρχισυνάγωγος	170
ἄσυλος	35-36
ἀσύνκριτος	142, 148-50
ἀτιμάζω	237-39
ἀτιμία	237-40
ἄτιμος	237, 239
ἀφθονία	125
ἄφθονος	259-60
ἀφθόνως	93
ἁψίς	96-97
γενερῶσος	135
γραμματεία	141
γραμματεύς	142-48, 154-55, 181, 287
γραμματεύω	141, 288
δεχυείρος	272, 277
διακομίζω	205
διαμονή	107-8
διάταγμα	271, 273, 287
δόξα	79, 81, 120, 192, 204, 235-37, 239-40
ἔθος	47
ἔκστασις	353
ἐνάργεια	68, 74
ἐνάργημα	78-79
ἐναργής	65, 67-68, 71
ἐνεδρεύω	272, 276, 278
ἔννοια	247
ἐνύπνια	353
ἐπιτελειόω	47-48, 66, 72
ἐπιφαίνω	73, 79
ἐπιφάνεια	65, 67-68, 70, 73, 75-76, 79-82
ἐπιφανής	71-72, 75, 77, 287
ἐργαστήριον	20, 272, 276, 278
ἐργαστηριάρχης	272, 278
ἑταιρία	271, 277
εὐγενής	135-36, 138
εὐχαριστῶ	298-99
εὔχομαι	259-60
ἡγεμονία	107
θάνατος	80, 341
θόρυβος	271-73
θρασύνω	271, 277
θυσία	72
θυσιαστήριον	169
ἱεράομαι	323
ἱερατεύω	73
ἱερεύς	127, 170, 187
ἱερεύω	117, 126
ἱέρεια	294, 300
ἱερίς	47
ἱερομνία	66-67
ἱερόν	38, 65, 67, 125, 157

Word Index

ἱεροπρεπώς	73	σοφία	93, 100
ἱερός	38–39, 183	συγγραμματεύς	142
ἱεροφαντέω	117	συγκρίνω	149
ἱεροφάντης	272	σύλλογος	271, 273–74
ἱερωσύνη	126	συναθροίζω	274
καθιέρευσις	43	συνέρχομαι	271, 273
καρπός	52–53	σύνθρονος	117–18
καρποφορέω	53	συνφυλάσσω	127
καρποφόρος	47, 51–52	σωτήρ	73, 80, 284
καρτερός	96–97	σωτηρία	221
κατ' ὄναρ	347–51, 353	σωφρονίζω	271, 276
καυτήριον	277	ταμιεία	272
κινήσω	290, 334	τάραχος	271, 273
κτίστης	87, 95, 284	τέμενος	35–37, 42–43, 58, 65, 67
λιμήν	187, 284–88	τόπος	76, 197
μέγας	79, 96, 141, 161, 181, 262	ὑπογραμματεύς	142
μεσότοιχος	43–45	φιλόκαισαρ	157–59, 161–63
μεταπέμπω	271–72, 276	φθονερία	248
μυστήριον	47–48, 79, 296-97	φθόνος	248–49
ναός	38, 65, 67, 72, 197, 294, 311	φιλοσέβαστος	158, 161–62, 187, 189, 211
νεωκόρος	97, 181, 230, 310	φύκτιμος	36
νικάω	181–82, 185	χαρακτήρ	232, 277
νόμιμος	47	χάρις	81, 225
ὁμόνοια	108, 144, 211–13, 216–17, 219–26	χαριστήριον	73, 262
		χήρα	129–30
ὀπτασία	353	χολόω	347–48
ὅραμα	353	ὥρα	341
ὅρασις	353		
οὐρέω	347–48	**Latin**	
παραβαίνω	35–36	aeternitas	110, 115
παραφυλακή	95–96	amicus	130, 160, 179
παραφυλάσσω	98	amicitia	161, 179
περίβολος	35–37	coetus	273
πληρόω	72, 293–96, 298–99, 301, 303, 305, 307–9, 311–13	collegium	172, 274, 278
		concordia	212–16, 219, 225, 227–29
πλήρωμα	293, 303–4, 311, 312–13	cura annonae	260, 262, 268–69
πρεσβευτής	38–39, 135	cursus honorum	58, 146, 150, 154, 172, 189, 245, 249–50, 255
πρεσβεύω	180–81, 187, 189		
πρόθυμος	93, 182	damnatio memoriae	18–19, 22, 236–37
προΐστημι	67, 271, 277–78	divi augusti	19
πρόσοδος	38	divi filius	38
προσσημειόω	272, 277	invidia	10, 18, 222, 243–44, 246–50
προστάτης	57–58, 221	pistrinum	276
σμικρολόγος	273	providentia	110, 115
σκαιολόγος	273		

Subject Index

aeternitas, 110. *See also* Hadrian
agora, 15–17, 20, 40, 42–43, 45, 141
agoranomos, 96, 125, 137, 189, 275
ambassadors, 5–6, 179–94, 218
    Paul's self-designation as, 189–92
    philosophers as, 179
    reciprocity in relations, 182
    theorodokoi list of Delphi, 180
    theoroi, 180
    to Rome, 179–80
    visits, 184–86
Anatolian mother goddess Cybele, 2, 119, 121
Androklos, founder of Ephesus, 87–101
    Basilid descendants of, 2
    epigraphic evidence, 93–98
    founder traditions, 97
        Paul and, 98–101
    frieze on temple of Hadrian, 90
    guards and restoration of statue, 95, 98
    heroon and fountain, 2, 89–90
    homonoia coins, 92
    statue
        in hall of baths of Vedius, 91–92
        procession of, 87
        Trajan's nymphaeum (hunter), 91
    transitions of government, 2
anti-imperial, 76–77, 113, 326
Antinous, paramour of Hadrian
    enthroned with Egyptian gods, 118
Aphrodite, 9–10, 16, 59–60, 235, 324
Apollo, 36, 76, 91, 94, 111, 119, 121, 184–86, 218, 222
apparitores, 137
Apollonius of Tyana at Ephesus, 13

aqueducts, 16, 20
Artemis
    Artemis Ephesia, 17, 19, 162, 218–19
    asylia, 35, 41
    celebration of mysteries, 40, 72, 297
    chrysophoroi, 21
    epiphany, 3, 65–81
    festival days, 66
    Hadrian's beneficence, 283
    kosmeteira ("adorner"), 211–12
    kouretes, 40, 94
    "manifest goddess," 71–72, 77
    neopoios, 323
    patroness, 310, 351
    priestess, 137, 211
    processional sacred way, 21, 87
        restoration of, 16
    prytaneis, 94
    sacred estates, 19–20
    sacred boundary markers, 20
    sacred herald of, 137
    soteriological deliverance, 3
    statuary in sanctuary, 58
    temenos, 35–46, 58
Artemision, 3–6, 16, 18, 44, 127, 309–10
asiarch, 144, 148, 174, 182, 189, 191, 288, 296
Asklepios Soter, 73, 161, 174, 218
associations, 46, 200, 275, 296–98, 301
    bakers, 274–75
    Demetriasts, 49
    Dionysiac artists, 50, 119, 248
    Dionysos inscription, 117–18
    epithets of deities, 48
    Kouretes, 297

Subject Index 401

associations (cont.)
  neoi, 15
  nut-sellers, 248
  physicians, 174
  rivalries for civic status, 50
  Sarapis, Thessalonian, 50
  silversmiths, 222, 238, 273–74, 276–78, 288, 352
  woolworkers, 245
Athena, 88, 118, 324
  Julia Livilla as Athena Pollias, 118
Augusteum, 18, 37–38, 41–42, 107
bakers' disturbance, 271–78
  horrific conditions of, 276
  threatened punishments, 277
  relevance for Acts 19:23–20:1, 278
bankers, 8, 246
benefactor, 58, 91–92, 96, 147–48, 150, 157, 161–62, 182, 189, 199–200, 204, 206–7, 219, 221–22, 235–37, 244–47, 283–84, 288, 310, 328
  as savior, 9, 17, 58, 73, 118, 284, 288
  dark underside of, 244–45
  Gaius Sterinius Orpex, 136
  grudging hospitality of, 335
  invidia
    Claudius Aristion and, 246–47
    Flavius Philippus and, 246
    Vedius Papianus Antoninus and, 243–48
  proconsul Passienus, 157–58
  resources of, 207
bequest of C. Vibius Salutaris, 20, 137, 213
  procession of statues, 87, 96
  statue bases and social hierarchy, 198
boasting, 113, 149–52, 158–59, 226, 238, 252, 327
choral praise of emperor. *See also* imperial cult
  epheboi, hymnodes, 21, 23, 119–20
Christology, 62, 66, 71, 74–81, 99, 192, 352
  messianic Son, 112
  heavenly high priest, 112, 114
  heavenly Lord, 114, 352

Christology (cont.)
  Pastoral Epistles and epiphany, 74–82
conventus, 17
cursus pudorum, 150
cursus honorum, 58, 137, 146, 150, 172, 189, 245, 249–50
Cybele, 2, 119, 121
damnatio memoriae, 18–19, 22, 236–37
Demeter Karpophoros and Thesmophoros, 19, 47–54
  celebration of the mysteries, 47–49
  Ephesian Demetriasts association, 49
  other epithets for, 49–50
  patronage of, 52
  worship as fertility goddess, 48
Dionysos, 117–22
  Attalids and patronage of, 50
  C. Fl. Furius Aptus as priest of, 322–33
  Hadrian enthroned with, 118
  mystai, 21, 117, 323
  new Dionysos
    Antony as, 323
    Hadrian as, 118, 323
  wine drinking and, 324
dishonor, 231–42
  corroded statues, 233–35
  inappropriate dedication of statue, 235
  recycling honorific statues, 235–37
  Paul's language of, 237–40
  removal of honorific inscription, 247
dream revelation, 50, 191, 348–51, 352
economics and the New Testament
  Paul's benefaction hermeneutic, 206–7
  Rome's supply of wheat, 259–69
  Ephesus bakers' strike, 271–78
  Terrace House 2 expenditure lists, 327–39
elites, civic, 15, 93, 98, 136–37, 145, 189, 205, 207, 219, 222, 234, 240, 249–50, 290, 350. *See also* Ephesus: elites
Embolos (Kuretes Street), 19, 188
enchainment in prison and custody, 190–91
enthronement rituals, New Testament, 117–23

Ephesus
  agora, Lower and Upper, 274
  arrival of first Christians at, 12
  demos, 211–27
  elites, 135–39, 141–55, 157–67, 169–77, 179–94
  harbor, silting of, 283–91
  Hellenistic citizenship decrees, 6
  Hestia as goddess of, 41, 43, 94–95, 100, 299
  Library of Celsus, 20, 94, 247
  Mazaeus-Mithridates gate, 15, 347, 348
  monument of Memmius to Sulla, 11–12, 188
  Mousseion, 174, 246
  neokorate temple, 18, 211, 216–17, 310
  peribolos wall, 37, 40–41, 44–45
  public offices of, 95–96
Ephesus, history
  first site and settlement (1000–550 BCE), 1–3
  second period (550–300 BCE), 3–6
  Hellenistic period (300–31 BCE), 6–12
    epigraphic evidence, 8–11
  Julio-Claudian period (31 BCE–68 CE)
    epigraphic evidence, 14–18
  Flavian period (69–138 CE)
    epigraphic evidence, 18–21
epigraphic studies, methodological limitations, xxvi–xxvii
epiphany. *See also* Artemis
  defensive and competitive contexts, 68
  enargeia, 74
  epigraphy of, 70–74
  glory, 67–68, 74, 79, 81
  grace epiphany, 81
  imperial connections of, 71
  in Pastoral Epistles, 75–78, 80–81
  of Hygeia, 73–74
  protocols, 68–70
  variegated patterns, 74
epitropos, 158, 162

equestrians, 122, 135–36, 199, 252, 323
eternal Rome. *See* Rome: eternal
eternity, language of, 107–8, 188, 222–23
evil eye, 248
festivals and games, 12–14, 19, 66–68, 74, 120, 180, 182
  agonothetês, 145, 147
  Artemisia, 41, 183
  athletes, 37, 92
  Augustus foundation, 43, 110
  Dionysia, 323
  Ephesia, the boxer, 71
  gladiators, 329–30
  great Ephesia, 148, 183
  gymnasiarch, 8, 108, 145–47, 181–82, 187–89, 299
  panegyriarch, 141, 146–48, 181–83
  Pasithia, 183
  Thesmophoria, 48
fides to citizens, 22
financial corruption, 128–30
fountain, Sextillius Pollio, 19
freedmen, 13, 203–9
  equestrian, 136
  imperial, 14–15, 35
  seafarers, 21
friendship, 137, 157–67
  amicus, amicitia, 160–61, 179
  in John 19:12b, 163–64
  Herodian coins, 161
  philokaisar, 159, 161–63
  philosebastos, 161–62
  Pilate as, 160
fruitfulness terminology, New Testament, 51–54
fullness metaphor, Ephesians, 293–317
  body of Christ/temple, 309–14
  plēroō/ma, 302–9
gerousia, 15–16, 21, 143, 146, 231, 275
  secretary of, 143
glory, divine and human, 50, 53, 67–68, 74, 79, 81, 91, 101, 112, 114, 120–21, 128, 152, 189, 192, 236–38, 240, 246, 251, 312–14, 337
gods, man-made, 23

Subject Index 403

graffiti, 321–45, 347–55
grain supply for Rome. *See* Rome: grain supply
grammateus, 141–52
guilds. *See* associations
gymnasium, 8, 15, 41, 92, 98, 174, 188, 218, 222, 245–47, 334, 339
  ephebes, 222
  neoi, 15
  paideia, 8
Hadrian
  aeternitas, 110
  creation of Panhellenion, 21
  as new Dionysos, 118, 323
  temple of, 21
  Zeus Olympios, 21
harbor toll house, 17–18, 49–50
Harmonia and marriage, 57–62
  blessing of, 59–60
  gymnasium ethical curriculum, 62
  Neopythagoreans and Stoics, 62
  visual evidence, 60
  popular philosophers on, 60–61
  Paul on, 61–62
homonoia/concord, 211–30
  and New Testament
    absent from, 212–27
    scholarship on, 223–24
  Aristides's treatises on, 213
  Augustus and imperial, 213
  Cicero, 214
  coinage, 215–16
  competition of city-states, 217–19
  epigraphic phrases, 219–23
  goddess Homonoia, 212–13
  temple of Concordia, 213–14
honor, 197–209. *See also* Pontius Pilate
  Ephesian epigraphic context of, 235–37
  epigraphic places of, 197–98
  Paul and rhetoric of imperial, 206
  rhetoric of praise, 206–7
  Sadducees and ancestral, 252–53
  seating priority
    early church on, 201–2
    at Qumran, 200–1

honor: seating priority (*cont.*)
  in antiquity, 198–99
  New Testament critiques, 199–201
incomparability, biblical, 149–52
imperial convoys accompanying Hadrian, 205
imperial cult. *See also* friendship; Hadrian
  Augusta Demeter Karpophoros, 49
  Augustiani and New Testament, 122
  divi Augusti, 19, 41, 47, 97, 100, 217, 288
  enthronement of ruler with deities, 119
  epiphany, 71
  household gods, 120
  Julia Livilla enthroned, 118
  Julius Caesar's descent, 9
  sale of Artemis priesthoods, 17, 125–31
  sebastoi, 174
  thea Sabina Augusta, 21
  titles
    god Augustus/son of a god, 14–15, 38–39
    god made manifest (Julius Caesar), 9, 16
    god Tiberius, 120
    god Nerva, 20
    god Vespasian, 18, 113
  Hera Sabina, Sebasta, 21
  manifest god (Caligula), 9, 16
  veneration of Caesars, 42
  worship of Julia Livilla, 118
  worship of Julia Domna, 118
invidia, 222, 243–56. *See also* benefactor
  papyrological evidence for, 248–49
  of the chief priests, 250–53
Jewish physicians at Ephesus, 169–77
  archaeological evidence, 169–70
  Jewish inscriptions, 170–71
  Julius the *archiatros*, 171–75
  medical competitions, 173–74
  New Testament evidence, 175
Nile, epigraphic prayer to, 260, 264
"noble" and "well born"
  Corinthian church, 138
  epigraphic evidence, 135–38

nymphaeum
  Traiani, 19, 20
  in honor of Domitian, 19
Odeion, 40, 41
patrons, patronage, 12, 58, 89, 91, 97, 135–37, 144, 162, 179, 221
  Sejanus as conduit for imperial patronage, 160
  Apollo, patron god of Hierapolis, 218
  Artemis, patroness of Ephesus, 310
Paul, apostle
  cruciform theology, 61, 114, 150, 159, 224, 226, 239–40, 334, 340, 352
    Christian symbol of the cross, 170
    crucified messianic pretender, 114, 163, 189, 253
  soteriology, 3, 81, 98–99, 112, 149–50, 192, 239, 337–38
  eschatology, 53–54, 76, 78, 100, 150, 192, 240, 290
  pneumatic perspective, 52–53, 61–62, 100, 129–30, 226–27, 240, 311, 324, 340, 343, 353
  evil spirits, 312
pax deorum, 108
petitions in antiquity, 204–5
Pontius Pilate, 157–64
  and Roman honor, 351–52
proconsuls, 7, 10, 15–17, 19–22, 38–39, 47, 49, 66, 97, 127, 146, 157–60, 188, 231, 233, 235, 273, 283, 285–86, 288
Providentia, 110
prytaneis, 94, 143
Prytaneion, 40, 43, 49, 94, 110, 274, 299
reciprocity, 163, 179, 182, 310
  balanced, 207
  cycle of *charis* and the Charites, 225
  ingratitude, 236–37, 245, 335
  Paul and rituals of Charites, 235
Roma, cult of, 42–43, 188, 223–24, 351–52
Rome
  eternal, 107, 109, 199
    critiques of, 112–13
  grain
    distribution, 260–62

Rome: grain (*cont.*)
    free market, 264–65
    goddess Annona, 265
    latifundia, 108, 267
    main centers, 260
    wheat shortages, 266–67
scatological humor. *See also* Terrace House 2
  ambiguity in, 341–43
  Stoic graffito, 339–40
  host-guest relations, 333–36
  Ostia, 333–34
  Pauline ethical imprint, 337–41
shame, 22, 80, 114, 149–51, 192, 237, 239, 249, 334–36, 338
slaves, 160, 267, 276–77 351–52
  familia Caesaris, 352
soothsayers (*haruspices*), 136–37
sophist
  Hadrianus of Tyre, 58–59
stadium, 17–18, 199
  Circus Maximus at Rome, 114
statues, corroded, 233–35
strategoi, 144, 145
synagogues, 113, 169, 175
  seating priority, 199
  ruler of, 170
temenos, 36–37, 39, 42. *See also* Artemis
Temple of Roma and Augustus, 110
terrace houses, 16, 107
Terrace House 2, 321–32
  curse against adulteress, 324–25
  drawings, 329–30
  expenditure lists, 327–39
  gematria puzzles, 325–26
  gods and goddesses, 324, 326
  owner of Unit 6, 322–23
  philosophers, 326–27
  satirical humor, 327
  scatological humor, 329
theater, 20–21, 97, 119
Titus, triumphal arch of, 113–14
urban elites. *See* elites, civic
urination curses, 347–55
  apotropaic contexts, 351–52

urination curses (cont.)
    divine threats, 348–49
    dreams and curses, 349–51
Varius (Scholastica) baths, 19, 20, 141, 147–48
Vedius bath-gymnasium complex, 245, 247–48
Vesta, 110–11
warning in Herodian Jerusalem temple, 36
Zeus, 324, 326, 348
    Olympios, 21
    Philios, 222–23
    priest of, 51

www.ingramcontent.com/pod-product-compliance
Lightning Source LLC
Chambersburg PA
CBHW020544300426
44111CB00008B/788